Frontiers in Credit Risk

Concepts and Techniques for Applied Credit Risk Measurement

Frontiers in Credit Risk

Concepts and Techniques for Applied Credit Risk Measurement

Editor

Gordian Gaeta

Co-Editors

Shamez Alibhai and Justin Hingorani

John Wiley & Sons (Asia) Pte Ltd

This publication is designed to provide accurate and authoritative information in regard to the subject
matter covered. It is sold with the understanding that the publisher is not engaged in rendering
professional services. If professional advice or other expert assistance is required, the services of a
competent professional person should be sought.

Other Wiley Editorial Offices

John Wiley & Sons, Inc., 111 River Street, Hoboken, NJ 07030, USA
John Wiley & Sons Ltd, The Atrium, Southern Gate, Chichester P019 8SQ, England
John Wiley & Sons (Canada) Ltd, 22 Worcester Road, Rexdale, Ontario M9W 1L1, Canada
John Wiley & Sons Australia Ltd, 33 Park Road (PO Box 1226), Milton, Queensland 4064, Australia
Wiley-VCH, Pappelallee 3, 69469 Weinheim, Germany

Library of Congress Cataloging-in Publication Data:
ISBN: 0471-47906-3

Typeset in 10.5/13 points, Times Roman by Linographic Services Pte Ltd
Printed in Singapore by Saik Wah Press Pte Ltd.
10 9 8 7 6 5 4 3 2 1

Contents

v

About the contributors

SCOTT D. AGUAIS

Scott Aguais is Senior Director and responsible for managing, marketing and developing Algorithmic's substantial product efforts for BIS II, Economic Capital and Credit Valuation. Prior to joining Algorithmics, Dr. Aguais was a Senior Manager in KPMG's Risk Solutions Practice focusing on credit risk management issues including analytic model development, business process design and technology linkages. He also headed KPMG's global Loan Analysis SystemSM (LAS) initiative. Dr. Aguais has extensive consulting experience in financial services including loan pricing, commercial default modeling, portfolio management strategy and policy design, credit card loan loss forecasting and credit risk MIS implementation. Prior to joining KPMG, he worked for AMS in New York and DRI/McGraw-Hill in Boston. Dr. Aguais education includes, University of Colorado, B.A. in Economics Cum Laude, and a Boston University, M.A. and Ph.D. in Economics.
email: saguais@algorithmics.com

SHAMEZ ALIBHAI

Shamez Alibhai works with Barclays Group Plc in London in the Retail Portfolio Management Unit. Mr. Alibhai is responsible for developing credit risk measurement approaches and risk transfer strategies for the groups' retail portfolio. Prior to joining Barclays, he was a director of Simplex Credit Advisory in Hong Kong, providing credit risk management technologies and solutions. Mr. Alibhai holds Master of Science degrees from McGill and Yale Universities and graduated with an Honours degree in Computer Engineering from the University of Waterloo, Canada.
email: s2alibhai@yahoo.com

EDWARD I. ALTMAN

Edward I. Altman is the Max L. Heine Professor of Finance at the Stern School of Business, New York University. Since 1990, he has directed the research effort in Fixed Income and Credit Markets at the NYU Salomon Center and is currently the Vice-Director of the Center. He received his MBA and Ph.D. in Finance from the University of California, Los Angeles. Professor Altman's primary areas of research include bankruptcy analysis and prediction, credit and lending policies, risk management in banking, corporate finance and capital markets. He has been a consultant to several government agencies, major financial and accounting institutions and industrial companies and has lectured to executives in North America, South America, Europe, Australia-New Zealand, Asia and Africa.

Professor Altman is also one of the founders and an Executive Editor of the international publication, the *Journal of Banking and Finance* and Advisory Editor of a publisher series, the *John Wiley Frontiers in Finance Series*. Professor Altman has published or edited almost two dozen books and over 100 articles in finance, accounting and economic journals including his most recent works on *Managing Credit Risk: The Next Great Financial Challenge (1998)* and *Bankruptcy, Credit Risk and High Yield Junk Bonds (2002)*. His work has also appeared in many languages including French, German, Italian, Japanese, Korean, Portuguese and Spanish.
email: ealtman@stern.nyu.edu

NISSO BUCAY

Nisso Bucay is a Senior Manager in Group Risk Management at Royal Bank Financial Group where he is responsible for research and methodologies of portfolio credit risk models. Prior to joining RBC Mr. Bucay was a senior financial engineer at Algorithmics where he worked in credit risk research and client projects. Before joining Algorithmics, Mr. Bucay was a senior vice-president at Grupo Financiero Banamex-Accival, the largest financial group in Mexico. He also gained experience in modeling mortgage and retail loan portfolios and sundry debtor relief programs undertaken by the Mexican government. He has an M.A. in Economics from Harvard University.
email: nisso.bucay@rbc.com

KEVIN S BUEHLER

Kevin S. Buehler is a principal at McKinsey & Company, where he co-leads the Firm's North American risk management practice. Mr. Buehler's thinking on the topic of risk management can be found in the *Wall Street Journal, Euromoney, Risk Magazine,* and *The McKinsey Quarterly.* Previously, Dr. Buehler served as the Chief Operating Officer of International Equity Partners, L.P., an emerging markets private equity firm. Mr. Buehler received his J.D., *magna cum laude,* from Harvard Law School, where he served as an editor of the *Harvard Law Review,* and his A.B. in Economics, *summa cum laude,* from Harvard College.
email: kevin_buehler@mckinsey.com

EDUARDO CANABARRO

Eduardo Canabarro is the Head of Credit Quantitative Risk Modeling at Goldman Sachs. He is responsible for designing and engineering the quantitative models for measuring, pricing and managing the counterparty risk of various Goldman Sachs' businesses, in particular, over-the-counter derivatives. Prior to that position, he was the quant strategist for fixed-income derivatives (1999), Co-Head of the Fixed Income Quantitative Modeling Group (1998-1999) and a member of that group since 1995 when he joined Goldman Sachs from Salomon Brothers Inc. Dr. Canabarro holds Ph.D. (1993) and MS (1990) degrees in Business Administration (Finance) from the University of California, Berkeley, USA, as well as MBA (1988) and Electrical Engineering (1980) degrees from UFRGS, Brazil.
email: eduardo.canabarro@gs.com

JOHN B. CAOUETTE

John B. Caouette is Vice Chairman of the MBIA Assurance S.A. based in London where he oversees the company's international financial guarantee business and new business development. He joined MBIA in 1998 with the merger of MBIA Inc. and CapMAC Holdings Inc., of which Mr. Caouette had been Chairman and Chief Executive Officer since its inception in 1987. Prior to founding CapMAC, he served in a variety of capacities at Citicorp including as executive director of the Asia Pacific Capital Corporation in Hong Kong, a Citibank subsidiary, and as Vice President and General Manager in the Swaps and Eurosecurities Department. Mr. Caouette was Senior Vice President and General Manager of the Foreign Exchange and Money Market Division of the Continental Grain Company. Mr. Caouette

is lead author of the book *Managing Credit Risk: The Next Great Challenge*, published by John Wiley & Sons in October 1998.
email: jack.caouette@mbia.com

CHRISTOPHER C. FINGER

Christopher C. Finger is Head of Credit Products at the RiskMetrics Group. He is primarily responsible for development of the CreditGrades, CreditManager and CDOManager product lines. Prior to his current position, Dr. Finger headed the research group, where he also has contributed to research into market risk, simulation methods, and the application of risk models in emerging markets. In addition, he has served as editor of the *RiskMetrics* Journal, formerly the *RiskMetrics and CreditMetrics Monitor*. Dr. Finger is a regular speaker at conferences on risk management, and is the author of numerous articles in the field. Before joining the RiskMetrics Group, Dr. Finger worked in Risk Management Services at J.P. Morgan, where he co-authored the CreditMetrics Technical Document, contributed to the RiskMetrics Technical Document, and wrote various articles pertaining to the two methodologies. He also worked on advisory assignments, implementing risk management methodologies for J.P. Morgan clients. Dr. Finger holds a Ph.D. in Applied Mathematics from Princeton University, and a B.S. in Mathematics and Physics from Duke University.
email: chris.finger@riskmetrics.com

LAWRENCE (LARRY) FOREST, JR

Lawrence (Larry) Forest, Jr, is a senior financial engineer in the Research Group. Since joining Algorithmics in 2000, Dr. Forest has worked on new credit applications such as the Credit Valuation System. He has over 10 years of experience in credit research, and has worked previously at KPMG, AMS, DRI/McGraw-Hill, and the Federal Reserve Board. Dr. Forest has a Ph.D. in Economics from the University of California, Berkeley.
email: lforest@algorithmics.com

GORDIAN GAETA

Gordian Gaeta is a director and founder of a range of consulting and advisory firms as well as private equity investment companies in services and light industries predominantly in Europe and Asia. He specializes in developing and implementing analytical solutions for complex strategic issues in financial services and other industries undergoing significant change or being exposed to intricate risk issues.

Two years ago, he co-founded Simplex Credit Advisory, a specialized quant based consulting and applied systems development firm in the area of credit risk measurement using a core model developed by Simplex Risk. In the area of credit and business risk, he brings a wealth of analytical and practical experience as an investor and having been a partner of Booz.Allen & Hamilton Inc dedicated to financial services and strategy related assignments, both at micro and macro economic level. Previously an academic and a bank executive in several countries, Gordian Gaeta holds a doctorate and master in law from the universities of Vienna and Salzburg and read Business Administration at the Zurich Institute of Technology and mathematics at the Vienna Institute of Technology. For the past twenty years, he has been living in Asia but has worked in most developed economies globally.

email: gaetag@netvigator.com

JAMES M. GERARD

Jim Gerard is a Senior Quantitative Analyst in the Fixed Income Division of Fidelity Investments. At Fidelity, Dr. Gerard has worked on mortgage securities valuation models, active portfolio risk exposure analysis and optimization and, most recently, on joint market/credit risk management analytics for the Money Markets Division. Prior to joining Fidelity, Dr. Gerard was a quantitative research analyst at Morgan Stanley in New York. He began his work in finance as an assistant professor of economics at Rutgers University. He holds a B.A. in Physics with a secondary specialization in applied mathematics from Northwestern University, and an M.A. and Ph.D. degree in applied economic theory from the California Institute of Technology.

email: james.gerard@fmr.com

TOM HESKES

Tom Heskes received M.Sc. and Ph.D. degrees in physics from the University of Nijmegen, The Netherlands, in 1989 and 1993, respectively. After one year postdoctoral work at the Beckman Institute in Champaign-Urbana, Illinois, he (re)joined the Dutch Foundation for Neural Networks (SNN) at the University of Nijmegen, where he is currently an assistant professor. Since 1997, Dr. Heskes runs the company SMART Research BV. SMART stands for Statistical Modeling and Artificial Reasoning Technology

and builds intelligent solutions for finance, forecasting, pattern recognition, and decision support in many different application areas. He is a member of the editorial board of *Neurocomputing* and serves as a referee for many international journals on neural networks and machine learning. His research interests are on the interplay between artificial intelligence and statistics.
email: tom@snn.kun.nl

JUSTIN HINGORANI

Justin Hingorani works with Maple Securities (UK) Ltd. in London developing both bespoke structured credit products for clients and Maple's internal credit research practice. Maple is a global financial services company with headquarters in Toronto and offices in London, Jersey City, Frankfurt, Milan and Amsterdam. Mr. Hingorani was formerly a director of Simplex Credit Advisory in Hong Kong, providing credit risk management technologies and solutions. Prior to that he worked with Simplex Risk Management in Hong Kong and Tokyo as well as KPMG in Toronto. He is a designated Chartered Accountant who graduated with a Masters in Accounting, Bachelor of Mathematics and minor in Computer Science from the University of Waterloo, Canada.
email: jhingora@yahoo.co.uk

SEAN C. KEENAN

Sean C. Keenan is currently a Vice President in Citigroup's Risk Architecture Group. He is involved in the development of quantitative tools and methodologies for assessing credit risk including debt rating models for C&I lending, default prediction and early warning systems for large corporate obligors, and risk assessment methodologies for a variety of asset-backed and structured loan products. Prior to joining Citigroup, Dr. Keenan was with Moody's Risk Management Services, where was involved in the development and validation of quantitative credit scoring and default prediction, and default-rate forecasting models, and was the primary author of several Moody's annual corporate bond default studies. Dr. Keenan holds a Ph.D. in Economics from New York University.
email: sean.keenan@citigroup.com

JONGWOO KIM

Jongwoo Kim is Director of the Asian Market at the RiskMetrics Group. He is responsible for developing business and providing risk management research and consulting services to institutions throughout the Asian market. Prior to his current position, he worked in research, where he developed methodologies for long horizon VaR, conditional transition matrices of credit ratings, hypothesis tests of default correlations, and risk management for individual investors. Before joining the RiskMetrics Group, Dr. Kim worked in the Risk Management Services Group at J.P. Morgan, as a researcher and a junior economist in the Monetary Management Department of the Bank of Korea, the central bank in Korea. He holds a Ph.D in Economics from Rutgers University, a M.A. in Finance and a B.Sc. in Business from Seoul National University.
email: jongwoo.kim@riskmetrics.com

SERGEY LYALKO

Sergey Lyalko is a Consultant Software Developer in the Risk Management Department, responsible for quantitative analysis in credit risk. He is employed by Fidelity since 1998. Prior to his role in financial research, he worked as an applied mathematician in several companies abroad and in the US. He received his B.Sc., M.Sc. and Ph.D. in Mathematics from Kiev University in the Ukraine.
email: sergey.lyalko@fmr.com

PAUL NARAYANAN

Paul Narayanan is a credit and financial risk consultant to major financial institutions in the US and abroad on credit and portfolio risk. He has developed and implemented credit risk models and worked in Chase Manhattan Bank, Bank of Boston, Meritor PSFS, and the Resolution Trust Corporation. Mr Narayanan has authored articles in the *Journal of Banking and Finance* and *Financial Analysts Journal*. He has been a speaker in various forums including NYU Stern School, and The Wharton School. He has taught at Drexel University where he also presented a seminar on Financial Dimensions of e-Commerce. He is a co-builder of the Zeta credit risk model, and coauthor of *Managing Credit Risk - The Next Great Financial Challenge*.
email: pauln@mcr2000.com

W. RANDALL PAYANT

Randy Payant an experienced banker, author and consultant, joined The IPS-Sendero Institute in 1993. He conducts research in emerging financial risk management concepts, teaches A/L management workshops, and consults on financial management issues. He has spoken at industry workshops and conferences in over 72 countries worldwide. Before joining IPS-Sendero, he was a senior vice-president with a US-based bank - eight years in credit management and six years in investment and funds management. Mr. Payant graduated from the University of Wisconsin and completed the Stonier Graduate School of Banking program in 1988 where he has returned to the school as a faculty member. He is a guest lecturer at the BAI Graduate School of Banking, the Financial Managers Society and several universities. He also holds the designation of a Certified Risk Professional.
email: randy.payant@ips-sendero.com

MANFRED PLANK

Manfred Plank is a Director in the Credit and Country Risk Measurement Group at UBS AG. Before that, Dr. Plank worked for two years in the Credit Portfolio Management Unit of UBS Switzerland. Prior to joining UBS AG in 2000, Dr. Plank spent three years as a bank regulator. He was member of the working group on the New Capital Accord in Brussels. He holds a Ph.D. in mathematics from the University of Vienna and worked there for four years as an Assistant Professor at the Department of Mathematics and Finance. Dr. Plank has published papers in mathematics, physics, operations research and economics in several academic journals and spoke at a number of conferences.
email: manfred.plank@ubs.com

DAN ROSEN

Dan Rosen is Vice President of Marketing at Algorithmics Incorporated. His responsibilities include setting the strategic direction of Algorithmics' solutions, as well as solutions management, strategy, and marketing communications. Prior to his current role, Dr. Rosen was VP Research and New Solutions. Since joining Algorithmics in 1995, he has headed the design of various market risk management tools, credit risk methodologies, advanced simulation and optimization techniques, as well as their application to several industrial settings. Dr. Rosen is an Adjunct Professor at the University of Toronto's program in Mathematical Finance. He holds

several degrees, including an M.A.Sc. and a Ph.D. in Applied Sciences from the University of Toronto.
email: drosen@algorithmics.com

PAUL S. SERFATY

Paul Serfaty is a director of Asian Capital Partners, an investment bank, and of Vietnam Enterprise Investments Ltd., a Dublin-listed direct investment fund. Based in Hong Kong, he has extensive experience in acquiring debt and equity linked portfolios in the Asian region and managing them from credit and profit centre perspectives. Mr. Serfaty has worked as a banker, lawyer, consultant and entrepreneur, initially in Europe but for the last 14 years in Asia. He established the Asian corporate banking business of Creditanstalt, was its Chief Representative in Tokyo and later General Manager in Hong Kong of Bank Austria. Mr. Serfaty has degrees in science and law from Trinity College, Cambridge and is a barrister.
email: yenji@consultant.com

J. LEE SCOGGINS

J. Lee Scoggins is Managing Director of Transparent Solutions, a risk technology company currently developing new methods for measuring operational and credit risk. Previously, Mr. Scoggins worked with McKinsey & Company as a member of the firm's Risk Management Practice where he worked with major investment banks and insurance firms. Mr. Scoggins has worked closely with the Federal Reserve Board of Governors and the Office of Comptroller of Currency on matters of credit cycles, risk measurement, and bank regulation. Prior to McKinsey, Mr. Scoggins developed neural network technology for measuring corporate credit risk. Mr. Scoggins' work on credit risk has appeared in *The Wall Street Journal*, the *McKinsey Quarterly*, and *The International Herald Tribune*.
email: leescoggins@att.net

ROMAN SCOTT

Roman Scott is a Vice President in the Boston Consulting Group's Singapore office and a senior member of BCG's global financial services practice with over 16 years of experience across 50 financial institutions and agencies. He started work in the UK financial markets, and has since lived and worked in Europe, South Africa, Japan and South East Asia. Mr. Scott leads BCG's

banking risk management and crisis restructuring work in the region. Besides risk management, his expertise also includes corporate strategy, privatization of state owned banks, and private banking. His previous work in Japan's insurance market was the subject of a best-selling business book. He has advised the Singapore Government and Australia's Finance Ministry on capital markets operations. More recently, he has been an advisor to the Indonesian government/IBRA on bank restructuring, and is currently involved in the restructuring, risk management efforts and privatization preparation of the top four banks in Indonesia. Mr. Scott holds an M.Phil. from Pembroke College, Oxford University, and a B.Sc. (Hons) from Manchester University.
email: scott.roman@bcg.com

MARK D. SHAPIRO

Mark D. Shapiro is a Director in McKinsey & Company's New York office where he serves clients in the financial services and professional services industries. Mr. Shapiro has been active in shaping corporate strategy for several major investment banks and was instrumental in founding McKinsey's Risk Management Practice. Mr. Shapiro's work on credit risk has appeared in *The Wall Street Journal*, the *McKinsey Quarterly*, and several leading financial publications. Mr. Shapiro received an M.B.A. degree from Harvard Business School, where he was a Fulbright Scholar. He also holds an M.A. degree in philosophy and economics from the University of Oxford.
email: mark_shapiro@mckinsey.com

JORGE R. SOBEHART

Jorge R. Sobehart is a vice president at Citigroup's Risk Architecture. He is currently involved in the probabilistic assessment of credit risk for portfolio risk management. Previously, he was a member of Moody's Standing Committee on Quantitative Tools and VP/Senior Analyst in Moody's Risk Management Services, where he developed and validated two credit risk models: RiskCalc for public firms and RiskScore. Dr. Sobehart has advanced degrees in Physics and postdoctoral experience at the Los Alamos National Laboratory (a US nuclear-weapons facility). During his career, he has worked and acted as scientific consultant for several prestigious companies and institutions. He has tens of refereed articles, contributions to

conferences, and technical reports in different fields, and acted as referee for several professional journals.
email: jorge.r.sobehart@citigroup.com

JAN-JOOST SPANJERS

Jan-Joost Spanjers received his M.Sc. degree in physics from the University of Nijmegen in 1999. After this, he joined the Dutch Foundation for Neural Networks (SNN) to work on the application of neural network technology to real-world problems. Under contract by SMART Research BV, he researched and implemented applications of neural networks for credit risk analysis and sales forecasting.
email: janj@snn.kun.nl

ROGER M. STEIN

Roger Stein currently heads Moody's development of quantitative and predictive models in credit analysis since joining in 1989. Prior to that he worked rating CBOs and other structured transactions and developing various quantitative methodologies for a number of credit applications at Moody's. Mr. Stein lectures frequently at the NYU Stern School of Business, has published numerous articles and chaired academic and professional conferences on quantitative modeling and data mining. His recent research emphasis includes methodologies for validating the predictive power of quantitative credit models and co-chairing Moody's Academic Advisory and Research Committee.
email: roger.stein@moodys.com

ROBERT J. TUCKETT

Robert Tuckett, who joined Fidelity in 1984, is the Director of Counterparty Research and has been managing the Counterparty Research Group since 1995. Prior to his current position, Mr. Tuckett was a fixed income research analyst, covering financial institutions for Fidelity's money market and corporate bond funds. From 1993 to 1995, he was the Director of Fixed Income Research. Before joining Fidelity, Mr. Tuckett worked for six years at the Federal Reserve Bank of Boston, in the Bank Credit Analysis section. He received his B.Sc. from Northeastern University, and earned his M.B.A. at Boston University.
email: bob.tuckett@fmr.com

MARKUS UNTERHOFER

Markus Unterhofer is an Associate Director in the Alternative Investments Unit of UBS Wealth Management & Business Banking. Prior to this, he spent over two years in the Credit Portfolio Management of UBS, responsible for managing credit risks in the Swiss loan portfolio. There the focus was on risk transformation via secondary market transactions and securitization of parts of the portfolio. Before starting to work for UBS, Mr. Unterhofer was a risk controller for market and credit risks at ABB World Treasury Center in Switzerland, and a portfolio management assistant at Erste Bank AG in Austria. He has two master's degrees from the University of Vienna, one of which in mathematics.

email: markus.unterhofer@ubs.com

Preface

When we were asked to pull together and edit a book on credit risk measurement, we planned a publication that would harness a wide spectrum of topics covering both the analytical aspects and the practicalities of the subject. This should best serve the goal of stimulating and progressing the discussion, criticism and ultimately adoption of credit risk measurement among the credit risk community.

As with any relatively new theme or intellectual progress, many approaches are possible. Differing or overlapping, even contradictory perspectives are commonplace. However, they each contribute in their own way to the furthering of the subject of risk measurement and thus should be considered in support of the objectives for this book. Equally, some contributions have already appeared – in specialized journals – but not including them would deprive the reader from a rounded set of themes.

Conversely, gaps may be perceived as were by some referees. They argued for an inclusion of Basel and the central banks as well as up-to-date data on some of the time series. We countered that structural and forward-looking concepts and ideas do not necessarily extend to multiple areas of implementation or short-term data validation. The longevity and power of the concepts should stand up for itself.

As a result, contributions from a variety of authors with varying points of view, inevitably lack the coherence of a traditional monograph. The subtitle "Concepts and Techniques" already indicates that not all aspects or indeed every particular aspect is fully or comprehensively treated. Yet, the resulting publication covers a wide range of important topics that should be interesting to all parties involved in the credit management process. If we have only contributed in some small way to progressing the views, perspectives and opinions of the reader, our objective is accomplished.

As always, there are a lot of people to thank for their efforts. Most importantly, we thank our publisher John Wiley & Sons, in particular Nick Wallwork, who once he proposed the idea, relentlessly pursued us in keeping to the timetable – which we did not keep even remotely – and forgave us on the way all idiosyncracies that are germane to practitioners, analysts and thinkers alike. Our thanks also go to Janis Soo for the publishing and patient administrative work and support. Given the diverse nature and origin of the contributions, consistency in presentation and language is a formidable challenge for both the editor and the publisher. Thus in many cases concessions had to be made along the principle "where necessary unity but in doubt freedom".

We extend our appreciation and respect to Prof. Dr. Francis Longstaff who was at the origin of the fundamental, structured SCA model approach. In this vein, Simplex Risk Management with Yoshihiro Mikami, Dr. Pratap Soudhi and others contributed greatly to these concepts from which we benefitted.

However, all contributors together have shouldered the largest part of the burden. Thank you for being part of this effort and we hope you are pleased with the outcome. To the many who could not participate, we wish the very best of luck in their efforts to bringing this necessary subject to a wider audience.

Gordian Gaeta, Editor
Shamez Alibhai & Justin Hingorani, Joint Co-Editors
Hong Kong, May 2002

Introduction and Overview

Gordian Gaeta

The book follows a simple logic: from making a case for credit risk measurement and answering the question 'why bother' in part one, part two picks up on some of the yet unresolved issues, suggests some solutions, and covers aspects of the validation of models. This gives some sense of comfort to users that results are not only intuitive but also numerically accurate. Finally, part three collects a range of contributions on practical applications of various credit risk measurement and management approaches.

For non-mathematically inclined readers, most contributions can be read and understood by the text only. It may require several readings and a focus on the conclusions but the key messages generally are there in plain text. The formulas and statistical considerations are often of a higher order but the results and evidence stand up from the graphs or the examples. Only those wishing to fully understand the conceptual rationale will require a serious grounding in mathematics and statistics. For such readers, the proposed solutions could be a valuable contribution to their own research.

In the vein of allowing readers without mathematical inclination to benefit from all contributions, we have included a demo-CD. This CD is meant to give readers the opportunity to test a particular model even without fully knowing the underlying mathematics. The model shows the power of risk measurement as a complement to other existing approaches.

Finally, an extensive bibliography is designed to provide everyone with an opportunity to deepen their knowledge in selected areas of credit risk management.

The following is an overview of the various contributions to the book.

PART 1: THE CASE FOR CREDIT RISK MEASUREMENT AS A NECESSARY BUT NOT SUFFICIENT CONDITION FOR CREDIT RISK MANAGEMENT

This first part of the book makes a case for considering credit risk measurement as a necessary complement to other widely used credit risk management techniques. The case is made on two fronts: one – based on the changing nature of the markets both on the supply and on the demand side and two – based on the deficiencies and failures of incumbent credit risk management tools in financial institutions. Academics, practitioners, and risk product architects agree that these developments have created a gap in the risk management arsenal of most institutions.

Altman and colleagues argue the case from the capital market and credit structuring points of view. Looking at the demand side for credit risk, in essence those willing to buy and hold all or parts of a credit risk, significant structural changes have led to a huge market for credit risk transfer and mitigation. This in turn has prompted the further development of a range of risk assessment, validation, and measurement processes to harness such transactions. Altman and colleagues review the range of available instruments and their underlying philosophy.

In the same vein, Serfaty, looks at the changes in credit relationships and banking from a universal bank point of view. His contention is that due to the changes in the capital markets and the behavior of banks, the nature of credit risk assessment is fundamentally altered from an ex post to an ex ante perspective. This echoes the views of Altman and colleagues who essentially argue that the dominant influence of capital markets over the originators of credit will create a new order. Serfaty recognizes the challenges inherent in the necessary cultural and process changes that commercial banks are likely to face.

Alibhai and colleagues look at the issue from a result perspective. They contend that credit risk management to date is inadequate and review the practices and deficiencies that have led to many credit loss surprises announced by financial institutions in recent times. The regulator's absence in pushing for a more sophisticated approach is noted. To resolve some of the issues identified, the authors propose a concept and model of risk measurement, an abstract and objective measure of the inherent risk in an instrument, obligor or portfolio. The case as a different yet complementary instrument is made and the failure of half-hearted substitutes is explained. Overcoming fallacious industry concerns and gaining practical application experience seems to be at the heart of the problem, not the potential weaknesses of credit risk measurement as a benchmark and complement to other credit risk management techniques.

Finally Payant summarizes the practicalities of using more deterministic approaches and sounds a warning to analytical junkies while encouraging the considerate and calculated use of analytical techniques as a useful but not sufficient set of tools.

PART 2: CONCEPTS AND ISSUES OF CREDIT RISK MEASUREMENT

Having made a case for credit risk measurement as another tool in the armory of risk-takers and managers, part two of this book outlines some of the analytical issues in measuring credit risk. They all deal with factor uncertainties faced by credit risk measurement approaches and seek to import some degree of determinism in otherwise unpredictable outcomes. The issues addressed range from variable cash flows and unpredictable events over implied equity market volatility and asset values to distress measurement under multiple time horizons. Validation of accuracy and performance of such models completes this part.

Aguais and colleagues start the ball rolling by presenting a loan valuation (measurement) framework. They base their analyses on embedded options that are typical for most loan structures and argue the case for capturing state contingent cash flows. To model such embedded options, the authors review the various credit risk measurement models and opt for a ratings-based approach. Applying a state of creditworthiness concept to credit risk measurement leads the authors to recommend a multi-state model incorporating stochastic interest rates and a systemic risk factor.

The notion of events, sudden, unexpected changes in any one factor affecting credit risk, has been largely ignored in most models. In risk measurement they do, however, form an integral part for a forward-looking model. Hingorani and colleagues outline a model to capture and treat events – a separate, random event generator based on historic volatilities of a company's asset values. They conclude that events – both positive and negative, although not symmetric in their occurrence (i.e., bad news events are larger and slightly more frequent than good news events) – must be treated separately. Using a mixture of two normal distributions, however, already approximates event risk. Adding dynamic volatilities and a separate but non-normal event distribution would further enhance the model results. An addendum analyzing the Enron case demonstrates the predictive power of event-based models.

Correlations between assets are another factor strongly affecting the prediction value and measurement of credit risk. Kim and Finger deploy a predictive stress test methodology and use several methodologies to test the correlation breakdown in unusual situations. The correlations of two assets can change significantly – depending on the methodology deployed – more so in hectic day situations with differing distributions and volatility than in quiet periods. The authors argue that the broken arrow test yields a simple one-figure result, and a more reasonable loss figure than other approaches for the most volatile periods.

Overcoming the limitations imposed by the unavailability of equity market information for non-traded or illiquid companies is the goal of the neural networks developed by the team around Spanjers and Heskes. Using a variety of neural networks and network ensembles that replicate the underlying non-linear relationships, the research team concludes that current neural networks can mirror future company equity market data with an error rate of 20–35% with a limited set of balance sheet data. Both market capitalization and volatility can be approximated by these networks across industries, although quarter on quarter fluctuations represent the greatest and yet unsolved challenge.

The contribution of Finger on model comparison deals with multiple time horizons and potentially varying default risk measurements. He reviews the possibilities for extending four single-period models to incorporate multiple time horizons. This investigation is motivated by the rapid growth in structured credit products that not only require default probabilities but also the timing of a potential default. The resulting default distributions demonstrate significant differences, expressed in ratings standards of up to three classes. This would invalidate any of the results of one-time models for multiple-time uses. The author concludes that the choice of a default measurement model is critical to avoid model errors. He proposes the copula method as the most practical choice for multiple time horizons.

Sobehart and colleagues develop a validation framework for evaluating the performance of credit risk measurement models. Undoubtedly, they have set a global standard by introducing a range of logic measures. Adequate validation of default risk models remains the core requirement for practitioners. Not only will high-performing models drive uptake but they will also define the key application areas for credit risk measurement models. Model accuracy, sensitivity and performance are incorporated into three key measures: cumulative accuracy profile, accuracy ratios, and conditional information entropy. These measures allow users to determine more precisely the value derived from credit risk measurement models.

Gerard takes a practical approach in evaluating a specific model – the SCA model – whereby the evaluation approach is more relevant than the model itself. Many of the proposed measures by Sobehart and colleagues are used. Gerard analyzes two distinct data samples used as tests and compares the risk measurement model with the ratings agencies' perspective. He shows the need and a way to evaluate models before buying into their results, regardless of the actual performance on the data sample. With their inherent bias, models tend to perform better in certain segments than in others – the model under consideration is no different. Adjusting the various models to end-user needs will become the key differentiating factor in selecting and using such models.

PART 3: EXTENSION AREAS FOR MEASUREMENT APPROACHES TO CREDIT RISK

As the mechanics and validation of credit risk measurement have been dealt with, this third and last part of the book discusses a wide array of application possibilities and practical issues involving credit risk management and measurement.

Altman and Karlin have been analyzing the US high-yield bond market for some time. The review of the year 2000 is relevant to the credit risk measurement process as the default loss rate was significantly above the weighted annual average of the previous years and a record number of 183 issues from 106 companies defaulted. This marked a period of growing defaults and the contribution sets the tone for an area urgently in need of improved credit risk measurement. Not only are there hardly any benchmarks, but the volume of outstanding and newly issued high-yield debt and consequently their potential loss make this arena a major area of application for credit risk measurement.

OTC derivatives and their embedded credit risk are the focus of the contribution by Canabarro. He explores the differing nature of the credit risk in OTC derivatives and develops models to simulate future credit exposures. Exposure profiles for single-traded and multiple-traded portfolios are reviewed and credit pricing discussed. The author concludes with some observations on risk mitigation and stress-testing.

Buehler, Shapiro and Scoggins explore internal corporate credit portfolios, such as supplier credit, an area hereto largely unmanaged when compared to the efforts of risk management in financial institutions. The treatment of corporate credit portfolios is becoming increasingly important and the authors make a strong argument on the link between internal credit risk and shareholder value. Application of advanced credit risk management methods will become an important factor for industries loaded with vendor finance.

Extending commercial credit risk portfolio techniques to estimating retail portfolio credit loss distribution is the tenor of Bucay and Rosen. They test three default models and capture the correlation of default rates to various macroeconomic factors. Their models measure expected and unexpected loss risk and decompose credit risk in its various sources to provide a better base for managing retail credit portfolios.

The economic rationale for collateralized loan obligations and synthetic transactions are the starting point for Plank and Unterhofer. They review market conditions for structuring and tranching such transactions. The risk economics of such transactions covering internal credit risk models and external ratings for counterparty evaluation, show the differences between internal and external risk assessments. This makes a forceful case for the granularity of internal credit risk measurement models.

Lyalko and Tuckett consider an approach to forecasting worst loss in counterparty exposure. This approach combines a default probability approach, settlement exposure with the credit risk assessment of a portfolio of brokers. The formula presented allows a real worst case replacement cost to be calculated against a set of trades made with several brokers.

Expanding on the contribution by Spanjers and Heskes earlier on, Alibhai and colleagues develop an approach to extending the SCA public company default risk measurement model to private firms. The authors discuss types and existing solutions for private firm credit risk measurement and argue the case for a more structured model. Despite some of the limitations given by the lack of data, the results of private firm credit risk measurement within the SCA framework show interesting and valuable relationships. Although results are outside desired error thresholds, the result of 61% accuracy would justify further suggested improvements and the use of some of the results as a benchmark to currently more qualitative risk assessment methods.

In a more radical extension of the subject, Gaeta applies the structured, fundamental SCA credit risk measurement model to opportunity analysis. By treating potential stock returns as an upside risk and adjusting for investor parameters, the contribution concludes that opportunity assessments are significantly more complex than risk measurements. Nevertheless, a rational application of risk measurement to upside development, yields interesting results. Not only are the probabilities of a particular return veridical over a number of time periods, but the model also provides differentiating and nonlinear probability depending on the target return analyzed. While the model alone seems alone unfit to select stock or determine choice of timing, the results provide a benchmark, validation and structural analysis of investments or portfolios.

Finally, Scott explores from a practical perspective the lessons learnt from the Asian financial crisis with respect to credit risk. Based on extensive experience in advising financial institutions, he outlines practical applications for choosing risk indicators. Reviewing the problems of VaR in emerging markets, the author concludes that refining the traditional credit assessment processes is the first step to improved credit risk management.

Better industry ratings, improving credit officer skills, validating credit manuals, and tightening the decision-making model are all critical parts of the necessary arsenal for emerging markets institutions. Risk management and risk-reporting conclude the prescriptive contribution with respect to emerging markets credit risk management.

SCA CREDITVISION MODEL

The CreditVision model is explained in simple user terms as to their toolbars and screens covering the default risk analysis, the default frequencies and the stock data. This introduction should allow every reader to perform a limited amount of testing using the enclosed CD. The SCA model is but one of the possiblities of measuring credit risk and should only be seen as an example to support the case.

Part 1

**The Case for Credit Risk Measurement
as a Necessary but Not Sufficient Condition
for Credit Risk Management**

CHAPTER 1

Credit Risk Measurement and Management: The Ironic Challenge in the Next Decade

Edward I. Altman, John B. Caouette, and Paul Narayanan
New York University

Interest and concern with credit risk management is escalating, as credit risk management emerges as the next great financial challenge. Lending institutions, primarily commercial banks, have reached a certain maturation stage whereby they no longer simply want to make loans (buy) and hold them either to maturity or charge-off. Stimulated by pressures from regulators, dynamic trading markets, and internal return on equity objectives, banks are increasingly willing to consider transacting their assets in counterparty arrangements whereby the credit risk exposure is shifted with the reduction in total risk of the original lender. Because the markets in which credit assets are hedged or sold are quite young, still fairly illiquid, and probably inefficient, banks and their counterparties are struggling to amass the information and analytical foundations for valuing the underlying assets in some form of meaningful risk-return framework.[1]

This motivation has helped to stimulate the congruent coming of age of four important ingredients for the sophisticated treatment of corporate credit evaluation and management:

- stand-alone valuation techniques;
- attempts to resolve the portfolio credit risk problem;
- comprehensive and fairly reliable relevant databases; and
- the advent and impressive early growth of the structuring and trading of credit risk derivatives and various types of credit insurance and guarantees.

By being more sophisticated in the assessment and laying off of credit risk-related securities and assets, financial institutions can be more aggressive in the creation and trading of new products (e.g., structured instruments). Before addressing these points, one should examine the economic environment that both predates and now surrounds the current surge of interest and activity in credit risk issues.

CREDIT RISK MANAGEMENT AND THE ECONOMIC ENVIRONMENT

Strong emphasis on credit risk management received significant attention throughout most of the world with the structural increase in defaults in the late 1980s and early 1990s. The United States led the way with record bank loan and public corporate bond defaults caused by many ill-fated, highly leveraged restructurings of the mid and late 1980s, an economic recession and the inability of marginal firms to refinance their obligations. Specific sector problems (e.g., in real estate, retailing, deregulated finance, and transport) compounded default problems of the early 1990s.

The junk bond default rate jumped to more than 10% in 1990 and 1991, and many skeptics argued that high credit risk markets, such as leveraged bank lending and junk bond financing, were likely to disappear. This surmise proved to be far from the reality, as new issuances in both of these lending markets has reached record levels in each of the past few years. Indeed, in 1996, high-yield public bond issuance was $66 billion and leveraged loan (low-quality) new issue volume reached $135 billion.

Although these events heightened concern about established credit risk management techniques and the lack of a meaningful credit culture within the world's largest financial institutions, we did not yet witness a pervasive interest in the creation and evaluation of new valuation techniques. What we observed was the occasional stand-alone valuation model, continued refinement of some relevant databases (first established in the mid 1980s), and surveys by regulators and consultants of existing techniques. The surveys invariably reached the conclusion that credit cultures of financial institutions and their lending strategies needed to be rethought and possibly redesigned (see, for example, Wuffli and Hunt 1993).

These calls for reassessment have come at a time of increased competition in lending markets as more varied type of firms are intermediating credit. Corporations no longer need to go to many different types of institutions for their complex borrowing needs. Banks are underwriting credits of all maturities, and securities firms are making loans, as well as underwriting bonds. The concept of a one-stop financial conglomerate has arrived, and with it the reduction of profit margins on traditional lending as the market becomes more competitive.

On the demand side, some investors in credit instruments are trying to enhance their yields by switching to non-traditional markets, such as emerging market debt and asset-backed vehicles, as well as moving down the credit-quality spectrum. In addition, the greater risk that investors are now willing to take, and the low interest rate environment creates greater vulnerability to market risk and, combined with credit-risk migration concerns (i.e., the risk that a firm's credit rating will drift downward), can result in mark-to-market losses, even if default incidence continues to be low. Recent default related losses in the Collaterized Debt Obligation (CDO) market have underscored the vulnerability of mark-to-market positions of leading financial institutions.[2]

STAND-ALONE RISK PROCEDURES

The foundation for any comprehensive treatment of a credit portfolio of loans and/or bonds is the initial assessment of the risk of each asset in the portfolio on a stand-alone basis. If the analysis is faulty or incomplete as to the default and credit migration risk of the underlying entity, then no matter how sophisticated the portfolio algorithm, the end result will be of little use. Stand-alone credit risk measurement involves a growing array of analytical techniques from univariate, qualitatively weighted quantitative systems, and qualitative variable credit-scoring systems to an increasing number of more sophisticated procedures. These other approaches have included multivariate regression, discriminate and logit statistical models, models based on contingent claims and market price proxies for asset value coverage of debt obligations, and finally, artificial intelligence procedures to either predict default or replicate the bond rating results of established bond rating agencies. The latter objective is critical because it is directly related to one of the caveats on any credit evaluation system: Regardless of the credit scoring system used, the results should be linked to capital market indicators and experience. We suggest that the appropriate capital market indicators are bond ratings. Not because we believe that the rating agencies have the best models and results with respect to default likelihood, but because the relevant databases on default and migration risk patterns are primarily based on the bond rating of the underlying credit. Hence, if the data that we used is based on ratings, then the scoring system should be tied to ratings.

We have mentioned several times the notion of credit risk migration. In essence, the ultimate negative migration is from some initial state to a default (i.e., from a performing asset to one that either has missed a periodic interest payment or for which a distressed restructuring is accomplished whereby the creditor receives a lower interest payment, an extension of the time period for repayment, and/or a more risky claim on the asset than the initial contract specified). In addition, credit risk involves the possibility that the inherent risk of the asset migrates to a lower quality level, thereby resulting in lower security values in a mark-to-market pricing environment.

The final ingredient of the credit risk assessment of individual loans/bonds is the loss to the creditor if the asset quality deteriorates or if it actually defaults. This step mainly involves assessing the impact of the recovery level given a default, although the impact of a change in credit quality on the security's value is also relevant. The recovery rate concept is extremely important, but it is given small, if any, consideration in traditional bond rating systems. Some rating agencies adjust for expected recoveries by reducing the senior unsecured bond rating equivalent for bonds of lower seniority levels and explicitly consider recovery levels in the bank loan rating programs. Other agencies state that recoveries are explicitly considered.

On the other hand, financial institutions of all types and the rating agencies themselves realize that the recovery on defaulted assets plays an important role in assessing credit-risk loss, and we can expect increased research and resources to be spent on the empirical investigation of historical recovery experience, particularly of non-publicly traded private debt.[3]

To summarize, the stand-alone, individual asset ingredient in credit risk management systems involves credit-scoring procedures, assessments of negative event probabilities, and the consequent losses given these negative migration or default events. Although for many years we have been emphasizing the important link between credit scoring procedures and capital market experience, an institution that ties its own scoring system to its own portfolio's historical experience is certainly justified in using its own files to assess risk and losses. The experience of the bank, however, or several banks that agree to pool their data, must be rich enough in terms of statistical quantity and data reliability to provide meaningful future estimates.

PORTFOLIO MODELS

The return distribution on risky debt assets is not nearly as normal as it is on equities. Whereas the debt investor is usually limited to the promised yield or slightly higher returns (given positive credit migration), the potential downside is total. The expected return distribution is, therefore, skewed toward lower than promised returns with a fairly large (fat) tail at default forward/levels. Hence, traditional mean return variance of return models are not appropriate, although they may be robust enough to use over the short term (e.g., one month or one quarter) measurement periods.

The search for alternative portfolio schemes seems to be heading either in two directions: Monte Carlo simulation of possible returns on a credit portfolio, or using a proxy-measure of risk, other than the variance of return, in a return-risk trade-off measure. One proxy that has received increased attention of late is the unexpected loss on individual loans or portfolios of loans based on some estimated distribution around the expected loss. In this approach, the expected loss estimate can be used in adjusting the promised yield to obtain the expected return. The unexpected loss is a by-product of this analysis and is an outcome that requires capital reserves. In all portfolio models, however, the illusive ingredient is to properly and reliably estimate risky-event correlations between assets. Little agreement exists as to how this estimate should be achieved, although meaningful attempts are being made by analyzing the time-series correlations of rating series, equity prices, or variables that explain equity prices and/or defaults.

DATABASES

In both the stand-alone and portfolio treatment of fixed-income assets, the solutions are dependent on the methodology used and the data inputs to the models. Among the most important data inputs are the expected default rates and migration (drift) patterns from the asset's internal credit rating. Fairly comprehensive databases exist on these inputs, the criteria being the bond rating from Moody's Investor Service or Standard & Poor's Corporation, either from original issuance or based on a basket of bonds at some point in time and then observed for subsequent years. Databases are available covering default and migration experience back to at least 1970.

In addition to default and migration rates, a third important input is the recovery rate on defaults, for which the critical distinguishing feature of the bond or loan is its seniority. Although data for recoveries on bonds are fairly comprehensive, data for recoveries on defaulted bank loans are quite inferior, and this statistic needs more study. Although financial institutions may choose to use their own databases, rather than rely on rating agency inputs, the reality is that few institutions have extensive historical data that is based on the credit scoring system currently in place. Hence, reliance on public data is likely to be the route that most decision-makers will take, at least in the near future.

CREDIT RISK DERIVATIVES AND CREDIT ENHANCEMENT MECHANISMS

The final factor related to the increased motivation for creating sophisticated credit evaluation and management techniques is the advent of and impressive early growth in the credit risk derivative and the corporate credit enhancement/financial guarantee markets. Selling a credit asset outright is no longer necessary if, for some reason, the original lender no longer wants to assume the credit risk. Relatively simple and also more complex financial instruments are being devised to set up a type of insurance mechanism for transferring the risk of default and also the risk of migration in the case of total return derivatives. These instruments have created new and dynamic counterparty exposures.

The credit derivatives market is growing as banks, securities firms, corporations, and other institutions seek to hedge their credit exposures or realign their lending portfolios. In the past five years, this market has grown considerably, with many of the major securities firms providing the liquidity by immediately finding counterparties or taking on the insurance risk themselves, confident that a counterparty will soon be found (see Parsley 1996 and McDermott 1997). The derivative seller provides insurance against any event (e.g., default) that changes the value of the underlying asset. In all of these cases, the relationship between the original borrower and lender is preserved.

Financial guarantees provide, in some cases, a leaner, less ambiguous form of credit derivative because no question arises of a change in ownership of the asset if some credit event occurs. The guarantor simply pays off the original lender based on some predetermined formula. This arrangement is particularly useful in the case of a non-transferable loan.

The seller counterparties in credit risk derivative transactions, or the more traditional credit insurance providers, are increasingly mindful of managing and trading their own credit portfolios. Hence, these institutions are particularly interested in techniques that combine the stand-alone and portfolio aspects of their revenue-based assets. The credit risk derivative and credit enhancement markets have been improving, and will continue to improve, the credit market's liquidity and vice versa. This development, in turn, will require more accountability and will also motivate attempts to price the products more profitably.

CONCLUSION

We are witnessing an impressive escalation in analytical resources devoted to more effective management of credit risk. The primary motivating factors include refinements of traditional techniques to evaluate the default likelihood of individual assets, new analytical solutions to credit portfolio management, larger and improved databases to translate risk ratings into expected losses, and the dynamics of market mechanisms such as credit derivative and credit enhancement techniques. When and if defaults increase in the near future, we can expect even more refinements and perhaps further breakthroughs in credit portfolio management.

NOTES

[1] This article is based on the author's book, *Managing Credit Risk: The Next Great Financial Challenge*, from John Wiley & Sons, 1998.

[2] In a related report, we estimated that US public bond defaults will approximate $22 billion (face value) in the 1997–1999 period. See Altman, Schimpf and Seltzer (1997).

[3] Many studies have documented the recovery experience on corporate bonds, including Altman and Eberhart (1994), Altman and Kishore (1996), Carty and Lieberman (1997), and Standard & Poor's Corporation (1997). Moody's Investor Service also has estimated the recovery rate on a small sample of defaulted corporate bank loans in Carty and Lieberman (1996). A study by Altman and Suggitt (1997) documents the recent default rate experience on bank commercial and industrial loans.

CHAPTER 2

The Changing Nature of Credit Relationships and Banking

Paul S. Serfaty
Creditanstalt-Bank Austria

TRANSITION FROM RELATIONSHIP TO MARKET-BASED CREDIT RISK MANAGEMENT

Historically, credit-oriented banking has been primarily relationship driven rather than quantitative in character. The traditional view that the character of the borrower was more important than its reported financial position is reflected in the maxim that "character is the foundation of credit". This view has only gradually been supplanted with the growth of computing power and the resultant ability to apply progressively more sophisticated statistical analyses to companies, markets, large numbers of individual borrowers, industries, and portfolios.

However, when the availability of data is compromised in quantity or quality, then credit risk management is necessarily more dependent on the subjective elements of credit assessment. Traditionally, the credit quality of a portfolio was the result of a series of micro decisions about borrowers (Figure 2.1). These were hedged by relatively gross controls such as single obligor, country and industry limits.

Today, the banking industry is undergoing a radical transformation in which relationship and origination ceases to be a core activity of the business, and portfolio management becomes its defining characteristic instead. This change has been made possible by the growth of data driven analytical tools, credit agency ratings, credit scoring and statistical risk management techniques that can be continually validated against real-world experience. In other words, origination activity now responds to the search for a superior trade-off between earnings volatility and the cost of capital. This means that the risk return trade-off that is attractive to a financial institution (FI) and its shareholders is defined *ex ante* rather than emerging

FIGURE 2.1 Relationship-based credit cycles tend to reinforce existing patterns

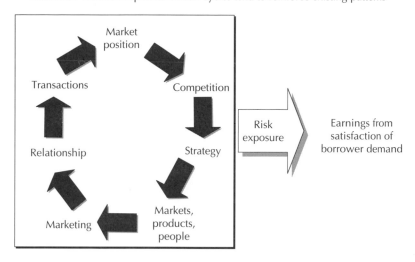

ex post from the FI's marketing. This shift is gradual only and depends on the specific circumstances of the financial institution.

Thus, for a small Indonesian bank with significant exposure to retail clients and small, private businesses, it is unlikely that the key risk questions will be answered by reference to statistical models on a client's financial standing. The problems of data collection, data reliability and data comparability are all quite obvious, and the importance in traditional communities of reputation, social networks, and other cultural factors is very much more important than the balance sheet or cash flow statement.

By contrast, a global commercial/investment bank such as JP Morgan Chase deals in markets that, on the whole, offer extremely reliable financial information, available in acceptably long time series and relating to a sufficiently broad and diverse range of client and product types. This allows the advantages of statistical analysis and the benefits of eliminating correlation risks. In addition, the scale and complexity of this analytical process calls for a very significant commitment of intellectual and financial capital, not easily available, or even acceptable in a smaller bank.

Even for a global commercial/investment bank, the constraints imposed by imperfections in available data remain quite real. For example, it is extremely difficult to find, across Asian markets, the range and reliability of data enjoyed in the markets of North America. Therefore, while considerable value added is brought to the risk/return profile of a major global lender through the application of statistical processes, it remains necessary to retain the capacity to evaluate risk according to qualitative methods. The option also exists for an FI to exclude itself from participating in markets where the internal risk/credit management practices of the FI do not fit its strategic outlook, or capacities.

Whether or not a process of self-exclusion takes place, the shift in focus away from a micro, relationship-based credit management process towards a portfolio-driven approach to banking, has induced many major banks, despite their still substantial balance sheets, to consider themselves temporary warehouses for assets. In their "new world", originated assets would be traded through to other distributors and investors with varied appetites for different forms of risk.

A NEW RISK PORTFOLIO WITH DIFFERENT MANAGEMENT REQUIREMENTS

The role of the bank then becomes to bundle and classify a wide range of credit risk exposures into pools of exposures for distribution to a global investor base. The origination function is thus driven by the distribution function, and the distribution function in turn by the risk appetite of the ultimate investor (Figure 2.2). Under this model, the investor rather than the borrower is the _de facto_ primary client, even in the commercial banking system.

This process is not limited to the allocation of simple types of debt obligation of a given credit class, but it also results in the creation of different classes of obligations in relation to the same borrower or class of borrower. This again emphasizes the subordination of the borrower relationship to the imperatives of distribution.

The majority of more traditional banking institutions (smaller origination banks in Asia, mid-size European banks, etc.) continue to be dominated by the marketing relationship function. In larger institutions of a more global nature, an internal dynamic – even tension – is built up and not yet fully

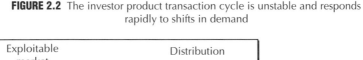

FIGURE 2.2 The investor product transaction cycle is unstable and responds rapidly to shifts in demand

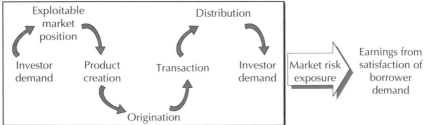

resolved between the long-established credit evaluation functions and the risk management perspective.

The distinction between risk assessment and risk management has tended to become more important as the risk measurement tools become more precise and better validated. This reinforces the trend toward the dominance of quantitative measures of risk and toward a more homogenous treatment of market segments having similar financial characteristics.

The tendency of human thought is to give more weight to what is capable of measurement than to what cannot easily be represented in figures or precise language. This means that, as institutions develop more sophisticated models and as managers in those institutions invest more in the mastery of those models, institutions will tend to service markets in ways that offer the best fit with their risk assessment processes. In the final analysis, if a product or a market does not fit the process or model, then institutions tend to avoid participating in that area of business, rather than sacrifice the comfort provided by the model.

Further, as institutions use the power of data management offered by progressively more powerful computer systems, there is a tendency to centralize the application of systems on a uniform basis across a wide range of geographies and products. Other changes reinforce this trend, particularly the push towards mark-to-market valuation of financial assets including loans, because any deviation from anticipated values has an immediate impact on the institution's profit and loss account.

The risk management of institutions is thus increasingly driven by models based on the statistical variability of net asset values implied by the financial structure of the business concerned. Whatever might be the detailed differences within each model, an institution's response to market opportunities will be driven by its appetite for a risk forward/return trade-off defined *ex ante*.

For banks, as for large investing institutions, it is difficult to lift performance above the average when using similar mathematical models for risk management (because the similarity of the models results in similar decision-making outcomes). The core of the business is then defined by strategic resource allocation decisions, reducing the scope at any given level of management for independent commercial decision-making, and emphasizing instead the institutionalized application of detailed rules. This in turn implies a gradual unbundling of product and services and the abandonment of business lines that do not offer adequate returns on capital or fit the perceived cultural buyers of the organization.

Thus, instead of being client-centered and operating a product development cycle designed to deliver services to a customer based on the asset side of the bank's balance sheet, institutions become oriented toward a product cycle that services a potentially variable investor basis. Thereby, institutions become driven by the demands of short-term relationships and counterparties to whom the traditional intermediate roles of banks are irrelevant.

Traditional lending institutions then become a holder of buffer stock for investors, and their client base becomes a source of raw material for restructuring and packaging different investment pools for the end-buyer of financial products. This necessarily shifts the culture of the credit institutions much more toward that of an investment bank, where risk is passed to investors and not held. Insofar as a credit institution accepts exposure to risk, the risk is evaluated as a trading risk, where issues of liquidity and market value are far more critical than the underlying financial strength of the borrower/issuer.

It is true that a market price will in principle reflect all material issues relating to financial strength and therefore the credit institutions and its credit relationship to its client should not be affected by whether risk is measured by qualitative/quantitative combinations or by the price/yield indicator. However, where market measures predominate, the credit relationship ceases to be the relevant one and only the market's view matters.

We therefore have the paradox that the development of progressively more sophisticated management tools helps convert parts of the banking sector from a customer-centered, credit-providing model to a market-driven trading model. Consequently, risk assessment models developed by individual institutions may be valued most not because they help to avoid credit risk as such, but because they help to avoid the adjustment of price that is the reflection of credit risk as seen through the markets.

The above changes represent significant progress, in that they should in principle allow the financial system, through specialization, to deliver a wider range of products with greater efficiency, reducing transaction costs in the allocation and distribution of capital between providers and users of capital.

CHAPTER 3

Credit Risk Measurement: A Necessary Dimension of Credit Risk Management

Shamez Alibhai, Gordian Gaeta and Justin Hingorani
Simplex Credit Advisory Ltd

Credit risk is inadequately managed today. The evidence can be found regularly in the announcements and results of major banks and financial institutions. What these institutions are often missing is an objective and forward-looking dimension to complement the existing credit risk management culture. Having an abstract benchmark and quantifying the propensity of an unexpected loss is a pressing need for today's financial institutions. Regulators are not helpful in fostering a new approach.

Credit risk measurement, still in its infancy, provides such a necessary tool. Risk measurement takes an unbiased view of credit risk by using quantitative and objective data input — no risk, return trade-offs and no qualitative factors are considered. Models are independent from an institution's credit franchise and competence.

An additional and abstract measure invariably leads to significant cultural and managerial resistance. Such concerns are unwarranted. Credit risk measurement only represents a complement or necessary dimension to existing processes, not a substitute.

THE CURRENT STATE OF CREDIT RISK MANAGEMENT

Credit risk management starts invariably with the origination of credit driven by an institution's appetite for loan assets. Once assets are booked, risk assessment and mitigation processes are applied to track and adjust developments in the credit profile, estimate expected losses and safeguard the capital deployed. Most of the steps in credit origination, underwriting, and reviews are based on judgment. While spreadsheet analyses and direct customer information form the analytical starting point, grading and pricing is a judgmental activity drawing on historic experience and best efforts on looking over the term of the loan. This comes with the nature of customers and competition. Customer relationships are built on mutual understanding and realistic forecasts, competition for good credit is fierce and institutions differentiate themselves by their credit culture — the cumulative experience and process integrity of an organization.

As it is the role of financial institutions to provide credit, there are many incentives to build the credit portfolio and, in the absence of external benchmarks, credit culture becomes a competitive advantage. This capability is invariably linked to judgment.

Unfortunately, the strong emphasis on credit risk assessment processes as a key input to the risk management process invariably leads to risk management processes that do not portray a complete picture of an institution's risk position.

Risk assessment, monitoring, and improvement strategies and tools are closely linked to present-state analyses. Their goal is to optimize current revenues from the existing portfolio in light of the best available information and market conditions. After all, yearly results drive stock price, determine the value of executive stock options and are the base for compensating staff. Together this cements a present-time and short-term perspective.

To cover the short-term downside, potential event risk is covered by stress-testing and scenario analysis. Typically, intuition or some heuristic method is used to test possible conditions and gauge how the relationship reacts. The lack of knowledge on the likelihood and amplitude of occurrence of the tested factors is the very weakness of experience-based stress tests.

Similarly, scenario analysis is fraught with problems. While the likelihood of scenarios materializing is a valid judgment made by the institution – indeed not much different than the judgment made for the institution's strategy overall – the potential impact on the instrument, obligor or portfolio is highly uncertain.

Consequently, risk management processes are biased toward the shortcomings in the institution's risk assessment process. Generally, these processes, supported by increasingly uniform regulatory requirements, share a number of generalized deficiencies.

Obligor Risk Analysis

The assessment and management of risk at the obligor level is an important component of the credit origination process and represents the first opportunity to control the risk profile (see Figure 3.1).

To this effect, banks develop limit systems and underwriting standards. Limit systems for credit risk are fairly similar across institutions. They define

FIGURE 3.1   Credit risk management today focuses on obligor origination

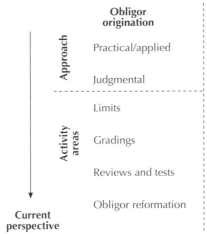

the maximum acceptable exposure within a geography, an industry, particular credit ratings, or grades. Generally, banks do not have a dynamic limit system whereby changing one limit would affect another limit to reflect correlation risks. They are typically independent maximum exposure boundaries.

Within limits, which are reviewed regularly, underwriting standards determine the type and nature of business to be accepted. Authority levels required for each facility and rules for covenants are defined. The most important underwriting standard consists of grading or rating each facility or customer. In this respect, banks and other financial institutions vary considerably in their approach — first, as to what they grade and second, on how they grade.

The majority of players grade customers or groups rather than facilities. There are also differences with respect to the inclusion of collateral in the credit grade and a differing perspective on grading customer default probability or likely loss in the event of default. A number of players adopt the rating agency approach and disallow higher grades for customers or facilities than the underlying risk domicile or sovereign.

There are three generic approaches to customer gradings: purely qualitative, mixed, and purely quantitative. The vast majority of banks have a mixed approach differentiated by the relative weight of analytical and qualitative factors and the degree of influence given to specific factors. On one side of this spectrum are institutions with a rigorous balance sheet model, including external rating comparisons, whereby the resulting grade can only be moderately varied by qualitative factors, say, for example, the assessment of management of the obligor.

On the other side of the spectrum, grades are the result of individual credit staff assessments of the customer's market potential, management competence, and technology resources with very limited useful balance sheet information. For Internet, new technologies, or innovation-based companies this is often the only possible approach. Regardless, of the specific credit grading process, gradings mostly represent a point-in-time assessment of the obligor based on available, current, or projected information.

To date, facility and obligor gradings are reviewed regularly, at least annually, and periodically when new information warrants such a review. The risk-monitoring process is intended to provide a dynamic perspective on the obligor or facility and cumulative risks taken at any point in time. Leading institutions may review the risk grade of their major customers or facilities in difficult times more than 10 times a year and thus have an up-to-date handle on the perceived risk. Certainly, most institutions review outstanding credits of customers below acceptable grade more than once a year.

A common, in some countries, obligatory practice of obligor risk assessment validation is the external credit review. They provide the board or credit committee with an external and professional assessment on the adequacy of typically the largest credits, albeit within the framework set by the organization.

Reviews are often combined with intuitive stress-testing. For example, banks often model within a worst case (imaginable) scenario the interest coverage against interest rate changes. These stress tests add to the realism of the risk assessment and to the soundness of continuing a credit relationship. Some banks also use scenario techniques to model external variables and estimate the potential impact on the obligors of their credit portfolio. Unfortunately, both approaches suffer from the need to have a good likelihood of occurrence and cause and effect understanding as to the sensitivity of customers to these potential changes. Generally, this information is not forthcoming as many companies do not know themselves. Thus, the true impact of an abrupt change in external variables on credit risk remains largely qualitative in nature. Few, if any banks, have institutionalized this testing process at obligor level.

The final measure, obligor default projections, is by no means ubiquitous in financial institutions. If they exist, projections are made on the basis of matching credit grades allocated to obligors or facilities with internal or rating agency default data. Increasingly, financial institutions are trying to adopt the loss history of these rating agencies for each grade. The result is a historic default rate that is common to all obligors in the same credit class.

Currently, most institutions compute their loss risk to selected obligors. Depending on the level and nature of collateral or security held, recovery rates based on experience are established and the net remaining exposure level is calculated. This net exposure can then be multiplied by the historic default rate of the credit grade assigned to the obligor to arrive at a loss projection.

Portfolio Risk Analysis

The second pillar of risk-related credit management is focused around the risk profile of the institution or portfolio (see Figure 3.2). This process generally starts with setting credit strategy and policy. Banks use several variations of model portfolios for planning purposes: some have a bucket system whereby aggregate risks, for example by maturity, geography, industry and asset class, are evaluated and budgeted for the institution as a whole. This comes close to defining a target portfolio based on credit grades and secondary market liquidity.

More advanced variations of credit portfolio planning utilize matrices that match obligor categories by risk grade with risk capital requirements based on historical defaults.

Portfolio analyses and loss estimation constitute the final and most critical element of credit management. Almost all financial institutions have some databases on their overall credit loss history. Although their memories may be short, their data shows losses by grade, industry, and sometimes segments or asset classes over a long time period. These historic losses were incurred within a specific macroeconomic or monetary context and can be calibrated against these external variables. Thus both volatility and an apparent cause and effect relationship between losses and the economic environment can be established. The volatility of provisions and write-offs

FIGURE 3.2 Portfolio management is an emerging, but as yet exploratory, perspective

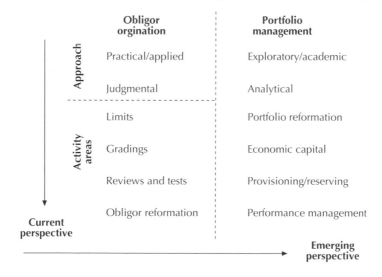

as a percent of assets forms the first line of planning and defining expected portfolio losses.

A complementary activity takes the average credit grade of the portfolio in comparison with historic losses and volatilities in light of prevailing macroeconomic conditions. Analysis of specific obligors in the current portfolio is not required. The averaging of past experience implies that aggregate models cannot, in general, take account of obligor specific factors. This average approach will include some adjustment for the structure or potential distribution of the portfolio with reference to historic losses.

Overall macroeconomic and industry analyses are used to make qualitative adjustments to the level of expected portfolio losses. These overall analyses also tend to be used in assessing the systematic risk of the portfolio defined as the risk resulting from the interdependence of market-wide macroeconomic and fundamental factors. The measure of impact is generally based on historic experience and long time series with arguably fairly constant correlations.

More advanced variations of credit portfolio analysis utilize credit transition matrices that estimate risk capital requirements based on historical defaults. The sophisticated mathematics that govern these models use ad-hoc and/or simplified assumptions about correlations between obligors. The portfolio is divided into smaller buckets based on common characteristics. The inter- and intra-bucket correlations are calibrated from historical default data and can be used to simulate future default or credit transition events.

Unfortunately, no matter how much credit assessment tools are honed, they always fall short of delivering an objective and abstract benchmark or risk measure at both obligor and portfolio level.

Regulator Approaches

No single approach to ensuring adequate capital adequacy is common to regulators. In each market, the regulatory approach is influenced by the legal, market, and political forces at play. In particular, the risk management approach is greatly determined by the sophistication of risk management practices at banks in the regulator's jurisdiction. In more developed banking economies, the regulatory approach to credit risk management lags the best practices of the most sophisticated banks.

Against this backdrop of varying standards and approaches, the Basel Committee has approached the problem of ensuring uniformity and consistency across markets by establishing guidelines and standards of best practice for its member and participating countries. In light of the responsibility of regulators to market participants and the Committee's need to satisfy a range of constituents, the recommendations of the Basel Committee tend to take a conservative approach and lag market developments in the area of credit risk measurement.

The first Basel Capital Accord applied an ad-hoc and experience-based approach to measuring credit risk — whereby the credit risk of a counterparty was derived from the type of credit it represented. This first attempt at setting a common standard had the side-effect of charging too much capital to the best credits and not enough capital to the worst credits. In response to this situation, financial institutions have engaged in forms of regulatory arbitrage that in some cases compromised their credit risk worthiness.

The subsequently proposed Capital Adequacy Approach makes a stronger attempt at linking the risk associated with a counterparty to the amount of regulatory capital that is required. At the heart of this approach, is the alignment of the risk assessment to the required regulatory capital. While the proposed accord does allow for a variety of approaches in assessing risk, based on either a bank's internal processes or external ratings, the idea of risk assessment is still central to the approach.

In the proposed accord, financial institutions will be allowed to select their risk management approach from a menu of options. At the highest level, institutions must choose from either the "standardized approach" or the "Internal Ratings Based" (IRB) approach.

For institutions without the capability to measure credit risk on their own, the accord proposes a "standardized approach", whereby the financial institution can rely on ratings provided by external rating agencies. The onus is upon the regulator to map the agency ratings into capital requirements through setting average default probabilities.

The IRB approach allows banks to apply their own internal ratings. Banks adopting the IRB approach will assign default probabilities to counterparties based on internal credit grades assigned. The proposal recognizes three techniques for mapping the risk grade to a default probability:

1. historical average default probabilities based on internal default experience;
2. mapping internal grades to external rating agencies;
3. statistical default models.

The emphasis on the risk grade is maintained even in those instances where the financial institution would be capable of assigning individual default probabilities for each borrower. In such cases, the proposed accord requires that the default probability of the grade, computed as an average of the individual default probabilities, be applied in computing the risk-weighted assets.

For both the standardized and the IRB approaches, the default probability for a single firm is a function of its risk assessment, either externally or internally derived. This approach reflects the processes applied by most of banks in the OECD and by the leading non-OECD banks.

As a consequence of the proposed accord, the regulator's mandate will be broadened to ensure the validity of the processes and techniques used to estimate default probabilities. The philosophy of the regulatory approach in measuring credit risk is summarized in the directive provided to banks in estimating default probabilities (PD):

"Each estimate of PD must represent a conservative view of a long-run average PD for the borrower grade in question and thus must be grounded in historical experience and empirical evidence. At the same time, these estimates must be forward looking."[1]

While the intent of the directive is well-meaning it is inherently flawed. There exists an incongruity between a process that is grounded in historical experience and one that attempts to be forward-looking. The distinction between frequency, derived from historical occurrence, and probability, based on a model of future events, needs to be recognized if the regulator and their constituents are to fulfill this "mission impossible".

SUMMARY DEFICIENCIES OF CURRENT PRACTICES

The credit risk management practices used by financial institutions are dependent upon their risk assessment practices. Furthermore, the evolving regulatory opinion is also being steered in this direction. With current risk assessment practices deeply rooted in the credit culture and experience of an institution, they fail in two key respects. They are:

- not objective or abstract;
- insufficiently predictive.

They are inherently judgmental and history-based (see Figure 3.3).

FIGURE 3.3   The current procedure to estimate losses is wanting

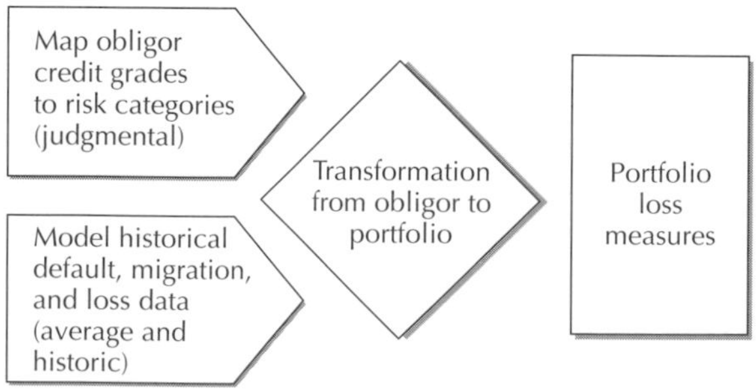

Without an impartial view of credit risk, event and systemic portfolio risks are obfuscated. The extent to which these shortcomings manifest themselves in the credit risk management activities of financial institutions tends to vary. In their different forms, however, they conspire to undermine effective credit risk management by obscuring the level of risk and potential loss facing an institution. This reduces efficient capital management. Emergency action to cover unexpected losses and less than required capital adequacy can be the consequence. Moreover, credit profitability potentially suffers.

These shortcomings also effect the regulator's ability to provide an independent and objective assessment of an institution's credit risk. The consequences for the financial system are more severe as the risk for the entire industry may be incorrectly represented. Unfortunately, given current directives, the possibility that the mandated regulatory capital is underestimated will only be known after a crisis. These potential consequences are not the result of poor competence or even poor judgment, but are a result of the inherently experience-oriented credit management and regulatory processes applied to credit risk management.

THE CRITICAL ROLE OF RISK MEASUREMENT

Risk assessment and risk measurement are two separate activities. The former is based on judgment and "soft" concerns, while the latter is a numeric concept.

Risk measurement takes an unbiased view of an institution's credit risk. Consequently, the inputs to risk measurement are quantitative and objective – they exclude "soft" factors. Additionally, the models and computations are different – they are abstract from the institution's other credit processes.

Using the same analyses for risk assessment and risk measurement fails simply because the former is designed to address the "soft factors" of the credit book and preserve the integrity of the process with all its implied judgments and preferences.

Conversely, risk measurement models can hardly be used to address the needs of the credit assessment function. Any impartial risk-based system would reject many of the assets in a credit book based on some future danger signal. For example, an institution may accept potentially large risks in order to maintain a strategic presence. Similarly, competition among the commercial banks has forced an easing of underwriting standards, although the credit quality of obligors may be worsening. Lastly, companies in "sunset" industries or smaller, volatile firms would be starved across the board.

The main characteristics of risk assessment and risk measurement show these differences (see Table 3.1):

TABLE 3.1   Differences between risk assessment and measurement

Risk assessment	Risk measurement
• Specific	• Abstract
• Qualitative/Quantitative	• Quantitative
• Internal data	• External data
• Current state	• Predictive
• Imaginable	• Unthinkable
• Perceived	• Actual
• Revenue generation	• Risk reduction

What is absent today, is a measurement dimension and approach that:

• uses different data and considerations than the original analyses to provide an objective perspective;
• ignores the qualitative attributes of a credit to be as abstract as possible with respect to each facility and obligor.

Used as a benchmark, such a measurement process provides an independent and numeric decision support tool to validate credit policy and credit decisions, and act as an arbiter in capital and reserving decisions.

THE FAILURE OF CURRENT MEASUREMENT SUBSTITUTES

Attempts to move from a judgmental risk assessment approach to an objective and abstract measure does not provide a solution. Independent models are the only valid development.

Common practice to map from a subjective ordinal grading system into a numeric concept of risk cannot be considered risk measurement. The grading-to-risk mapping process as a measure fails for four reasons:

1. gradings are based on subjective assessment;
2. gradings tend to blur the differences between obligors;
3. the mapping outcome is not predictive;
4. mapping internal grades to agency ratings is error-prone.

A measure of risk is by its nature a numeric and objective construct. Therefore, there exists a fundamental incompatibility in trying to convert a grading that was based upon subjective concerns into an independent measure. The acceptance of a bank's internal risk assessment as a base for a risk measure level is allowing "the fox to guard the hen house" or creating a serious moral hazard problem.

Second, the grading process is inherently coarse. In the United States, the average number of credit classes for non-loss obligors is five. If the number of classes was increased substantially, it would render the grading process too difficult for the subjective assessment used by credit officers. Thus we must accept that the number of grading classes must be small. As a consequence of coarse grading classes, individual differences between obligors are smoothed out. Each obligor in the same credit grade is necessarily assigned the same risk measure. In effect, we treat the risk contribution from each obligor identically.

To convert a grade into a risk measure, that is a default probability, requires the availability of a large database of obligor default histories. Historical data by its nature is backward-looking and can only reflect a change in a situation after it has happened. It has no recognizable value for looking into the future. In emerging economies, the difficulties with using historical data are compounded by the fact that there is less historical data available. Most agency data or third-party databases consist of companies based in the United States or Western Europe. For example, in 1998 over half of the defaulters recorded by Moody's were in Asia, but the Moody's database only contains well less than 5% of Asia domiciled-bond issuers out of a possible 4,500 issuers.[2]

To map internal credit grades to ratings provided by external agencies is prone to significant errors. Most banks use a point-in-time evaluation while rating agencies tend to use a through-cycle evaluation of a firm's credit risk. The difference between point-in-time and through-cycle ratings can often result in significant errors in estimating the probability of default, on the order of 3%.[3] The errors induced by the difference in perspective are more severe in companies with poor credit quality. Over an economic cycle, the default probabilities associated with a poor agency rating tend to fluctuate more than for a good rating. Unfortunately, this is exactly the level of credit grade where accuracy in the default estimation is important. Estimating the company position in the business cycle and using agency default data that reflects this equivalent period may just compound the judgment error.

A FRAMEWORK FOR RISK MEASUREMENT

The default event has been the focus of most approaches to credit risk management. However, this preoccupation with the default event belies the importance other factors may have on the credit risk faced by an institution. An obligor in distress may be in a position to fulfill its debt obligations to certain counterparties at the expense of others. Therefore, there is a need to shift both the nomenclature and more importantly the perspective from default risk to distress risk. For a financial institution with exposure to a counterparty, the distress event occurs when the obligor is in a position where the fulfillment of its contractual obligation to that financial institution is imperiled. Therefore, the distress event serves as a generalization of the default event.

In a distress situation, the loss incurred by the financial institution is affected by a plurality of circumstances of which relationship, seniority of the contract, contract provisions, and other affected lenders play a critical role. The consequential recovery rate varies across financial institutions and industries.

Therefore, the credit risk faced by a financial institution is the product of two constituents, the distress probability and the recovery rate. The former is specific to an obligor, independent of the credit relationship, and exhibits itself before the distress event. By contrast, the recovery rate is the consequence of a complex web of interests and agreements that come into play after the distress event has occurred. Monetization of the distress risk based on expected recovery rates results in a distribution of possible future loss values in monetary values.

Risk measurement deals with the probability of distress events. The specific nature of the distress event, its presence in all credit-related transactions and its primacy in the chain of events makes it the most acceptable indicator and measure of credit risk.

There are three common approaches to measuring the distress (default) risk of a financial institution:[4]

1. relative value models;
2. averaged fundamental value models;
3. specific fundamental value models.

Relative value models imply the distress risk of a firm from the prices of traded market securities. As the probability of a distress event increases, the market expects to be rewarded for holding this extra risk.

The early work in this area focused on using corporate debt to compute the distress probabilities. Subsequent work has expanded the possible range of instruments to include equities. These later advances have dramatically increased the applicability of this modeling approach. However, the distress risk computed by these approaches is based on an instrument's price process and includes the impact of liquidity, market asymmetry, and recovery expectations. This limits the applicability of the models.

In contrast, fundamental value models infer the distress risk from projecting the company's asset value. The approach dates back to Merton (see Note 5 of this chapter and bibliography) who saw equity as an option of the company. If the company's debts exceed the asset value of the firm, the equity owners choose not to exercise their control of the company and the firm is passed on to the debt holders. Thus, in fundamental models, if company assets cross a defined threshold, the system records a distress event. The distress probability is computed as the total number of crossings divided by the total number of simulations.

Fundamental value models project asset values based on an assumed relationship between the equity and asset dynamics of a company. This assumed relationship is the most contentious aspect of this approach.

Within the family of fundamental value approaches there are two main schools. The first, averaged relative value models, computes the distress risk as a two-step process. The first step computes an intermediate distress measure that is then translated into a distress frequency. This mapping from intermediate distress measure to distress frequency is done by regressing the intermediate default probability against observed historical default. The dependence on a historical database in the process compromises the forward-looking nature and the specificity of the risk measure.

The second approach, specific fundamental value models, computes the distress probability of a firm directly from imputed future asset values and the observed number of distress events without regressing the distress probability against historical default data. Consequently, the approach preserves the forward-looking and company-specific nature of the distress probability.

Whatever the model chosen, any risk measurement system must identify possible future outcomes that have a material effect on the credit quality of a counterparty or portfolio. Most significantly, in so doing, the risk measure must also remain independent of a subjective or qualitative assessment of future outcomes.

Essentially, a risk measurement framework must fulfill four properties:

- forward looking – considers relevant potential risks that affect credit quality
- event inclusive – quantifies outcomes that are unforeseeable;
- objective – input data restricted to observable phenomena;
- specific – exclusive to the risk of individual counterparties.

This poses a considerable challenge to any credit risk measurement model.

A MODEL FOR RISK MEASUREMENT

To demonstrate the application of the above criteria, we present a model of obligor default probabilities based on a fundamental value model that is an extension of the Merton approach.[5] The system computes the likelihood of possible future asset values of a company and compares this to a pre-assigned distress threshold. Additionally, the model incorporates an event generator that randomly introduces jumps of varying size. The inclusion of event risk creates a fat-tail distribution in the probability distribution of future asset values.

In its simplest form, the model randomly (or linked to some proxy for volatility) projects the asset value of the obligor in relation to its distress threshold (see Figure 3.4).

FIGURE 3.4   Analysis starts with asset value simulation

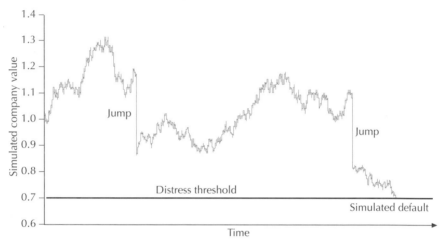

The simulation of thousands of possible future outcomes results in a distribution of asset values and simulated distress events for a given time horizon. From there, both the probability of distress occurrence can be derived without any input on cause and effect (see Figure 3.5).

In the above example, the dynamics of the asset values were calibrated to the historic behavior of equity price returns. Therefore, we are not modeling default patterns, but rather an intermediate variable, the asset value, which can generate default patterns that have not existed before. The computed default probability remains specific since the input data is limited to the equity history of the specified obligor.

The importance of incorporating event risk, simulated by jumps in asset value, is of crucial importance. Figure 3.6 shows the calculations for one obligor with and without event risk. The result speaks for itself.

No reference to a credit grade is necessary for computing the distress probability, nor is there any reference to an institution's specific loss experience. The calculations are objective and abstract. This stands to reason. The likelihood of distress by a company does not depend at all on

FIGURE 3.5 Simulating paths of the asset value results in a probability of default

FIGURE 3.6 Forward-looking simulation combined with event risk provides early warning of credit quality decay

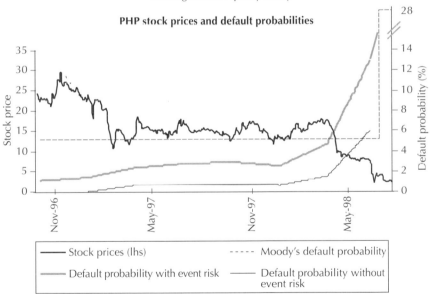

Sources: Bloomberg, AAII, Simplex Credit Advisory analysis

the assessment of credit management, but rather on factors intrinsic to the company, which may or may not have been detected by the credit units.

Used as a benchmark, a risk measurement process provides an independent and numeric decision support tool to validate credit policy and credit decisions. Deviations between the risk measure and the risk assessment should be addressed as a necessary part of the risk management function. In the end, the choice to take a punt on a credit lies with management; however, this decision can now be made in reference to a fixed mark.

In addition to its role as a benchmark, the risk measurement tool can be applied within a risk management process to:

1. objectively differentiate between companies based on their sensitivity to risk factors;
2. perform proforma analysis without appealing to cause and effect models.

At the simplest level, the default probability force ranks companies from best quality to worst. While forced rankings are useful inputs for investment decisions, relying on a projected default probability at the margin is overly simplistic. Two companies with similar one-year default probabilities will have risk profiles that differ along other dimensions besides time. The differences along these other dimensions are material in the credit decision.

The non-linearity of a company's default probability to risk factors besides time is an effective tool in selecting firms that are in accord with the credit policies of an institution. For a given credit risk tool, the inputs to the model are the risk factors along which the company is analyzed.

A "risk web" illustrates the effect of a change on the model's inputs on the default probability. Figure 3.7 shows the risk web for two companies, Crown Resources Corporation and Air Canada, using the credit risk model defined. Both companies have similar default probabilities as of June 30 1998. However, the risk webs for both companies are substantially different. The default probabilities computed for Crown Resources Corporation are strongly affected by changes in the default threshold, asset volatility, event frequency, and event size. In contrast, the default probability computed for Air Canada is not materially altered by a 20% change in the event size or event frequency. This difference in default probability profile suggests that Air Canada may have been a better credit risk in June 1998 if the risk manager believed that the market was entering a period of crisis.

The risk measurement tool can also be used to conduct structured scenario analysis for a firm. The effect of the risk measure on changes to the inputs can be measured across companies, industries, or geographies. The application of the model to US industries between 1996 to 1998 reflects intuitive results: services, basic materials, transportation, and utilities have low event size, while health care, consumer cyclicals, and technology have high event values with all industries roughly the same base volatility and event frequency. Only energy shows a high event frequency driven by the deregulation of the market. For a more detailed discussion, see the later contribution: "Measuring the unexpected: events in credit risk" by Alibhai, Gaeta, and Hingorani.

FIGURE 3.7 Sensitivity to risk factors differentiates between risks at the margin

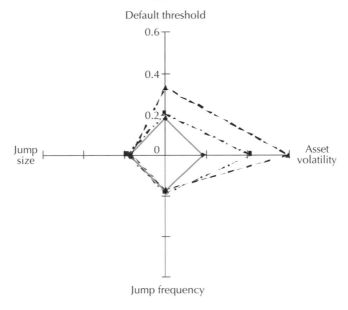

Air Canada, June 30 1998

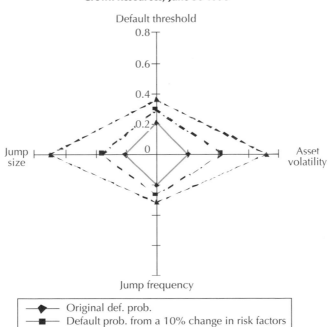

Crown Resources, June 30 1998

Sources: Bloomberg, AAII, Simplex Credit Advisory analysis

MEASUREMENT SYSTEMS IN PRACTICAL APPLICATION

Whatever the cultural challenges, financial institutions (FIs) should find ways to apply these new mechanisms to facilitate the practical measurement of risk within their organizations. A credit risk measurement system will provide management with tools that can:

- act as a sanity check for credit judgments;
- enable differentiation between otherwise broadly equivalent credits;
- anticipate shifts in loan/asset values;
- provide lead time for mitigation action.

In the course of implementation of a particular program in a major international bank, a highly adaptable approach was taken by the relevant FI that resulted in the inputs of management experience in specific markets being incorporated into the testing of the models.

This not only validated many of the subjective judgements held up by the relative managers, but also acted as a valuable cross-border educational understanding of the need to avoid applying in one market presumptions developed through experience in another. Specifically, it transpired that the best retrospective matching of computed risk levels to actual experience resulted from the differential weighting of three major components of the risk model: net worth, cash flow, and profits according to geographical region of business.

In the case of continental European companies, a very materially higher weighting was ultimately given to net worth, while in Asia, the key element was cash flow, and in the UK/US arena, profit was the prime rate driver of the credit risk model.

It seems models may require quite significant adjustment as against the framework developed prior to their adaptation by individual institutions. This enables the FI to preserve a core culture that balances marketing with risk awareness, in the specific geographies in which the FI operates.

Ultimately, the logic of such continuing refinement would lead to a credit process in which data is automatically accessed through the Internet, and continuously integrated into the model in real time with only limited human intervention to mitigate the inevitable loss of finer human judgment of specific but difficult-to-define credit factors.

Thus, even where the new measurement tools are applied with appropriate care and discrimination, it is clear that a significant cultural shift will still occur within organizations, bringing to the corporate field the same depersonalization of the interface with the client seen in the area of retail credit. However, if it enables an enhancement of the product range, it is not a total loss.

To the extent that this encourages a new focus on the quality of service and fee-based product, the average impact on the banking system should be favorable. As pointed out earlier, these changes act as a further stimulus to the unbundling of banking products and should continue to drive efficiency gains within the financial system as a whole.

INDUSTRY CONCERNS ARE NOT JUSTIFIED

The need for abstract risk measurement seems compelling. Yet, the financial industry at large and many of the regulators voice concerns. These concerns fall into three categories: first and generally, there is strong resistance to de-couple any critical part of credit risk management from the credit judgment used by those who are trained and qualified to take credit decisions. That is to say, abstract models have no place in relationship-based credit. Many industry participants, in particular credit staff, argue that the key asset of any financial institution providing credit is its credit culture. It represents a capability that creates a competitive advantage. This credit culture is largely based on the quality and competence of the staff and executives dealing with credit decisions. A model that can be replicated, would invalidate the base upon which banks compete today – such is the argument.

Second, the argument is made that in wholesale lending with fewer borrowers and large amounts, statistics cannot usefully supplement judgment. Every company and every market has different and unique characteristics that need to be considered when providing credit. These particularities play an important role in any credit decision. Statistics, on the other hand, work on abstract distributions and averages based on mathematical laws of probability. Statistics can therefore never "understand" wholesale credit.

Finally, the aversion toward statistical models also arises because they are often shrouded in mathematical abstraction. This abstraction does not allow the credit manager to apply his or her judgment toward assessing the plausibility of the model's conclusions. Moreover, results and implications may not easily be accepted by credit staff even if action based on abstract numbers is sometimes fairly unconvincing and hard to defend.

All of these concerns are admirably documented in a leading bank's annual report (condensed by the authors). Their risk management philosophy is based on eight principles – with a clear primacy of judgment and the avoidance of statistical models:

- experience, judgment and communication;
- vigilance, discipline and awareness;
- clear leadership in committing capital;

- policies and procedures;
- the need to probe and test for potential losses;
- reporting on exposures;
- flexibility of process;
- the need to minimize the possibility of incurring unacceptable loss.

Such unacceptable losses usually arises from unexpected events that most statistical model-based risk methodologies cannot predict.

The need for an objective benchmark and an abstract measure of the unexpected loss are largely ignored. "Models cannot compensate for the direct customer contact and information – they do not apply to wholesale credit" summarizes the general position of many credit professionals.

This statement is incomplete and seeks to force an exclusive choice between two independent and different activities where no choice is required or even warranted. Statistical models provide an invaluable decision-making tool in support of all existing credit selection and management processes. Models do not replace or invalidate traditional credit evaluation processes but they complement them.

For the banking institutions concerned, however, the shift to include a risk measurement approach will represent a major cultural adjustment that would better be consciously embraced rather than accidentally fallen into. Market practitioners are well aware of the very substantial differences in mind set, risk horizon, risk appetite, and risk management that exist between traders, investment, and commercial bankers. Indeed, they face different sets of risks but ultimately have the same tools and techniques at hand to manage their exposures. Anecdotal evidence demonstrates the major managerial challenges when such adaptation is made or attempted.

When an institution adopts a risk measurement process, there is a profound change in the internal culture that is very likely to overwhelm the traditional lending culture a bank.

TABLE 3.2 Three-tier approach to risk management

Tier	Risk management approach	Players
One	Strongly quantitative, balanced with qualitative assessments	Select group of institutions in the OECD
Two	Qualitative assessments with quantitative approaches limited to scenario/stress-testing	Majority of institutions in the OECD and leading regional players
Three	Largely qualitative and based on experience/relationship of analysts	Majority of regional/local banks in less-developed economies

ADOPTION OF RISK MEASUREMENT CONCEPTS TO DATE

The reluctance to employ quantitative approaches to credit risk management is not shared by all institutions. Financial institutions can be categorized into three tiers according to the sophistication of their risk management approach (see Table 3.2).

Demand for improved tools to manage credit risk has come from the tier one institutions. These leading institutions are the first to partner with academic institutions and maintain an impressive army of quantitative staff dedicated to advancing the cause. For these institutions, advances in managing credit risk represent a competitive advantage over their peers. A number of tier one players have started to apply risk measurement techniques in their risk management practices. The risk measure is applied to obligors on a case-by-case basis, to specific products and portfolios often in addition to traditional subjective analysis.

Tier two institutions typically adopt a more cautious approach and move forward once a technology has a substantial track record. These institutions usually do not maintain a large team of quantitative specialists and look for market approval when deciding on new initiatives. At present, tier two players are applying risk grades or external ratings to manage their risks. They have invested significant efforts in developing databases that can facilitate the grade-to-risk mapping. In addition, many of these institutions have purchased commercially available credit risk tools. These tools are usually applied on an ad-hoc or experimental basis and are not incorporated into the risk management practices of the institution as a whole. Unfortunately, the difficulty in using some of the early generation tools has reinforced the skepticism toward quantitative models among early adopters.

The tier three players do not place any strong emphasis on improving their risk management practices. Typically, these institutions have implicit government guarantees or have not adopted appropriate disciplines in managing their credit exposures. The impetus for change arises from intervention by supra-national organizations or from national bodies and regulators.

The regulatory approach to credit risk measurement is more cautious and tends to lag the newest market development in risk management (see Figure 3.8).

Pressure to advance the leading edge of the regulatory approach is strongly influenced by the approaches that the market has adopted. In markets where tier one players are present, regulators are well placed to evaluate the approaches used by the leading players. In markets lacking tier one players, regulators are generally adopting an approach on par with the capabilities of tier two institutions. In other markets, it is the role of the

FIGURE 3.8 There exists a push–pull relationship between financial institutions and the regulators

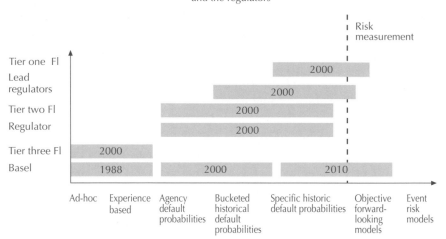

regulator to motivate tier-three institutions to improving their risk management practices.

The recommendations of the Basel Committee reflect this categorization. Most OECD financial institutions have adopted risk management practices reflective of tier two players. The proposed regulatory approach has legitimized the risk management practices of these institutions. The proposed approach lags the practices of the tier one players and has only partially moved toward accepting the risk management practices of these institutions in determining the level of regulatory capital.

CONCLUSION

Current credit risk management practices rely too heavily on historic and judgmental approaches. They fail because true risk is measured by a probability distribution of possible future outcomes and not by reviewing history or our perceptions. Thus, the case for objective, abstract, forward-looking risk measurement that includes event and correlation risk is compelling. Such a numerical tool will not invalidate judgment, nor supplement credit assessments made the traditional way.

Risk measurement offers a new and necessary way to enhance the toolkit of credit management, ultimately of corporate management. Ignoring the potential of developing proprietary risk measurement models will cause financial institutions to miss the opportunity of dramatically enhancing their capital efficiency and protecting shareholders and customers from the potential of failure or large losses.

The adoption of a risk measurement system will have a considerable impact on current credit management activity areas in two ways:

- as a complement to existing credit management activities;
- as a new and independent support and decision-making tool.

In both areas conceptual, organizational, and procedural changes will be required.

Risk measurement will sharpen the ability to set appropriate credit strategy. Different model portfolios proposed by line management now can be measured and benchmarked as to their inherent risks. As a result, credit portfolios should become more sharply managed and, depending on the chosen structure, result in risk reduction through better management.

With a correlation model, limit systems will become more dynamic and as limits change, the potential impact to be considered for other limits will be quantified. Moreover, the model will be able to reflect the impact of limit changes on the potential portfolio risk profile. This will give management a fine tool to manage short-term necessities and to send direct signals to line functions to effectively shift the structure of the portfolio.

At obligor level, facility grades now are much more accurate. Pricing benefits from an independent benchmark. Huge inconsistencies by risk grade and within each grade of the past can be reduced, if not eliminated. This would not disallow overriding judgment to reflect relationship tenor and value or competitive pressure, but would make the pricing process more transparent and credit staff more accountable.

Without abandoning intuitive tests at relationship level, institutions can now test a range of unforeseeable states, and measure their impact on obligors without resorting to detailed cause and effect analyses or estimating the likelihood of change. Portfolio tests are another enhancement derived from the model. As each major obligor is subjected to a numerically integral test, the resulting impact on the portfolio can be effectively determined.

Most importantly, all of the credit sensitive contracts of an institution can be severally and jointly measured, benchmarked, and tested in all possible directions. This should give management the ideal base to make the right decisions on capital deployment, capital adequacy planning, and reserving. Faster reaction in reforming and protecting the credit portfolio by understanding the impact of still unpredictable external events could represent a new competitive advantage and risk capability hereto underutilized.

Successful implementation requires proper technology, procedural, and organizational infrastructure to be developed. This must assure timeliness and accuracy of the rather extensive inputs that are needed, as well as the numerically intensive analyses as output.

Once the organizational, procedural, and technology requirements have been met to support the asset-based framework, a comprehensive decision support Management Investment System (MIS) can be defined for all levels of management. A detailed specification of the MIS is necessarily institution-specific reflecting, as it must, the business franchise, organizational structure, and policy parameters mandated by management.

NOTES

[1] Basel Committee on Banking Supervision, *The New Basel Capital Accord*, Basel Committee on Banking Supervision, January 2001.

[2] Moody's Investors Service. *Historical Default Rates of Corporate Bond issuers, 1920–1998.* January 1999.

[3] Treacy, W.F. and Carey, M.S. *Credit Risk Rating at Large U.S. Banks.* Federal Reserve Bulletin, Federal Reserve Board, United States, November 1998.

[4] See Duffie, D. and Singleton, K.J. "Modeling Term Structure of Defaultable Bonds." Graduate School of Business, Stanford University, July 1, 1998; Geske, R. "The Valuing of Corporate Liabilities as Compound Options." *Journal of Finance and Quantitative Analysis*, 12, pp. 541–552; Longstaff, F.A. and Schwartz, E.S. "A Simple Approach to Valuing Risky Fixed and Floating Debt." *Journal of Finance*, July 1995, pp. 789–819; and Zhou, C. *A Jump-diffusion Approach to Modeling Credit Risk and Valuing Defaultable Securities.* Board Of Governors Of The Federal Reserve System. Finance and Economics Discussion Series. No. 1997–15. March 1997.

[5] Merton, R.C. "On the Pricing of Corporate Debt: The Risk Structure of Interest Rates." *The Journal of Finance*, May 1974, pp. 449–570.

CHAPTER 4

The Forsaken Side of Risk Management: Have Deterministic Approaches Gone Too Far?

W. Randall Payant
The IPS-Sendero Institute

"It was the best of times, it was the worst of times, it was the age of wisdom, it was the age of foolishness." No, British author Charles Dickens was not writing about contemporary risk management, but he very well could have been. For all those affected by this evolving discipline, Dickens' words could aptly be describing the current state of financial risk management.

Financial risk is nothing new. Risk and its consequences have been around since the dawn of banking. JP Morgan and its RiskMetrics™ development staff did not discover risk measurement, although they did popularize it. Value-at-risk is not an innovative concept, despite rhetoric to the contrary. Even our own organization, General Association of Risk Professionals (GARP), has at times promoted the view that we are at the dawn of a new profession, the risk profession.

For those of us old enough to have grappled with managing credit and investment portfolios, one can't help but notice that the often-neglected RISK side of the risk/return relationship is now receiving long overdue attention. Quantifying and managing risk is not a new profession, but it's certainly a concept undergoing meteoric change.

The rapid changes in risk measurement and management affect financial institutions, industrial organizations, investors, shareholders, regulators, governments and their minions, virtually all economies, societies, and communities. Advances in data-gathering, computer technology, applied mathematics, and statistics have all contributed to the creation of increasingly complex financial structures and their inherent risks.

Financial innovation has created a continuous spectrum of investment contracts that make distinctions between risk-free debt and risk-capital (equity) largely irrelevant. Investment bankers continue to underwrite and distribute new classes of financial instruments, decomposed and reformulated from the same old financial raw material.

New equity class issues track segments of business, attempting to uncover value not found in the host corporation's stock market capitalization figure. Mortgage loans are stripped to their bare essentials, and sold off in tranches at premium prices. Ambiguous cash flows in proprietary written financial contracts are divided and subdivided among various investors. The contract's anticipated but indeterminable gains are capitalized on the belief that their future earnings potential has a deterministically quantifiable value today. Derivatives, well need I say more. There are now increased numbers of ways to assume risk, rather than to manage it.

Coupling these financial transaction trends to decompose and reformulate cash flows are new words like securitization, risk-controlled arbitrage, delta-neutral, portfolio insurance, and long-term hedge – terms that attempt to take the sting out of the idea of potential financial loss.

Sophisticated, multi-faceted trading strategies are developed and tested with the aid of computer models that attempt to quantify return and risk exposures. The global financial web continuously shifts, with lightning speed, the fuels of regional economic engines, capital, currencies, debt, and commodities. The speed of global communications and the free flow of capital have led to the growth of loosely regulated financial casinos, where market players can place customized bets on perceived financial market anomalies.

While our global village has clearly benefited from these advances in financial risk management for many players, the bets have turned sour, creating billions of losses. These losses have trickled down from investors to the general public, humbling scores of emerging economies and causing great social tragedy.

Numerous governments, and international financing agencies, have had to bail out financial risk management gone wrong. Adding insult to injury, in many cases the market players' ultimate losses have not been commensurate with the amount of risk assumed. Some who have bet big and lost have been bailed out, and are allowed to play the game again. Some who had nothing at risk have experienced loss. In our attempt to divide and conquer risk, one has to wonder if we have inadvertently created more.

So how have we arrived at where we are today in risk management? I believe there are three factors that have shaped the good, the bad, and the ugly in contemporary risk management.

1. There has been a paradigm shift from too little data to too much data in risk management. The availability of too much data has led to increasingly finer divisions of risk and reward.

Humanity has continuously faced the financial repercussions of an uncertain future. To help understand the probable outcomes of the future, man began observing and tracking past patterns of behavior. By tracking the past, humanity was able to instinctually gain intuition about probable future financial outcomes.

Slowly humanity began converting its instinctual understanding of past behavior to a more rational view of the probable consequences of the future. In order to place a value on yet unknown outcomes, the probability of achieving any single outcome had to be quantified. Much of this rationalization rested on advances in the mathematical sciences.

One of the first recorded applications of mathematics to model uncertainty was in 1654 when Baisle Pascal and Pierre de Fermat arrived at a probability-based solution to a simple game of chance. Their collaboration rested on understanding all possible outcomes of a game, and then determined the probability of any one outcome occurring. They mathematically quantified uncertainty, and thus laid the seeds for our modern risk quantifying techniques. Their work was based on organizing and interpreting data derived from patterns of behavior. Many others improved on this early work, pushing the mathematics of probability-based solutions to quantify and value risk even further.

Harry Markowitz built on these mathematical approaches with his 1950s work on risk and reward relationships, giving us concepts of diversification, correlation of outcomes, and modern portfolio management theory. Others have contributed by refining mathematically based approaches to value uncertainty – the science of quantifying risk. In the 1970s, Fischer Black and Myron Scholes provided us the framework for option pricing models, a real test of measuring the value of uncertainty.

Mathematical deterministic techniques to quantify risk have been available for years, but what was often lacking was the behavioral data necessary to determine probabilities of outcomes across numerous financial dimensions and markets simultaneously. This is where recent technology and communications advances have changed the paradigm.

With the abundance of increasingly granular data and its transformation into information, updated continuously, risk managers are able to disaggregate financial transactions to their simplest elements and track the elements' individual market volatility. The more minutely data is tracked, the more apparent its underlying volatility becomes. Increased volatility means increased risk.

As disaggregation of behavior patterns continues to its most minute elements, the benefit of diversification ceases. Risk-reducing benefits on uncorrelated risk elements are lost when tracked individually. The sum of all individual risk elements inherent in highly complex financial transactions is much greater than the risk in the underlying transactions from which it's created. Thus, the more finely risk is quantified and traded, the greater in aggregate it becomes.

2. Many investors rely almost exclusively on a limited number of deterministic risk measures that they don't truly understand.

Quantifying risk using increasingly complex model algorithms has reached a point that only the model's designers understand its inner workings, and therefore its strengths and weaknesses. Not all risk modelers use the same approaches, nor start with the same sets of data, although they are measuring the same risk. Even worse, rarely do different models provide comparative measurement results. So what *is* the appropriate measure of risk?

In an effort to come up with simple measures of risk, modelers often force reality to fit the model, rather than the other way around. Behavior patterns are forced to be normally distributed; correlations across behavioral factors are held constant; and the law of large numbers minimizes the impact of catastrophic disasters. Many modelers assume arrogance in their analysis, only to sheepishly blame factors outside their model when unanticipated losses occur. The best we can do with modeling is create resemblances of behavior, but we can't determine the reality of behavior.

Risk measurement is not only highly dependent on the model, but also on the underlying historical date used to create the assumption sets necessary in the measurement process. But this is data of past behavior, not of future behavior.

What are left out of deterministic approaches to risk-quantifying are the structural shifts of behavior patterns caused by factors not considered in the model's equations. Advances in technology, communications, delivery channels, regulation, accounting rules, and other barrier breakthroughs to commerce dynamically shift behavior patterns of economies and markets.

Correlation and auto-correlation of short-term observations of static risk elements cannot capture behavior-changing undercurrents that haven't surfaced yet. Looking only at the past blinds one to paradigm shifts in behavior. Behavior is not deterministic. Maybe risk managers have relied too heavily on mathematicians and financial engineers, and not enough on sociologists, psychologists, and other behavioral scientists.

The growing complexity of risk models has left many ultimate users of the model's results lacking an instinctual understanding of the measurement process and the underlying premises on which it relies. But this hasn't deterred market players from placing blind faith in the invincibility of these risk-quantifying tools. Mathematical risk quantification has become a pseudo religion that pacifies our insecurity, caused by our lack of clairvoyance. Models have become sacred pagan gods, but God's wrath can change.

The numbers and techniques only provide a representation of what "might" happen, not what "will" happen. As Peter Bernstein stated, "Numbers are the tools of our discipline, not its soul." It is a lack of an instinctual understanding of the tools' shortcomings that has left many losers in the risk-taking game wondering what went wrong. Most lament that, "If I had only known of a model's fallacies, I would have reacted differently." Based on observations collected over time, this conjecture itself is probably false. Greed and blind faith often win out over fear and skepticism in the financial risk-taking business.

3. For many investors, short-term valuation, and VAR measures have completely replaced the long-term focus on earnings, earnings-at-risk, and liquidity.

Risk only relates to something that has value. Value is determined at a point in time. Changes in value occurring over time create earnings opportunities. The mesmerizing fixation with value-at-risk concepts has shifted our focus away from managing earnings accumulation and liquidity over time.

Value can decline drastically in the short term, especially in illiquid markets, due to temporary abnormalities in market behavior patterns. But the underlying question is: who determines value, markets, or models?

Liquid markets allow players to enter and exit transactions relatively friction free, providing diversification of timing. The ability to diversify market timing creates liquidity. Diversification doesn't insure against loss, only against losing everything immediately. With sufficient liquidity, temporary downturns in value can be weathered, sometimes without negatively affecting earnings. Liquidity is found only in markets, not in models.

Models don't calculate market value, rather they attempt to explain value, based on observations of price behaviors of market-traded instruments. Models calculate model value, and too often models assume a static continuation of liquidity in their calculations. It is rare to find a VAR model that considers the changing breadth and depth of market liquidity as a factor in determining overall risk.

Too often financial bets are placed on monetary values that are determined only with valuation models, not from prices directly observed in liquid markets. For a growing number of the structured transactions, a party to one side of the transaction controls the model and the market, and therefore the sole determinate of value. These transactions have no observable market price and no liquidity. Casino owners, who control the game and its pay-off odds, rarely allow their players to leave without suffering loses. If market participants have sufficient external sources of liquidity, they can weather short-term market price turbulence. Those who can't, go broke.

What I have described does not speak well of the profession in which we participate. With too much data, a limited understanding of the limitations of the data, and a growing focus on the short term only, how can we, as risk managers and modelers, bring true value to our profession?

For answers to this question, we need to turn to the principles of risk management as outlined in the Basle Committee's works. While there are eleven principles, I would like to paraphrase those that relate to the risk measurement process:

1. Risk measures must identify and address all major sources of risk.
2. Risk measurement processes must be reasonable and transparent, with the underlying assumptions used to quantify risk understood by those relying on the measures.
3. The risk measures must consider possible breakdown of key assumptions, particularly the liquidity of markets, on the measured results.

The essence of the principles establishes the recommended standards for all risk measures. While these principles shouldn't create descent from risk modelers, the manner in which they are adhered to has not been established or formalized. This is where GARP can improve the stature of the risk profession discipline. GARP should adopt a standardized "risk measurement disclosure statement." A disclosure statement would provide decision-makers with the information necessary to understand the measurement process and the degree of confidence they choose to place in its results.

Without specifying format or content detail, a disclosure statement should include at minimum the following five items:

1. Definition of the risk(s) being measured and which risks are not being considered in the measurement process. The definition should include what is being risked, who is financially affected directly by the risk, and the time period the risk is assumed to exist.
2. Description of the risk measurement framework used, including the specific sources of risk considered in the measurement process. Known sources of risk not formally addressed in the measurement process should be disclosed.
3. Description of the behavioral data used in the assumption determination phase of the measurement process, including the length of any look-back period used to derive the measurement assumptions.
4. Identification of the critical measurement assumptions and the degree of sensitivity each key assumption has on the measured results. The

key assumptions' sensitivity should be disclosed without regard to correlation.

5. Disclose the weakest known link in the risk measurement framework.

Whether or not a disclosure statement is ever adopted, everyone assuming financial risk should have a clear understanding of the underlying premises on which the risk analysis is based. By doing so, risk-takers should not be lulled into a false sense of security. Quantifying risk is a necessary part of managing risk, but so is having an instinctual understanding of the dynamics of risk.

There is real danger in relying solely on deterministic approaches to risk measurement. We must take their results, understand them, and use them in conjunction with our own experience and intuition. We still need these measurement tools, as they are the only approach we have to determine, *relatively*, the degree of possible negative consequences of the uncertain future.

Part 2

Concepts and Issues of Credit Risk Measurement

CHAPTER 5

Building a Credit Risk Valuation Framework for Loan Instruments

Scott Aguais, Lawrence (Larry) Forest, Jr, and Dan Rosen
Algorithmics

W e present a general option valuation framework for loans that provides valuation information at loan origination and supports mark-to-market analysis, portfolio credit risk, and asset and liability management for the entire portfolio. We describe, in detail, the main structures found in commercial loans and the practical assumptions required to model the state-contingent cash flows resulting from these structures. The characteristics of the credit risk model necessary to capture the main features of the problem are described. Finally, we discuss the families of credit models appropriate for pricing, the data required for their calibration and reasonable criteria for choosing the sophistication of the model. We propose a multi-state, ratings-based credit model with three credit drivers: the credit state of the obligor, the level of risk-free rates, and the spreads. Though we focus primarily on large corporate and middle-market loans, the approach is applicable more generally to bonds and credit derivatives.

Since its application to derivatives valuation in the early 1970s, no-arbitrage pricing has become the basis for managing the risk of the trading and investment books of financial institutions. No-arbitrage techniques are used to price and hedge securities such as bonds and derivatives, to mark-to-market (MtM) portfolios, and to measure risk.

The application of option valuation techniques to bank loans has been much slower in developing. Most banks today manage the credit risk of their loan books in fairly simple and basically static ways. Perhaps the most prevalent method for pricing and managing loans applies the concept of RAROC (risk-adjusted return on capital). The RAROC approach attempts to distribute aggregate risk costs down to businesses, products customers, and, ultimately, individual transactions. Measures of static, marginal risk contributions are used in the RAROC approach to allocate capital costs directly to individual loans in relation to the firm's aggregate debt and equity costs.

Since RAROC is not a no-arbitrage technique, it does not reconcile the prices of loans with those of similar securities available in the market (such as bonds, other loans, and credit derivatives). Hence, it cannot assess comparative business opportunities and arbitrage-like situations arising from relative price mismatches. In addition, it is unable to capture the natural hedges that often motivate the creation of new credit securities. Finally, while several of the financial principles behind RAROC seem generally sound, there are many limitations in its implementation, as has been pointed out in the literature (Shearer and Forest 1998). For example, the approach neglects the state contingency of many loan cash flows, takes a static view of credit risk, generally considers an arbitrary fixed horizon in pricing credit risk, and uses highly subjective parameters in practice.

Many financial institutions today are considering a move toward mark-to-market (MtM) approaches for managing their traditional lending business. An MtM approach for loans can facilitate better pricing and structuring of credit risky instruments, more flexible and dynamic management of credit portfolios, and greater exploitation of arbitrage opportunities. With wholesale bank loans, corporate bonds, and credit derivatives together accounting for more than $30 trillion (all amounts is USD) in exposures worldwide, better valuation and risk-management techniques hold the potential for enormous business benefits. Those who stand to benefit the most are the institutions that take advantage of an MtM approach to understand the effects of structure and embedded optionality on the value of credit instruments.

We present a general option-valuation framework for loans. While we focus primarily on large corporate and middle-market loans, the approach is applicable more generally to bonds and credit derivatives. This framework provides key valuation information during loan origination, and it supports MtM analysis, as well as the portfolio credit risk and asset and liability management functions.

We emphasize the modeling of key product-specific features of loans and not the simple application of a specific type of pricing model to the problem. To make an effective choice of underlying credit risk model with broad applicability, one must understand these features of loans and have an informed practical view of the market and the data available. While this may seem obvious from a practitioner perspective, most of the academic literature has steered clear of many of the complications of loan structures. Instead, many papers focus on building new and improved credit risk pricing models, and illustrate their applications with simple instruments such as straight bonds and simple credit derivatives, thereby avoiding many of the details needed in practice, (e.g., Jarrow and Turnbull 1995; Jarrow et al. 1997; Madan and Unal 1998; Jarrow and Turnbull 2000). These papers offer no solutions to practitioners choosing and adapting these models to price their generally complex credit instruments, and calibrating them to available data.

One can readily find articles and books describing the features of credit derivatives and their application (e.g., Das 1998; Tavakoli 1998). However, it is more difficult to find work that describes the structures of loans, their embedded optionality, the data available for pricing these assets, and the choice of appropriate pricing models. Early research in this type of application was performed at Citibank (Asarnow 1994; Ginzburg et al. 1994) and was continued by Aguais et al. (1998) and Aguais and Santomero (1998). While our discussion falls short of a comprehensive survey of loan instruments, we present a framework that incorporates several main structures encountered in practice and describes a consistent approach to modeling the underlying risk factor processes.

We lay a tripartite foundation to motivate the general valuation framework:

- *The main structures* found in commercial loans, such as utilization of credit lines and options to prepay. We describe these structures and outline the practical assumptions required to model the resulting state-contingent cash flows.

- *The credit model characteristics* that are necessary to capture the main features of the problem. Three factors are generally required to model the state contingency of cash flows in a reasonable way. These three factors explain the creditworthiness of the borrower, the level of risk-free interest rates, and the level of credit spreads. All three factors can, in principle, be stochastic.

- *The families of pricing models and the data required for their estimation.* We discuss existing credit models that are appropriate for these problems, as well as reasonable criteria for choosing the model based on a trade-off between speed, complexity, data availability, and accuracy.

The rest of the chapter is organized as follows. The next section serves as background, describing briefly why option valuation techniques are gaining practical status and acceptance for loan portfolios. Thereafter, we present examples of loan structures and describe the optionality embedded in these structures. The following section describes various models that capture these structures, and the rationale for several economic and behavioral assumptions. Following a brief discussion of the characteristics of appropriate credit risk pricing models, we motivate the use of various families of models, outline the data required and discuss practical limitations. As a result, we describe a general framework for implementing these models.

APPLYING OPTION VALUATION TECHNIQUES
TO CREDIT RISK

While the application of option valuation to securities with underlying credit risk was originally envisioned by Merton over 25 years ago (Merton 1974), it was only in the late 1980s that credit risk option valuation models began to appear in applications. Three main factors contributed to this long delay. First, credit risk modeling is complex and, hence, has trailed behind that of market risk (including equities, foreign exchange, and risk-free interest rates). Second, many have accepted the pessimistic view that the standard assumptions made for tractability in no-arbitrage models (such as continuous trading, complete markets, no-frictions, and the like) generally do not apply when valuing credit risky instruments. Finally, consistent with this view, financial institutions have, by and large, opted for static management of their (illiquid) credit risks.

Financial institutions, however, are being forced to reconsider these practices and move towards MtM approaches for managing their bank loans for several reasons:

- *Evolution of credit risk markets.* The 1990s saw the development of stronger bond markets, secondary loan markets, and a tendency for these two markets to converge. Furthermore, the credit derivatives industry has burgeoned, resulting in enhanced liquidity to support the needs of market participants to transfer credit risk.
- *Advances in credit risk models.* Several decades of research have resulted in a better understanding of the nature of credit risk and in various practical pricing and risk management models that can be calibrated to observable prices and historical data.
- *Integration of market and credit risk.* The advent of credit derivatives to support the transfer of credit risk and the convergence of credit markets are compelling financial institutions to manage the risk in the banking and trading books in a more unified manner. The assumption that credit risk cannot be traded actively is being reconsidered, and the application of no-arbitrage models seems more realistic. This trend has led also to the development of pricing and portfolio models that integrate market and credit risk (e.g., Das and Tufano 1996; Jarrow and Turnbull 2000; Iscoe et al. 1999).
- *Trends in regulation and best practices.* Although a market-based valuation and assessment of credit risk is not yet required, both regulatory trends and best practices point in that direction in the long term. This is evident from the proposal of the Bank for International Settlements (BIS 1999) to amend the regulatory regime and the

various discussion papers that have appeared in response to it, as well as the disclosure of loan MtM practices by several institutions.

- *Improvements in technology.* The advent of computational technology provides ready access to non-traditional institutions and investors in the credit markets, and allows the application and delivery of more sophisticated computational tools to price and manage credit risk. Furthermore, the availability of Internet tools provides an effective means to distribute online credit information and valuation tools to a large number of users.

COMMON TYPES OF CREDIT INSTRUMENTS

The vast majority of credit instruments involve a mixture of standard types that lend themselves to a rather straightforward specification. These types include:

- bond
- term loan
- revolver
- financial letter of credit
- banker's acceptance
- default swap
- total return swap
- multi-option facility.

General descriptions of these standard credit instruments appear in Appendix 5.1.

To illustrate the state contingency embedded in credit instruments, we provide four examples.

Large Corporate Term Loan

Consider a recent syndicated deal of $115 million to help fund the acquisition of PlayCore Holdings Inc., an unrated holding company with interests in the sporting and games industries. The agreement closed on April 14, 2000.

The deal includes a $30 million revolver, a $25 million term loan (A) and a $60 million term loan (B). Credit is secured by a borrowing base composed of 85% of eligible accounts receivable, 60% of eligible inventories, plus $3,000 monthly prepayments from November through March. Covenants require, among other things, hedging of some interest rate risk, maintenance of minimum fixed-charge coverage ratios, limitations on dividends, and use of excess cash flow, debt or equity issuance, or insurance proceeds to retire outstanding credit under this agreement. Pricing is tied to the ratio of funded debt to EBITDA (earnings before interest, taxes, depreciation, and amortization). In default, pricing increases by 200 basis points (bps). The contract allows prepayment without penalty at any repricing date.

We describe the term loan B component, which is marketed to loan funds. The final maturity of the loan is July 1, 2006 – 87 months after the April 14, 2000 closing. The 20 quarterly payments of $150,000, starting on October 1, 2000, are followed by eight quarterly payments of $7,125. The loan amortizes over several quarters. Initially, at contract closing, this facility is priced at the prime lending rate + 225bps or London Interbank Offered Rate (LIBOR) + 400bps. Thereafter, the pricing grid, summarized in Table 5.1, determines pricing on the basis of the company's ratio of indebtedness to cash flow as shown in the most recent financial statement. The current pricing corresponds to a ratio between 4.25 and 4.75, as shown in the second row of Table 5.1.

Large Corporate Revolving Line

Consider another recent syndication. The entire $150 million package closed on March 29, 2000; final maturity is March 29, 2003. It provides working capital for Rollins Truck Leasing, which is a BBB+ rated company in the truck rental and leasing business.

The deal includes two $75 million revolvers, one with a 364-day term and the other with a three-year term. Credit is secured by 90% of the net equipment value of all motor vehicle equipment. Covenants include a maximum ratio of funded debt to adjusted tangible net worth and material restrictions on dividends. Pricing is tied to the company's senior debt rating. In default, pricing steps up by 200bps or to the prime lending rate + 200bps, whichever is greater. The agreement includes a letter of credit (LC) option. The contract allows prepayment without penalty at any repricing date.

The three-year facility is a bullet bond that expires in its entirety at term.

TABLE 5.1   Pricing grid of PlayCore term loan B (LPC Gold Sheets 2000a)

Level	Debt to cash flow ratio	Prime + (bps)	LIBOR + (bps)
1	4.75 or greater	250	425
2	[4.25, 4.75]	225	400
3	less than 4.25	200	375

Through September 30, 2000, this loan has a price of LIBOR + 75bps, a commitment fee (CF_{CF}) of 17.5bps annually, and a letter of credit fee (CF_{LC}) of 12.5bps at issuance plus 75bps annually. Thereafter, beginning on the date set by the contract, the grid, summarized in Table 5.2, sets pricing on the basis of the company's most recent senior unsecured debt rating established by Standard and Poor's (S&P). Thus, for example, if the company is downgraded to BBB, the loan moves to LIBOR + 95bps, a commitment fee of 20bps annually, and a letter of credit fee of 12.5bps annually, as given in the third row of Table 5.2.

TABLE 5.2 Pricing Grid of Rollins' 36-month revolver (LPC Gold Sheets 2000b)

Level	Senior rating	Prime + (bps)	LIBOR + (bps)	Commitment fee, CF (bps)	Letter of credit, LC (bps)
1	A− or better	0	60	15.0	12.5 + 60
2	[BBB+, A−)	0	75	17.5	12.5 + 75
3	[BBB, BBB+)	0	95	20.0	12.5 + 95
4	worse than BBB	0	115	25.0	12.5 + 115

Middle-market Revolving Line

Relatively few of the larger middle-market loans involve syndicates. As is typical of middle-market loans today, the term is shorter and the structure simpler than most large corporate instruments. However, middle-market loans are becoming more complex, and some of the larger ones now include three- to seven-year terms, commitment fees and pricing grids.

To illustrate a typical middle-market loan, we consider a bilateral deal involving one bank but, for confidentiality, change the borrower's name and some of the less important details of the agreement. This one-year $8.5 million revolving line supports the working capital needs of NE Timber, which is in the logging business. According to the bank's internal credit rating system, NE has an S&P-equivalent rating of B.

A borrowing base composed of cash plus 80% of zero- to 90-day receivables, plus 60% of inventory, plus 40% of raw timber secures credit under the agreement. The contract includes the standard covenant package, which limits dividends, requires maintenance of a minimum ratio of operating cash flow to debt, and prescribes that any new debt be used first to retire credit under this agreement. Pricing is at the prime lending rate + 250bps, with no fee on unused amounts, as summarized in Table 5.3.

Prepayment involves no penalty at repricing dates, and a 2% hedge-breakage fee at other times. The loan matures 12 months after closing. The commitment amortization is a bullet bond.

TABLE 5.3 Pricing grid of NE's line of credit

Price level	Prime + (bps)
1	250

Credit Default Swap

Consider an agreement providing protection against default by a Latin American country. Under the terms of the five-year contract, the protection buyer owes a fee of 250bps per annum payable quarterly, in advance, on a notional principal of $25 million. The protection seller owes nothing unless the country defaults, with default defined by standard documentation. Broadly, default occurs if the Latin American country misses a senior debt payment or offers a distressed exchange of assets, or if the market value of the underlying asset identified in the contract falls by more than a specified amount.

In case of default, the protection seller pays par for $25 million at face value of the underlying USD-denominated asset, if available, to the protection buyer. Alternatively, if the underlying asset is unavailable, a fair net cash settlement is paid as determined by the calculation agent identified in the contract. The contract terminates within a specified short period following default, and the protection buyer has the right to cancel the agreement at any time.

CASH FLOW TIMING AND COMPONENTS

As illustrated above, the embedded options and other features characteristic of most credit agreements cause the associated cash flows to vary over time and with changes in the state of the world necessitating a cash-flow modeling approach that accounts for state dependency. We start by describing the calculation of cash flows at a given state and time, then discuss the modeling of credit-line usage and prepayment behavior. These features substantially affect the cash flows and the value of credit contracts at each state and time.

We assume a series of discrete time steps though, for ease of exposition, we focus on a single time step. All the contingent cash flows whose contractual values depend on the state at the beginning of the time step are modeled. However, payments may occur either at the beginning or the end of the time step.

The cash flows realized depend on certain contingencies:

- The payments at the end of the period vary, depending on whether the borrower defaults during the time step.
- The payments both at the beginning and end of the period vary, depending on whether the borrower chooses to prepay.

Since the main objective is valuation, formulas are developed to express all these cash flows aggregated on a discounted basis at the beginning of the period. The cash flows for a simple bond and a default swap are described first, and then the more involved case of a complex credit facility.

Bond

Consider the simplest case of a bond. At each state and time step, some of the cash flows occur at the beginning of the period (in advance) and some occur at the end (in arrears).

The bond's cash flows are expressed as:

$$CF_B = \begin{cases} AC + CF_{PP} & \textit{if prepayment occurs} \\ 0 & \textit{otherwise} \end{cases} \tag{1}$$

$$CF_E = \begin{cases} 0 & \textit{if prepayment occurs} \\ CF_1 + CF_P & \textit{if no prepayment and} \\ & \textit{no default occurs} \\ (1 - L)(CF_1 + AC) & \textit{if no prepayment and} \\ & \textit{default occurs} \end{cases} \tag{2}$$

where CF_B denotes cash flow at the beginning of the period; CF_E is the cash flow at the end of the period; AC is the commitment amount (which, for a bond, equals the principal outstanding); CF_{PP} is a prepayment penalty; CF_1 is the cash interest payment; CF_P is the principal repayment owed; and L is the loss severity rate.

Equations (1) and (2) show that if the borrower prepays, the holder of the security immediately receives the outstanding principal plus any applicable prepayment fee. Otherwise, the cash flow received at the end of the period depends on whether the borrower defaults during the time step. If the borrower does not default before interest and principal come due, the holder of the security receives the amounts owed in full at the end of the period over which those charges accrue. Alternatively, if the borrower defaults, the holder of the security receives only a portion $(1 - L)$ of the interest and principal owed. The timing of these cash-flow components is illustrated in Figure 5.1.

FIGURE 5.1 Usual timing of cash flow components
for a bond

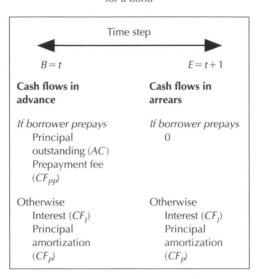

This method of representing default proceeds is called the *recovery of par* or *legal claims approach* (see, for example, Duffie and Singleton 1999; Jarrow and Turnbull 2000). There are other conventional ways of modeling default losses. In the *recovery of treasury approach*, losses (or recoveries) are expressed as a fraction of the value of a risk-free bond (Jarrow and Turnbull 1995). In the *recovery of market value approach*, losses are expressed as a fraction of the value of the instrument just prior to default (Duffie and Singleton 1999). The remainder of this chapter focuses on the legal claims approach.

For valuation, the cash flows at the beginning and end of the time step in Equations (1) and (2) can be combined on a discounted basis, using the discount rate known in the state at the beginning of the time step. The discounted cash flows at the beginning of the period are then given by:

$$
DCF = \begin{cases}
AC + CF_{PP} & \text{if prepayment occurs} \\
(1 + R)^{-1}(CF_1 + CF_P) & \text{if no prepayment and default occurs} \\
(1 + R)^{-1}(1 - L)(CF_1 + AC) & \text{if no prepayment and default occurs.}
\end{cases}
$$

(3)

Here, *DCF* denotes discounted cash flow and R the applicable one-period (simple) discount rate, conditional on the state of the world at the beginning of the time step.

Assume that, at the beginning of the time step, default has not occurred and that, based on the time and state of the world, we know:

- the risk-neutral prepayment probability, P_P;
- the risk-neutral probability that default occurs during the time step, conditional on no prior default and all prior information, P_D.

Then, the risk-neutral expected value of cash flows discounted over the time step can be obtained by taking the expectation in Equation (3) with respect to the (one-period) risk-neutral default and prepayment probabilities to derive the expected discounted cash flow of a bond at the beginning of the period:

$$ECF = (AC + CF_{PP}) \cdot P_P + [(1 - R)^{-1}((1 - P_D)(CF_1 + CF_P)$$
$$+ P_D \cdot (1 - L)(CF_{IS} + AC))] \cdot (1 - P_P). \tag{4}$$

Equation (4) applies also to the risk-taking side of a total return swap with the bond as the underlying.

In the next two examples, we simplify the presentation by focusing only on expected discounted cash flows. In practice, all the conditional cash flows must be captured, without consolidation.

Credit Default Swap

The one-period expected discounted cash flow of a credit default swap is given by:

$$ECF = CF_{PP} \cdot P_P + (CF_{DS} - CF_C - (1 + R)^{-1}P_D \cdot L \cdot AC)$$
$$\times (1 - P_P). \tag{5}$$

Equation (5) can be understood as follows: a prepayment in this credit default swap means that the protection buyer cancels the agreement. This event has a probability P_P. In this case, the seller might receive a cancellation fee (CF_{PP}). Otherwise, if the contract continues, the buyer pays a premium at the start of the period (CF_{DS}) and the seller incurs servicing and monitoring costs (CF_C). If default occurs, the protection seller pays compensation $(L \cdot AC)$ to the buyer at the end of the period, where AC is the committed amount.

Bank Credit Facility

Bank credit facilities sometimes allow the borrower to obtain credit by choosing from among a set instrument types. In the most general case, the borrower obtains credit by means of:

- a term loan;
- a funded revolving line;

- a letter of credit;
- banker's acceptance.

Although it is rare for a single credit agreement to grant the borrower the option of choosing from among all of these instruments, the simultaneous use of all of these instruments leads to payments of interest and several different kinds of fees. The complexity of the resulting cash flows illustrates the required flexibility of the model. The timing of cashflow components for a bank credit facility is illustrated in Figure 5.2.

In bank credit agreements other than straight, term loan facilities, the borrower has discretion, within limits, in choosing when to obtain credit, when to repay it and in what amounts. For modeling purposes, we assume that the borrower chooses the desired draw on a credit line at the beginning of each period and repays or cancels in full at the end of the period (as illustrated in Figure 5.3). This approach, in effect, treats the varying outstanding amounts in a credit line as a time series of differently sized one-period term loans. While this payment-and-draw pattern may not mirror the

FIGURE 5.2   Usual timing of cash flow components for a bank credit facility

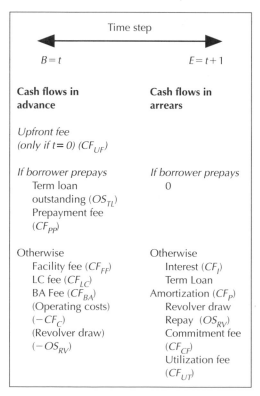

actual sequence of transactions, the state-contingent draws at the beginning of each time step offset any overstatement of repayment at the end of the preceding time step.

Tables A1 to A5, in Appendix 5.2, summarize the relevant balances, bank cash flows, pricing rates, cost rates, and utilization rates for a bank credit facility.

The cash flows from a bank credit facility include the following items paid at the beginning of the period:

- For a new facility ($t = 0$), the borrower may owe an "upfront" fee, CF_{UF}, at other times, $CF_{UF} = 0$.
- In the case of prepayment, the borrower returns the outstanding principal, OS_{TL}, and pays any applicable prepayment penalty, CF_{PP}. Thus, with probability P_P, prepayment occurs and leads to a total cash flow of:

$$CF_{UF} + OS_{TL} + CF_{PP}.$$

Note that, under this end-of-period revolver repayment convention, only the outstanding term loan amount is repaid at the beginning of the time step if prepayment occurs (see Figure 5.3). If no revolver draw occurs at the beginning of a period in which the borrower prepays, the repayment of the term loan reduces the outstanding balance to zero.

- If the credit facility continues, the borrower owes, at the start of the period, any applicable facility fees, CF_{FF}, letters of credit fees, CF_{LC}, and banker's acceptance fees, CF_{BA}. The borrower's draw of funds on a credit line, OS_{RV}, and the lender's expenses, CF_C, occur in advance. These items create cash outflows, which appear as negative entries. Thus, with probability $1 - P_P$, there is a total beginning-of-period cash flow of:

FIGURE 5.3 Modelling credit-line usage

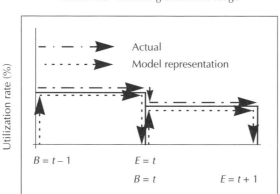

$$CF_{UF} - CF_{FF} + CF_{LC} + CF_{BA} - OS_{RV} - CF_C.$$

If the credit facility continues, several additional cash flows occur in arrears and the amounts realized depend on whether the borrower defaults.

- Interest, CF_I, commitment fees, CF_{CF}, utilization fees, CF_{UT}, and principal repayment, CF_P, come due at the end of a period. Also, by modeling convention, the funded revolving amount, OS_{RV}, is paid at the end of a period. Thus, in the absence of default, the total cash flow at the end of the period is:

$$CF_I + CF_{CF} + CF_{UT} + CF_P + OS_{RV}.$$

- In default, we assume that the borrower pays only the portion $(1 - L)$ of those amounts owed. The loss-in-event-of-default rate (L) reflects the seniority of the obligation, strength of covenant protection, the value and type of any collateral, and the protection afforded by subordinated debt. Also, in default, the creditor receives only the portion $(1 - L)$ of the principal outstanding. Thus, all together, the cash flows at the end of the period if default occurs are

$$(1 - L)(CF_I + CF_{CF} + CF_{UT} + CF_P + OS_{RV}).$$

- For credit lines with commitments available (i.e., when $AC > OS_{TL}$), the outstanding principal can rise as the borrower goes into default. The loan equivalency of the commitment, $LEQAC$, and the normal utilization rate, REU, determine the amount of this additional draw. Specifically, the funded outstanding amount in default is the sum of the normally drawn amount $(AC \times REU)$ and the normally undrawn amount, weighted by the $LEQAC$ factor $(AC \cdot (1 - REU) \cdot LEQAC)$. The additional draw in default is then given by the expected outstanding amount in default, which is the sum of two terms:

$$(AC \cdot REU + AC \cdot (1 - REU) \cdot LEQAC)$$

less the *funded* outstanding balance at the beginning of the period,

$$OS_{TL} + OS_{RV}.$$

This contributes to an additional cash flow loss at the end of the period:

$$L[AC(REU + (1 - REU)LEQAC) - OS_{TL} - OS_{RV}].$$

This expression adjusts for the *additional* draw on a credit line that frequently happens as a borrower goes into default. For time steps as long as one year, this adjustment is needed to represent accurately the amount that will be outstanding and thus vulnerable to loss in default. For time steps as short as one month or one quarter, the *LEQAC* adjustment may be inappropriate.

Suppose that, during the year leading up to default, borrowers make additional draws of about 40% of the *original* commitment less the amount typically drawn; then, for an annual time step, *LEQAC* = 40%. Assuming the normal utilization rate *REU* = 30% (which implies a normally undrawn fraction of $1 - REU = 70\%$), the expected usage in default is $0.30 + 0.70 \times 0.40 = 0.58$. The additional draw in default is thus $0.58 - OS_{TL} - OS_{RV}$.

The loan equivalency factor, *LEQAC*, measures the proportion of normally undrawn balances that have been drawn and thus are vulnerable to loss in the event of default. Thus, it reflects two competing effects:

- the deteriorating borrower's attempt to draw additional funds to cover an increasing cash flow deficiency;
- the lender's attempt to reduce the commitment available to a deteriorating borrower who predictably violates some loan covenants.

Weighting by the appropriate probabilities and discounting the cash flows occurring at the end of the period, all of these components are consolidated to obtain the expected discounted cash flow of the credit facility:

$$
\begin{aligned}
ECF = {}& (CF_{UF} + OS_{TL} + CF_{PP}) \cdot P_P \\
& + [(CF_{UF} + CF_{FF} + CF_{LC} + CF_{BA} - OS_{RV} - CF_C) \\
& + (1 + R)^{-1}\{(1 - P_D)(CF_I + CF_{CF} + CF_{UT} + CF_P + OS_{RV}) \\
& + P_D (1 - L) (CF_I + CF_{CF} + CF_{UT} + OS_{TL} + OS_{RV}) \\
& - P_D \cdot L \cdot (AC \cdot (REU + (1 - REU) \cdot LEQAC) \\
& - OS_{TL} - OS_{RV})\}] \times (1 - P_P).
\end{aligned} \tag{6}
$$

The *LEQAC* factor controls explicitly the usage of the credit line in default Equation (6). Moreover, it also controls the maximum usage of the credit line in non-default. Thus, it also affects several cash flows and outstanding amounts in Equation (6), through the credit line usage model. The *LEQAC* factor is further explained in the next section. Since one expects that the incentive to draw will be highest as the borrower goes into default, our assumptions do not allow usage in default to rise higher than that in a non-default situation.

Note that *LEQAC* measures the exposure in default as a fraction of the original, and not of the terminal, commitment. Its value can be imputed from market pricing of undrawn commitments or from past evidence on the usage of normally undrawn amounts in default. For example, suppose that market credit spreads on undrawn balances average about 25% of those on drawn balances. This motivates a *LEQAC* value of 25%. Alternatively, suppose that past data show that, in default, borrowers end up drawing about 50% of the commitment that was unused early in the life of the facility before any substantial decline in creditworthiness. This suggests $LEQAC = 50\%$. Studies typically estimate $LEQAC$ well below 100% and the Bank for International Settlements capital adequacy guidelines (BIS 1988) prescribes a value of 50% for undrawn commitments extended for one year or more. The concept of a loan equivalency factor is familiar to practitioners exposed to BIS and internal capital allocation schemes. An alternative and more direct approach to using $LEQAC$ is to model the credit line that the lender predictably achieves as the borrower's risk rating degrades. This can be seen as a lender's "option to reduce the line." Thereafter, the borrower is free to use the whole amount of the reduced commitment.

Several standard accounting relationships and other formulas ultimately tie the cash flow components shown previously to model inputs that describe the pricing and structure of the credit facility, market conditions, and borrower behavior. Most of these primary relationships determine cash flows as the product of rates and balances. For example:

- The interest payable, CF_I, equals the product of the contractual interest rate, R_I, and the outstanding funded balance, using the proper day count and compounding conventions.
- The interest rate, R_I, equals either a specified fixed rate or the current value of the relevant floating rate computed as the sum of a base rate and a spread.
- In the case of a choice among varied floating rates, the option that provides the lowest rate, or the lowest rate that falls between an interest rate floor and ceiling, determines the floating rate.
- The spreads valid at the current time and state depend on the pricing grid, if there is one. Similar considerations arise in determining other cash-flow components.

To conclude this section, note that two different assumptions on operating costs may give rise to different expected cash flows and the value of the loan at each state and time. Operating costs can be seen from the perspectives of the market and the lender. The costs of efficient credit providers can be imputed from market spreads on loans. These market-derived costs affect market values, which, in turn, affect prepayment behavior. Prepayment depends on the borrower's opportunities in the market as compared with the given loan. On the other hand, the lender's costs, as estimated possibly from activity-based studies, can differ from market-derived costs. In that case, the value of a loan from the viewpoint of the lender differs from its competitive market value. Assessing the difference between these two prices is an important exercise for the lender. We elaborate further on these two perspectives when discussing the prepayment modeling.

MODELING THE EMBEDDED OPTIONS

Equations (4) to (6) describe the expected discounted cash flows for a bond, a default swap, and a general bank credit facility, at a given point in time and state of the world. Embedded in these formulas are three types of options that depend on credit events:

With a *default option*, the borrower may not pay an obligation in full in the event of default. The expected cash flows of the bond, credit default swap, and bank-credit facility are affected explicitly by this option through the probability of default, P_D, in Equations (4) to (6).

With a *prepayment option*, the obligor has the right to prepay commitments or cancel the contract at specified times before maturity. Prepayment generally depends on whether it is cheaper for the obligor to cancel the deal and enter into an identical one in the market, netting for cancellation costs and fees. This occurs when the market conditions (interest rates and spreads) move sufficiently in the obligor's favor, or if there is a substantial improvement in creditworthiness, thus allowing the obligor to negotiate lower spreads.

The value of this option depends directly on both the market conditions and the creditworthiness of the obligor. In this sense, the option is contingent on credit events other than default (credit migrations). The expected cash flows in Equations (4) to (6) are explicitly contingent on prepayment through the probability of prepayment, P_P, which, in turn, is dependent on the credit state of the obligor, as well as the level of risk-free interest rates and spreads. With a *credit line utilization option*, an obligor has the right to choose the usage level of a given commitment. Of the three examples, only the bank credit facility offers this option. It is generally the case that as an obligor's creditworthiness diminishes, the draw on the credit line increases. Therefore, as with the prepayment option, the credit line utilization contains an embedded option on credit events other than default, such as credit downgrades.

This option makes several terms in Equation (6) contingent on the state of the world, which now includes the credit state of the obligor as well as market conditions. The terms that are affected by utilization are the cash flows CF_{LC}, CF_{BA}, CF_C, CF_I, CF_{CF} and CF_{UT}, as well as the outstanding amounts OS_{RV}, OS_{LC}, and OS_{BA}.

Default probabilities and credit migration are captured through the underlying credit model. The necessary characteristics of the credit risk model are described in the next section. In what follows, we describe the modeling of prepayment and line utilization, which occur simultaneously in a comprehensive framework. Hence, many of the same cost considerations apply in both cases.

Prepayment

It seems plausible to assume that the borrower will exercise the option to prepay a loan instrument if the market value of the loan, *VNM*, conditional on it continuing, rises high enough above par to pay for:

- any prepayment penalty, given by a prepayment rate times the committed amount, $R_{PP} \cdot AC$;
- refinancing transactions costs of the borrower, given by fixed and variable costs of searching for and negotiating a new loan, $FTC_{PP} + MTC_{PP} \cdot AC$;
- origination costs, which are the (fixed and variable) costs that an efficient lender in the primary market incurs in originating a new facility, $FC_{ORIGM} + MC_{ORIGM} \cdot AC$.

Combining these three items, we obtain the total transaction cost of prepayment (TC_{PP}):

$$TC_{PP} = R_{PP} \cdot AC + FTC_{PP} + MTC_{PP} \cdot AC + FC_{ORIGM} + MC_{ORIGM} \cdot AC.$$

We assume that, in a given state of the world, the borrower will prepay if, in switching to a new loan with a competitive value of par in the secondary market, the savings relative to the existing above-par loan more than cover the transactions cost. Thus, the probability of prepayment in a state of the world, P_P, can assume only the values of zero or one and simply becomes an index of the prepayment event:

$$P_P = \begin{cases} 1 & \text{if } VNM - OS_{TL} > TC_{PP} \\ 0 & \text{otherwise.} \end{cases}$$

Although one could more generally model P_P as a continuous monotonic function of the predicted prepayment savings ($VNM - OS_{TL} - TC_{PP}$); in practice, it is difficult to obtain data to calibrate this function to actual borrower behavior.

As an example, consider the workings of the prepayment model in the case of a $10 million facility. Suppose that as a result of an upgrade in creditworthiness, the facility's *NPV* in the market, conditional on no prepayment, rises to $150,000. Assume that, in refinancing the loan, an efficient lender will incur origination costs of $40,000, and that the borrower will incur search and negotiation costs of $15,000. Assume, further, that there is no prepayment fee. The total transaction cost of $55,000 falls short of the $150,000 gross savings that the borrower can realize from refinancing. The model will predict prepayment.

To implement this approach and ultimately determine the credit facility's value to a particular lender, both the lender's and the market's costs of originating and of servicing loans must be estimated. By "market" costs we mean those of competitive providers of credit. Borrower costs of transacting a new loan must also be determined. These estimates come from varied sources as described further in the data calibration section.

Credit Line Utilization

In bank credit agreements other than straight, term-loan facilities, the borrower has the option to choose the usage of the line. Obviously, the line utilization is realized only in the event that the borrower does not prepay the facility. The usage of a line influences both the payments that the borrower owes to the creditor, as well as the amount of exposure that the creditor bears. In Equation (6), the usage of the line affects several cash flows and outstanding amounts as described below.

The amount outstanding as a term loan, OS_{TL}, is fixed by the loan contract. Any remaining commitment above that amount is available to the borrower, assuming compliance with the loan covenants. The compliant borrower may use this amount in varying degrees from 0% to 100%. The usage model determines two components:

- the overall usage, $RUACA$, of the available commitment;
- the relative usage of the different instrument options: the funded revolver, the letter of credit, and the banker's acceptance.

The overall and relative utilization rates determine, in Equation (6), cash flows CF_{LC}, CF_{BA}, CF_C, CF_I, CF_{CF}, and CF_{UT}, as well as the outstanding amounts OS_{RV}, OS_{LC}, and OS_{BA}. The cash flows are obtained by multiplying contractual pricing rates by the corresponding drawn (outstanding) or undrawn (commitment less outstanding) balances. The outstanding amounts also influence operating costs and exposure.

We now describe the models for the overall and relative usage rates.

Overall Usage Rate, RUACA

The borrower's usage of the available commitment amount is modeled as a function of the net credit line cost. This can best be explained in several steps.

We start by defining the available commitment. Term loans basically involve a known schedule of outstanding amounts; hence, they are deterministic. All of the other bank loan types – funded revolvers, letters of credit, bankers' acceptances – involve outstanding balances that may fluctuate randomly. Thus, to determine the range of possible random variation in credit outstanding, we need to identify the commitment amount in excess of that set aside for a term loan.

The available commitment, *ACA*, given by the total commitment, *AC*, less any term loan outstanding amount, OS_{TL}, can also be expressed as a proportion of the total commitment:

$$ACA = AC - OS_{TL} = AC \cdot (1 - REUTL) \tag{7}$$

where *REUTL* denotes the portion of the facility devoted to a term loan. This is an attribute of the loan contract. In many cases, REUTL = 0% – a pure revolving line – or REUTL = 100% – a straight, term loan. Equation (7) also describes the case of a multi-instrument facility that includes a term loan as a component.

Then, the amount of available commitment that is outstanding, *OSACA*, is given by the product of the available commitment and its usage rate, *RUACA*:

$$OSACA = RUACA \cdot ACA.$$

Usage rates vary widely, depending on the purpose of a facility. A back-up line generally has low usage rates, while an operating line has relatively high rates. The normal usage pattern is assumed to be provided by the user who knows the facility's purpose.

We assume that the borrower tries to minimize the costs of required credit. This suggests that the usage rate, *RUACA*, rises above its anticipated value if the marginal cost of drawing credit becomes cheap, and falls if the marginal cost becomes expensive. "Cheap" and "expensive" mean "low" and "high," respectively, relative to the market par cost of obtaining credit. If the cost of obtaining additional credit under the existing line rises far above the market par cost, then the borrower should be able to find cheaper credit elsewhere. The borrower would logically curtail usage of the credit line. If the cost under the existing line falls far below the market par cost, the borrower would tend to draw on the line and reduce the use of alternative credit.

Let *CC* represent the marginal cost of credit under the existing credit line and let *MC* denote the market cost, with both expressed in basis points. We define the net credit-line cost, *N* as:

$$N = CC - MC.$$

Appendix 5.3 explains how the marginal cost of credit, *CC*, and the market cost of credit, *MC*, can be computed in a given state of the world and time step.

As a practical matter, major changes in the net cost of drawing credit mostly reflect shifts in creditworthiness. One might expect the borrower to draw the maximum amount possible whenever the net cost falls below zero and draw nothing whenever it rises above zero. However, the available evidence generally suggests a less extreme reaction, where usage rises rather continuously as the credit rating degrades. Thus, a plausible model expresses usage as a logistic function of net credit line cost, *N*, as shown in Figure 5.4.

When the net cost is at zero, or at some other near par value established by assumption, the usage rate equals the anticipated value for the facility; that is, $RUACA = REU$ (see Equation (6)). As shown in Figure 5.4, when the net cost falls sufficiently below par, the logistic function is capped to reach a maximum, through the use of the loan equivalency of undrawn commitments ($LEQAC$). Usage reaches a minimum when the net cost rises well above par. The parameters of the logistic curve allow for calibration to the limited information on utilization patterns.

Recall that the $LEQAC$ rate controls both the maximum usage in non-default and the usage in default. It represents, roughly, the effect of lender options to reduce a credit line as a borrower with deteriorating creditworthiness violates covenants.

If the contractual pricing of the facility does not itself depend on usage, then we obtain directly a single value for the net cost of a draw, N. The logistic function capped by the $LEQAC$ factor in Figure 5.4 determines directly the usage, $RUACA$. Mathematically, we express this as:

$RUACA = U(N)$

where $U(N)$ denotes the usage function in Figure 5.4.

However, some credit instruments include utilization fee schedules that assess incremental charges on usage in excess of specified thresholds. For example, a utilization fee schedule could specify no fee on utilization less than 33%, a 5bps surcharge on usage above 33% up to 50%, and an additional 5bps (for a total of 10bps) on incremental usage above 50%. In this case, a numerical algorithm must be used to solve simultaneously for the net cost, N, and the usage rate, $RUACA$.

FIGURE 5.4 Capped logistic usage function

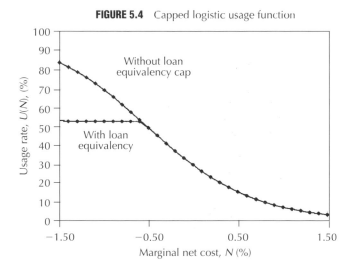

Relative Usage Rates of Different Instruments

The usage model also deals with a general, multi-option facility in which the borrower has the right to draw credit as a funded balance, a letter of credit or a banker's acceptance. To model the relative usage of these different instrument options, one starts by determining which, if any, offers the cheapest cost of drawing credit. Then, relative to its anticipated value, the usage of any less economical instrument drops as its cost spreads relative to the minimum cost option grows. Figure 5.5 gives an example of the relative usage function. The relative usage for a given instrument is given as a decreasing function of the spread gap to the minimum cost option.

This model of line usage accounts for the price of credit in contrast with approaches that tie usage only to the borrower's credit grade (CreditMetrics 1997). Such approaches imply that usage is the same at a risk grade regardless of the cost of obtaining credit and, hence, may not be very realistic.

Information on relative usage of alternative instrument options is very limited. The basic economic incentives faced by a borrower motivate the approach here. Parameters that limit the intensity of this economic incentive effect can be established if other considerations determine a borrower's relative usage of the different instrument options.

CREDIT RISK VALUATION FRAMEWORK

As illustrated above, most credit agreements include key embedded options, notably the borrower's option to prepay or cancel a contract, and to draw on

FIGURE 5.5 Example of relative usage schedule for instrument option

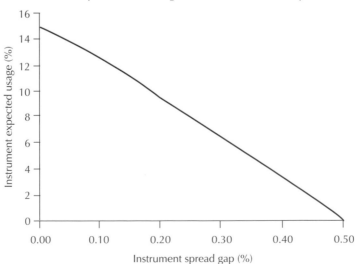

a credit line. As a result of these options, the cash flows from credit facilities vary with time, borrower creditworthiness (e.g., risk rating), interest rates, and credit spreads. In particular, a decrease in interest rates or credit spreads or an improvement in borrower risk rating may trigger prepayment, drastically changing cash flows. Furthermore, more complex credit facilities also include additional features such as pricing grids, graduated utilization fees, and amortization schedules that amplify the state and time dependency of cash flows.

In essence, we require an underlying credit risk model that describes each state of the world by:

- the creditworthiness of the obligor (perhaps as given by a discrete set of credit ratings and default probabilities);
- the term structure of default-free interest rates;
- the term structures of credit spreads for non-defaulted securities.

In principle, each of these sets of variables can vary stochastically through time. Intuitively, one would expect that at least three factors are required to capture this stochasticity in a reasonable way (e.g., a credit rating index, the risk-free short rate or forward rate, and a systemic factor affecting credit spreads). The choice of the model, however, depends on trade-offs between the generality, complexity, speed, data requirements, and accuracy of the model. For example, if one is interested in valuing floating rate instruments, then an assumption of deterministic risk-free interest rates and spreads may be appropriate and a one-factor model may be used. However, for fixed-rate instruments, it is important to have a stochastic model describing the evolution of risk-free interest rates. This can be done generally through a one-factor term-structure model. Although it may be tempting to use multi-factor models that better describe the evolution of the term structure, this may lead to an overall credit valuation model of dimensionality that is too high to be practical.

In what follows, some of the issues that influence the choice of the underlying credit risk model, the data required, and the basic structure of the underlying pricing framework are highlighted.

Choice of Underlying Credit Risk Model

Credit risk pricing models are broadly classified in the literature into two main categories: the so-called structural approach and the reduced-form, or intensity-based, approach. See Das (1998), Duffie and Lando (1997), and Jarrow and Turnbull (2000) for comprehensive descriptions of the two approaches. (The reader is also referred to Aziz 1999a, 1999b, 2000) for some simple practical explanations of the general principles underlying these models.) Appendix 5.4 provides a brief review of these credit risk approaches.

In general, cash flows for loans vary with changes in the creditworthiness of a non-defaulting borrower; that is, movements between the various ratings grades short of default. Therefore, models that distinguish among many possible credit states, not just default and non-default, are required. Multi-credit state (rating-based) models seem particularly suitable for this problem (e.g., Jarrow, Lando, and Turnbull 1997 (JLT); Lando 1998). In terms of applications specific to the loan market, rating-based models were first used in Ginzberg et al. (1994). Aguais et al. (1998), and Aguais and Santomero (1998) also describe valuation applications that use a multi-state model for evaluating the embedded options and other structural features found in loan instruments.

The potentially high dimensionality of rating-based models presents various theoretical and practical challenges. For example, in the most general case, a rating system with n credit states implies the need to calibrate on the order of n^2 parameters (rating transitions) per time step. Clearly, some reasonable structure to reduce the dimensionality of the problem must be added. The JLT model presents one such approach and Lando (1998) discusses more generally a number of additional practical approaches.

In general (assuming complete markets), no-arbitrage models require only pricing data for calibration. Rating-based models, in contrast, start by using real transition matrices (like those provided by S&P and Moody's) to describe the high-dimensional, discrete-transition probability space. One usually assumes that the evolution of the obligor's creditworthiness follows a time-homogeneous Markov process (in the real measure). A low-dimensional process is then applied to modify the transition matrix in order to fit to the observed term structure of market spreads. This yields the so-called risk-neutral measure. Typically, this calibration step may convert the process into a time-inhomogeneous Markov process (under the risk-neutral measure).

One can use the JLT or Lando low-dimensional process transformations to fit the observed credit spreads. However, in practice, this choice is not obvious. For example, since the JLT approach involves a proportional scaling of the transitions, it sometimes leads to numerical problems when applied in practice. Lando's approach using eigenvalue decomposition can also lead to practical numerical problems. Moreover, in both cases, the transformations are chosen for mathematical tractability and are not derived from underlying financial principles.

Note that by defining credit states as arising from an underlying process of the value of the firm, structural models can also be useful for this type of problem. However, these models may be difficult to fit to market data (particularly short-term spreads) and their use, in practice, may require some extra level of sophistication for modeling cash flows such as those found in loan instruments. A mixed model that combines functional parts of reduced form and structural models provides a sensible alternative.

The mixed approach assumes that there is an (unobserved, perhaps) underlying structural process, referred to as the creditworthiness index (CWI), determining a firm's credit state. This approach was first advanced in the CreditMetrics methodology (CreditMetrics 1997). As in the Merton model, default occurs when the CWI falls below a given threshold or default boundary. Also, one may define multiple thresholds that determine various credit states.

In the CreditMetrics approach, the default and migration thresholds are fit directly to match observed (one-year) rating migrations and default probabilities. Assuming that the underlying index is Gaussian, simple closed-form solutions can be obtained for one-period problems. As shown in Gordy (2000), Koyluoglu and Hickman (1998), and Belkin et al. (1998a,1998b), the model leads naturally to the modeling of stochastic default probabilities and transitions as a function of systemic risk factors. The CreditMetrics methodology solves the problem only for a single step. Multi-step versions of the methodology are presented in Iscoe et al. (1999) and Li (2000).

In summary, one may obtain a sensible underlying credit risk model for elaborating on the three factors outlined above:

- *Factor 1: borrower creditworthiness,* as designated by a set of discrete credit ratings.
- *Factor 2: default-free short rate* or *continuous forward rate,* as determined by an HJM model or *discrete forward rate,* driven by a Brace-Gatarek Musiela (BGM) model (at a higher computational cost, one may choose a higher dimensional model of the default-free term structure.)
- *Factor 3: systemic factor describing stochastic credit spreads,* from a stochastic intensity model or as the systemic component of a structural creditworthiness index.

Calibration Data for the Credit Model and the Cost Models

The data required for calibrating the underlying credit risk model depends on its level of sophistication. For a model with deterministic spreads (two-factor model), the data for calibration include:

- default-free term structure of interest rates;
- defaultable term structure of interest rates (spreads) for each rating class derived from a combination of bond and loan data;
- current transition matrix (as estimated, for example, from historical data as with ratings agencies or from a market-based model such as that of KMV or Moody's);
- recovery rates for each seniority and collateral class, as well as by advance rate.

To include further stochastic spreads in the model, one also requires implied spread volatilities from traded instruments or, if these are not available, a time series of historical spreads or default/transition data.

To obtain a correlated model of default-free and defaultable rates, one requires time series of default-free interest rates and spreads or, alternatively, observed default probabilities, to estimate correlations.

Ideally, we calibrate the model to prices of liquid, frequently traded credit instruments representing the economic regions, sectors, and risk grades and terms needed for a comprehensive description of credit risk. It is important to note that one must extract option-adjusted spreads from the raw pricing information, to obtain the zero spreads used to calibrate the credit model. Recovery rates used in this calibration are usually drawn from bond and loan recovery studies (see, for example, Brand and Bahar (1998) and Eales and Bosworth (1998)). Finally, under the best circumstances, time series of credit prices to estimate spread are gathered.

Pricing data from both the bond and loan markets are used. Unlike bond spreads, loan spreads comprise an implicit cost component paid out of designated margins. As mentioned earlier, to determine the credit facility's value to a particular lender, one requires a model for both the lender's and the market's cost of originating and servicing loans. "Market" costs are those of competitive providers of credit. One also needs to estimate borrower costs of transacting a new loan. The estimates of lender, market, and borrower costs come from varied sources.

For a particular lender, the cost information could derive from proprietary studies of credit activities at the institution. These costs might differ from market implied costs. While sometimes difficult in practice, market costs can be imputed from observed prices of loans and other instruments such as bonds. We illustrate this process with several examples:

- Suppose, in the secondary market, high-grade term loans have option-adjusted spreads that exceed those of comparable bonds by 45bps. That value might be taken as an estimate of the cost of servicing and monitoring those loans. In loans, the spreads pay for those costs, whereas in bonds they do not. Alternatively, if the servicing tranches on collateralized loan agreements offer spreads of about 40bps, that might be taken as a general estimate of servicing loans.

- With regard to origination costs, suppose that, following payment of reported upfront fees averaging 40bps, term loans in the secondary market trade at an average of 99.8% of par. We might conclude, therefore, that it costs lenders about 20bps to originate loans. Assuming that loans typically originate at par and solving for origination costs:

$$100\% + FC_{ORIG} - CF_{UF} \times 0.4\% = 99.8\%. \tag{9}$$

- Suppose that the combined selling and underwriting expense of bond issuance are reported to average 40bps. This can be used as an approximation of origination costs for syndicated loans.

- If almost no loan in the secondary market trades higher than 100.6% of par, an estimate of 60bps for the total of borrower transactions costs and lender origination costs might seem reasonable. Then, given a value of 35bps for competitive origination costs (in Equation (9)), the borrower cost of searching for and negotiating a new loan is 25bps.

In most cases, these factors can be estimated only roughly, given the state of the current data. In particular, due to non-reporting of some upfront payments to lead arrangers, the available data could well understate lender origination costs. All such estimates of operating costs and of pure credit spreads (excluding costs) need, together, to reconcile with market pricing.

The loan market data cover mostly large syndications, with occasional sketchy reports on general trends in the US middle market. Data on investment-grade, syndicated loans come mostly from the primary market. Only speculative-grade loans trade enough for compilation of reasonably reliable secondary-market prices. Loan pricing vendors currently provide benchmark prices by credit grade for only two broad maturity bands: 364 days and multi-year (four to six years on average). One vendor provides such pricing information for several industry groups. As suggested earlier, extracting the zero-rates term structure (plain vanilla structure) from the raw prices may not be easy due to the complex structure and embedded optionality in loans. This process of adjustment depends on the model itself and can be complex.

Credit Risk Valuation Architecture

We now describe the overall architecture required to support the pricing and structuring of loan instruments.

From a business perspective, the architecture must support the primary requirements of valuing each individual transaction at origination and MtM for an entire portfolio of credit instruments. The support of loan valuation over a set of future scenarios (Dembo et al. 2000) is also required for advanced portfolio credit risk solutions.

In terms of technology support for these two business objectives, valuation at origination requires pricing and structuring decision support for a large number of users in the front office, while MtM analysis typically requires middle-office, batch-mode analysis for an entire loan portfolio. Recent advances in technology, such as Web-based tools, provide a platform for the deployment of this type of valuation framework, by placing decentralized valuation analysis much closer to the customer, while providing centralized management and control of complex analytics, key calibration parameters, and credit data.

In Figure 5.6 we highlight the overall architecture needed to support implementation of this credit valuation approach, including five key components:

- *Credit risk calibration data*: this includes market data for bonds and loans (spreads), current credit data (default probabilities, transition matrices, and recovery rates), and spread volatility data.

FIGURE 5.6   Overall architecture

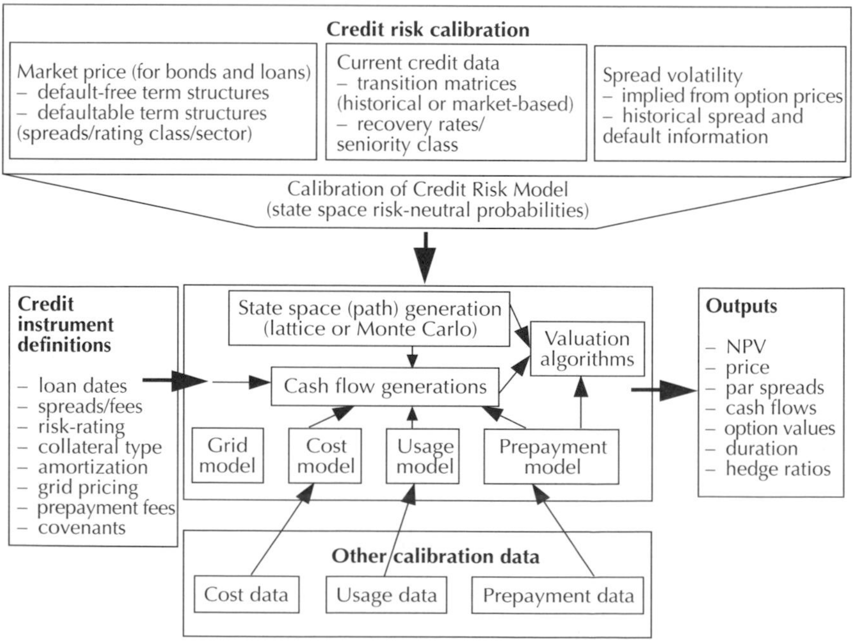

- *Usage, prepayment, and cost calibration data*: this includes data to support the calibration of behavioral options components such as line utilization and prepayment. In addition, operating costs, which are part of the overall loan spread as highlighted, are determined by market-based information or a bank's own internal cost assessments.
- *Core analytics*: the core analytics include modules that determine option-exercise behavior and the generation of state-contingent cash flows. These are combined with the valuation algorithm, using either Monte Carlo or lattice-based methods.
- *Credit instrument definitions*: the specific terms and conditions of each credit instrument are inputs; the valuation outputs describe the loan's risk-adjusted characteristics.
- *Output reports*: these include prices, par spreads, cash flows, sensitivities, "what if" analyses, and so on.

The pricing algorithm can be based on either a lattice-based or Monte Carlo-based approach. When working with up to three factors, lattice-based valuation methods are probably the most appropriate. In this case, a state-space lattice provides the framework that combines the cash flow generating modules, which include the behavioral option-exercise logic, with the backward recursion algorithm that determines expected values. In particular, given that prepayment exercises depend on the actual value of the contract to the holder at a given state of the world and time, lattices provide a natural way to compute exercise boundaries (as is common, for example, with American options).

When the dimensionality of the model is higher, Monte Carlo methods are generally necessary to solve for the loan prices. These methods further allow for the handling of more complex path-dependent instruments, as well. However, Monte Carlo pricing usually has a high computational cost. Furthermore, as with American options, the practical implementation of the prepayment logic is more difficult in this case.

CONCLUSION

We present a general option valuation framework for loans. While the focus is primarily on large, corporate, and middle-market loans, the approach is applicable more generally to bonds and credit derivatives. This framework provides key valuation information during loan origination, and it supports MtM analysis for the entire loan portfolio, portfolio credit risk, and asset and liability management. We emphasize the modeling of key product-specific features of loans and not the simple application of a specific type of pricing model to the problem. We describe the main structures found in commercial loans, such as utilization of credit lines and options to prepay, as well as outline the practical assumptions required to model the state-contingent cash flows resulting from these structures. The credit risk model characteristics necessary to capture the main features of the problem are also defined. Finally, we discuss briefly the families of credit models that may be appropriate for pricing, the data required for their estimation and reasonable criteria for choosing the sophistication of the model.

The proposed multi-state, ratings-based credit modeling approach with three factors captures the main characteristics of loans. By incorporating a stochastic interest rate factor, the model also values both floating-rate and fixed-rate credit instruments. Stochastic credit spreads can be supported by incorporating a systemic risk factor, which also captures the business cycle. This point is key since a prepayment-option exercise is driven by both movements between credit states and changes in the level of the term structure of credit risk.

As financial institutions progress toward applying MtM valuation to loans to support trading and credit risk transfer, this type of framework represents a key step forward. For those institutions that understand the arbitrage opportunities available in the loan market, the business benefits will be substantial. Implementation of valuation methods that incorporate detailed, state-contingent loan structures will also support improved estimates of portfolio credit Value-at-Risk.

APPENDIX 5.1   STANDARD CREDIT INSTRUMENTS

The simplest type of credit instrument is the (bullet) corporate bond (BD) in which the issuer obtains cash from the initial investors at origination and, in return, agrees to make payments of interest and, at maturity, of principal to holders of the securities. Some bonds include sinking fund or redemption provisions basically equivalent to amortization of principal. Most allow prepayment after a period of call protection. The bond's comparative simplicity makes it more readily marketable than other credit agreements that, in contrast, often include clauses proscribing or limiting assignments.

A *term loan* (TL) is a credit contract in which the borrower receives funds from the creditor(s) at contract closing or usually over a short period following closing and, in return, agrees to make payments of interest, fees, and principal based on formulas and schedules specified in the agreement. Term loans can be quite complicated, involving amortization of principal, differing levels of seniority, posting of collateral, detailed covenant restrictions, prepayment penalties, and interest and fees that may vary with the borrower's risk-rating or financial performance. Term loans, however, account for a minority share of the lending by commercial banks.

A *revolver* (RV), or credit line or revolving line, is a credit agreement in which the borrower has the right to choose when to obtain funds and when to repay funds and how much to borrow, within limits set by the contract. These limits typically stipulate a maximum borrowing amount (commitment), the date by which all borrowed funds must be repaid, and the covenants that the borrower must satisfy to qualify for receiving funds. In some cases, the agreement requires that the borrower periodically "cleans up" (pays down to a specified level) the facility before re-borrowing. The revolving line involves all of the complications of the term loan plus the added feature of granting the borrower the right to choose when to borrow and in what amounts.

Different types of revolving lines account for the major share of bank lending to businesses. By providing funds virtually on demand, the revolver allows a business to meet its working capital needs and to manage the liquidity risk created by volatile cash flows. By pooling revolvers across many businesses, a bank eliminates through diversification most of the liquidity risk that it inherits from customers.

Revolvers and term loans cover most of the lending that requires the creditor's money. Other standard types of credit instruments do not normally involve the bank or non-bank creditor actually lending money.

In a *financial letter of credit* (LC), the creditor guarantees the repayment of a counterparty's obligation and, in return, receives a one-time or periodic fee. Thus, a bank could issue a financial LC in support of a customer obtaining short-term cash from a money market fund that offers an attractive rate. In a financial LC, the bank essentially provides credit insurance. The instrument's contingent pay-offs mirror those of a credit default swap.

A *banker's acceptance* (BA) is another type of payment guarantee. In a BA, the bank certifies that it will stand behind time drafts (post-dated cheques) issued by a customer. The customer may then sell drafts endorsed as accepted by the bank at a discount to a funding source that does not want to bear the issuer's credit risk.

LC and BA facilities usually allow the borrower to choose when to make use of the credit support offered by the bank. Thus, the outstanding amount under these instruments may "revolve" in the same way as disbursed balances in a funded revolving line.

In a *credit-default swap* (DS) the buyer pays a one-time or periodic fee to the seller of protection for the right, in the case of default by a particular borrower, to receive cash compensation or to sell a credit instrument issued by the borrower at a specified price (near par). In contracts with extremely low-risk counterparties, this instrument offers basically the same state-contingent cash flows as a financial LC. Otherwise, the instrument involves counterparty risk as well as the risk of the underlying instrument. As with a financial LC and insurance contracts in general, the protection buyer in a DS typically has the right of cancelling (prepaying) the agreement.

In a *total-return swap* (RS) the protection buyer exchanges the total returns on a specified underlying debt instrument for a set of stable cash flows. The protection seller receives cash flows that match the interest and principal payments, plus the gains (minus the losses) of the underlying instrument. As in the DS, the RS can involve counterparty risk in addition to the risk of the underlying instrument. Also, as in the DS, the RS usually allows the protection buyer to cancel the agreement.

We turn lastly to the most complex case, the *multi-option credit facility* (MOF). In a MOF, the borrower has access to a range of instrument types within a single facility or contract. In this case, the creditor commits to provide credit up to a maximum amount, which can amortize over time, to be drawn on in various ways largely at the borrower's discretion. In a more general case, the borrower can receive a term loan and then, as needed, obtain additional credit up to the remaining commitment amount. This additional credit can take the form of additional funded balances (revolvers), letters of credit, bankers' acceptances, or some combination of these types. Of course, a MOF can offer less than the full menu of instrument types.

APPENDIX 5.2   SUMMARY OF RELEVANT CASH FLOWS

TABLE A1   Selected balances affecting bank loan cash flows and exposures

Variable	Description	Revolving (Y/N)	Derivation
AC	commitment amount	N	loan attribute from contract
OS	total outstanding amount	Y	$OS_{TL} + OS_{RV} + OS_{LC} + OS_{BA}$
OS_{TL}	term loan outstanding amount	N	$RU_{TL} \times AC$
OS_{RV}	revolver outstanding amount	Y	$RU_{RV} \times AC$
OS_{LC}	LC outstanding amount	Y	$RU_{LC} \times AC$
OS_{BA}	BA outstanding amount	Y	$RU_{BA} \times AC$

TABLE A2 Selected bank loan cashflow components

Variable name	Description	Timing (beginning or end of period)	Derivation
CF_{UF}	upfront fee	beginning	upfront fee rate $\times$ commitment amount
CF_{PP}	prepayment penalty	beginning	prepayment penalty rate $\times$ commitment amount
CF_{FF}	facility fee	beginning	facility fee rate $\times$ commitment amount
CF_{LC}	LC fee	beginning	LC fee rate $\times$ LC outstanding amount
CF_{BA}	BA fee	beginning	BA fee rate $\times$ BA outstanding amount
CF_C	operating costs	beginning	origination costs ($t = 0$) + servicing costs + collateral monitoring cost origination costs = fixed origination costs + marginal origination cost rate $\times$ commitment amount servicing costs = fixed servicing costs + marginal cost rate on outstanding $\times$ total outstanding amount + marginal cost rate on undrawn $\times$ (commitment amount − total outstanding amount) collateral monitoring cost = fixed collateral monitoring cost + marginal cost rate on collateralized outstanding $\times$ collateralized outstanding amount
CF_I	interest	end	contractual interest rate $\times$ (term loan outstanding amount + revolver outstanding amount)
CF_{CF}	commitment fee	end	commitment fee rate $\times$ (commitment amount − total outstanding amount)
CF_{UT}	utilization fee	end	total outstanding amount $\times$ blended utilization fee rate
CF_P	principal repaid (drawn)	end	term loan outstanding end of period − term loan oustanding beginning of period; determined by loan contract

TABLE A3 Selected pricing rates affecting bank loan cash flows

Variable	Description	Derivation
R_I	contractual interest rate	contractually specified fixed rate or minimum rate of floating rate options
R_{UF}	upfront fee rate	contractually specified
R_{CF}	commitment fee rate	contractually specified
R_{FF}	facility fee rate	contractually specified
R_{LC}	LC fee rate	contractually specified
R_{BA}	BA fee rate	contractually specified
R_{UT}	blended utilization fee rate	computed from contractually specified utilization fee schedule and current utilization as determined by usage model
R_{PP}	prepayment fee rate	contractually specified

TABLE A4 Selected cost rates affecting bank loan cash flows

Variable	Description	Derivation
FC_{ORIG}	fixed cost of loan origination	estimated from pricing of small loans
MC_{ORIG}	marginal origination cost rate	imputed from secondary loan prices
FC_{SERV}	fixed cost of loan servicing	imputed from pricing of small loans
MC_{SERVOS}	marginal servicing cost rate on total outstanding amount	imputed from pricing of low-risk term loans
MC_{SERVAC}	marginal servicing cost rate on undrawn amount	imputed from undrawn pricing of low-risk loans
FC_{COLL}	fixed cost of collateral monitoring	imputed from pricing of small, secured loans
MC_{COLL}	marginal cost rate of collateral monitoring	imputed from default rates and pricing of secured and unsecured loans

TABLE A5 Selected utilization rates affecting bank loan cash flows

Variable	Description	Derivation
RU_{TL}	term loan outstanding as percentage of commitment amount	loan attribute specified by contract
RU_{RV}	funded revolver outstanding as percentage of commitment amount	determined by usage model as influenced by the relative costs and anticipated usage rates of the different draw options
RU_{LC}	LC outstanding as percentage of commitment amount	determined by usage model as influenced by the relative costs and anticipated usage rates of the different draw options
RU_{BA}	BA outstanding as percentage of commitment amount	determined by usage model as influenced by the relative costs and anticipated usage rates of the different draw options
REU_{RV}	anticipated revolver outstanding as percentage of commitment amount	loan attribute entered by analyst
REU_{LC}	anticipated LC outstanding as percentage of commitment amount	loan attribute entered by analyst
REU_{BA}	anticipated BA outstanding as percentage of commitment amount	loan attribute entered by analyst

APPENDIX 5.3   MARGINAL AND MARKET COST OF CREDIT

Let CC represent the marginal cost of credit under the existing credit line and let MC denote the market cost, both expressed in basis points. The net credit-line cost, N, is:

$$N = CC - MC.$$

We compute MC by solving for the spread that implies an NPV of zero on a one-period term loan issued by the borrower:

$$0 = \frac{(1 + R + MC)(1 - PD \cdot L)}{1 + R} - 1 - MCOS$$

where *MCOS* denotes the per-dollar cost of servicing and monitoring the term loan, as inferred from market pricing. Solving, we obtain:

$$MC = (PD \cdot L + MCOS) \frac{1+R}{1-PD \cdot L}. \tag{A1}$$

Equation (A1) shows that *MC* equals the sum of market-based credit and servicing costs, with some minor adjustments for payment timing and exposure to default.

The credit-line cost, *CC*, reflects the terms of the loan contract. Consider, for example, a revolver with a drawn spread over the risk-free discount rate of *RS*, a commitment fee of *RCF* and no other charges:

$$CC = RS - RCF.$$

When the borrower draws, the interest-spread payments increase and commitment-fee payments simultaneously decrease. The marginal cost, *CC*, is computed by netting the two rates.

Suppose, alternatively, that the credit line is an *LC* facility, with an *LC* fee of *RLC* and a facility fee of *RFF*. Then:

$$CC = RLC \frac{1+R}{1-PD \cdot L}.$$

The factor applied to the *RLC* adjusts for that fee being paid in advance rather than in arrears. The facility fee is not substituted, since, unlike commitment fee payments, facility fee payments do not decline with increasing line usage.

Suppose that $R = 6\%$, $RS = 175\text{bps}$, $RCF = 45\text{bps}$, $PD = 2.5\%$, $L = 30\%$, and $MCOS = 50\text{bps}$. Then:

$$CC = 0.0175 - 0.045 = 0.0130$$

$$MC = (0.025 \cdot 0.3 + 0.005) \frac{1+0.06}{1-0.025 \cdot 0.3} = 0.01335$$

$$N = CC - MC = -0.00035.$$

Therefore, $N = -3.5$ bps, which indicates a small incentive to raise usage above initial expectations.

APPENDIX 5.4   CREDIT RISK MODELING APPROACHES

There are two common approaches to credit risk modeling. The *structural approach*, originally developed by Merton (1974), treats the firm's asset-value process and its capital structure as the underlying determinants of expected default rates. Equity and debt of the firm are seen as options on the underlying firm's value. These models assume that default occurs if the firm's asset value falls sufficiently below the value of its debt. Instruments with credit risk to the firm are modeled as derivatives of the firm's asset value, and can therefore be priced using the Black–Scholes–Merton approach. Early research in this area focused on developing explicit valuation formulas, given particular assumptions on the asset-value process and capital structure, and on comparing the values from those formulas with available market prices. More recent research attempts to explain features of market pricing by introducing jumps and informational imperfections into the valuation model (see, for example, Leland (1994); Longstaff and Swartz (1995a, 1995b); Duffie and Lando (1997); Madan and Unal (1998)).

The alternative *reduced-form* or *intensity-based approach* does not specify an underlying model of asset value and capital structure. Instead, default is modeled as an unpredictable jump event governed by a stochastic intensity process. The stochastic intensity processes describing default events or, more generally, credit-state transitions, are directly calibrated to market prices. By defining recovery rates in the event of default exogenously, no particular assumptions on the capital structure of the firm or priority in bankruptcy are required. Furthermore, given their mathematical tractability and similarities to terms structure models, the intensity models lead in an elegant way to Heath–Jarrow–Morton no-arbitrage conditions for defaultable debt (see, for example, Duffie and Singleton (1999); Madan and Unal (1998)).

The earliest reduced-form models deal with just two credit states (default and no-default). They make particular assumptions in order to obtain closed-form solutions for bond prices and facilitate model calibration to observed credit spreads (e.g., Jarrow and Turnbull (1995); Duffie and Singleton (1999)). Lando (1994), Jarrow, Lando, and Turnbull (1997) (JLT), and Lando (1998) extend the reduced-form approach to the case of multiple, discrete, credit states or ratings. These models are sometimes referred to as *rating-based models*.

Under the JLT model, spreads are deterministic since both the migration probabilities and the recovery rates are also deterministic. Das and Tufano (1996) (DT) extend the JLT model to allow for stochastic credit spreads that may also exhibit correlation to the risk-free term structure. For mathematical simplicity, DT assume that transition probabilities are deterministic and that recoveries follow a mean-reverting process.

The intuition behind the DT model is that stochastic credit spreads arise when the underlying default probabilities (or the intensities) and/or the recovery rates are stochastic. Either one of these two conditions alone can be used to fit the model to observed spread volatilities. Instead, Lando (1998) and Jarrow and Turnbull (2000) use Cox processes to obtain stochastic intensities that also lead to stochastic spreads. Gaussian models generally are used only for tractability, although they may lead to negative intensities in practice. Alternatively, Duffie and Singleton (1999) propose modeling the intensities directly as a stochastic mean-reverting process (perhaps with jump terms).

CHAPTER 6

Measuring the Unexpected: Events in Credit Risk

Justin Hingorani, Gordian Gaeta, and Shamez Alibhai
Simplex Credit Advisory Ltd

EVENTS: A CRITICAL BUT IGNORED ELEMENT OF CREDIT RISK

Risk is the assignment of probabilities to expected or anticipated future outcomes. On this basis we generally manage risk. However, it is the assumption that future outcomes are known that compromises the effectiveness of credit risk management practices. Significant losses are not caused by outcomes we expect, but rather by the unexpected events that catch us off guard. The Russian crisis, the Asian financial crisis and the development hedge funds are but some of the more recent examples of unexpected events with dire consequences for credit risk management. Events are thus critical, yet largely ignored elements of managing credit risk.

The industry at large reconciles this dilemma by assigning responsibility for expected losses to provisions and the prudent management of a financial institution. Unexpected losses are covered by capital adequacy or reserves mandated by the regulator.

With this division of labor, it is not surprising that regulators continuously refine capital adequacy rules as they update their perception of the unexpected while being cautious to accept internal credit risk measurement models as a basis for capital adequacy.

The inability to predict the future does not imply that we cannot manage it. Uncertainty differs substantially from risk in that future outcomes and their associated probabilities are both unknown. To shift from a situation governed by uncertainty to one characterized by risk, requires a formalized understanding, a model of dealing with uncertainty. Such a model can be a factor model based on large-scale causal relationships and predictions or on abstract possibilities. Both models are the focus of current risk measurement technologies.

Yet, few models for credit risk are effective in considering all possible future states of the world and assigning a probability measure to each state. The two substitutes used are intuition or historical correlation and normality.

The first approach uses the experience of the analyst to determine future scenarios and their effect on credit risk – the result is a subjective assessment. Consequently, the risk measurement process is a function of the imaginable and not of all possible future states. In a more formal setting, a set of explanatory variables is related to historical instances of default through statistical methods. While this quantifies some subjective or coincidental relationships, it fails to consider the effect of the unexpected. The outcomes used by the model for calibration are historical and without any basis for predicting future states.

The second approach in risk measurement differs fundamentally from the first, in that all possible outcomes are considered without appealing to models of cause and effect. With such an abstract model one is able to objectively consider and quantify a large number of possible events at various times and magnitudes, and their resulting affect on the credit risk of the company. This provides a more complete measurement of the impact event risk can have on the credit risk of a company, rather than relying on ad hoc considerations. Stress-testing and scenario analysis can then be layered on top of such a model to test changes in the model's event characteristics as further explored in other contributions.

An acceptable risk measurement system must reduce the overall uncertainty in the system. Progress can be made by using an abstract and objective event generator, or a method of generating unexpected outcomes to adequately capture the effect of unexpected events. While this does not quantify uncertainty, it does allow analysis of the effect of uncertainty on future outcomes. Moreover, it is a starting point to including the unthinkable in credit risk measurement.

To move towards this goal, the following section starts by examining events and their characteristics. This will define the requirements of the model. Two alternative models are considered to serve as basis of comparison. The proposed model is then used to highlight the information and benefits provided by quantifying event risk and is finally extended to include remaining requirements of events; namely, dynamic volatilities and non-normality.

CHARACTERIZING EVENTS

An event is an occurrence that causes a sudden, unexpected change in any one factor affecting credit risk. If the impact is of significance, the event is termed a "jump". A jump's significance is measured relative to the underlying volatility at that point in time and thus its size varies in magnitude.

Although the notion of a jump is intuitively simple, it is difficult to quantify objectively. Off-hand, one would consider a 50% change in a company's value to be a jump. In fact, a 50% change in value would have been considered significant for Hong Kong conglomerate Hutchison Whampoa at the start of 1997, when it had an approximate annualized asset volatility of 20%. But at the onset of the Asian crisis, Hutchison's asset volatility rose to 38%, reducing the significance of a 50% change. Thus, jumps must be defined in relative terms, in this case to the period of volatility in which they occur.

Jumps occur infrequently and when they do they are typically followed by a period of increased volatility of the underlying measure. After an unexpected and strong event has shocked the company, a period of increased uncertainty causes added volatility. How long the volatility takes to revert to previous levels, if it ever does, varies. However, an increase in volatility does not necessarily occur before a jump. As the event is unexpected it catches people off-guard, so a jump can occur during a period of relatively low volatility.

A jump is a large infrequent change identified relative to the volatility of the surrounding period and is measured in terms of number of standard deviations. Specifically, for purposes of the analysis, a jump is defined as greater than +3 or less than −3 standard deviations. Under an assumption of normality, which most current commercial approaches base their calculations on, this assigns a 0.2% probability of a jump occurring.

Consider these characteristics within the context of PHP Healthcare. In May of 1998, the market learned that the US Securities and Exchange Commission was investigating PHP Healthcare's accounting practices. Shortly thereafter, a class action suit was filed on behalf of PHP shareholders, alleging that PHP had been disclosing fraudulent information to inflate results. PHP's stock price crashed from USD 17 5/16 to USD 7 6/16 and on November 19, 1998 PHP filed for bankruptcy protection.

Figure 6.1 shows the daily returns for PHP's stock price divided by their relevant volatilities.

The number of jumps, as given in Figure 6.2, and their frequencies of occurrence can be calculated.

Clearly jumps are infrequent, but a probability of 0.2% severely underestimates the chance of jumps occurring. PHP's jump frequency rose to over 5% during the company's disastrous year of 1998. Experience suggests that, across the board, an assumption that possible future outcomes have a normal distribution tends to understate the probability and thus effect

FIGURE 6.1 Jumps are identified relative to the surrounding period's volatility

PHP stock prices and standardized returns (1994 to 1999)

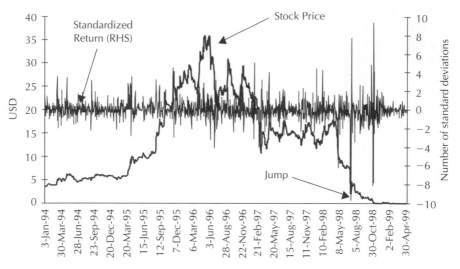

Source: Bloomberg, Simplex Credit Advisory analysis

FIGURE 6.2 Jumps occur more frequently than implied by a normal distribution

Actual PHP jump frequency and intermediate changes

	Jumps	Intermediate changes
1994	1.19%	9.52%
1995	1.98%	18.25%
1996	1.57%	23.23%
1997	2.37%	23.72%
1998	5.20%	26.40%
Normal distribution	0.2%	31.7%

Sources: Bloomberg, Simplex Credit Advisory analysis

of events. Therefore, this approach to measuring risk is skewed towards a view on the plausible and does not adequately incorporate the unexpected.

On May 18, 1998 PHP's stock price fell 23.57% or 6.23 standard deviations, coinciding with the announcement of the SEC investigation. The unexpected nature of this was characterized by the fact that the volatility over the preceding one month was 50%, but the event was followed by a one-month volatility of 71% – calculated excluding the event day. Overall, PHP had a relatively constant volatility of 60% during the first half of 1998 but as the stock price crashed, volatility increased to 133% by July 1998.

Volatility or even collective market information was not expecting the event and reacted strongly afterwards.

Not considering the risk of unexpected events or the characteristics of events will inaccurately estimate a company's risk. Jumps need to be incorporated not only as an event but also with their specific characteristics.

CAPTURING AND TREATING EVENTS

When including events, two problems arise: how to generate events (size, timing, frequency, and so on) and how to treat them within a model. In most approaches, events are an integral part of the computation methodology and not an explicit exogenous factor.

A first step for capturing events is the rather over-simplistic use of a single normal distribution of possible outcomes, say, from a complete credit loss to no credit loss at all. As shown earlier, a single normal distribution significantly underestimates the chance of a jump occurring. However, jumps have another ramification. When calculating the size of the distribution using a set of returns, jumps in the data cause the distribution to widen as it attempts to fit large events into its realm of possible changes. The result is a model that exaggerates intermediate movements.

Consider intermediate movements to be those relative changes in value which are between $+1$ and $+3$, or -1 and -3 standard deviations in size. In a standard normal distribution, such movements have just over a 30% chance of occurring. However, Figure 6.2 shows that the annual frequency of intermediate movements was much less at 10% in 1994 and didn't start to approach a 30% level until the panic period of 1998. Exaggeration of intermediate movements' likelihood through a normal distribution can result in overestimating a company's underlying risk and does nothing for projecting the recurrence or magnitude of a future event.

Numerous methods, proposed for explicitly capturing the characteristics of jumps, have been attempted. Jump-diffusion is one approach that combines a single distribution to capture the "normal" diffusion in value along with a distribution for modeling rare events – the Poisson distribution – that induces a jump every now and then. Such a rare event is considered as something that could cause a change in the magnitude of 10 standard deviations, like 1987's Black Monday. The problem is, how does one tune a model to event data that only occurs maybe once per year? For example, in PHP's data there are no changes greater than six standard deviations for 1994 to 1997 and in 1998 there are only seven. Such infrequent data is not statistically significant and thus reduces the confidence in the accuracy of the result.

None of the methods satisfactorily solve the problem of event generation. Events are therefore best modeled by treating them for what they are; namely, unexpected infrequent, and unpredictable changes in value. They cannot be defined at the outset, as they would then no longer differ from expected changes.

A framework to create an event generator and distribution is proposed. Historical changes of the chosen variable are reverse engineered into two distributions, one base distribution and one event distribution, the artificial training set for the unexpected. The resulting coefficients are optimized to fit the historical change distribution via maximum log likelihood.[1] This process creates several new coefficients that determine the shape of both the base and event distributions, and the propensity of a change resulting from the base distribution, the event distribution, or the event frequency. This idea has been used by institutions to model foreign exchange rates, as well as a way to enhance VAR calculations (Zangari 1996).

USING DISTRIBUTIONS

Consider an application for simulating future company value. A base distribution and a separate event distribution are combined to model the daily percentage change in a company's returns. The base distribution is defined as the returns that occur on a frequent basis, and the event distribution is defined as a set of larger, less frequent changes in the company's value, including jumps. The event frequency defines the chance of a day's return being selected from the event distribution instead of the base distribution. For return r the equations can be expressed as:

$$r = \begin{cases} \phi(\mu_B, \sigma_B^2) & \text{with probability } (1 - \lambda), \text{ or otherwise} \\ \phi(\mu_E, \sigma_E^2) & \text{with probability } \lambda \end{cases} \qquad (1)$$

where $\phi(\mu, \sigma^2)$ is a normal distribution distributed with mean μ and variance σ^2, $\{\mu_B, \sigma_B\}$ and $\{\mu_E, \sigma_E\}$ are the mean and volatility/size of the base and event distributions respectively, and λ is the event frequency.

A return drawn from either the base or event distribution is multiplied by the company's current value to project the next day's value. This process is conducted for the length of the simulation period. Repeating this random process thousands of times generates a distribution of possible values in the future, which can be used in risk measurement.

Introducing a separate event distribution containing jumps enables the volatility characteristics before and after a jump to be replicated. Immediate and significant jumps in value from positions of low volatility can be increased in frequency by instantly moving to the event distribution.

A separate event distribution provides another crucial benefit. Due to the infrequency of jumps by nature, it becomes extremely difficult to calibrate the characteristics of a distribution of jumps. How does one accurately calculate the likelihood of future jumps for a company when there have only been three large movements in the past five years? By considering jumps as part of a larger and more frequent set of events, characteristics of an event distribution (or jump-implied distribution) can be calculated. Kim and Finger (2000) calculate that when the size of a change in the S&P 500 is greater than or less than $+3$ or -3, respectively, there is almost a 100% chance the change was drawn from an event distribution (or what the authors call a "hectic day"). Thus, the measurement of jumps occurs indirectly through the event distribution. When the event distribution is used to describe a movement in the underlying risk variable, there is a chance that the movement may be a jump.

INTUITIVE COMPANY AND INDUSTRY RESULTS

Events are not limited to any specific geographies or industries. They are significant global factors. Explicit inclusion of events allows a model to remain firm-specific, making clear distinctions between different companies, even within the same industry and geography. Event parameters also provide an additional dimension to characterize industries and identify periods of increased uncertainty not evident from a single volatility. Such characteristics can be tracked over time to identify shifts or trends within the industries.

Take Polaroid and Kodak, companies operating in similar industries. At the measurement date, volatility of both companies was 20%. However, Polaroid's event size was 49% compared to Kodak's 70%, while Polaroid's event frequency was 20% and Kodak's 6%. Though both companies' values show similar risk on most days, Polaroid is subject to more frequent, large changes. On the occasion that an event manages to strike Kodak it does so with more impact. This clearly indicates the different risk profiles of both companies.

Differing equity dynamics result in a varying impact of jumps in an event-enhanced model (Figure 6.3).

Depending on the frequency and severity of the event, the model trades off its impact on volatility, frequency, and size of events.

Trade off is evident in an analysis of the US airline industry before and after the tragedies of September 11, 2001. Before that date, the S&P 500 Airline Subindex traded at a level around 275. However, when the markets re-opened on September 17, it had dropped 39% to 186. The future of the US airline industry was in question. This was only slightly reflected by a moderation in base volatility from 30% to 35%, but was clear in the shift of

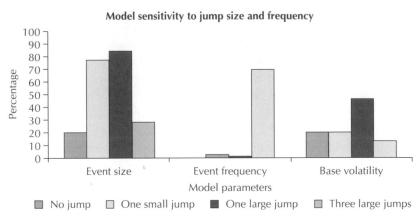

FIGURE 6.3   Parameters in the model trade-off to reflect equity dynamics

Source: Bloomberg, Simplex Credit Advisory analysis

the event risk parameters. Event size exploded from 47% to over 300%, while event frequency dropped from 17% to below 1%.

To show the importance of events outside individual companies, the approach was calibrated to numerous companies across several US industries. The parameters were averaged within each industry to identify the dynamics of each. Results reflect what one might intuitively expect. At one end of the spectrum the health care and technology industries show significant volatility with large events, whereas the stable, regulated utilities industry yields minimal volatility with smaller events. Event frequency remains fairly stable across the board (Figure 6.4).

Consider, specifically, two of these industries: energy and technology. In recent history both have undergone significant shifts in structure as well as incurring numerous events. To examine this, two stock indices are used, the Dow Jones 15 Utilities and the Nasdaq, representing the energy and technology industries respectively. Two models are fit to the indices' data and the resulting model parameters compared to reflect different information content. The first model consists of a single normal distribution (a univariate model) and the second model is the mixture of two distributions (a mixture model) described thus far.

The only parameter in the univariate model is the size of the distribution, or the volatility. This volatility is referred to as an unconditional volatility because it is not conditional on time or being in a base or event state, as in the mixture model. As mentioned earlier, the three parameters of the mixture model are base volatility, event frequency, and event size.

In a third case, this type of analysis is extended to the stock indices of Hong Kong, Singapore, South Korea, and Thailand during the Asian crisis

FIGURE 6.4 Volatility and event frequency describe US industries

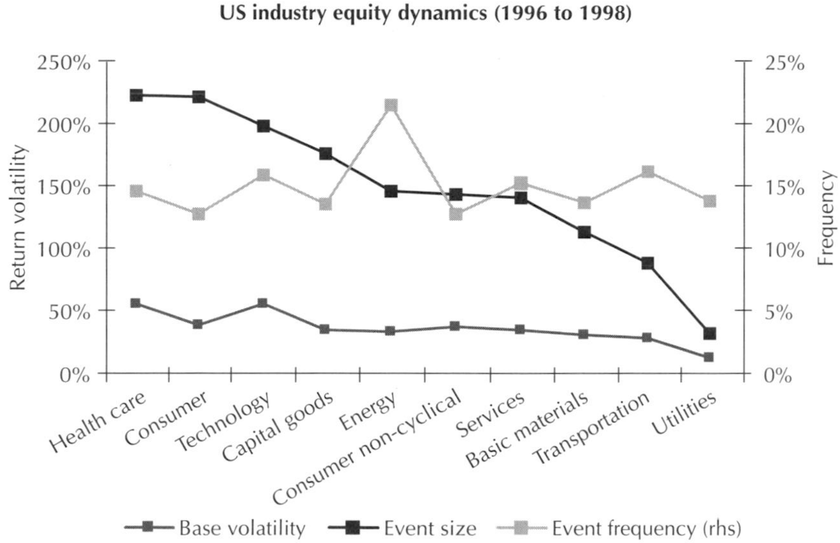

US industry equity dynamics (1996 to 1998)

Source: Bloomberg, Simplex Credit Advisory analysis

---

of 1997 and 1998. The results provide a rich perspective of the risk that existed during this time.

Case 1 The Energy Crisis

A trend to deregulate energy providers swept across the United States during the late 1990s. In September 1996, legislation was approved to open California's $20 billion electricity market to competition under the premise that deregulation would lower bills for all. Subsequently, in January 1998, deregulation bills approved by state lawmakers took effect, including a rate cap imposed on utilities until they had divested themselves of their generation plants. As a result, utilities immediately began their asset disposals. From Figure 6.5 we see that the parameters remained fairly stable until the end of 1998, except for the daily event frequency, which bounced around a level of 22.5%.

In July 1999, San Diego Gas & Electric (SDG&E) was the first California utility to deregulate. With the company no longer restricted by a price cap, SDG&E passed on high wholesale costs to consumers, which had been driven up by low energy supply relative to demand. Bills effectively doubled from an average residential bill of $49 to about $100 by May 2000, and by mid-summer customers' bills had tripled.

FIGURE 6.5   With the onset of the energy crisis event risk increased through 1999

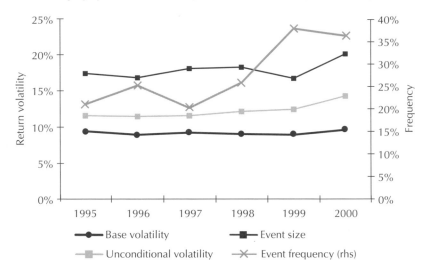

Equity dynamics of the Dow Jones 15 Utilities Index (1995 to 2000)

Source: Bloomberg, Simplex Credit Advisory analysis

On May 22, 2000 the California Independent System Operator (ISO) declared the first of 36 alerts, when power reserves dropped below 5 percent, followed by rolling blackouts (June 15, 2000) and an emergency on December 7, 2000, when power reserves fell below 1.5 percent. During this time, average wholesale power prices, which were $12 in mid-1988, hit $120 a megawatt-hour in June 2000 and surpassed $1,000 by December 2000.

Clearly, significant events affected the energy sector during this time. In the univariate model, the situation was reflected by a gradual increase in the unconditional volatility from 12% to 14.3%; a rise in uncertainty but not at all near the degree one would expect from the significance of the above events. On the other hand, the mixture model conveyed the situation by a dramatic increase in event risk. The event frequency shot up from 26% at the end of 1998 to around 37% by the end of 1999 and throughout 2000. Similarly, the event size rose from 17% in 1999 to 20% in 2000 while base volatility remained fairly stable, only slightly rising in the end. By breaking apart the event risk, we are provided with a clearer picture of the severity of the situation and the potential risks involved.

Case 2 New Dynamics of the "New Economy"

A great source of uncertainty is exploration of the unknown and the technology bubble of the 1990s is an example of such. In a matter of few years, the Internet evolved from a communication tool for governmental and educational institutions to an electronic wealth of graphical and textual information and finally a fertile breeding ground for business coined as e-commerce. This latter use spawned companies that were said to be a part of the "new economy" as people were uncertain as to how their business models would evolve. But uncertainty did not stop them from pouring in unprecedented amounts of capital.

The new economy was seeded by a series of developments starting in 1993 when Mosaic, the first graphics-based Web browser, became available and traffic on the Internet expanded at a 341,634% annual growth rate. In 1994 Netscape Communications Corp was formed and by 1995 the Web comprised the bulk of Internet traffic. In 1996, e-business was in full bloom with Web addresses dotting the US landscape, annual global Internet Service Provider (ISP) revenue approaching $3 billion and approximately 40 million people going online with more than $1 billion per year changing hands at Internet shopping malls (PBS 1997).

Overall, the technology industry analyzed through the dynamics of the Nasdaq Index 1995–2000 was growing and moving into new and uncertain territory. In the univariate model, all of these events were reflected by a slight increase in unconditional volatility not much of an indicator for a period of evolutionary change. However, in the mixture model, base volatility and event size increased from 1996 to 1997, balanced by a decrease in event frequency (Figure 6.6).

FIGURE 6.6   The new economy required a clear distinction between daily and event risk

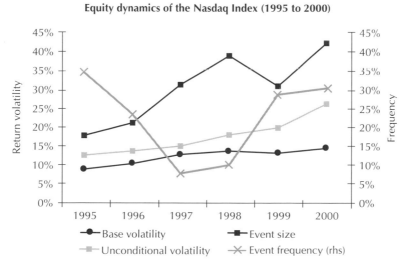

Equity dynamics of the Nasdaq Index (1995 to 2000)

Source: Bloomberg, Simplex Credit Advisory analysis

This reflected an overall increase in the day-to-day risk combined with the potential larger impact from uncertain events as technology started to become a larger, but yet unknown force in the economy.

This initial outstanding growth only continued through 1997. But in 1998 people were reminded of the uncertainty behind the new technologies with numerous announcements of job cuts at several leading companies including Intel, National Semiconductor, Compaq, and Motorola, who announced plans on June 4 to layoff 10% of its workforce, or about 15,000 workers. With this combination of growth and uncertainty, on July 16, 1998 Nasdaq inched over 2,000 for the first time, soon followed (August 31, 1998) by a fall of 140.43, its worst point drop ever at that time.

The potential impact of events started to be realized. The univariate model portrayed such events as an overall increase in risk with unconditional volatility further increasing. In contrast, the mixture model took a different view on matters. It showed daily risk to have leveled out (base volatility flattened) at around 14%, with the real source of risk being the uncertainty of events shown by both event size and event frequency climbing 8% and 2%, respectively, from 1997. Not only was there a greater chance of events occurring but the possible impact was larger.

The worries of 1998 did not stop the new economy as the Nasdaq continued to rocket skywards in 1999 while technology companies reaped the benefits of increased Y2K spending. After Y2K turned out to be a non-event, celebration of the digital economy's marvels still continued climaxing at the Nasdaq's peak of 5,000 in March 2000. After that a downward spiral began as the Nasdaq plunged more than 500 points and billions of dollars of investments were wiped out on April 14, 2000 when the Nasdaq tumbled almost 10%. At the end of 2000, the Nasdaq finished its worst year ever at about half of the peak and down 30% or so for the year, fueled by a rash of poor earnings announcements and "dot-com" bankruptcies. Layoffs increased to almost 10,000, totaling over 45,000 job cuts at almost 500 companies with about 100 of these no longer existing.

To measure this impact, the univariate model drove its unconditional volatility upwards during 1999 and 2000, showing overall risk continuing to rise. However, the market's final actualization of the event risk was reflected in the mixture model with base volatility continuing fairly level, event size bouncing around 30%, and the event frequency still rising but starting to plateau. Event risk forecasted last period was now being realized. Once again the primary risk source was not daily changes in value but events with chain effects. Large pieces of the technological wall were crumbling and taking other pieces with them.

Case 3 Taming the Asian tiger

Event characteristics are not restricted to the US markets. The mixture model's parameters can help dissect risks that existed during the Asian crisis and would not be evident from a simple univariate model. Figures 6.7a and 6.7b examine three countries greatly affected – Thailand, South Korea, and Indonesia – and uses Singapore, which weathered the crisis relatively well, as a basis of comparison.

Up until 1997 the countries' risk indicators showed fair stability. However, after more than a decade of substantial growth in Asia, the Asian Tiger's roar was muzzled in 1997. It began immediately in January with the first default ($6 billion) in over ten years of a leading Korean chaebol, soon followed by Thailand's first company to default on foreign debt payments and the subsequent collapse of another Korean chaebol, Sammi Steel.

Two days after the Thai Prime Minister's June 30 announcement that their currency would not be devalued, the Bank of Thailand was forced to devalue once foreign reserves were depleted. The devaluation was precipitated by hedge funds who cashed in with bets on the baht's decline. From that point onwards Southeast Asian currencies tumbled one by one. In July, the Singapore dollar dropped to its lowest level since February 1995, the Malaysian ringgit hit a 38-month low and Hong Kong spent US $1 billion over a two-hour period to defend its currency. In August, the Indonesian rupiah plunged to a new historic low and between October to December the Korean won fell to more than one half of its value.

As a result, all countries' event size shot up with Indonesia's doubling from 20% and Korea's jumping from 32% to over 50%, compounded by a 3.5% increase in event frequency. Thailand's rise was little more moderated as its event size and frequency were already at lofty heights. Though Singapore was not forgotten, it stood its ground with event size only increasing to 30%, event frequency dropping below those of the other Asian countries and base volatility just slightly rising from 9.5% to 10.5%. In fact, the base volatility risk rose moderately for all four of the countries with the majority of the risk being reflected in events.

Though Korea's base volatility and event size remained solid, 1998's event likelihood steadily rose to over 22% by the end of the year. This punishing year started in December 1997 with a glimmer of hope when the IMF provided South Korea with a record $57 billion bailout package. But this was not enough and by the end of 1997 bad loans at South Korean banks had almost quadrupled, totaling $6 billion, or 2.7% of all loans. In 1998, a third of South Korea's 30 merchant banks were forced to close and warnings of soaring inflation, record-high unemployment, and recession resounded with more than 10,000 firms defaulting (Roubini 1998).

FIGURE 6.7a The univariate model did not reflect the event risk of the Asian economic crisis but the mixture model did, through increased event sizes

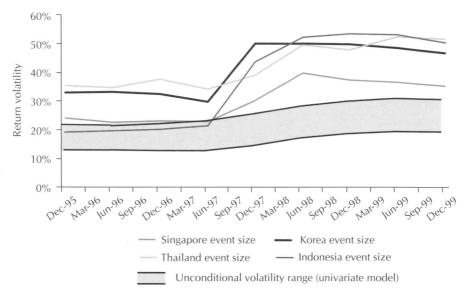

Event sizes and unconditional vol. range of four Asian indices (1995 to 1999)

Source: Bloomberg, Simplex Credit Advisory analysis

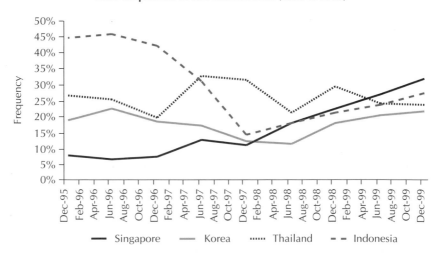

FIGURE 6.7b Event frequencies adjusted accordingly

Event frequencies of four Asian indices (1995 to 1999)

Source: Bloomberg, Simplex Credit Advisory analysis

Indonesia's event frequency moved alongside Korea's with its event size continuing to climb to over 53%. Market selling that continued into January 1998, along with a lack of confidence in Indonesia, crashed its stock market down 18.5% in one day and the rupiah dropping 26% in a single session, down more than 70% since July of 1997. By February when President Suharto first came to power, riots broke out and announcements declared the economy on the brink of hyper-inflation, with prices soaring at rates not seen since the mid-1960s. This was compounded by wage freezes and higher unemployment.

Singapore continued to be battered by contagion effects, particularly from Indonesia and Malaysia, with its event frequency reversing direction and increasing by 6%. However, always a pillar of strength, its base volatility only climbed slightly and its event size plateaued at less than 40%, far below rival countries. In fact, the political upheaval in Indonesia unnerved investors in markets as far away as Russia, Brazil, and Mexico, arousing fears the deepening economic troubles in Asia could become global in scope.

Overall, the univariate model reflected the crisis risk as a steady increase of about 10% on average over 1997 and 1998. But this did not reflect the sudden onslaught of risk that occurred in the latter half of 1997 as evident by the jump in the mixture model's event size; nor did the univariate convey the magnitude of the situation mirrored by the doubling in the potential size of events. The single measure of the univariate model also masked the fact that the majority of the risk was due to an environment conducive to increased event risk and not just a general increase in day-to-day fluctuations in value.

THE NON-NORMALITY OF EVENTS

What is the shape of events? So far we have assumed events to be normally distributed – i.e., to randomly occur positively or negatively with similar possible impacts. However, are these infrequent changes in value actually symmetrical or can they have a recurring bias or even a bias at a point in time, such as during a bear or bull market? For example, in 2000 the markets were in a severe downturn. This downturn may have been due to a string of bad events or the markets simply drifting downwards as a flow of pessimistic information was released.

This investigation can be broken down into two questions:

- Does bad news occur more often than good or vice versa?
- Are bad news events generally larger than good news events or even possibly the reverse?

To examine these questions we conduct two tests on each of the S&P 500 and Nasdaq. The first uses a distribution with an adjustable skew to model events. The skew of a distribution measures the amount of bias present. A negative skew means that bad events have a greater chance of occurring and/ or a greater magnitude of impact, whereas a positive skew reflects more and/ or larger good events.

To examine the extent of skew in events, a mixture model is applied to both the S&P 500 and Nasdaq. However, for this analysis a beta distribution is used to model events instead of a normal. The beta distribution has the density functional form:

$$f(x \mid a, b) = \frac{\Gamma(a+b)}{\Gamma(a) \cdot \Gamma(b)} \, x^{a-1}(1-x)^{b-1}, \text{ for } 0 < x < 1 \text{ and zero otherwise}$$

(2)

where $f(x \mid a, b)$ is the probability of x occurring given parameters $\{a, b\}$ and $\Gamma(\cdot)$ is the gamma function.[2] To accommodate beta's restrictions on x, a transformation is performed on the stock returns so that they map into the interval between 0 and 1.

This functional form contains two parameters $\{a, b\}$ that determine beta's shape, allowing it to have a positive skew, negative skew, or be perfectly symmetrical. Figure 6.8 demonstrates the different shapes the beta distribution can assume. As the parameters increase in value and are equal,

FIGURE 6.8   The beta distribution provides a flexible shape

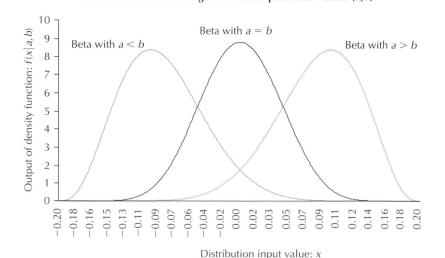

Beta distributions resulting from various parameter values {a,b}

Source: Bloomberg, Simplex Credit Advisory analysis

the beta distribution serves as a close approximation to the normal distribution. The flexibility of beta's shape will enable us to determine if the event distribution is best modeled with a skew or if events are symmetrical.

Figures 6.9 and 6.10 show the maximum log-likelihood estimation (MLE) results for both normal and beta event distributions calibrated to the S&P 500 and Nasdaq at various times over data sets extending from March 25, 1994 to March 23, 2001. In all calibrations, the MLE results are equally accurate for the normal and beta event distributions as indicated by the sum of the log likelihoods. This is because the beta parameters $\{a, b\}$ for all calibrations are approximately equal, suggesting that events are evenly distributed and not positively or negatively skewed. In fact, with the beta distributions approximating normals, the event frequencies, sizes, and means for both beta and normal event distributions are approximately equal.

Thus, the only bias is evident by the non-zero means of the base and event distributions. To determine whether these means are statistically different from zero we perform a z-test[3] under the hypothesis that the true mean is zero. A Z-score greater than 1.96 or less than -1.96 for any of the dates rejects the hypothesis with 95% confidence.

For the S&P 500 the corresponding z-scores (Figure 6.9) show with greater than 95% confidence that the base mean is consistently non-zero, whereas the hypothesis cannot be rejected for the event distribution, except on December 31, 1998. For the Nasdaq (Figure 6.10), using the Z-scores, it is clear that both the base and event means are non-zero.

Thus, generally, the base distributions tend to have a positive bias whereas the event distributions are often negatively biased. In other words, for events, bad events are larger and occur a little more frequently than good events. But around these distributions' shifted means, the data occurs randomly above and below with little or no skew.

Another angle to investigate this issue from is to examine the raw data directly. The second test calibrates a mixture of normals to the S&P 500 and Nasdaq index returns. From these parameters, the probabilities of a return, conditioned on the size of the return given, having been a simple daily change or having occurred during an event are calculated. Namely,

$$f(event \mid x_t) = \frac{\lambda \cdot f(x_t \mid \mu_{event}, \sigma^2_{event})}{(1 - \lambda) \cdot f(x_t \mid \mu_{base}, \sigma^2_{base}) + \lambda \cdot f(x_t \mid \mu_{event}, \sigma^2_{event})} \quad (3)$$

where $f(event \mid x_t)$ is the probability of the return x_t having been drawn from the event distribution given the value of x_t (Kim and Finger 2000). Similarly for $f(base \mid x_t)$, just substitute the numerator with $(1 - \lambda) \cdot f(x_t \mid \mu_{base}, \sigma^2_{base})$.

With these conditional probabilities, historical return data is randomly divided into base and event distributions and the first four moments – mean,

FIGURE 6.9 Beta's parameters approximate a normal distribution for the S&P 500

Normal and beta distribution results for the S&P 500 (1997 to 2001)

	Base mean		Base volatility		Event frequency		Event mean		Event size	
	Normal event	Beta event	Normal event	Beta event	Normal event	Beta event	Normal event	Beta event	Normal event	Beta event
23-Mar-01	0.11%	0.10%	10.25%	10.36%	31.82%	30.59%	−0.06%	−0.07%	25.62%	26.00%
31-Dec-00	0.10%	0.10%	10.20%	10.31%	31.08%	29.81%	−0.03%	−0.03%	25.33%	25.72%
30-Jun-00	0.11%	0.11%	10.27%	10.39%	27.68%	26.36%	−0.02%	−0.02%	25.94%	26.40%
31-Dec-99	0.12%	0.12%	10.07%	10.21%	25.30%	23.76%	−0.03%	−0.04%	24.87%	25.41%
30-Jun-99	0.12%	0.12%	9.90%	10.03%	23.69%	22.30%	−0.04%	−0.05%	25.37%	25.92%
31-Dec-98	0.12%	0.12%	10.16%	10.25%	14.96%	14.08%	−0.14%	−0.15%	28.80%	29.48%
30-Jun-98	0.12%	0.11%	9.46%	9.82%	16.75%	12.92%	−0.08%	0.00%	23.00%	25.17%
31-Dec-97	0.11%	0.11%	8.81%	9.31%	19.82%	14.45%	−0.05%	−0.09%	22.28%	25.08%
30-Jun-97	0.11%	0.11%	7.18%	7.26%	36.20%	34.68%	0.03%	0.02%	15.58%	15.81%

	Beta parameters		Base mean Z-score		Event mean Z-score		Sum log likelihoods	
	a	b	Normal event	Beta event	Normal event	Beta event	Normal event	Beta event
23-Mar-01	73.8	74.3	6.84	6.72	−1.67	−1.78	5635.8	5634.7
31-Dec-00	75.6	75.8	6.51	6.39	−0.67	−0.78	5483.2	5482.2
30-Jun-00	71.7	71.9	6.57	6.48	−0.40	−0.56	5112.8	5111.8
31-Dec-99	77.4	77.7	7.04	6.92	−0.75	−0.96	4788.8	4787.8
30-Jun-99	74.3	74.7	7.09	6.97	−1.00	−1.21	4392.8	4391.9
31-Dec-98	57.0	57.9	6.54	6.44	−2.69	−2.88	4047.8	4046.5
30-Jun-98	79.1	79.1	6.36	6.03	−1.70	0.00	3720.8	3719.5
31-Dec-97	79.3	80.0	6.08	5.66	−1.06	−1.83	3309.8	2944.0
30-Jun-97	201.3	200.8	6.87	6.85	0.82	0.65	2956.8	2956.2

Source: Bloomberg, Simplex Credit Advisory analysis

FIGURE 6.10 Beta's parameters approximate a normal distribution for the Nasdaq

Normal and beta distribution results for the Nasdaq (1997 to 2001)

	Base mean		Base volatility		Event frequency		Event mean		Event size	
	Normal event	Beta event	Normal event	Beta event	Normal event	Beta event	Normal event	Beta event	Normal event	Beta event
23-Mar-01	0.21%	0.22%	13.70%	13.70%	34.77%	34.77%	-0.25%	-0.30%	42.82%	42.81%
31-Dec-00	0.21%	0.21%	13.41%	13.46%	34.33%	33.98%	-0.21%	-0.21%	40.64%	41.02%
30-Jun-00	0.22%	0.21%	13.27%	13.66%	31.14%	28.62%	-0.15%	-0.17%	37.77%	39.00%
31-Dec-99	0.22%	0.21%	11.99%	13.05%	35.04%	26.58%	-0.09%	-0.15%	29.42%	32.65%
30-Jun-99	0.19%	0.19%	12.72%	12.82%	26.37%	25.47%	-0.19%	-0.20%	31.30%	31.73%
31-Dec-98	0.16%	0.16%	13.22%	13.35%	13.65%	12.60%	-0.41%	-0.43%	35.24%	36.32%
30-Jun-98	0.16%	0.15%	12.46%	12.69%	13.81%	11.40%	-0.41%	0.48%	26.08%	27.31%
31-Dec-97	0.14%	0.14%	12.12%	12.37%	13.83%	11.40%	-0.37%	-0.48%	26.46%	27.31%
30-Jun-97	0.18%	0.18%	9.94%	10.08%	34.29%	32.31%	-0.13%	0.15%	19.51%	19.76%

	Beta parameters		Sum log likelihoods		Base mean Z-score		Event mean Z-score	
	a	b	Normal event	Beta event	Normal event	Beta event	Normal event	Beta event
23-Mar-01	26.6	27.4	4840.1	4834.8	10.33	10.50	-3.95	-4.62
31-Dec-00	29.1	29.8	4760.2	4757.5	10.35	10.21	-3.37	-3.35
30-Jun-00	32.4	32.9	4544.2	4542.1	10.28	9.81	-2.48	-2.83
31-Dec-99	46.4	47.1	4385.6	4384.7	11.13	9.56	-1.80	-2.70
30-Jun-99	49.1	50.0	4039.4	4038.3	8.75	8.60	-3.44	-3.58
31-Dec-98	36.9	38.5	3770.2	3769.2	6.80	6.61	-6.36	-6.59
30-Jun-98	65.4	68.7	3500.3	3499.9	6.75	6.34	-8.27	-9.15
31-Dec-97	65.4	68.7	3114.0	3113.6	5.84	5.58	-6.90	-8.61
30-Jun-97	127.6	129.5	2742.0	2742.0	8.38	8.14	-3.14	-3.49

Source: Bloomberg, Simplex Credit Advisory analysis

variance, skew, and kurtosis – calculated for each subset of data. Random splitting of the data is repeated multiple times to obtain a range of values for each distribution's moments. Each moment's range of values for the base and event distributions will be used to see if each the moments lie within possible values that may have been generated by normal distributions.

To demonstrate, we randomly generate a return series using a mixture of distributions. The base distribution used is normal but the event distribution is taken to be a Gumbel distribution. We will call these the "true base" and the "true event" distributions.

A Gumbel distribution, shown in Figure 6.11, is skewed and is used in extreme value theory because the tails of the distribution can vary significantly in thickness, encompassing a range of other distributions – e.g., normal, exponential, and lognormal. The Gumbel's probability density function has the form:.

$$f(x_t \,|\, l, s) = \frac{1}{s}\, e^{\,=[\frac{x_t - l}{s} + e^{-\left(\frac{x_t - l}{s}\right)}]}$$

with mean $E(x) = l + \gamma s$ and variance $Var(x) = \frac{1}{6}\pi^2 s^2$ (4)

where l is the location parameter, s is the scale parameter, and γ is the Euler constant.[4] In this form, the skew is positive. To make it negative we multiply each x_t by -1 before calculating its density value.

FIGURE 6.11 The Gumbel distribution provides a significant skew for modelling events

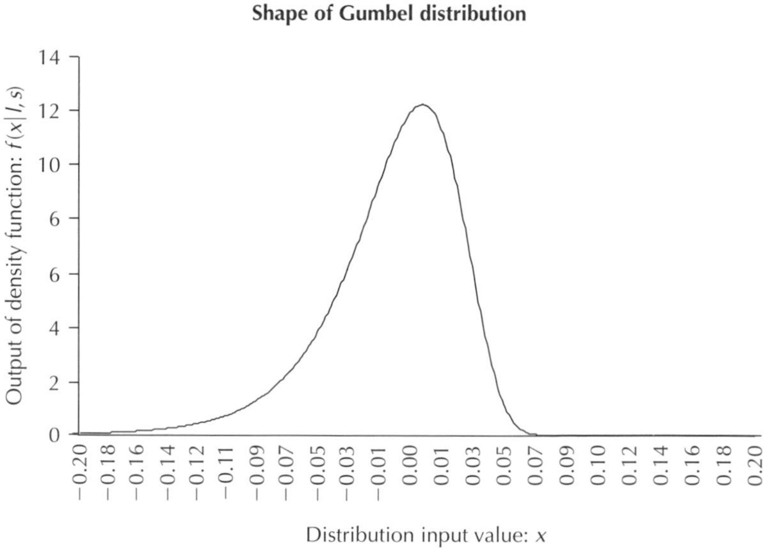

Shape of Gumbel distribution

Source: Bloomberg, Simplex Credit Advisory analysis

The normal distribution used has a mean of 0% and a daily volatility of about 0.63% (10% annually). The Gumbel distribution's location parameter l is set to 0, with a scale s of 0.0123 and a daily event frequency of 15%. Using these two distributions in a mixture model we generate a sample return series with the sample moments indicated by the dots in Figure 6.12.

After generating the return series from a normal Gumbel mixture we fit a mixture of normals to the series; namely, the "fitted base" and "fitted event" distributions. The result is a fitted base distribution with a mean of 0.02% and an annualized volatility of 11.83%. The fitted event distribution occurs with a daily frequency of about 1%, mean of −3.87%, and an event size of 20.64%.

Separating the raw data as above we have the 95% confidence intervals and means of each of the first four moments as given in Figure 6.12. The first thing to note is that the event frequency has decreased from 15% to 1%. As the normal event distribution is unable to mimic the skew of the Gumbel it has focused on picking up the returns generated by the negative tail of the true event distribution and has largely ignored the majority of the mass of the Gumbel as well as its positive tail. This resulted in a decrease in event frequency and significantly shifted the mean of the event distribution so the 95% confidence interval lies far from the true mean of 0.04%.

The base normal distribution must now encompass the positive returns of both the true base, as well as the true event distribution slightly skewing it positive instead of being symmetrical. On the other hand, the fitted event is skewed negative like the true event as it tries to capture the fatter tail of the Gumbel.

With respect to kurtosis the mixture of normals completely falters. Left with capturing 99% of the returns, the base distributions kurtosis signficantly increases towards the kurtosis of the entire data series, 7.97, but not completely as the majority of the kurtosis was a result of the Gumbel's negative tail, being modeled by the shifted fitted event distribution. In contrast, the event distribution's kurtosis fluctuates wildly as one large return can have a significant impact on a small sample only including 1% of the returns. Thus, from examining the raw data we can immediately see that two normals provide a poor fit. More specifically, the negative mean and skew of the fitted event distribution show us that there is a bias in the true event distribution towards bad events. The kurtosis demonstrates that the tails of the base and event normals are insufficient to capture the full range of returns in the data series. Thus, though the mixture of normals does not correctly represent the underlying data, using them as a basis to separate the data into two distributions provides a framework for analysis that can guide us towards a better model.

FIGURE 6.12 A clear negative bias appears in the fitted event distribution as it tries to model large events

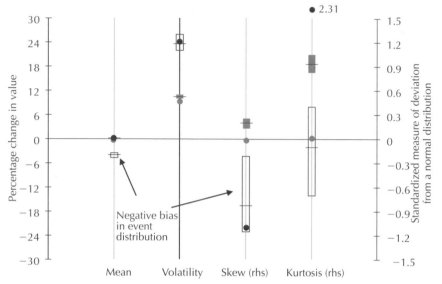

Distribution characteristics of the true and fitted distributions

Source: Bloomberg, Simplex Credit Advisory analysis

Figures 6.13 and 6.14 show the results of calibrating a mixture of normals on Nasdaq and S&P 500 returns from March 25, 1994 to March 23, 2001. These charts show the 95% confidence intervals and averages for the first four moments of each of the base and event data series. If the data series were generated by normal distributions with zero means it is possible that the resulting data may have non-zero means, skews, and kurtosis for the base and event distributions due to sampling error.

To determine a 95% confidence interval of calculation errors for each of the first four moments we generated multiple data series from a normal distribution with zero mean. The curly braces in Figures 6.12 and 6.13 show these confidence intervals. Thus we can see that both Nasdaq and S&P 500 have statistically significant non-zero base and event distribution means, which lie outside of the error range for a zero-mean normal. Specifically, the base distribution has a positive mean while the event distribution's mean is negative for both Nasdaq and S&P 500. However, the base distribution's skew and kurtosis significantly overlap with the error range. Thus, we cannot reject the hypothesis that base distribution's skew and kurtosis are both zero.

We can more confidently reject the hypothesis for the event distribution. Nasdaq's skew lies just above its error range and S&P 500's skew lies just below it, though it does slightly overlap. Thus, it is possible for the event distribution to have a slight skew that can be positive or negative. However, overall the event distribution is biased toward bad events as both indices have negative mean. It's just that the negative shift in S&P 500 is less than Nasdaq's, so a negative skew is required to capture the remaining bad events.

The kurtosis of the event distribution lies far above the error range, indicating significant fat tails that cannot be captured by a normal distribution. Overall, both indices have a base distribution approximated very well by a normal distribution. The skew for both indices is not large and could be ignored. However, the event distribution could use a model distribution that can incorporate fat tails. One way is to use a fat-tailed

FIGURE 6.13   Large events in the Nasdaq occur more frequently than in a normal distribution

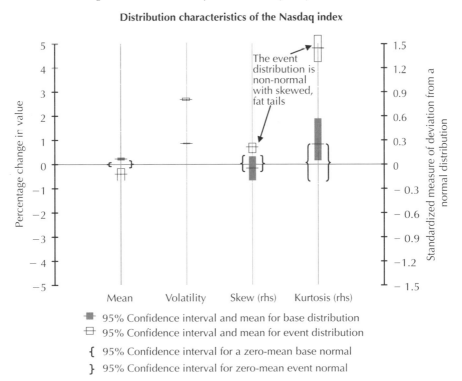

Distribution characteristics of the Nasdaq index

Source: Bloomberg, Simplex Credit Advisory analysis

FIGURE 6.14   ... and similarly for the S&P 500

Distribution characteristics of the S&P 500 index

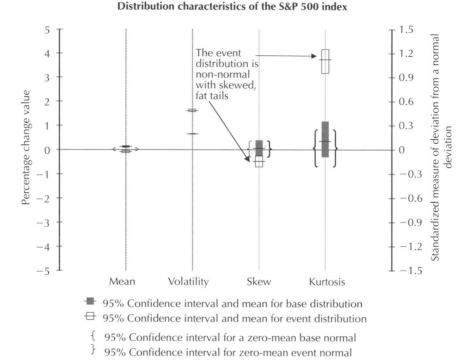

Source: Bloomberg, Simplex Credit Advisory analysis

distribution such as Student's T-Distribution. Another is to model volatilities changing over time.

DYNAMIC VOLATILITIES

In characterizing events we noted that volatilities and event size change over time. This was evident from the changing base volatilities and event size of the Dow Jones 15 Utilities index as we re-trained the mixture model to the index over time. PHP Healthcare showed that the change in volatility can be quite significant after an event, possibly taking some time before it returns to pre-event levels.

To capture these properties we incorporate a time-varying volatility into the mixture model; namely, GARCH (Generalized Autoregressive Conditional Heteroskedasticity). GARCH applies a deterministic process to weight a combination of constant value, the volatility predicted by GARCH for the last period, and the error from last period's prediction. Specifically, the equation is:

$$\sigma_t^2 = \alpha\sigma_{t-1}^2 + \beta X_{t-1}^2 + \varpi \tag{5}$$

where σ_t^2 is the volatility for the upcoming period, σ_{t-1}^2 is the volatility from the previous period, X_{t-1}^2 is the error in the last period's prediction of the return, ϖ is a constant, and α and β are parameters for weighting the impact of σ_{t-1}^2 and X_{t-1}^2.

In simulating a company's value over time a return is drawn from the mixture distribution. This return then feeds into the time-varying volatilities to calculate the volatility for the next day, thus allowing volatilities to change over time. The time-varying volatilities are not used explicitly to capture events, but rather to provide a dynamic basis for defining events. A dynamic basis is essential, as a constant event size cannot allow for a changing definition of a jump that coincides with a company's changing volatility as demonstrated by the Hutchison Whampoa example.

Incorporating GARCH with a separate event distribution replicates characteristics of volatilities after a jump. Empirical observation shows that volatilities in the aftermath of a large event do not immediately drop to pre-jump levels; rather they taper off as the market continues to reel from the shock. GARCH also maintains the higher level of volatilities in the aftermath of a jump since its calculation includes last period's error – i.e., the jump size. However, the volatilities are able to taper off at a reasonable rate by moving out of the event distribution.

Consider fitting the model parameters of a mixture of normal models with and without dynamic volatilities to the S&P 500 and Nasdaq on March 23, 2001 using maximum loglikelihood estimation. Since we are trying to maximize the loglikelihood, the larger the sum of loglikelihoods the better the fit. The model using a constant volatility produces sum of loglikelihoods for the S&P 500 and Nasdaq of 5635 and 4840, respectively. Incorporating GARCH results in increased sums of 5780 and 5167 for the S&P 500 and Nasdaq. Thus, as GARCH is able to better capture properties of volatilities we are able to improve the fit of the model to the data.

CONCLUSION

In current credit risk management processes, the likelihood and impact of events have largely been ignored. However, their impact has been felt globally through significant losses. To measure risk they must be considered and quantified.

To model events one must consider their characteristics, namely that they are sudden, unexpected changes, which can be quite significant in magnitude relative to the underlying volatility of the company's value. A single normal distribution is insufficient to encompass events and day-to-day changes in value because it ends up underestimating large changes and exaggerating the occurrence of intermediate movements. To capture events they should be modeled explicitly.

A mixture of distributions enables the modeling of events within their own distribution so that specific characteristics can be captured. Using a simple mixture of two normal distributions is sufficient to produce highly intuitive and informative results that can identify differences in risk between seemingly like companies, characterize industries, and distinguish changes in risk due to daily movements versus events. Enhancing this with dynamic volatilities and a non-normal event distribution that can capture the fat tails of events, e.g., Student's T-Distribution, enables changing event size and more frequent jumps to also be incorporated and improves model fit to historical data.

Thus, with an accurate model of fluctuations in company value that explicitly measures event risk we have a basis for measuring obligor credit risk in a fundamental framework.

NOTES

[1] Maximum Loglikelihood Estimation (MLE) is a process for adjusting the parameters of a distribution D so the probability of the data series $x = \{x_1, x_2, \ldots, x_n\}$ having occurred is maximized given x was distributed $\sim D$. For further explanation see Hamilton (1994).

[2] The gamma function $\Gamma(n)$ is used to calculate the factorial $(n - 1)!$

[3] This z-test examines the normally distributed sample means around zero where the z-score is the number of standard deviations a given sample mean is from the hypothesized "center", zero, of the normal distribution. The z-score is calculated by taking the distance the sample mean is from the theoretical mean ($\mu_s - 0$) and dividing by the size of a standard deviation ($\sigma_s / \sqrt{N}$) where σ_s is the daily return volatility and N is the number of stock returns in the data set. If the z-score lies outside of the range $[-1.96, 1.96]$ we can reject the hypothesis that the sample mean is statistically equal to zero with 95% confidence.

[4] The Euler constant is $\gamma = \lim_{n \to \infty} \sum_{i=1}^{n} \frac{1}{i} - \ln(n) \approx 0.5772$.

Addendum: The Case of Enron

Gordian Gaeta and Justin Hingorani

The power of event-based risk models and their predictive value is well demonstrated by the three case examples in the preceding article. However, the dramatic events around Enron have prompted us to demonstrate the concept and model with Enron data having, of course, the advantage of hindsight.

The late 1990s spelt the glory days of Enron. The company established itself as a leader in innovation, redefining its business as an energy trader and expanding into new areas such as weather derivatives and broadband. The result was a steady increase in stock price. As Figure 6.15 shows, the stock price experienced a steady increase up to the end of 1999. During the first quarter of 2000, Enron's market capitalization doubled and the stock continued its upward move until August 2000 when another significant hike drove the stock toward its high of US$90. From the first quarter 2001 onwards, the stock price essentially declined with increasing speed towards its ultimate doom in December 2001. A number of events are marked along the time axis in Figure 6.15 showing key announcements and stock price benchmarks.

Any investor or lender will also have considered the credit risk of such a booming investment. The traditional measure of volatility is typically computed to assess the risk. In essence, volatility measures the variances of stock returns and thus indicates, when measured over longer periods of time, the historic risk of share price changes. Figure 6.16 shows both base volatility and unconditional volatility. Base volatility is defined as the change that occurs on a frequent basis, while unconditional volatility is independent of any time, base or event conditions, as outlined in the previous section.

Despite the rapid increase in share price, both volatility measures remain relatively stable with the exception of a step in the first quarter of 2000.

FIGURE 6.15   Enron's stock price developments did not foreshadow its rapid demise

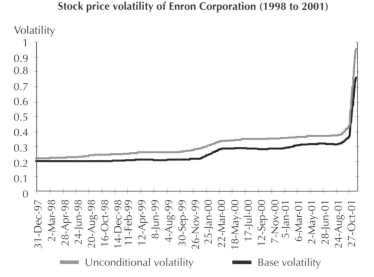

Stock prices of Enron Corporation (1998 to 2001)

US$/share

① June 1, 2000
EnronOnline
has handled
$50 billion in
transactions

② Aug. 17, 2000
Enron stock
price hits $90

③ Mar. 9, 2001
Enron-
Blockbuster
deal falls
through

④ Aug. 13, 2001
Jeff Skilling,
Enron
president and
CEO, resigns

⑤ Sept. 18, 2001
Enron stock
price drops
below $30

⑥ Oct. 2001
Oct. 16 – Enron announces
$618 million loss
Oct. 22 – SEC inquiry
announced
Oct. 24 – Fastow , CFO,
ousted
Oct. 29 – Moody's
downgrades Enron to
Baa2

⑦ Dec. 2, 2001
Enron files
for Chapter
11
Bankruptcy
two days
after stock
price hits
26¢

Source: Bloomberg, Simplex Credit Advisory analysis

FIGURE 6.16   Volatility measures remained steady over the entire trouble period

Stock price volatility of Enron Corporation (1998 to 2001)

Volatility

━━━ Unconditional volatility   ━━━ Base volatility

Source: Bloomberg, Simplex Credit Advisory analysis

Also, both volatility measures move symmetrically, and albeit on a steady increase, this would indicate a potential downward exposure of 20–40% in 2000 but on a much higher share price. Overall, this would suggest an investment or portfolio holding with a manageable downside-risk. Only towards the final stages of the drama – at the time Enron announced its loss, authorities started to get interested and Moody's reacted – did both volatility measures increase dramatically.

Without the inclusion of an event-based or mixed model as outlined previously, the volatility measure did not in any discernable way foreshadow the catastrophe to come. We therefore include event measures for the period under review.

Figure 6.17 shows event size and event frequency – in addition to both volatility measures – up to the end of 1999; that is, the period of steady but fairly stable stock price increases. While event size remains constant if not declining, event frequency shows a marked rise from well below 10% at the start of 1998 to around 40% by the end of 1999. This indicates that there was a growing probability that events – either favorable or unfavorable – would affect the company, although the impact of any one of these events would remain relatively controllable. Up to the end of 1999 there was thus a growing chance that the company's fortunes would be impacted by events of smaller and manageable size.

This indicator alone demonstrated, at a time of bullish market developments, that indeed the risk was increasing.

Enron entered the year 2000 with a "bang" as its stock price jumped numerous times rising from $40 to around $70 by the end of January 2000. Enron continued to announce rising revenues with the help of its creative

FIGURE 6.17 Enron phase one volatility and event measures compared: 1997–1999

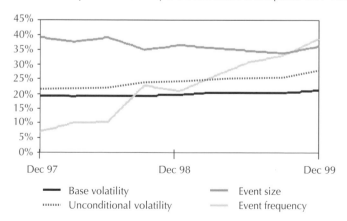

Source: Bloomberg, Simplex Credit Advisory analysis

accounting and in June 2000 it announced that EnronOnline, its online market place that the company had formed in November 1999, had handled $50 billion in transactions. As the share price continued to climb – albeit with some minor corrections – the second half of 2000 saw a record price of US$90. Figure 6.18 shows continued moderation of volatility measures, but a marked impact on event risk measures.

Over the year 2000, potential event size almost doubled while event frequency declined to around 20%, still double pre-1998 levels. This meant that the likelihood of an event was decreasing but that any event would have a much bigger impact – approximately double – than in the previous period. While from the perspective of an investor, the stock price was hitting its peak in August and hype was abundant, a careful event risk analysis would have indicated a real concern of a potentially threatening event to Enron's well-being.

The year 2001 marked the decline of the energy giant in terms of stock price, yet volatility measure persisted only with a slow, steady climb. Event risk measures, however, noticeably sharpened their trend from 2000 and showed yet another increase in potential event size with declining event frequency, well ahead of the continued share price decline. By October 2001, just ahead of the disastrous chain of events, event risk had moved sharply upwards leaving little doubt of the risk for a potentially serious problem.

The model did not predict any event but it indicated a measure of likelihood and severity. Thus, the veridical risk was highlighted. This would have been sufficient for an investor to take an educated decision on holding,

FIGURE 6.18   Enron phase two volatility and event measures compared: 2000

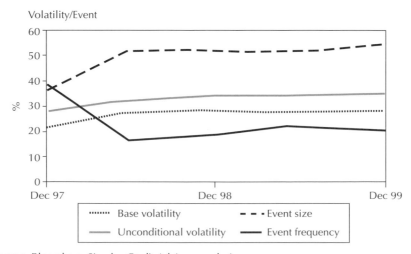

Source: Bloomberg, Simplex Credit Advisory analysis

FIGURE 6.19   Overall volatility and event measures compared: 1998–2001

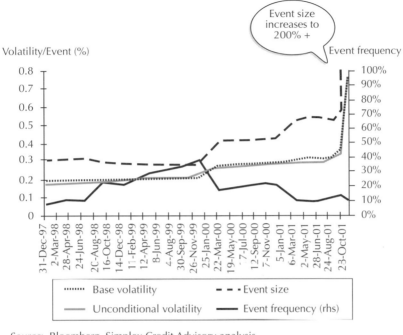

Source: Bloomberg, Simplex Credit Advisory analysis

hedging, or disposing of the stock. The volatility measures did not signal anything of that order. Once the more traditional measures reacted, the rest was already history. In October, Enron reported a $618 million third-quarter loss, the SEC enquiry was announced and Enron's credit rating was lowered. Much too late for any investor or lender to react.

The prediction that such a disastrous event would eventually strike is not part of the model capabilities, only the quantification of the potential danger. Companies with similar measures can survive equally well but for the lending and investing community, the risk measures go a long way of harnessing the potential risk.

Event measures, however, show the risk of an important event on the horizon and should have cautioned any investor as early as the first quarter of 2000 or some fifteen months in advance of the drama – also well in advance of the more dramatic stock price decline.

The trade-off between event size and event frequency by the model allows a differentiated perspective on risk. A lower likelihood of a bigger event may be preferable to some investors than the higher likelihood of a smaller event. By taking a punt that a future event will not happen, investors and credit professionals can make a conscious decision based on the

FIGURE 6.20 The differing dynamics of price returns and event risk provide an excellent risk measure

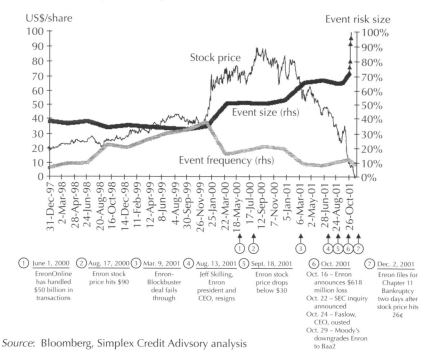

Stock price developments and event measures (1998 to 2001)

① June 1, 2000	② Aug. 17, 2000	③ Mar. 9, 2001	④ Aug. 13, 2001	⑤ Sept. 18, 2001	⑥ Oct. 2001	⑦ Dec. 2, 2001
EnronOnline has handled $50 billion in transactions	Enron stock price hits $90	Enron-Blockbuster deal fails through	Jeff Skilling, Enron president and CEO, resigns	Enron stock price drops below $30	Oct. 16 – Enron announces $618 million loss Oct. 22 – SEC inquiry announced Oct. 24 – Faslow, CEO, ousted Oct. 29 – Moody's downgrades Enron to Baa2	Enron files for Chapter 11 Bankruptcy two days after stock price hits 26¢

Source: Bloomberg, Simplex Credit Adivsory analysis

veridical risk inherent in a company. Without these additional risk measures, companies with similar stock price returns and consequently volatility measures cannot be properly differentiated.

Although the model feeds on equity dynamics, event risk measures are by no means a reflection of stock price returns. When comparing the event risk measures with the stock price developments, a clear differentiation becomes evident. The trade-off by the model is explained in the previous section but in this case, the model correctly indicated a low risk of a major event.

The predictive and analytical power of an event-based or mixed credit risk model demonstrated by the recent surprising downfall of Enron, suggests yet again the importance of including abstract risk measures into any risk management system.

CHAPTER 7

A Stress Test to Incorporate Correlation Breakdown

Jongwoo Kim and Christopher C. Finger
RiskMetrics

The authors introduce the broken arrow stress test, in which they estimate correlation levels in stress situations and apply these correlation levels to arrive at the expected loss for the peripheral assets in the stress test. To identify correlation in stress situations, the joint distribution of core and peripheral assets is specified as a mixture of normals. For the majority of cases, the asset returns are drawn from a normal distribution with lower volatility and one level of correlation; on rarer hectic days, the asset returns are drawn from a different normal distribution, with higher levels of volatility and a second correlation level. In the example presented, stressed correlation levels illustrate significant changes in correlation for four of the 18 markets examined. The broken arrow stress test produces a more reasonable expected loss estimate than other parametric methods and does not present the problem with idiosyncrasies seen with historical stress tests.

> Furthermore, joint distributions estimated over periods without panics will misestimate the degree of correlation between asset returns during panics. Under these circumstances, fear and disengagement by investors often result in simultaneous declines in the values of private obligations, as investors no longer realistically differentiate among degrees of risk and liquidity, and increases in the values of riskless government securities. Consequently, the benefits of portfolio diversification will tend to be overestimated when the rare panic periods are not taken into account.
>
> *Remarks by Federal Reserve Bank Chairman, Alan Greenspan* (1999)

INTRODUCTION

Stress tests are a common counterpart to the objective models used for day-to-day risk monitoring. One example of the objective models is Value-at-Risk (VaR). The objective models typically forecast worst case losses conditional on markets behaving generally as they have in the recent past. To make accurate forecasts, these models rely on a relatively short (one year at most) history of market factor returns. While certain models will extrapolate from these returns and forecast losses greater than those observed in the historical period, the loss forecasts are always restricted by the historical returns. Stress tests – point estimates of portfolio losses based on market factor returns that have never occurred, or that occurred outside of the relevant historical period for the model – complement the objective model forecasts by providing a notion of losses deemed implausible by the model, but which certainly could occur.

The Basle Committee on Banking Supervision (1996) requires banks that use the internal models approach for market risk capital requirements to implement a rigorous and comprehensive stress-testing framework. Further, the BIS and the Technical Committee of the International Organization of Securities Commissions (1998) oblige institutions with significant trading activities to execute stress tests on a regular basis, using a variety of assumptions that cover both hypothetical and historical events. The President's Working Group on Financial Markets (1999), formed after the bail-out of Long Term Capital Management, emphasizes that, in addition to routine risk management, banks need to stress test credit, as well as market risk profiles in order to evaluate the potential impact of adverse market conditions on cash flows and asset/collateral values supporting trading transactions.

Generically, stress tests involve the specification of adverse market moves (scenarios) and the revaluation of the portfolio under these moves (Laubsch 1999). To specify scenarios, it is first necessary to select which market factors (the core assets) to stress, then define the amount by which to stress them, and the time period over which the stress move will take place. For the remaining (peripheral) assets, there are a number of methods to specify the moves that would coincide with moves in the core assets.

The simplest specification for peripheral asset moves is to simply assume no change (call this the "zeroed-out" stress test). A second specification (the predictive stress test) utilizes current estimates of volatility and correlation to estimate the conditional expectation of peripheral asset moves given the stress moves in the core assets. See Kupiec (1998) for more details. A third specification (historical stress test) applies the moves in the peripheral assets that have coincided with large moves in the core assets historically. We summarize the three stress test methodologies in Table 7.1.

TABLE 7.1 Assumptions on peripheral assets in alternative stress tests

Stress test	Return of peripheral assets	Benefit	Drawback
Zeroed-out	Zero return	Implementation is quite easy	Ignoring co-movement is unrealistic
Predictive	Expected return based on correlation	Idiosyncratic errors are averaged out	Correlation is calculated in the normal situation
Historical	Actual return of the specific historical event	The stress situation is easily incorporated	Idiosyncratic errors of the historical event cannot be removed

Of the three methods, the predictive stress test appears most attractive, if we can justify the contention that standard volatility and correlation estimates will produce good stress forecasts of the peripheral asset moves. Though Kupiec (1998) does show that this contention tends to hold up in practice, the sentiment expressed by Chairman Greenspan remains, and is supported by a number of empirical observations of "correlation breakdown." See Longin and Solnik (1999) for an example. With this breakdown in mind, it is tempting to filter the data and compute correlations based only on days that, in retrospect, appear most volatile. Boyer, Gibson, and Loretan (1999) issue an explicit warning against this practice, citing the bias it introduces, and state in their conclusion:

> In order to carry out a valid test, we argue that it is necessary that the researcher begins with a data-coherent model of the data generating process that builds in the possibility of structural changes, estimate the model's parameters, and only then decide whether the estimated parameters imply changing correlations.

In this chapter, we introduce the broken arrow stress test, in which we apply the predictive stress methodology, but using an estimate of correlation in stress situations. For one core and one peripheral asset, we will specify the joint distribution as a mixture of bivariate normals. For the majority of cases (quiet days), the asset returns are drawn from a normal distribution with lower volatility and one level of correlation; on rarer hectic days, the asset returns are drawn from a different normal distribution with higher levels of volatility and a second correlation level. Using historical data on the core asset, we identify the ex post conditional probabilities that a given day's returns were drawn from a quiet or hectic distribution. With these conditional probabilities, we compute the correlation levels for the quiet and hectic periods, and test for the significance of the difference of these two levels. We finish by applying the predictive stress-testing methodology with our estimates of hectic correlation levels.

IDENTIFYING STRESSED SITUATIONS

To identify the distinct correlation levels in stressed and non-stressed situations, we stipulate that the asset return distribution for a given day depends explicitly on whether the day is quiet or hectic. Specifically, we let two asset returns, x (core asset) and y (peripheral asset) follow a mixture of two multivariate normal distributions:[1]

$(x, y) \sim$

$$
\begin{cases}
MVN\left(\begin{bmatrix} \mu_{x1} \\ \mu_{y1} \end{bmatrix}, \begin{bmatrix} \sigma_{x1}^2 & \sigma_{x1}\rho_1\sigma_{y1} \\ \sigma_{x1}\rho_1\sigma_{y1} & \sigma_{y1}^2 \end{bmatrix}\right) & \text{with probability } 1 - \omega \text{ (quiet days)} \\[2em]
MVN\left(\begin{bmatrix} \mu_{x2} \\ \mu_{y2} \end{bmatrix}, \begin{bmatrix} \sigma_{x2}^2 & \sigma_{x2}\rho_2\sigma_{y2} \\ \sigma_{x2}\rho_2\sigma_{y2} & \sigma_{y2}^2 \end{bmatrix}\right) & \text{with probability } \omega \text{ (hectic days)}
\end{cases}
$$

(1)

where MVN denotes multivariate normal distribution and the core asset is more volatile in the hectic days than quiet days; that is, $\sigma_{x2} > \sigma_{x1}$.

We begin by estimating the marginal distribution of the core asset. Thus, the unknown parameters ω, μ_{x1}, σ_{x1}, μ_{x2}, and σ_{x2} are estimated from the marginal distribution of x:

$$
x \sim \begin{cases}
UVN(\mu_{x1}, \sigma_{x1}^2) \text{ with probability } 1 - \omega \text{ (quiet days)} \\
UVN(\mu_{x2}, \sigma_{x2}^2) \text{ with probability } \omega \text{ (hectic days)}
\end{cases}
$$

(2)

where UVN denotes a univariate normal distribution. For our example, we set USD S&P 500 as the core asset, and utilize daily returns from August 23, 1996 to July 13, 1999. As a reference, we fit the unconditional normal distribution (i.e., $x \sim UVN(\mu_x, \sigma_x^2)$ with probability (1) to the USD S&P 500 data. We then estimate the mixture of two normal distributions using the maximum likelihood estimation (MLE).[2] The results for both distributions are presented in Table 7.2.

In Figure 7.1, we compare the distribution of the USD S&P 500 data and the two conditional distributions.[3] It is worth noting that our MLE results

TABLE 7.2 Estimation of mixture of two normal distributions

Model	Probability	Mean	STD	Loglikelihood
Unconditional (one normal)	1.00	0.0971	1.1329	−469.94
Conditional on quiet	0.92	0.1236	0.9209	
Conditional on hectic	0.08	−0.2078	2.4877	−426.47

FIGURE 7.1 Mixture of two normal distributions

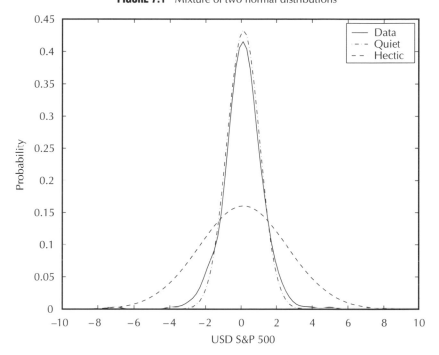

match two typical features of equity index distributions: fat tails and a right skew. The volatility of the hectic distribution is more than two times larger than that of the quiet distribution. This means that there exists a small number of outliers that account for the fat tails of the sample data. Furthermore, the mean of the hectic distribution is smaller than that of the quiet distribution, reflecting a skew to the right.

In Figure 7.2, we plot the kernel density of our data, along with the two assumed distributions. The mixture of two normal distributions seems to fit the high peak and fat tails on both sides better than the single normal distribution. To test this hypothesis formally, we implement a likelihood ratio (LR) test. The null hypothesis is that the data-generating process is a single normal distribution. The LR test statistic is computed by:

$$-2 \ln \lambda = -2(\ln L_c - \ln L_u)$$
$$= -2[(-469.94) - (-426.47)] = 86.93 \qquad (3)$$

where $\ln L_c$ denotes the log likelihood value under the constraint of the null hypothesis (one normal distribution model) and $\ln L_u$ denotes the log likelihood value in the unconstrained case (mixture of two normal distributions model).

With mixture models, standard regularity conditions, under which the asymptotic null distribution of the LR test statistic is chi-squared with degrees of freedom equal to the difference in the number of parameters in the two hypotheses, do not hold. To overcome this, we utilize a modified LR test suggested by Wolfe (see McLachan and Basford (1988)). The test statistic is modified as:

$$-2c \ln \lambda \sim \chi^2_{df} \qquad (4)$$

where now the degree of freedom df is twice the difference in the number of parameters in the two hypotheses, excluding the mixing probabilities. The parameter c is equal to $(N - 1 - p - 0.5g)/N$, where N, p, and g are the sample size (753), the dimension of the data (1), and the number of distributions in the mixture model (2), respectively.

FIGURE 7.2 Goodness-of-fit: one normal versus mixture of two normals

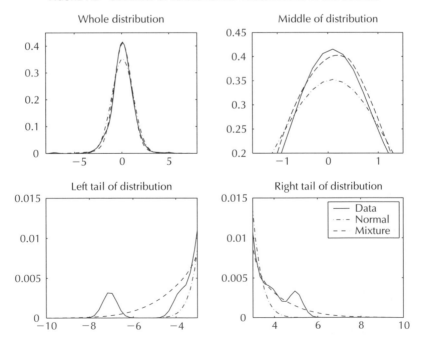

Our modified LR test statistic is 86.58, while the critical value of the modified LR test is $\chi^2(\alpha = 0.01, df = 4) = 13.28$. We are able to reject the null hypothesis at the 1% significance level, meaning that the mixture of two normal distributions fits the data better than one normal distribution, even accounting for the loss of degrees of freedom in the mixture model.

ESTIMATING CONDITIONAL CORRELATIONS

Using the estimated marginal distribution of the core asset, we can identify the likelihood that a given day's return came from the hectic or quiet distribution. Let $\alpha(x_t)$ be the conditional probability that a given day was hectic, given our observation of the core asset return x_t on that day. Recall that the *unconditional* probability (i.e., the probability before we know the asset return) that a given day is hectic is ω. Using Bayes' rule, we have:

$$\alpha(x_t) = \frac{\omega\phi(x_t \mid \mu_{x2}, \sigma_{x2}^2)}{(1-\omega)\phi(x_t \mid \mu_{x1}, \sigma_{x1}^2) + \omega\phi(x_t \mid \mu_{x2}, \sigma_{x2}^2)} \quad \text{for } t = 1, \ldots, N, \text{ (5)}$$

where $\phi(\cdot \mid \mu, \sigma^2)$ denotes the normal PDF with mean μ and variance σ^2. The conditional probability that day t was quiet is then $1 - \alpha_t$.

In Figure 7.3, we plot $\alpha(x_t)$ as a function of the core asset return on each day. Note that days on which the core asset experienced more than a three standard deviations move ($= -3\sigma_x = -3 \times 1.1329 = -3.3987$) are nearly certain to have been hectic days. For the purposes of stress-testing, where the core asset move will be at least this great, only the hectic conditional distribution is relevant.

Given the conditional hectic and quiet probabilities, we can estimate the remaining parameters (ie., the conditional volatilities for the peripheral asset, and the conditional correlation levels) in the multivariate mixture model. For instance, to estimate the conditional mean for y in hectic periods, we observe that the expectation of $\alpha(x) \cdot y$ is $\omega\mu_{y2}$. Thus:

$$\frac{1}{N} \sum_{t=1}^{N} \alpha(x_t) y_t \tag{6}$$

is an unbiased estimator of $\omega\mu_{y2}$. Observing also that:

$$\frac{1}{N} \sum_{t=1}^{N} \alpha(x_t) \tag{7}$$

is an unbiased estimator of ω, we see that:

FIGURE 7.3 Conditional probabilities of hectic days, as a function of core asset return

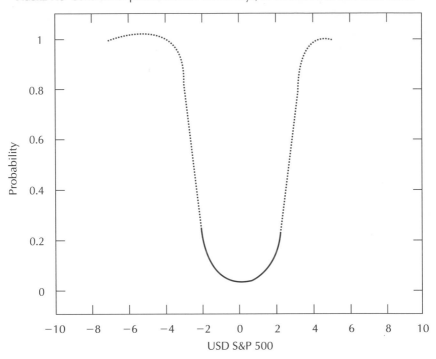

$$\frac{\sum\limits_{t=1}^{N} \alpha(x_t) y_t}{\sum\limits_{t=1}^{N} \alpha(x_t)} \tag{8}$$

is a reasonable estimator for μ_{y2}. This expression has a nice interpretation as the average of the observed peripheral asset returns, weighted by each day's probability of having come from the hectic distribution, conditional on the core asset return.

The weighted average estimator applies to the other parameters as well. The conditional correlation given a hectic day, or ρ_2, is the conditional expectation of $(x - \mu_{x2}) \cdot (y - \mu_{y2})$, normalized by the conditional volatilities σ_{x2} and σ_{y2}. We estimate ρ_2 by:

$$\rho_2 = \frac{\sum\limits_{t=1}^{N} \alpha(x_t)(x_t - \mu_{x2})(y_t - \mu_{y2})}{\sigma_{x2}\sigma_{y2} \sum\limits_{t=1}^{N} \alpha(x_t)}. \tag{9}$$

The estimate of ρ_2 is the standard estimate of correlation, with each data point weighted by the likelihood that it came from the hectic distribution.

As an example, we estimate the multivariate mixture model for USD S&P 500 and CAD TSE100. Figure 7.4 shows a scatter plot of the actual data, data generated by a single normal distribution, and data generated from the mixture distribution, conditional on quiet and hectic periods. We see in particular that the mixture of the two conditional distributions replicates more closely the severe returns in the actual data.

We repeat our estimation for 18 assets across foreign exchange rates, mid- and long-term government bond prices, equity indices, and commodity prices, maintaining the USD S&P 500 as the core asset. The estimation results appear in Table 7.3.[4]

In order to ascertain the significance of our results, we apply two tests to our correlation estimates. For the first test, we construct 90% confidence intervals for the correlation in the unconditional (one normal) distribution using Monte Carlo simulations and compare our hectic correlation to these confidence intervals. The comparisons are illustrated in Figure 7.5, which plots correlations on hectic and on a 90% confidence interval of unconditional correlation based on one normal distribution. For 13 of the 18 peripheral assets, the hectic conditional correlations lie outside of the confidence interval.

FIGURE 7.4 Conditional correlations

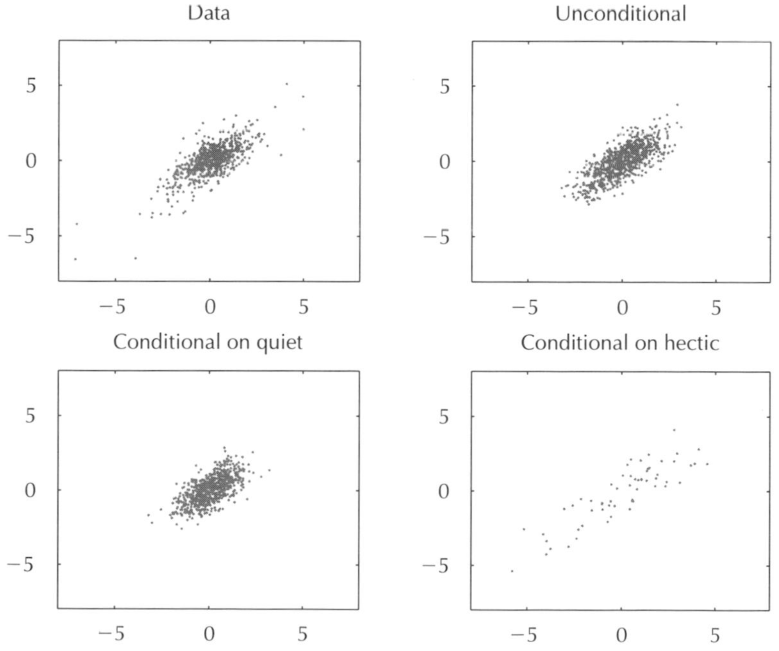

TABLE 7.3 Alternative correlations

	Correlation of USD S&P500 and	Unconditional	Quiet	Hectic
1	USD 2yr T-Bond	−0.0819	0.0569	−0.4366
2	USD 30yr T-Bond	0.0568	0.1615	−0.2623
3	USD/EUR Spot FX	−0.2059	−0.215	−0.1914
4	DEM DAX	0.3302	0.2903	0.4424
5	DEM 2yr T-Bond	0.0117	0.0534	−0.1289
6	DEM 30yr T-Bond	0.0627	0.1383	−0.1873
7	USD/JPY Spot FX	−0.0315	−0.0542	0.0593
8	JPY Nikkei 200	0.2843	0.2485	0.4711
9	JPY 2yr T-Bond	−0.0786	−0.0507	−0.2179
10	JPY 20yr T-Bond	−0.0834	−0.0591	−0.2023
11	USD/CAD Spot FX	0.0378	0.0215	0.0852
12	CAD TSE 100	0.7299	0.6346	0.8713
13	CAD 2yr T-Bond	0.1269	0.0669	0.2541
14	CAD 30yr T-Bond	0.0774	0.1513	−0.1482
15	Aluminum Spot	0.0021	−0.0351	0.1477
16	Copper Spot	0.0268	0.0124	0.0816
17	Crude Oil Future	0.0201	0.0117	0.0577
18	Heating Oil Future	0.0169	0.0063	0.0681

Our second test is motivated by the observation in Boyer, Gibson, and Loretan (1990) that correlations estimated on truncated datasets are subject to significant bias. Though we have not truncated our data explicitly, our weighting by α_t in estimates such as Equation (9) is effectively a smooth way of truncating. We would like to assure that the differences between our quiet and hectic correlation estimates are not simply an artifact of our conditioning. Thus, we construct a hypothesis test where the null hypothesis is that the core and peripheral assets do follow the mixture model specified in Equation (1), but with $\rho_1 = \rho_2$; that is, with the quiet and hectic correlations equal.

To set up the test, we observe that in our mixture model, conditional on the core asset return x_t, the peripheral asset follows a mixture of univariate normal distributions. In particular:

$$y_t \mid x_t \sim \begin{cases} UVN(\mu_{y1t}, \sigma^2_{y1t}) \text{ with probability } 1 - \alpha(x_t) \text{ (quiet days)} \\ UVN(\mu_{y2t}, \sigma^2_{y2t}) \text{ with probability } \alpha(x_t) \text{ (hectic days)} \end{cases} \tag{10}$$

where $\alpha(x_t)$ is given by Equation (5):

$$\mu_{y1t} = \rho \frac{\sigma_{y1}}{\sigma_{x1}} (x - \mu_{x1}) + \mu_{y1}, \tag{11}$$

FIGURE 7.5 Significance test of hectic correlation estimate based on a single normal distribution. Core asset: USD S&P 500. Box: 90% confidence intervals for the correlation in the unconditional distribution. Circle: point estimate for the hectic correlation

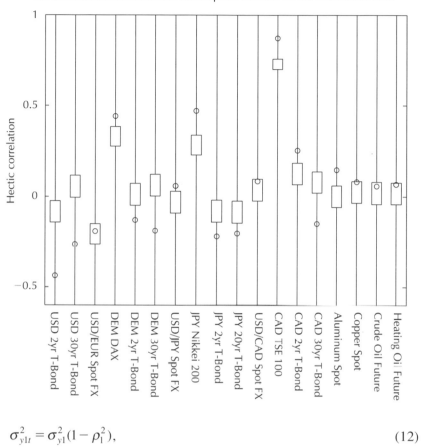

$$\sigma^2_{y1t} = \sigma^2_{y1}(1 - \rho^2_1),$$ (12)

and μ_{y2t} and σ_{y2t} are computed similarly. For each day t, we generate a Monte Carlo sample $\hat{y}_t$ of the peripheral return by drawing from the conditional distribution in Equation (10), with both ρ_1 and ρ_2 set to the unconditional correlation between the core and peripheral returns. Once we have a sample $\hat{y}_t$ for each day, we pair these Monte Carlo returns with the actual core returns and estimate a quiet and hectic correlation as above. Repeating this process gives us conditional correlation estimates under the null hypothesis to which we can compare our conditional correlation estimates from the true data.

To illustrate our test, we present Monte Carlo results in Figure 7.6, with a USD two-year Treasury Bond as the peripheral asset. For reference, we also plot the unconditional correlation and our conditional correlation estimates. The conditional correlations obtained under the null hypothesis form a cloud around the unconditional correlation, and there is a large

FIGURE 7.6 Monte Carlo test of correlation estimates for USD S&P 500 versus USD two-year T-bond

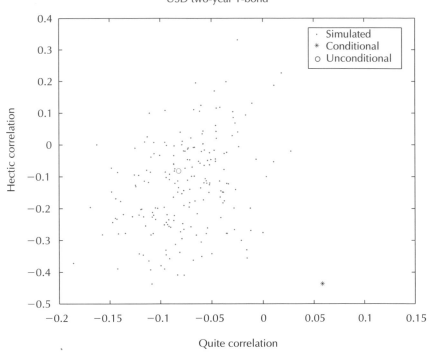

amount of variation in these estimates. Our conditional correlation estimates, however, lie significantly outside of the cloud, indicating that we should reject the null hypothesis of a constant correlation for this peripheral asset.

To test our results more formally, we compare our hectic correlation estimates with confidence intervals on the hectic correlation from the Monte Carlo procedure. These results are presented in Figure 7.7. The confidence intervals here are typically wider than those in Figure 7.5, and now only four of the 18 hectic correlation estimates (USD two-year T-bond, USD 30-year T-bond, DEM 30-year T-bond, and CAD 30-year T-bond) lie outside the confidence intervals. For these four peripheral assets, we can reject the null hypothesis of constant correlation and conclude that the assets' correlation with the USD S&P 500 is different in hectic periods.

IMPLEMENTING CONDITIONAL CORRELATIONS IN STRESS TESTS

To illustrate the application of the conditional correlation estimates to stress-testing, we will perform stress tests on a sample portfolio where the move in the USD S&P 500 is set to -3.4% (three unconditional daily standard deviations) and the moves in the remaining (peripheral) assets are set

FIGURE 7.7 Significance test of hectic correlation estimate based on mixture of two normal distributions. Core asset: USD S&P 500. Box: 90% confidence intervals for the hectic correlation assuming the quiet and hectic correlations equal. Circle: point estimate for the hectic correlation

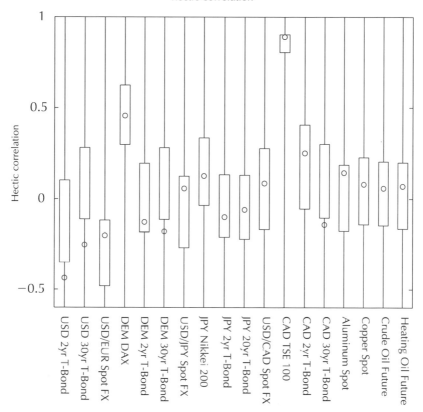

according to a variety of methods. Our sample portfolio consists of USD 1MM invested in each of the 19 assets. We choose the sign of each position based on its hectic period correlation with USD S&P 500, to insure that the most common large asset moves do not offset one another. For example, since in hectic periods the USD two-year T-bond is negatively correlated to the USD S&P 500 while the DEM DAX is positively correlated, we ensure that the positions in these two peripheral assets are opposite. The positions are listed in Table 7.4.

We examine four methods to fix the peripheral asset returns. In the *zeroed-out* stress test, the peripheral asset returns are all set to zero. In the *historical* stress test, we identify the dates where the USD S&P 500 fell by 3.4% or more, and apply the actual peripheral asset returns on these dates.[5] For our historical period, there are four such dates and thus, four sets of peripheral asset returns to apply.

TABLE 7.4 Example stress tests, USD S&P as core asset

Asset	Position USD	Zeroed out	Predictive	Broken arrow	Returns, %		Historical	
					27-Oct-97	4-Aug-98	27-Aug-98	31-Aug-98
0 USD S&P	1 m	−3.3986	−3.3986	−3.3986	−3.3986	−3.3986	−3.3986	−3.3986
1 USD 2yr	−1 m	0	0.0271	0.113	0.133	0.0555	0.3052	0.1103
2 USD 30yr	−1 m	0	−0.1995	0.6348	0.2533	0.3805	1.1615	1.1695
3 USD/EUR	−1 m	0	0.3174	0.2824	0.4969	0.062	0	0.3517
4 DEM DAX	1 m	0	−1.4719	−1.6884	−2.0697	−0.0411	−2.8828	−1.5678
5 DEM 2yr	−1 m	0	−0.0008	0.0248	0.0303	0.0161	0.0902	0.0229
6 DEM 30yr	−1 m	0	−0.2286	0.3837	−0.4646	0.6927	3.3618	0.3701
7 USD/JPY	1 m	0	0.0694	0.1018	−0.1857	0.4149	1.1856	0.7068
8 JPY Nikkei	1 m	0	−1.386	−1.2327	−2.0793	−0.1807	−3.0553	0.887
9 JPY 2yr	−1 m	0	0.0165	0.02	0.0163	−0.023	0.0659	−0.0116
10 JPY 20yr	−1 m	0	0.3122	0.3336	0.3864	0.0263	1.073	−0.0208
11 USD/CAD	1 m	0	−0.0492	−0.074	−0.2158	0.0365	−1.0951	0.4421
12 CAD TSE	1 m	0	−2.3285	−2.7801	−3.127	−3.2596	−5.6316	−2.0318
13 CAD 2yr	1 m	0	−0.0613	−0.0972	0.1162	−0.0328	−1.0143	−0.5957
14 CAD 30yr	−1 m	0	−0.2124	0.5189	2.0998	0.3555	−1.1577	1.3441
15 Aluminum	1 m	0	−0.0099	−0.2605	−0.9969	1.2034	−0.2565	0
16 Copper	1 m	0	−0.1485	−0.3827	−0.744	−0.508	0.4925	0
17 Crude Oil	1 m	0	−0.1583	−0.2985	0.2273	0.3354	−2.2681	−0.5753
18 Heating Oil	1 m	0	−0.1321	−0.1701	0.5911	1.0988	−2.3739	0.4395
Portfolio (%)	3 m	−1.1329	−3.0356	−4.1974	−4.9446	−1.9658	−8.3993	−3.01
Portfolio (USD)	3 m	−33,986	−91,068	−125,920	−148,339	−58,974	−251,979	−90,301

The remaining two methods (*predictive* and *broken arrow* stress tests) utilize the conditional expectation of the peripheral asset returns, given that the core asset (the USD S&P 500) falls by 3.4%. In both cases, we rely on a linear relation between the peripheral (y_t) and core (x_t) asset returns:

$$\frac{y_t - \mu_y}{\sigma_y} = \rho \left(\frac{x_t - \mu_x}{\sigma_x} \right) + \sqrt{1 - \rho^2} \, \varepsilon_t \tag{13}$$

where ε_t is a random error term, with zero mean and unit variance. The conditional expectation of the peripheral asset return, given the core asset return, is then:

$$E[y_t | x_t] = \mu_y - \left(\frac{\rho \sigma_y}{\sigma_x} \right) \mu_x + \left(\frac{\rho \sigma_y}{\sigma_x} \right) x_t . \tag{14}$$

Under the predictive stress test, we will set the peripheral asset returns using Equation (14), with the five parameters (μ_x, μ_y, σ_x, σ_y, and ρ) set to their unconditional values. Under the broken arrow stress test, we use Equation (14), but substitute the hectic conditional parameters (μ_{x2}, μ_{y2}, σ_{x2}, σ_{y2}, and ρ_2).

Consider an example with the USD S&P 500 as the core asset and the USD 30-year Treasury Bond as the peripheral asset. Figure 7.8 illustrates the linear relationship between the two assets using the unconditional, quiet, and hectic parameters. The slopes of the unconditional and quiet conditional lines are both slightly positive, while the slope of the hectic conditional line is negative. The interpretation is that these two markets tend to move together, but move opposite each other when volatility is high. This is consistent with the notion of "flight to quality" in volatile periods.

The returns for each peripheral asset, along with the portfolio return, under the four stress test methods are reported in Table 7.4. Note that for the historical stress test, we have presented the results for each of the four days in which the USD S&P 500 experienced a three standard deviation loss or more.

Clearly, the zeroed-out stress test represents a significant underestimation of expected loss. Further, since the hectic correlation is stronger for all assets than the unconditional correlation, our broken arrow stress test shows a larger loss estimate than the predictive case. The four historical loss estimates are likely to be of little use as a risk statistic, since the four days seem fairly idiosyncratic and produce a large range of loss estimates.

FIGURE 7.8 Conditional linear relations

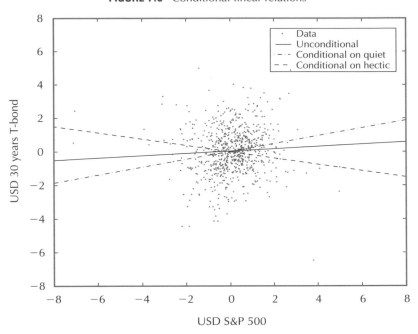

CONCLUSION

We have introduced the broken arrow stress test, in which we estimate correlation levels in volatile periods and apply these correlation levels to arrive at the expected loss for the peripheral assets in our stress test. Our method to estimate stressed correlation levels is straightforward and illustrates significant changes in correlation for four of the 18 markets we examine. Since stress tests seek to depict losses in the most volatile periods, the broken arrow stress test produces more reasonable loss figures than those based on no peripheral asset moves (the zeroed-out stress test) or based on peripheral asset moves consistent with unconditional correlations (the predictive stress test). Additionally, the broken arrow stress test yields one loss figure rather than the set of idiosyncratic figures presented by the historical stress test.

NOTES

[1] Zangari (1996) uses a mixture of two normal distributions to incorporate fat tails in the VaR calculation.

[2] Since the gradient of ω has several local maxima, we apply a grid search to ω. We restrict ω between 0.01 and 0.49.

[3] To smooth the curve for the actual data, we use a Gaussian Kernel Density with the bandwidth, $h = cN^{-r}$, where N is number of samples and the two parameters, c and r are set to $1.06\sigma_x$ and 0.2, respectively. See Silverman (1986) for further details.

[4] As in Kupiec (1998), we added a one-day lag to JPY Nikkei200, JPY two-year T-bond, and JPY 20-year T-bond in order to synchronize the return data.

[5] In practice, to facilitate comparison with the other methods, we scale the historical returns to the base USD S&P 500 return of -3.4%. Thus, for a day where the USD S&P 500 return was -6.8%, we apply the base -3.4% return to the USD S&P 500 and for each peripheral asset, apply the actual return scaled down by a factor of two.

CHAPTER 8

Neural Networks for Modeling Volatility and Market Capitalization

Jan-Joost Spanjers and Tom Heskes
SMART Research BV

A fundamental, structured model of credit risk uses equity market information as one of its inputs.[1] This restricts the use of the model to exchange-traded companies. To extend a structured approach to measuring the credit risk of private companies, surrogate inputs are needed in place of the missing equity market data. This chapter describes research undertaken to develop neural networks to estimate equity market data (namely, market capitalization and volatility), for use as surrogates, using data that would be available for a private companies; for example, financial statements.

Initial neural network investigation was done using public companies financial and market data. For a discussion of extending the research to private company data and the neural networks' use in calculating default probabilities see Alibhai, Gaeta, and Hingorani (2001). Financial data was obtained from the American Association of Individual Investors' (AAII) US financial database. The financial information covered eight quarters, between 1996 and 1998, of companies from four industries, specifically services, technology, healthcare, and basic materials. The data were compiled into more than 180 financial ratios, including quarterly dollar and percentage changes in data, calculated for over 1700 companies and index statistics including volatility and index level. However, industry information did not significantly improve neural network performance, so this discussion focuses on financial statement inputs.

Neural networks developed in the study are treated as statistical tools for pattern recognition, more complex than, but not principally different from more classical approaches (Bishop 1995; Duda, Hart, and Stork 2000). To implement the neural networks and produce final estimations, numerous steps are followed:

- a functional form is selected for the components of the network;
- an optimization methodology is chosen to calculate weightings of the components;
- error functions are formulated to train the networks and analyze results;
- data are scaled to manage outliers;
- optimization is performed across an ensemble of networks to stabilize performance;
- the architecture is modified to improve training results;
- the total number of inputs is reduced to a set of 20.

The following expands on each of these steps.

MULTI-LAYERED PERCEPTRONS

The neural networks used in this study are so-called multi-layered perceptrons, which contain one or more layers of hidden units with sigmoidal (hyperbolic tangent) transfer functions (Rumelhart et al. 1986). In the simplest case, a network with a single layer of hidden units, where y is the output predicted by the network given inputs x_i, reads:

$$y = \sum_j w_j \tanh\left[\sum_i v_{ji} x_i + v_{j0} \right] + w_0 \tag{1}$$

with v the weight from input to hidden units and w the weights from hidden to output units. Thus, calculation of an output y given a set of inputs x_i $\{i = 1, 2, \ldots, N\}$ can be broken down as follows:

- when input x_i enters the neural network as an input to hidden unit h_j it is first multiplied by the weight v_{ji};
- inside h_j the weighted inputs $v_{ji} x_i$ are summed and input into a hyperbolic tangent function so that the resulting value of h_j lies between -1 and 1:

$$h_j = \tanh\left(\sum_i v_{ji} x_i + v_{j0} \right) \tag{2}$$

- when the result h_j exits the hidden unit it is multiplied by a weight w_j before it exits the neural network;
- the final output y sums up all weighted hidden units $w_j h_j$ to get the final estimation:

$$y = \sum_i w_j h_j + w_0 . \tag{3}$$

Given a data set of P pairs of input (x^μ) and target output (t^μ) combinations ($\mu = 1 \ldots P$), training basically means fitting the parameters v and w such that the predicted output $y(x^\mu)$ best matches the target output t^μ. In this, "best matches" means minimizing (under some constraints) an error function $E(Y, T)$, where $Y = \{y(x^1), \ldots, y(x^P)\}$ and $T = \{t^1, \ldots, t^P\}$.

In this study, we use market capitalization and volatility of public companies as target output t, and the available data from public information for the companies as input x.

OPTIMIZATION

The available data set is subdivided into a training set and a second set for testing, which is only used after training the network. The first set is used for training the networks and therefore gives in-sample results, which are not a good indication of the generalization ability of the networks. The test set is used to compute out-of-sample results that indicate how good the predictions will be on any (comparable) data set. Generally, about half of the data are left aside for testing and half are used for training.

Neural networks are trained using conjugate gradient optimization, which is a fast and stable routine for training neural networks and does not require difficult parameter settings (Press, Teukolsky, Vetterling, and Flannery 1992). The "backpropagation rule" (Rumelhart et al. 1986) is used to compute the gradient of the error, which is passed to the optimization procedure.

During initial training, the model provides excellent estimations for a training set, but performance on a testing set is extremely poor. This is because the model is over-fitting the training data so the relationship it captures does not apply to data outside of a training set.

To prevent over-fitting, the original training set is divided into a new training set and a validation set. While optimizing on the new training set, the error on the validation set is monitored. Training errors decrease, as they should, but validation errors at some point start to increase, indicating that the model is starting to over-fit. When validation errors start to increase, training is stopped and the network that yields the lowest validation error is chosen. This regularization procedure is sometimes referred to as "early stopping" or "stopped training" (Finnoff 1994), and is a common technique to prevent over-fitting.

ERROR FUNCTION

To evaluate performance of the network(s) a relative error is computed:

$$r^{\mu} = \left| \frac{y^{\mu}}{t^{\mu}} - 1 \right| \tag{4}$$

where y^{μ} is the prediction for data pair μ and t^{μ} the target output for that pair. This formulation implies that an error of 0.5 means the prediction is either 50% too high or 50% too low.

To evaluate the performance on a data set with many patterns the average of the error measure in Equation (4) would be the obvious choice. However, the average of r^{μ} is extremely sensitive to outliers. Therefore, the median error is used instead of the mean:

$$R(Y, T) = \operatorname*{median}_{\mu} r^{\mu}. \tag{5}$$

From a statistical viewpoint, the error equation used for training is not necessarily equal to the error equation used for evaluation, but should rather correspond to the statistical properties of the data (Bishop 1995). Analyzing residuals between target and predictions suggests that logarithms of market captilization and volatility are more or less normally distributed. Thus, to represent the statistical form of the data in the optimization an error function of the following form is minimized:

$$E(Y, T) = \sum_{\mu} [\log(y^{\mu}) - \log(t^{\mu})]^2 = \sum_{\mu} \left[\log\left(\frac{y^{\mu}}{t^{\mu}} \right) \right]^2 \tag{6}$$

where μ indicates that $\{t^{\mu}, y^{\mu}\}$ is a pair of corresponding targets and neural network outputs. Taking logarithms also normalizes the data, making it easier for a neural network to train. Since the difference between two logarithms is equal to the logarithm of the quotient, as shown in Equation (6), the percent by which a neural network output deviates from a target output is minimized. Different error functions, including r^{μ} of Equation (4), were tried, but this one yields the best and most stable results.

SCALING DATA

Financial ratios are the key inputs to the neural networks but they have a tendency to generate extreme outliers. This is especially a challenge when a denominator's value can be positive or negative, thus passing through zero where a ratio's value is undefined. When calibrating a neural network, outliers can overshadow all other numbers in an input set. To limit the effect of outliers, inputs are transformed by squeezing them between -1 and 1 with a hyperbolic tangent:

$$x_{new} = \tanh(ax + b). \tag{7}$$

Parameters a and b are chosen such that the mean and standard deviation equal 0 and 0.3, respectively, so the data are reasonably distributed around the range of -1 to 1. Figure 8.1 shows a histogram of unscaled inputs with many outliers.

After squeezing these inputs through a hyperbolic tangent, the histogram on the right side of Figure 8.1 is obtained, which is much more bell-shaped or normally distributed.

Similarly, financial statement numbers like total assets and current liabilities figure a large range of values. This too can cause a neural network to overcompensate for large values in the training set. To overcome this, the data distribution is also changed to a bell-shaped pattern, which serves as a good starting point for training neural networks. The distributions are transformed logarithmically:

$$x_{new} = \log(x). \tag{8}$$

They are then scaled linearly to have a zero mean and unit standard deviation. Logarithmic scaling is also done for market capitalization and volatility outputs, as explained earlier in the description of the error function, Equation (6). The result for both inputs and outputs is a bell-shape similar to Figure 8.1.

NETWORK ENSEMBLES

The current standard is not to train a single neural network, but instead an "ensemble" of them, each of them using a slightly different training set and different initial conditions (see e.g., Breiman 1996 and Heskes 1997). After

FIGURE 8.1   Unscaled inputs of the left histogram show outliers (crosses), whereas the scaled right histogram is bell-shaped.

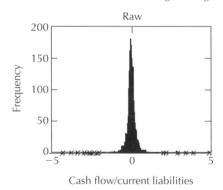
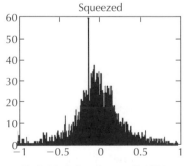

training, an outcome to a given input set is found by a weighted averaging over the network outputs within the ensemble. It is known that such an ensemble is much more stable and leads to a better generalization performance.

For each network in the ensemble a slightly different training set is generated using a method called naive bootstrapping (Efron and Tibshirani 1993). Suppose that the original training set consists of P pairs of inputs and outputs. Bootstrapping then draws P pairs, with replacement, from this set and puts them in the new training set. Pairs that are not part of the new training set, about 37%, can be used for validation.

The actual bootstrapping procedure taken here has two layers. Residuals (difference between target and prediction) for the same company across different quarters are highly correlated. Therefore, for a fair and appropriate subdivision of data in training and validation, we bootstrap companies rather than individual data points. This method is referred to as the "block bootstrap" (Efron and Tibshirani 1993) and is often applied in the context of time series.

After training and validating each of the networks, they are combined to generate a final answer. Many different suggestions on this issue have been made in literature, ranging from simple equal averaging, so-called bagging (Breiman 1996) to keeping the single best network, and so-called bumping (Tibshirani and Knight 1995). We use a weighting scheme called balancing, which takes the best of both worlds. It puts higher weight on the best networks and generally outperforms both bagging (a little) and bumping (a lot) (Heskes 1997).

ARCHITECTURE

In searching for the best architecture (number of hidden layers; number of hidden units), a brute force trial-and-error approach is used. From experience, a single layer of hidden units is sufficient to model most real-world data sets. Therefore, networks with a single layer of hidden units are first considered, and the number of units are varied from 1 to 10. Ensembles of 250 networks are trained. To obtain out-of-sample results, half of the data set is used for training and the other half for testing. After this, the training and test sets are reversed and another set of ensembles are computed, completing out-of-sample results for all companies in the original training set. The results are shown in Figure 8.2. Here the median error $R(Y; T)$ is plotted as a function of the number of hidden units. The baseline, the median error with "0 hidden units", is the performance obtained on linear models without a hidden layer. It can be seen that, for modeling both the volatility and the market capitalization, the optimal number of hidden units is two.

FIGURE 8.2   Median error drops off after two hidden units for both market capitalization
(left-hand side) and volatility (right-hand side)

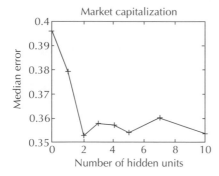
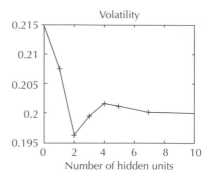

This refers to out-of-sample performance on companies not in the training set. Without early stopping, a network with 10 hidden units can easily reach a training error that is order of magnitudes lower than this. In other words, the neural networks are sufficiently powerful to fit non-linearities in the training data. The issue, however, is much more to grasp non-linearities that translate to the test set.

Architectures with a second hidden layer are also tried, but do not obtain better performance. The conclusion is that two hidden units are enough, both for volatility and for market capitalization. It should be noted that the fact that a neural approach achieves better performance than a simple linear model is not obvious. For example, in a comparison test on a similar problem related to predicting company failure, neural networks did not outperform a simpler linear discrimant solution (Altman, Marco, and Varetto 1994). The interpretation is that the data have a "weak nonlinear" tendency: the difference with a linear model is significant, yet not enormous and a neural network with two hidden units is sufficiently complex to achieve this improvement. State-of-the-art techniques, like ensembles and appropriate optimization tools, are required to make this difference.

INPUT SELECTION

An important issue is which inputs to include for the final neural networks. This approach starts with a neural network trained using all available inputs. Iteratively, the least relevant input is eliminated. To estimate which input is least relevant, a method called "partial retraining" is applied (see e.g., Van de Laar and Heskes 1999). The basic idea is to leave out a particular input, and adapt the weights from the input to hidden units such as to compensate for the lack of this input. The performance of the "partially retrained" network is then computed on the validation set. The least relevant input will yield the smallest decrease (or perhaps even slight increase) in performance. This so-called backward elimination process is repeated on all networks in the ensemble independently.

Graphs are used to visualize the performance as a function of the number of inputs taken into account, a typical example of which is shown in Figure 8.3 for market capitalization.

Here performance is defined as the percentage of explained variance. A model without any inputs (the left corner of the graph), explains no variance. 100% explained variance corresponds to a perfect fit with no residuals. The full model explains about 92% of the variance (in the logarithms of the market capitalization). There is a direct relationship between this percentage of explained variance and the error $E(Y, T)$. Reading the graph from right to left, the effect of leaving out the least relevant input on the percentage of explained variance can be seen. Here, things really do not start to happen until there are fewer than 30 inputs. A fairly safe assumption is that eliminated inputs are largely irrelevant, leaving at most 20 relevant inputs.

Backward elimination, as described in the previous steps, is notoriously unstable (Breiman 1996); that is, for the various networks in the ensemble, there can be different orderings of inputs. The performance graphs, however, are all quite similar. To get a final ordering of relevant inputs, a new network is trained to fit the predictions of the ensemble and apply the backward elimination procedure to this network. As a result, a set of the 20 most relevant inputs were found and used in the rest of the study.

There is no "golden truth" here. Many of these inputs can be replaced with others and yield roughly the same performance. A final set of 20 inputs was settled on after examining variations and possible substitutes.

FIGURE 8.3   Changes in the percentage of explained variance occur when there are fewer than 30 inputs remaining (the right plot is an inset of the left)

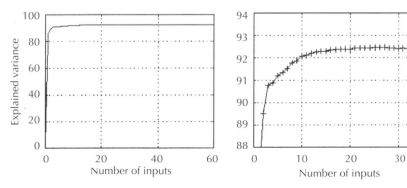

The results of the neural networks for input data are given in Figure 8.4 for both volatility and market capitalization prediction. Though separate neural network inputs were initially selected for volatility and market capitalization prediction, performance does not differ significantly when the market capitalization input set is used in volatility prediction and vice versa; in large part this is due to the ability of financial ratios to substitute for each other. Thus, a single input set is used for both target outputs to simplify matters.

PERFORMANCE

Using the inputs from Figure 8.4 we trained two ensembles of 250 networks for each industry, one predicting volatility and one predicting market capitalization. These ensembles are trained using half of the data available for the target industry, leaving the other half of the data for test results. We will refer to these ensembles as (industry) specialized ensembles. We also trained ensembles on a combined data set of all the industries together, which we will call (industry) general ensembles.

Figure 8.5 visualizes the results for the basic materials industry. The left-hand scatter plots show the actual market capitalization and volatility as a function of the predicted market capitalization and volatility. The right-hand error plots are cumulative plots of the relative error r defined in Equation (4). Specifically, for each r on the horizontal axis, the percentage of predictions with errors less than or equal to r are given on the vertical access. The dark solid line indicates results for the ensemble that was trained

FIGURE 8.4   The final 20 inputs cover most ratio types

Company size

| Total assets |
| Capital invested |
| Cash |
| Free cash flow |

Debt level or leverage

| Total debt/Capital invested |
| Total liabilities/Total assets |
| Long-term debt/Working capital |
| Current liabilities |

Debt servicing

| Cash flow/Current liabilities |
| Cash flow/Capital invested |

Profitability

| Gross operating income/Total assets |
| Net income/Sales |
| Net income/Total liabilities |
| Sales |
| Gross profit margin |

Liquidity

| Quick assets/Total assets |
| Cash/Total assets |
| Accounts receivable turnover |
| Free cash flow/Equity |
| Working capital/Total assets |

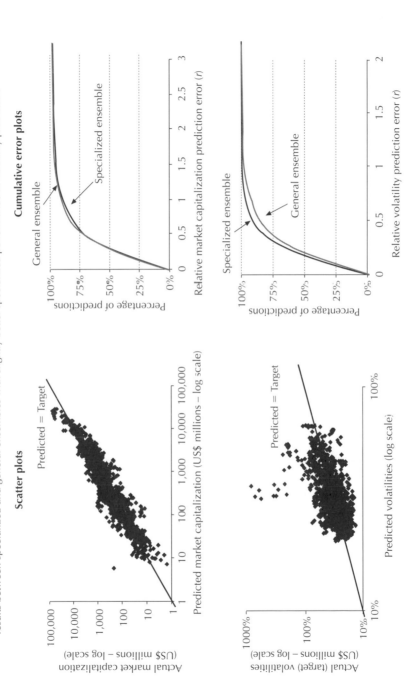

FIGURE 8.5 For the basic materials industry, predictions trend around the diagonal in the scatter plots and the error plots show similar market capitalization results between specialized and general ensembles with slightly better specialized performance in volatility prediction

on the basic materials industry only; the specialized ensemble. The lighter line represents results on companies from the basic materials industry predicted by the general ensemble. It appears that (for this industry) the results do not improve significantly by training ensembles specialized on this industry. The median relative error r is 0.31 for market capitalization, and 0.18 for volatility (Table 8.1).

Figures 8.6, 8.7, and 8.8 show results for the other industries. Again, there is no significant improvement by using the specialized ensembles. For the healthcare industry the general ensemble even gives significantly better results for market capitalization. This is probably a consequence of the small sample size of the training set for this industry.

ERROR ANALYSIS

To understand the nature of the remaining errors, we performed the following error analysis. For simplicity of notation, t_i refers to the logarithm of the market capitalization for a particular company in quarter i and y_i to the logarithm of the corresponding predictions. We consider the sum-squared error as in Equation (6) for a single company, averaged across eight quarters. It can be decomposed as:

$$E = \frac{1}{8} \sum_i (t_i - y_i)^2 = (\bar{t} - \bar{y})^2 + \frac{1}{8} \sum_i [(t_i - \bar{t})^2 - (y_i - \bar{y})^2] \tag{9}$$

with:

$$\bar{t} = \frac{1}{8} \sum_i t_i \quad \text{and} \quad \bar{y} = \frac{1}{8} \sum_i y_i.$$

The first term gives the error between the "average" target and the "average" prediction. Averaged over all companies it amounts to about 75% of the total error. The remaining 25% is caused by the second term, which

TABLE 8.1 Median errors are around 35% for market capitalization predictions and 20% for volatility predictions

Industry	Market capitalization	Volatility
Basic materials	0.31	0.18
Technology	0.33	0.21
Healthcare	0.38	0.16
Services	0.41	0.20
All	0.35	0.20

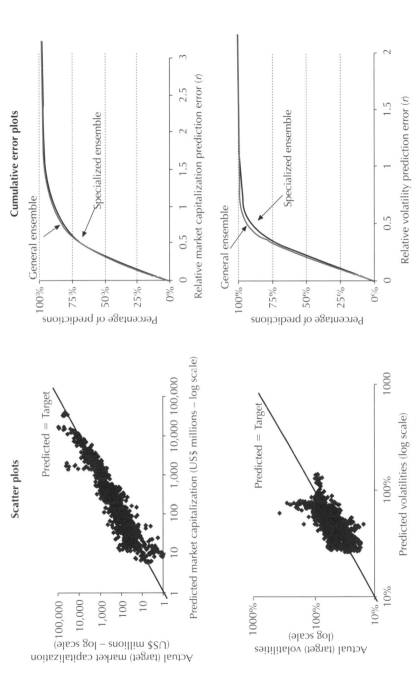

FIGURE 8.6 Technology industry predictions also trend around the diagonal with near identical results between general and specialized ensembles

FIGURE 8.7 Similar prediction results exist for the healthcare industry, except the general ensemble outperforms the specialized ensemble in predicting market capitalization

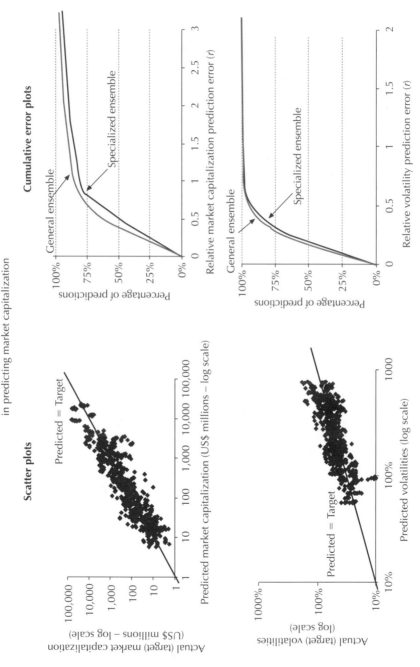

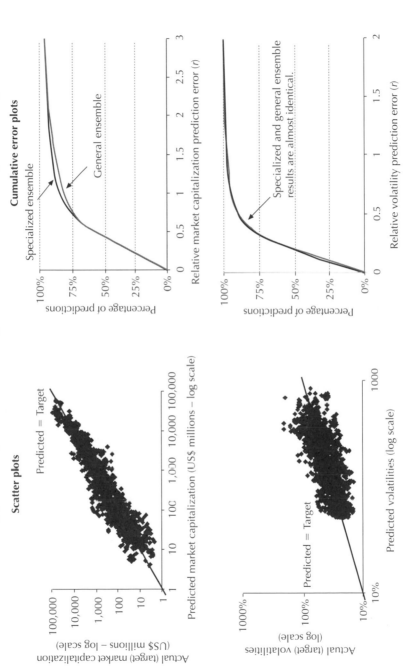

FIGURE 8.8   For the services industry, predictions again trend around the diagonal with similar results between specialized and general ensembles

measures how well the difference between quarters are predicted. Focusing on this second term, it appears that (on average):

$$\frac{1}{8}\sum_i [(t_i - \bar{t}) - (y_i - \bar{y})]^2 \approx \frac{1}{8}\sum_i (t_i - \bar{t})^2 \tag{10}$$

that is, none of the fluctuations between quarters is explained by the models. The typical picture is illustrated in Figure 8.9: the predictions tend to either underfit or overfit the targets for all eight quarters (the largest part of the error between targets and predictions). Directions between different quarters are not grasped either.

ERROR BARS

Outputs of the neural networks can be interpreted as estimates of the average market capitalization and base volatility for a company with given balance sheet information. Error bars can be computed to give an indication of the accuracy of these outputs in estimating the true market capitalization and volatility. As discussed before, the residuals for the logarithms of market capitalization and volatility appear to be more or less normally distributed. Computation of error bars then amounts to computation of the variance s^2 of these residuals (in log scale).

The approach we took follows from Heskes (1997). Part of a new network is trained to fit the variance of the residuals as a function of the inputs. The resulting error bars are visualized in Figure 8.10 as the solid

FIGURE 8.9   Quarterly predictions tend to consistently underfit (as in this illustration) or overfit target values and fluctuations in predicted values do not correlate with target fluctuations

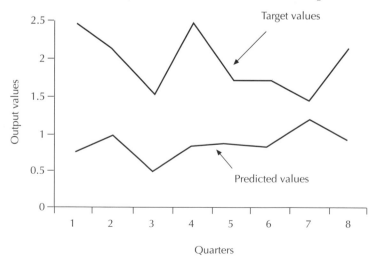

lines, and defined as predictions plus or minus two times standard deviation computed by the new network. Figure 8.10 also plots predicted values versus target values scaled by taking the logarithm of the market capitalization or volatility and normalized to a mean zero and unit standard deviation. Targets in each plot well outside of the band formed by the error bars can be considered outliers.

From Figure 8.11 it seems that the error bars are, relatively speaking, somewhat larger for smaller market capitalizations and larger volatilities. In other words, predictions for smaller size companies are somewhat less accurate.

FIGURE 8.10   Error bars define a boundary for outliers

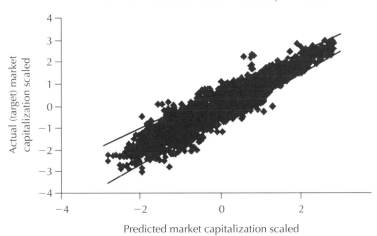

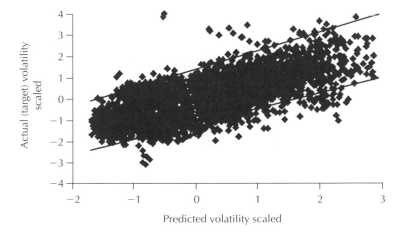

Error bars help define the distribution of market capitalization and volatility predictions. In a final implementation in conjunction with a credit risk model, this is valuable in determining a distribution of possible default probabilities for a company given the company's financial statement information, rather than calculating a credit risk measure based on point estimates of the market capitalization and volatility.

CONCLUSION

The neural network structure used is a single layer of weighted, hidden units. Hidden units or nonlinear functions contribute to a neural network's ability to replicate nonlinear relationships between inputs and outputs. Weightings determine how much the results of hidden units contribute to the final value of a network's output. The weightings are optimized on target outputs using conjugate gradient optimization, a fast and stable routine. Optimization occurs for an ensemble of networks, each of them using slightly different sets of input and output data for training, and different initial conditions; that is, initial guesses for the weightings. Thereafter, a result to a given input set is obtained by taking a weighted average over the networks' outputs within the ensemble to produce a result with better, generalized performance.

Around 20 inputs appear sufficient to maximize predictive power of the neural networks. In fact, many of the inputs used in the top 20 are interchangeable so that the same set of inputs can be used for both market capitalization and volatility calculations. Inputs are not industry specific either. Predictions of neural networks specialized on industry specific data do not outperform a general neural network trained across industries.

The results are neural network predictions for market capitalization and volatility with errors on the order of 35% and 20%, respectively. In many cases, predictions overestimate (or underestimate) actual values consistently across quarters and are not able to reflect the fluctuations in target values between quarters.

The level of errors produced is significant and areas for improvement do exist. These include resolving deficiencies in the data used and other enhancements explored in Alibhai, Gaeta, and Hingorani 2001. However, though the performance is not desirable it is very promising and serves as an excellent initial base for a private company credit risk model.

NOTE

[1] For a description of such a model, see Gaeta, Alibhai, and Hingorani 2000.

CHAPTER 9

A Comparison of Stochastic Default Rate Models

Christopher C. Finger
RiskMetrics

Collateralized debt obligations have sparked interest in portfolio default models over multiple horizons. For these, in contrast to single-period models, there is little understanding of the impact of model assumptions. We investigate four multiple-horizon models, each calibrated to the same set of input data. Our results show a significant disparity, showing that the issue of model choice is more consequential here than in the single period case.

INTRODUCTION

In recent years, models of defaults in a portfolio context have been well studied. Three separate approaches (CreditMetrics, CreditRisk+, and CreditPortfolioView[1]) were made public in 1997. Subsequently, researchers have examined the mathematical structure of the various models.[2] Each of these studies has revealed it is possible to calibrate the models to each other, and the differences between the models lie in subtle choices of the driving distributions and in the data sources one would use to feed the models.

Common to all of these models and the subsequent examinations thereof is the fact that the models describe only a single period. In other words, the models describe, for a specific risk horizon, whether each asset of interest defaults within the horizon. The timing of defaults within the risk horizon is not considered, nor is the possibility of defaults beyond the horizon. This is not a flaw of the current models, but rather an indication of their genesis as approaches to risk management and capital allocation for a fixed portfolio.

Not entirely by chance, the development of portfolio models for credit risk management has coincided with an explosion in issuance of collateralized debt obligations (CDOs). The performance of a CDO structure depends on the default behavior of a pool of assets. Significantly, the dependence is not just on whether the assets default over the life of the structure, but also on when the defaults occur. Thus, while an application of the existing models can give a cursory view of the structure (by describing, for instance, the distribution of the number of assets that will default over the structure's life), a more rigorous analysis requires a model of the timing of defaults.

In this chapter, we will survey a number of extensions of the standard single-period models that allow for a treatment of default timing over longer horizons. We will examine two extensions of the CreditMetrics approach: one that models only defaults over time and a second that effectively accounts for rating migrations. In addition, we will examine the copula function approach introduced by Li (1999) and Li (2000), as well as a simple version of the stochastic intensity model applied by Duffie and Garleanu (1998).

We will investigate the differences in the four approaches that arise from model – rather than data – differences. Thus, we will suppose that we begin with satisfactory estimates of expected default rates over time and of the correlation of default events over one period. Higher order information, such as the correlation of defaults in subsequent periods or the joint behavior of three or more assets, will be driven by the structure of the models. The analysis of the models will then illuminate the range of results that can arise given the same initial data. Nagpal and Bahar (1999) adopt a similar approach in the single-horizon context, investigating the range of possible full distributions that can be calibrated to first- and second-order default statistics.

In the following section, we present terminology and notation to be used throughout. We proceed to detail the four models. Finally, we present two comparison exercises: in the first, we use closed-form results to analyze default rate volatilities and conditional default probabilities, while in the second, we implement Monte Carlo simulations in order to investigate the full distribution of realized default rates.

NOTATION AND TERMINOLOGY

To compare the properties of the four models, we will consider a large homogeneous pool of assets. By homogeneous, we mean that each asset has the same probability of default (first-order statistics) at every time we consider; further, each pair of assets has the same joint probability of default (second-order statistics) at every time.

To describe the first-order statistics of the pool, we specify the *cumulative default probability*, q_k, the probability that a given asset defaults in the next k years – for $k = 1, 2, \ldots T$, where T is the maximum horizon we consider. Equivalently, we may specify the *marginal default probability* p_k – the probability that a given asset defaults in year k. Clearly, cumulative and marginal default probabilities are related through:

$$q_k = q_{k-1} + pk, \text{ for } k = 2,...,T. \tag{1}$$

It is important to distinguish a third equivalent specification: *conditional default probabilities*. The conditional default probability in year k is defined as the conditional probability that an asset defaults in year k, given that the asset has survived (that is, has not defaulted) in the first $k = 1$ years. This probability is given by $p_k/(1 - q_{k-1})$.

Finally, to describe the second-order statistics of the pool, we specify the *joint cumulative default probability* $q_{j,k}$ – the probability that for a given pair of assets, the first asset defaults sometime in the first j years and the second defaults sometime in the first k years. Equivalently, we can specify the *joint marginal default probability* $p_{j,k}$ – the probability that the first asset defaults in year j and the second defaults in year k. These two notions are related through:

$$q_{j,k} = q_{j-1,k-1} + \sum_{i=1}^{j-1} p_{i,k} + \sum_{i=1}^{k-1} p_{j,i} + p_{j,k}, \text{ for } j,k = 2,...,T. \tag{2}$$

In practice, it is possible to obtain first-order statistics for relatively long horizons, either by observing market prices of risky debt and calibrating cumulative default probabilities as in Duffie and Singleton (1999), or by taking historical cumulative default experience from a study such as Keenan et al. (2000) or *Ratings Performance 1999: Stability & Transition* (2000). Less information is available for second-order statistics, however, and therefore we will assume that we can obtain the joint default probability for the first year $(p_{1,1})$,[3] but not any of the joint default probabilities for subsequent years. Thus, our exercise will be to calibrate each of the four models to fixed values of $q_1, q_2, \ldots q_T$ and $p_{1,1}$, and then to compare the higher order statistics implied by the models.

The model comparison can be a simple task of comparing values of $p_{1,2}$, $p_{2,2}$, $q_{2,2}$, and so on. However, to make the comparisons a bit more tangible, we will consider the distributions of *realized default rates*. The term "default rate" is often used loosely in the literature, without a clear notion of whether default rate is synonymous with default probability, or rather is itself a random variable. To be clear, in this article, the default rate is a random variable equal to the proportion of assets that default in a portfolio. For instance, if the random variable $X_i^{(k)}$ is equal to one, if the ith asset defaults in year k, then the year k default rate is equal to:

$$\frac{1}{n} \sum_{i=1}^{n} X_i^{(k)}.$$ (3)

For our homogeneous portfolio, the mean year k default rate is simply p_k, the marginal default probability for year k. Furthermore, the standard deviation of the year k default rate (which we will refer to as the *year k default rate volatility*) is:

$$\sqrt{p_{k,k} - p_k^2 + (p_k - p_{k,k})/n}.$$ (4)

Of interest to us is the large portfolio limit (that is, $n \to \infty$) of this quantity, normalized by the default probability. We will refer to this as the *normalized year k default volatility*, which is given by:

$$\frac{\sqrt{p_{k,k} - p_k^2}}{p_k}.$$ (5)

Additionally, we will examine the *normalized cumulative year k default volatility*, which is defined similarly to the above, with the exception that the default rate is computed over the first k years rather than year k only. The normalized cumulative default volatility is given by:

$$\frac{\sqrt{q_{k,k} - q_k^2}}{q_k}.$$ (6)

Finally, we will use Φ to denote the standard normal cumulative distribution function. In the bivariate setting, we will use $\Phi_2(z_1, z_2; \rho)$ to indicate the probability that $Z_1 < z_1$ and $Z_2 < z_2$, where Z_1 and Z_2 are standard normal random variables with correlation ρ.

In the following four sections, we describe the models to be considered and discuss in detail the calibration to our initial data.

DISCRETE CREDITMETRICS EXTENSION

In its simplest form, the single-period CreditMetrics model calibrated for our homogeneous portfolio can be stated as follows:

1. define a default threshold α such that $\Phi(\alpha) = p_1$;
2. to each asset i, assign a standard normal random variable $Z^{(i)}$, where the correlation between distinct $Z^{(i)}$ and $Z^{(j)}$ is equal to ρ, such that:

$$\Phi_2(\alpha, \alpha; \rho) = p_{1,1};$$ (7)

3. asset i defaults in year 1 if $Z^{(i)} < \alpha$.

The simplest extension of this model to multiple horizons is to simply repeat the single-period model. We then have default thresholds α_1, $\alpha_2, \ldots, \alpha_T$ corresponding to each period. For the first period, we assign standard normal random variables, $Z_1^{(i)}$ to each asset as above, and asset i defaults in the first period if $Z_1^{(i)} < \alpha_1$. For assets that survive the first period, we assign a second set of standard normal random variables, $Z_2^{(i)}$, such that the correlation between distinct $Z_2^{(i)}$ and $Z_2^{(j)}$ is ρ, but the variables from one period to the next are independent. The asset then defaults in the second period if $Z_1^{(i)} < \alpha_1$ (it survives the first period) and $Z_2^{(i)} < \alpha_2$. The extension to subsequent periods should be clear. In the end, the model is specified by the default thresholds $\alpha_1, \alpha_2, \ldots, \alpha_T$ and the correlation parameter ρ.

To calibrate this model to our cumulative default probabilities q_1, $q_2, \ldots, q_T$ and joint default probability, we begin by setting the first period default threshold:

$$\alpha_1 = \Phi^{-1}(q_1). \tag{8}$$

For subsequent periods, we set α_k such that the probability that $Z_i^{(k)} < \alpha_k$ is equal to the conditional default probability for period k:

$$\alpha_k = \Phi^{-1}\left(\frac{q_k - q_{k-1}}{1 - q_{k-1}}\right). \tag{9}$$

We complete the calibration by choosing ρ to satisfy Equation (7), with α replaced by α_1.

The joint default probabilities and default volatilities are easily obtained in this context. For instance, the marginal year two joint default probability is given by (for distinct i and j):

$$\begin{aligned} p_{2,2} &= \mathbf{P}\{Z_1^{(i)} > \alpha_1 \cap Z_1^{(j)} > \alpha_1 \cap Z_2^{(i)} < \alpha_2 \cap Z_2^{(j)} < \alpha_2\} \\ &= \mathbf{P}\{Z_1^{(i)} > \alpha_1 \cap Z_1^{(j)} > \alpha_1\} \cdot \mathbf{P}\{Z_2^{(i)} < \alpha_2 \cap Z_2^{(j)} < \alpha_2\} \\ &= (1 - 2p_1 + p_{1,1}) \cdot \Phi_2(\alpha_2, \alpha_2; \rho) \end{aligned} \tag{10}$$

Similarly, the probability that asset i defaults in the first period and asset j in the second period is:

$$\begin{aligned} p_{1,2} &= \mathbf{P}\{Z_1^{(i)} < \alpha_1 \cap Z_1^{(j)} > \alpha_1 \cap Z_2^{(j)} < \alpha_2\} \\ &= (p_1 - p_{1,1}) \cdot (q_2 - p_1)/(1 - p_1). \end{aligned} \tag{11}$$

It is then possible to obtain $q_{2,2}$ using Equation (2) and the default volatilities using Equations (5) and (6).

DIFFUSION-DRIVEN CREDITMETRICS EXTENSION

By construction, the discrete CreditMetrics extension does not allow for any correlation of default rates through time. For instance, if a high default rate is realized in the first period, this has no bearing on the default rate in the second period, since the default drivers for the second period (the $Z_2^{(i)}$ mentioned previously) are independent of the default drivers for the first. Intuitively, we would not expect this behavior from the market. If a high default rate occurs in one period, then it is likely that those obligors that did not default would have generally decreased in credit quality. The impact would then be that the default rate for the second period would also have a tendency to be high.

In order to capture this behavior, we introduce a CreditMetrics extension where defaults in consecutive periods are not driven by independent random variables, but rather by a single diffusion process. Our diffusion-driven CreditMetrics extension is described by the following process:

1. define default thresholds $\alpha_1, \alpha_2, \ldots, \alpha_T$ for each period;
2. to each obligor, assign a standard Wiener process $W^{(i)}$, with $W_0^{(i)} = 0$, where the instantaneous correlation between distinct $W^{(i)}$ and $W^{(j)}$ is ρ^4;
3. obligor i defaults in the first year if $W^{(i)} < \alpha_1$;
4. for $k > 1$, obligor i defaults in year k if it survives the first $k - 1$ years (that is, $W_1^{(i)} > \alpha_1, \ldots, W_{k-1}^{(i)} > \alpha_{k-1}$) and $W_k^{(i)} < \alpha_k$.

Note that this approach allows for the behavior mentioned above. If the default rate is high in the first year, this is because many of the Wiener processes have fallen below the threshold α_1. The Wiener processes for non-defaulting obligors will have generally trended downward as well, since all of the Wiener processes are correlated. This implies a greater likelihood of a high number of defaults in the second year. In effect, then, this approach introduces a notion of credit migration. Cases where the Wiener process trends downward, but does not cross the default threshold can be thought of as downgrades, while cases where the process trends upward are essentially upgrades.

To calibrate the first threshold α_1, we observe that:

$$\mathbf{P}\{W_1^{(i)} < \alpha_1\} = \Phi(\alpha_1) \tag{12}$$

and thus, that α_1 is given by Equation (8). For the second threshold, we require that the probability that an obligor defaults in year two is equal to p_2:

$$\mathbf{P}\{W_1^{(i)} > \alpha_1 \cap W_2^{(i)} < \alpha_2\} = p_2. \tag{13}$$

Since $W^{(i)}$ is a Wiener process, we know the standard deviation of $W_t^{(i)}$ is $\sqrt{t}$ and for $s < t$, the correlation between $W_s^{(i)}$ and $W_t^{(i)}$ is $\sqrt{s/t}$. Thus, given α_1, we find the value of α_2 that satisfies:

$$\Phi\left(\frac{\alpha_2}{\sqrt{2}}\right) - \Phi\left(\alpha_1, \frac{\alpha_2}{\sqrt{2}}; \frac{\sqrt{1}}{2}\right) = p_2. \tag{14}$$

For the kth period, given $\alpha_1, \ldots, \alpha_{k-1}$, we calibrate α_k by solving:

$$\mathbf{P}\{W_1^{(i)} > \alpha_1 \cap \ldots \cap W_{k-1}^{(i)} > \alpha_{k-1} \cap W_k^{(i)} < \alpha_k\} = p_k \tag{15}$$

again utilizing the properties of the Wiener process $W^{(i)}$ to compute the probability on the left-hand side.

We complete the calibration by finding ρ such that the year one joint default probability is $p_{1,1}$:

$$\mathbf{P}\{W_1^{(i)} > \alpha_1 \cap W_1^{(j)} < \alpha_1\} = p_{1,1}. \tag{16}$$

Since $W_1^{(i)}$ and $W_1^{(j)}$ each follow a standard normal distribution and have a correlation of ρ, the solution for ρ here is identical to that of the previous section.

With the calibration complete, it is a simple task to compute the joint default probabilities. For instance, the joint year two default probability is given by:

$$p_{2,2} = \mathbf{P}\{W_1^{(i)} > \alpha_1 \cap W_1^{(j)} > \alpha_1 \cap W_2^{(i)} < \alpha_2 \cap W_2^{(j)} < \alpha_2\} \tag{17}$$

where we use the fact that $\{W_1^{(i)}, W_1^{(j)}, W_2^{(i)}, W_2^{(j)}\}$ follow a multivariate normal distribution with covariance:

$$\text{Cov}\{W_1^{(i)}, W_1^{(j)}, W_2^{(i)}, W_2^{(j)}\} = \begin{pmatrix} 1 & \rho & 1 & \rho \\ \rho & 1 & \rho & 1 \\ 1 & \rho & 2 & 2\rho \\ \rho & 1 & 2\rho & 2 \end{pmatrix}. \tag{18}$$

COPULA FUNCTIONS

A drawback of both the CreditMetrics extensions above is that in a Monte Carlo setting, they require a stepwise simulation approach. In other words, we must simulate the pool of assets over the first year, tabulate the ones that default, then simulate the remaining assets over the second year, and so on. Li (1999) and Li (2000) introduce an approach wherein it is possible to simulate the default times directly, thus avoiding the need to simulate each period individually.

The normal copula function approach is as follows:

1. specify the cumulative default time distribution F, such that $F(t)$ gives the probability that a given asset defaults prior to time t;
2. assign a standard normal random variable $Z^{(i)}$ to each asset, where the correlation between distinct $Z^{(i)}$ and $Z^{(j)}$ is ρ;
3. obtain the default time τ_i for asset i through:

$$\tau_i = F^{-1}(\Phi(Z^{(i)})). \tag{19}$$

Since we are concerned here only with the year in which an asset defaults and not the precise timing within the year, we will consider a discrete version of the copula approach:

1. specify the cumulative default probabilities $q_1, q_2, \ldots, q_T$ as in the section on notation and terminology;
2. for $k = 1, \ldots, T$ compute the threshold $\alpha_k = \Phi^{-1}(q_k)$. Clearly, $\alpha_1, \alpha_2, \ldots, \alpha_T$. Define $\alpha_0 = -\infty$;
3. assign $Z^{(i)}$ to each asset as above;
4. asset i defaults in year k if $a_{k-1} < Z^{(i)} \leqslant \alpha_k$.

The calibration to the cumulative default probabilities is already given. Furthermore, it is easy to observe that the correlation parameter ρ is calibrated exactly as in the previous two sections.[5]

The joint default probabilities are perhaps simplest to obtain for this approach. For example, the joint cumulative default probability $q_{k,l}$ is given by:

$$q_{k,l} = \mathbf{P}\{Z^{(i)} < \alpha_k \cap Z^{(j)} < \alpha_l\} = \Phi_2(\alpha_k, \alpha_j; \rho). \tag{20}$$

STOCHASTIC DEFAULT INTENSITY

Description of the Model

The approaches of the three previous sections can all be thought of as extensions of the single-period CreditMetrics framework. Each approach relies on standard normal random variables to drive defaults and calibrates thresholds for these variables. Furthermore, it is easy to see that over the first period, the three approaches are identical; they only differ in their behavior over multiple periods.

Our fourth model takes a different approach to the construction of correlated defaults over time and can be thought of as an extension of the single period CreditRisk+ framework. In the CreditRisk+ model, correlations between default events are constructed through the assets' dependence on a common default probability, which itself is a random variable.[6] Importantly, given the realization of the default probability, defaults are conditionally independent. The volatility of the common default probability is in effect the correlation parameter for this model; a higher default volatility induces stronger correlations, while a zero volatility produces independent defaults.[7]

The natural extension of the CreditRisk+ framework to continuous time is the stochastic intensity approach presented in Duffie and Garleanu (1998) (hereafter DG) and Duffie and Singleton (1998). Intuitively, the stochastic intensity model stipulates that in a given small time interval, assets default independently, with probability proportional to a common default intensity.[8] In the next time interval, the intensity changes, and defaults are once again independent, but with the default probability proportional to the new intensity level. The evolution of the intensity is described through a stochastic process. In practice, since the intensity must remain positive, it is common to apply similar stochastic processes as are utilized in models of interest rates.

For our purposes, we will model a single intensity process h. Conditional on h, the default time for each asset is then the first arrival of a Poisson process with arrival rate given by h. The Poisson processes driving the defaults for distinct assets are independent, meaning that given a realization of the intensity process h, defaults are independent. The Poisson process framework implies that given h, the probability that a given asset survives until time t is:

$$\exp\left[-\int_0^t du\, h_u\right].$$

(21)

Furthermore, because defaults are conditionally independent, the conditional probability, given h, that two assets both survive until time t is:

$$\exp\left[-2\int_0^t du\, h_u\right].$$

(22)

The unconditional survival probabilities are given by expectations over the process h, so that in particular, the survival probability for a single asset is given by:

$$1 - q_t = \mathbf{E}\,\exp\left[-\int_0^t du\, h_u\right].$$

(23)

For the intensity process, we assume that h evolves according to the stochastic differential equation:

$$dh_i = -\kappa(h_t - \bar{h}_k)dt + \sigma\sqrt{h_t}\,dW_t \tag{24}$$

where W is a Wiener process and $\bar{h}_k$ is the level to which the process trends during year k. (That is, the mean reversion is toward $\bar{h}_1$ for $t < 1$, toward $\bar{h}_2$ for $1 \leqslant t < 2$, and so on.) Let $\bar{h}_0 = \bar{h}_1$. Note that this is essentially the model for the instantaneous discount rate used in the Cox–Ingersoll–Ross interest rate model. Note also that in DG, there is a jump component to the evolution of h, while the level of mean reversion is constant.

In order to express the default probabilities implied by the stochastic intensity model in closed form, we will rely on the following result from DG.[9] For a process h with $h_0 = \bar{h}$ and evolving according to Equation (24) with $\bar{h}_k = \bar{h}$ for all k, we have:

$$\mathbf{E}_t\left[\exp\left[-\int_t^{t+s} du\, h_u\right]\exp[x + yh_{t+s}]\right] = \exp[x + \alpha_s(y)\bar{h} + \beta_s(y)h_t] \tag{25}$$

where $\mathbf{E}_t$ denotes conditional expectation given information available at time t. The functions α_s and β_s are given by:

$$\alpha_s(y) = \frac{\kappa}{c}s + \frac{\kappa(a(y)c - d(y))}{bcd(y)}\log\left[\frac{c + d(y)e^{bs}}{c + d}\right], \text{ and} \tag{26}$$

$$\beta_s(y) = \frac{1 + a(y)e^{bs}}{c + d(y)e^{bs}} \tag{27}$$

where:

$$c = \frac{\kappa + \sqrt{\kappa^2 - 2\sigma^2}}{2} \tag{28}$$

$$d(y) = (1 - cy)\frac{\sigma^2 y - \kappa + \sqrt{(\sigma^2 y - \kappa)^2 - \sigma^2(\sigma^2 y^2 - 2\kappa y - 2)}}{\sigma^2 y^2 - 2\kappa y - 2} \tag{29}$$

$$a(y) = (d(y) + c)y - 1 \tag{30}$$

$$b = \frac{-d(y)(\kappa + 2c) + a(y)(\sigma^2 - \kappa c)}{a(y)c - d(y)}. \tag{31}$$

Calibration

Our calibration approach for this model will be to fix the mean reversion speed κ, solve for $\overline{h}_1$ and σ to match p_1 and $p_{1,1}$, and then to solve in turn for $\overline{h}_2, \ldots, \overline{h}_T$ to match $p_2, \ldots, p_T$. To begin, we apply Equation (23) and Equation (25) to obtain:

$$p_1 = 1 - \exp[\alpha_1(0)\overline{h}_1 + \beta_1(0)h_0] = 1 - \exp[[\alpha_1(0) + \beta_1(0)]\overline{h}_1]. \qquad (32)$$

To compute the joint probability that two obligors each survive the first year, we must take the expectation of Equation (22), which is essentially the same computation as above, but with the process h replaced by $2h$. We observe that the process $2h$ also evolves according to Equation (24) with the same mean reversion speed κ, and with $\overline{h}_k$ replaced by $2\overline{h}_k$ and σ replaced by $\sigma\sqrt{2}$. Thus, we define the functions $\hat{\alpha}_s$ and $\hat{\beta}_s$ in the same way as α_s and β_s, with σ replaced by $\sigma\sqrt{2}$. We can then compute the joint one-year survival probability:

$$\mathbf{E} \exp\left[-2\int_0^t du\, h_u\right] = \exp\left[2\left[\hat{\alpha}_1(0) + \hat{\beta}_1(0)\right]\overline{h}_1\right]. \qquad (33)$$

Finally, since the joint survival probability is equal to $1 - 2p_1 + p_{1,1}$, we have:

$$p_{1,1} = 2p_1 - 1 + \exp\left[2\left[\hat{\alpha}_1(0) + \hat{\beta}_1(0)\right]\overline{h}_1\right]. \qquad (34)$$

To calibrate σ and $\overline{h}_1$ to Equation (32) and Equation (34), we first find the value of σ such that:

$$\frac{2\left[\hat{\alpha}_1(0) + \hat{\beta}_1(0)\right]}{\alpha_1(0) + \beta_1(0)} = \frac{\log[1 - 2p_1 + p_{1,1}]}{\log[1 - p_1]} \qquad (35)$$

and then set:

$$\overline{h}_1 = \frac{\log[1 - p_1]}{\alpha_1(0) + \beta_1(0)}. \qquad (36)$$

Note that though the equations are lengthy, the calibration is actually quite straightforward, in that we only are ever required to fit one parameter at a time.

In order to calibrate $\overline{h}_2$, we need to obtain an expression for the two-year cumulative default probability q_2. To this end, we must compute the two-year survival probability:

$$1 - q_2 = \mathbf{E} \exp\left[-\int_0^2 du\, h_u\right]. \tag{37}$$

Since the process does not have a constant level of mean reversion over the first two years, we cannot apply Equation (25) directly here. However, Equation (25) can be applied once we express the two-year survival probability as:

$$1 - q_2 = \mathbf{E} \exp\left[-\int_0^1 du\, h_u\right] \mathbf{E}_1 \exp\left[-\int_1^2 du\, h_u\right]. \tag{38}$$

Now given h_1, the process h evolves according to Equation (24) from $t = 1$ to $t = 2$ to with a constant mean reversion level $\bar{h}_2$, meaning we can apply Equation (25) to the conditional expectation in Equation (38), yielding:

$$1 - q_2 = \mathbf{E} \exp\left[-\int_0^1 du\, h_u\right] \exp[\alpha_1(0)\bar{h}_2 + \beta_1(0)h_1]. \tag{39}$$

The same argument allows us to apply Equation (25) again to Equation (39), giving:

$$1 - q_2 = \exp[\alpha_1(0)\bar{h}_2 + [\alpha_1(\beta_1(0)) + \beta_1(\beta_1(0))]\bar{h}_1]. \tag{40}$$

Thus, our calibration for the second year requires setting:

$$\bar{h}_2 = \frac{1}{\alpha_1(0)} \{\log[1 - q_2] - [\alpha_1(\beta_1(0)) + \beta_1(\beta_1(0))]\bar{h}_1\}. \tag{41}$$

The remaining mean reversion levels $\bar{h}_3, \ldots, \bar{h}_T$ are calibrated similarly.

Joint Default Probabilities

The computation of joint probabilities for longer horizons is similar to Equation (34). The joint probability that two obligors each survive the first two years is given by:

$$\mathbf{E} \exp\left[-2\int_0^2 du\, h_u\right]. \tag{42}$$

Here, we apply the same arguments as in Equation (38) through Equation (40) to derive:

$$\mathbf{E} \exp\left[-2\int_0^2 du\, h_u\right] = \exp[2\hat{\alpha}_1(0)\bar{h}_2 + 2[\hat{\alpha}_1(\hat{\beta}_1(0)) + \hat{\beta}_1(\hat{\beta}_1(0))]\bar{h}_1]. \tag{43}$$

For the joint probability that the first obligor survives the first year and the second survives the first two years, we must compute:

$$\mathbf{E}\exp\left[-\int_0^1 du\, h_u\right]\exp\left[-\int_0^2 du\, h_u\right]=\mathbf{E}\exp\left[-2\int_0^1 du\, h_u\right]\exp\left[-\int_1^2 du\, h_u\right].$$

(44)

The same reasoning yields:

$$\mathbf{E}\exp\left[-\int_0^1 du\, h_u\right]\exp\left[-\int_0^2 du\, h_u\right]$$

$$=\exp[\alpha_1(0)\bar{h}_2+2[\hat{\alpha}_1(\hat{\beta}_1(0)_2)+\hat{\beta}_1(\hat{\beta}_1(0)_2)]\bar{h}_1].$$

(45)

The joint default probabilities $p_{2,2}$ and $p_{1,2}$ then follow from Equation (43) and Equation (45).

MODEL COMPARISONS: CLOSED FORM RESULTS

Our first set of model comparisons will utilize the closed form results described in the previous sections. We will restrict the comparisons here to the two-period setting and to second-order results (that is, default volatilities and joint probabilities for two assets); results for multiple periods and actual distributions of default rates will be analyzed through Monte Carlo in the next section.

For our two-period comparisons, we will analyze four sets of parameters: investment and speculative grade default probabilities, each with two correlation values.[10] The low and high correlation settings will correspond to values of 10% and 40%, respectively, for the asset correlation parameter ρ in the first three models. For the stochastic intensity model, we will investigate two values for the mean reversion speed κ. The "slow" setting will correspond to $\kappa = 0.29$, such that a random shock to the intensity process will decay by 25% over the next year; the "fast" setting will correspond to $\kappa = 1.39$, such that a random shock to the intensity process will decay by 75% over one year. Calibration results are presented in Table 9.1.

We present the normalized year two default volatilities for each model in Figure 9.1. As defined in Equation (5) and Equation (6), the marginal and cumulative default volatilities are the standard deviation of the marginal and cumulative two-year default rates of a large, homogeneous portfolio. As we would expect, the default volatilities are greater in the high correlation cases than in the low correlation cases. Of the five models tested, the stochastic

TABLE 9.1 Calibration results

	Investment grade		Speculative grade	
Parameter	Low correlation	High correlation	Low correlation	High correlation
Inputs				
p_1	0.16%	0.16%	3.35%	3.35%
p_2	0.33%	0.33%	3.41%	3.41%
$p_{1,1}$	0.0007%	0.01%	0.18%	0.52%
Discrete CreditMetrics extension				
α_1	−2.95	−2.95	−1.83	−1.83
α_2	−2.72	−2.72	−1.81	−1.81
ρ	10%	40%	10%	40%
Diffusion CreditMetrics extension				
α_1	−2.95	−2.95	−1.83	−1.83
α_2	−3.78	−3.78	−2.34	−2.34
ρ	10%	40%	10%	40%
Copula functions				
α_1	−2.95	−2.95	−1.83	−1.83
α_2	−2.58	−2.58	−1.49	−1.49
ρ	10%	40%	10%	40%
Stochastic intensity – slow mean reversion				
κ	0.29	0.29	0.29	0.29
σ	0.1	0.37	0.28	0.76
$\overline{h}_1$	0.16%	0.16%	3.44%	3.67%
$\overline{h}_2$	1.47%	1.58%	6.06%	12.10%
Stochastic intensity – fast mean reversion				
κ	1.39	1.39	1.39	1.39
σ	0.14	0.53	0.4	1.12
$\overline{h}_1$	0.16%	0.16%	3.44%	3.68%
$\overline{h}_2$	0.53%	0.55%	4.00%	5.02%

intensity model with slow mean reversion seems to produce the highest levels of default volatility, indicating that correlations in the second period tend to be higher for this model than for the others.

It is interesting to note that of the first three models, all of which are based on the normal distribution and default thresholds, the copula approach in all four cases has a relatively low marginal default volatility but a relatively high cumulative default volatility. (The slow stochastic intensity model is in fact the only other model to show a marginal volatility less than the cumulative volatility.) Note that the cumulative two-year default rate is the sum of the first- and second-year marginal default rates, and thus that the two-year cumulative default volatility is composed of three terms: the first- and second-

FIGURE 9.1   Marginal and cumulative year two default volatility

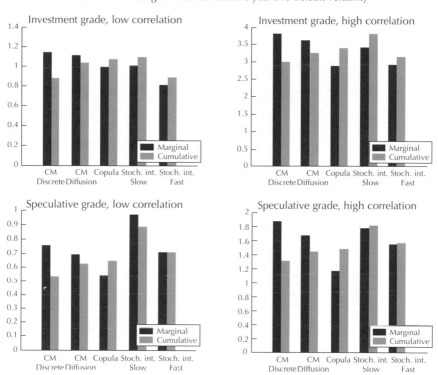

year marginal default volatilities and the covariance between the first and second years. Our calibration guarantees that the first-year default volatilities are identical across the models. Thus, the behavior of the copula model suggests a stronger covariance term (that is, a stronger link between year one and year two defaults) than for either of the two CreditMetrics extensions.

To further investigate the links between default events, we examine conditional probability of a default in the second year, given the default of another asset. To be precise, for two distinct assets i and j, we will calculate the conditional probability that asset i defaults in year two, given that asset j defaults in year one, normalized by the unconditional probability that asset i defaults in year two. In terms of quantities we have already defined, this normalized conditional probability is equal to $p_{1,2}/(p_1 p_2)$. We will also calculate the normalized conditional probability that asset i defaults in year two, given that asset j defaults in year *two*, given by $p_{2,2}/p_2^2$. For both of these quantities, a value of one indicates that the first asset defaulting does not affect the chance that the second asset defaults; a value of four indicates that the second asset is four times more likely to default if the first asset defaults than it is if we have no information about the first asset. Thus, the probability

FIGURE 9.2 Year two conditional default probability given default of a second asset

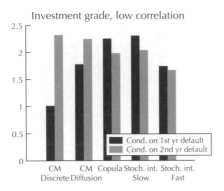

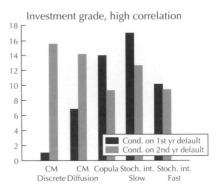

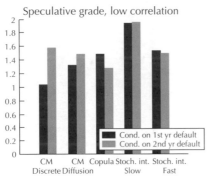

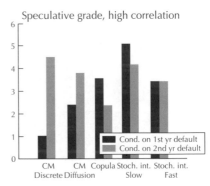

conditional on a year two default can be interpreted as an indicator of contemporaneous correlation of defaults, and the probability conditional on a year one default as an indicator of lagged default correlation.

The normalized conditional probabilities under the five models are presented in Figure 9.2. As we expect, there is no lagged correlation for the discrete CreditMetrics extension. Interestingly, the copula and both stochastic intensity models often show a higher lagged correlation than contemporaneous correlation. While it is difficult to establish much intuition for the copula model, this phenomenon can be rationalized in the stochastic intensity setting. For this model, any shock to the default intensity will tend to persist longer than one year. If one asset defaults in the first year, it is most likely due to a positive shock to the intensity process; this shock then persists into the second year, where the other asset is more likely to default than normal. Further, shocks are more persistent for the slower mean reversion, explaining why the difference in lagged and contemporaneous correlation is more pronounced in this case. By contrast, the two CreditMetrics extensions show much higher contemporaneous than lagged correlation. This lack of persistence in the correlation structure will manifest itself more strongly over longer horizons.

To this point, we have calibrated the collection of models to have the same means over two periods and the same volatilities over one period. We have then investigated the remaining second-order statistics – the second-period volatility and the correlation between the first and second periods – that depend on the particular models. In the next section, we will extend the analysis on two fronts: first, we will investigate more horizons in order to examine the effects of lagged and contemporaneous correlations over longer times; second, we will investigate the entire distribution of portfolio defaults rather than just the second-order moments.

MODEL COMPARISONS: SIMULATION RESULTS

In this section, we perform Monte Carlo simulations for the five models investigated previously. In each case, we begin with a homogeneous portfolio of 100 speculative-grade bonds. We calibrate the model to the cumulative default probabilities in Table 9.2 and to the two correlation settings from the previous section. For over 1,000 trials, we simulate the number of bonds that default within each year, up to a final horizon of six years.[11]

The simulation procedures are straightforward for the two CreditMetrics extensions and the copula approach. For the stochastic intensity framework, we simulate the evolution of the intensity process according to Equation (24). This requires a discretization of Equation (24):

$$h_{i+\Delta t} - h_t \approx \kappa(h_t - \overline{h}_k)\Delta t + \sigma\sqrt{h_t}\sqrt{\Delta t}\varepsilon \tag{46}$$

where ε is a standard normal random variable.[12] Given the intensity process path for a particular scenario, we then compute the conditional survival probability for each annual period as in Equation (21). Finally, we generate defaults by drawing independent binomial random variables with the appropriate probability.

The simulation time for the five models is a direct result of the number of timesteps needed. The copula model simulates the default times directly and is, therefore, the fastest. The two CreditMetrics models require only annual timesteps and roughly 50% more runtime than the copula model. For

TABLE 9.2 Moody's speculative-grade cumulative default probabilities

Year	1	2	3	4	5	6
Probability	3.35%	6.76%	9.98%	12.89%	15.57%	17.91%

Source: Figure 9.1, Keenan et al. (2000)

FIGURE 9.3   Normalized cumulative default rate volatilities – speculative grade

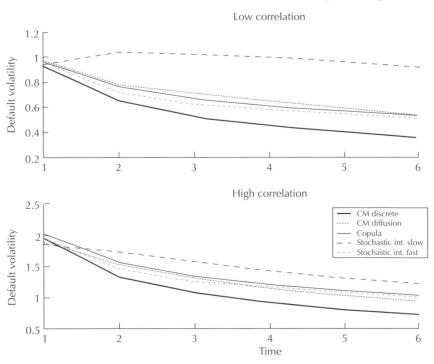

the stochastic intensity model, the need to simulate over many timesteps produces a runtime over 100 times greater than the simpler models.

We first examine default rate volatilities over the six horizons. As in the previous section, we consider the normalized cumulative default rate volatility. For year k, this is the standard deviation of the number of defaults that occur in years one through k, divided by the expected number of defaults in that period. This is essentially the quantity defined in Equation (6), with the exception that here we consider a finite portfolio. The default volatilities from our simulations are presented in Figure 9.3. Our calibration guarantees that the first-year default volatilities are essentially the same. The second-year results are similar to those in Figure 9.1, with slightly higher volatility for the slow stochastic intensity model and slightly lower volatility for the discrete CreditMetrics extension. At longer horizons, these differences are amplified: the slow stochastic intensity and discrete CreditMetrics models show high and low volatilities, respectively, while the remaining three models are indistinguishable.

Though default rate volatilities are illustrative, they do not provide us with information about the full distribution of defaults through time. At the one-year horizon, our calibration guarantees that volatility will be consistent

TABLE 9.3 One-year default statistics – speculative grade portfolio

Statistic	CreditMetrics discrete	CreditMetrics diffusion	Copula	Stoch. int. slow	Stoch. int. fast
Low correlation					
Mean	3.37	3.36	3.51	3.2	3.2
St. dev.	3.15	3.27	3.4	3.03	3.05
Median	3	2	3	3	2
5th percentile	10	9	10	9	10
1st percentile	14	15	15	13	14
High correlation					
Mean	3.62	3.24	3.72	3.69	3.56
St. dev.	7.08	6.32	7.52	6.84	6.73
Median	1	1	1	1	1
5th percentile	19	15	19	19	16
1st percentile	37	32	34	30	35

TABLE 9.4 Six-year cumulative default statistics – speculative grade portfolio

Statistic	CreditMetrics discrete	CreditMetrics diffusion	Copula	Stoch. int. slow	Stoch. int. fast
Low correlation					
Mean	17.72	16.93	18.04	17.34	18.1
St. dev.	6.4	8.68	9.66	16.15	9.73
Median	17	16	17	12	16
5th percentile	29	33	37	52	37
1st percentile	34	42	47	73	49
High correlation					
Mean	18.41	17.28	18.61	19.81	20.41
St. dev.	13.49	17.41	19.27	24.37	19.36
Median	15	12	12	9	13
5th percentile	45	54	63	82	62
1st percentile	59	73	78	98	86

across the five models; the distribution assumptions, however, influence the precise shape of the portfolio distribution. We can see in Table 9.3 that there is actually very little difference between even the first percentiles of the distributions, particularly in the low correlation case. For the full six-year horizon, Table 9.4 shows more differences between the percentiles. Consistent with the default volatility results, the tail percentiles are most extreme for the slow stochastic intensity model and least extreme for discrete CreditMetrics. Interestingly, though the CreditMetrics diffusion model shows similar volatility to the copula and fast stochastic intensity models, it produces less extreme percentiles than these other models. Note also that among distributions with similar means, the median serves well as an indicator of skewness. The high correlation setting generally, and the slow stochastic intensity model in particular, show lower medians. For these cases, the distribution places higher probability on the worst default scenarios, as well as the scenarios with few or no defaults.

The cumulative probability distributions for the six year horizons are presented in Figures 9.4 through 9.7. As in the other comparisons, the slow stochastic intensity model is notable for placing large probability on the very low and high default rate scenarios, while the discrete CreditMetrics extension stands out as the most benign of the distributions. Most striking, however, is the similarity between the fast stochastic intensity and copula models, which are difficult to differentiate even at the most extreme percentile levels.

As a final comparison of the default distributions, we consider the pricing of a simple structure written on our portfolio. Suppose each of the 100 bonds in the portfolio has a notional value of $1 million, and in the event of a default, the recovery rate on each bond is 40%. The structure is composed of three elements:

1. *First loss protection.* As defaults occur, the protection seller reimburses the structure up to a total payment of $10 million. Thus, the seller pays $600,000 at the time of the first default, $600,000 at the time of each of the subsequent fifteen defaults, and $400,000 at the time of the seventeenth default.

2. *Second loss protection.* The protection seller reimburses the structure for losses in excess of $10 million, up to a total payment of $20 million. This amounts to reimbursing the losses on the seventeenth through the fiftieth defaults.

3. *Senior Note.* Note with a notional value of $100 million maturing after six years. The note suffers a principal loss if the first and second loss protection are fully utilized; that is, if more than 50 defaults occur.

FIGURE 9.4 Distribution of cumulative six-year defaults – speculative grade, low correlation

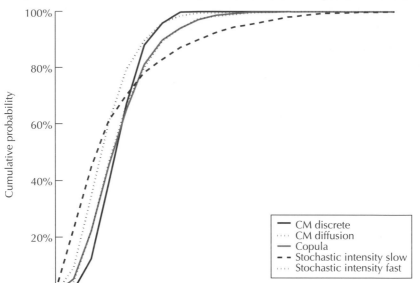

FIGURE 9.5 Distribution of cumulative six-year defaults, extreme cases – speculative grade, low correlation

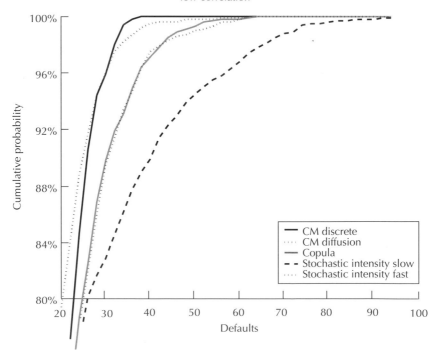

FIGURE 9.6   Distribution of cumulative six-year defaults – speculative grade, high correlation

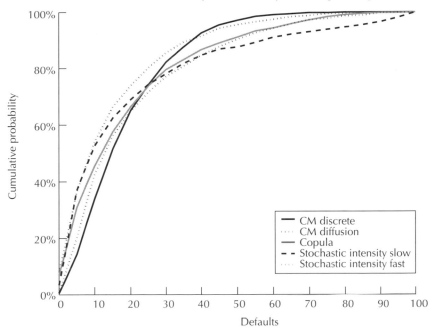

FIGURE 9.7   Distribution of cumulative six-year defaults, extreme cases – speculative grade, high correlation

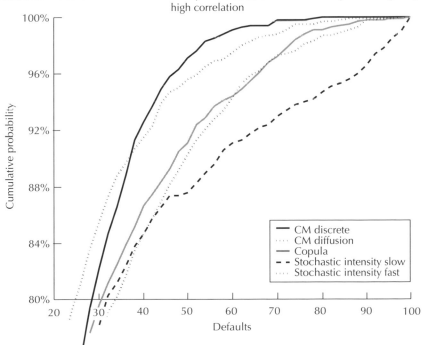

TABLE 9.5   Target expected losses for
six-year maturity

Rating	Expected loss
Aaa	0.002%
Aa1	0.023%
Aa2	0.048%
Aa3	0.101%
A1	0.181%
A2	0.320%
A3	0.500%
Baa1	0.753%
Baa2	1.083%
Baa3	2.035%

Source: Chart 3, Cifuentes et al. (1998)

For the first- and second-loss protection, we will estimate the cost of the protection based on a constant discount rate of 7%. In each scenario, we produce the timing and amounts of the protection payments, and discount these back to the present time. The price of the protection is then the average discounted value across the 1,000 scenarios. For the Senior Note, we compute the expected principal loss at maturity, which, along with Table 9.5, is used by Moody's to determine the note's rating. Additionally, we compute the total amount of protection (capital) required to achieve a rating of A3 (an expected loss of 0.5%) and Aa3 (an expected loss of 0.101%).

We present the first and second loss prices in Table 9.6, along with the expected loss, current rating, and required capital for the Senior Note. The slow stochastic intensity model yields the lowest pricing for the first-loss protection, the worst rating for the Senior Note, and the highest required capital. The results for the other models are as expected, with the copula and fast mean reversion models yielding the most similar results.

CONCLUSION

The analysis of collateralized debt obligations and other structured products written on credit portfolios requires a model of correlated defaults over multiple horizons. For single-horizon models, the effect of model and distribution choice on the model results is well understood. For the multiple-horizon models, however, there has been little research.

We have outlined four approaches to multiple horizon modeling of defaults in a portfolio. We have calibrated the four models to the same set of input data (average defaults and a single-period correlation parameter)

TABLE 9.6 Results for structure written on speculative grade collateral ($ millions)

	First loss	Second loss	Exp. loss	Rating	Senior notes Capital (Aa3)	Capital (A3)
Low correlation						
CM discrete	7.227	1.35	0.00%	Aaa	17.3	13.8
CM diffusion	6.676	1.533	0.02%	Aa1	21.6	15.9
Copula	6.788	1.936	0.02%	Aa1	24.5	18
Stoch. int. – slow	5.533	2.501	0.47%	A3	39.8	29.4
Stoch. int. – fast	6.763	1.911	0.04%	Aa2	25.7	18.3
High correlation						
CM discrete	6.117	2.698	0.16%	A1	32.3	23.6
CM diffusion	5.144	2.832	0.51%	Baa1	41.1	30.2
Copula	5.21	3.2	0.82%	Baa2	43.7	34.4
Stoch. int. – slow	4.856	3.307	1.90%	Baa3	54.5	46.1
Stoch. int. – fast	5.685	3.5	0.92%	Baa2	45.9	35.2

and have investigated the resulting default distributions. The differences we observe can be attributed to the model structures and, to some extent, to the choice of distributions that drive the models. Our results show a significant disparity. The rating on a class of Senior Notes under our low correlation assumption varied from Aaa to A3, and under our high correlation assumption, from A1 to Baa3. Additionally, the capital required to achieve a target investment grade rating varied by as much as a factor of two.

In the single period case, a number of studies have concluded that when calibrated to the same first- and second-order information, the various models do not produce vastly different conclusions. Here, the issue of model choice is much more important, and any analysis of structures over multiple horizons should heed this potential model error. Furthermore, because the copula method requires significantly fewer calculations and produces results in the middle of the range observed, it is the most practical choice of the models tested for simulating defaults over multiple horizons.

NOTES

[1] See respectively Gupton et al. (1997), *CreditRisk+* (1997), and Wilson (1997a) and Wilson (1997b).

[2] See Finger (1998), Gordy (2000), and Kolyoglu and Hickman (1998).

[3] This is a reasonable supposition, since all of the single-period models mentioned previously essentially require $p_{1,1}$ as an input.

[4] Technically, the cross variation process for $W^{(i)}$ and $W^{(j)}$ is ρdt.

[5] Details are presented in Li (1999) and Li (2000).

[6] More precisely, assets may depend on different default probabilities, all of which are correlated.

[7] See Finger (1998), Gordy (2000), and Kolyoglu and Hickman (1998) for further discussion.

[8] As with our description of the CreditRisk+ model, this is a simplification. The DG framework provides for an intensity process for each asset, with the processes being correlated.

[9] We have changed the notation slightly from the DG result in order to make more explicit the dependence on $\bar{h}_2$.

[10] Taken from Exhibit 30 of Keenan et al. (2000).

[11] As we have pointed out before, it is possible to simulate continuous default times under the copula and stochastic intensity frameworks. In order to compare with the two CreditMetrics extensions, we restrict the analysis to annual buckets.

[12] Note that while Equation (24) guarantees a non-negative solution for h, the discretized version admits a small probability that $h_{t+\Delta t}$ will be negative. To reduce this possibility, we choose Δt for each time step such that the probability that $h_{t+\Delta t} < 0$ is sufficiently small. The result is that while we only need 50 time steps per year in some cases, we require as many as 1,000 when the value of σ is large, as in the high correlation, fast mean reversion case.

CHAPTER 10

Complexities and Validation of Default Risk Models

J. R. Sobehart*, S. C. Keenan*, and R. Stein[1]
Citigroup*
Moody's[1]

This chapter presents a summary of an approach used to validate and benchmark quantitative default risk models for corporate obligors. We discuss performance measurement and sampling techniques, as well as other practical considerations associated with performance evaluation for quantitative credit risk models. This framework specifically addresses issues of data sparseness and the sensitivity of models to changing economic conditions. Our model validation approach continues to evolve and is used extensively for evaluating internal and external quantitative models.

Credit risk can be defined as the potential that a borrower or counterparty will fail to meet its obligations in accordance with the terms of an obligation's loan agreement, contract, or indenture. For most individual and institutional investors, bonds and other tradable debt instruments are the main source of credit risk. In contrast, for banks, loans are often the primary source of credit risk.

Since banks often lend to firms not rated by rating agencies, they often have the need of supplementary credit assessments. However, since a bank's individual exposures to such firms are often relatively small, it is typically uneconomical for borrowers to pay to obtain an agency rating or for banks to devote extensive internal resources to the analysis of a particular borrower's credit quality. Not surprisingly, these economic factors have caused banking institutions to be among the earliest adopters of quantitative credit risk models.

A major challenge in developing models that can effectively assess the credit risk of individual obligors is the limited availability of high-frequency objective information to use as model inputs. In cases where no historical data are available at all, both model development and validation must rely on heuristic methods and domain experts. However, when historical data are available, model validation can proceed in a more objective and rigorous context. The approach we present in this chapter is an example of such a validation strategy.

Most models estimate the creditworthiness over a period of one year or more, which often implies a need for several years of historical financial data for each borrower.[2] While reliable and timely financial data can usually be obtained for the largest corporate borrowers, they are difficult to obtain for smaller borrowers, and are particularly difficult to obtain for companies in financial distress or default, which are key to the construction of accurate credit risk models. The scarcity of reliable data required for building credit risk models stems from the highly infrequent nature of default events.

As institutions become more familiar with credit-modeling technology, their focus is widening to include a much higher level concern with model validation. In its recent reports on credit risk modeling, the Basle Committee on Banking Supervision (1999, 2000) highlighted the relatively informal nature of the credit model validation approaches at many financial institutions. The Committee specifically emphasized data sufficiency and model sensitivity analysis as significant challenges to validation. More precisely, the Basle Committee (1999) has identified validation as a key issue in the use of quantitative default models concluding that "... the area of validation will prove to be a key challenge for banking institutions in the foreseeable future."

Because of the unique nature of default risk, it is often not clear how to evaluate and compare various credit models and frameworks. In order to improve an institution's competitive advantage in the area of risk management, new methods and technologies must be developed capable of detecting a richer spectrum of credit failure patterns. There is no shortage of theoretical models for credit risk assessment to choose from as well as a steadily growing body of academics and practitioners with experience in the development of credit risk models. However, the true performance of default risk models is not a theoretical, but an empirical issue. Default risk models that perform well over a given historical data set may not perform accurately under the situations found in practice with real portfolios of credit instruments, and where data on credit events are limited, sparse, or unreliable. Because of this, model validation and calibration is far more difficult for credit risk models than for market risk models.

This chapter describes several of the techniques that we have found useful for accurate and objective quantitative default model validation and benchmarking. More precisely, we focus on (a) the segmentation of data for model validation and testing; and (b) several robust measures of model performance and inter-model comparison that we have found informative and currently use. The techniques we present are especially useful in domains where the sparseness of default data makes standard statistical approaches unreliable. We also address the two fundamental issues that arise in validating and determining the accuracy of a default risk model:

1. *what is measured,* or the metrics by which model "goodness" should be defined; and
2. *how it is measured,* or the framework that should be used to ensure that the observed performance can reasonably be expected to represent the behavior of the model in practice.

MODEL SELECTION

Models are mathematical abstractions of reality. As such they represent only a partial and codified view of the problem they describe. This limitation is particularly important for modeling default risk, where models are usually estimated with sparse data on credit events. If an unreliable or unsound model is used, then inference based on the model and its underlying data will often be poor. Therefore, it is important to select an appropriate model for the analysis of a specific data set.

There are three basic aspects of valid inference in default risk modeling: (1) model specification and selection; (2) estimation of the model parameters; and (3) estimation of the precision of the parameters. There are literally many books and countless articles in professional journals on model fitting and parameter estimation (items (2) and (3) above). In contrast, relatively little has appeared in the area of default risk model concerning item (1): model specification (what candidate models to consider) and modeling selection (what models to use for inference). Because model specification and selection are usually believed to be outside the field of mathematical statistics, most of the practical work on this area has been related to hypothesis-testing as a means of selecting a model.

In its widest sense, model specification and selection is conceptually more difficult than estimating the model parameters and their precision. Model specification and selection is the point where economic and financial arguments formally enter the research. Because in practice data are sparse, unreliable and nonexistent, default risk models often depend on significant subjectivity both, in determining relevant financial variables and determining the relationships between those variables. Thus, even default risk models based on structural models or statistical regressions often depend on significant judgment of analysts and modelers. Theoretically sound model selection methods are still required and, particularly, methods that are easy to use and widely applicable. "What default risk model to use?"

remains the key question in making a valid inference from data on default and credit events.

In this chapter we provide practical advice for the analysis of default risk models, focusing mainly on robust performance measures for selecting and benchmarking models. A detailed technical discussion on the issues we describe here can be found in Burnham and Anderson (1998) and references therein.

MODEL ACCURACY

Although accuracy is only one dimension of model quality,[3] it is often the most prominent one in discussions of credit risk models. Because credit risk models are often used to generate opinions of credit quality on which investment decisions are taken, prices are set, or risk capital is reserved, it is important to understand each model's strengths and weaknesses. When used as classification models, default risk models can err in one of two ways. First, the model can indicate low risk when, in fact, the risk is high. This is referred to as Type I error, and corresponds to the assignment of a high ranking (low credit risk) to issuers who nevertheless default or come close to defaulting in their obligations. The cost to the investor can be the loss of principal and interest that was promised, or a loss in the market value of the obligation. Second, the model can assign a low ranking (high credit risk) when, in fact, the risk is low. This case is referred to as Type II error. Potential losses resulting from Type II error include the loss of return and origination fees when loans are either turned down or lost through non-competitive bidding. In the case of tradable loans or securities, Type II error may result in the selling of obligations that could be held to maturity, at disadvantageous market prices.

These accuracy and cost scenarios are described schematically in Figures 10.1 and 10.2.

Because it is possible for some risk models to commit less of one type of error than another, investors and financial institutions usually seek to keep models where the probability of making *either* type of error is as small as possible. Unfortunately, minimizing one type of error usually comes at the expense of increasing the other type of error. That is, the probability of making a Type II error increases as the probability of a Type I error is reduced.

The issue of model *error cost* is a complex and important one. It is often the case, for example, that a particular model will out-perform another under one set of cost assumptions, but will be disadvantaged under a different set of assumptions.[4] Since different institutions have different cost and pay-off structures, it is difficult to present a single cost function that is appropriate

FIGURE 10.1 Types of errors

Actual		Low credit quality	High credit quality
Model	Low credit quality	Correct prediction	Type II error
	High credit quality	Type I error	Correct prediction

FIGURE 10.2 Costs of errors

Actual		Low credit quality	High credit quality
Model	Low credit quality	Correct assessment	Opportunity costs and lost and potential profits. Lost interest income and origination fees. Premature selling at disadvantageous prices.
	High credit quality	Lost interest and principal through defaults. Recovery costs. Loss in market value.	Correct assessment

across all companies. For this reason, in the tests described in this chapter, we use cost functions related only to the information content of the models.

A VALIDATION FRAMEWORK FOR QUANTITATIVE DEFAULT MODELS

When evaluating default risk models, it is reasonable to question whether the relationships implied by the models and the assumptions that underlie them are actually useful in predicting default events rather than just describing them. Although the adequacy of default risk models rests on the performance of the different key success factors chosen to assign risk, and the reliability of the financial and market information available to create the models, a major issue is the performance of distress event prediction. Verification of predicted distress events can be challenging, since statistical tests of model performance have extremely low power to detect poorly performing models and consequently require many events to produce reliable results. However, an understanding of the issues associated with model validation can help address some of these limitations and lead to more useful and well-informed analysis. Irrespective of the validation approach undertaken, there are some basic tenets that should be kept in mind when comparing two or more default risk models:

- *Compare models on the same data set*: Due to the sparseness of credit event data, performance statistics are sample dependent. This means that differences in sample composition can result in differences in model performance even for two models that are expected to perform similarly.

- *Avoid using the same data or time period to test a model that was used to build the model*: Particularly for models that are calibrated to historical data, it is important to understand how the model will perform in practice. Typically, this means that the model will be used in a time period subsequent to the one in which it is developed or calibrated, and on different firms. Testing the use of subsequent periods (out-of-time validation[5]) and independent data contemporaneous with the data set used to build the model (out-of-sample validation) should highlight the limitations of the model. These crucial testing procedures will make overfit models less appealing since the performance estimates from out-of-time and out-of-sample validation are done using new data that can show the true performance of the model.

- *Avoid relying only on anecdotal analysis; compare performance in aggregate*: It has become common practice among commercial vendors to look for examples of adverse credit events, such as high visibility defaults, and to examine a model's performance on these events retrospectively. While such analysis can be reassuring from an intuitive perspective, it often obscures the true performance of a model since it misses Type II errors. It is often more instructive to examine aggregate measures such as Receiver Operating Characteristics (ROC) and Cumulative Accuracy Profiles (CAP) curves (also known as power curves or dubbed curves), and their summary statistics that describe both Type I and Type II errors.

- *Understand the variability and robustness of performance estimates*: In very small samples, a handful of records can account for a large difference in some performance measures. In order to understand the sensitivity of a test's outcome to this, techniques such as resampling (or bootstrapping) can be very valuable. These techniques provide estimates of the variability of a performance measure, given the sample at hand.

Since performance statistics for default risk models can be highly sensitive to the data sample used for validation, in order to avoid embedding unwanted sample dependency, models should be developed and validated using some type of out-of-sample, out-of-universe, and out-of-time testing approach on panel or cross-sectional data sets.[6] However, even this seemingly rigorous approach can generate false impressions about a model's reliability if done incorrectly. Hold-out testing can easily miss important model problems, particularly when processes vary over time, as credit risk does.[7]

The statistical literature on model selection and model validation is quite broad. While we will not attempt to exhaustively cover this topic, the methodology described here brings together several streams of the validation literature that we have found useful in evaluating quantitative default models. Here we describe a validation framework that accounts for variations across both time and across the population of obligors. In doing so, it can provide important information about the performance of a model across a range of economic environments.[8] A schematic of the framework is shown in Figure 10.3. The figure breaks up the model testing procedure along two dimensions: (a) time (along the horizontal axis); and (b) the population of obligors (along the vertical axis). The least restrictive validation procedure is represented by the upper left quadrant, and the most stringent by the lower right quadrant. The other two quadrants represent procedures that are more stringent with respect to one dimension than another.

FIGURE 10.3 Model validation techniques. Testing strategies are broken out based on whether they account for variances across time (horizontal axis) or across the data universe (vertical axis, boxes A and B). Dark circles represent data used for model fitting and white circles represent testing data. Gray circles represent data that may or may not be used for model validation

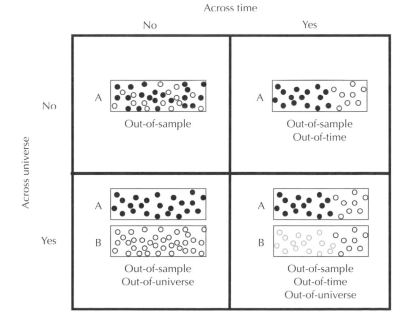

The upper left quadrant describes the approach in which the testing data for model validation is chosen completely at random from the full model fitting data set. This approach to model validation assumes that the properties of the data remain stable over time (stationary process). Because the data are drawn at random, this approach validates the model across the population of obligors preserving its original distribution.

The upper right quadrant describes one of the most common testing procedures. In this case, data for model fitting are chosen from any time period prior to a certain date and testing data are selected from time periods only after that date. A model constructed with data from 1980 through 1990 and tested on data from 1991 through 2000 is a simple example of this out-of-time procedure. Because model validation is performed with out-of-time samples, the testing assumptions are less restrictive than in the previous case and time dependence can be detected using different validation sub-samples.

The lower left quadrant represents the case in which the data are segmented into two sets containing no companies in common, one set for building the model and the other for validation. In this general situation the testing set is out-of-sample. If the population of the validation set is different from that of the set used for building the model, the data set is out-of-universe. An example of out-of-universe would be a model that was built on manufacturing firms but tested on multiple industries. Because the temporal nature of the data is not used for constructing this type of out-of-sample test, this approach validates the model homogeneously in time and will not identify time dependence in the data. Thus, the assumption of this procedure is that the relevant characteristics of the population do not vary with time.

Finally, the most robust procedure is shown in the lower right quadrant and should be the preferred sampling method for default risk models. In addition to being segmented in time, the data are also segmented across the population of obligors. Non-overlapping sets can be selected according to the peculiarities of the population of obligors and their importance (out-of-sample and out-of-universe sampling). An example of this approach[9] would be a model constructed with data for all rated manufacturing firms from 1980 to 1990, and tested on a sample of firms in the service sector rated Ba1 or lower for 1990 to 2000.

It is common to validate a default risk model by using observed data on historical defaults. However, model validation based solely on predicted default events can be problematic because statistical tests for samples with low default rates often have extremely low power[10] and, consequently, would require many default events to produce reliable results. To illustrate this point, Figure 10.4 shows monthly time series of default events only for firms with agency ratings. The top figure shows the aggregated number of monthly defaults for all industries. The other figures show the monthly number of default events for a handful of specific industries. It is clear from the figure that data sparseness could be a serious problem for validating default risk models.

A common solution is to use relatively long time horizons (e.g., 10 or 20 years of data) to create large panel data sets. Unfortunately, this approach may introduce bias in the testing procedure due the high temporal correlation of the model outputs and the low number of credit events. Temporal correlation in the data cannot be ignored since it violates the assumptions of many standard statistical tests of model performance (e.g., the Kolmogorov–Smirnoff test). On the other hand, if a hold-out sample is selected over a relatively short time frame (to avoid aggregation issues), tests based on this sample may incorrectly disqualify relatively accurate models and certify the accuracy of many relatively poor models due to insufficient data.

Because default events are rare and default model outputs for consecutive years are highly correlated, it is often impractical to create a model using one data set and then test it on a separate "hold-out" data set composed of completely independent cross-sectional data. While such out-of-sample and out-of-time tests would unquestionably be the best way to compare models' performance if default data were widely available, this is usually not the case. As a result, most institutions face the following dilemma:

1. If too many defaulters are left out of the in-sample data set, estimation of the model parameters will be seriously impaired and overfitting becomes likely.
2. If too many defaulters are left out of the hold-out sample, it becomes exceedingly difficult to evaluate the true model performance due to severe reductions in statistical power.

An effective approach is to "rationalize" the default experience of the sample at hand by combining out-of-time and out-of-sample tests. The procedure we describe is often referred to in the trading model literature as "walk-forward" testing.

The walk-forward procedure works as follows:

1. select a year, for example, 1989;
2. fit the model using all the data available on or before the selected year;
3. once the model's form and parameters are established for the selected time period, generate the model outputs for all the firms available during the following year (in this example 1990). Note that the predicted model outputs for 1990 are out-of-time for firms existing in

FIGURE 10.4 Monthly observations of default events for rated firms only. The upper figure shows the aggregated number of defaults for all industries. Lower figures show the defaults for the following specific sectors: (a) consumer products, (b) media, (c) retail, and (d) technology

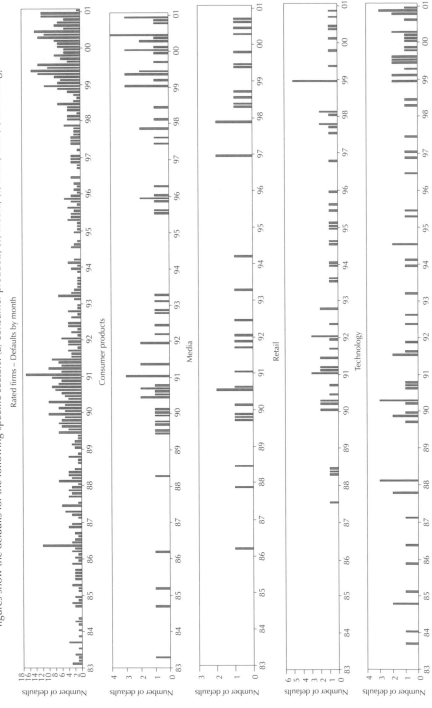

previous years, and out-of-sample for all the firms whose data become available after 1989;

4. save the prediction as part of a *result set*;
5. now move the window up one year (e.g.: to 1991) so that all the data through that year can be used for fitting and the data for the following year can be used for testing;
6. repeat steps 2 to 5 adding the new predictions to the result set for every year.

Collecting all the out-of-sample and out-of-time model predictions produces a set of model performances. This validation result set can then be used to analyze the performance of the model in more detail. Note that this approach simulates, as closely as possible given the limitations of the data, the process by which the model will actually be used in practice. Each year, the model is refit and used to predict the credit quality of all known credits, one year hence. The walk-forward validation process is outlined in Figure 10.5.

FIGURE 10.5 Validation methodology: end-to-end. We fit a model using a sample of historical data on companies and test the model using both data on those companies one year later, and using data on new companies one year later (upper portion of figure). Dark circles represent data for fitting the model and white circles represent validation data. We perform "walk-forward testing" (bottom left) by fitting the parameters of a model using data through a particular year, and testing on data from the following year, and then inching the whole process forward one year. The results of the testing for each validation year are aggregated and then resampled (lower left) to calculate particular statistics of interest

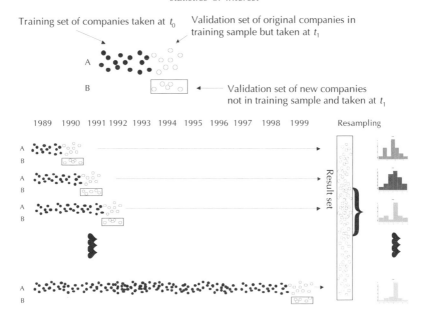

For example, for Moody's RiskCalc™ default risk model for public firms we selected 1989 as the first year for which to construct the validation result set (prior to 1989 we did have enough data to build a sufficiently reliable model). Following the above procedure, we constructed a validation result data set containing over 54,000 observations (company-years), representing about 9,000 different companies (rated and unrated), and including over 530 default events from Moody's extensive database. Once a result set containing all the predictions from different time periods has been produced, a variety of performance measures of interest can be calculated (we suggest several in the section "model performance and benchmarking").

Note that this approach has two major benefits. First, it allows us to get a realistic view of how a particular model would perform over time. Second, it allows us to leverage the available data to a higher degree. However, before turning to model performance evaluation, it is important to note that the result set is itself a sub-sample of the population and, therefore, may yield spurious model performance differences based only on data anomalies. A common approach to addressing this problem, and one used extensively in our research, is to use one of a variety of *resampling* techniques to leverage the available data and reduce the dependency on the particular sample at hand.[11]

Resampling

It is important to realize that, because of the sparseness of defaults in most credit data, accuracy statistics may sometimes yield spurious model performance differences based only on data anomalies. To avoid these problems we suggest the use of the above performance measures combined with *resampling* techniques to leverage the available data and reduce the dependency on the particular sample at hand. A typical resampling technique[12] proceeds as follows. From the result set, a sub-sample is selected at random. The performance measure of interest (e.g., number of defaults correctly predicted) is calculated for this sub-sample and recorded. Another sub-sample is then drawn, and the process is repeated. This continues for many repetitions until a distribution of the performance measure is established. The mean standard error and other statistics of the distribution then becomes the reported performance measures. A schematic of the resampling process is shown in Figure 10.5.

Resampling approaches provide two related benefits. First, they give an estimate of the variability around the actual reported model performance. In those cases in which the distribution of means converges to a known distribution, this variability can be used to determine whether differences in model performance are statistically significant using familiar statistical tests. In cases where the distribution properties are unknown, non-parametric permutation type tests can be used instead. Second, because of the low numbers of defaults, resampling approaches decrease the likelihood that individual defaults (or non-defaults) will overly influence a particular model's chances of being ranked higher or lower than another model. For example, if model A and model B were otherwise identical in performance, but model B, predicted a default where none actually occurred for a particular company in the sample as predicted by model A, we might be tempted to consider model B inferior to model A. However, a resampling technique like the one we use might show that the models were virtually equivalent. In our testing, 85% of the result set was drawn at random (resampled) 100 times and the metric of interest (and its distribution) was calculated taking into account the correlation of the estimates. In model performance and benchmarking we use this approach to compute the values of several specific performance measures that we have found to be particularly valuable in evaluating quantitative default risk models.

MODEL COMPLEXITY

It is extremely important to the user of a default risk model derived from multivariate analysis of market and accounting data to know whether the model is sensitive to violations of the underlying modeling assumptions. That is, is the model's mathematical complexity adequate to describe the data at hand? When determining one or more of the assumptions of the model is not valid, methods of correcting for these violations must be established. We briefly discuss some of these issues in the following.

To illustrate our ideas, assume we are fitting a simple multivariate model to our default data. Let y_k denotes the k-th dependent variable of a sample $k = 1, \ldots, N$. The dependent variable can take only two possible values: $y_k = 1$ when the firm risk exceeds certain (random) threshold level leading to default during a time period T, and $y_k = 0$ if the firm remains viable. Let ξ_k denote the threshold response level for firm k. Now if $z_k = AX_k$ denotes the risk exposure of the firm, where $X_k = \{x_{k1}, \ldots, x_{kM}\}$ is a vector of the M regression variables of the model and A is a vector of unknown coefficients, then $y_k = 1$ if $z_k > \xi_k$ and $y_k = 0$ if $z_k \leq \xi_k$. We now need to determine how y_k and ξ_k are related in probabilistic terms. This is done by introducing the cumulative distribution function (CDF), $F(z)$, of the random threshold ξ_k given the model inputs X_k:

$$\Pr(y_k = 1) = \Pr(\xi_k > AX_k \mid X_k) = F(AX_k)$$
$$\Pr(y_k = 0) = 1 - F(AX_k). \tag{1}$$

Once the functional form of $F(z)$ is specified, the model reduces to finding the coefficients A such that:

$$E(y) = \Pr(y = 1) = F(AX) . \tag{2}$$

Here the coefficients A can be estimated, for example, using the maximum likelihood function:

$$L = \prod_{k=1}^{N} F(AX_k)^{y_k} (1 - F(AX_k))^{1-y_k} . \tag{3}$$

When the model selected for the firm's risk exposure $z(X)$ is more complex than the simple multivariate linear model $z = AX$ described previously, other techniques such as error minimization, information entropy, Bayesian methods, and cross-validation-based methods can also be used to estimate the parameters of the model. For a technical discussion on alternative methods see, for example, Press (1977), Cox and Tiao (1992), Burnham and Anderson (1998), and references therein.

Let us abstract from the functional form of the model for the company's risk exposure $z(X)$ and focus on the function $F(z)$. When $F(z)$ is taken to be the normal cumulative distribution function, the method is called *probit* analysis.

$$F(z) = \Phi(z) = \int_{-\infty}^{z} \frac{e^{-x^2/2}}{\sqrt{2\pi}} \, dx . \tag{4}$$

For the probit model, the estimation by maximum likelihood is straightforward but computationally difficult since $F(z)$ has no simple analytical representation. A more appealing alternative is to select a CDF that has a tractable form such as the logistic distribution (or *logit* analysis).

$$F(z) = \frac{1}{1 + e^{-z}} . \tag{5}$$

The logistic and Normal CDFs are numerically close to each other except in their tails. Because logistic representations are analytically more convenient than the cumulative normal, they are one of the most popular fitting models.

Although there is a variety of natural extensions to the logit model, neural networks with sigmoidal transformations of variables represent perhaps one of the most widely used alternatives (Herzt, Krogh, and Palmer (1991)). These particular neural networks are nested logit regressions where the output of each logit regression (or node) serves as the input to other logit regressions. Because the logistic function saturates for large values of its input, nested logistic regressions allow both thin-tail and fat-tail distributions at the expense of additional mathematical complexity. Figure 10.6 shows the difference between a probit model, a logit model, and a simple neural network composed of two layers of nested logit models:

$$F(z) = \frac{1}{1 + e^{-G(z)}}, \qquad G(z) = \frac{a}{1 + e^{-\alpha z + \beta}} + \frac{b}{1 + e^{-\gamma z + \delta}} + c. \qquad (6)$$

The parameters of the nested models 1 and 2 in Figure 10.6 have been selected to show thin-tail and fat-tail distributions. Note that this type of model provides greater flexibility at the expense additional mathematical complexity.

One of the most common misconceptions among practitioners is that models based on neural networks (or nested regressions) are complex "black boxes" with hidden relationships. As we explained above, a neural network can be seen simply as a higher order regression technique based on conventional statistical methods. Instead of creating a single regression equation, several coupled equations are created. These regression equations need to be solved simultaneously. The regression coefficients of the model are found with iterative methods that exploit the mutual feedback of the intermediate regressions (known as "nodes"). The hybrid nonlinear model described in the next section (RiskCalc for public firms) has been developed using a similar nested regression method to capture nonlinear relationships in the data.

Other advanced computational techniques such as adaptive neural networks, tree structures, fuzzy logic, genetic algorithms, and statistical

FIGURE 10.6 Probit model, logit model, and nested logit regressions with thin-tail and fat-tail distributions

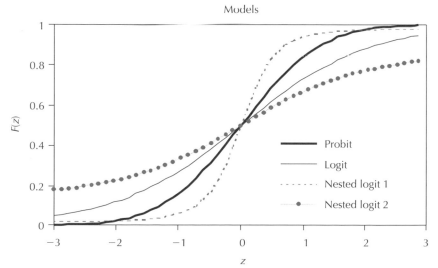

Models

Bayesian methods are also useful for modeling default risk at the cost of adding additional mathematical complexity. While we do not discuss these models in this chapter, the literature on model complexity has increased substantially in the past decades. Technical discussions on complex models and their applications can be found in Hertz, Krogh, and Palmer (1991), Refenes (1995), Burhman and Anderson (1998), and references therein. The reader is referred to those sources for more detailed treatment.

Regardless of the complexity of the selected default risk model, a quick and frequent way of checking whether or not the default risk model is mispecified is to plot the output of the model against the observed frequency of default events (quantile–quantile plot or Q–Q plot). If the points fall along a straight line, the model assumptions are acceptable. If the points follow a straight line for the central portion but they tend to tail off towards the horizontal, the underlying distribution might be fat-tailed relative to the distribution assumed for the model. In contrast, if the points tend to tail-off towards the vertical, the underlying distribution is thin-tailed. In either case, the assumed distribution is not justified and some type of "correction" must be imposed. If the actual underlying distribution can be found from the data, it may be possible to make statistical inference based on it. Transformation of data can also be carried out to reduce the impact on model performance and produce a better fitting. Often, however, this type of problem can not be eliminated completely.

When the discrepancies between the observed and the theoretical default probabilities are small, or when it is not possible to find a more appropriate model specification, a simple approach is to create a mapping $M_T^*(F)$ between the observed frequency of default events $f(z)$ and the model estimate $F(z)$ for each time period T. Then the estimated probability of default (PD) for firm k during period T is reported as the mapped value of the model output $PD_k(T) = M_T^*(F(z_k))$. This correction represents a final reality check on the selected model and it is usually referred in the literature as to the "default probability mapping" (see, for example, Sobehart, Stein, Mikityanskaya, and Li (2000) and Falkenstein, Boral, and Carty (2000)).

MODEL PERFORMANCE AND BENCHMARKING

In this section we introduce objective metrics for measuring and comparing the performance of credit risk models and analyzing information redundancy. This entails the following:[13]

1. cumulative accuracy profiles;

2. accuracy ratios;
3. conditional information entropy ratios.

These techniques are quite general and can be used together with standard statistical tools to compare different types of models, even when the model outputs differ and are difficult to compare directly. Furthermore, categorical outputs, such as the credit ratings produced by rating agencies, can be evaluated side by side with continuous score values generated by a quantitative model.

In order to demonstrate the applicability of the methodology described here, we compared six univariate and multivariate models of credit risk using Moody's proprietary database of default events. We compared the following models:

1. A simple univariate model based on return on assets (adjusted ROA);
2. Reduced Z-score model[14] (1993);
3. Z-score model (1993);
4. A hazard model[15] (1998);
5. A variant of the Merton model based on deviations from the default point;[16]
6. Moody's RiskCalc default risk model for public firms (2000).

These models represent a wide range of modeling approaches listed in order of complexity. Model 1 consists simply in ordering firms according to their profitability (adjusted ROA). Models 2, 3 and 4 are multivariate models that use accounting and market information. Model 5 is a variant of the contingent claims approach proposed by Merton (1973, 1974). Model 6 combines the structural approach of model 5 with nonlinear statistical regressions of ratings, accounting, and market information.

Inter-model comparison is essentially the comparison of prediction errors for each model. Unfortunately, a large segment of the validation research found in the literature can be viewed as "residual error diagnostics" (e.g., t-statistics) that are of limited practical use for model comparison. Many of the assumptions that underlie residual diagnostics are frequently violated in practice.[17] Although it is not difficult to determine to what extent these assumptions are violated in each case, it is exceedingly difficult to determine *how to correct* the t-statistics figures or other statistics that authors cite in recommendation of their models.

The techniques discussed below are useful not only because of their power and robustness, but because they can be used to compare default prediction models, even when data are correlated or otherwise "messy", or when their true statistical properties are unknown. Comparing the performance across different default prediction models is challenging since the models themselves usually measure slightly different aspects of the default events and time horizons, and may be expressing a quantification of credit risk using different types of outputs. For example, some models calculate an explicit probability of default, or expected default frequency, which is a number between zero and one, and is usually reported to several decimal places. Others, such as agency ratings, rank risk using a coarser scale, but incorporate other aspects of default, such as recovery and expected losses. Moreover, agency ratings are intended to endure normal economic cycles and, therefore, place a premium on stability over long time horizons. In contrast, some models are designed to react sharply to potential changes in short-term creditworthiness and market conditions. An attractive feature of these validation measures, not discussed in detail in this chapter, is that they can also provide estimates of a model's *precision*. Although model outputs are often given as "continuous" variables, in reality, due to data limitations and statistical significance, all models that are econometrically calibrated to historical default frequency will exhibit some underlying granularity in their outputs. This is true for most statistical models and also of structural models (e.g., contingent claims models) when they are adjusted to reflect historical default experience. A key issue in model comparison is to determine whether a higher degree of refinement in the scale of a given model's output represents any additional "precision" supported by statistical evidence, or whether small increments in estimated risk just reflect random noise. For example, is there a statistically meaningful difference between a model default prediction of 2bps and 3bps? For these tests, the minimum finite precision that produces a significant difference in the performance of the model determines the precision of the model output.

The Meaning of Cumulative Accuracy Measures

Let us begin our description[18] of model performance by assuming two models being tested on a population of borrowers. It is the task of the models to distinguish defaulters (right distribution) from non-defaulting borrowers (left distribution), as shown in Figure 10.7. The population of defaulters has been exaggerated for illustration purposes. In practice, defaulters are a small fraction of the borrowers and the two populations overlap considerably for risky borrowers. Figure 10.7a shows a hypothetical decision axis that represents one situation in our example. This axis is conceptualized as the output of model 1 that represents the borrower's credit quality. In Figure 10.7a it is assumed that the criterion C_1 (cut-off point) adopted by a user for classifying a borrower as a defaulter has been established at a fairly high value along the model decision axis. In this example, the selected cut-off

FIGURE 10.7 Panels (a) and (b) show the hypothetical decision axis for model 1 adopting either a lax criterion C_1 or a strict criterion C_2. Panels (c) and (d) show the hypothetical decision axis for model 2 adopting either a lax criterion C_3 or a strict criterion C_4. The population of non-defaulters is on the left, and the population of defaulters, exaggerated for illustration purposes, is on the right.

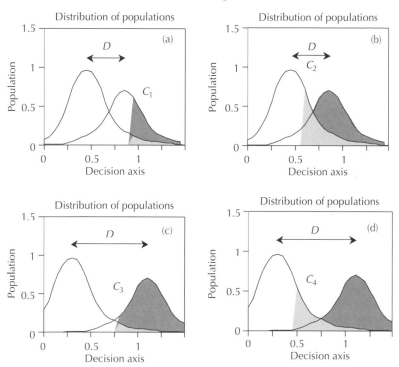

point C_1 is in compliance with the decision to be lax in judging the credit quality of a borrower. Borrowers whose risk scores are above C_1 should be classified as likely defaulters. This criterion results in a small fraction of defaulters being classified correctly (Type I error). In Figure 10.7b the user is shown to have adopted a lower cut-off, C_2, in accordance with instructions to assume a strict criterion in judging the borrower's credit quality. This criterion results in a large fraction of non-defaulters being classified incorrectly (Type II error). In Figures 10.7c and 10.7d, the user of model 2 is seen to have adopted somewhat different, but corresponding criteria, C_3 and C_4, under these same guidelines.

For each borrower, there are four possible outcomes in the identification of defaulters:

1. *Hit:* the model correctly classifies the borrower as a defaulter.
2. *Miss:* the model assigns low risk to a defaulter.
3. *False alarm:* a low-risk borrower is classified as a defaulter.

4. *Correct rejection:* the model assigns low risk to a high-quality borrower.

The proportions of these possible outcomes depend on two aspects of the decision-making situation: (1) the cut-off C, which the user uses to classify borrowers, and (2) the separation D of the population of defaulters and non-defaulters along the decision axis. The latter depends on the model's ability to differentiate the populations.

Figure 10.7 indicates how the cut-off C and the separation D contribute to the proportion of behaviors occurring in each possible contingency. In Figures 10.7a and 10.7b, D is fairly small as the populations of defaulters and non-defaulters overlap along the decision axis. In Figure 10.7c and 10.7d, the populations are separated by a greater amount indicating that model 2 can differentiate risky borrowers better than model 1.

In each panel of Figure 10.7 the shaded area under the population of defaulters represents the proportion of hits attained. The cross-hatched area represents the proportion of false alarms generated by the model in response to the risk characteristics of the borrower. The unshaded area under the population of defaulters represents misses occurring when the model assigns low risk to a defaulter. Finally, the unshaded area under the non-defaulter population represents correct rejections.

A key question about model performance is how effectively a model separates the two populations for different decision cut-offs. The separation of populations is related to both, the selected cut-off C and the distance D. This relation is easily represented in curves known[19] as the receiver operating characteristics (ROC)[20] and the closely related cumulative accuracy profiles (CAP)[21] described in the following sections.

Receiver Operating Characteristic (ROC) Curves

The ordinate of the ROC curve is scaled as the *hit rate* (proportion of hits attained for all borrowers). The abscissa is scaled as the *false alarm rate* (proportion of false alarm responses for all borrowers). The formula for the hit rate (HR) is:

$$HR(C) = \frac{H(C)}{H(C) + M(C)}. \tag{7}$$

Here $H(C)$ is the number of hits and $M(C)$ is the number of misses for a cutoff C. Note that $H + M$ is the total number of defaulters. The formula for the false alarm rate (FAR) is:

$$FAR(C) = \frac{F(C)}{F(C) + R(C)}. \tag{8}$$

Here $F(C)$ is the number of false alarms and $R(C)$ is the number of correct rejection for a cut-off C. Note that $F + R$ is the total number of non-defaulter obligors. Using $HR(C)$ and $FAR(C)$ we can construct the ROC curves shown in Figure 10.8.

Notice that the main problem of model comparison is the fact that different models produce different score scales, so the value of cut-off criterion may differ. To compare different models, one needs a framework independent of the absolute value of the model scores and cut-off. The ROC curves eliminate the dependence on the absolute value of the cut-off by plotting hit rate $HR(C)$ versus false alarm rate $FAR(C)$.

The departure of a model's ROC curve from a chance performance line (diagonal $HR = FAR$) is a measure of the model's ability to separate the two populations. The curves in Figure 10.8 show that model 2 is more sensitive at identifying defaulters than model 1 for the same level of false alarms. It is clear from Figures 10.7 and 10.8 that minimizing one type of error usually comes at the expense of increasing the other type of error; that is, the probability of making a Type II error increases as the probability of a Type I error is reduced.

Since the upward-sloped diagonal $HR = FAR$ represents the case where the population of defaulters and healthy firms overlap completely (non informative case), one may wonder if the downward-sloped diagonal $HR = 1 - FAR$ also provides information on the separation of the populations. In fact, the distance along this diagonal is a measure based on the local properties of the ROC curve. Let C^* define the cut-off value for which the ROC curve (the hit rate $HR(C)$) intersects the diagonal $1 - FAR(C)$ as shown in Figure 10.8. Using Figure 10.7 as a guiding tool, the cut-off C^* represents the point where the shaded area under the normalized population of defaulters equals the unshaded area under the normalized population of non-defaulters. The distance between the model's ROC curve and the uninformative ROC, measured along this diagonal, defines a natural *local* statistic:

$$L = \sqrt{\left(HR(C^*) - \frac{1}{2} \right)^2 + \left(FAR(C^*) - \frac{1}{2} \right)^2}. \tag{9}$$

Distance L is composed of two contributions. The first term is the difference between the median of the population of defaulters and the cumulative fraction of defaulters correctly classified by the model at cut-off

FIGURE 10.8   ROC curves for models 1 and 2 based on the hypothetical decision axes and criteria of Figure 10.7. The distance L between the model's ROC curve and the uninformative (random) ROC defines a local (less powerful) measure of the separation between the population of defaulters and healthy firms

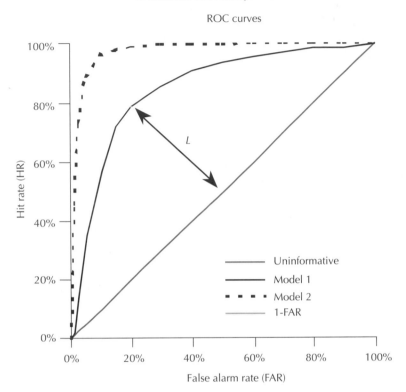

C^* (the shaded area under the distribution of defaulters in Figure 10.7). The second term is the difference between the median of the non-defaulter population and the cumulative fraction of false alarms at cut-off C^* (the shaded area under the distribution of healthy firms in Figure 10.7). Predictive models will be able to separate the two populations and, therefore, will have $HR(C^*)$ close to 1 and $FAR(C^*)$ near 0. Poorly performing models will confuse the two populations and, therefore, will have both $HR(C^*)$ and $FAR(C^*)$ near 1/2. Thus, risk measures with L close to 0 display little advantage over a random assignment of risk scores while those with L near $1/\sqrt{2}$ indicates a good separation of the populations of defaulters and healthy firms.

Cumulative Accuracy Profiles (CAP)

Cumulative accuracy profiles (CAP) provide an insightful visual assessment of model performance. While similar tools exist under a variety of different names (lift-curves, dubbed-curves, receiver-operator curves, power curves, and so on), we use the term CAP when the curve represents the cumulative fraction of defaults over the *entire* population, as opposed to the non-defaulting population only as in ROC curves. This form of the plot is particularly useful in that we can construct curves for Type I and Type II errors.

In contrast to ROC curves, the abscissa of a CAP curve is scaled as the fraction of all borrowers ordered by model output. Because defaulters usually represent a small fraction of the population of borrowers, ROC and CAP curves will look similar. However, ROC curves for an ideal model that produces perfect predictions are not well defined, while CAP curves are steep but well-defined.

To plot cumulative accuracy profiles, companies are first ordered by model score, from riskiest to safest. For a given fraction $X\%$ of the total number of companies, a CAP curve is constructed by calculating the percentage $Y(X)$ of the defaulters whose risk score is equal to or lower than the one for fraction X. Figure 10.9 shows an example of a CAP plot.

A good model concentrates the defaulters in the riskiest scores so the percentage of all defaulters identified (the y axis in the figure above) increases quickly as one moves up the sorted sample (along the x axis). If the model were totally uninformative, if, for example, it assigned risk scores randomly, we would expect to capture a proportional fraction $X\%$ of the defaulters with about $X\%$ of the observations, generating a straight line or *random CAP* (the dotted line in Figure 10.9). A perfect model would produce the *ideal CAP*, which is a straight line capturing 100% of the defaults within a fraction of the population equal to the default rate of the sample. Because the historical default rate is usually a small number, the ideal CAP would look like a vertical line at the point in the plot where the percentage of remaining firms was equal to the actual number of defaults.

A good model also concentrates the non-defaulters at the lowest riskiness. Therefore, the percentage of all non-defaulters $Z(X)$, whose score is lower or equal to X, should increase slowly at first. One of the most useful properties of CAP curves is that they reveal information about the predictive accuracy of the model over its entire range of risk scores for a particular time horizon.

Figure 10.10 shows the CAP curves for the models described in this section using the validation sample (out-of-sample and out-of-time) described in the section on a validation framework for quantitative default models. The values plotted represent the mean values of the resampling tests. Similar results are obtained for the in-sample tests.[22] Note that Moody's RiskCalc model for public firms (hybrid regression model) appears to outperform all of the benchmark models consistently.

FIGURE 10.9   Type 1 CAP curve. The dark curved line shows the performance of the model being evaluated. It depicts the percentage of defaults captured by the model (vertical axis) versus the model score (horizontal axis). The dotted line represents the uninformative case (random assignment of scores). The upper light line represents the case in which the model is able to discriminate perfectly and all defaults are captured at the lowest model output

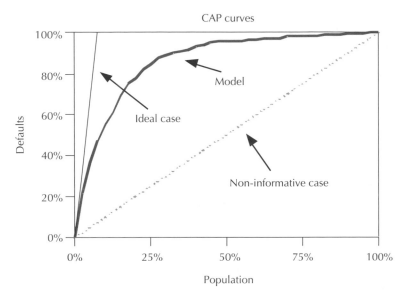

Accuracy Ratios (ARs)

While CAP plots are a convenient way to visualize model performance, it is often convenient to have a single measure that summarizes the predictive accuracy of each risk measure for both Type I and Type II errors into a single statistic. We obtain such a measure by comparing the CAP plot of any set of risk scores with the ideal CAP for the data set under consideration; the closer the CAP is to its ideal, the better the model performs. In principle, we could calculate a summary statistic by defining a local measure such as the distance L in Figure 10.8. Importantly, because L is only a local measure, it does not provide an unambiguous absolute ranking of model performance when ROC and CAP curves have irregular shapes or cross each other. Given that L is measured at only one point along the curve, a higher L does not necessarily indicate a greater ability to distinguish between defaulters and healthy firms for the entire range of credit scores. Thus it is important to define global statistics of model performance. To calculate the global summary statistic, we focus on the area that lies *above* the random CAP and is *below* the model CAP. The more area there is below the model CAP and above the random CAP, the better the model is doing overall (see Figure 10.9).

FIGURE 10.10 CAP curves for the selected models. All models were tested on the same data set. The 45° dashed gray line represents the non-informative case. All models perform considerably better than random; however, the nonlinear hybrid model clearly outperforms all others and is much better at discriminating defaults in the middle ranges of credits

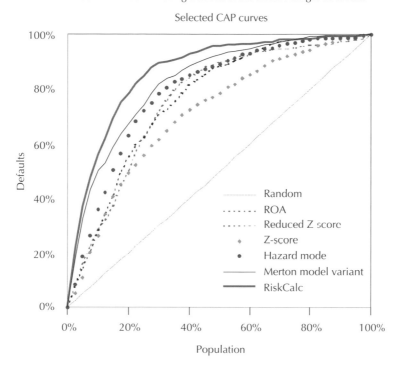

The maximum area that can be enclosed above the random CAP is identified by the ideal CAP. Therefore, the ratio of the area between a model's CAP and the random CAP to the area between the ideal CAP and the random CAP summarizes the predictive power over the entire range of possible risk values. We refer to this measure as the accuracy ratio (AR), which is a fraction between 0 and 1. Risk measures with ARs close to 0 display little advantage over a random assignment of risk scores while those with ARs near 1 display almost perfect predictive power. The accuracy ratio can be envisioned as the ratio of area A to area A + B in Figure 10.11.

Mathematically, the AR value is defined as:

$$R = \frac{2\int_0^1 Y(x)dx - 1}{1 - f} = \frac{1 - 2\int_0^1 Z(x)dx}{f}. \tag{10}$$

Here $Y(X)$ and $Z(X)$ are the Type I and Type II CAP curves for a population X of ordered risk scores, and $f = d/(n + d)$ is the fraction of defaults, where

FIGURE 10.11 The accuracy ratio is the ratio of the performance improvement of the model being evaluated over the non-informative model (area A) to the performance improvement of the ideal model over the non-informative model (areas A + B)

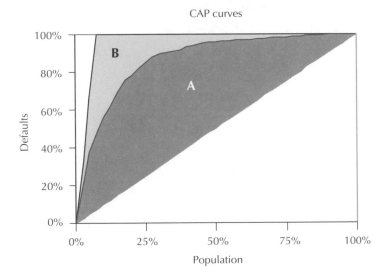

d is the total number of defaulting obligors and n is the total number of non-defaulting obligors. Note that our definition of AR provides the same performance measure for Type I and Type II errors.

Table 10.1 shows AR values for the tested models for in-sample and validation tests (out-of-sample and out-of-time) for annual observations. Most of the models we tested had ARs in the range of 50% to 75% for out-of-sample and out-of-time tests. The results we report here are the product of the resampling approach described in the resampling section. Thus, in addition to the reported value, we are also able to estimate an error bound of the statistic. We found that the maximum absolute deviation of the AR is of the order of 0.02 for most models.[23] Not surprisingly, we found that accuracy of the estimates deteriorates for small samples. In a loose sense, AR is similar to the commonly used Kolmogorov–Smirnov (KS) test

TABLE 10.1 Selected accuracy ratios

Selected model	In-sample AR	Validation AR
ROA	0.53	0.53
Reduced Z-score	0.56	0.53
Z-score	0.48	0.43
Hazard model	0.59	0.58
Merton model variant	0.67	0.67
Moody's model	0.76	0.73

designed to determine if the model is better than a random assignment of credit quality. However, AR is a global measure of the discrepancy between the CAPs while the KS test focuses only on the maximum discrepancy. Since the KS focuses only on a single maximum gap, it can be misleading in cases where two models behave quite differently as they cover more of the data space from low-risk model outputs to high-risk model outputs. Also notice that, because the comparison of ARs is relative to a data set, our definition of the AR is not restricted to having completely independent samples as in the KS test.[24]

To confirm the validity of the AR figures in Table 10.1, we also checked if a particular model differed significantly from the one ranked immediately above it by calculating a KS statistics tests using a sub-sample of over 9,000 independent observations selected from the (out-of-sample/out-of-time) validation set. KS tests support the AR results on the validation sample. More precisely, KS tests showed that only the reduced Z-score and ROA were not significantly different.

Similarly to the definition of global summary statistics for CAP curves, we define summary statistics for ROC curves. More precisely, we focus on the area that lies *above* the uninformative diagonal line and is *below* the model ROC. The more area there is below the model ROC and above the uninformative line, the better the model is doing overall (see, for example, Hanley and McNeil 1982). The maximum area that can be enclosed above the uninformative ROC curve is identified by the ideal ROC and its value is 1/2. Therefore, the ratio of the area between a model's ROC and the uninformative ROC to the area between the ideal ROC and the uninformative ROC summarizes the predictive power over the entire range of possible risk values. To be consistent with our previous notation, we refer to this measure as the ROC Accuracy Ratio (RAR):

$$RAR = 2 \int_0^1 HR(FAR)d(FAR) - 1. \tag{11}$$

RAR is a fraction between 0 and 1. Risk measures with RARs close to 0 display little advantage over a random assignment of risk scores, while those with RARs near 1 display almost perfect predictive power. RARs are global performance statistics similar to the CAP accuracy ratios (AR).

Information Entropy (IE)

Another measure used to determine the power of a model is based on the information about defaults contained in the distribution of model scores, or *information entropy*. The information entropy (IE) is attractive since it is applicable across all types of model outputs, and is a powerful way of objectively measuring how much real information is contained in a set of risk scores.

Information entropy (IE) is a summary measure of the "uncertainty" that a probability distribution represents. This concept has its origin in the fields of Statistical Mechanics and Communication Theory.[25] Intuitively, the information entropy measures the overall "amount of uncertainty" represented by a probability distribution.

We define information entropy as follows. Assume the existence of an event with only two possible outcomes: (A) issuer defaults with probability p, and (B) issuer does not default with probability $1 - p$. The amount of additional information an investor requires to determine which outcome actually occurred is defined as:

$$\text{Information} = -\log_2 (p) \tag{12}$$

where $\log_2 (p)$ is the logarithm of p in base 2.

If only the first outcome is possible with certainty, then $p = 1$ and the information required is: $\log_2 (p) = 0$ (bit). In this case, there is no uncertainty about the outcome and, therefore, there is no relevant information that was not previously known. If the two events are equally likely for the investor (uninformative case), then $p = 1/2$ and the amount of information required reaches a maximum value of $-\log_2 (p) = 1$ (bit). Exactly 1 bit of information (the equivalent to a yes–no-type of answer) is the information required by the investor to know which of the two equally likely possibilities have occurred.

The use of two as the logarithmic base has certain advantages for this example but any base can be used. Usually, the natural logarithms are used for convenience. Note, however, that the amount of information depends upon what logarithmic base is used which determines the unit of measure of information.

The information entropy of the event is defined as:

$$H_0 = -[p \log(p) + (1 - p) \log(1 - p)]. \tag{13}$$

Figure 10.12 shows the information entropy as a function of p (Equation (13)). Note that the entropy reaches its maximum (1 bit $=$ log 2) when the probability is $p = 1/2$. This is a state of absolute ignorance because both possibilities are equally likely for the investor. If the assigned probability of an event is lower than 1/2, one outcome is more likely to occur than the other; that is, the investor has less uncertainty on the possible outcomes. The reduction in the uncertainty of the outcomes is reflected in the reduction of entropy.

Consider again the two mutually exclusive outcomes of an event: (A) issuer defaults and (B) issuer does not default; one of which must be true.

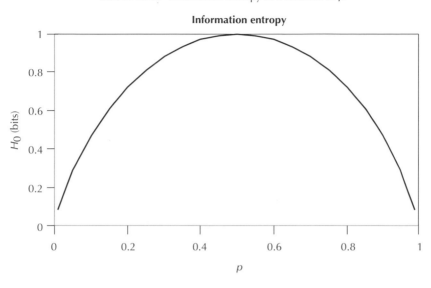

FIGURE 10.12   Information entropy as a function of *p*

Given a set of risk scores $S = \{R_1, \ldots, R_n\}$ produced by a model, the conditional entropy that measures the information about the propositions A and B for a specific risk score R_j is:

$$h(R_j) = -(P(A \mid R_j) \log P(A \mid R_j) + P(B \mid R_j) \log P(B \mid R_j)) \tag{14}$$

where $P(A \mid R_j)$ is the probability that the issuer defaults, given that the risk score is R_j and $P(B \mid R_j) = 1 - P(A \mid R_j)$. This value quantifies the average information gained from observing which of the two events A and B actually occurred.

The average overall possible risk scores is the conditional information entropy:

$$H_1(s, \delta) = H_1(R_1, \ldots, R_n, \delta) = \sum_{k=1}^{n} h(R_k) P(R_k). \tag{15}$$

For models with continuous outputs, the most straightforward way to estimate the quantities defined in Equations (14) and (15) is to use a bin-counting approach. The range of the model output is divided into a number of bins of size δ – related to the accuracy of the output. Because Equation (15) requires estimating the conditional distributions of defaults and non-defaults, the bins of size δ has to be bigger than the actual precision of the model outputs if entropy is to provide a meaningful statistic. For illustration, we use $\delta = 5\%$ of the model output range for each model.[26] Thus, the IE defines an absolute measure of the amount of uncertainty contained in the models as long as all the models' outputs describe the same data set.

Conditional Information Entropy Ratio (CIER)

In the same way we reduced CAP and ROC curves to a single statistic in order to have a measure that lends itself to comparison across models, we can use IE to produce another summary statistic for how well a given model can predict defaults. This is done via the conditional information entropy ratio (CIER). The CIER compares the amount of "uncertainty" there is about default in the case where we have no model (a state of more uncertainty about the possible outcomes) to the amount of "uncertainty" left over after we have introduced a model (presumably, a state of less ignorance). This measure is related to the Kulbach–Leibler entropy statistic (see Burnham and Anderson (1998)).

To calculate the CIER, we first calculate the IE $H_0(p)$, where p is the default rate of the sample. That is, without attempting to control any knowledge that we might have about credit quality, we measure the uncertainty associated with the event of default. This entropy reflects knowledge common to all models; that is, the likelihood of the event given by the probability of default. We then calculate the IE $H_1(S_1, \delta)$ after having taken into account the predictive power of the model. The CIER is one minus the ratio of the latter to the former; that is:

$$CIER(S, \delta) = \frac{H_0 - H_1(S_1, \delta)}{H_0}. \tag{16}$$

If the model held no predictive power, the CIER would be 0. In this case the model provides no additional information on the likelihood of the outcomes that is not already known. If it were perfectly predictive, the conditional information entropy ratio would be 1. In this case, there would be no uncertainty about the outcomes and, therefore, a perfect default prediction. Because the information entropy measures the reduction of uncertainty, a higher CIER indicates a better model. Table 10.2 shows the CIER results. CIER errors are of the order of 0.02 and are obtained with a bootstrap scheme similar to the one described for the AR measure.

TABLE 10.2   Selected entropy ratios

Selected model	In-sample CIER	Validation CIER
ROA	0.06	0.06
Reduced Z-score	0.10	0.09
Z-score	0.07	0.06
Hazard model	0.11	0.11
Merton model variant	0.14	0.14
Moody's model	0.21	0.19

CONCLUSION

The benefits of default risk models cannot be fully realized without a deep understanding of how accurately any given model represents the dynamics of default risk. This makes reliable validation techniques crucial for both commercial and regulatory purposes. In this chapter we have presented a set of measures and a testing approach that we have found useful for benchmarking default models and validating their performance.

The framework presented in this chapter uses a combination of statistical and computational approaches that address the type of data problems that often present themselves in the validation of credit risk models. Our approach to data segmentation is flexible and permits the calculation of many performance measures of interest. It facilitates direct statistical comparisons of models that produce quite different outputs. More precisely, our approach allows researchers and analysts to make use of sparse default data for both model development and testing.

In the course of our research into default risk modeling, we have found that simple statistics (such as the number of defaults correctly predicted) are often inappropriate in the domain of default risk models. As a result, we have developed several useful metrics that give a sense of the value added by a quantitative risk model. In this chapter, we described four such measures: cumulative accuracy profiles (CAP), receiver-operating characteristics (ROC), accuracy ratios (AR and RAR), and conditional information entropy ratios (CIER). This last measure is interesting in that it permits analysts to assess the amount of additional predictive information contained in one default risk model versus another. In situations where a specific model contains no additional information relative to another, the less informative should be discarded in favor of the more informative. In the special case where *both* models contribute information to each other, users may wish to combine the two to garner additional insight.

The approach we describe here is an effective way to benchmark internal and external default risk models where data permits. In that regard, we believe that it begins to address several of the Basle Committee's concerns regarding model validation.

NOTES

[1] The authors thank E. Ibarra for providing the monthly observations of default events.

[2] See, for example, Herrity, Keenan, Sobehart, Carty, and Falkenstein (1999); Crouhy, Galai, and Mark (2001).

[3] See, for example, Dhar and Stein (1997, 1998) and Burnham and Anderson (1998).

[4] See, for example, Provost and Fawcett (1997) or Hoadley and Oliver (1998).

[5] Out-of-sample refers to observations for companies that are not included in the sample used to build the model. Out-of-universe refers to observations whose distribution differs from the population used to build the model. Out-of-time refers to observations that are not contemporary with the training sample.

[6] A panel data set contains observations over time on many individuals. A cross-sectional data set contains one observation on many individuals.

[7] See, for example, Mensah (1984).

[8] The presentation of the validation framework follows closely that of Sobehart, Keenan, and Stein (2000) with additional clarifications and enhancements.

[9] This case is particularly important when one type of error is more serious than another; that is, there are cost structures associated with different errors. To illustrate these ideas, an error of two notches for an Aa-rated credit is generally less costly than a similar error for a B-rated credit, given the latter's relative proximity to default. The cost structure depends, among other things, on the action taken as a result of accepting or rejecting obligors based on the outputs of the models.

[10] Recall that statistical power refers to the probability that a statistical test at a particular significance level will unintentionally confirm the null hypothesis when in fact an effect is present. While significance gives information about Type II error, power gives information on Type I error. For an overview see Cohen (1988).

[11] Data bootstrap (e.g., Efron and Tibshirani (1993)), randomization tests (e.g., Sprent, (1998)), and cross-validation (*ibid.*) are all examples of resampling tests.

[12] A practical application is discussed in Herrity, Keenan, Sobehart, Carty, and Falkenstein (1999).

[13] See Keenan and Sobehart (1999).

[14] For the definition of the original Z-score and its various revisions Z' see Altman (1968) and Caouette, Altman, and Narayanan (1998).

[15] For simplicity we selected the model based on Zmijweski's variables described in Shumway (1998).

[16] For this research, Moody's has adapted the Merton model (1973, 1974) in a similar fashion to which KMV has modified it to produce their public firm model (see Vasicek (1984), McQuown (1993), and Crouhy, Galai, and Mark (2001)). More specifically, we calculate the *distance from default* based on equity prices and the company's liabilities. For an exact definition of Moody's distance from default measures see Sobehart, Stein, Mikityanskaya, and Li (2000).

[17] In particular, independence of samples or the Gaussian distribution of errors does not typically hold.

[18] Our presentation follows closely that of Burton (1972), Keenan and Sobehart (2000) and Sobehart and Keenan (2001).

[19] These curves are also known as dubbed curves and power curves.

[20] Burton (1972), Swets (1988), Provost and Fawcett (1997), and Hoadley and Oliver (1998).

[21] Keenan and Sobehart (1999).

[22] Here *in-sample* refers to the data set used to build Moody's nonlinear model.

[23] Due to the high levels of correlation in the resampling, the maximum absolute deviation gives a more robust estimate of an error range than a corrected standard error.

[24] In fact, AR based on panel data sets will provide aggregated information about the time correlation of the risk scores.

[25] See Shannon and Weaver (1949), Jaynes (1957), and Pierce (1970).

[26] This resolution can allow an easy comparison with agency ratings whose precision is $1/21 \approx 5\%$.

CHAPTER 11

A Fundamental Credit Model: Review of Preliminary Test Results

James Gerard
Fidelity

In the fall of 1999, several practitioner conferences on quantitative approaches to credit risk were held under the auspices of the *Risk* magazine and the Society of Quantitative Analysts. A main topic of these meetings was the attempt to translate academic progress in understanding the dynamics of obligor credit into practical, empirically implementable models of use to financial professionals. Most of the talks dealt with so-called *reduced form* credit models, which are applicable to problems such as the valuation of credit derivatives. A second thread of research, of more direct interest to a variety of buy-side credit concerns, involves *fundamental* models of credit, in which the company's financial data (equity prices and balance sheet entries) are used to estimate the future dynamics of the firm's total asset value. This literature, dating to Robert Merton's pathbreaking 1974 paper has been refined over recent years to the point that it has served as the basis for several empirically based models of credit risk.[1]

At the *Risk* conference, a new variation on a fundamental model was introduced that has the additional advantages of transparency and user customizability; that is, compared to existing commercially available systems, the Simplex Credit Advisory (SCA) model was designed to be tailored to a variety of end uses. After some preliminary discussion, it was decided that Fidelity's Fixed Income Division and Risk Management Group (RMG) would jointly undertake preliminary trials of the SCA model. From FID's perspective, the model offers the potential for both the bond and the money markets to create an independent, quantitative benchmark for relative obligor credit quality that directly makes use of inputs from our credit analysts.

The two Fidelity groups had different goals in their test protocols. RMG set out to test the Simplex model's ability to screen a medium-sized,

($N = 87$) highly diverse group of companies by credit risk on a one-year horizon. They provided Simplex with equity price histories and balance sheet data up through the end of 1998, and then asked the model to estimate default risks for the firms through 1999. The default probability results could then be compared with actual default events and Moody's ratings actions occurring in 1999. The FID trial was designed to explore the time series information in Simplex's estimated default probabilities over a smaller set of (mostly higher credit quality) obligors. Accordingly, the FID data sample provides 10 quarterly snapshots of the firms' balance sheets (beginning in the second and third quarters of 1997), and daily equity price data beginning five to seven years prior to the first balance sheet data. One goal of the FID study was to follow the financial firms in the data set through the Russian/ LTCM crisis of 1998 to compare the stress levels captured by the estimated default probabilities.

The second section of this chapter lays out a description of the internals of the Simplex model, and notes the model's points of departure from the pre-existing literature and modeling strategies. We then discuss the preparation of the trial data and examine the model's performance on the RMG and FID data sets.

SIMPLEX MODEL BACKGROUND

In a fundamental credit risk model, the probability of a default event is derived from an estimation of the likelihood of the firm's total asset value falling below the outstanding amount of its fixed liabilities over a given horizon. Nothing is assumed about market credit spreads or the relationship of spreads to implied bankruptcy risk; rather, bankruptcy risk is derived directly from model inferences about the future dynamics of the firm's asset value. The key, of course, is that the day-to-day market value of a firm's assets is, strictly speaking, unobservable. Asset paths for a given firm are typically constructed from a combination of balance sheet information and historical equity price data. The model stands or falls on the assumptions used to construct asset dynamics.

The Simplex model begins with the definition of the *default threshold*, the asset level for the firm that, if hit, results in default. If the simulation date is time 0, the company's (face value) of long-term debt is D_0, and the level of current assets and liabilities are CA_0 and CL_0, respectively, the default threshold is defined as:

$$K = D_0 + \max[CL_0 - CA_0, 0]. \tag{1}$$

Thus, the default threshold is entirely a function of balance sheet quantities.[2]

The accounting model underlying the definition of K is that short-term liability claims are satisfied out of current assets, where possible, but that excess current assets do not offset long-term liabilities.[3] The initial value of the firm, V_0, is then defined as $K + N_S S_0$, where N_S is the number of outstanding equity shares, and S_0 is the initial share price. (In other words, the value of the company is assumed to be the sum of the default threshold and the total equity market capitalization.) During the simulation period (for example, a one-year horizon beyond the simulation date), the company assets evolve according to a statistical model of the company equity dynamics (the rate of drift and the volatility of the firm's stock price), "deflated" by the company time 0 leverage ratio $L_0 = N_S S_0 / (K + N_S S_0)$. The higher the company debt load, the more volatile is the company's underlying equity compared to its asset base.

The evolution of the company equity is represented by a specialized random process similar to the one introduced by Black and Scholes to price options. If ΔS_t stands for the change in the equity price over a short time interval (say, a day), then the daily equity return $\Delta S_t / S_t$ is assumed to move according to:

$$\frac{\Delta S_t}{S_t} = \alpha \Delta(t) + \sigma_t \Delta W_t + \gamma_t \Delta Q_t. \tag{2}$$

This equation defines a process in which the equity price is distributed lognormally, with a constant "drift" rate α, and a (possibly time-varying) volatility σ_t per unit time. (The ΔW_t term stands for a draw from standard normal distribution with mean zero and standard deviation 1). Superimposed over this drifting random walk is a discontinuous "jump" process (represented by the Q_t term), that very occasionally (that is, on time scales long compared to one day) moves the stock price up or down by a large amount. "Jump-diffusion" models such as this one have been found to fit empirical observations of financial data such as credit spreads better than models without jumps.[4] The Simplex model features a neat implementation of the mixed continuous-jump process that overcomes some of the statistical problems that are typical in estimating the model's parameters.[5]

Once the Simplex model estimates the critical parameters of the equity process, the asset volatility and jump intensity are derived from the equity parameters by dividing them by the leverage factor, L_0. Sample paths of company assets can then be generated out to the chosen simulation horizon, starting from the initial asset level V_0. At each time step t on each path, the model checks whether $V_t > K$; if the asset level is above the default threshold, the simulation path continues, if not, it terminates. After a large number of sample path simulations (~10–50,000), the fraction of terminated paths gives the estimated default probability for that obligor.

Simplex does not represent its model as a predictor of rating changes, but, given the speed with which the equity markets discount information about companies' prospects (as well as the temporal lag of the rating process), default probabilities often exhibit trend changes prior to rating actions. In other instances, the Simplex model simply disagrees with the risk level implied by the company's current rating. For example, a company taking on debt to finance a new acquisition may trigger a "reflexive" downgrade by a rating agency. If, however, the equity markets "approve" of the acquisition's effects on the company's long-term earnings prospects, the asset value of the company may rise without a significant increase in asset volatility. The apparent default risk of the firm might actually fall in conjunction with the ratings downgrade.[6] The Simplex model tends to attach very low default probabilities to companies in industries with historically low equity volatilities (such as regulated utilities), even when such companies operate with significant financial leverage.

RISK MANAGEMENT GROUP TEST AND RESULTS

The RMG test data consists of financial data and stock price histories on 87 companies, spanning Moody's ratings Aa1 to Ca as of the end of 1998. The RMG sample of companies is biased towards lower (and deteriorating) credit quality in comparison with Fidelity's high-grade bond and money market investment universe. Of the 87 sample firms, 31 are foreign, with Japan most frequently represented. The data consists of a balance sheet snapshot at or near December 31, 1998, the end-of-1998 Moody's rating for each firm, a sample of daily equity prices prior to December 31, 1998 (of variable length), along with equity price data through 1999, and the Moody's rating change through the end of 1999. Nineteen of the companies in the sample saw no ratings change in 1999; six firms were upgraded (most by multiple steps), while 62 firms saw downgrades, including seven that entered bankruptcy during the year.[7] The RMG list of firms, their 1999 ratings activity and Simplex model results are available from the author on request.

Given the diversity and credit rating span of the companies in the RMG sample, it is not surprising that some of the chosen companies present difficulties for fundamental credit models. In general, major corporate reorganizations (mergers, acquisitions, and spin-offs) pose modeling challenges in creating a representative equity price history for the emergent company (assuming that a pro forma balance sheet can be constructed). Several companies in the RMG sample underwent ratings changes that occurred because they became acquirers or targets in merger transactions. Moreover, some companies balance sheets do not readily lend themselves to "generic" treatment in the calculation of the default threshold – industry-specific tailoring of the accounting inputs must take place, particularly for insurance, broker/dealer, and some banking companies. Table 11.1 details the companies in the RMG sample that were either particularly "non-generic" or underwent extraordinary transactions during or just before the analysis period (December 1998 – December 1999):

TABLE 11.1 RMG sample companies with simplex model data issues shown with Moody's 1999 rating actions

Firm	Moody's		Comment
	Dec. 98	Dec. 99	
Credit Foncier de France	A3	Aa3	During 1999, the bank was 90% purchased by CC-CEP, and thus, in effect, assumed the sovereign credit rating of France. Model analysis reflects Credit Foncier as a stand-alone credit.
Time Warner	Baa3	Baa3	Merger with AOL during analysis period.
America Online	Ba3	Ba1	Merger with TWX during analysis period.
Broadwing	A3	Ba2	Spinoff of Cincinnati Bell, November 1999; previously a regulated utility (spanning whole equity price history), now a voice/wireless/Internet solutions company.
MMI Companies	Baa1	Ba1	Multiline insurer with zero long-term debt; default threshold zero – no recognition of reserve trends.
Samsonite Corp.	B1	B3	Executed self-tender for 51% of shares, June 1998; biased equity jump process.
Insilco Holding	Caa1	Caa1	Equity data sample too sparse for parameter estimation.
Pioneer American	Ba1	Ba2	Equity data sample too sparse for parameter estimation.

FIGURE 11.1 Simplex default probabilities versus initial/final 1999 MDY ratings; $N = 87$

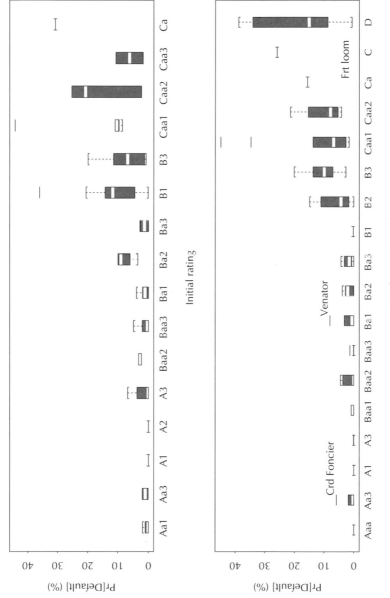

The following charts provide an overview of the Simplex model results.[8] Figure 11.1 offers two views of the calculated Simplex default probabilities versus Moody's (fully disaggregated) rating categories. The top chart plots Simplex default probabilities against *initial* (that is, Dec. 1998) Moody's ratings, while the bottom chart plots the same data against *final* (Dec. 1999) Moody's ratings. In both cases the default probabilities are calculated as of the end of 1998 (period 2 in the RMG sample). The charts thus show the migration of Moody's ratings over the year against the (constant) Simplex default probabilities.

The Simplex default probabilities define a risk index that is generally consistent with long-term Moody's rankings; but more importantly, the coherence of the Simplex ranking increases over the 1999 analysis period, as we move from the top to the bottom panel of Figure 11.1. In other words, the end of 1998 Simplex default probability "forecasts" the direction of a significant number of ratings moves during 1999. On the high-quality end of the spectrum, for example, the long-term, historical one-year default rate of firms rated A or higher by Moody's is essentially zero. However, the RMG sample contained a number of firms for which Simplex derived default probabilities significantly above zero at the end of 1998 (note particularly the A3-rated firms in the top panel of Figure 11.1). By the end of 1999, almost all of the A3 firms had exited the category, with seven of the 11 firms downgraded.[9]

Another outlier in the top panel of Figure 11.1 is the Ba2 category, which exhibits anomalously high Simplex default probabilities compared to the rating categories around it. The bottom panel shows that many of the companies in this category were in fact in transition; by the end of 1999, all of the initially Ba2-rated firms had been downgraded three to four notches. Further down the credit spectrum, the B1 category as of the end of 1998 contained a number of companies with extremely high default probabilities; all of these firms had been downgraded during 1999, with three of them defaulting or ceasing operations.[10] Figure 11.2 shows the end-of-1998 Simplex default probabilities plotted against (end-of-1999) Moody's aggregate ratings (that is, [Baa1, Baa2, Baa3] mapped to B+).

Given the relatively small total number of firms analyzed, the sample of distressed and defaulting companies is smaller still, but the Simplex one-year horizon default probabilities are in reasonable agreement with the empirically observed default frequencies in the sample. For example, the actual default rate among the companies with Simplex default probabilities 0–4.9% was one in 55, or 1.8%; for companies with Simplex probabilities between 5–15% it was 2 in 16 (12.5%), and for companies with Simplex probabilities >15%, the fraction actually defaulting was four in eight (50%). It should also be noted that several of the companies in the sample in the

FIGURE 11.2 RMG trial results: simplex default prob. (period 2) versus final Moody's ratings (*N* = 87)

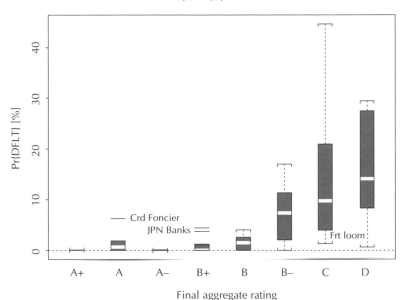

upper end of the default probability range ceased operations or were delisted from their exchanges during or just after the end of the analysis period (December 31, 1999).[11]

SIMPLEX COMPARATIVE ACCURACY

Judging the accuracy of the Simplex credit model over a particular set of sample data presents a number of challenges, not the least of which is deciding what is meant by "accuracy". In the context of investment-grade credit analysis (particularly for money market funds), "accuracy" is typically synonymous with low Type I error; that is, the model must identify distressed credits accurately, even to the point of incorrectly identifying some performing credits as distressed. Further, a good model should be able to risk-rank companies across the credit spectrum over a horizon relevant to money management (e.g., six months to one-and-a-half years ahead). A more delicate issue is the notion of relative accuracy. All of the public domain or commercially available credit models make accuracy claims supported by statistical testing, undertaken with varying degrees of rigor. Unfortunately, very little true out-of-sample testing of competing models has been published. Making a rigorous comparison of a group of widely used credit models over a large, unbiased sample of firms would be an important step toward sorting out the strengths and weaknesses of different modeling approaches. For the present, however, we restrict attention to some illustrative results for the Simplex model.

Toward that end, Fidelity's Risk Management Group suggested a comparison of the Simplex model's credit separation capability on the RMG dataset with the corresponding results of a benchmark credit scoring model, the Altman Z-score.[12] In a way, the comparison is not really fair, since the Altman model was designed to distinguish financially distressed companies from "healthy" ones, not to make relative credit comparisons across the full range of credit states. Still, contrasting the two models provides an illustration of some of the issues involved in model selection.

The Altman Z models are examples of so-called *linear discriminant models*, which use a series of observable variables to separate a sample population into discrete sub samples. Potential sets of discriminatory variables are tested until the routine settles on one that does the "best" job of categorical sorting on the original population. Altman Z models use this technique to sort an arbitrary set of companies into "distressed" and "non-distressed" categories on a one- to five-year horizon, using financial statement information to construct discriminators. The revised Altman model (from 1995) applied here can be written:

$$Z'' = 6.56X_1 + 3.26X_2 + 6.72X_3 + 1.05X_4 \tag{3}$$

where X_1 is the ratio of working capital (current assets minus current liabilities) to total (book) assets; X_2 is the ratio of retained earnings to total assets; X_3 is the ratio of EBIT to total assets; and X_4 is the ratio of the (book) value of equity to the book value of total liabilities. The financial ratios selected into the model are diagnostic of the earning power and liquidity reserves of a firms assets. Sustained negative values of these ratios have been shown to be highly correlated with corporate failures. This model produced a classification accuracy of 95% on Altman's (relatively small) original development sample of companies, over a one-year horizon prior to default.

In the initial analysis of the RMG dataset, it was found that, indeed, the Altman Z mean scores (calculated using late 1998 financial information) for defaulting and non-defaulting firms were statistically different from each other at the 95% level of confidence.[13] RMG went on to show that the same result could be obtained using the Simplex period 2 default probabilities.[14] Even allowing for the downward-biased credit distribution of the RMG sample, statistical results on means for sample sizes less than 10 are not very robust. More relevant to the task of sorting companies by credit would be a demonstration that a model can rank-order companies by credit quality along a continuum.

A number of non-parametric techniques exist for making global comparisons of alternative model's discriminatory power. Probably the simplest, and the easiest to interpret, is the *cumulative accuracy profile* (CAP).[15] Plotting a CAP curve for a model begins with sorting the model risk statistics from the sample from worst to best. For a given fraction f of the entire sample, a Type I CAP curve depicts the fraction $d(f)$ of the target subset (for example, the distressed credits) that have risk score lower than or equal to the score for percentile f in the overall population. Thus, if the true fraction of distressed companies in the sample is D, a perfect model would order risk scores such that $d(D) = 1$; in other words, the worst $D\%$ of the risk scores would reveal 100% of the distressed firms. Alternatively, a model with no ability to sort by credit would tend to detect just $f\%$ of the distressed companies in the same fraction of the overall population. Figure 11.3 plots the CAP curves for the Altman and Simplex models over a portion ($N = 76$) of the RMG data set. Excluded were the companies with data issues as detailed in Table 11.1, as well as several others for which balance sheet data required for Z-score calculations was missing. Figure 11.3 was created with the target, or distressed population defined as all companies rated Caa1 or lower at the end of 1999.[16]

For the restricted RMG data set, the distressed fraction was 20/76, or 0.263. The ideal Type I CAP curve is shown in Figure 11.3 as the upper dotted line; the "naive" model line is the 45-degree lower dashed line. The

FIGURE 11.3 RMG trial: simplex versus Altman Z-score Type I cumulative accuracy profiles ($N = 76$)

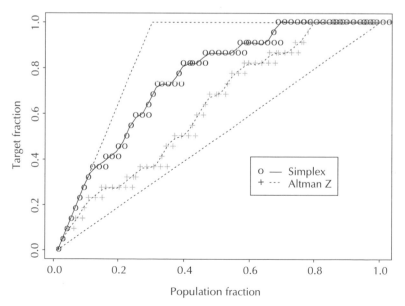

CAP-related measure of accuracy is the area between the ideal line and the model's CAP curve; the smaller the discrepancy, the higher is the discriminatory power of the model. Note that the Simplex model consistently identifies a higher fraction of the distressed companies, over a narrower range of the population sample, than does the Altman model. The implication is that Simplex's credit ordering of the companies, on a one-year horizon, reveals more coherent information about the likelihood of credit distress (or, more generally, about the likelihood of credit state changes) than the Altman Z ranking does. As previously noted, it is in the mid-range of the credit population that the extra discriminatory power of the Simplex model shows itself; the Altman model is relatively insensitive in this region.[17]

FIXED INCOME DIVISION TRIAL RESULTS

In contrast to the cross-sectional credit trial undertaken by the Risk Management Group, the Fixed Income Division sought to explore the time series properties of a smaller set of quarterly Simplex default probability estimates. The FID trial was meant to simulate the way the tool might actually be used, with sequential updates of equity prices and balance sheet information through time (unlike the RMG trial, companies' balance sheet information was updated quarterly during the test period). Results for the FID firms are collected the next series of charts. The companies in the sample ($N = 10$) were selected to represent a mixture of high-quality financial and industrial names commonly held by the bond and money markets funds.[18]

The FID sample of companies is too small for statistical analysis of the results, but the charts reinforce some of the model tendencies glimpsed in the RMG data set. First, the dynamic range of default probabilities among financial companies is larger and more volatile than that of the industrial companies – even though the financial companies are of equal or higher credit quality (at least according to Moody's ratings). This may indicate that the interpretation of balance sheet inputs to the default threshold calculation needs to be customized for the financial *versus* industrial sectors. Another potential modeling problem for financial companies is the simple measure of leverage used to transform the estimated equity process to the corresponding value process for the company. To the extent that many financial companies (banks and, especially, broker/dealers) may operate at higher effective leverage than is expressed by this measure, the estimated volatility of the company's value process would be biased upwards, and hence, so would the number of simulated default scenarios.

A second area of interest was the model's ability to react (but not overreact) to information in equity prices, in conjunction with balance sheet changes. The test event in the FID sample was the Russian currency/Long Term Credit Management (LTCM) crisis in the fall of 1998. The banking firms in Figure 11.4 show the response of the sector to the crisis, as well as the varying rates of recovery from the financial stress of the LTCM failure. Note that the bank with the largest dealer franchise, JP Morgan, was the clear risk outlier in the top chart, but looks to be more in the risk range of Merrill Lynch when plotted in Figure 11.5. Note also the change of scale needed to accommodate the relative default risk of Lehman Brothers – as well as the comparatively slower recovery of its default probability to pre-1998 third quarter levels. Finally, Figure 11.6 shows the onset of a slow deterioration in credit quality across a diverse group of industrial names. Again, only quarterly estimates are shown; if the equity price series updates had been make more frequently, additional resolution could be achieved.

Significantly, Moody's has begun testing a quantitative credit model, partially based on Merton distance-to-default techniques, whose output can be directly compared to the Simplex model results.[19] Although again, the overlap sample is too small to allow for strong conclusions, the general trend and magnitude of the two models' default probabilities are fairly similar. Unfortunately, the Simplex model trial ends during the third quarter of 1999, and subsequent credit action in several of the names (for example, Rite Aid) has been dramatic. Still, there is evidence that the Simplex model is producing similar results to a model that purports to have addressed a number of the shortcomings of pure Merton-based, time-to-default models.

FIGURE 11.4   Bank EDF monthly timeseries: October 1997–December 1999

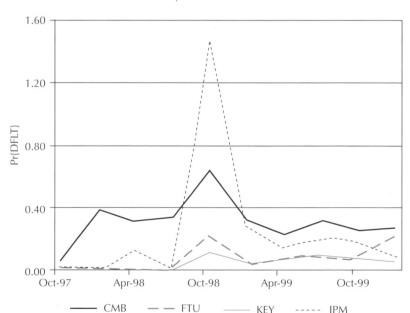

FIGURE 11.5   Broker/Deler DEF monthly timeseries: October 1997–December 1999

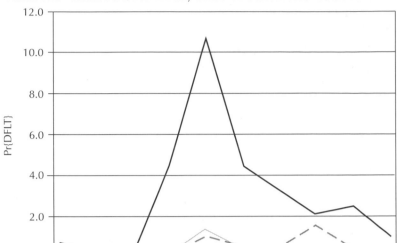

FIGURE 11.6   Non-financial EDF monthly timeseries: October 1997–December 1999

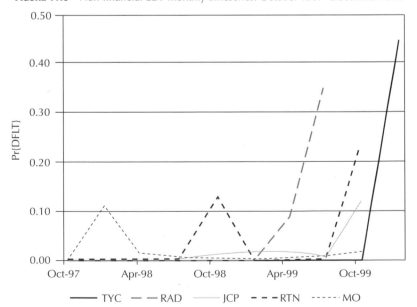

CONCLUSION

The Simplex credit risk model represents, in many ways, a return to the pure, classical option pricing approach to the problem of assessing the creditworthiness of debt claims. A number of other models make use of Merton's approach, but then find it necessary to appeal to historical data and other post-processing in order that the model's default estimates "square up" with market experience. While such techniques can be defended, the result is a loss of model transparency. By contrast, the Simplex model makes a simple claim: the key to making the fundamental approach work is a more empirically realistic model of the dynamics of equity prices, and, the implied value of the company (any company) can be expressed as a simple transformation of those enhanced equity dynamics. This report has attempted to test a working model built on this claim. In general, the model performed well under what could be easily interpreted as adverse testing conditions. With continuing refinements, it seems likely that a model like the one Simplex proposes could fill a crucial role in credit risk assessment.

Because of its open architecture, the Simplex model inputs and outputs can be tailored to meet the demands of a range of modeling credit modeling tasks. As a long-range credit distress screen for analyst discussion at research meetings, or as an alternative source of forced rankings for approved companies, analysts could directly explore how the model's input assumptions affected risk rankings, and how sensitive the answers were to different assumptions. Iterated, this process creates a quantitative metric that parallels the credit analyst's current thinking on a particular company. These quantitative likelihood measures can then be used in risk analytics, and applied to risk simulations of fund portfolios.

Our preliminary testing has identified a number of issues requiring attention in ongoing model development. Chief among these is the amount and nature of industry-specific input customization that will be required to derive consistent default probabilities across industry groups. We have observed that financial and non-financial companies seem to operate in different default probability regimes. An alternative hypothesis, given the relatively small trial size, is that the model treats high- and low-credit quality companies differently. Default probabilities for companies far from default may not fully take into account options companies have for renegotiating debt or rearranging assets to forestall default. Further, the model does not treat off-balance-sheet holdings, both a source and a mitigator of risk, particularly for financial companies. Given the preponderance of high credit quality financial firms held in investment-grade bond funds, these concerns need to be addressed in the course of further model development. Overall, however, the trial has suggested that Simplex offers a viable modeling approach that has the added advantage of being highly customizable to the needs of asset managers.

NOTES

[1] The most commercially successful of these models to date is produced by KMV Corporation (principals Kealhofer, McQuown, and Vasicek); their public company model is a hybrid of a Merton distance-to-default approach and a database that relates default distance measures with historically observed credit performance.

[2] Simplex uses the face value of debt for convenience; clearly, as the value of the company approaches the default threshold, (and control of the firm begins to pass to the debtholders), the relative priority and the market value of the outstanding debt become more important. For most of the companiess of interest to FID, the difference between par and the market value of debt may not be significant.

[3] The KMV model uses a default point defined loosely as the sum of short-term debt and one-half the book value of long-term debt. This is an attempt to recognize the "softness" of the actual default threshold in empirically observed default events. In practice, the value of a firm's assets may decline below the total outstanding debt level without triggering default, if, for example, outstanding long-term liabilities can be reorganized by creditors, or if creditors can force asset sales to secure the repayment of the firm's obligations.

[4] A problem with continuous diffusion models is that they predict credit spreads that should diminish to zero for short-maturity corporate debt; more generally they tend to underestimate default probabilities in real-world settings. Adding the jump term implies that there is a small, but non-zero chance in any time interval of a sudden jump that could render the firm insolvent.

[5] In effect, the model replaces the last two stochastic terms of the $\Delta S_t/S_t$ equation above with a mixture of two normal distributions having different standard deviations. One distribution's σ is the continuous standard deviation, while the other (typically larger), represents the "jump" return. The two distributions are mixed at the jump frequency λ. When a jump occurs, the return standard deviation does not return instantly to the continuous level; rather, the asset σ reverts towards its long-run value at a speed controlled by a GARCH model.

[6] Part of the disagreement comes from the difference in time horizon implied in agency ratings and the output of a simulation model such as Simplex. Rating agencies like to represent their ratings as long- (or at least, indeterminate) term, extending across changes in business cycles. A Merton-variant fundamental model is specified with an explicit estimate horizon, as detailed above. Fundamental models are thus more "reactive" to changes in the firm's asset level and volatility.

[7] Companies in the default sample were (1998 Moody's rating and default date in parentheses): Service Merchandise (Caa2, 3/27/99), AMF Bowling (Caa1, 7/28/99), TransTexas Gas (B1, 4/23/99), Axiohm Solutions (B1, 11/8/99), Royal Oak Mines (B3, 2/16/99), Mariner Post Acute Network (B1, 10/5/99), and Fruit of the Loom (Ba1, 12/30/99).

[8] Figure 11.1 is a *boxplot*, designed to reveal information about the scatter of the default data in each rating category. The white bar in the center of the boxes

marks the median observation in the category, and the "box" (shaded in grey) denotes the 25th and 75th percentiles of the observations. The horizontal bars (connected by dotted lines) show the 1.5 × quartile ranges, and the "whiskers" far outside of the boxes indicate extreme values. When the sample size in a given category is low, not all of the components of the box plot may be present, but the chart gives a good overall impression of the range, dispersion, and symmetry about the median of the categorized model results.

[9] One exception was the upper outlier, Credit Foncier, upgraded by virtue of its absorption into the French national banking system; another outlier was Broadwing, also noted in Table 11.1 above.

[10] Finally, there are several firms whose default probabilities remain stubbornly high for their "final" ratings; see, for example in the lower panel, the Baa2 category. The companies responsible for this category's dispersion turn out to be the two Japanese banks, IBJ and Dai-Ichi Kangyo; the Simplex model attaches 1999 failure probabilities to these banks that are more consistent with Ba-level ratings.

[11] Companies whose equity effectively ceased trading for reasons other than default (with date of last trades in parentheses) were: Novacare Inc. (11/29/99), American Architectural Products (6/01/00), and Pediatric Services of America (5/15/00).

[12] Altman's original research was reported in Altman, E (1968). The revised version utilized here is discussed in Caouette, Altman, and Narayanan (1998), Chapter 10.

[13] Croft J, "Simplex: Quantitative Credit Risk Modeling", RMG Group report, 2000.

[14] Croft concluded from his review of these difference-of-means tests that differences in one-year predictive accuracy between the Simplex and Altman models were insignificant. However, these t-statistic-based tests fail to say much about the relative accuracy of the two models. Evaluating a model as an *ex-ante* screen for adverse credit events implies a different statistical approach than does the task of verifying a model's *ex post* ability to sort companies, in the mean, into distressed and non-distressed subsets.

[15] An excellent review of several of these non-parametric techniques is Keenan, S C, and Sobehart, JR (1999).

[16] This was done to raise the size of the target sample; the demarcation in credit quality between lower B and "junk" status is fairly well-defined. A larger universe of companies would allow the "distressed" sample to be limited to those firms actually defaulting.

[17] Although, somewhat surprisingly, the Simplex model also outperforms in the lowest quality tier of firms, at least for this particular sample.

[18] The list displayed in the Figures 11.4–11.6 is: JP Morgan [JPM], Chase Manhattan Bank [CMB], First Union Bank [FTU], Keycorp [KEY], Merrill Lynch [MER], Lehman Brothers [LEH], JC Penney [JCP], Rite Aid Corp [RAD], Raytheon Co. [RTN], Phillip Morris Cos. [MO], and Tuco International [TYC].

[19] The Moody's variant, known as RiskCalc, is a nonlinear, multivariate model incorporating distance to default, balance sheet, ratings history, and equity trend information to create estimates of one-year expected default frequencies. The current version in testing covers only industrial companies; a financial company variant of the model is due to be released during 2001. For a discussion of the model and its estimation and validation, see Sobehart and Stein (2000).

Part 3

**Extension Areas for Measurement
Approaches to Credit Risk**

CHAPTER 12

Measuring Default Risk in the US High-Yield Bond Market

Edward I. Altman with Brenda Karlin
New York University

The year 2000 was one of the most difficult years for the high-yield bond market in the United States, since we began studying this market – a sample period of 30 years. Total returns were a dismal –5.68%, second only to the poorest absolute return year of 1990 (–8.46%), and the return spread of –20.13% was easily the worst in history. New issuance of high-yield bonds dropped considerably from 1999's impressive level and was reduced to a trickle by the end of the year as promised yields soared to about 14.5%, almost 9.5% above the risk-free rate – again the highest since 1990.

Defaults registered a second straight record year in terms of absolute amounts and topped $30 billion for the first time. Still, the default rate, though rising to about 5.0%, was just half that of the record years of 1990 and 1991. Combined with a relatively low recovery rate of 26.4%, also second lowest to 1990, the default loss rate was 3.9%, above the weighted average annual rate of about 2.5% and about double the arithmetic average of about 2.0% per annum. Average annual return spreads (above the risk-free rate) dropped to below 2.0% per annum, still quite decent but almost a full percentage point per annum less than just one year ago.

This chapter documents the high-yield bond market's risk and return performance by presenting traditional and mortality default rate statistics and providing a matrix of performance data over the market's evolution and growth. Our analysis covers the 1971–2000 period for default and the 1978–2000 period for returns. In addition, we present our annual forecast of expected defaults in 1999. Although we expected high defaults in 1999, we underestimated just how difficult the year would be as several new industries emerged as troubled, asbestos-related defaults re-emerged after being dormant for many years, and the flight to quality continued for the third year in a row (since August 1998).

231

For 2001, we were concerned about the proportion of the market that appeared to be distressed and also a softening economy. We expected defaults to again set a record absolute level and perhaps to rise to above $40 billion and the default rate to 6.5–7.0%. Although there were several parallels in 2000 to 1990, the default carnage was not expected to reach such a "lofty" rate as a decade earlier. When this became apparent in 2001, or perhaps even before the peak of defaults, we expected a reversal in total returns and return spreads. Required yield spreads at the end of the year appeared to be factoring in default rate expectations that were higher than we expected. Indeed, the default rate increased to 9.8% in 2001 and will certainly top that in 2002, producing a record level and rate of default.

DEFAULT LEVELS AND RATES

In 2000, a record $30.25 billion of developed country high-yield straight bonds defaulted or restructured under distressed conditions. This amount comprised 183 issues from 106 defaulting companies and resulted in a default rate of 5.07%. This compares to $23.5 billion on 149 issues from 100 companies in 1999. A list of 2000 defaults appears in Appendix 12.1.[1] The 2000 default rate is somewhat higher than last year's rate (4.15%), above the historic weighted average annual rate from 1971–2000 of 3.48% per annum (2.7% arithmetic average rate), and is also above the median annual rate (1.66%) over the same 30-year period (Figures 12.1 and 12.2). The face value of defaults reached record levels, topping the 1999 amount by almost $7 billion and exceeding 1991's previous record by almost $12 billion. Of course, the high-yield market is now about three times larger than it was in 1991. The default rate calculation is based on a mid-year population of high-yield bonds, estimated to be $597.2 billion. The default rate in 2000 provided a two-year string of record defaults and higher-than-average default rates, which followed a six-year period of below-average rates. We will return shortly to a discussion of this sizeable increase.

QUARTERLY DEFAULTS

In Appendix 12.2 and Figure 12.3, we present default rates on a quarterly basis from 1990 to 2000. It can be observed that the quarterly default levels and rates in 2000 were consistently high (except perhaps in the third quarter) with the second and fourth quarters' levels at about $10 billion each; both were around 1.65%. Quarterly rates are not usually indicative of trends, except possibly back in the 1990–1991 period when default rates skyrocketed to record levels over several consecutive quarters. Yet in 2000,

FIGURE 12.1 Historical default rates – straight bonds only excluding defaulted issues from par value outstanding (1971–2000) ($ millions)

Year	Par value outstanding (a) $	Par value defaults $	Default rates %	
2000	597,200	30,248	5.065	
1999	567,400	23,532	4.147	
1998	465,500	7,464	1.603	
1997	335,400	4,200	1.252	
1996	271,000	3,336	1.231	
1995	240,000	4,551	1.896	
1994	235,000	3,418	1.454	
1993	206,907	2,287	1.105	
1992	163,000	5,545	3.402	
1991	183,600	18,862	10.273	
1990	181,000	18,354	10.140	
1989	189,258	8,110	4.285	
1988	148,187	3,944	2.662	
1987	129,557	7,486	5.778	
1986	90,243	3,156	3.497	
1985	58,088	992	1.708	
1984	40,939	344	0.840	
1983	27,492	301	1.095	
1982	18,109	577	3.186	
1981	17,115	27	0.158	
1980	14,935	224	1.500	
1979	10,356	20	0.193	
1978	8,946	119	1.330	
1977	8,157	381	4.671	
1976	7,735	30	0.388	
1975	7,471	204	2.731	
1974	10,894	123	1.129	
1973	7,824	49	0.626	
1972	6,928	193	2.786	
1971	6,602	82	1.242	Standard deviation
Arithmetic average default rate		1971 to 2000	2.713%	2.484%
		1978 to 2000	2.948%	2.683%
		1985 to 2000	3.719%	2.829%
Weighted average default rate (b)		1971 to 2000	3.482%	2.558%
		1978 to 2000	3.503%	2.563%
		1985 to 2000	3.582%	2.565%
Median annual default rate		1971 to 2000	1.656%	

Notes

(a) As of mid-year.

(b) Weighted by par value of amount outstanding for each year.

Source: Authors' compilation and Salomon Smith Barney estimates

FIGURE 12.2 Historical defaults rates (1972–2000)

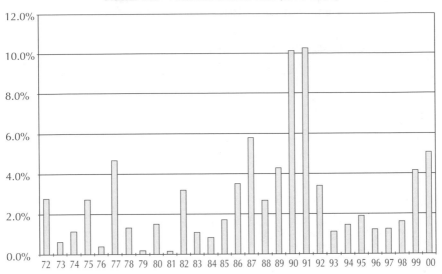

each quarter's default rate was greater than 1.0% (except in the third quarter) and showed a consistently higher level than any quarter since early in 1992 and the second quarter of 1999.

OUR DEFAULT RATE VERSUS MOODY'S

There has been considerable discussion in recent years about how the Altman-NYU Salomon Center default rate calculations differ from Moody's (New York) results. Analysts point out that the Moody's rate, especially in recent years, is consistently higher. This can be seen in the last two columns of Appendix 12.2. These results represent our 12-month moving average (or to be precise, last-four-quarter) default rates compared with Moody's 12-month moving average rate. One can observe that Moody's rate is, for the most part, higher since, essentially, 1992. The main reason for this is that Moody's includes emerging market corporate and quasi-municipal bond defaults while we do not. Our calculation essentially has been a domestic default rate calculation.[2] Note that Moody's ended 2000 at a 6.02% 12-month moving average rate compared to our 5.06% rate, about a 1% differential.

In order to analyze the differences in these two calculations, we constructed a moving four-quarter Altman/SC rate and compared it to Moody's 12-month moving averages, at the relevant quarterly dates. As noted above, Moody's rates are, for the most part, higher. But, when we ran a correlation of these absolute quarterly rates over the sample period (41 observations), we find (Appendix 12.2 continued) that the correlation is 0.97

FIGURE 12.3 Quarterly default rate and 12-month moving average (1992–2000)

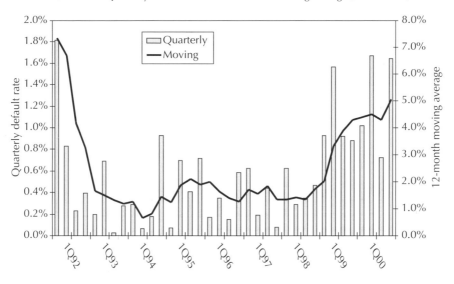

and the R-Square (proportion of one default rate "explained" by the other) is a huge 0.94. Even when we ran the regression based on either first differences in the change in the quarterly default rates or the percentage change in the rates, the correlations were high (0.77 and 0.57, respectively). In other words, both default rate measures are depicting very similar trends and directions of default rates. Moody's predicted default rate of 9.5% by the end of 2001 was considerably higher, however, than our 6.5–7.0% rate (see discussion below).

DEFAULT LOSSES AND RECOVERY AT DEFAULT

Default losses also rose substantially in 2000 versus 1999 and 1998 (3.94% versus 3.21% and 1.10%), and were substantially above the 1978–2000 average of 1.95% per year – 2.45% weighted (by the amount of bonds outstanding) average annual rate. Figure 12.4 shows the 2000 loss rate, which includes the loss of half of the average annual coupon. Default losses for the last 23 years are shown in Figure 12.5.

The average recovery rate on the issues for which we had prices just after default was 26.4%, the lowest since 1990, far below the venerable 40%–42% historical average recovery rate (Figures 12.5 and 12.6) and just below last year's figure (27.9%). This was less surprising this year than last, since the majority of the 164 defaulting issues with prices were subordinated (see Figure 12.6). Still, the low recovery rate is important since it reflects supply and demand conditions for defaulted bonds and lower expected

---

FIGURE 12.4 Default loss rate (2000)

Background data	
Average default rate 2000	5.065%
Average price at default (a)	26.396%
Average loss of principal	73.604%
Average coupon payment	8.539%
Default loss computation	
Default rate	5.065%
× Loss of principal	73.604%
Default loss of principal	3.728%
Default rate	5.065%
× Loss of 1/2 coupon	4.269%
Default loss of coupon	0.216%

Default loss of principal and coupon	**3.944%**

Note

(a) If default date price is not available, end-of-month price is used.

Source: Authors' compilation and Various Dealer Quotes

reorganization values. It is also consistent with our empirical observation of a strong negative correlation between concurrent levels of default and recovery rates.

Seventeen of the defaults were discount bonds, where we use accreted values as the base to determine recovery rates, as well as in our default total and rate calculations. The number of discounted defaulting issues was the highest ever.

About 70% of all new issuance in the high-yield market since 1991 has been senior in priority. But, the issuance of even more senior bank debt and secured bonds has lowered the priority of much of the defaulted public debt in the last two years, adding to the downward pressure on recovery rates. The much lower than average 1999 and 2000 recovery rates are a caution to investors who cannot assume that senior bonds will always result in above-average recovery rates and junior bonds average recoveries. Figure 12.6 lists the recovery rates (prices just after default) by seniority for 2000 and for the previous 22 years. For example, the senior secured recovery rate in 2000 was only 39.6% versus an historical average of more than 53.7%, and the senior unsecured average recovery rate slumped to just 25.4%, compared to a two-decade average of close to 44%. All of the seniority levels recovered lower amounts in 2000 than the historical average, except for the discounted bond group, which represents bonds of all seniorities. The overall arithmetic average 23-year recovery rate dipped below 40% (37.2%) and is now based on 1,102 issues (41.2% average, weighted by the amount outstanding in each year and a median rate of 40.7%).

FIGURE 12.5 Default rates and losses (a) (1978–2000)

Year	Par value outstanding (a) ($ millions)	Par value of default ($ millions)	Default rate (%)	Weighted price after default ($)	Weighted coupon (%)	Default loss (%)
2000	597,200	30,248	5.06	26.4	8.54	3.94
1999	567,400	23,532	4.15	27.9	10.55	3.21
1998	465,500	7,464	1.60	35.9	9.46	1.10
1997	335,400	4,200	1.25	54.2	11.87	0.65
1996	271,000	3,336	1.23	51.9	8.92	0.65
1995	240,000	4,551	1.90	40.6	11.83	1.24
1994	235,000	3,418	1.45	39.4	10.25	0.96
1993	206,907	2,287	1.11	56.6	12.98	0.56
1992	163,000	5,545	3.40	50.1	12.32	1.91
1991	183,600	18,862	10.27	36.0	11.59	7.16
1990	181,000	18,354	10.14	23.4	12.94	8.42
1989	189,258	8,110	4.29	38.3	13.40	2.93
1988	148,187	3,944	2.66	43.6	11.91	1.66
1987	129,557	7,486	5.78	75.9	12.07	1.74
1986	90,243	3,156	3.50	34.5	10.61	2.48
1985	58,088	992	1.71	45.9	13.69	1.04
1984	40,939	344	0.84	48.6	12.23	0.48
1983	27,492	301	1.09	55.7	10.11	0.54
1982	18,109	577	3.19	38.6	9.61	2.11
1981	17,115	27	0.16	12.0	15.75	0.15
1980	14,935	224	1.50	21.1	8.43	1.25
1979	10,356	20	0.19	31.0	10.63	0.14
1978	8,946	119	1.33	60.0	8.38	0.59
Arithmetic average 1978–2000:			2.95	41.2	11.22	1.95
Weighted average 1978–2000:			3.50			2.45

Notes
(a) Excludes defaulted issues.
Source: Figures 1 and 4

FIGURE 12.6 Weighted average recovery rates on defaulted debt by seniority per $100 face amount (1978–2000)

Default year	Senior secured		Senior unsecured		Senior subordinated		Subordinated		Discount and zero coupon		All seniorities	
	No.	$	No.	$	No.	$	No.	$	No.	$	No.	$
2000	13	39.58	47	25.40	61	25.96	26	26.62	17	23.61	164	25.83
1999	14	26.90	60	42.54	40	23.56	2	13.88	11	17.30	127	31.14
1998	6	70.38	21	39.57	6	17.54	0	0	1	17.00	34	37.27
1997	4	74.90	12	70.94	6	31.89	1	60.00	2	19.00	25	53.89
1996	4	59.08	4	50.11	9	48.99	4	44.23	3	11.99	24	51.91
1995	5	44.64	9	50.50	17	39.01	1	20.00	1	17.50	33	41.77
1994	5	48.66	8	51.14	5	19.81	3	37.04	1	5.00	22	39.44
1993	2	55.75	7	33.38	10	51.50	9	28.38	4	31.75	32	38.83
1992	15	59.85	8	35.61	17	58.20	22	49.13	5	19.82	67	50.03
1991	4	44.12	69	55.84	37	31.91	38	24.30	9	27.89	157	40.67
1990	12	32.18	31	29.02	38	25.01	24	18.83	11	15.63	116	24.66
1989	9	82.69	16	53.70	21	19.60	30	23.95			76	35.97
1988	13	67.96	19	41.99	10	30.70	20	35.27			62	43.45
1987	4	90.68	17	72.02	6	56.24	4	35.25			31	66.63
1986	8	48.32	11	37.72	7	35.20	30	33.39			56	36.60
1985	2	74.25	3	34.81	7	36.18	15	41.45			27	41.78
1984	4	53.42	1	50.50	2	65.88	7	44.68			14	50.62
1983	1	71.00	3	67.72			4	41.79			8	55.17
1982			16	39.31			4	32.91			20	38.03
1981	1	72.00									1	72.00
1980			2	26.71			2	16.63			4	21.67
1979							1	31.00			1	31.00
1978			1	60.00							1	60.00
Total/Average median	126	53.73 59.08	365	44.28 42.54	299	31.27 31.91	247	31.03 32.91	65	20.83 17.50	1102	37.17 40.67

Source: Authors' compilation from various dealer quotes

FIGURE 12.7 Average price after default by original bond rating (1971–2000)

Rating	No. of observations	Average price ($)	Median price* ($)	Std. dev.* ($)	Minimum price ($)	Maximum price ($)
AAA	7	68.34	71.88	20.82	32.00	97.00
AA	20	59.59	54.25	24.59	17.80	99.88
A	65	62.07	62.00	24.86	10.50	100.00
BBB	117	37.54	46.00	23.79	2.00	103.00
BB	108	32.78	37.00	22.05	1.00	98.75
B	589	30.83	33.00	24.66	0.50	112.00
CCC	133	48.78	31.00	27.18	1.00	103.25
Total	1039	48.56	36.50	25.76	0.50	112.00

* The median and standard deviation figures are from 1971–1999 only.

Source: Authors' compilation

In Figure 12.7, we list the average recovery at default stratified by original bond rating for the period 1971–2000. The weighted recoveries for the A-rated categories of bonds definitely show higher recovery rates than for non-investment grade debt, but the three non-investment-grade bond classes, and also BBB-rated bonds, continue to show very little differences. This is also true after adjusting for seniority bias.

Figure 12.8 lists the original Standard & Poor's ratings of defaulting issues, as well as the one-year and six-months-prior-to-default ratings. Of the 1,039 issues tabulated, 79.4% were original issue high-yield bonds, and 20.6% were originally rated as investment grade but eventually defaulted; 9.0% of the defaulted issues were still rated investment grade one year before default and 7.6% six months prior (multiple issues from a few large high-grade issuers, for example, Columbia Gas System, however, accounted for a large proportion of the 12- and six-month-prior investment grade defaults) and most of these were BBB. These 12- and six-months-prior statistics were up from the previous year's results since several BBB-rated bonds at these intervals did eventually default. This reflects the precipitous drops in credit quality, recently, of investment-grade bonds. If the California public utility bonds default by June 30, 2001, those issues will add to the investment-grade original rating proportion, as well as the six-month and 12-month categories when the bonds were rated AA– to A+.

Figure 12.9 shows that the time it takes for an issue to default compared to its issuance date makes virtually no difference in the recovery rate. Most weighted recoveries by year after issuance are in the low to mid $30s range.

FIGURE 12.8 Rating distribution of defaulted issues (a) at various points prior to default (1971–2000)

	Original rating		Rating one year prior to default		Rating six months prior to default	
	Number	Percentage	Number	Percentage	Number	Percentage
AAA	5	0.5	0	0.0	0	0.0
AA	25	2.4	0	0.0	0	0.0
A	69	6.6	12	1.3	2	0.2
BBB	115	11.1	72	7.7	65	7.4
Total investment grade	214	20.6	84	9.0	67	7.6
BB	118	11.4	90	9.7	81	9.2
B	569	54.8	478	51.3	444	50.6
CCC	134	12.9	248	26.6	236	26.9
CC	4	0.4	22	2.4	43	4.9
C	0	0.0	8	0.9	7	0.8
D	0	0.0	1	0.1	0	0.0
Total noninvestment grade	825	79.4	847	91.0	811	92.4
Total	1039	100	931	100	878	100

(a) Based on Standard & Poor's bond ratings

Source: Authors' compilation

FIGURE 12.9 Average price at default by number of years after issuance (1971–2000)

Years to default	No. of observations	Average price ($)	Median price* ($)	Standard deviation* ($)
1	81	32.30	31.75	24.45
2	183	30.60	31.30	22.30
3	194	29.97	34.31	25.83
4	150	36.36	39.00	24.90
5	124	34.44	36.50	27.30
6	92	49.90	36.25	26.33
7	62	36.92	37.75	24.16
8	39	30.80	27.50	27.07
9	20	36.01	33.00	27.34
10	28	28.83	32.00	22.78
All	973	34.61	35.00	25.15

* The median and standard deviation figures are from 1971–1999 only.
Source: Authors' compilation

DETERIORATION IN ORIGINAL ISSUANCE CREDIT QUALITY

One apparent reason for the sizeable amount of defaults in 2000 is the deterioration in credit quality of new issuance in recent years. This is demonstrated by the significant increase in the percentage of bonds that defaulted in the first three years after issuance. From Figures 12.10 and 12.11, we observe that in 2000, 19 of the 183 issues defaulted within 12 months (10%), 70 (38%) defaulted within 24 months, and 126 (69%) within 36 months. This compares with 9%, 30%, and 51%, respectively, for the 1971–2000 period (Figure 12.10); and about 4%, 17%, and 20% for the 1991–1998 period.[3] Hence, a sizeable increase in one-, two- and three-year defaults is observed in the 1999 and 2000 cohort. The 10% one-year proportion, however, is down from the record 26% in 1999.

We observe that in Figure 12.12, the 1999 new issue cohort had an approximate 0.49% (BBB), 1.50% (BB), 1.62% (B), and 63.1% (CCC) default rate,[4] which are higher than the one-year rates from 1971–2000 (see our mortality rate data in Figure 12.14). These higher marginal default rates in 2000 are also manifested in the second and third years after issuance (1998 and 1997 cohorts), especially for all three B-rated categories. In order to better understand these statistics, however, we need to analyze the purpose of the financing (for example, growth versus refinancing versus Leveraged Borrowing Obligations (LBOs)), to see if the one to three years aging results are symptomatic of credit quality drift or of other things (see our following discussion).

FIGURE 12.10   Distribution of years to default from original issuance date (by years of default) (1989–2000)

Years to default	1989		1990		1991		1992		1993/1994		1995	
	No. of issues	% of total	No. of issues	% of total	No. of issues	% of total	No. of issues	% of total	No. of issues	% of total	No. of issues	% of total
1	4	6	3	3	0	0	0	0	3	8	1	3
2	12	18	25	23	18	13	0	0	6	16	9	28
3	15	23	23	21	26	19	7	13	5	14	7	22
4	13	20	18	17	29	21	10	19	2	5	3	9
5	1	2	23	21	35	26	8	15	4	11	1	3
6	7	11	5	5	10	7	12	22	8	22	2	6
7	7	11	5	5	4	3	5	9	7	19	2	6
8	2	3	4	4	10	7	4	7	0	0	2	6
9	1	2	1	1	3	2	0	0	0	0	4	13
10	3	5	1	1	2	1	8	15	2	5	1	3
Total	65	100	108	100	137	100	54	100	37	100	32	100

Years to default	1996		1997		1998		1999		2000		1989–2000	
	No. of issues	% of total	No. of issues	% of total	No. of issues	% of total	No. of issues	% of total	No. of issues	% of total	No. of issues	% of total
1	2	8	5	20	2	6	32	26	19	10	71	9
2	3	13	4	16	5	15	37	30	51	28	170	21
3	3	13	4	16	10	30	15	12	56	31	171	21
4	8	33	9	36	3	9	14	11	14	8	123	15
5	1	4	3	12	10	30	7	6	13	7	106	13
6	5	21	0	0	2	6	8	6	5	3	64	8
7	0	0	0	0	1	3	10	8	12	7	53	6
8	0	0	0	0	0	0	2	2	4	2	28	3
9	0	0	0	0	0	0	0	0	3	2	12	1
10	2	8	0	0	0	0	0	0	6	3	25	3
Total	24	100	25	100	33	100	125	100	183	100	823	100

Source: Authors' compilation

FIGURE 12.11 Percentage defaults in 2000 by year from issuance

Time	# of issues	Percentage (%)
1st year	19	10
2nd year	51	28
3rd year	56	31
4th year	14	8
5th year	13	7
6th year	5	3
7th year	12	7
8th year	4	2
9th year	3	2
10th (+) year	6	3
Total	183	100

Source: Authors' compilation

DEFAULTS IN 1990 VS 2000

In a prior study, we observed that defaults resulting from highly leveraged restructuring (LBOs, recaps, and so on) accounted for about $20 billion in 1990–1992, about 46% of total defaults in those years. In contrast, the most recent years' results show that defaults from highly leverage restructurings in 1999–2000 did not account for any material amount and the outlook is for this source to continue not to be very important. We assessed the proportion of total new high-yield bonds issued for a number of stated reasons, including acquisitions, leverage restructurings, capital expenditure and other general corporate investments, and the refinancing of existing debt. The latter category has been the most important use of new debt financing every year since our data series began (1986–1999). The levels of refinancing in 1997–1999 were not exceptionally high – in fact, they were below the average over this 14-year period. One reason for this is that, although Treasury rates did fall in these years from 1996 levels, the yields on high-yield debt actually increased, making refinancing actually more expensive. Even so, the refinancing proportion of 40%–45% of the more than $100 billion of new issues in each year is a great deal of financing that did not provide new cash to the issuer.

Overall, we find that in the years 1995–1999, about 20% of high-yield bond new issuance was used for acquisitions and only 4%–5% for leveraged restructurings. This compares to 10%–15% for acquisitions and well over 30% for LBOs and recapitalizations in the years leading up to the market's problems a decade ago. Since leveraged restructurings can lead to unsustainable levels of debt and possible financial distress, we feel that at least in terms of this important factor, the new issue market was decidedly more risky in the earlier period.

FIGURE 12.12 Year 2000 defaults by rating and age

One-year defaults – bonds issued 1999

Original rating in 1999	Defaults ($ mm)	# issues	Amount issued ($ mm)	# issues	Dollar default rate %	Issue default rate %[1]
BBB	482.14	1	99,468.50	683	0.485	0.161
BB	439.59	2	29,311.80	160	1.500	1.375
B	973.92	5	60,108.60	295	1.620	1.864
CCC	853.20	3	1,352.00	7	63.106	47.143

Two-year defaults – bonds issued 1998

Original rating in 1998	Defaults ($ mm)	# issues	Amount issued ($ mm)	# issues	Dollar default rate %	Issue default rate %[1]
A						
BBB	1,453.49	5	112,914.60	672	1.287	0.818
BB	1,147.68	5	44,569.10	209	2.575	2.632
B	6,445.16	34	73,427.00	450	8.778	8.311
CCC	116.28	1	7,976.90	39	1.458	2.821

Three-year defaults – bonds issued 1997

Original rating in 1997	Defaults ($ mm)	# issues	Amount issued ($ mm)	# issues	Dollar default rate %	Issue default rate %[1]
A						
BBB	1,068.04	4	75,331.70	477	1.418	0.922
BB	1,296.14	5	28,674.30	176	4.520	3.125
B	6,094.10	27	67,450.30	425	9.035	6.988
CCC	183.40	1	2,846.30	18	6.443	6.111

Four-year defaults – bonds issued 1996

Original rating in 1996	Defaults ($ mm)	# issues	Amount issued ($ mm)	# issues	Dollar default rate %	Issue default rate %[1]
A						
BBB	207.79	1	48,353.70	299	0.430	0.368
BB	311.69	1	17,420.20	114	1.789	0.965
B	3,102.98	14	36,339.10	220	8.539	7.000
CCC						

Five-year defaults – bonds issued 1996

Original rating in 1995	Defaults ($ mm)	# issues	Amount issued ($ mm)	# issues	Dollar default rate %	Issue default rate %[1]
A						
BBB	599.35	4	37,877.60	267	1.582	1.648
BB						
B	2,375.09	8	16,806.40	102	14.132	8.627
CCC						

(1) With 10% adjustment to number of issues defaulted due to incomplete default sample.
Source: Authors' compilation, Thomson Financial Securities Data

Still, the high-yield bond industry's enthusiasm for new issuance in 1996–1998, and the apparent deterioration in credit quality, needs to be monitored closely. This deterioration in credit quality undoubtedly contributed to recent default growth, but the added factor of earlier defaults exacerbated the 1999–2000 numbers. Investors will need additional promised yields to achieve return spreads comparable to the performance data of the past two decades (see our data involving return spreads, especially Figure 12.16).

OTHER REASONS FOR THE INCREASE IN DEFAULTS

In addition to the deterioration in credit quality and the earlier occurrence of defaults, a number of other factors contributed to the sizeable increase in 2000. These are (1) the increased dollar amount of recent new issuance, (2) the vestige of Russia's default in 1998, (3) a number of "sick" industries despite the economy's apparent overall strength (now being questioned for 2001), and (4) banks' reluctance to refinance marginal clients.

We have already noted the huge new issuance years of 1997–1999 and the expected increase in dollar defaults as these new issues age. This simple mortality idea is the primary basis for our forecasted default numbers and percentages, which we will discuss at a later point. If nothing else, a regression to the mean would have caused the 2000 default amounts and default rate to increase vis-à-vis prior years.

The increase in the bond default rate to more than 5%, however, was caused by additional factors. One intangible, but important, factor is the ability of distressed firms to refinance their indebtedness, especially with funding from the commercial banks. Refinancing occurred with increasing difficulty in the aftermath of Russia's default and the flight-to-quality that ensued. Although this occurrence is mainly anecdotal, we are convinced that without the Russian contagion, the default rate would have been lower.

In 2000, bank loan defaults of rated loans (by S&P) were about $16 billion and Maden, Horowitz, and O'Connor estimate that bank loan defaults overall were $23 billion in 2000 and reached $33 billion in 2001 (Salomon Smith Barney Equity Research: US report, January 9, 2001).

INDUSTRY DEFAULTS

We continue to observe pockets of defaults in either chronically or newly ailing industrial sectors. Appendix 12.3 lists the 2000 defaults by major industrial sectors, as well as the industry default data since 1970. In 2000, in addition to general manufacturing and miscellaneous industries (23 and 34 defaulting issuers), such sectors as leisure/entertainment (9), communications (8), retailing (7), healthcare (6), real estate (6), and financial services (6) were most prominent. Some particularly hard hit categories were movie theatre chains and steel. Indeed, the former "industry" realized more than a 50% failure rate in recent years and the latter had two large Chapter 22s (LTV and Wheeling Pittsburgh). Hence, despite an ebullient economy for most of the year, driven by technology and productivity growth, a number of sectors have been ailing, and some will continue to do so going forward. Others, like energy and shipping, which were big "contributors" in 1999, fell to just one default in each sector in 2000. As points of reference, Grossman and Verde concluded that retail, insurance, supermarkets, drug stores, and textiles/furniture had the highest default rates in the 1991–1999 period.

Appendix 12.4 lists the 2000 defaults by more precise industry classifications for the individual defaulting issuers, and Appendix 12.5 provides an update on the recovery rates by sector for 1971–2000.

RECOVERY RATES FOR COMMUNICATION COMPANIES

Recently, a great deal of attention has been given to recovery rate experience and expectations of recoveries for defaults in particular industrial sectors. This is particularly important for an industry such as the communications sector, especially the telecommunication segment, which has been a major issuer of new high-yield bonds in recent years. These data are relevant not only for traditional investors (mutual and pension funds) in high-yield debt, but also for specialized investors and insurers of such instruments as collateralized bond/loan obligations and writers of credit derivatives. Figure 12.13 shows the default recovery experience for communication companies on defaults since 1987, mostly in the last five years. Note that the weighted average recovery rate at default for 91 issues and 41 issuers was about 28%, with a standard deviation of about 20%. The relatively low recovery rate for communication defaults is indicative of recent overall recovery experience in the high-yield bond market, perhaps reflecting low asset values.

If one wants to highlight specific segments within the communications sector, the compilation in Figure 12.13 permits you to do so. We intend to provide this analysis for other sectors in the future.

MORTALITY RATES AND LOSSES

Updated mortality rates and losses for 1971–2000 are reported in Figures 12.14 and 12.15. Total defaulted issues that had a rating on issuance and a price at default were 953 and 845, respectively. The methodology for

FIGURE 12.13 Recovery rates for communications industry (1987–2000)

Issuer	Bond	Coupon	Issue size	Default date	Default price ($)
Western Union Telegraph	SF Deb 5/15/97	7.90	5.000	1/11/1987	39.00
SCI Television	Sub Deb '99	17.50	128.000	1/8/1989	20.00
SCI Television	Sr ExtNts '90	15.50	200.000	1/8/1989	65.00
SCI Television	Sr Sr Deb '97	16.50	100.000	1/8/1989	33.00
Metropolitan Broadcasting	Jr Sub Deb 9/30/06	16.50	70.200	12/10/1989	57.75
Metropolitan Broadcasting	Sr Sub 9/30/06	13.25	65.000	12/10/1989	84.50
Olympic Broadcasting	Sr Sub Deb '96	13.38	17.400	1/11/1989	64.00
Univision Holdings	Sub Deb '99	13.38	105.000	1/2/1990	37.00
Univision Holdings	Sr Sub Disc Nts '98	0.00	160.000	1/2/1990	65.00
Western Union Corp.	SF Debs 3/15/96	8.45	8.100	15/6/1990	18.00
Western Union Corp.	SF Debs '8/15/93	8.10	7.700	15/6/1990	20.88
Western Union Corp.	SF Debs 3/1/92	5.00	8.000	15/6/1990	21.00
Western Union Corp.	SF Debs 12/1/97	9.25	1.400	15/6/1990	22.50
Western Union Corp.	Sub Deb '97	10.75	14.500	15/6/1990	19.50
Olympic Broadcasting	Sr Sr Deb '96	14.38	23.400	1/12/1990	11.00
Price Communications	Sub Nts '96	13.00	93.000	15/1/1991	7.88
Price Communications	Sub Nts '95	11.75	52.500	15/2/1991	6.50
Star Cable Vision	Sr Sub Debs '02	13.50	21.000	15/2/1991	50.00
Price Communications	Sub Deb '00	14.63	66.600	15/3/1991	6.50
Western Union Corp.	Sr Sec Rst Nts '12/15/92	19.25	201.700	15/6/1991	39.25
Western Union Tel.	Notes '6/15/91	16.00	23.800	15/6/1991	35.00
Western Union Tel.	SF Deb 10/1/08	13.25	30.300	15/6/1991	27.00
Gillett Holdings	Sr Sr Deb 8/1/98	12.63	250.400	25/6/1991	25.00
Gillett Holdings	Sr Nts E Zero cpn93	0.00	75.000	25/6/1991	39.00
Gillett Holdings	Sub Deb 8/15/99	13.88	170.000	25/6/1991	20.00
Gillett Holdings	Sr Nts F Zero cpn94	0.00	61.900	25/6/1991	39.00
Gillett Holdings	Sr Nts D Zero cpn92	0.00	75.000	25/6/1991	40.50
Burnham Broadcasting	Sub Deb '99	13.88	32.000	1/9/1991	20.00

FIGURE 12.13 (*cont.*)

Issuer	Bond	Coupon	Issue size	Default date	Default price ($)
Western Union Tel.	Notes 3/15/94	13.63	6.300	15/9/1991	22.13
Telemundo Group 46	Sr Zero Cpn Nts '8/15/93	0.00	55.000	15/1/1992	46.00
Telemundo Group (JohnBlair)	Sub Debs '98	13.63	47.000	15/1/1992	30.00
Telemundo Group33	Sr Zero Cpn Nts '8/15/92	0.00	55.000	15/1/1992	33.00
AR CableServices	Sub Deb 12/30/97	16.75	134.300	28/1/1992	77.50
SPI Holdings	Sub Debs '02	14.75	75.000	1/4/1992	89.00
SPI Holdings	Sr Sub Reset Nts '99	14.88	221.200	1/4/1992	97.00
Telemundo Group	Jr Sub Dis Nts '01	12.00	21.300	15/5/1992	15.00
Great American Comm. Company	Sr Sub Notes '99	14.38	40.500	14/4/1993	35.00
GACC Holding Company	Sr Nts '96	14.13	32.200	15/4/1993	38.00
GACC Holding Company	Sr Ext'd Rst Nts '95	20.50	4.600	15/4/1993	36.00
Maryland Cable	Sr Sub Disc Nts '98	15.38	162.000	15/3/1994	32.00
Spectravision	SrDiscNts'01	11.50	178.300	1/6/1995	20.00
Spectravision	SrSubReset'95	11.65	313.400	1/6/1995	7.00
Scott Cable Communications	SubDebs '01	12.25	50.000	15/2/1996	65.50
Mobilemedia Communications	SrSubNts '11/07	9.38	250.000	1/11/1996	54.20
Mobilemedia Communications	SrSubNts '12/03	10.25	210.000	1/11/1996	44.19
In-Flight Phone Corp.	Senior Discount Notes	14.00	285.800	24/1/1997	4.50
Australis Holdings	Senior Discount Notes	0.00	193.100	8/4/1998	18.00
Australis Holdings	Senior Discount Notes	0.00	80.200	8/4/1998	33.00
Heartland Wireless Communications, Inc.	Senior Notes 4/15/03	13.00	100.000	15/4/1998	30.00
Heartland Wireless Communications, Inc.	Senior Notes 10/15/04	14.00	125.000	15/4/1998	28.50
American Telecasting	Senior Discount Notes	0.00	135.900	13/5/1998	15.00
American Telecasting	Senior Discount Notes	0.00	141.000	13/5/1998	19.60
Geotek Communications, Inc.	Senior Discount Notes	0.00	207.000	30/6/1998	17.00
CAI Wireless Systems, Inc.	Senior Notes	12.25	275.000	30/7/1998	24.00
CAI Wireless Systems, Inc.	Senior Notes	12.00	30.000	30/7/1998	24.00
International Wireless Communications Hldgs	Senior Secured Discount Notes	0.00	139.000	3/9/1998	10.00

FIGURE 12.13 (cont.)

Issuer	Bond	Coupon	Issue size	Default date	Default price ($)
Ionica Group PLC	Senior Notes	13.50	150.000	28/9/1998	30.00
Ionica Group PLC	Senior Discount Notes	0.00	250.000	28/9/1998	3.00
PhoneTel Tech.	Guaranteed Senior Notes	12.00	125.000	15/1/1999	35.00
Telegroup, Inc.	Senior Dicount Notes	0.00	85.600	10/2/1999	34.00
Wireless One, Inc.	Sen or Discount Notes	0.00	175.100	11/2/1999	9.57
Wireless One, Inc.	Senior Notes	13.00	150.000	11/2/1999	10.00
USN Communications	Senior Discount Notes	0.00	123.700	18/2/1999	9.00
FWT, Inc.	Senior Subordinated Notes	9.88	105.000	16/4/1999	7.00
Teletrac, Inc.	Senior Subordinated Notes	14.00	98.400	9/6/1999	25.00
ICO Global Comm. Services, Inc.	Eurobonds	15.25	107.100	1/7/1999	47.00
ICO Global Comm. Services, Inc.	Senior Notes	15.00	460.000	1/7/1999	44.00
Iridium LLC/Capital Corp.	Senior Notes	11.25	5.600	15/7/1999	19.00
Iridium LLC/Capital Corp.	Senior Notes	13.00	0.300	15/7/1999	19.00
Iridium LLC/Capital Corp.	Senior Notes	10.88	350.000	15/7/1999	19.00
Iridium LLC/Capital Corp.	Senior Notes	14.00	500.000	15/7/1999	19.00
TeleHub Network Services Corp.	Senior Unsecured Discount Notes	13.88	79.100	27/10/1999	13.00
Optel, Inc.	Senior Notes	11.50	200.000	28/10/1999	33.00
Optel, Inc.	Senior Notes	13.00	225.000	28/10/1999	33.00
Paging Network, Inc.	Senior Subordinated Notes	10.00	500.000	1/2/2000	39.70
Paging Network, Inc.	Senior Subordinated Notes	10.13	400.000	1/2/2000	39.70
Paging Network, Inc.	Senior Subordinated Notes	8.88	300.000	1/2/2000	39.70
CellNet Data Systems	Senior Discount Notes	0.00	452.600	4/2/2000	17.34
CellNet Data Systems	Senior Discount Notes	0.00	223.300	4/2/2000	12.63
GST Telecommunications, Inc.	Senior Discount Notes	0.00	289.800	17/5/2000	24.80
GST Telecommunications, Inc.	Senior Subordinated Accrual Notes	12.75	165.300	17/5/2000	6.75
GST Telecommunications, Inc.	Senior Secured Notes	13.25	265.000	17/5/2000	45.00
GST Telecommunications, Inc.	Senior Discount Notes	0.00	370.400	17/5/2000	56.70
Central Euro Media Entertainment	Senior Notes	8.13	65.396	15/8/2000	30.00

FIGURE 12.13 (cont.)

Issuer	Bond	Coupon	Issue size	Default date	Default price ($)
Central Euro Media Entertainment	Senior Notes	9.38	100.000	15/8/2000	35.00
Orbcomm Global LP	Senior Notes	14.00	170.000	15/8/2000	15.00
ICG Communications Corp.	Senior Discount Notes	0.00	320.039	14/11/2000	8.00
ICG Communications Corp.	Senior Discount Notes	0.00	393.970	14/11/2000	8.00
ICG Communications Corp.	Senior Discount Notes	0.00	521.611	14/11/2000	12.00
ICG Communications Corp.	Senior Discount Notes	13.50	584.300	14/11/2000	12.00
ICG Communications Corp.	Senior Discount Notes	0.00	151.724	14/11/2000	8.00
41 Firms/91 Issues			14,098.340 Average price		$ 29.87
			Weighted average price		$ 28.08
			Standard deviation		$ 19.68

Source: Prior annual reports and various dealer quotes

FIGURE 12.14 Mortality rates by original rating – all rated corporate bonds[1] (1971–2000)
Years after issuance (in percentage)

		1	2	3	4	5	6	7	8	9	10
AAA	Marginal	0.00	0.00	0.00	0.00	0.03	0.00	0.00	0.00	0.00	0.00
	cumulative	0.00	0.00	0.00	0.00	0.03	0.03	0.03	0.03	0.03	0.03
AA	Marginal	0.00	0.00	0.35	0.19	0.00	0.00	0.00	0.00	0.03	0.02
	cumulative	0.00	0.00	0.35	0.54	0.54	0.54	0.54	0.54	0.57	0.59
A	Marginal	0.00	0.00	0.02	0.07	0.03	0.08	0.05	0.09	0.06	0.00
	cumulative	0.00	0.00	0.02	0.09	0.12	0.20	0.25	0.34	0.40	0.40
BBB	Marginal	0.12	0.48	0.55	0.59	0.56	0.58	0.72	0.15	0.05	0.26
	cumulative	0.12	0.60	1.14	1.73	2.28	2.85	3.55	3.70	3.75	3.98
BB	Marginal	0.96	1.65	3.15	1.54	2.15	0.95	1.65	0.45	1.75	3.75
	cumulative	0.96	2.59	6.50	7.12	9.12	9.98	11.47	11.87	13.41	16.66
B	Marginal	1.60	4.94	5.95	6.72	5.94	4.15	3.12	2.10	1.65	0.85
	cumulative	1.60	6.46	12.03	17.85	22.73	25.94	28.25	29.76	30.92	31.51
CCC	Marginal	4.35	13.26	14.84	8.15	3.02	9.15	4.56	3.26	0.00	4.15
	cumulative	4.35	17.03	31.00	36.62	38.53	44.15	46.70	48.44	48.44	50.58

(1) Rated by S&P at issuance.
Based on 933 issues.
Source: Standard & Poor's (New York) and authors' compilation

FIGURE 12.15 Mortality losses by original rating – all rated corporate bonds[1] (1971–2000)
Years after issuance (in percentage)

		1	2	3	4	5	6	7	8	9	10
AAA	Marginal	0.00	0.00	0.00	0.00	0.00	0.00	0.00	0.00	0.00	0.00
	cumulative	0.00	0.00	0.00	0.00	0.00	0.00	0.00	0.00	0.00	0.00
AA	Marginal	0.00	0.00	0.06	0.06	0.00	0.00	0.00	0.00	0.02	0.02
	cumulative	0.00	0.00	0.06	0.12	0.12	0.12	0.12	0.12	0.14	0.16
A	Marginal	0.00	0.00	0.01	0.04	0.02	0.05	0.02	0.04	0.04	0.00
	cumulative	0.00	0.00	0.01	0.05	0.07	0.12	0.14	0.18	0.22	0.22
BBB	Marginal	0.10	0.35	0.37	0.36	0.42	0.43	0.50	0.10	0.04	0.18
	cumulative	0.10	0.45	0.82	1.18	1.60	2.02	2.51	2.61	2.63	2.81
BB	Marginal	0.57	0.99	2.45	1.10	1.12	0.66	1.03	0.25	0.95	1.75
	cumulative	0.57	1.55	3.96	5.02	6.08	6.69	7.68	7.89	8.77	10.37
B	Marginal	1.12	3.70	4.60	4.67	4.50	2.49	1.87	1.42	0.85	0.61
	cumulative	1.12	4.78	9.16	13.40	17.30	19.36	20.87	21.97	22.65	23.12
CCC	Marginal	2.82	10.60	11.39	6.52	2.27	6.40	3.64	2.65	0.00	3.10
	cumulative	2.82	13.12	23.02	28.04	29.67	34.17	36.57	38.25	38.25	40.16

(1) Rated by S&P at issuance.
Based on 799 issues.
Source: Standard & Poor's (New York) and authors' compilation

these calculations comes from Altman (1989). It is interesting to note that bond calls in 2000 were again extremely low as interest rates in the high-yield market increased throughout the year and the end-of-year promised yield to maturity on noninvestment grade issues was 14.56%, compared to 11.41% one year earlier. Treasury Bond yields decreased, however, over the same period, from 6.44% to 5.12%. As with actuarial insurance experience calculations, our mortality method measures default experience for major rating categories from the "birth" of the issue and is market value (not issuer) weighted. As such, it clearly adjusts for the aging bias, and the marginal default rate experience can also be analyzed. This becomes particularly relevant as we experience earlier defaulting issues, as we have in 1999 and 2000.

As noted earlier, 2000 defaults were distinctive in their higher than average number and rate, as well as in their relatively early incidence. Indeed, in Figure 12.10 we observe that almost 70% of the defaults took place within three years of issuance. The early default phenomenon manifests clearly in our mortality rate compilations. We observe that the first-, second-, and third-year marginal rates of default for single B securities in the period 1971–2000 were 1.60%, 4.94%, and 5.95%, respectively, compared with 1.58%, 3.92%, and 4.88% for the period 1971–1999 (see Peters and Altman 2000). The same trend is observed in Figure 12.14 for BB defaults (0.96%, 1.65%, and 3.15% versus 0.71%, 0.81%, and 2.65%, measured last year). For BBB defaults, as well, this higher and earlier default trend is clearly observed.

We also note that there is a marked increase in the first three years' marginal and cumulative mortality rates in this current report. The same observations can be made for our mortality loss compilations in Figure 12.15. Again, the higher early mortality loss rates are a function primarily of earlier defaults but are also caused by lower recovery rates.

RETURNS AND RETURN SPREADS

Figures 12.16–19 document total returns and spreads on high-yield bonds versus 10-year US Treasuries for the period 1978–2000, inclusive. Figure 12.16 shows each year's absolute return and return spread, as well as the promised yield to maturity and yield spread at year-end. The high-yield bond market's return spread over US Treasuries was a dismal –20.13% in 2000, bringing the arithmetic average annual spread for the last 23 years to 1.88%, versus 2.88% for data through 1999. The compound average annual spread, assuming reinvestment at the end of each year, is now 1.90% per year, versus 2.96% one year earlier. Hence, the low absolute returns on high-yield

FIGURE 12.16 Annual returns, yields[1] and spreads on ten-year treasury (TREAS) and high-yield (HY) bonds (1978–2000)

	Return (%)			Promised yield (%)		
Year	HY	TREAS	Spread	HY	TREAS	Spread
2000	(5.68)	14.45	(20.13)	14.56	5.12	9.44
1999	1.73	(8.41)	10.14	11.41	6.44	4.97
1998	4.04	12.77	(8.73)	10.04	4.65	5.39
1997	14.27	11.16	3.11	9.20	5.75	3.45
1996	11.24	0.04	11.20	9.58	6.42	3.16
1995	22.40	23.58	(1.18)	9.76	5.58	4.18
1994	(2.55)	(8.29)	5.74	11.50	7.83	3.67
1993	18.33	12.08	6.25	9.08	5.80	3.28
1992	18.29	6.50	11.79	10.44	6.69	3.75
1991	43.23	17.18	26.05	12.56	6.70	5.86
1990	(8.46)	6.88	(15.34)	18.57	8.07	10.50
1989	1.98	16.72	(14.74)	15.17	7.93	7.24
1988	15.25	6.34	8.91	13.70	· 9.15	4.55
1987	4.57	(2.67)	7.24	13.89	8.83	5.06
1986	16.50	24.08	(7.58)	12.67	7.21	5.46
1985	26.08	31.54	(5.46)	13.50	8.99	4.51
1984	8.50	14.82	(6.32)	14.97	11.87	3.10
1983	21.80	2.23	19.57	15.74	10.70	5.04
1982	32.45	42.08	(9.63)	17.84	13.86	3.98
1981	7.56	0.48	7.08	15.97	12.08	3.89
1980	(1.00)	(2.96)	1.96	13.46	10.23	3.23
1979	3.69	(0.86)	4.55	12.07	9.13	2.94
1978	7.57	(1.11)	8.68	10.92	8.11	2.81
Arithmetic annual average:						
1978–2000	11.38	9.51	1.88	12.90	8.14	4.76
Compound annual average:						
1978–2000	10.73	8.83	1.90			

(1) End of year yields.

Source: Salomon Smith Barney Inc.'s High Yield Composite Index

bonds and the significant increase in returns on default risk-free 10-year Treasuries, 14.45%, resulted in the average historical return spread's falling by a full percentage point (100 bps) in one year. Figures 12.17 and 12.18 show these absolute and relative returns and spreads for various starting and ending years over the 1978–2000 period. And, Figure 12.19 indicates that a $1,000 investment in high-yield bonds would have aggregated to more than $10,400 by 2000, compared to $7,000 for 10-year Treasuries.

As noted above, high-yield returns were exceptionally poor in 2000 and the yield spread versus 10-year Treasuries widened by almost 450 bps in just 12 months – from 4.97% to 9.44% (Figure 12.16). This change in spread of

FIGURE 12.17 Compound average annual returns of high-yield bonds (%) (1978–2000)

Base period (Jan. 1)	Terminal Period (December 31)																						
	1978	1979	1980	1981	1982	1983	1984	1985	1986	1987	1988	1989	1990	1991	1992	1993	1994	1995	1996	1997	1998	1999	2000
1978	7.57	5.61	3.36	4.39	9.48	11.45	11.02	12.80	13.21	12.31	12.58	11.65	9.96	12.05	12.46	12.82	11.85	12.41	12.35	12.45	12.03	11.54	10.73
1979		3.69	1.32	3.36	9.97	12.24	11.61	13.57	13.93	12.85	13.09	12.03	10.16	12.41	12.82	13.18	12.12	12.70	12.62	12.71	12.26	11.73	10.88
1980			(1.00)	3.19	12.14	14.48	13.26	15.30	15.47	14.05	14.18	12.90	10.77	13.17	13.55	13.89	12.71	13.29	13.23	13.17	12.73	12.15	11.82
1981				7.56	19.36	20.17	17.14	18.87	18.47	16.38	16.24	14.56	12.02	14.55	14.86	15.12	13.76	14.32	14.12	14.13	13.54	12.89	12.54
1982					32.45	27.01	20.52	21.88	20.79	17.92	17.53	15.47	12.53	15.27	15.54	15.77	14.25	14.81	14.57	14.55	13.91	13.19	12.83
1983						21.80	14.96	18.55	18.04	15.21	15.22	13.23	10.26	13.51	13.98	14.37	12.85	13.56	13.39	13.45	12.84	12.15	11.77
1984							8.50	16.96	16.81	13.62	13.94	11.86	8.70	12.51	13.10	13.73	12.07	12.90	12.77	12.88	12.26	11.57	11.17
1985								26.08	21.20	15.38	15.35	12.54	8.73	13.14	13.65	14.24	12.43	13.31	13.13	13.22	11.56	10.83	10.36
1986									16.50	10.37	11.98	9.39	5.56	11.07	12.07	12.84	11.01	12.10	12.02	12.21	11.56	11.16	10.40
1987										4.57	9.78	7.12	2.99	10.01	11.35	12.32	10.35	11.62	11.59	11.83	11.16	10.40	9.91
1988											15.25	8.41	2.47	11.42	12.76	13.67	11.20	12.54	12.39	12.58	11.78	10.90	10.36
1989												1.98	(3.38)	10.17	12.14	13.35	10.53	12.16	12.04	12.29	11.43	10.51	9.93
1990													(8.46)	14.50	15.75	16.39	12.33	13.95	13.56	13.65	12.54	11.41	10.76
1991														43.23	30.16	26.09	18.23	19.05	17.71	17.21	15.48	13.86	13.13
1992															18.29	18.31	10.90	13.67	13.18	13.36	11.98	10.64	9.84
1993																18.33	7.38	12.17	11.94	12.40	10.96	9.59	8.68
1994																	(2.55)	9.21	9.89	10.97	9.54	8.20	7.15
1995																		22.40	16.69	15.88	12.80	10.49	9.21
1996																			11.24	12.74	9.77	7.70	6.14
1997																				14.27	9.04	6.54	4.49
1998																					4.04	2.88	(0.09)
1999																						1.73	(4.05)
2000																							(5.68)

Source: Salomon Smith Barney Composite Index; Edward I. Altman, New York University Salomon Center

FIGURE 12.18 Compound annual returns spreads between high-yield and LT government bonds (%) (1978–2000)

Base period (Jan. 1)	Terminal Period (December 31)																						
	1978	1979	1980	1981	1982	1983	1984	1985	1986	1987	1988	1989	1990	1991	1992	1993	1994	1995	1996	1997	1998	1999	2000
1978	8.68	6.60	5.01	5.51	3.17	5.82	4.13	3.10	1.99	2.57	3.15	1.64	0.19	1.77	2.43	2.66	2.88	2.67	3.15	3.14	2.57	2.96	1.90
1979		4.55	3.23	4.48	1.71	5.22	3.32	2.23	1.08	1.84	2.55	0.94	(0.57)	1.19	1.95	2.23	2.49	2.29	2.81	2.83	2.24	2.67	1.57
1980			1.96	4.45	0.67	5.39	3.05	1.79	0.51	1.46	2.30	0.54	(1.08)	0.88	1.73	2.04	2.34	2.14	2.70	2.72	2.10	2.56	2.01
1981				7.08	(0.13)	6.74	3.36	1.75	0.22	1.37	2.35	0.36	(1.43)	0.77	1.70	2.05	2.36	2.15	2.75	2.77	2.42	2.60	2.05
1982					(9.63)	6.49	1.93	0.18	(1.39)	0.29	1.59	(0.58)	(2.46)	0.07	1.16	1.58	1.97	1.76	2.44	2.48	1.79	2.33	1.78
1983						19.57	6.62	2.97	0.39	1.94	3.13	0.49	(1.73)	0.96	2.05	2.42	2.75	2.48	3.14	3.13	2.37	2.90	2.23
1984							(6.32)	(5.94)	(6.48)	(2.59)	(0.22)	(2.73)	(4.76)	(1.40)	0.08	0.68	1.23	1.04	1.87	1.96	1.22	1.86	1.18
1985								(5.46)	(6.56)	(1.30)	1.34	(2.00)	(4.50)	(0.69)	0.89	1.47	1.98	1.72	2.55	2.60	1.76	2.40	1.66
1986									(7.58)	0.48	3.28	(1.26)	(4.32)	(0.00)	1.67	2.22	2.68	2.33	3.18	3.17	2.24	2.88	2.00
1987										7.24	8.04	0.61	(3.61)	1.38	3.08	3.51	3.84	3.34	4.16	4.06	2.98	3.61	2.58
1988											8.91	3.00	(7.41)	(0.24)	2.15	2.82	3.31	2.80	3.78	3.71	2.56	3.28	2.23
1989												(14.74)	(15.07)	(3.32)	0.44	1.58	2.38	1.93	3.14	3.14	1.93	2.77	1.64
1990													(15.34)	2.59	5.68	5.82	5.82	4.76	5.73	5.41	3.80	4.52	3.21
1991														26.05	18.45	14.26	11.80	9.40	9.72	8.78	6.51	6.98	5.51
1992															11.79	9.06	7.84	5.83	6.94	6.32	4.14	4.98	3.23
1993																6.25	6.00	3.87	5.76	5.25	2.89	4.05	2.06
1994																	5.74	2.76	5.61	5.01	2.26	3.71	1.29
1995																		(1.18)	5.50	4.69	1.22	3.23	0.78
1996																			11.20	7.29	1.93	4.17	0.51
1997																				3.11	(2.93)	1.83	(2.58)
1998																					(8.73)	1.25	(5.82)
1999																						10.14	(6.43)
2000																							(20.13)

Source: Salomon Smith Barney Composite Index; Edward I. Altman, New York University Salomon Center

FIGURE 12.19   Cumulative value of $1,000 investment (1978–2000).
High-yield bonds vs 10-year US T-bonds

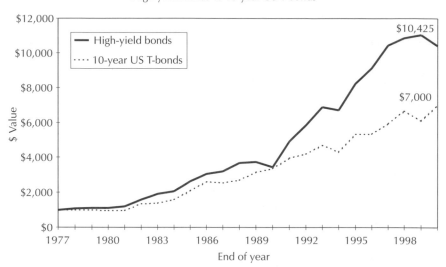

447 bps was the largest increase for any annual period, including the 326 bps increase in 1990. Interest rates on high-yield bonds averaged 18.57% at the end of 1990, however, compared to 14.56% in 2000. Clearly, the market is putting an enormous required risk premium on high-yield bonds today, the primary cause of which is the market's concern about future default rates (see our breakeven discussion below) fueled by the observation of the record level of defaults in 2000, the sizeable increase in the distressed bond population to more than 30% of the high-yield market as of December 31, 2000, and the uncertain state of the economy going forward. All of these things have caused an enormous liquidity and default risk premium imbedded in the required yield.

It should be noted that about 30% (132 bps) of the increase in yield spread in 2000 was owing to the *lowering* of the yield-to-maturity on 10-year US Treasuries as fixed-income investors fled-to-quality throughout the year and the supply/demand equation for long-term government bonds, like 10-year notes, changed dramatically due to the budget surplus and unusually high redemptions.[5] In 1990, by contrast, interest rates on 10-year Treasuries actually increased slightly by 14 bps. That's a swing of 146 bps owing to monetary condition differences from a decade ago. If rates on 10-year Treasuries had not changed in either 1990 or 2000, the spread change would have been +315 bps in 2000 versus +338 bps in 1990.

To reflect on the almost 2% annual return spread advantage, one must assess whether this result is sufficient to compensate for both the higher liquidity risk of high-yield bonds versus Treasuries and the fact that one might not achieve the average absolute return each year (11.38%). Although we see only four instances over the last 23 years of negative returns (see Figure 12.16), it is clear, especially based on 2000 experience, that there is a possibility of unexpected losses, and investors must be compensated for this risk. Unexpected losses can occur in years of unexpected lackluster performance or when a portfolio is not well diversified and results fall short of average market performance.

Publicly regulated and insured financial institutions typically are required to allocate capital against unexpected loss possibilities while prudence guidelines for unregulated investors, such as mutual and pension funds, suggest professional standards for portfolio diversification and liquidity policies. Optimum portfolio analysis has recently become an important effort for the world's commercial banks in their trading and bank-lending books,[6] but little work has been published and tested for other credit asset portfolios, such as corporate bonds. As we noted last year, we expect that greater emphasis will be put on formal portfolio models for bond investors in the coming years.

BREAKEVEN AND RISK PREMIUM ANALYSIS

In a number of earlier papers, we have shown that a relatively simple analysis can be constructed that shows the breakeven yield (BEY) that investors must be promised in order to compensate for actual or expected default and recovery rates.[7] The end result is a comparison between actual yields at a point in time and the breakeven yield. This difference is the yield premium (if any) at any point in time (that is, the amount to compensate investors for risks, other than expected default risk; for example, liquidity, unexpected losses, flights to quality, and so on).

When we calculate the yield premium above the breakeven yield as of December 31, 2000, assuming a range of 4% to 10%, default rates, various recovery rates, a risk-free rate = 5.12%, an average coupon of 10% and an average high yield-to-maturity rate of 14.56% (Figure 12.16), we get the results shown in Figure 12.20.

We observe that if the market requires a risk premium above the breakeven rate of between 2–3%, the implied default rate is between 7.5% and 8.5%, and a recovery rate of 30%. The 2–3% risk premium is selected to conform with historical total return spreads that have been earned by high-yield investors over the last two decades – depending on whether the last year of our time series is 1999 or 2000. This analysis is sufficiently robust to accommodate more optimistic or pessimistic assumptions about expected default or recovery rates. Since we are expecting default rates in

FIGURE 12.20 Breakeven yields and yield premiums for various
assumptions of expected default and recovery rates
(December 31, 2000)

	Breakeven rates	
Expected default rates (%)	Expected recovery rates (%)	
	30	40
4	8.46	8.04
5	9.34	8.81
6	10.23	9.60
7	11.15	10.40
8	12.09	11.22
9	13.04	12.05
10	14.02	12.91

	Yield premiums	
Expected default rates (%)	Expected recovery rates (%)	
	30	40
4	6.10	6.52
5	5.22	5.75
6	4.33	4.96
7	3.41	4.16
8	2.47	3.34
9	1.52	2.51
10	0.54	1.65

Source: Authors' compilation

the next year or two to be in the 6.5–7.0% range, and a 30% recovery seems
reasonable to us, the current yield premium seemed quite attractive relative
to historic return spread performance. For example, a 7.0% default rate and
a 30% recovery rate estimate results in a yield premium of 3.41%. Note that
the yield premium jumps to 4.16% if we assume a 40% recovery rate.

DEFAULT FORECAST FOR 2001

Forecasting defaults is always a tricky exercise, but one that is necessary in
order to understand the dynamics of a risky security market, such as high-
yield bonds. One might try to forecast micro- and macroeconomic variables,[8]
as well as the term structure of default rates, or simply examine the historical
experience that we can observe and therefore feel more confident about. We
essentially embrace the latter methodology in our attempt to forecast default

levels and rates. We also consider the size of the distressed bond market. Figure 12.21 shows the size of the distressed and defaulted bond market as a percentage of the high-yield bond market from 1990–2000. We define distressed bonds, as we have since 1990, as those whose yield-to-maturity exceeds the 10-year Treasury Note by 10% (1,000 bps). As shown earlier in Figure 12.16, the spread for the entire market widened dramatically in 2000 to 944 bps and the proportion greater than 1000 bps had grown to about 31% at the end of 2000. The proportion of distressed debt was just 9% one year earlier and 17% by mid-year. If US Treasuries had not *fallen* by 1.32% in 2000, the proportion of bonds with at least a 1000 bps spread would still have been very large, 27%, and comparable to the level in 1990.

To provide our forecast of default rates, we observe the amount of new issuance by initial bond rating over the last 10 years and apply these amounts to the marginal mortality rates from Figure 12.14. We then consider the current market's distressed proportion (27–31%) and conclude that something like half of that cohort will default over the next two years. Combining these two methods results in a forecast of a 6.5–7.0% default rate in 2001.[9] This will add a considerable amount of debt to the defaulted debt segment, perhaps $42–45 billion – at least $12 billion more than in 2000. We expect that the size of the high-yield bond market will swell by mid-2001 to perhaps $650 billion as we add the huge amount of new fallen angels to our base, plus new issuance that picked up in early January 2001. Estimates are that as much as $70 billion of these bonds were downgraded to

FIGURE 12.21 Distressed* and defaulted debt as a percentage of total high-yield debt market

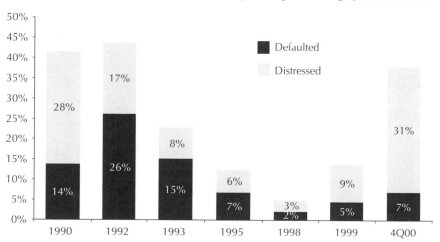

* Defined as yield-to-maturity spread greater than or equal to 1,000 bps over comparable treasuries.

Source: Salomon Smith Barney and NYU Salomon Center

non-investment-grade status, most in the second half of 2000. Of course, a great deal will depend upon the level of the economy and whether the nation enters a recession or not. A few very large defaults would swell our default numbers as well. For example, defaults by Finova, Southern California Edison, and Pacific G&E could increase our statistics considerably.[10]

SIZE OF THE DEFAULTED AND DISTRESSED DEBT MARKET

The current size of the defaulted and distressed debt markets is the largest we have ever recorded. Our estimate, shown in Figures 12.22 and 12.23, is that public defaulted bonds are about $47 billion face value and public distressed debt about $186 billion (assuming a 30% proportion on a $615 billion high-yield bond market). We have revised our private to public debt ratio down from 2:1 to 1.8 due to more recent observations of defaulted company balance sheets. Still, the enormous increase in defaulted and distressed bonds result in an estimate of more than $650 billion (face value) of public and private, defaulted, and distressed debt. Our market value estimates are also extremely high although we reduced our estimates of the market to face value ratio to 25% (public defaults), 50% (public distressed),

FIGURE 12.22 Estimated face and market values of defaulted and distressed debt (December 31, 2000) ($ billions)

Public debt	Face value ($)	Market value ($)
Defaulted[1]	47.0	11.8 (0.25 × FV)
Distressed[2]	186.0	93.0 (0.50 × FV)
Total public	233.0	104.8
Private debt[3]		
Defaulted	84.6	50.8 (0.60 × FV)
Distressed	334.8	251.1 (0.75 × FV)
Total private	419.4	301.9
Total public and private	**652.4**	**406.7**

Notes

(1) Updated from 1998 and includes $23.5 billion of defaults in 1999 and $30.2 billion of defaults in 2000. The total is also adjusted for bonds that have emerged from Chapter 11 bankruptcies in 2000.

(2) Distressed debt is defined as YTM >10% (1,000 bps) above the Treasury 10-year bond rate. This amount is estimated to be 31% of the high-yield bond market ($600 billion).

(3) Assumes 1.8 to 1.0 ratio of private to public debt. Based on recent sample of defaulting company balance sheets in 1997–1999 and several prior similar studies by the author.

Sources: Estimated by Professor Edward Altman, NYU Stern School of Business from Salomon Smith Barney's High Yield Bond DataBase, NYU Salomon Center Defaulted Bond DataBase, New Generation Research Corporation

FIGURE 12.23 Size of defaulted and distressed debt market now exceeds record levels of early 1990s

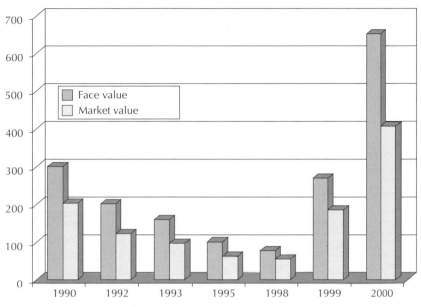

Source: E. Altman, NYU Salomon Center

60% (private defaults), and 75% (private distressed). All together, we estimate about a $400 billion (market value) defaulted and distressed debt market. Note that the 2000 estimates are more than double the amounts, for both face and market values, of the previous highest year (1990).

HIGH-YIELD MARKET RETURNS

Estimates of returns for 2001 were also very difficult due to the many factors that could trigger a substantial turnaround or a continuation of the recent past downward spiral. Looking dispassionately at the aforementioned breakeven analysis (Figure 12.20) and the historical co-movement of default rates and total annual returns (Figure 12.24), we actually were quite optimistic about returns in 2001, as long as default rates do not exceed 8% this year. At 8% and a recovery rate of 30%, the yield-to-maturity of 14.56 (and the yield-to-worst of 13.75%) as of December 31, 2000 provided a substantial cushion over the breakeven rate. This "cushion," at 2.47%, compares quite closely with actual historical return spreads that investors have apparently been content with in the past. Since we are actually predicting lower default rates than 8%, the outlook is even more positive.

FIGURE 12.24   High-yield bond market default rates versus returns

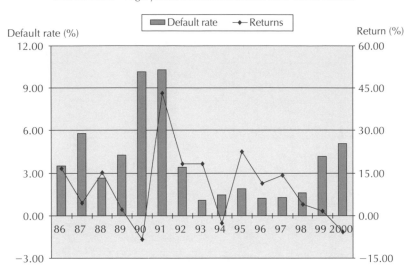

Source: E. Altman, NYU Salomon Center

The average high-yield bond market's yield spread tightened considerably in the first two weeks of January 2001, by about 60 bps, as returns moved positively for the first time in a long time. We are quite sanguine about the possibility of another reversal as new bad news may manifest about defaults in general, or high-profile names becoming distressed or actually failing, or if the economy falters more than expected. If we look at the historical relationship (shown in Figure 12.24), we could very well see a reversal similar to, although not as spectacular as, 1991, albeit with more volatility as the market has changed since the early 1990s. The question, of course, is when the reversal or turnaround will take place on a fairly consistent basis.

NOTES

[1] We do not include emerging market defaults in these calculations. All defaults were in the United States, Canada, Australia, or offshore US dollar-denominated issues from domestic companies. European company defaults, denominated in non-USD currencies totaling 738 million Euros are not included. If they were included, as well as the Euro-high-yield population of over $30 billion, the default rate would be 4.93% (see Newman and Crawley (2001) and Schroder Salomon Smith Barney (2001)). In addition, consistent with our past approach, we do not include those issues that missed interest payments in 2000 but cured their delinquencies within the typical 30-day grace period and we indicate (Appendix 12.1) those that missed their payment in December.

[2] There are other differences in the two calculations, for example, we do not include cured defaults, and their rated population is somewhat different, but these are minor compared to the emerging market bias.

[3] Grossman and Verde 1999, FITCH/IBCA.

[4] The CCC default rate is based on a very low new issuance of $1.35 billion. The default amounts and rates are adjusted slightly for the fact that we could not locate an original issue rating on a small number of defaults.

[5] There are some observers who now question the usefulness of 10-year Notes as a benchmark for the default risk-free market owing to this supply versus demand imbalance. We prefer to retain the same historical data series but need to point out the costs of doing so.

[6] See Saunders (1999); and Caouette, Altman, and Narayanan (1998).

[7] This formula is as follows: $BEY = \dfrac{R_f + D_f(1 - \text{Re } c) + (D_f xHYC/2)}{1 - D_f}$. See Altman and Bencivenga (1995) and *the Financial Analysts Journal*, September/October 1995.

[8] This is essentially Moody's (1999) approach. The resulting expected default rate on all of their rated debt was 9.5% by the end of 2001 (revised up from 9.1% on January 25, 2001 from their year-end forecast).

[9] This is an increase of 1% over our mid-year 2000 forecast, mainly owing to the increase in the size of the distressed market and the sudden vulnerability of heretofore investment-grade public utilities and financial companies that have become fragile fallen angels.

[10] Indeed, Southern California Edison announced in mid-January that it had defaulted on its $32 billion line of Commercial Paper. If the bonds of these California electric and gas utilities default, they may add to our default totals. But, in reality, no high-yield bond dedicated portfolios actually have invested in these bonds since they were downgraded only in early 2001. Indeed, Pacific G&E and Southern California Edison were AA- and A-rated as late as the end of 2000. Hence, these bonds do not appear in our high-yield population at the end of the year and cannot be part of any first quarter 2001 default rate.

APPENDIX 12.1
Defaulted corporate straight debt (2000)
(By date of default)

Company	Bond issue	Coupon (%)	Maturity date	Outstanding amount ($ mm)	Default date
Altiva Financial Corporation	Subordinated Notes	12.500	12/1/02	31.0	1/1/00
Imperial Home Decor Group	Guaranteed Senior Subordinated Notes	11.000	3/15/08	125.0	1/5/00
PennCorp Financial Group, Inc.	Senior Subordinated Notes	9.250	12/15/03	150.0	1/10/00
Safety Components International, Inc.	Senior Subordinated Notes	10.125	7/15/07	90.0	1/15/00
Ameriserve – Ameriserve Foods, Inc.	Guaranteed Senior Notes	8.875	10/15/06	350.0	1/31/00
Ameriserve – Ameriserve Foods, Inc.	Guaranteed Senior Subordinated Notes	10.125	7/15/07	500.0	1/31/00
Ameriserve – Ameriserve Financial (n)	Senior Secured Notes – Euro-Dollar	12.000	9/15/06	205.0	1/31/00
Ameriserve – Nebco Evans Holding Co. (a)	Senior Discount Notes	12.375	7/15/07	74.5	1/31/00
Phase Metrics, Inc.	Senior Notes	10.750	2/1/05	110.0	2/1/00
Paging Network, Inc.	Senior Subordinated Notes	8.875	2/1/06	300.0	2/1/00
Paging Network, Inc.	Senior Subordinated Notes	10.000	10/15/08	500.0	2/1/00
Paging Network, Inc.	Senior Subordinated Notes	10.125	8/1/07	400.0	2/1/00
Pen-Tab Industries, Inc.	Senior Subordinated Notes	10.875	2/1/07	75.0	2/1/00
Canadian Airlines (b)	Senior Notes	10.000	5/1/05	175.0	2/1/00
Canadian Airlines	Senior Notes	12.250	8/1/06	100.0	2/1/00
CellNet Data Systems (c)	Senior Discount Notes	0.000	6/15/05	223.3	2/4/00
CellNet Data Systems (d)	Senior Discount Notes	0.000	10/1/07	452.6	2/4/00
Paracelsus Healthcare Corp.	Senior Subordinated Notes	10.000	8/15/06	325.0	2/15/00
Prime Succession, Inc.	Senior Subordinated Notes	10.750	8/15/04	100.0	2/15/00
Eagle Food Center, Inc.	Senior Notes	8.625	4/15/00	100.0	2/29/00
Superior National Insurance	Guaranteed Senior Notes	10.750	12/1/17	105.0	3/8/00
United Homes, Inc.	Debentures	11.000	3/15/05	6.8	3/9/00
LaRoche Industries, Inc.	Senior Subordinated Notes	9.500	9/15/07	175.0	3/15/00
Crown Vantage, Inc.	Senior Subordinated Notes	11.000	9/1/05	250.0	3/15/00
Crown Vantage, Inc.	Senior PIK Notes	11.450	12/31/07	110.1	3/15/00

APPENDIX 12.1 *(cont.)*

Company	Bond issue	Coupon (%)	Maturity date	Outstanding amount ($ mm)	Default date
President Casinos	Guaranteed Senior Notes	13.000	9/15/01	75.0	3/15/00
President Casinos	Senior Secured Notes	12.000	9/15/01	25.0	3/15/00
Key Plastics, Inc.	Guaranteed Senior Subordinated Notes	10.250	3/15/07	125.0	3/23/00
ContiFinancial Corp.	Senior Notes	7.500	3/15/02	200.0	3/30/00
ContiFinancial Corp.	Senior Notes	8.125	4/1/08	200.0	3/30/00
ContiFinancial Corp.	Senior Notes	8.375	8/15/03	300.0	3/30/00
Genesis Health (e)	Senior Subordinated Notes	9.250	10/1/06	125.0	4/1/00
Genesis Health	Senior Subordinated Notes	9.750	6/15/05	120.0	4/1/00
Genesis Health	Senior Subordinated Notes	9.875	1/15/09	125.0	4/1/00
Genesis Health	First Mortgage Bonds	9.250	9/1/07	25.0	4/1/00
Genesis Health – Multicare Co.	Senior Subordinated Notes	9.000	8/1/07	250.0	4/1/00
CHS Electronics, Inc.	Guaranteed Senior Notes	9.875	4/15/05	200.0	4/4/00
Vista Eyecare, Inc.	Senior Notes	12.750	10/15/05	125.0	4/5/00
Dimac Direct, Inc. – Dimac Holdings Corp.	Senior Subordinated Notes	12.500	10/1/08	100.0	4/6/00
Medical Resources, Inc. (s)	Senior Notes	7.770	2/20/05	75.0	4/7/00
Uniforet, Inc. (b)	Senior Secured Notes	11.125	10/15/06	125.0	4/10/00
Hedstrom Holdings, Inc.	Guaranteed Senior Subordinated Notes	10.000	6/1/07	110.0	4/11/00
Hedstrom Holdings, Inc. (f)	Senior Discount Notes	0.000	6/1/09	36.5	4/11/00
Silver Cinemas International, Inc.	Senior Subordinated Notes	10.500	4/15/05	99.6	4/15/00
Employee Solutions	Guaranteed Senior Notes	10.000	10/15/04	85.0	4/15/00
Glenoit Corp.	Guaranteed Senior Subordinated Notes	11.000	4/15/07	100.0	4/15/00
United Artists Theatre (k)	Senior Subordinated Notes	10.415	10/15/07	50.0	4/15/00
United Artists Theatre	Senior Subordinated Notes	9.750	4/15/08	225.0	4/15/00
United Artists Theatre	Pass Thru Certs	9.300	7/1/15	107.7	4/15/00
Clark Material Handling Co.	Guaranteed Senior Notes	10.750	11/15/06	150.0	4/17/00
Zeta Consumer Products	Senior Notes	11.250	11/30/07	85.0	4/25/00
Kitty Hawk, Inc.	Senior Secured Notes	9.950	11/15/04	340.0	5/1/00

APPENDIX 12.1 (*cont.*)

Company	Bond issue	Coupon (%)	Maturity date	Outstanding amount ($ mm)	Default date
Pathmark Stores	Senior Subordinated Notes	9.625	5/1/03	438.8	5/1/00
Pathmark Stores	Junior Subordinated Notes	10.750	11/1/03	225.3	5/1/00
Packaging Resources	Senior Secured Notes	11.625	5/1/03	110.0	5/1/00
Stellex Technologies, Inc.	Senior Subordinated Notes	9.500	11/1/07	100.0	5/1/00
Cambridge Industries, Inc.	Senior Subordinated Notes	10.250	7/15/07	100.0	5/10/00
American Eco Corp.	Guaranteed Senior Notes	9.625	5/15/08	120.0	5/15/00
Sunterra Corp.	Senior Notes	9.250	5/15/06	140.0	5/16/00
Sunterra Corp.	Senior Subordinated Notes	9.750	10/1/07	200.0	5/16/00
GST Telecommunications, Inc. (g)	Senior Discount Notes	0.000	5/1/08	370.4	5/17/00
GST Telecommunications, Inc. (h)	Senior Subordinated Accrual Notes	12.750	11/15/07	165.3	5/17/00
GST Telecommunications, Inc.	Senior Secured Notes	13.250	5/1/07	265.0	5/17/00
GST Telecommunications, Inc. (i)	Senior Discount Notes	0.000	12/15/05	289.8	5/17/00
Morris Material Handling, Inc.	Guaranteed Senior Notes	9.500	4/1/08	200.0	5/17/00
Laidlaw, Inc. (b)	Debentures	6.500	5/1/05	200.0	5/18/00
Laidlaw, Inc.	Debentures	6.650	10/1/04	225.0	5/18/00
Laidlaw, Inc.	Debentures	6.700	5/1/08	100.0	5/18/00
Laidlaw, Inc.	Debentures	6.720	10/1/27	200.0	5/18/00
Laidlaw, Inc.	Notes	7.050	5/15/03	100.0	5/18/00
Laidlaw, Inc.	Notes	7.650	5/15/06	400.0	5/18/00
Laidlaw, Inc.	Debentures	7.700	8/15/02	200.0	5/18/00
Laidlaw, Inc.	Debentures	7.875	4/15/05	150.0	5/18/00
Laidlaw, Inc.	Debentures	8.250	5/15/23	100.0	5/18/00
Laidlaw, Inc.	Debentures	8.750	4/15/25	150.0	5/18/00
Laidlaw, Inc. (j)	Debentures – CAD	8.500	12/16/02	66.7	5/18/00
Laidlaw, Inc. (j)	Debentures – CAD	10.950	4/16/01	83.4	5/18/00
Safety-Kleen Corp.	Guaranteed Senior Notes	9.250	6/1/08	325.0	5/18/00
Safety-Kleen Corp.	Guaranteed Senior Notes	9.250	5/15/09	225.0	5/18/00

APPENDIX 12.1 (cont.)

Company	Bond issue	Coupon (%)	Maturity date	Outstanding amount ($ mm)	Default date
American Architectural Products Corp.	Senior Notes	11.750	12/1/07	125.0	6/1/00
Fine Air Services, Inc.	Guaranteed Senior Notes	9.875	6/1/08	200.0	6/1/00
Master Graphics – Premier Graphics, Inc.	Guaranteed Senior Notes	11.500	12/1/05	130.0	6/1/00
Mediq, Inc.	Senior Subordinated Notes	11.000	6/1/08	190.0	6/1/00
Mediq, Inc. (m)	Senior Discount Notes	0.000	6/1/09	87.0	6/1/00
Stage Stores – Specialty Retailers, Inc.	Guaranteed Senior Notes	8.500	7/15/05	200.0	6/1/00
Stage Stores – Specialty Retailers, Inc.	Guaranteed Senior Subordinated Notes	9.000	7/15/07	100.0	6/1/00
Stage Stores – 3 Bealls Holding Corp.	Notes	12.000	12/31/02	6.0	6/1/00
Iowa Select Farms	Senior Subordinated Notes	10.750	12/1/05	130.0	6/1/00
Cuddy Int'l Corp.	Senior Notes	10.750	12/1/07	75.0	6/1/00
Gothic Energy Corp. (l)	Senior Discount Notes	0.000	5/1/06	80.4	6/5/00
Safelite Glass Corp.	Senior Subordinated Notes, Ser. B	9.875	12/15/06	100.0	6/9/00
Safelite Glass Corp.	Senior Subordinated Notes, Ser. D	9.875	12/15/06	55.0	6/9/00
Pathmark Stores	Subordinated Notes	11.625	6/15/02	199.0	6/15/00
Pathmark Stores	Subordinated Notes	12.625	6/15/02	95.8	6/15/00
Bulong Operations (b)	Senior Secured Notes	12.500	12/15/08	185.0	6/15/00
Flooring America, Inc.	Senior Notes	9.250	10/15/07	71.0	6/16/00
All Star Gas Corp.	Debentures	9.000	12/31/07	9.7	6/30/00
Waxman Industries, Inc.	Senior Notes	12.750	6/1/04	92.8	7/10/00
Waxman USA, Inc.	Senior Notes	11.125	9/1/01	35.9	7/10/00
Reliant Building Products, Inc.	Senior Subordinated Notes	10.875	11/1/02	25.0	7/11/00
GNI Group, Inc.	Senior Unsecured Notes	10.875	7/15/05	75.0	7/15/00
All Star Gas Corp. – Empire Gas Corp.	Senior Secured Notes	12.875	7/15/04	127.2	7/15/00
Carmike Cinemas, Inc.	Senior Subordinated Notes	9.375	2/1/09	198.0	8/1/00
Heilig-Meyers Co. – MacSaver Fin'l	Unsecured Notes	7.400	2/15/02	100.0	8/1/00
Heilig-Meyers Co. – MacSaver Fin'l	Unsecured Notes	7.600	8/1/07	175.0	8/1/00
Heilig-Meyers Co. – MacSaver Fin'l	Unsecured Notes	7.875	8/1/03	200.0	8/1/00

APPENDIX 12.1 *(cont.)*

Company	Bond issue	Coupon (%)	Maturity date	Outstanding amount ($ mm)	Default date
Tokheim Corp. (n)	Senior Subordinated Notes	11.375	8/1/08	8.3	8/1/00
Tokheim Corp.	Guaranteed Senior Subordinated Notes	11.375	8/1/08	114.7	8/1/00
Globe Manufacturing Corp.	Guaranteed Senior Subordinated Notes	10.000	8/1/08	150.0	8/1/00
Globe Manufacturing Corp. – Globe Hldgs (o)	Senior Discount Notes	0.000	8/1/09	34.4	8/1/00
Anacomp, Inc.	Senior Subordinated Notes, Ser. D	10.875	4/1/04	135.0	8/3/00
Anacomp, Inc.	Senior Subordinated Notes, Ser. B	10.875	4/1/04	200.0	8/3/00
Coram Healthcare Corp. (s)	Subordinated Notes	11.500	5/15/01	168.4	8/8/00
Anchor Advanced Products, Inc.	Senior Notes	11.750	4/1/04	50.0	8/8/00
Orbcomm Global LP	Senior Notes	14.000	8/15/04	170.0	8/15/00
Central European Media Enterprises, Ltd (q)	Senior Notes	8.125	8/15/04	65.4	8/15/00
Central European Media Enterprises, Ltd	Senior Notes	9.375	8/15/04	100.0	8/15/00
Styling Technology Corp.	Guaranteed Senior Subordinated Notes	10.875	7/1/08	100.0	8/31/00
Plainwell, Inc.	Senior Subordinated Notes; Ser. B	11.000	3/1/08	130.0	9/1/00
Amer Reefer Company, Ltd	1st Mortgage Notes	10.250	3/1/08	100.0	9/1/00
AMF Bowling Worldwide	Guaranteed Senior Subordinated Notes	10.875	3/15/06	250.0	9/15/00
AMF Bowling Worldwide (p)	Senior Discount Notes	0.000	3/15/06	333.0	9/15/00
Resort at Summerlin	Senior Subordinated Notes	13.000	12/15/07	120.2	9/15/00
SFAC New Holdings (t)	Senior Secured Discount Notes	0.000	6/15/09	336.0	9/18/00
SFAC New Holdings	Senior Notes	11.250	8/15/01	170.8	9/18/00
SFAC New Holdings	Senior Subordinated Notes	13.250	8/15/03	201.0	9/18/00
Dyersburg Corp.	Guaranteed Senior Subordinated Notes	9.750	9/1/07	125.0	9/25/00
Galaxy Telecom L.P.	Senior Subordinated Notes	12.375	10/1/05	120.0	9/28/00
Kasper ASL, Ltd	Senior Notes	13.000	3/31/04	110.0	9/30/00
Owens-Corning – Fiberglass (u)	Debentures	5.375	11/26/00	7.1	10/5/00
Owens Corning	Notes	7.000	3/15/09	250.0	10/5/00
Owens-Corning – Fiberglass (v)	Debentures	7.250	12/2/00	57.8	10/5/00
Owens Corning	Notes	7.500	5/1/05	300.0	10/5/00

APPENDIX 12.1 (*cont.*)

Company	Bond issue	Coupon (%)	Maturity date	Outstanding amount ($ mm)	Default date
Owens Corning	Bonds	7.500	8/1/18	400.0	10/5/00
Owens Corning	Notes	7.700	5/1/08	250.0	10/5/00
Owens-Corning – Fiberglass	Debentures	8.875	6/1/02	40.0	10/5/00
Owens-Corning – Fiberglass	Debentures	9.375	6/1/12	7.0	10/5/00
Owens-Corning – Fiberglass	Bonds	9.900	5/15/15	69.2	10/5/00
OC Funding BV	Guaranteed Subordinated Notes	10.000	6/1/01	42.4	10/5/00
Drypers Corp.	Senior Notes	10.250	6/15/07	145.0	10/10/00
Indesco International, Inc.	Senior Subordinated Notes	9.750	4/15/08	145.0	10/15/00
Compass Aerospace Corp.	Guaranteed Subordinated Notes; Ser. D	10.125	4/15/05	19.0	10/15/00
Compass Aerospace Corp.	Guaranteed Subordinated Notes; Ser. B	10.125	4/15/05	110.0	10/15/00
Talon Automotive Group, Inc.	Senior Subordinated Notes	9.675	5/1/08	120.0	11/1/00
Decora Industries, Inc.	Senior Secured Notes	11.000	5/1/05	112.8	11/1/00
Colorado Prime Corp.	Senior Notes	12.500	5/1/04	100.0	11/1/00
Global Health Sciences	Senior Notes	11.000	5/1/08	225.0	11/1/00
ICG Communications Corp. – ICG Holdings, Inc.	Senior Discount Notes	13.500	9/15/05	584.3	11/14/00
ICG Communications Corp. – ICG Holdings, Inc. (w)	Senior Discount Notes	0.000	5/1/06	521.6	11/14/00
ICG Communications Corp. – ICG Holdings, Inc. (x)	Senior Discount Notes	0.000	3/15/07	151.7	11/14/00
ICG Communications Corp. – ICG Services, Inc. (y)	Senior Discount Notes	0.000	2/15/08	394.0	11/14/00
ICG Communications Corp. – ICG Services, Inc. (z)	Senior Discount Notes	0.000	5/1/08	320.0	11/14/00
Pillowtex Corp.	Guaranteed Senior Subordinated Notes	10.000	11/15/06	125.0	11/14/00
Pillowtex Corp.	Guaranteed Senior Subordinated Notes	9.000	12/15/07	185.0	11/14/00
Sunbeam Corporation	Senior Discount Notes	0.000	5/15/01	3.2	11/15/00
Park 'N' View, Inc.	Senior Notes	13.000	5/15/08	75.0	11/15/00
Reliance Group Holdings, Inc.	Senior Notes	9.000	11/15/49	291.0	11/15/00
Reliance Group Holdings, Inc.	Senior Subordinated Debentures	9.750	11/15/03	174.0	11/15/00
Lodestar Holdings, Inc.	Senior Notes	11.500	5/15/05	150.0	11/15/00
Wheeling-Pittsburgh Corp.	Senior Notes	9.250	11/15/07	274.5	11/16/00

APPENDIX 12.1 (cont.)

Company	Bond issue	Coupon (%)	Maturity date	Outstanding amount ($ mm)	Default date
Wheeling-Pittsburgh Corp.	Senior Notes	10.500	4/15/05	302.0	11/16/00
Metal Management, Inc.	Senior Secured Notes	12.750	6/15/04	30.0	11/20/00
Metal Management, Inc.	Guaranteed Senior Subordinated Notes	10.000	5/15/08	180.0	11/20/00
Big V Supermarkets	Senior Subordinated Notes	11.000	2/15/04	80.0	11/22/00
Lernout & Hauspie Speech Products N.V.	Guaranteed Senior Subordinated Notes	11.750	8/1/05	200.0	11/29/00
Regal Cinemas, Inc.*	Senior Subordinated Notes	9.500	6/1/08	600.0	12/1/00
Gorges/Quick-to-Fix Foods, Inc.	Senior Subordinated Notes	11.500	12/1/06	52.0	12/4/00
RBX Corp.	Senior Secured Notes	12.000	1/15/03	100.0	12/7/00
RBX Corp.	Guaranteed Senior Subordinated Notes	11.250	10/15/05	100.0	12/7/00
Regal Cinemas, Inc.*	Senior Subordinated Notes	8.875	12/15/10	200.0	12/15/00
Imperial Sugar Co.*	Guaranteed Senior Subordinated Notes	9.750	12/15/07	250.0	12/15/00
Quentra Networks – Diane Corp.	Debentures	11.250	1/1/02	1.3	12/15/00
Pioneer Americas Acquisition Corp.*	Senior Secured Notes	9.250	6/15/07	200.0	12/15/00
Worldtex, Inc.*	Senior Notes	9.625	12/15/07	175.0	12/15/00
Global Telesystems, Inc.*	Senior Notes	10.875	6/15/08	150.0	12/15/00
Global Telesystems, Inc.* (aa)	Senior Notes	11.000	6/15/08	68.6	12/15/00
Northwestern Steel & Wire Company	Senior Notes	9.500	6/15/01	115.0	12/15/00
Outboard Marine Corp.	Medium Term Notes	8.675	3/15/01	5.0	12/22/00
Outboard Marine Corp.	Guaranteed Senior Notes	10.750	6/1/08	160.0	12/22/00
Outboard Marine Corp.	Debentures	9.125	4/15/17	57.6	12/22/00
REV Holdings, Inc.	Senior Discount Notes	0.000	3/15/01	770.0	12/25/00
LTV Corp.	Guaranteed Senior Notes	8.200	9/15/07	300.0	12/29/00
LTV Corp.	Guaranteed Senior Subordinated Notes	11.750	11/15/09	275.0	12/29/00
			Total	30,247.8	

Notes

Armstrong World defaulted on $50 million in commercial paper on 11/23/00. This triggered a cross-default with $450 million credit facility. Armstrong is not included in 2000 calculations because the company was still rated "investment grade" as of 9/30/00. As of 11/23/00, the company had $832.185 million in bonds outstanding.

(*) Coupon payment is under grace period.

(a) Zero coupon until 7/02, 12.375% thereafter. Face value $100.4 million. Accreted value at default $74.5 million. Subsidiary of Ameriserve Foods

(b) Yankee Bond.

(c) Zero coupon until 6/15/00. 13% thereafter. Face value $235 million. Accreted value at default approximately $223.3 million.

(d) Zero coupon until 10/02. 14% thereafter. Face value $654.1 million. Accreted value at default $452.6 million.

(e) Forebearance granted until 6/30/00.

(f) Zero coupon until 6/02, 12% thereafter. Face value $44.612 million. Accreted value at default approximately $36.5 million.

(g) Zero coupon until 5/03, 10.5% thereafter Face value $500 million. Accreted value at default $370.4 million.

(h) Outstanding amount includes $40.286 million accrued interest not paid-out in cash. Par value $125 million.

(i) Zero coupon until 12/00, 13.875% thereafter. Face value $312.448 million. Accreted value at default $289.8 million.

(j) Securities are denominated in Canadian Dollars. Outstanding amounts are CAD$100 million and CAD$125 million, respectively. USD amount is based on 5/18 CAD spot rate of 1.499.

(k) Coupon rate is based on three-month LIBOR + 437.5 bps. The business day following default, the coupon reset to 10.65625%.

(l) Zero coupon until 5/02, 14.125% thereafter. Face value $104 million. Accreted value at default $80.423.

(m) Zero coupon until 6/03, 13% thereafter. Face value $140.885 million. Accreted value at default $87.027.

(n) Euro-Dollar market issue.

(o) Zero coupon until 8/03, 14% thereafter. Face value $49.086 million. Accreted value at default approximately $34.424 million.

(p) Zero coupon until 3/01, 12.25% thereafter. Face value $451.5 million. Accreted value at default $333 million.

(q) Securities are denominated in Deutsche Marks. Outstanding amount is DEM140 million. USD amount is based on 8/15 spot rate of 2.1408.

(s) Private placement.

(t) Zero coupon until 6/04, 13% thereafter. Face value $569.636 million. Accreted value at default approximately $336.045 million.

(u) Securities are denominated in Swiss Francs. Outstanding amount is CHF12.52 million. USD amount is based on 10/05 spot rate of 1.7522.

(v) Securities are denominated in Deutsche Marks. Outstanding amount is DEM130 million. USD amount is based on 10/05 spot rate of 2.2501.

(w) Zero coupon until 5/01, 12.5% thereafter. Face value $550.300 million. Accreted value at default $521.611 million.

(x) Zero coupon until 3/02, 11.675 thereafter. Face value $176 million. Accreted value at default $151.724 million.

(y) Zero coupon until 2/03, 10% thereafter. Face value 490 million. Accreted value at default $393.970 million.

(z) Zero coupon until 5/03, 9.875% thereafter. Face value $405.250 million. Accreted value at default $320.040 million.

(aa) Securities are denominated in Deutsche Marks. Outstanding amount is DEM150 million. USD amount is based on 12/15 spot rate of 2.1858.

APPENDIX 12.2a

Quarterly default rate comparison:
Altman/SBC versus Moody's high-yield debt market (1990–2000)

Quarter		Par value debt outstanding ($ billions)	Debt defaulted by quarter ($ billions)	Quarterly default rates (%)	Altman/SBC 12M moving average	Moody's 12M moving average
1990	1Q	$185.00	$4.16	2.25%		
	2Q	$185.00	2.51	1.36%		
	3Q	$181.00	6.01	3.32%		
	4Q	$181.00	<u>5.67</u>	3.13%	10.06%	8.83%
			18.35			
1991	1Q	$182.00	$8.74	4.80%	12.61%	10.62%
	2Q	$182.00	2.75	1.51%	12.77%	11.57%
	3Q	$183.00	5.01	2.74%	12.18%	10.58%
	4Q	$183.00	<u>2.36</u>	1.29%	10.34%	9.65%
			$18.86			
1992	1Q	$183.20	$3.33	1.82%	7.35%	7.17%
	2Q	151.10	1.26	0.83%	6.67%	5.55%
	3Q	163.00	0.37	0.23%	4.16%	4.69%
	4Q	151.89	<u>0.59</u>	0.39%	3.26%	3.94%
			$5.55			
1993	1Q	$193.23	$0.38	0.20%	1.65%	3.78%
	2Q	193.23	1.33	0.69%	1.50%	3.23%
	3Q	206.91	0.05	0.03%	1.30%	3.08%
	4Q	190.42	<u>0.52</u>	0.27%	1.19%	3.06%
			$2.29			
1994	1Q	$232.60	$0.67	0.29%	1.28%	2.49%
	2Q	230.00	0.16	0.07%	0.65%	1.44%
	3Q	235.00	0.41	0.17%	0.80%	2.18%
	4Q	235.00	<u>2.18</u>	0.93%	1.46%	1.93%
			$3.42			
1995	1Q	$240.00	$0.17	0.07%	1.24%	1.20%
	2Q	240.00	1.68	0.70%	1.88%	2.17%
	3Q	240.00	0.98	0.41%	2.11%	2.41%
	4Q	240.00	<u>1.72</u>	0.72%	1.90%	3.30%
			$4.55			
1996	1Q	$255.00	$0.44	0.17%	2.00%	3.48%
	2Q	$255.00	$0.89	0.35%	1.64%	2.86%
	3Q	$271.00	$0.41	0.15%	1.39%	2.19%
	4Q	$271.00	<u>$1.59</u>	0.59%	1.26%	1.66%
			$3.34			
1997	1Q	$296.00	$1.85	0.63%	1.71%	1.60%
	2Q	$318.40	$0.60	0.19%	1.55%	1.61%
	3Q	$335.40	$1.48	0.44%	1.84%	2.27%
	4Q	$335.40	<u>$0.27</u>	0.08%	1.34%	2.03%
			$4.20			

APPENDIX 12.2a *(cont.)*

Quarter		Par value debt outstanding ($ billions)	Debt defaulted by quarter ($ billions)	Quarterly default rates (%)	Altman/SBC 12M moving average	Moody's 12M moving average
1998	1Q	$379.00	$2.37	0.63%	1.34%	2.38%
	2Q	$425.70	$1.22	0.29%	1.43%	3.01%
	3Q	$465.50	$1.62	0.35%	1.34%	2.73%
	4Q	$481.60	$2.26	0.47%	1.73%	3.46%
			$7.46			
1999	1Q	$515.00	$4.76	0.92%	2.03%	3.89%
	2Q	$537.20	$8.42	1.57%	3.31%	4.74%
	3Q	$567.40	$5.24	0.92%	3.88%	5.89%
	4Q	$580.00	$5.11	0.88%	4.30%	5.51%
			$23.53			
2000	1Q	$584.00	$5.96	1.02%	4.39%	5.64%
	2Q	$595.60	$9.95	1.67%	4.50%	5.43%
	3Q	$597.50	$4.32	0.72%	4.30%	5.13%
	4Q	$608.15	$10.02	1.65%	5.06%	6.02%
			$30.25			

Source: Altman (1990–2000), Salomon Smith Barney, and Moody's (New York)

APPENDIX 12.2b

Comparing Altman/SBC moving average default rates with Moody's (1990–2000)

Absolute numbers		First differences		Percentage differences	
Altman 12M moving average (%)	Moody's 12M moving average (%)	Altman 12M moving average (%)	Moody's 12M moving average (%)	Altman 12M moving average (%)	Moody's 12M moving average (%)
10.06	8.83				
12.61	10.62	2.55	1.79	25.39	20.27
12.77	11.57	0.15	0.95	1.22	8.95
12.18	10.58	−0.58	−0.99	−4.56	−8.56
10.34	9.65	−1.84	−0.93	−15.13	−8.79
7.35	7.17	−2.99	−2.48	−28.89	−25.70
6.67	5.55	−0.68	−1.62	−9.25	−22.59
4.16	4.69	−2.51	−0.86	−37.62	−15.50
3.26	3.94	−0.90	−0.75	−21.57	−15.99
1.65	3.78	−1.62	−0.16	−49.55	−4.06
1.50	3.23	−0.14	−0.55	−8.64	−14.55
1.30	3.08	−0.20	−0.15	−13.39	−4.64
1.19	3.06	−0.12	−0.02	−9.05	−0.65
1.28	2.49	0.09	−0.57	7.62	−18.63
0.65	1.44	−0.62	−1.05	−48.68	−42.17
0.80	2.18	0.15	0.74	22.75	51.39
1.46	1.93	0.65	−0.25	81.40	−11.47
1.24	1.20	−0.22	−0.73	−14.77	−37.82
1.88	2.17	0.63	0.97	50.95	80.83
2.11	2.41	0.23	0.24	12.39	11.06
1.90	3.30	−0.21	0.89	−10.03	36.93
2.00	3.48	0.10	0.18	5.31	5.45
1.64	2.86	−0.35	−0.62	−17.64	−17.82
1.39	2.19	−0.26	−0.67	−15.51	−23.43
1.26	1.66	−0.13	−0.53	−9.21	−24.20
1.71	1.60	0.45	−0.06	35.86	−3.61
1.55	1.61	−0.16	0.01	−9.31	0.62
1.84	2.27	0.29	0.66	18.62	40.99
1.34	2.03	−0.51	−0.24	−27.54	−10.57
1.34	2.38	0.00	0.35	−0.02	17.24
1.43	3.01	0.10	0.63	7.33	26.47
1.34	2.73	−0.09	−0.28	−6.55	−9.30
1.73	3.46	0.39	0.73	28.96	26.74
2.03	3.89	0.30	0.43	17.28	12.43
3.31	4.74	1.28	0.85	63.22	21.85
3.88	5.89	0.58	1.15	17.40	24.26
4.30	5.51	0.41	−0.38	10.65	−6.45
4.39	5.64	0.10	0.13	2.23	2.36
4.50	5.43	0.10	−0.21	2.34	−3.72
4.30	5.13	−0.20	−0.30	−4.44	−5.52
5.06	6.02	0.77	0.89	17.83	17.35

APPENDIX 12.2b *(cont.)*

Absolute numbers regressions		First differences regressions		Percentage differences regression	
Regression statistics		*Regression statistics*		*Regression statistics*	
Multiple R	0.969785946	Multiple R	0.76820831	Multiple R	0.567898832
R Square	0.940484781	R Square	0.590144007	R Square	0.322509083
Adjusted		Adjusted		Adjusted	
R Square	0.93895875	R Square	0.579358323	R Square	0.304680375
Standard error	0.008448828	Standard error	0.006061656	Standard error	0.224030916
Observations	41	Observations	40	Observations	40

APPENDIX 12.3

Corporate bond defaults by industry
(Number of companies)

Industry	1970–82	1983	1984	1985	1986	1987	1988	1989	1990	1991	1992	1993	1994	1995	1996	1997	1998	1999	2000	Total
Auto/Motor carrier	3								3	3				1				1		11
Conglomerates								3	1	4	2				1		1		1	13
Energy	3	3	5	7	12	2	4	11										13	1	61
Financial services	4	1	1	1			7	11	7	14	6	4	2	2	1			1	6	67
Leisure/Entertainment						5	4	4	8	2	4	3	3	1	1	5	5	8	9	62
General manufacturing	9	1	1	2	6	3	1	5	8	8	7	3	3	8	6	7	6	16	23	123
Healthcare									2	1			2	2	1	2	2	8	6	26
Miscellaneous industries	3	1	2	6	3				4	4	4	1	1	1		3	3	16	34	86
Real estate/Construction	7		1	1	3	1		2	5	5	1	1	1	2		2	1	4	6	43
REIT	11	1						1												13
Retailing	6	1	1	1			1	2	6	15	6	4	3	6	3	6	6	12	7	86
Communications	7	2	1	1	1	3		2	3	4	1	1	3	2	2	1	6	11	8	59
Transportation (non-auto)	4	2			1			1		2			2	2		2	1	8	5	30
Utilities									1						1	1	1			5
Total	57	12	12	19	23	15	24	26	47	62	34	22	19	28	15	29	37	98	106	685

APPENDIX 12.4
Defaults by industry (2000)

Company	Industry
All Star Gas Corp.	Retail – Propane distribution
Altiva Financial Corporation	Finance – Consumer loans
American Architectural Products Corp.	Miscellaneous manufacturer
American Eco Corp.	Remediation services
Ameriserve	Food – Wholesale/Distribution
Amer Reefer Company, Ltd	Transport – Marine
Anchor Advanced Products, Inc.	Cosmetics and toiletries
AMF Bowling Worldwide	Recreational centers
Anacomp, Inc.	Computers – Memory devices
Big V Supermarkets	Food – Retail
Bulong Opeations	Metals/Minerals
Cambridge Industries, Inc.	Miscellaneous manufacturer
Canadian Airlines	Airlines
Carmike Cinemas	Theatres
CellNet Data Systems	Wireless equipment
Central European Media Enterprises, Ltd	Television
CHS Electronics, Inc.	Distribution/Wholesale
Clark Material Handling Co.	Machinery – Construction and mining
Colorado Prime Corp.	Diversified mfg. op.
Compass Aerospace Corp.	Aerospace/Defense equip.
ContiFinancial Corp.	Finance – Mtge loan/Banker
Coram Healthcare Corp.	Healthcare services
Crown Vantage, Inc.	Paper and related products
Cuddy Int'l Corp.	Poultry
Decora Industries, Inc.	Miscellaneous manufacturer
Dimac Direct, Inc.	Direct marketing
Drypers Corp.	Cosmetics and toiletries
Dyersburg Corp.	Textile – Products
Eagle Food Center, Inc.	Retail – Hypermarkets
Employee Solutions	Human Resources
Fine Air Services, Inc.	Transport – Air freight
Flooring America, Inc.	Retail – Floor coverings
Galaxy Telecom L.P.	Telecom Services
Genesis Health	Medical – Nursing homes
Glenoit Corp.	Textile – Products
Global Health Sciences	Medical Products
Global Telesystems, Inc.	Telephone – Integrated
Globe Manufacturing Corp.	Textile – Products
GNI Group, Inc.	Hazardous waste disposal
Gothic Energy Corp.	Oil – US royalty trusts
GST Telecommunications, Inc.	Telecommunication equip.
Hedstrom Holdings, Inc.	Miscellaneous manufacturer
Heilig-Meyers Co. – Macsaver Fin'l	Finance – Consumer loans
ICG Communications Corp.	Satellite telecomm
Imperial Home Decor Group	Home decoration products
Imperial Sugar Company	Sugar
Indesco International, Inc.	Consumer products – Misc.
Iowa Select Farms	Agricultural operations
Kasper ASL, Ltd.	Apparel manufacturers
Key Plastics, Inc.	Chemicals – Plastics
Kitty Hawk, Inc.	Transport – Air freight
Laidlaw, Inc.	Transport Services
LaRoche Industries, Inc.	Chemicals – Specialty
Lernout & Hauspie Speech Products N.V.	Communications Software

APPENDIX 12.4   *(cont.)*

Company	Industry
Lodestar Holdings, Inc.	Diversified operations
LTV Corp.	Steel producers
Master Graphics – Premier Graphics, Inc.	Printing – Commercial
Medical Resources	Medical laboratories
Mediq, Inc.	Medical products
Metal Management, Inc.	Recycling
Morris Material Handling, Inc.	Bldg and construct. products
Northwestern Steel & Wire Company	Steel producers
Orbcomm Global LP	Telecom services
Outboard Marine Corp.	Recreational vehicles
Owens Corning	Bldg. and construct. products
Packaging Resources	Containers – Paper/Plastic
Paging Network, Inc.	Wireless equipment
Paracelsus Healthcare Corp.	Medical – Hospitals
Park 'N' View, Inc.	Retail – Misc./Diversified
Pathmark Stores	Food – Retail
PennCorp Financial Group, Inc.	Life/Health insurance
Pen-Tab Industries, Inc.	Misc. manufacturer
Phase Metrics	Data processing/mgmt
Pillowtex Corp.	Textile – Apparel
Pioneer Americas Acquisition Corp.	Chemicals – Diversified
Plainwell, Inc.	Paper and related products
President Casinos	Gambling (non-hotel)
Prime Succession, Inc.	Funeral services
Quentra Networks, Inc – Diane Corp.	Telecommunication equip.
Gorges/Quick-to-Fix Foods, Inc.	Food – Misc./Diversified
RBX Group, Inc.	Misc. manufacturer
Regal Cinemas, Inc.	Theatres
Reliance Group Holdings, Inc.	Property/Casualty insurance
Reliant Building Products, Inc.	Prod – Doors and windows
Resort at Summerlin	Resorts/Theme parks
REV Holdings, Inc.	Cosmetics and toiletries
Safelite Glass Corp.	Housewares
Safety Components International, Inc.	Misc. manufacturer
Safety-Kleen Corp.	Non-hazardous waste disposal
SFAC New Holdings	Food – Misc./Diversified
Silver Cinemas International, Inc.	Motion pictures and services
Stage Stores – Specialty Retailers, Inc.	Retail – Apparel/Shoe
Stellex Technologies	Aerospace/Defense
Styling Technology Corp.	Cosmetics and toiletries
Sunbeam Corporation	Leisure and rec. products
Sunterra Corp.	Resorts/Theme parks
Superior National Insurance	Property/Casualty insurance
Talon Automotive Group, Inc.	Auto/Trk. Prts. and Equip.
Tokheim Corp.	Machinery – Gen'l. industry
Uniforet, Inc.	Building prod. – Wood
United Artists Theatre	Motion pictures and services
United Homes, Inc.	Building – Res./Comm.
Vista Eyecare, Inc.	Retail – Vision service ctr.
Waxman Industries, Inc.	Bldg. and construct prod. – Misc.
Wheeling-Pittsburgh Corp.	Steel producers
Worldtex, Inc.	Textile – Apparel
Zeta Consumer Products	Containers – Paper/Plastic

Appendix 12.5

Weighted average recovery rates by industry (1971–2000)

Industry	Sample	Weighted avg. price ($)	Avg. price	Price range Low ($)	Price range High ($)	Std. dev. ($)	Median ($)
Mining	69	33.51	34.65	9.50	99.00	17.19	32.50
Food and kindred products, tobacco	37	43.73	47.38	10.00	98.00	25.50	44.50
Textile mill, apparel and related products	55	29.50	29.83	0.75	89.30	18.97	29.00
Lumber, wood products, furniture and fixtures, paper and allied products	20	26.70	30.07	2.00	75.00	22.90	27.50
Chemical, petroleum and energy, rubber, plastic and leather products	48	65.73	53.55	3.00	107.75	31.48	60.50
Stone, clay, glass, concrete, metals and fabricated products	85	26.61	35.77	1.75	101.50	24.35	30.00
Machinery, electrical, electronic and transportation equipment, instruments and related products	70	34.18	39.41	3.00	86.00	22.45	38.25
Miscellaneous ad diversified manufacturing	12	36.26	34.09	0.75	88.00	29.89	31.19
Transportation (rail road, bus, air, water, freight), pipeline and transporation services	78	38 15	38.83	5.00	103.25	26.49	34.25
Printing and publishing, communication, and movie production	133	27.79	30.65	3.00	97.00	19.71	28.83
Utilities	62	54.77	67.01	2.00	99.88	23.15	77.38
Wholesale and retail trade	176	33.00	34.82	0.50	98.50	22.27	31.25
Finance, insurance and real estate	132	33.94	35.52	1.00	103.00	26.75	30.00
Services	98	38.14	39.73	0.75	112.00	29.87	34.50
Total	1075	35.75	38.26	0.50	112.00	25.58	33.50

Source: Appendices 12.1 and 12.3 and Figure 12.5

CHAPTER 13

Credit Risk Embedded in Over-the-Counter Derivatives

Eduardo Canabarro
Goldman Sachs

FUNDAMENTAL CONCEPTS AND DEFINITIONS

C redit exposure (sometimes referred to as **counterparty exposure**) is the *positive* marked-to-market value of the portfolio of positions with a counterparty (including collateral holdings/postings and taking enforceable netting rights into account) that a party would lose if its counterparty were to default and the recovery rate were zero. Netting reduces credit exposures because it allows for the offsetting of positive- and negative-value positions in determining net amounts payable or receivable. Collateral received reduces the credit exposure to the counterparty. Collateral posted creates credit exposures to the counterparty. Credit exposures created by OTC derivatives are usually only a small fraction of the total notional amount of trades with a counterparty.

Current exposure (CE) is the value of the credit exposure today (that is, at $t = 0$).

Potential future exposure (PFE) or, simply, potential exposure (PE) is the maximum amount of exposure expected, with a high degree of statistical confidence, to occur at a certain date in the future. The curve $PE(t)$ is sometimes referred to as the *potential exposure profile*. It represents the PEs for all dates in the future up to the final maturity of the portfolio of OTC derivatives with the counterparty. The PEs are usually computed through Monte Carlo simulation models: the value of the portfolio of trades with a counterparty is simulated over time and, for each future date, the 95- or 99-percentile of the distribution of exposures is picked to represent the PE at that date. The peak PE over the life of the portfolio, that is the highest PE on the PE profile, is sometimes referred as *maximum potential exposure*

(MPE). PE(t) and MPE are contrasted with credit limits in the process of approving trades.

Expected positive exposure (EPE) or, simply, expected exposure (EE) is the expected (average) exposure at a certain date in the future. The curve EE(t) is sometimes referred to as the *expected exposure profile*. It represents the EEs for all dates in the future up to the final maturity of the portfolio of OTC derivatives with the counterparty. The EEs are usually computed through Monte Carlo simulation models: the value of the portfolio of trades with a counterparty is simulated over time and for each future date the exposures are averaged out. The EE(t) curve is sometimes referred to as *the credit-equivalent or the loan-equivalent exposure curve*. Its main application is for credit pricing as we will see later in this chapter.

Right-way/wrong-way exposures are the ones in which there is strong correlation between credit exposure and credit quality of the counterparty. Those exposures have low/high expected credit losses associated with them. In some cases the directionality is obvious; for example, selling local currency for dollars to an emerging country bank is clearly a wrong-way trade. In other cases, it is not so obvious; for example, buying gold forwards from a gold miner. One would think that this would be a right-way trade but this may not be the case because of the specific hedging strategy followed by the miner.

The explosive growth of OTC derivatives markets over the last 10 years has drawn the attention of risk managers to the credit risk faced by the derivatives counterparties. The total credit risk in the OTC derivatives portfolio can be particularly large in long-dated books like interest-rate and cross-currency swaps. For large derivatives dealers and end-users, the credit risk embedded in their OTC derivatives positions could be equivalent to multi-billion-dollar holdings of default-risky bonds. When measured on a mark-to-market basis, the credit risk embedded in OTC derivatives is an important component of the overall market risk of those firms.

WHAT IS SPECIAL ABOUT THE CREDIT RISK EMBEDDED IN OTC DERIVATIVES?

The simplest, most traditional and known vehicles of credit risk are loans and bonds. The main characteristics of the credit exposures created by those instruments are:

- the credit exposure is *unilateral*; that is, only the lender faces credit risk with respect to the borrower;

- the credit exposures, computed at risk-free rates, are mostly *constant* over the life of the instrument, fluctuating around the face value of the loan or bond.

In more elaborate credit facilities (for example, commitments to lend or revolving lines of credit) the exposures can vary quite a lot over time: from zero to the maximum drawing amount allowed by the facility. The credit risk is still unilateral though: one party is the potential lender and the other party is the potential borrower.

In OTC derivatives, the credit exposures faced by the parties *vary* according to the movements of the underlying market prices/rates. Moreover, in many OTC derivatives (for example, futures, forwards, swaps) the credit risk is *bilateral*: either party can find itself in a lending or borrowing position depending on the marked-to-market value of the derivative.

The correlation between the underlying market factors and the credit quality of the counterparties becomes important. Consider a forex trade where a G7-based-bank buys the hard currency forward from an emerging market bank. The scenario where the emerging market currency suffers a major devaluation would correspond to the G7-based-bank having exposure to the emerging market counterparty. Now, one could construe that, following a major devaluation of the local currency, the local financial system would be under stress and that the credit quality of the local bank would have deteriorated. In such case, the G7-based-bank would have exposure to the local bank at the worst possible circumstance.

The risk of a portfolio of exposures reflects the correlations among the credit qualities of the various borrowers. Concentrations of borrowers in a single industry or geographical region tend to increase the *tail-risk* of the portfolio. In the case of a portfolio of credit exposures created by OTC derivatives it is important to consider various correlations: a) correlations among the credit qualities of the counterparties; b) correlations among the market-driven exposures to counterparties; c) correlations between exposures and credit qualities.

CREDIT RISK MITIGANTS

Netting Agreements

Legally enforceable netting agreements are powerful credit risk mitigants. They allow positions to be netted before settlement upon the default of one of the counterparties. Without netting, the non-defaulting party would have to make full payment on the trades with negative value but receive only the recovery value on the trades with positive value. With netting, positives and negatives are added first to determine the net payment due. Exposure calculators need to compute exposures with and without netting since the enforceability of netting is a legal issue that cannot be determined with 100% certainty.

Collateral Agreements

Collateral agreements are powerful credit mitigants too. They require counterparties to mark-to-market periodically their positions and to post collateral (that is, transfer the ownership of assets) to each other as exposures exceed pre-established thresholds. Usually, the threshold schedule is a function on the credit ratings of the counterparties. Counterparties with high (low) credit ratings have to post collateral if amounts due exceed high (low) threshold values. Collateral agreements do not eliminate all the credit risk. A counterparty may fail to post collateral when called upon. There is also the risk that a counterparty would default while retaining an excess amount of collateral posted.

Under mark-to-market and collateral agreements the positions are marked to market daily and, to the extent that their aggregate value exceeds a pre-specified threshold (which may decrease as the credit quality of the counterparty deteriorates), a call is made for additional collateral. If the counterparty cannot post the amount of collateral called within a contractually specified period of time, the derivatives positions are closed and the collateral value is applied against the amount owed by the counterparty.

What are the components of credit risk under collateral agreements?

- exposures below the threshold beyond which collateral is called;
- market movements that could increase the value of the derivatives portfolio between the time collateral is called and the time the positions are closed;
- the collateral received (posted) depreciates (appreciates) in value during that period of time.

Early Termination Clauses

Liquidity puts and credit triggers also reduce credit exposures by shortening the effective maturity of trades. Liquidity puts give the parties the right to terminate trades and settle at-market at pre-specified dates in the future. Credit triggers specify that trades have to be settled if the credit rating of either party falls below pre-specified thresholds.

Cross-product Netting

Some counterparties trade many derivative types with a dealer, for example, interest rate swaps, foreign exchange forwards and options, commodity swaps. The ability to net across products is desirable for the reasons mentioned above. Legal issues with respect to the enforceability of netting arise when a dealer books trades at different subsidiaries (legal entities), possibly based in different jurisdictions.

In terms of the exposure measurement system, cross-product aggregation of exposures (with or without netting) requires that the same set of market scenarios be applied uniformly across all trades.

NUMERICAL AND GRAPHICAL EXAMPLES

Below, we illustrate the computation of the exposures for a one-market scenario (one market path) and then we show the expected and potential exposures (95-percentile) for the full set of simulated market scenarios. The exposures curves are shown in current dollars; that is, the future exposures are discounted to present using the LIBOR curve.

MODELS TO SIMULATE FUTURE CREDIT EXPOSURES

OTC derivatives generate credit exposures that are driven by the underlying market factors' movements. In general, the credit exposures created by OTC derivatives are bilateral; that is, each party can be potentially exposed to the other on a future date. The magnitude of the potential future credit exposures depends on:

- the size (notional amount) of the trades;
- the sensitivity of the value of the trades to underlying market factors;
- the volatility of the market factors affecting the values of the trades;
- the existence (or not) of credit-risk mitigants like netting agreements, collateral agreements, liquidity puts, or credit triggers.

The estimation of the PEs requires sophisticated Monte Carlo simulation models to generate the exposures across many market scenarios on various future dates. Various simulation models could be developed to produce substantially different results. The choice of model is of paramount importance for the assessment of the PEs. Below, we discuss various possibilities of model specification and we highlight the various choices and trade-offs involved. Ultimately, one should realize that, despite the large amount of mathematics, statistics, probability, financial engineering, and computer science involved, the modeling of PEs is largely an art; good

TABLE 13.1 Computation of credit exposures for a portfolio of ten traces on various points along one market path
(Trade values in $ mm)

Time (years)	0	1	2	3	4	5	6	7	8	9	10
trade 001	0.0	-0.1	0.1	0.0	-0.3	-1.8	-2.8	-2.2	-2.7	-3.5	-5.3
trade 002	0.0	2.2	2.5	1.3	-0.8	-0.2	0.9	-0.8	-0.9	0.8	0.7
trade 003	0.0	0.3	0.7	-0.4	-1.8	-2.9	-2.6	-1.8	-1.2	-0.9	-3.2
trade 004	0.0	0.6	-0.4	-0.6	1.8	2.4	2.1	2.0	3.7	4.0	4.4
trade 005	0.0	-0.1	-0.6	-1.9	-2.7	-3.1	-3.2	-4.2	-4.6	-5.0	-6.4
trade 006	0.0	-1.2	-0.6	-0.7	0.0	-0.2	0.6	2.3	4.0	5.4	6.0
trade 007	0.0	-0.5	-0.4	-0.3	-0.2	-0.2	-0.5	0.8	-0.4	0.0	0.9
trade 008	0.0	-0.8	-1.5	-0.1	0.6	1.9	0.9	2.3	2.6	2.5	2.5
trade 009	0.0	-0.7	-0.7	-0.4	-0.7	-1.0	-3.2	-3.3	-4.8	-7.5	-7.0
trade 010	0.0	2.3	3.6	3.1	2.9	1.3	0.5	0.1	2.2	2.9	2.9
Exposure											
– without netting	0.0	5.5	6.8	4.5	5.4	5.6	4.9	7.6	12.5	15.5	17.4
– with netting	0.0	2.1	2.7	0.1	0.0	0.0	0.0	0.0	0.0	0.0	0.0

FIGURE 13.1   Potential and expected exposure curves for the full set of 2,000 simulated market paths (with netting in $ mm)

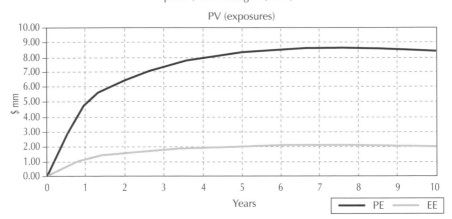

judgment plays a key role in the construction of useful exposure measurement systems.

Stochastic Processes Driving the Risk Factors

Different classes of market prices (that is, interest rates, foreign exchange rates, equity and commodity prices, and option implied volatilities) require the specification of different stochastic processes to characterize their evolutions through time.

Interest rates in major currencies are usually modeled as *normal or lognormal diffusion processes*. When interest rates are low (for example, 1% to 3%) the normal diffusion appears to be more appropriate. When interest rates are at more usual levels (e.g., 4% to 8%), the lognormal diffusion seems more appropriate.

The stochastic processes for major currencies (e.g., JPY, EUR, and CAD) are usually modeled as diffusions. This is in contrast with the emerging market currencies where jumps (discontinuities) in prices can occur. It is common practice to use jump-diffusion processes to characterize the movements of those currencies. The occurrence of jumps can produce very high exposures over very short periods of time. Some analysts would argue that the stochastic processes followed by the emerging market currencies are not Markovian. That is, the recent history (path) of the exchange rates affects the likelihood of a large devaluation: if a currency has not been devaluated for a long period of time it is more likely to be devaluated in the future. Immediately after a devaluation, the likelihood of another one would be small.

The shorter the time horizon over which the exposure is computed the larger the importance of jumps in determining the potential exposures. For longer horizons, jumps tend to dissipate and cannot be easily distinguished from diffusions. This suggests that the modeler has to consider the horizon at which the exposures are being analyzed. For the estimation of short-dated exposures (for example, some created by forex, equity, and commodity derivatives) it is absolutely necessary to specify the jump process where required.

Commodities, and equities' prices are usually modeled as lognormal diffusions. However, there is well-documented evidence of jumps (positive and negative) in their prices: oil crises, sensitive political/economic situations causing the demand for gold to increase, and so on.

Sometimes the risk factor to simulate is not a single price but rather a string of prices. Examples are interest rate curves and commodity forward curves. In those cases, the simulation model has to be elaborate enough to generate consistent changes along the entire curve; for example, changes in level, slope, and curvature. Arbitrage-free, multi-factor term structure models have been applied to simulate the evolution of interest rate and commodity curves.

Some prices display mean-reverting characteristics. For example, very high and very low interest rates are unlikely to persist for long periods of time in well-functioning economies. Mean-reversion is an important feature to incorporate in the stochastic processes, especially those aimed at generating long-dated exposures. If mean reversion (or some other mechanism to achieve volatility compression) is not incorporated, unrealistic levels of exposures could be estimated at long time horizons.

Calibration of the Parameters of the Stochastic Models

The calibration of the parameters of the simulation models is an important step in model building. The future values of the market risk factors (for example, interest rates, foreign exchange rates, equity, and commodity prices) are fundamentally determined by the choice of the calibration scheme.

Models calibrated to historical data tend to project future values based on the statistical regularities observed in the past. Models calibrated to a cross-section of market prices (for example, current forward curves and option implied volatilities) tend to reflect forward-looking views shared by market participants. One can find positive and negative aspects in each form of calibration. Historical calibration implies that the process generating future market behavior is the same that was observed in the past. The model may be slow to react to changes in market conditions and market structures even if some sort of time decay factor is used to overweight the more recent observations. On the other hand, market prices contain components that are not the result of market participants' expectations about the future (for example, risk and liquidity premia, carrying costs/benefits, and so on).

The objective of the simulation model is to project as accurately as possible the future developments in the markets being simulated. In that sense, the models should operate under the true probability measures. The only justification to use the risk-neutral measure is that, to some extent, it contains the consensus expectations of market participants of future levels, variances, and so on, of the risk factors.

Correlations among Market Risk Factors

The correlations among market risk factors are the most important determinants of the potential credit exposures created by large and well-diversified portfolios of trades. Highly positively correlated positions tend to exacerbate credit exposures. Yield curve models are necessary to create the appropriate correlation among the various sectors of the yield curves. Yield curves tend to move subject to restrictions that guarantee positive forward rates. Also, the short-term rates and the long-term rates tend to have different correlations across various currencies. We find that long-term rates tend to be more correlated than short-term rates among G-7 economies.

Re-pricing Trades on Each Scenario

Once a future market scenario is generated, all trades held with the counterparty have to be priced. That task uses an enormous amount of computational resources. Just imagine a typical swap dealer's book with 50,000 trades with average maturity of 7 years, 2,000 market scenarios generated every 3 months:

$$50,000 \times 2,000 \times 7 \times 4 = 2.8 \text{ billion re-pricings.}$$

If each re-pricing takes one mili-second of CPU time:

$$2,800,000,000 \times 0.001 = 2,800,000 \text{ seconds} = 778 \text{ hours.}$$

Clearly, a good amount of financial/software engineering and/or CPU power is required. Some banks have retained super-computers for the computation of the credit exposures generated by their portfolios of OTC derivatives. Others have developed heavily engineered algorithms to economize on the computation time (for example, price grids, sophisticated interpolation schemes in both time and space dimensions, and so on).

Unnecessary analytical complexity should be avoided: one should avoid refining within the margin of error. This is particularly important for long-dated exposures: the volatilities, correlations, and probabilistic assumptions used in constructing such long-dated scenarios are themselves surrounded by considerable uncertainty. Constructing highly accurate (and computationally intensive) trade valuations conditional on such uncertain market conditions certainly qualifies as refining within the margin of error.

How Many Simulations?

Table 13.2 illustrates the accuracy of estimation of the quantiles of a standard normal distribution with 2,000 and 500 simulations. Notice that the standard deviation of the 95-percentile estimate is 0.0473 and 0.0916 for the cases with 2,000 and 500 simulations (that is, roughly 2.9% and 5.8% of the 95-percentile, respectively).

Technological Issues

The collection and integration of market data, trades, netting, and collateral agreements plus other information required to compute credit potential exposures requires access to various front- and back-office systems spread throughout the organizations. The level of cooperation among various departments has to be high. Indeed, the data-integration challenge is an important reason why many first-tier financial institutions have not succeeded in evolving their systems to measure potential exposures beyond the BIS mark-to-market plus add-on approach. In addition to data collection and integration, there is the need to develop and implement analytical tools to perform the simulations and presentation tools to deliver the resulting information to various levels of decision-makers in a timely and clear fashion.

TYPICAL EXPOSURE PROFILES FOR SINGLE-TRADE PORTFOLIOS

There are two general types of PE/EE profiles created by OTC derivatives. I will refer to them as *amortizing* and *cliff* exposure profiles. In order to understand the differences, let's analyze the main determinants of the PE/EE profiles:

- volatility effect;
- aging effect;
- discounting to present value.

TABLE 13.2 Accuracy in estimating quantiles of standard normal distributions with 2,000 and 500 simulations

	5%	10%	25%	50%	75%	90%	95%
Exact	−1.6449	−1.2816	−0.6745	0.0000	0.6745	1.2816	1.6449
2,000 simulations							
mean	−1.6471	−1.2825	−0.6753	−0.0014	0.6729	1.2808	1.6414
standard deviation	**0.0463**	**0.0377**	**0.0291**	**0.0279**	**0.0321**	**0.0390**	**0.0473**
skewness	−0.0436	−0.0328	−0.0602	0.1616	−0.0167	−0.0265	−0.0238
kurtosis	0.2810	0.2690	−0.1218	0.0488	0.0004	−0.0736	0.1781
minimum	−3.1156	−3.5802	−3.6864	−3.0482	−3.6142	−2.8420	−3.0392
maximum	3.5176	3.4199	2.6106	3.1444	3.1747	3.0315	3.7556
500 stimulations							
mean	−1.6569	−1.2886	−0.6793	−0.0028	0.6697	1.2736	1.6291
standard deviation	**0.0984**	**0.0767**	**0.0613**	**0.0553**	**0.0600**	**0.0729**	**0.0916**
skewness	−0.1828	−0.1094	−0.1319	0.0489	0.0068	0.0091	0.0683
kurtosis	0.1112	−0.1601	0.1138	0.0087	0.0194	−0.0942	−0.1226
minimum	−3.6794	−2.7244	−3.5157	−2.9103	−3.2471	−3.0216	−2.8715
maximum	2.9186	2.9740	3.0964	3.1411	3.5856	3.4693	3.1281

All three effects are related to time. As the horizon at which exposures are computed increases, the dispersion of the probability distribution of the underlying risk factors increases (that is, volatility accumulates); the number of remaining cash flows of the aging trades decrease; and the discounting of exposures to present value is heavier.

Interest rate, commodity, and equity swaps generate exposure profiles of the amortizing type. The volatility effect is counteracted by the aging and discounting effect as the horizon time increases. The general shape of the profile of an at-market swap is represented in Figure 13.2.

Interest rate, commodity, and equity forwards and options generate exposure profiles of the cliff type. There is no aging affect to counteract the volatility effect. The discounting effect is not strong enough over short- and mid-range maturities. Thus, PEs tend to increase monotonically up to the expiration date. Figure 13.3 shows the exposure profile for an at-market forward contract expiring in 10 years.

Exposure Profiles for Single-trade Portfolios with Collateral

Mark-to-market and exchange of collateral tend to reduce credit exposures dramatically. The exposures are not completely eliminated though: it takes time to close out positions after a counterparty's failure to fulfill a margin call. During the period between the margin call and the final closing out,

FIGURE 13.2 Uncollateralized exposures – amortizing type $100 mm notional, at-market, 10-year interest rate swap pay USD float, receive USD fixed

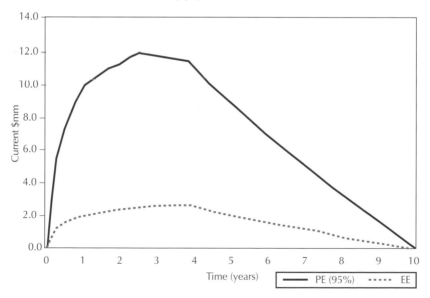

FIGURE 13.3 Uncollateralized exposures – cliff type $100 mm notional, at-market, 10-year cross-currency swap pay USD float, receive USD fixed

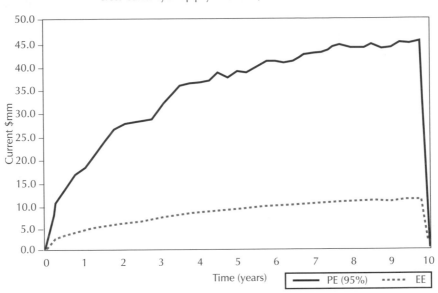

markets can move and exposures can be created. Figures 13.4 and 13.5 show the exposures created by 10-year interest rate and cross-currency swaps when there is a zero-threshold collateral agreement between the counterparties. Compare the levels of exposures in Figures 13.2 and 13.3 with the levels in Figures 13.4 and 13.5.

Exposure Profiles of Multiple-trade Portfolios

The peak exposure and the overall exposure profiles of derivative portfolios reflect various attenuating effects that operate at the portfolio level:

- offsetting and netting;
- diversification across multiple underlying risk factors;
- diversification of peak-exposure times.

All those effects tend to make the total exposure of the portfolio much smaller than the sum of the exposures created by individual trades.

Offsetting is the effect related to trades that have opposite sensitivity to the same underlying risk factor. For example, a long and a short position on the same forward contract. Even in the absence of enforceable netting rights, opposite trades cannot create credit exposure simultaneously.

To the extent that the underlying risk factors are not perfectly correlated, there will be a diversification effect acting upon the total exposure of the

FIGURE 13.4   Collaterized exposures – amortizing type $100 mm notional, at-market, 10-year interest-rate swap pay USD float, receive USD fixed

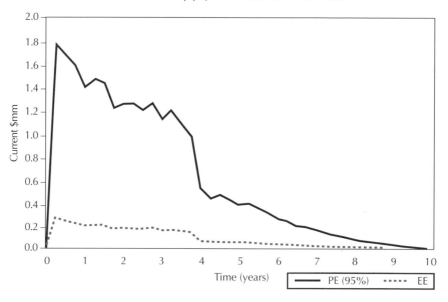

FIGURE 13.5   Collaterized exposures – cliff type $100 mm notional, at-market, 10-year cross-currency swap pay USD float, receive EUR fixed

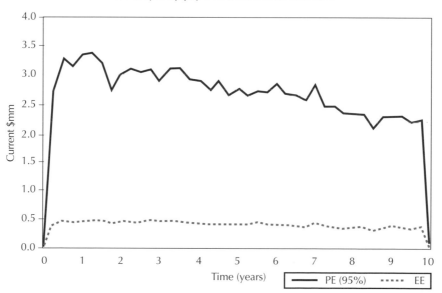

portfolio. For example, suppose that a portfolio is comprised of two trades with the same expiration date and sensitive to two uncorrelated factors. Suppose that the PE of each trade is $5 mm. The PE of the portfolio is roughly equal to $7 mm (that is, 5 times the square root of two).

Potential exposure profiles of individual trades tend to peak at different points in time. Thus, the sum of the peak exposures (MPEs) of the individual trades tends to be much smaller than the peak exposure of the portfolio.

Figure 13.6 below shows the PE and EE for a portfolio of interest rate swaps.

CREDIT PRICING

Counterparty exposure profiles created by OTC derivatives can be priced similarly to bond and loan exposures. In the case of OTC derivatives, it is crucial to understand the settlement rules in the case of default of either counterparty. Under standard International Swaps and Derivatives Association (ISDA) settlement procedure, the counterparty that has not defaulted should collect at least four quotes from derivatives dealers, cut off the highest and lowest, and average out the remaining. The computed average would be the claim against or the amount to be paid to the defaulting counterparty.

Mid-market values of derivatives are computed by discounting expected cash flows using the LIBOR curve. Credit valuation adjustments (CVAs) to

FIGURE 13.6   Swaps counterparty exposures (total notional amount of swaps = $14,400 mm)

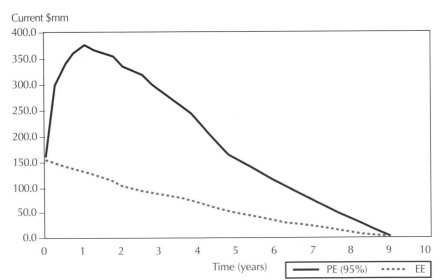

mid-market values are intended to reflect the market price of the credit risk of the counterparties.

An algorithm to compute the credit valuation adjustment[1] of a portfolio of derivatives with a counterparty is as follows:

- Simulate the paths of the short-term risk-free rate and underlying risk factors through maturity of the longest derivative.
- Compute the paths of the mid-market values of the portfolio for counterparty A, $V(t)$, and of the money market account value $B(t)$.
- Compute the paths of the credit exposures $Ea(t)$ and $Eb(t)$ faced by the parties A and B, respectively. Those exposures should reflect netting rights, collateral agreements, and other credit mitigants.
- Simulate the occurrence of default of the counterparties A and B and the recovery rates. The default intensities, default events, and recovery rates could be correlated.
- If counterparty B is the first to default at time t, accumulate $PV(\text{A\_Loss}) += Ea(t) \cdot (1 - R)/B(t)$.
- If counterparty A is the first to default at time t, accumulate $PV(\text{B\_Loss}) += Eb(t) \cdot (1 - R)/B(t)$.
- The fair value of the swap at $t = 0$ is: $V(0) - PV(\text{A\_Loss}) + PV(\text{B\_Loss})$

$PV(\text{B\_Loss}) - PV(\text{A\_Loss})$ is the credit valuation adjustment to be added to the mid-market value of the portfolio of derivatives of A with its counterparty B.

By marking-to-market credit exposures created by derivatives trans-actions we ensure that:

- the true economic values (including the valuation of credit risk) of the derivatives are reflected in the books and records;
- the correct economic incentives are put in place to induce beneficial trades and credit mitigation agreements;
- the correct risk measures are computed to hedge the overall market risks (including credit risk).

The prices of credit risk are obtained from credit markets (for example, bond spreads, prices of credit default swap prices, and so on). Usually, credit prices, as represented by spreads or prices of default swaps, are converted into risk-neutral default intensities by assuming a certain recovery rate.

Why Do We Have to Price the Bilateral Credit Risk?

The credit valuation adjustment (CVA) reflects the assignment value of the portfolio of trades with the counterparty assuming that: (a) the portfolio is an isolated netting set to the assignee and (b) the existing netting provisions are maintained.

Suppose that a single-A dealer has a receiver interest rate swap with a triple-B counterparty.

If the dealer were to assign its side of that swap to a triple-A dealer, the triple-B party would benefit from having now a triple-A counterparty and should pay for that benefit.

The following is a numerical example:

- receive-fixed-side expected exposure   = $70
- pay-fixed-side expected exposure   = $50
- mid-market PV (based on LIBOR curve) = $50
- the dealer receives fixed on the swap
- triple-A credit spread over LIBOR   = 0
- single-A credit spread over LIBOR   = +50 bps
- triple-B credit spread over LIBOR   = +80 bps

PV of the swap between single-A dealer and triple-B counterparty:
$18.9 + 0.0050 \times 50 - 0.0080 \times 70 = \$18.59$

PV of the assigned swap for the AAA dealer:
$18.9 + 0.0000 \times 50 - 0.0080 \times 70 = \$18.34$

So, when the single-A dealer assigns the swap, it should receive $18.34 from the triple-A dealer and $0.25 ($-18.34 + 18.59$) from the triple counterparty. The triple-B party should be willing to pay $0.25 for the improved credit quality of its counterparty, now a triple-A dealer.

CREDIT DERIVATIVES TO HEDGE CONTINGENT CREDIT EXPOSURES

Credit exposures created by OTC derivatives are, in general, dynamic; that is, as market prices change, derivatives go in and out of the money. Only in-the-money derivatives create credit exposures – if our counterparty defaults when the derivative is out-of-the-money to us, we do not incur any credit loss.

Default swaps provide market-level independent protection against default; that is, when we buy default protection we get paid upon default irrespective to the market scenario realized at the time of default. We may get paid in market scenarios where we do not have any exposure to the counterparty.

Figure 13.7 illustrates the potential exposures (95%, expected and the 95% seen by the counterparty) created by a $100 mm notional 10-year at-market interest rate swap.

FIGURE 13.7 $100 mm 10-year swap potential exposures

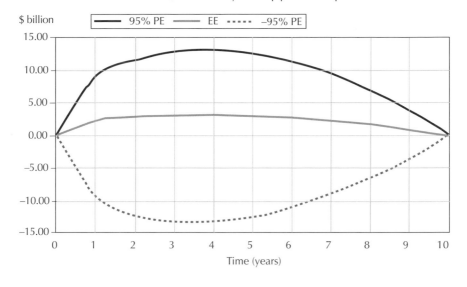

Assuming that the credit spread curve of the counterparty is flat at 100 bps over LIBOR, the credit charge associated with our exposures in the swap is $0.17 mm.

Suppose we buy credit protection on $10 mm in the form of a default swap. That protection would cost $0.74 mm.

Notice:

- the cost of the default swap is more than four times the value of the credit exposures created by the interest rate swap;
- even buying that amount of protection we would still face 95% residual potential exposures of the order of $3 mm in years 3–5.

The reasons why the default swap is so expensive are:

1. The default swap provides unconditional protection; that is, independent of market scenario. We pay for protection even in scenarios where the interest rate swap is out-of-the-money for us and we do not need protection.
2. The level of protection is constant over time.
3. The level of protection is high, close to the level of exposures that will occur only 5% of the time.

A possible alternative to reduce the cost of the credit protection would be to reduce the purchased notional amount of the default swap. The problem with that approach is that the residual potential exposures around years 3–5 could be large. For example, if we decided to buy $5 mm of protection (cost is $0.37 mm), the residual 95% potential exposures would grow to $8 mm in years 3–5.

Another alternative would be to stagger a portfolio of default swaps in order to match more closely the time profile of potential exposures. Figure 13.8 illustrates the approach.

The total cost of the default swaps in this case is $0.61 mm. That cost is still high relative to the credit risk content of the trade $0.17 mm because of steps 1 and 3 above.

The solution to the problem described above is: (a) the purchase of market-contingent credit protection (for example, in the form of a revolver facility referenced to the underlying interest rate swap); or (b) a dynamic credit/market risk hedging scheme that would synthesize the contingent protection. The market for contingent credit protection is still quite illiquid.

Stress Analysis

It is important to understand the sensitivity of the credit exposures to various market scenarios. Some market scenarios may generate large credit exposures. Understanding the concentration of the portfolio's exposures on the various risk factors is a crucial aspect of the risk management of credit risk embedded in OTC derivatives. Figure 13.9 illustrates the results of one such stress/sensitivity analysis. The graph shows the changes in the total portfolio exposures in various pre-specified market scenarios. It shows that the portfolio is most sensitive to market shock 2 where the total exposures increase by $4.6 billion. Scenario 2 could be a composite of various simultaneous, arbitrarily specified moves in market prices/rates. The definition of the scenarios can be quite arbitrary and will depend on the specific circumstances of the analysis. Designing the scenarios requires a good amount of understanding of the underlying portfolio and its interaction with market risk factors. It is much more art than science. Stress analysis has gained much consideration by portfolio managers, especially after the credit market events of 1997 (Asian crisis) and 1998 Long-term Capital Management (LTCM) debacle. Risk managers realized that they need to understand much more the components of the risk of the portfolio than it is possible via aggregate measures like VaR. They also realized that they need to stress the portfolios much beyond the regularities observed in the near past.

FIGURE 13.8 $100 mm 10-year swap potential exposures

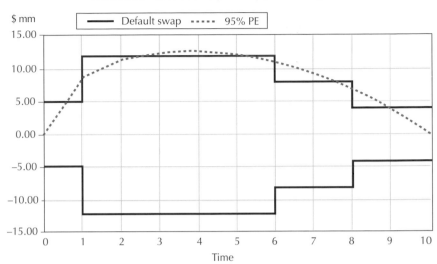

FIGURE 13.9 Change in current exposure when compared to the base case scenario

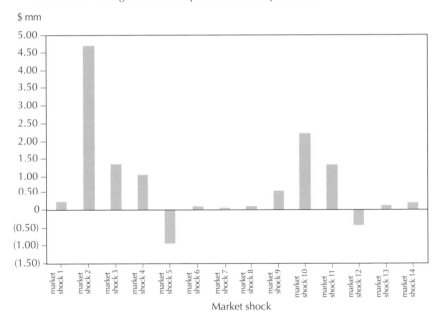

NOTE

[1] This algorithm assumes that the settlement value of the portfolio of derivatives upon the default of any of the parties is the mid-market value of the portfolio.

CHAPTER 14

Internal Corporate Credit Portfolios: The Next Frontier in Credit Risk

Kevin Buehler, Mark Shapiro, and Lee Scoggins*
McKinsey & Company
Transparent Solutions*

There has been important discussion on applying modern risk portfolio techniques to financial institutions in order to avoid credit crises and improve earnings. We suggest that, in the near future, internal credit portfolios of non-financial companies will benefit increasingly from the same techniques. Indeed, recent telecommunication sector troubles have dramatically evidenced the sudden and harsh impact of credit events. In this chapter, we make some recommendations for managers of internal portfolios. We underscore our recommendations by presenting recent research that suggests an important link between risk management and shareholder value.

THE HIDDEN WORLD OF INTERNAL CREDIT PORTFOLIOS

Large non-financial corporations, such as those with revenue of $100 million or greater, extend a tremendous amount of credit in the course of daily business. Credit exposures can range from relatively mundane receivables to large loans to clients, such as when energy firms install new HVAC systems to generate energy savings for their clients. Of the estimated 55,000 firms in North America with assets over $25 million, we estimate that the majority have material internal credit portfolios. Indeed, *Euromoney* magazine recently estimated that in Europe alone the largest 50 companies had a total of more than $50 billion of credit exposure on their books.

These internal corporate portfolios often exhibit a diversity of exposures across many geographies and industry sectors. Because non-financial companies typically do not have an ingrained "credit culture," these firms often manage these exposures on an ad hoc basis. Indeed, many corporations continue to extend credit beyond their own internal credit limits.

We believe the time has come to deploy techniques from the wholesale banking world to manage credit and other firm-wide risks. Exposures must be measured properly and forecasts must be developed that include sensitivities to changing economic cycles. We are starting to see some evidence that more sophisticated non-financial companies are adopting portfolio-based approaches to managing and pricing credit risk, but much work remains to be done. Recent troubles in the telecommunication industry highlight the importance of better risk strategies.

THE PAINFUL LESSONS OF VENDOR FINANCE

Vendor finance provides a particularly compelling illustration of the damage caused by poor credit practices at non-financial companies. A fair portion of the telecommunication industry's meteoric growth was propelled by financing that equipment providers extended to high-tech and telecom start-ups that are now having difficulty making their payments or, like Winstar, have spectacularly collapsed. Consequently, the earnings of the equipment providers, such as Cisco and Lucent, are also suffering.

Among the non-financial companies, the problem is hardly confined to the telecom sector. Xerox, for example, is struggling under the burden of the $11 billion it borrowed to help customers purchase its products. Managers in all kinds of industries assumed that if the cash on hand or the future cash flows of high-tech start-ups were not sufficient to finance their purchases of needed equipment, the capital markets and private equity firms would cooperate. But investors abandoned that faith many months ago.

How can vendors protect themselves in the future? It probably isn't necessary for them to drop the practice of financing their sales, but they will need to scrutinize borrowers more closely and to adopt better risk-management techniques.

During the good times, companies like Lucent and Nortel expanded their vendor financing at nearly triple-digit compound annual growth rates. By the end of last year, we estimate, there were at least $25.6 billion (estimate includes direct vendor loans and customer loan guarantees) worth of loans on the books of nine global telecom giants: Alcatel, Cisco, Ericsson, Lucent, Motorola, Nokia, Nortel, Qualcomm, and Siemens. This compares to $12.2 billion of such exposure in 1996. Total vendor financing by the five North American companies in that group equaled 123% of their pretax earnings in 1999. Approximately 35% of this credit has gone to telecom start-ups, including competitive local-exchange carriers (CLECs), digital local-exchange carriers (DLECs), competitive interexchange carriers (CIXCs), and fixed-wireless providers, many of them now reeling. Since loan losses in excess of reserves are charged to current earnings, high rates of default will have a substantial and immediate impact on the vendors' financial performance.

The true extent of the underlying credit problem is hard to determine, since companies are not obliged to report even the total amount of credit they have extended to customers, let alone the true level of non-performing assets; many companies incorporate their credit losses in a general restructuring expense. But from what we have been able to glean from company interviews and financial analysis, as much as 30 to 40% of the $25.6 billion outstanding is at risk, versus an estimated 10 to 20% at fiscal year end 1996.

Lucent, for example, took a $501 million charge to earnings in fiscal 2000 to reflect its customers' unpaid debts (equivalent to 41% of 2000 earnings). Although Cisco's financial statements provide little detail on its exposure, the company has an estimated $2.4 billion in vendor loans outstanding, and in 1999 it suffered a $60 million credit loss from a single customer. At Nortel, vendor financing represented almost 7% of revenue last year.

Telecom start-ups and "dot-coms" without earnings or credit histories managed to obtain significant credit from their equipment suppliers on terms they could never have obtained from a bank. Such loans were in effect a discount on the price of the equipment. Many of these uneconomic loans were motivated by fear of losing relationships with the likely purchasers of their next-generation equipment.

Most companies lack loan workout specialists and are able to recover only a small portion of the original loan when debts go bad. Repossessing the unpaid-for equipment barely offsets such losses, since it has in the meantime drastically depreciated in value. Cisco, for instance, estimated that assets it sold to obligor Digital Broadband would fetch only 10 cents in the dollar in a bankruptcy auction. In a recent liquidation, a Cisco 7500 Series router, which sells for $150,000 new and for $11,000 after being refurbished, fetched just $1,850. Even worse, the flood of used equipment on the market depresses sales of new equipment. The combination of reduced sales and massive write-offs will further batter the equipment providers' bottom lines.

RECOMMENDATIONS FOR MANAGEMENT

Much of the problem can be attributed either to the vendors' lack of awareness of best lending practices or to pressures to circumvent them. At most companies, vendor finance loans are initiated by the sales force; only then do credit underwriters assess the risk and set a price. But these underwriters often lack even basic tools, such as credit-scoring models. While it is not impossible for rigorous credit analyses to be conducted within a sales unit – provided its credit managers receive the independence, the authority, and the time they need – the soundest finance decisions are usually made by a separate treasury or finance department.

Prudent risk management mandates that companies maintain reserves for expected losses, just as banks do. These reserves should equal the amount of the loan multiplied by the probability of default multiplied by the loss given default. It is also necessary to maintain sufficient capital to withstand the unexpected losses that will periodically occur. The expected losses and the cost of the capital set aside for unexpected losses represent the economic cost of extending credit. Regrettably, few companies have taken this cost fully into account.

By taking advantage of new advances in credit derivatives and other hedging instruments offered by investment banks and brokers, companies can transfer at least some of their credit risk to investors. In effect, a vendor can insure against the bankruptcy of its largest customers, or it can offset its entire credit risk by purchasing a customized portfolio of so-called default swaps, so long as it does so before a major crisis makes the price of credit protection uneconomical – the situation of today's telecommunication companies.

Investors would benefit if companies reported the amount of their vendor finance outstanding (including future credit obligations and loan guarantees to customers), as well as the quality of their credit portfolios. Banks, for example, are required to publicly disclose their non-performing loans, declare their losses, and hold capital to cover potential loan defaults.

Although the total volume of vendor finance doesn't appear separately on the balance sheets of companies, Wall Street analysts should have noted with concern the explosive growth of receivables. Rating agencies downgraded several large telecom-equipment providers only last fall, well after they had taken on a huge exposure to risk. The telecom bond index, reflecting an assessment of increased risk, has risen by 300 basis points since April 2000, but vendor finance had started to explode back in 1997 and 1998. In coming months, the revenue of borrowers will be affected even more severely by the non-performance of outstanding loans and the abundance of used equipment for sale.

Specialized "vulture" investors can take advantage of the current troubles by purchasing vendor debt at steep discounts and then pursuing collections and arranging workouts. Several investment banks and financial boutiques have been looking at new ways to securitize and market such debt to a bearish investment community. Vendors will be grateful for the cash and for being freed from an operational burden.

Such steps would merely make a bad situation somewhat better, while the practice of vendor financing itself cries out for reform. It is understandable how telecom suppliers pursuing continued rapid growth would turn to vendor financing to stimulate sales and help fund customer's ambitious plans. Unfortunately, most lacked the risk management tools, organizational checks and balances, and credit culture needed to assess and manage the risk associated with the huge bets they were placing on their customers.

The Link between Risk and Value

The reader may ask "Why should the senior management team be concerned? Are not large credit events just part and parcel of a changing economic cycle?" The answer is yes, of course, but beyond just the ability to wipe out a year's income, these credit events can have a severe impact on a firm's market value. Recent Transparent Solutions research has highlighted the importance of deploying better risk techniques by looking purely at earnings volatility as a driver of company value.[1]

Let's examine earnings volatility to begin with. Specifically, we considered volatility to be the measured standard deviation of downside,

FIGURE 14.1 Downside deviation from trendline volatility (%)

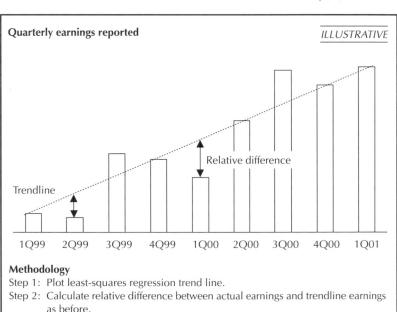

Quarterly earnings reported

ILLUSTRATIVE

Relative difference

Trendline

1Q99 2Q99 3Q99 4Q99 1Q00 2Q00 3Q00 4Q00 1Q01

Methodology

Step 1: Plot least-squares regression trend line.
Step 2: Calculate relative difference between actual earnings and trendline earnings as before.
Step 3: Set positive relative differences equal to zero.
Step 4: Calculate earnings volatility as standard deviation of relative differences.

relative variations in earnings from a linear trend line. This definition normalizes the measure by using relative earnings differences, it also smoothes out overall volatility by reducing the impact of outliers, and it measures only the downside portion of volatility. Figure 14.1 describes our methodology.

Why does earnings volatility matter? The answer lies within shareholder value creation (SVC), which is the best way to quantify risk-adjusted return and management performance. SVC looks specifically at the absolute change in equity market capitalization less the required return on the initial equity market capital less share issuances plus dividends, share buybacks, and spin-offs (all adjustments are compounded at the beta-adjusted market return). Transparent Solutions believes SVC is also a very good measure for management performance.

Our research has provided substantial evidence that companies and economic sectors that contain earnings volatility get penalized by the market. Transparent Solutions examined the top 350 North American public companies and regressed shareholder value creation to earnings growth, company beta, and earnings volatility over the period 1995–2001. Beta was

FIGURE 14.2   Earnings growth and downside volatility as driver of SCV (1995–2001)
Mean $ SVC per $ average market cap

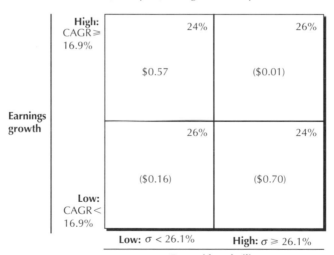

Note: 350 companies observed; all differences are statistically significant (at the 99% level), based on F-test except for one; mean of ($0.16) is not significantly different from ($0.01), based on the Tukey, e.g., Kramer test of multiple mean comparisons, which is plausible and shows that the trade-off between high growth/high volatility and low growth/low volatility is not straightforward from the perspective of shareholder value creation.
Source: Compustat; McKinsey analysis

found not to be statistically significant while earnings growth and volatility were strong drivers. Our conclusion is that companies that can manage their earnings volatility can increase abnormal returns.

The following chart shows the impact on shareholder value creation (adjusted to eliminate "size effects" by dividing with market capital) of earnings growth and downside volatility.

Perhaps more interesting is the high correlation of SVC/market capitalization and volatility among portfolios of companies with similar earnings volatility. In other words, substantial empirical evidence suggests shareholders of low volatility firms get rewarded through greater shareholder value.

In fact, there are examples that have created (destroyed) shareholder value through a decrease (increase) of their earnings volatility despite below-average (above-average) earnings growth.

Clearly, shareholders of companies with low earnings volatility get rewarded. Volatility can manifest itself in stock prices as abnormal changes in price from earnings surprises. We looked at abnormal changes from seven days prior to an earnings announcement and one day after the announcement. Figure 14.5 illustrates how varying stock analyst forecasts play a role.

FIGURE 14.3   Impact of earnings volatility* on shareholder value creation (1995–2001)
Mean volatility and SCV/Market cap for 13 portfolios of 27 companies with similar earnings volatility

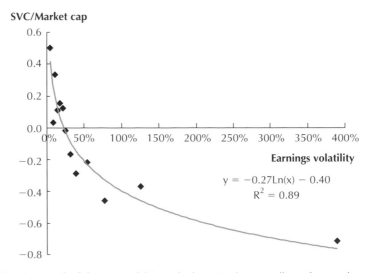

*Calculated as standard deviation of downside deviation from trendline of quarterly earnings numbers
Source: Compustat; McKinsey analysis

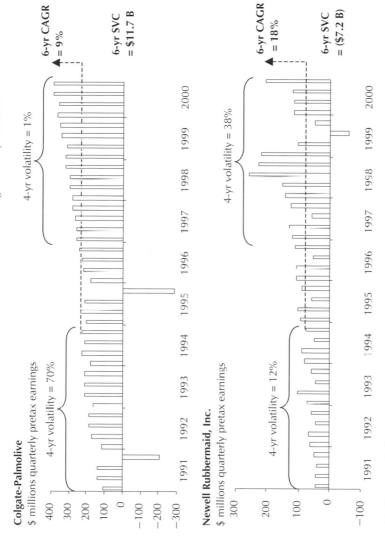

FIGURE 14.4 Shareholder value creation through volatility reduction

Source: Compustat; McKinsey analysis

FIGURE 14.5 Stock movement in response to earnings surprises as a manifestation of volatility

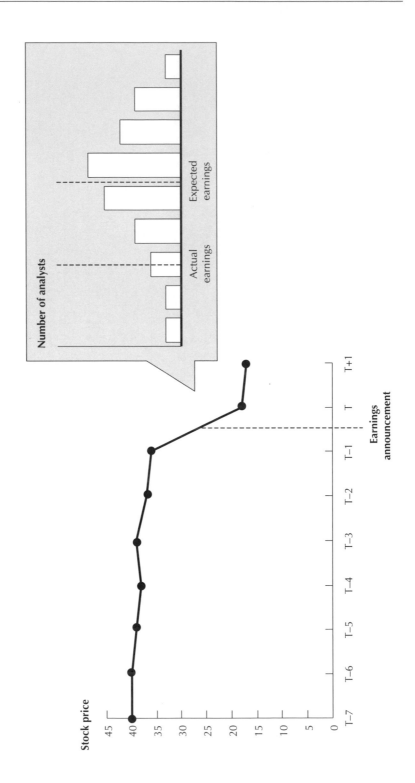

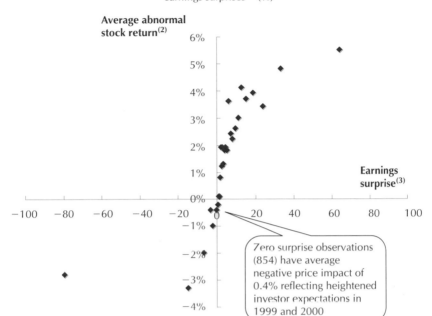

FIGURE 14.6 Effect of earnings surprises on stock prices
average abnormal stock returns for portfolios of observations of similar
earnings surprises[1] (%)

(1) 3,824 earnings announcement observations for S&P 500 companies in 1999 and 2000 were rank ordered by earnings surprises and then grouped into portfolios of 110 observations; zero surprise observations (854) were all put into one portfolio.

(2) Abnormal stock return is the stock return from seven days prior to one day after the earnings release return less CAPM-expected beta market return over same period; days are weekdays (including market holidays but not weekends).

(3) Earnings surprise = (actual EPS – expected EPS)/expected EPS.

Source: Zacks, BARRA, Bloomberg, McKinsey analysis

Investors are constantly reminded of the effect of earning surprises on stock prices. Figure 14.6 shows the abnormal stock return from seven days prior to one day after an earnings announcement less a CAPM-expected beta market return over the same period.

This shows that the relative impact on share prices is biggest for small surprises and diminishes for bigger surprises. The S-shaped relation between abnormal stock returns and earnings surprises demonstrates that the effect diminishes with larger surprises that are associated with high forecast variations and low analyst coverage. Large companies are particularly sensitive to even small surprises because they are generally well covered by analysts and enjoy higher forecast precision. Therefore, large companies in particular should be concerned about earnings predictability.

TABLE 14.1 Why manage risks?

Potential benefits	Explanation
Reduced tax liabilities	Tax benefit that can be secured by reducing the riskiness of earnings – Progressive tax structure – Increase in debt capacity, thereby capturing the incremental tax shield
Reduce/eliminate costs of financial distress	– Direct costs (e.g., legal, court, accounting) associated with bankruptcy – Shareholders' propensity for risk-taking is anticipated by creditors, which leads to higher cost of capital for the firm (asset substitution) – Shareholders choose not to pursue value-creating projects due to the asymmetric pay-offs to creditors and shareholders (underinvestment)
(post loss) Capital access	Costly capital access (after a loss) forces the firm to forgo some value-adding (when internal funding available prior to the loss) (re)investment opportunities
More effective compensation packages for managers	– Incentive compensation has to compensate for both performance and inherent risk – Reduce/eliminating the risk can therefore lower the level of compensation – Reduce/eliminating the risk that is outside the managers' control can also establish a closer link between profit of the firm and the managers' performance
Increasing earning predictability	Capital market awards stable earnings, also a signal of high-quality management
More efficient capital structure	Less risky firms have access to low cost debts

Source: Integrated Risk Management, NA, Doherty, FT Mastering Risk; McKinsey

Ultimately, managing earnings volatility is nothing but managing enterprise risk, but there are additional benefits to risk management as well. Table 14.1 details some potential benefits that can turn out to be material.

Companies have begun to realize that earnings predictability does matter and the interest in integrated risk solutions is growing and no longer just restricted among a few large and sophisticated players.

Since earnings and cash flow volatility is driven by many different risk types, as a first step, a company must identify all relevant risks it is exposed

FIGURE 14.7 Number of analysts as driver of earnings forecast precision

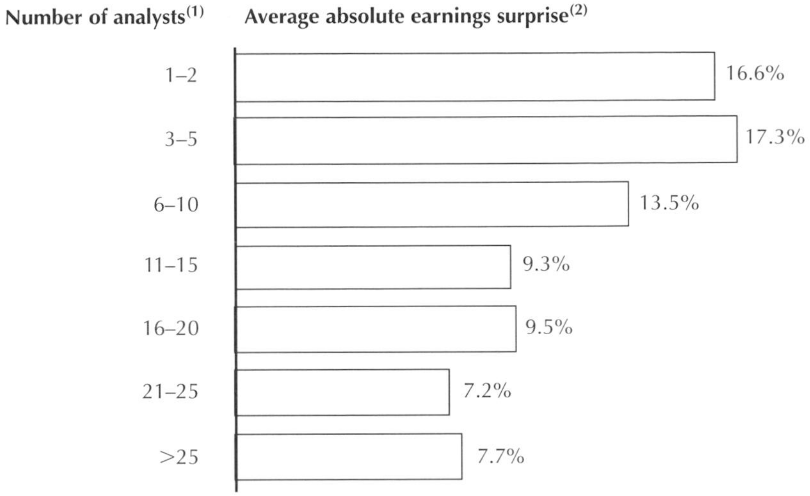

Number of analysts[1]   **Average absolute earnings surprise**[2]

Number of analysts	Average absolute earnings surprise
1–2	16.6%
3–5	17.3%
6–10	13.5%
11–15	9.3%
16–20	9.5%
21–25	7.2%
>25	7.7%

(1) Analysts making a forecast for the observed quarter.
(2) Based on 2,332 earnings announcement observations for S&P 500 companies in 1999 and 2000.
Source: Zacks, Compustat; McKinsey analysis

to. This should be followed by an assessment of each risk with respect to frequency and severity that leads to an initial risk profile for the company and helps prioritize risks. For the successful implementation of an enterprise-wide, holistic risk management program a number of critical questions then have to be answered that address risk appetite, risk management tools and measures, cost of risk management, and organizational and implementation approach.

At the end of the day, the benefits are clear. Senior management must focus more energy on managing risk enterprise-wide. Those that do so will be rewarded handsomely by the capital markets.

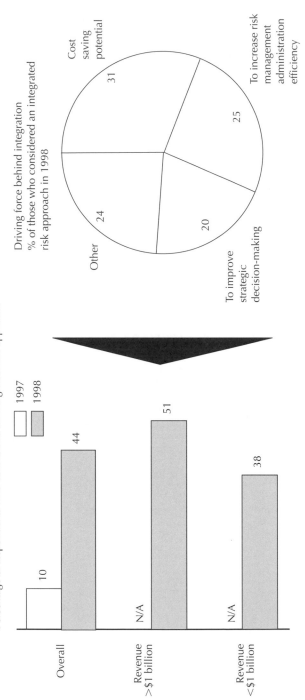

FIGURE 14.8 Growing interest in integrated risk management.

CHAPTER 15

Applying Portfolio Credit Risk Models to Retail Portfolios

Nisso Bucay and Dan Rosen
Algorithmics

W e present a simulation-based model to estimate the credit loss distribution of retail loan portfolios and apply the model to a sample credit card portfolio of a North American financial institution. Within the portfolio model, we test three default models that describe the joint behavior of default events. The first model is purely descriptive in nature while the other two models are causal models of portfolio credit risk, where the influence of the economic cycle is captured through the correlations of default rates to various macroeconomic factors. The results obtained using all three default models are very similar when they are calibrated to the same historical data. In addition to measuring expected and unexpected losses, we demonstrate how the model also allows risk to be decomposed into its various sources, provides an understanding of concentrations, and can be used to test how various economic factors affect portfolio risk.

In recent years several methodologies for measuring portfolio credit risk have been introduced that demonstrate the benefits of using internal models to measure credit risk in the banking book. These models measure economic credit capital and are specifically designed to capture portfolio effects and account for obligor default correlations.

Several portfolio credit risk models developed in the industry have been made public; e.g., CreditMetrics (Gupton et al. 1997), CreditRisk+ (Credit Suisse Financial Products 1997), and Credit Portfolio View (Wilson 1997a and 1997b). Others remain proprietary, such as KMV's Portfolio Manager (Kealhofer 1996). Although the models appear quite different on the surface, recent theoretical work has shown an underlying mathematical equivalence among them (Gordy 2000; Koyluoglu and Hickman 1998). However, the models differ in their distributional assumptions, restrictions, calibration, and solution. Also, empirical work shows that all models yield similar results if the input data are consistent (Crouhy and Mark 1998; Gordy 2000).

A limitation these credit risk models share is the assumption that, during the period of analysis, market risk factors, such as interest rates, are constant. While this assumption is not a major obstacle when measuring credit risk for portfolios of loans or floating rate instruments, it is not acceptable when a portfolio contains derivatives or instruments with embedded optionality. An example of an integrated market and credit risk model that overcomes this limitation is given in Iscoe et al. (1999). The authors extend the framework outlined by Gordy (2000) and Koyluoglu and Hickman (1998) by generating scenarios that include explicit market risk factors and credit drivers, and allowing for stochastic exposures in each scenario.

The general principles of portfolio credit risk models are equally applicable for both the commercial and the retail markets. However, most of the applications of these models in the literature have focused on portfolios of bonds or corporate loans (e.g., Carey 1998; Crouhy and Mark 1998; Bucay and Rosen 1999; Wilson 1997a and 1997b). The measurement of portfolio credit risk in retail loan portfolios has not received as much attention.

In this chapter, we develop a methodology to measure the credit risk of a retail portfolio. The method is based on the general portfolio credit risk framework described in Iscoe et al. (1999). We discuss the practical estimation and implementation of the model and demonstrate its applicability with a case study based on the credit card portfolio of a North American financial institution. Finally, we analyze the sensitivity of the results to various assumptions.

An important part of the framework is the model that describes the joint behavior of default events. We present and test three models to describe this joint default behavior and calibrate them using the same historical data. The first model is a *sector-based model*, which is purely descriptive in nature and makes no attempt to explain economic causality of credit distress. The other two models are *factor-based models* of portfolio credit risk. Factor-based models are *causal models*, in which the influence of the economic cycle is captured through the correlations of default rates to various macroeconomic factors. Both causal models use a multi-factor model that captures the systemic component of credit risk due to a set of macroeconomic factors. Therefore, the factor-based models are useful for further stress-testing and estimating conditional losses using economic scenarios. These two models differ in the mathematical function they use to relate the factors to the default probabilities.

The rest of the chapter is organized as follows. The next section briefly reviews the general quantitative framework for portfolio credit risk models. Thereafter, the credit risk models used in the case study are described, as well as the methodology for their estimation. Then the case study is presented in the following manner: first, the portfolio and the data are described together with assumptions made to measure the different inputs of the model; second, the estimation of the different parameters of the model are discussed; third, the results are presented and the models are compared; fourth, several stress tests are presented. Finally, some concluding remarks and directions for future research are discussed.

PORTFOLIO CREDIT RISK MODELING FRAMEWORK

Portfolio credit risk models can be understood within a general underlying framework (see Gordy (2000); Koyluoglu and Hickman (1998); Iscoe et al. (1999)). In this section, we introduce the basic components of the framework. Subsequently, we presented a model to assess the credit risk of a credit card portfolio.

We focus on default-mode portfolio credit risk models; i.e., on models that measure exclusively the losses due to default events. The framework also applies, more generally, to mark-to-market models, where losses due to credit migration are also considered.

Portfolio credit risk models consist of five parts:

- *Part 1: Description of the scenarios or state of the world.* This is a model of the evolution of the relevant "systemic" or sector-specific credit drivers that drive credit events, as well as those market factors driving obligor exposures, over the period of analysis.
- *Part 2: Correlated default model.* Default probabilities vary as a result of changing economic conditions. At each point in time, an obligor's default probabilities are conditioned on the state of the world. Default correlations among obligors are determined by how changes in credit drivers affect conditional default probabilities.
- *Part 3: Obligor exposures, recoveries, and losses in a scenario.* The credit exposure to an obligor is the amount the institution stands to lose should the obligor default. Recovery rates are generally expressed as the percentage of the exposure that is recovered through such processes as bankruptcy proceedings, the sale of assets, or direct sale to default markets. Exposures can be assumed to be constant in all scenarios for banking instruments without optionality as well as bonds, but not for derivatives or banking book products with credit-related optionality such as prepayment options.
- *Part 4: Conditional portfolio loss distribution in a scenario.* Conditional on a scenario, obligor defaults are independent. Based on this property, we can apply various techniques to obtain the conditional portfolio loss distribution (see, for example, Credit Suisse (1997); Finger (1999); Nagpal and Bahar (1999)).

- *Part 5: Aggregation of losses in all scenarios.* The unconditional distribution of portfolio credit losses is obtained by averaging the conditional loss distributions over all scenarios.

SINGLE-STEP PORTFOLIO CREDIT RISK MODEL FOR A RETAIL PORTFOLIO

We present a single-step, default-mode portfolio credit risk model. The model estimates the distribution of potential losses due to obligor defaults occurring during a single horizon. We assume that exposures and recovery rates at the end of the horizon are deterministic and do not vary with the state of the economy. This is a simplifying assumption that could be relaxed in future work.

Consider the single period $[t_0, t]$; specifically, assume $t = 1$ year. The portfolio contains N obligors or accounts; each obligor belongs to one of $N^s \leq N$ sectors. A sector is a group of obligors of similar characteristics and credit quality. Thus, it is assumed that obligors in a sector are statistically identical; i.e., they have the same probability of default, recovery, and exposure in each scenario.

Three variants of the model are presented: a sector-based logit model, a factor-based logit model, and a factor-based Merton model.

The scenarios in factor-based models are described by both systemic and sector-specific factors, while the scenarios in sector-based models are described by only sector-specific factors. Sector-based models are purely descriptive and make no attempt to explain the economic causality of credit distress. On the other hand, factor-based models are causal models of portfolio credit risk. In factor-based models, the influence of the economic cycle is captured through the use of multi-factor models, which capture the correlations of defaults to various systemic factors. Hence, factor-based credit risk models are useful for further stress-testing and estimating portfolio losses conditional on economic forecast scenarios.

The factor-based logit model and Merton model differ in the mathematical function used to describe conditional default probabilities for each sector. While the logit model uses a functional form purely for mathematical convenience, the Merton model uses a functional relationship derived from financial principles and a microeconomic view of credit.

In the following sections, the specific parts of the models are described.

Scenarios or States of the World

A scenario or state of the world at t is defined by the outcome of q systemic and sector-specific factors that influence the creditworthiness of the obligors in the portfolio. We refer to these factors as the credit drivers. Of the q credit drivers, there are q^M systemic drivers that represent macroeconomic, country, and industry factors; the remainder $q^S = q - q^M$ drivers are sector-specific factors.

Denote by x the vector of factor returns at time t; i.e., x has components $x_k = \ln\{r_k(t)/r_k(t_0)\}$, where $r_k(t)$ is the value of the k-th factor at time t. At the horizon, assume that the returns are normally distributed: $x \sim N(\mu, Q)$, where μ is a vector of mean returns, and Q is a covariance matrix. Denote by $\mathbf{Z}$ the vector of standardized factor returns with entries $Z = (x_k - \mu_k)/\sigma_k$. To distinguish between systematic macroeconomic factors and sector-specific factors we write the standardized factor returns as the row vector $\mathbf{Z} = (\mathbf{Z}^M, \mathbf{Z}^S)$ where $\mathbf{Z}^M = (\mathbf{Z}_1^M, \ldots, \mathbf{Z}_{qM}^M)$ represents the macroeconomic factors and $\mathbf{Z}^S = (\mathbf{Z}_1^S, \ldots, \mathbf{Z}_{qS}^S)$ the sector-specific factors.

Factor-based models attempt to explain partially the economic causality of credit losses. Therefore, scenarios include the realization of both the macroeconomic and sector-specific factors; i.e., they are defined on the whole vector $\mathbf{Z}$. In this case, it is common to assume also that the sector-specific factor returns are uncorrelated.

The sector-based model, on the other hand, is descriptive only and assumes that the states of the world are described by levels of sector-specific factors. Therefore, scenarios are represented only by realizations of the vector of sector-specific drivers, $\mathbf{Z}^S$. In this case, these factors are assumed to be correlated.

For mathematical convenience, it is common practice before the analysis to transform the factor returns to a vector of independent factors. This can be achieved, for example, by applying principal component analysis (PCA) to the original macroeconomic factor returns and the sector-specific factors as required. Hence, for ease of exposition, and without loss of generality, we assume that the standardized factor returns, $\mathbf{Z}$, are independent.

Joint Default Model

For each obligor, the joint default model consists of three components. The first is the definition of the unconditional probability of default. The second is the definition of a creditworthiness index and the estimation of the multi-factor model that links the index to the credit drivers. The third component is a model of obligor default that links the creditworthiness index to the default probability; the default model is used to obtain conditional default probabilities in each scenario. Each of these components is explained below.

Denote by τ the time of default of an obligor in sector j, and by p_j its unconditional probability of default by time t:

$$p_j = P_r\{\tau \leq 1\}$$

It is assumed that unconditional probabilities for each sector are known. The method used to obtain these probabilities from historical default experience is described in Appendix 15.1.

The second component of the joint default model is that the creditworthiness index. Consider a given obligor l in sector j. The obligor creditworthiness index, denoted by Y_l, is a continuous variable that determines an obligor's creditworthiness or financial health. The likelihood of the obligor being in default at time t can be determined directly by the value of its index. In general, Y_l is a standard normal variable (i.e., with zero mean and unit variance).

The creditworthiness index, Y_l, is related to the scenario $\mathbf{Z}$, through a linear multi-factor model:

$$Y_l = \sum_{k=1}^{q} \beta_{lk} Z_k + \sigma_l \varepsilon_l \tag{1}$$

where

$$\sigma_l = \sqrt{1 - \sum_{k=1}^{q} \beta_{lk}^2}$$

β_{lk} is the sensitivity of the index l to factor k, and the ε_l for each obligor index are independent and identically distributed standard normal variables (independent of Z_k) representing obligor-specific, or idiosyncratic, components.

All obligors in a sector share the first term in the right side of Equation (1). Also, all obligors in a sector, j, have a common σ_l, denoted by σ_j, where the subindex j denotes the sector to which obligor l belongs. However, each obligor has its own specific, uncorrelated component, ε_l. Thus, obligors in a given sector share the systemic component and have idiosyncratic components of similar magnitude. Hence, the index for any obligor in sector j is:

$$Y_l = \sum_{k=1}^{q} \beta_{jk} Z_k + \sigma_j \varepsilon_l .$$

An obligor creditworthiness index consists of three components: a systemic component driven by the macroeconomic factors, $\mathbf{Z}^M$; a sector-specific component driven by the sector-specific factors, $\mathbf{Z}^S$; and an obligor-idiosyncratic component. Thus Equation (1) can be rewritten as:

$$Y_l = \sum_{k=1}^{q^M} \beta_{jk}^M Z_k^M + \sum_{k=1}^{q^S} \beta_{jk}^S Z_k^S + \sigma_j \varepsilon_l \tag{2}$$

where

$$\sigma_j = \sqrt{1 - \left(\sum_{k=1}^{q^M} (\beta_{jk}^M)^2 + \sum_{k=1}^{q^S} (\beta_{jk}^S)^2 \right)}.$$

It is useful to write the index as:

$$Y_l = \beta_j^{S*} Y_j^S + \sigma_j \varepsilon_l \tag{3}$$

where

$$\sigma_j = \sqrt{1 - (\beta_j^{S*})^2}$$

Y_j^S denotes the sector creditworthiness index common to obligors in sector j and $(\beta_j^{S*})^2$ represents the percent of variance of the obligor index explained by the sector index. (The sector creditworthiness index is standard normal.) The logit model requires only sector creditworthiness indices, while the Merton model requires explicitly the obligor creditworthiness indices.

The sector creditworthiness index in a factor-based model contains both the systemic macroeconomic component and a sector-specific component. Furthermore, the only sector-specific factor that contributes to the financial health of an obligor in sector j is Z_j^S. Then, from Equation (2) and Equation (3), the sector creditworthiness index for a factor-based model becomes:

$$Y_j^S = \sum_{k=1}^{q^M} \beta_{jk}^{M*} Z_k^M + \beta_{jj}^{S*} Z_j^S$$

where

$$\beta_{jk}^{M*} = \beta_{jk}^M / \beta_j^{S*}, \quad k = 1, \ldots, q^M$$

and $\beta_{jj}^{S*} = \beta_{jj}^S / \beta_j^{S*}$.

On the other hand, in a sector-based model, the sector creditworthiness index does not include a macroeconomic component. Since, in this case, the sector-specific factors are correlated, the creditworthiness index for a sector-based model can be expressed as:

$$Y_j^S = \sum_{k=1}^{q^S} \beta_{jk}^{S*} Z_k^S.$$

The functional forms for the index used in each model are summarized in Table 15.1.

The third and final component of the joint default model is a model of obligor default used to obtain conditional default probabilities in each scenario.

TABLE 15.1   Creditworthiness indices in each model

Model	Index	Default model
Sector-based logit	sector	$Y_j^S = \sum_{k=1}^{q^S} \beta_{jk}^{S^*} Z_k^S$
Factor-based logit	sector	$Y_j^S = \sum_{k=1}^{q^M} \beta_{jk}^{M^*} Z_k^M + \beta_{jj}^{S^*} Z_j^S$
Factor-based Merton	obligor	$Y_j^S = \sum_{k=1}^{q^M} \beta_{jk}^{M^*} Z_k^M + \beta_{jj}^{S^*} Z_j^S$

The conditional probability of default of an account is the probability that an obligor defaults conditional on a scenario. Given the definition of the sectors and the scenarios, all obligors in a given sector share the same conditional default probabilities. Formally, the conditional probability of default of an obligor in sector j, $p_j(\mathbf{Z})$, is the probability that an obligor defaults conditional on the state of the credit drivers, $\mathbf{Z}$:

$$p_j(\mathbf{Z}) = Pr\{\tau \leq t \mid \mathbf{Z}\}.$$

In factor-based models, default probabilities are conditioned on both macroeconomic and sector-specific drivers. In the sector-based model, the probability of default of an obligor in sector j is conditioned on the sector factors only:

$$p_j(\mathbf{Z}) = p_j(\mathbf{Z}^S) = Pr\{\tau \leq t \mid \mathbf{Z}^S\}.$$

The computation of conditional probabilities requires a model that describes the functional relationship between the creditworthiness index (and, hence, the systemic and sector-specific factors) and obligor default probabilities. The functional relationship is a map of the index to the range [0, 1].

We consider two types of models: a logit model, as presented, for example, in Wilson (1997a), and a Merton model, as used in CreditMetrics. From an econometric perspective, the latter is usually referred to as a probit model.

In the logit model, the probability of default of an obligor in sector j is related to the sector creditworthiness index, Y_j^S, through:

$$p_j(Y_j^S) = \frac{1}{1 + a_j \exp(b_j Y_j^S)} \qquad (4)$$

where a_j and b_j are two strictly positive parameters of the model. Note that Equation (4) can alternatively be written as:

$$p_j(y_j^S) = \frac{1}{1 + \exp(y_j^S)}$$

where $y_j^S = \ln a_j + b_j Y_j^S$. That is, the logit model can also be expressed in terms of the non-standardized version of the creditworthiness index, $y_j^S \sim N(\ln (a_j), b_j^2)$. The variables y_j^S are referred to as the logit variables.

Based on Equation (4) and the definition of the sector indices, the conditional default probabilities, $p_j(\mathbf{Z})$, for the sector-based and the factor-based logit models are, respectively:

$$p_j(\mathbf{Z}) = \frac{1}{1 + a_j \exp\left(b_j \sum_k \beta_{lk}^{S^*} Z_k^S \right)}$$

$$p_j(\mathbf{Z}) = \frac{1}{1 + a_j \exp\left\{ b_j \left(\sum_k \beta_{lk}^{M^*} Z_k^M + \beta_{jj}^{S^*} Z_j^S \right) \right\}}.$$

In the Merton model (Merton 1974), default occurs when the assets of a company fall below a given boundary, generally defined by its liabilities. In this situation, an obligor's creditworthiness index, Y_l, can be considered to be the standardized returns of its asset levels. Since obligors in a sector are statistically identical, they share the same default boundary. Thus, default of an obligor l in sector j occurs when Y_l falls below a given sector boundary, α_j. Figure 15.1 provides a graphical representation of the model.

FIGURE 15.1 Merton model of default

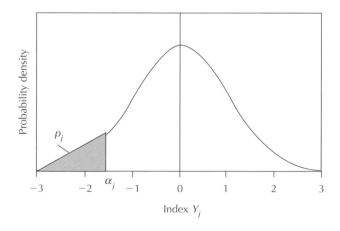

Since the indices are standard normal variables, the unconditional probability of default of obligor l in sector j can be expressed as:

$$p_j = Pr\{Y_l < \alpha_j\} = \Phi(\alpha_j) \tag{5}$$

where Φ denotes the normal cumulative density function and α_j is the unconditional sector threshold. The unconditional threshold is generally calculated by taking the inverse of Equation (5), $\alpha_j = \Phi^{-1}(p_j)$.

From Equation (5), the probability of default, conditional on the index itself, is either zero or one. However, given the factor model defined in Equations (1) to (3), the probability of default of an obligor in sector j, conditional on a scenario, $\mathbf{Z}$, is given by:

$$p_j(\mathbf{Z}) = Pr\{Y_l < \alpha_j \mid \mathbf{Z}\} \tag{6}$$

$$= Pr\left\{\sum_{k=1}^{q^M} \beta_{jk}^M Z_k^M + \beta_{jj}^S Z_j^S + \sigma_j \varepsilon_l < \alpha_j \,\middle|\, \mathbf{Z}\right\}$$

$$= Pr\left\{\varepsilon_l < \frac{\alpha_j - \left(\sum_{k=1}^{q^M} \beta_{jk}^M Z_k^M + \beta_{jj}^S Z_j^S\right)}{\sigma_j}\right\}$$

$$= \Phi\left\{\frac{\alpha_j - \left(\sum_{k=1}^{q^M} \beta_{jk}^M Z_k^M + \beta_{jj}^S Z_j^S\right)}{\sigma_j}\right\}$$

$$= \Phi(\tilde{\alpha}_j).$$

The conditional threshold $\tilde{\alpha}_j = \tilde{\alpha}_j(Z)$, is the threshold that the idiosyncratic component must cross for default to occur in the state of the world, $\mathbf{Z}$. Note that the set of q credit drivers includes both macroeconomic and sector-specific credit drivers.

The three default models are summarized in Table 15.2.

The logit function, Equation (4), and the formula for conditional default probabilities in the Merton model, Equation (6), have similar functional forms. This can be seen in Figure 15.2, which graphs the conditional default probabilities obtained from both models as a function of the sector creditworthiness index.

TABLE 15.2 Default models

Model	Conditional default probabilities
Sector-based logit model	$$p_j(\mathbf{Z}^S) = \frac{1}{1 + a_j \, \exp\left(b_j \, \sum_k \beta_{lk}^{S^*} Z_k^S \right)}$$
Factor-based logit model	$$p_j(\mathbf{Z}) = \frac{1}{1 + a_j \, \exp\left\{ b_j \left(\sum_k \beta_{lk}^{M^*} Z_k^M + \beta_{jj}^{S^*} Z_j^S \right) \right\}}$$
Factor-based Merton model	$$p_j(\mathbf{Z}) = \Phi\left(\frac{\alpha_j - \left(\sum_k \beta_{jk}^M Z_k^M + \beta_{jj}^S Z_j^S \right)}{\sigma_j} \right)$$

Finally, in the case of factor-based models, note that the correlations of creditworthiness indices are uniquely determined by the multi-factor model (which links the indices to the credit driver returns). The correlations of obligor defaults are then obtained from the functional relationship between the indices and the default probabilities, as determined by the Merton or logit model. Similarly, in sector-based models, default correlations are fully defined by the sector index correlations and the default model.

Obligor Exposures and Recoveries in a Scenario

The exposure to an obligor j at the horizon t, V_j, is the amount that can be lost in outstanding transactions with that obligor when default occurs (unadjusted for future recoveries). We assume that the amount that can be lost is deterministic and does not depend on the state of the world: $V_j \neq f(\mathbf{Z})$. Recoveries, in the event of default, are also assumed to be deterministic.

Therefore, the economic loss if an obligor in sector j defaults in any state of the world is:

$$L_j(\mathbf{Z}) = \begin{cases} V_j \cdot (1 - \gamma_j) & \text{with prob. } p_j(\mathbf{Z}) \\ 0 & \text{with prob. } 1 - p_j(\mathbf{Z}) \end{cases}$$

where γ_j is the recovery rate expressed as a fraction of the obligor's exposure. This does not necessarily mean that recovery occurs precisely at default, only that it is expressed as a fraction of the exposed value at default.

FIGURE 15.2 Logit model versus Merton model

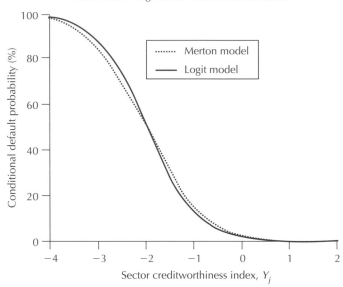

Conditional Loss Distribution in a Scenario

An important fact used for computation is that, conditional on a scenario, obligor defaults are independent. In the most general case, a Monte Carlo simulation can be applied to determine portfolio conditional losses; however, more effective computational tools exploit the property of obligor independence. For example, if a portfolio contains a very large number of obligors, each with a small marginal contribution, then the Law of Large Numbers (LLN) can be applied to estimate conditional portfolio losses. As the number of obligors approaches infinity, the conditional loss distribution converges to the mean losses over that scenario, and the conditional variance and higher moments become negligible. Hence, the conditional portfolio losses, $L(\mathbf{Z})$, are given by the sum of the expected losses of each obligor:

$$L(\mathbf{Z}) = \sum_j E\{L_j(\mathbf{Z})\} = \sum_j V_j \cdot (1 - \gamma_j) \cdot p_j(\mathbf{Z}). \tag{7}$$

The number of accounts in each sector is assumed to be sufficiently large to apply Equation (7). This assumption is made for computational efficiency and can easily be relaxed.

Other efficient methods to compute conditional portfolio losses include the application of the Central Limit Theorem (which assumes that the number of obligors is large, but not necessarily as large as that required for the LLN), the application of moment generating functions with numerical integration, and the application of probability generating functions with a discretization of exposures.

Aggregation of Losses in All Scenarios

Unconditional portfolio losses are obtained by averaging the conditional losses over all states of the world. Mathematically, the loss distribution is given by:

$$Pr\{L_p < \theta\} = \int_Z Pr\{L(\mathbf{Z}) < \theta\} \, dF(\mathbf{Z})$$

where L_p denotes the unconditional portfolio losses, θ denotes the level of losses, and $F(\mathbf{Z})$ is the distribution of $\mathbf{Z}$.

The integral is obtained by performing a Monte Carlo simulation. The Monte Carlo simulation process is performed by the following steps:

- generating a set of joint scenarios on $\mathbf{Z}$. In the factor-based model, scenarios are generated on $\mathbf{Z} = (\mathbf{Z}^M, \mathbf{Z}^S)$, while in the sector-based model scenarios are generated only on $\mathbf{Z}^S$;
- computing, under each scenario:
  - the conditional default probabilities for each sector (using either the logit or the Merton model)
  - the conditional portfolio losses (assuming that the LLN applies);
- obtaining the distribution of portfolio losses by averaging the distribution over all scenarios.

The methodology for calibrating each of these models is presented in Appendix 15.1.

CASE STUDY

In this case study we apply the credit risk models described in the previous section to a sample credit card portfolio of a North American financial institution. The analysis period is the first quarter of 1999.

The objective of the study is to compute the portfolio credit loss distribution of outstanding accounts over a one-year horizon and to analyze the various contributions to these losses. Credit losses are defined as those arising exclusively from the event of an obligor's default.

We describe the portfolio and historical data followed by some formal definitions and modeling assumptions. Thereafter, we present the macroeconomic factors and market data. For obvious reasons of confidentiality, the data presented have been normalized. However, this in no way affects the analysis or the conclusions that can be drawn from the results.

Portfolio Description

The data consist of account information for credit cards issued between the last quarter of 1995 and the first quarter of 1999. Accounts are grouped in terms of their cohort and risk class. A cohort is formed by all the credit cards issued in a particular month.

Cards are scored at acquisition. The score is an internal rating of the creditworthiness of a particular cardholder and assesses a borrower's future repayment performance (see, for example, Mays (1998); Lewis (1992)). Scoring models have been commonly used to measure credit risk in retail portfolios (see, for example, Richeson (1994)).

A risk class is formed by accounts with similar scores. Accounts in the portfolio were originally classified into 20 risk classes, 18 of which are scored. The other two classes correspond to two types of unscored accounts. They require special consideration because of their size and specific characteristics. The first class, "unscored_1," contains special accounts with cards issued directly to existing customers of the financial institution. The second class, "unscored_2," contains cards for which a reliable score is not available (e.g., cards that were not scored or cards for which the score was lost).

For modeling purposes, we construct sectors of similar accounts. Each sector must contain a large number of accounts in order to estimate the parameters of the model reliably. For this study, a sector is defined as all the accounts that belong to a specific risk class. Given that some risk classes in the low- and high-risk categories are very thinly populated, the number of sectors was consolidated from 20 to 11. With larger samples it is possible to group accounts in sectors by adding, for example, geographical or demographic information.

The sample portfolio contains between half a million and a million cards. Figure 15.3 presents the percentage of the total number of accounts in each sector and the percentage of the total credit limit available to each sector. Sector 1 contains the highest risk accounts (low scores), while sector 9 contains the lowest risk accounts (high scores). Note that the unscored sectors represent a large percentage of the sample portfolio when measured by the percentage of total accounts or total credit limits. As is expected, on a per card basis, the average credit limit generally increases with the score. At any point in time, accounts in the portfolio are classified as performing in default or closed. This data is used to estimate default rates. Figure 15.4

FIGURE 15.3 Composition of the portfolio

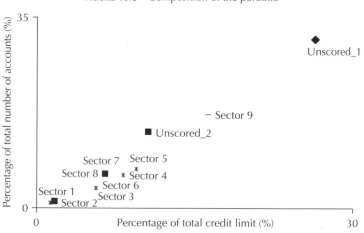

presents the cumulative percentage of accounts classified as either performing or in default, by sector.

Portfolio as of First Quarter, 1999

We measure the credit risk of all cards in the portfolio classified as performing at the end of the first quarter of 1999. Figure 15.5 shows the average balance per card and the utilization rate (given by the ratio of the current balance over the original credit limit). The average balance and the utilization rate are presented as deviations from the average balance per card and the utilization rate for the portfolio as a whole. For example, while the average balance per card in sector 1 is 30% above the average balance per card for the portfolio, the average balance per card in sector 9 is about 45% below.

Not surprisingly, high-risk accounts carry a larger average balance since accounts with low scores are expected to be credit takers, while cards in the high-score categories are expected to have a larger transactional component.

Modeling Assumptions and Data

All three models require:

- current ratings (or scores) for all accounts
- definition of sectors for analysis
- definition of default events
- default probabilities for each sector
- credit exposures
- recovery rates.

FIGURE 15.4 Cumulative percentage of performing and default accounts by sector

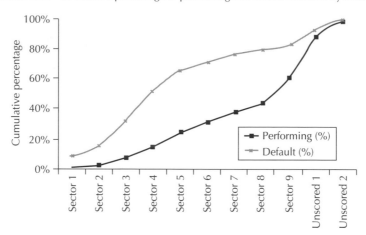

In addition, the factor-based models also require the definition of macroeconomic factors or credit drivers and their joint distribution. Below, we describe the assumptions and data used in the model.

Account Scores

The score of each account at the current time is required to classify accounts into sectors and to estimate the likelihood of each account defaulting in the following year. Since the sample data contains only the scores of the credit

FIGURE 15.5 Average balance per card

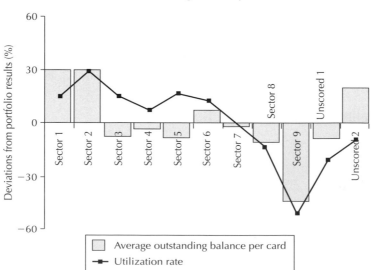

cards when they were issued, we assume that all outstanding accounts retain a score similar to the one they were originally assigned; hence, they remain in the same sector that they were assigned to at acquisition. More precisely, we assume that overall, the portfolio has the same proportion of accounts in each sector.

Sectors

As noted, 11 sectors are identified. The assumptions of the model are that a sector is homogeneous (i.e., accounts are approximately the same size) and all accounts within a sector are statistically identical.

Default Events

A default event occurs when a particular cardholder fails to pay three minimum monthly payments on the credit card balance (and the loan is eventually charged-off by the bank) or when the cardholder declares bankruptcy. Given the method for estimating probabilities of default, we also assume that all accounts classified as performing at the time of the analysis were performing in the previous months. This assumption may require further validation.

Probabilities of Default

In order to calibrate the joint default model, we require the one-year probabilities of default for all sectors and a description of how these default probabilities change through time.

For each month in the sample, default probabilities are estimated as the observed default rates over the following year of all new accounts issued for each sector. The one-year default rates for these cohorts are measured by the cumulative number of defaults (charge-offs and bankruptcies) one year after a specific cohort was formed, as a percentage of the number of accounts issued.

There are two reasons to estimate default rates from only the one-year default rates of accounts when they are issued. First, the only data available are the scores assigned to the cards on the issue date; second, using a new set of cards each month results in independent samples that can be used to estimate the distribution of default probabilities, even though the periods are overlapping. The latter is a subtle, yet important point in the estimation of the joint default model.

The time series contains 28 one-year default rates for each sector. Table 15.3 summarizes the statistics for these series. The median and

Table 15.3 Statistics for default probabilities time series

Sector	1	2	3	4	5	6	7	8	9	u_1	u_2
Median[1]	108	103	107	113	112	102	101	98	96	88	104
Standard deviation[2]	36	43	42	42	37	40	47	41	42	60	40
Excess Kurtosis	−0.55	−0.42	−0.95	−0.88	−0.90	−0.23	4.02	3.16	−0.37	0.82	−0.25
Skewness	−0.54	−0.50	−0.57	−0.54	−0.55	−0.13	1.39	1.31	0.24	1.08	−0.33
Chi-square statistic	6.5	2.5	11.5	5.5	5.0	2.0	2.5	7.5	2.5	10.1	2.0
Critical Chi-square	9.5	9.5	9.5	9.5	9.5	9.5	9.5	9.5	9.5	9.5	9.5
Test result	Accept	Accept	Reject	Accept	Accept	Accept	Accept	Accept	Accept	Reject	Accept

(1) ratio of median/mean rate (%)
(2) ratio of standard deviation/mean rate (%)

standard deviations are presented as a percent of the mean rate in each sector.

Average default probabilities decrease monotonically with the score of the sector. The average rates of sector unscored_1 and sector unscored_2 fall between the averages rates of sector 6 and sector 7.

Although it is difficult to assess accurately the distribution of default rates using only a few observations, the distribution of default rates in general appears to be close to normal. We test for the normality of the distribution of default rates by applying a Chi-square goodness-of-fit test with a 5% confidence level. This suggests that a direct simulation of joint default probabilities might be a simple alternative to other models.

Table A1 in Appendix 15.2 provides the sample correlations of default probabilities between sectors. Correlations between default rates in each sector are substantial (they range between −12% and 88%) and, hence, cannot be assumed to be independent.

Credit Exposures

Credit exposure is the amount the bank stands to lose in the event that a cardholder defaults, unadjusted for any recovery. Generally, when an account that has been performing accumulates missed payments prior to default, the outstanding balance quickly approaches the current credit limit (which for longstanding accounts may be different from the original credit limit). With timely updates on the evolution of credit limits, the credit exposure to an account that default is generally close to the last authorized credit limit.

We estimate the credit exposure of an account in default by the average utilization rate at the time of default (the product of the percentage by which the outstanding balance exceeds the original credit limit and the limit). Average exposures in each sector are shown in Figure 15.6 as deviations from average exposures for the portfolio.

Recovery Rates

In the case of retail loans, like credit cards, factors such as the lack of collateral, the small size of loans and the expense incurred in court proceedings contribute to low recovery rates, if recovery occurs at all. In this study, recovery rates are deterministic and are based on the average loss rate in each sector. The recovery rates are presented in Figure 15.6 as deviations from the average rate for the portfolio.

Credit Drivers

For the factor-based models, nine macroeconomic variables are considered to be the credit drivers that systemically drive the default probabilities of each sector. These credit drivers are:

1. industrial production
2. stock index
3. consumer price index
4. retail sales
5. unemployment level
6. three-month treasury bill at tender
7. short-term government bond yield
8. medium-term government bond yield
9. long-term government bond yield.

Monthly data for the credit drivers from December 1982 to March 1999 is obtained from the Standard & Poors' financial market and economic database (Standard & Poors' 1999).

CALIBRATION OF JOINT DEFAULT PROBABILITY MODELS

The estimation techniques used to calibrate the joint default probability models are presented in Appendix 15.1. In this section, we present the results as applied to the data in this case study.

FIGURE 15.6 Credit exposure and average recovery rate per sector

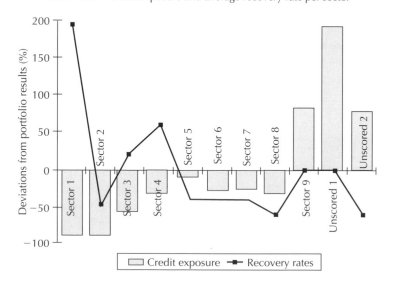

The data on default probabilities cover the period from the last quarter 1995 to the first quarter of 1998. Therefore, a time series of 28 monthly overlapping one-year returns on each of the nine macroeconomic factors $(x_k(t_i), i = 1, \ldots, 28, k = 1, \ldots, 9)$ is used to estimate the parameters of the joint default model.

Sector-based Logit Model

The statistics for the logit variables in each sector are presented in Table 15.4. As can be seen in it, the assumption of normality of the logit variables might not be accurate, particularly for sector 3, sector 4, and sector 5. However, additional data would be required to estimate this distribution with more confidence.

The correlation matrix of the logit variables is presented in Table A2 in Appendix 15.2. As is expected from the correlations of the default probabilities, correlations are substantial between the sector indices, ranging between −10% and 82%.

Factor-based Models

The factor-based models are based on factors that are independent standard normal variables. (This assumption is made for computational convenience and does not restrict the analysis.) Independent factors are obtained from the original macroeconomic factors using PCA (principal component analysis).

With PCA, the credit drivers are expressed as linear combinations of uncorrelated standardized random variables called principal components (PC). The use of principal components reduces the number of credit drivers used in the estimation of the model.

Figure 15.7 presents the percent variance that each of the principal components explains, as well as the cumulative variance. Note that five factors explain more than 95% of the joint movements of all nine macroeconomic factors. Figure 15.8 plots the weights in each factor for the first five principal components. For example, the first factor, which explains over half of the joint movements of the credit drivers, has positive weights on the retail sales, stock index, unemployment level, consumer price index and industrial production, and a negative weight on all interest rate credit drivers.

For each default model, the coefficients of the multi-factor model are estimated using regression as described in Appendix 15.1. In this exercise, the regressors are the principal components of the nine macroeconomic credit drivers. (Note that the factor-based models with nine principal components are likely to suffer from over-fitting, given the small number of

Table 15.4 Statistics of the time series of logit variables

Sector	1	2	3	4	5	6	7	8	9	u_1	u_2
Mean	2.5	3.1	3.6	3.7	3.9	4.2	4.5	4.8	5.8	4.3	4.4
Median	2.4	2.9	3.4	3.5	3.8	4.1	4.4	4.7	5.8	4.3	4.3
Standard deviation	0.5	0.5	0.6	0.6	0.5	0.5	0.4	0.4	0.5	0.5	0.6
Excess Kurtosis	0.69	0.58	2.31	0.45	0.73	3.0	1.3	1.1	−0.09	−0.43	3.26
Skewness	1.21	1.1	1.5	1.23	1.2	1.53	0.63	0.26	0.72	−0.32	1.7
Chi-square statistic	12.5	1.3	22.0	16.5	15.5	6.0	5.5	5.5	6.5	6.4	10.0
Critical Chi-square	9.5	6.0	9.5	9.5	9.5	9.5	9.5	9.5	9.5	9.5	9.5
Test result	Reject	Accept	Reject	Reject	Reject	Accept	Accept	Accept	Accept	Accept	Reject

observations. However, they will likely result in more conservative losses since they build higher correlations. For predictive purposes, and further risk decomposition, a model with fewer systemic factors is likely to be better behaved and more robust.)

Logit Model

The regression results are presented in Table A3 in Appendix 15.2. Note that some individual weights form the regression are not statistically significant, in part because of the small number of observations. Based on the

FIGURE 15.7   Percent of variance explained by PCA

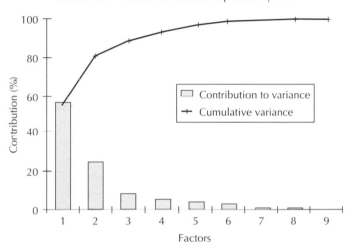

FIGURE 15.8   Factor weights for the first five principal components

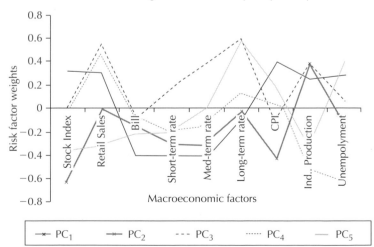

regression, estimates for the systemic and idiosyncratic components of the indices are presented in Table 15.5.

The credit drivers explain between 38% and 73% of the variance of the sector creditworthiness indices. Figure 15.9 shows the explanatory power of the credit drivers by plotting the systemic component and the historical realizations of the index in the period of estimation for selected sectors. Clearly, the systemic component tracks the main tendencies of the indices. Only four sectors are shown, but the results are similar for the remaining indices.

Factor-based Merton Model

The weights (β_{jk}) of the factor-based Merton model are summarized in Table A4 in Appendix 15.2. The systemic and sector-specific components of the indices are presented in the second and third row of Table 15.6. These are the relative sizes of the coefficients $\sum_{k} (\beta_{jk}^{M})^2$ and $(\beta_{jj}^{S})^2$ as defined in Appendix 15.1 (Equation A1 and Equation A2). The sector-specific component, σ_j^2, is presented in the last row of Table 15.6.

In the following sections we present the results of the analyses performed on the sample portfolio, considering first the portfolio loss distribution calculated according to each of the three models, followed by an analysis of risk contribution and marginal risk by sector and finally, stress-testing of some parameters of the model.

PORTFOLIO LOSS DISTRIBUTION

The portfolio loss distribution is estimated based on 5,000 Monte Carlo scenarios on the relevant credit drivers for each of the models. Scenarios on the logit variables for each sector, y_j^S, are used in the sector-based logit model; scenarios on the nine macroeconomic credit drivers and the 11 sector-specific credit drivers are used for the factor-based models. Scenarios are generated directly on the standardized independent returns, or first on the macroeconomic factors and then transformed into standardized independent variables. Given the independence of the sector-specific credit drivers, simulation could have been restricted to scenarios on the systemic credit drivers only.

Table 15.5 Specific and systemic risk in the factor-based logit model

Sector	1	2	3	4	5	6	7	8	9	u_1	u_2
Variance of logit variables	0.25	0.24	0.38	0.35	0.23	0.278	0.25	0.17	0.23	0.28	0.34
Percentage systemic	65.32	52.20	73.22	65.77	73.40	46.85	38.16	47.47	50.48	52.67	63.84
Percentage sector-specific	34.70	47.80	26.77	34.23	26.58	53.14	61.83	52.55	49.53	47.33	36.17

Table 15.6 Specific and systemic risk in the facto-based Merton model

Sector	1	2	3	4	5	6	7	8	9	u_1	u_2
Variance of inverse normal variables	0.0545	0.0470	0.0606	0.0552	0.0347	0.0388	0.0339	0.0220	0.0238	0.0429	0.0439
Percentage systemic	65.49	52.72	74.85	66.81	74.60	48.99	39.38	47.29	50.62	53.33	63.49
Percentage sector-specific	34.51	47.28	25.15	33.19	25.40	51.01	60.62	52.71	49.38	46.67	36.51
Percentage variance of sector-specific factors, σ_j^2	0.97	0.98	0.97	0.98	0.98	0.98	0.98	0.99	0.99	0.98	0.98

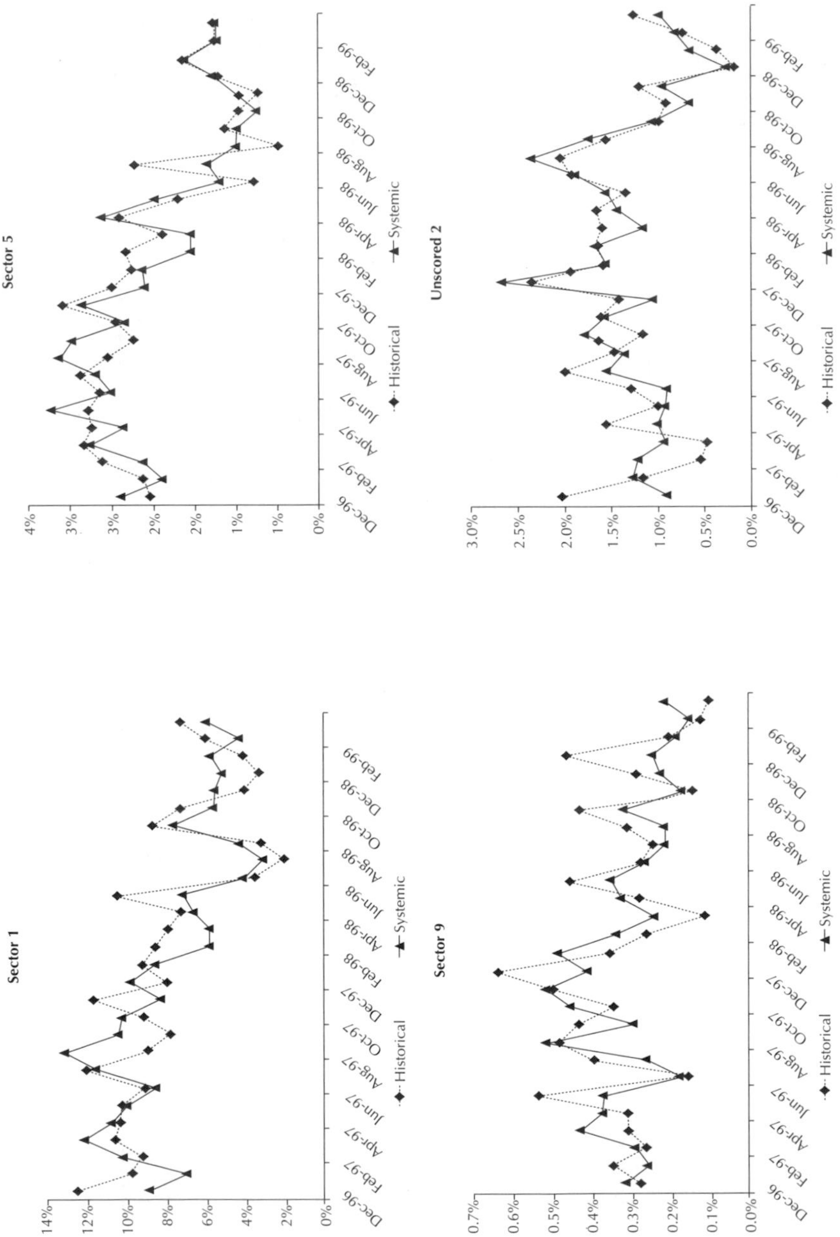

FIGURE 15.9 Systemic component and index over period of estimation for factor-based logit model

Sector-based Logit Model

The portfolio loss distribution is presented in Figure 15.10. The distribution is presented as deviations from the expected losses. As expected, this distribution is skewed and has a long fat tail on the left due to the nature of credit risk.

Table 15.7 presents the relevant statistics of the loss distribution, including the expected losses, standard deviation, maximum percentile losses, unexpected losses (Credit VaR), and expected shortfall at the 99.9^{th} percentiles for each of the models. Expected losses have been normalized to 1.0 and all the statistics are scaled to expected losses. Numbers in parentheses represent the number of standard deviation from the expected losses.

Credit VaR measures the capital required to cover unexpected losses (maximum percentile losses minus expected losses) at the chosen level (99% or 99.9%). In this case, capital is approximately 15% to 78% higher than the reserves, depending on the confidence level chosen. Note that Credit VaR (99%) is approximately three times the standard deviation; if the distribution were normal, Credit VaR would be only twice the standard deviation.

In addition to the most commonly known measures of risk, Table 15.7 also presents the expected shortfall (tail conditional loss). Expected shortfall measures the expected losses beyond a specified percentile of the distribution. By measuring the area under the tail of the distribution, expected shortfall provides a good measure of extreme losses, should they occur. On the other hand, maximum percentile losses are point estimates in the tail of the distribution and may present undesirable properties from a risk management perspective (see Artzner et al. (1998)).

FIGURE 15.10 Loss distribution for the sector-based logit model

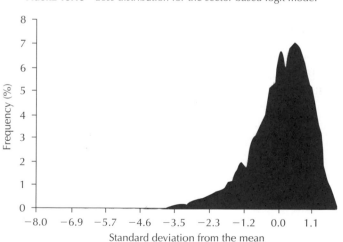

TABLE 15.7 Statistics for one-year loss distribution

	Sector-based logit model	Factor-based logit model	Factor-based Merton model
Expected losses	1.0	1.0	1.0
Standard deviation	0.4	0.3	0.3
Maximum losses (99%)	2.1	2.1	1.9
Credit VaR (99%)	1.1 (3.2)	1.1 (3.2)	0.9 (2.8)
Expected shortfall (99%)	2.4	2.3	2.2
Maximum losses (99.9%)	2.7	2.6	2.5
Credit VaR (99.9%)	1.8 (5.0)	1.6 (4.6)	1.6 (4.8)
Expected shortfall (99.9%)	3.1	3.0	2.8

Factor-based Logit Model

The relevant statistics for the loss distribution using the factor-based logit model are presented in Table 15.7. The results for the factor-based loss distribution are similar to those for the sector-based loss distribution. The loss distribution looks qualitatively similar to that in Figure 15.10. This implies that when scenarios are defined using explicit macroeconomic and sector-specific credit drivers, the joint behavior of default probabilities for each sector is largely accounted for.

The main differences arise in the extreme tail of the distribution. For example, at the 99.9^{th} percentile, expected shortfall is 5.6% lower in the factor-based model than in the sector-based model. This occurs because the sector-based model presents fewer correlations, since the model can only build correlations through the systemic credit drivers (the sector-specific factors are assumed independent).

Factor-based Merton Model

The relevant statistics for the loss distribution using the factor-based Merton model are reported in Table 15.7. Again, the results are very similar to those of the logit model, particularly to the factor-based logit model. The functional equivalence of the factor-based models is clear since the expected and unexpected losses (at the 99th and 99.9^{th} percentiles) in the logit and Merton model are similar.

Risk Contributions and Marginal Risk

Figure 15.11 presents the risk contributions of each sector. The graphs present the percentage decrease in the specified statistic if the accounts of the corresponding sector are eliminated. The risk contribution of any sector is roughly the product of the size of the sector and the marginal risk of increasing the exposure to a particular sector by one unit. Therefore, it is useful to understand whether the risk contribution of a particular score arises because a large portion of the portfolio falls in that sector, or because the sector has a high marginal risk. Figure 15.12 plots the marginal risk of every sector (marginal standard deviation as a percentage of mean exposure) against the mean exposure.

From a risk management perspective, it is desirable to have a small exposure to sectors with high marginal risk and a large exposure to sectors with low marginal risk. Sectors with high exposure and high marginal risk are outliers, as is the case, for example, for sector unscored_1. One sector dominates another sector if it has both higher exposure and marginal risk. For example, sector 5 dominates sector 6, and sector unscored_1 dominates sectors 6 through 9 and unscored_2. Dominant portfolios are outliers that may point to opportunities for effective restructuring.

Note in Figure 15.12 that, on a marginal basis, sectors 1 through 9 have progressively lower marginal risk, since, on average, accounts in these sectors have decreasing unconditional default probabilities. On a portfolio basis, however, correlations between obligor defaults may play a significant role. Therefore, one sector with a lower default probability than another may

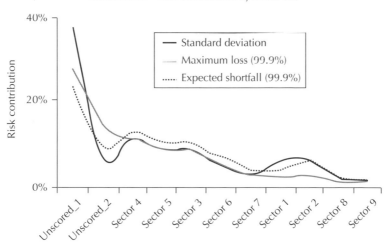

FIGURE 15.11   Risk contribution by sector (%)

FIGURE 15.12   Marginal risk versus average exposure

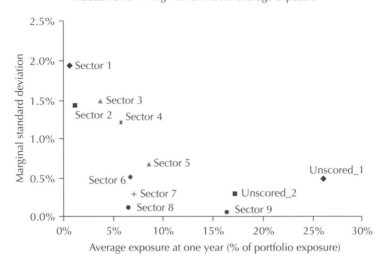

have a larger marginal contribution, since it has a higher correlation to the overall portfolio. This is the case, for example, for sector 2 and sector 3.

STRESS-TESTING

The results obtained using factor-based logit model (Table 15.7) are designated as the base case. Comparisons to the base case are used to test the sensitivity of the loss distribution to changes in various parameters of the model. Given the functional equivalence of the factor-based logit and Merton models, and the similarity of the results, the comparison could have been based on the result of either model.

We perform four tests. First, we assess the appropriateness of the Monte Carlo simulation by computing sampling errors for the distribution estimates and comparing the results to a simulation with a larger number of scenarios. Second, we assess the impact of concentration risk by assuming all sectors are independent. Third, we estimate a model of the credit driver evolution using a larger data sample that better captures the impact of the business cycle. Finally, we apply a weaker definition of default that results in higher default rates, and estimate the portfolio losses that result from this larger set of events.

Sampling Errors

The statistics in the base case are point estimates based on 5,000 Monte Carlo scenarios on both macroeconomic and sector-specific credit drivers.

These estimates can be characterized using probabilistic confidence bounds. Confidence bounds on the mean and standard deviation are estimated using standard methods found in most statistics texts; the bounds on percentiles are estimated using rank statistics (Pritsker 1997).

Table 15.8 presents the 95% confidence bounds for the expected losses, standard deviation, and maximum losses at the 99th and 99.9th percentiles. The statistics are presented relative to expected losses in the base case. The numbers in parentheses indicate the percentage deviation from the estimate. While the point estimate of the maximum losses (99%) is twice the level of the expected losses, with 95% confidence, the true losses are within 5% of this ratio. At higher percentiles, the confidence bounds widen. Hence, the certainty of the results diminishes.

Table 15.8 also summarizes the results of a simulation with 10,000 scenarios. Notice that the difference between the estimates of the two simulations is much smaller than the difference between the confidence bounds with 5,000 scenarios.

For example, while the bounds for the maximum losses (99%) scaled by expected losses are approximately 5% of the estimate, the difference between the two simulations is approximately 1%. In general, the non-parametric bounds on maximum losses are fairly conservative. The accuracy of the Monte Carlo simulation is inversely related to the square root of the number of scenarios. Therefore, using twice as many scenarios reduces the uncertainly in the results by a factor of about two.

Given the greater uncertainty in the estimation of the parameters of the model, these results suggest that increasing the number of scenarios may result in unnecessary additional computation.

TABLE 15.8 95% confidence bounds for the estimates

	Estimate with 5,000 scenarios			Estimate with 10,000 scenarios
	Lower bound	Estimate	Upperbound	
Expected losses	0.98 (1.5%)	1.00	1.02 (1.5%)	1.00
Standard deviation	0.34 (2.2%)	0.35	0.36 (4.4%)	0.35
Maximum losses (99%)	2.02 (4.3%)	2.11	2.22 (5.6%)	2.08
Maximum losses (99.9%)	2.46 (5.6%)	2.60	3.41 (31.2%)	2.67

Independent Defaults

We estimate the loss distribution assuming that defaults across sectors are uncorrelated and determined only the sector-specific factor.

Figure 15.13 illustrates the loss distribution assuming that sector defaults are independent. The distribution is graphed against deviations from expected losses in the base case. This loss distribution has a higher mass in the center and a tail that is not as fat as the distribution of the base. The fact that the base case has a fatter tail can also be concluded by noticing that the standard deviation is smaller if defaults are independent. Therefore, even though extreme losses have the same distance from the mean, economic capital is higher if defaults are correlated.

Table 15.9 presents the statistics for the case of independent defaults and compares them to those of the base case. The results are presented relative to the expected losses in the base case. The numbers in parentheses indicate the percentage deviation from the base case.

Expected losses are not affected by correlations, therefore, credit reserves are not affected. However, economic capital is very sensitive to correlations. Assuming independent defaults, Credit VaR with independent defaults is about 60% lower, compared to the base case. The ratio of the expected shortfall in the base case to the expected shortfall with independent defaults is between 70% and 75% for the 99th and 99.9[th] percentiles, respectively.

FIGURE 15.13   Loss distribution with independent defaults

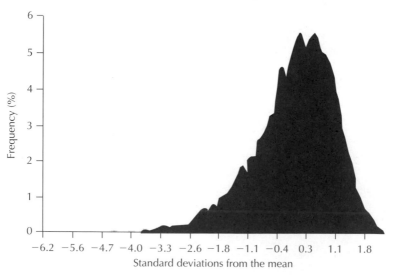

Standard deviations from the mean

Losses with Correlated Credit Risk Drivers

The parameters of the credit risk model are estimated based on data for defaults and credit drivers that spans a short, 28-month time period (from the last quarter of 1995 to the first quarter of 1998). Thus, the sample probably does not cover a full business cycle. One major advantage of the factor-based models in credit risk measurement is that data for the credit drivers are available for longer horizons. Thus, more information about the business cycle can be incorporated using factor-based models.

Recall that the default model with credit drivers consists of two parts: a multi-factor model that links the creditworthiness index of each sector (and hence the default probabilities) to the credit drivers, and a model for the evolution of the credit drivers. The results in the base case are obtained using data from the 28-month period to estimate both parts of the model. We can refine the estimates of portfolio losses by estimating the joint behavior of the credit drivers using data for longer horizons.

In this example, we perform the Principal Component Analysis (PCA) on the credit drivers using quarterly non-overlapping data from a period that extends from the first quarter of 1983 to the first quarter of 1999. The regression model is re-estimated with the newly transformed credit drivers, which are correlated during the estimation period of the default model. The simulation is performed using these new parameters. Figure 15.14 presents the resulting portfolio loss distribution. The distribution is graphed against deviations from expected losses in the base case.

The statistics for the loss distribution for the case of correlated credit drivers are presented in Table 15.10. The results presented are relative to the expected losses in the base case. The numbers in parentheses indicate the percentage deviation from the base case.

The expected losses are higher and the standard deviation is somewhat smaller than in the base case. Given that, the Credit VaR at the 99% level

TABLE 15.9 Statistics for independent defaults

	Base case	Independent defaults
Expected losses	1.0	1.0
Standard deviation	0.3	0.2
Maximum losses (99%)	2.1	1.6
Credit VaR (99%)	1.1 (3.2)	0.6 (3.0)
Expected shortfall (99%)	2.3	1.8
Maximum losses (99.9%)	2.6	2.0
Credit VaR (99.9%)	1.6 (4.6)	1.0 (4.5)
Expected shortfall (99.9%)	3.0	2.1

FIGURE 15.14   Loss distribution with correlated credit drivers

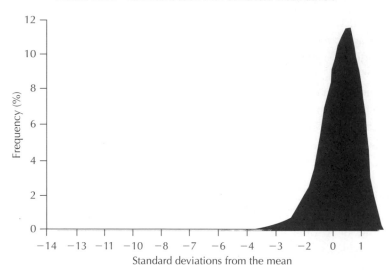

Standard deviations from the mean

TABLE 15.10   Statistics conditioned on correlated credit drivers

	Base case	**Correlated credit drivers**
Expected losses	1.0	1.1
Standard deviation	0.3	0.3
Maximum losses (99%)	2.1	2.1
Credit VaR (99%)	1.1 (3.2)	1.0 (3.0)
Expected shortfall (99%)	2.3	2.5
Maximum losses (99.9%)	2.6	3.2
Credit VaR (99.9%)	1.6 (4.6)	2.1 (6.7)
Expected shortfall (99.9%)	3.0	4.1

in both cases are very similar. However, the Credit VaR at the 99.9% level
is more than 25% higher for correlated credit drivers, due to the longer tail
associated with the distribution. In general, the statistics at the 99.9% level
are between 25% and 39% higher than those of the base case. One
explanation for these results is that the scenarios span a broader range of
market and economic changes that better capture the effect the economic
cycle has on consumer finance.

Default Losses with False-performing Accounts

At the end of each month, some accounts are classified as performing,
though they are actually in default. The default losses computed in the base
case do not incorporate the "potential" losses of these *false-performing*

accounts. Thus, it is useful to estimate the impact on the relevant default statistics of classifying these accounts as true defaults. To accomplish this, the parameters on the models must be estimated with new regressions.

The histogram of the loss distribution and the statistics of the distribution are shown in Figure 15.15 and Table 15.11, respectively. In both cases, the results are presented relative to the expected losses in the base case. The numbers in parentheses indicate the percentage deviation form the base case.

Note that while changing correlations affects only dispersion statistics, changing default frequencies severely impacts on the expected losses as well. Incorporating false-performing accounts increases the expected losses by 50% (because of the increase in estimated default probabilities) and increases economic capital by 45% to 55%, depending on the statistic and confidence level being used.

CONCLUSION

We have developed a simulation-based framework to estimate the one-period credit loss distribution of a retail loan portfolio, and demonstrated the usefulness of the model by estimating one-year credit losses for a credit card portfolio. The framework allows risk to be decomposed into its various sources, and provides further understanding of risk concentrations and the impact of economic factors on the portfolio.

We present and test three models to describe joint default behavior: a sector-based logit model, a factor-based logit model, and a factor-based

FIGURE 15.15 Loss distribution with false-performing accounts

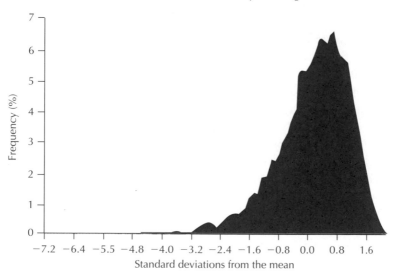

TABLE 15.11 Statistics including false-performing accounts

	Base case	False-performing accounts
Expected losses	1.0	1.5
Standard deviation	0.3	0.5
Maximum losses (99%)	2.1	3.1
Credit VaR (99%)	1.1 (3.2)	1.6 (3.1)
Expected shortfall (99%)	2.3	3.5
Maximum losses (99.9%)	2.6	4.0
Credit VaR (99.9%)	1.6 (4.6)	2.5 (4.8)
Expected shortfall (99.9%)	3.0	4.5

Merton model. While the sector-based model is purely descriptive, the factor-based models are causal models that capture the economic cycle through macroeconomic factors. Hence, the latter models are useful for further stress-testing and estimating conditional losses using economic scenarios.

All three default models yield comparable results when the same data are used. The discrepancies that arise are due to different distributional assumptions. The discrepancies observed are small, and are probably amplified by the scarcity of data. More statistical analysis is required to explore the difference between the models.

Several reasonable and commonly used assumptions may influence the results of the models. First, sector indices and factor returns are assumed to be joint normally distributed. Although this is common practice, it may be unrealistic; more research is required to determine the effect of this assumption. Second, the exposure and recovery rates per sector are deterministic; although this is common to most portfolio models today, it may be useful to explore the implication of stochastic exposures using an integrated market and credit risk model, such as that introduced in Iscoe et al. (1999). Finally, each sector is assumed to have a large, fully diversified sub-portfolio; this is reasonable given the large number of accounts in each sector, but may lead to some underestimation of credit risk. This assumption could be relaxed easily during the simulation.

One of the main limitations in the case study is that of data availability. Although the results are useful, a large amount of historical data may be required to obtain more robust estimations of joint default probability distributions and factor models. The lack of sufficient data leads to two problems.

The first problem is that the uncertainty associated with the parameters entering the model is quite large. This does not mean that the parameters should be discarded but, rather, that they should be treated as "best guesses", given the current information. Consequently, more stress-testing and sensitivity analysis must be performed. If conservative estimates of credit risk are required, one can apply the most conservative parameters obtained from the data.

The second problem is that given that the default data covers less than three years, the model may not capture the dependency of default frequencies on the economic cycle. In this case, data over a longer time horizon, which spans economic cycles, are required. We show how the impact of economic cycles can be addressed using multi-factor models. Of course, more work in this area is required.

Since data availability is often an issue, it is important, whenever possible, to complement the data used for estimation with external industry/agency data, as well as reasonable, conservative data acquired from internal experience.

The results from the case study clearly show that some refinement in the modeling of the portfolio may lead to the greatest improvements. For example, as expected, there is a large concentration of losses in the unscored sectors. These sectors are also the most likely to be inhomogeneous sectors; the use of historical data to estimate default rates for these sectors may be less accurate. Further refinement and classification of accounts in these sectors is likely to lead to substantial enhancements in the credit risk assessment of the portfolio.

In this study, the score of each card at acquisition is used as an indicator of default likelihood over the following year. This means that the results assume that the credit cards in the portfolio at the time of the analysis maintain the score they were assigned initially, or, alternatively, that migration across sectors is such that the net of migration across sectors is very small. This may be a strong assumption. A better way to address this problem is to use current, up-to-date scores and account characteristics to group obligors into sectors. However, for many institutions these data may not be readily available and acquiring them may be a costly proposition. An alternative in this case is to use Bayesian methods to refine the composition of the cards in each sector, given all historical default experience.

The methodology presented in this chapter can also be used to obtain risk management reports that include further sensitivity analysis and stress-testing, RAROC and risk-return analysis, systemic and idiosyncratic risk decomposition, risk contributions of economic factors and conditional credit risk calculation using factor-based models, and economic forecasts.

In conclusion, the application of portfolio credit risk models to retail portfolios is in its infancy and much more research is required. Of particular importance is the validation and backtesting of the models. This is an issue that was raised by the Basel Committee (1999) and work in this area will likely require extensive (external) data and intensive computation (see, for example, Lopez (2000)).

ACKNOWLEDGMENTS

We would like to thank David Dallaire, Alex Kreinin and Leonid Merkoulovitch for fruitful discussions and help provided in the estimation of the different models and Michael Zerbs for constructive feedback on the analysis of the results.

APPENDIX 15.1 CALIBRATION OF JOINT DEFAULT PROBABILITY MODELS

The parameters of the joint default probability models are estimated as follows.

Sector-based Logit Model

Data input: for each sector j, a time series of equally spaced observed default rates $p_j(t_i)$, $i = 1, \ldots, n$.

Output: joint distributions of the sector indices, Y_j^S.

Since the indices are assumed to be joint normal, we estimate the mean for each index and the covariance matrix. For each sector, the time series of default probabilities is transformed into a time series of logit variables:

$$y_j^S(t_i) = ln\left(\frac{1 - p_j(t_i)}{p_j(t_i)}\right), i = 1, \ldots, n.$$

The mean, volatility, and correlations of the indices are obtained from the sample mean, volatility, and correlations of this time series.

The indices, y_j^S, are assumed to be normal (not standard normal); they have a non-zero mean, μ_j^S, and non-unit standard deviation, σ_j^S. It is straightforward to express the model in terms of standard normal indices $Y_j^S = (y_j^S - \mu_j^S)/\sigma_j^S$.

Factor-based Models

Data input: a time series of equally spaced observed default rates for each sector j and of macroeconomic factors returns, $p_j(t_i)$, $x_k(t_i)$, $k = 1, \ldots, q^M$, $i = 1, \ldots, n$.

Output: the definition of the q independent credit drivers and the multi-factor model joining the indices to the credit drivers. Since the credit drivers include q^M macroeconomic factors and q^S sector-specific factors, the total number of credit drivers is $q = q^M + q^S$.

We write the (row) vector of uncorrelated standard credit drivers as $\mathbf{Z} = (Z_1^M, \ldots, Z_{q^M}^M, Z_1^S, \ldots, Z_{q^S}^S)$, where the Z_j^M and Z_j^S denote macroeconomic and sector-specific credit drivers, respectively. A sector-specific factor affects only a single sector. Thus, for a given obligor l in sector j, the creditworthiness index in Equation (2) can be written as:

$$Y_l = \sum_{k=1}^{q^M} \beta_{jk}^M Z_k^M + \beta_j^S Z_j^S + \sigma_j \varepsilon_l$$

where

$$\sigma_l = \sqrt{1 - \left(\sum_{k=1}^{q^M} \beta_{jk}^2 + (\beta_j^S)^2 \right)}.$$

A set of independent factors are constructed from the macroeconomic factors, as follows:

- First, obtain a time series of standardized factor returns for the macroeconomic credit drivers, $\hat{Z}_k(t_i) = (x_k(t_i) - \mu_k)/\sigma_k^x$, $k = 1, \ldots, q^M$, where μ_k and σ_k^x are the sample mean and standard deviation of each factor.
- Second, using principal component analysis (PCA), obtain a set of independent credit drivers as the linear combinations of the correlated macroeconomic factors. A brief overview of PCA is given in Kreinin et al. (1998).
- Third, construct a time series of the new uncorrelated standardized factors $Z_k(t_i) = \sum_{l=1}^{q} A_{kl} \hat{Z}_k(t_i)$, $i = 1, \ldots, n$, where the coefficients A_{kl} are determined from the eigenvalues and eigenvectors in the PCA.

The methods used to obtain the weights for the creditworthiness index of each model are outlined below.

From Tables 1 and 2, the model of the conditional probability of default for the factor-based logit model is:

$$p_j(\mathbf{Z}) = \frac{1}{1 + a \exp(bY_j^S)}$$

where

$$Y_j^S = \sum_{k=1} \beta_{jk}^{M^*} Z_k^M + \beta_{jj}^{S^*} Z_j^S$$

and

$$\sum_k (\beta_{jk}^{M^*})^2 + (\beta_{jj}^{S^*})^2 = 1.$$

The factor weights are calculated as follows:

- Similar to the sector-based model, from the time series of default rates in each sector, we obtain a time series of logit variables:

$$y_j^S(t_i) = Ln\left(\frac{1 - p_j(t_i)}{p_j(t_i)}\right), i = 1, \ldots, n.$$

Each logit variable has mean μ_j^S and standard deviation σ_j^S.

- The component of the multi-factor model that depends on the macroeconomic factors is estimated by minimum least squares using:

$$y_j^S(t_i) - \mu_j^S = \sum_{k=1}^{q^M} \tilde{\beta}_{jk}^M Z_k^M(t_i) + \xi_j(t_i)$$

where $\xi_j(t_i)$ are independent normal errors.

- The loading of the sector-specific factor, $\tilde{\beta}_{jj}^S$, is computed by matching the total volatility of the multi-factor model of the sector and the observed sample index volatility:

$$\tilde{\beta}_{jj}^S = \sqrt{(\sigma_j^S)^2 - \sum_k (\tilde{\beta}_{jk}^M)^2}.$$

- Finally, the parameters of the model are given by:

$$\beta_{jk}^{M^*} = \tilde{\beta}_{jj}^M / \sigma_j^S, \quad \beta_{jj}^{S^*} = \tilde{\beta}_{jj}^S / \sigma_j^S$$

$$a_j = \exp(\mu_j^S), \quad b_j = \sigma_j^S.$$

The process for the **factor-based Merton model** is similar to that described for the logit model. We estimate the parameters α_j, β_{jk}^M, β_{jj}^S, and σ_j, such that:

$$p_j(\mathbf{Z}) = \Phi\left(\frac{\alpha_j - \left(\sum_k \beta_{jk}^M Z_k^M + \beta_{jj}^S Z_j^S\right)}{\sigma_j}\right)$$

and

$$\sigma_j = \sqrt{1 - \left(\sum_k (\beta_{jk}^M)^2 + (\beta_{jj}^S)^2 \right)}.$$

These parameters are obtained as follows:

- From the time series of default rates in each sector we obtain a time series of inverse normal variables:

$$\tilde{\alpha}_j(t_i) = \Phi^{-1}\{p_j(t_i)\}, \quad i = 1, \ldots, n.$$

- For each sector j, we first apply minimum least squares to estimate $\hat{\alpha}_j$ and $\hat{\beta}_{jk}^M$ from the regression model:

$$\Phi^{-1}(p_j) = \tilde{\alpha}_j = \hat{\alpha}_j + \sum_{k=1}^{q^M} \hat{\beta}_{jk}^M Z_k^M + \xi. \tag{A1}$$

- Then, we obtain the sensitivity of the inverse standard normal variable of sector j to the sector-specific credit driver by the following relationship:

$$\hat{\beta}_{jj}^S = \sqrt{\sigma_{\alpha_j}^2 - \sum_{k=1}^{q^M} (\hat{\beta}_{jk}^M)^2}$$

where $\sigma_{\alpha_j}^2$ is the variance of $\tilde{\alpha}_j(t_i)$, which is the inverse standard normal variable for the sector over the period.

- The coefficients in the multi-factor model are then obtained by properly scaling the regression coefficients by the volatility of the idiosyncratic obligor component of the index:

$$\beta_{jk}^M = \hat{\beta}_{jk}^M \cdot \sigma_j$$

$$\alpha_j = \hat{\alpha}_j \cdot \sigma_j$$

$$\beta_{jj}^S = \hat{\beta}_{jj}^S \cdot \sigma_j$$

where the volatility is finally given by:

$$\sigma_j^2 = \frac{1}{1 + \sigma_{\alpha_j}^2}.$$

The derivation of these formulas is presented below. Recall from Equation (6) that the conditional default probabilities in the Merton model are given by:

$$p_j(\mathbf{Z}) = \Phi\left(\frac{\alpha_j - \left(\sum_{k=1}^{q^M} \beta_{jk} Z_k + \beta_j^S Z^S\right)}{\sigma_j}\right) \tag{A2}$$

From the time series of conditional default probabilities and macro-economic factors, we estimate the parameters α_j, β_{jk}, β_j^S, and σ_j in Equation (A2) with the extra constraint that:

$$\sigma_j = \sqrt{1 - \left(\sum_{k=1}^{q^M} \beta_{jk}^2 + (\beta_j^S)^2\right)}. \tag{A3}$$

Applying an inverse normal transformation and making the change of variables:

$$\hat{\alpha}_j = \alpha_j / \sigma_j, \quad \hat{\beta}_{jk} = \beta_{jk} / \sigma_j, \quad \hat{\beta}_j^S = \beta_j^S / \sigma_j \tag{A4}$$

Equation (A2) becomes the equation defined for the regression:

$$\Phi^{-1}(p_j) = \hat{\alpha}_j = \hat{\alpha}_j + \sum_{k=1}^{q^M} \hat{\beta}_{jk} Z_k + \hat{\beta}_j^S Z^S.$$

By regressing the inverse normal of the conditional default probabilities to the macroeconomic factors we obtain the parameters $\hat{\beta}_{jk}$, and the residual volatility gives the sensitivity of the inverse to the sector-specific factor:

$$\hat{\beta}_j^S = \sqrt{\sigma_{\alpha_j}^2 - \sum_{k=1}^{n} \hat{\beta}_{jk}^2} \tag{A5}$$

where $\sigma_{\alpha_j}^2$ is the variance of $\tilde{\alpha}_j(t_i)$.

The original parameters of the model are then obtained as follows. First the volatility σ_j can be estimated from Equation (A3), Equation (A4), and Equation (A5):

$$\sigma_j^2 = 1 - \left(\sum_{k=1}^{q^M} \beta_{jk}^2 + (\beta_j^S)^2\right) = 1 - (\sigma_j^2, \sigma_{\alpha_j}^2).$$

Therefore, $\sigma_j^2 = \dfrac{1}{1 + \sigma_{\alpha_j}^2}$.

Finally, α_j, β_{jk}, and β_j^S are obtained by simply substituting back in Equation (A4).

APPENDIX 15.2   ESTIMATION RESULTS

TABLE A1   Sample correlations of default rates per sector (%)

Sector	1	2	3	4	5	6	7	8	9	u_1	u_2
1	100										
2	37	100									
3	62	72	100								
4	76	57	88	100							
5	68	67	73	73	100						
6	37	35	57	62	56	100					
7	26	22	36	37	47	55	100				
8	13	43	41	19	33	8	9	100			
9	29	34	38	35	35	42	50	14	100		
u_1	35	14	35	45	44	52	−2	−6	8	100	
u_2	16	42	35	30	20	28	44	−12	16	−9	100

TABLE A2   Sample correlations of logit variables (%)

Sector	1	2	3	4	5	6	7	8	9	u_1	u_2
1	100										
2	32	100									
3	54	81	100								
4	69	721	82	100							
5	63	641	72	61	100						
6	38	25	37	58	40	100					
7	29	27	38	45	42	63	100				
8	30	52	45	34	37	−3	−10	100			
9	21	34	36	31	29	33	29	9	100		
u_1	49	21	41	44	48	48	4	1	8	100	
u_2	22	37	27	47	14	35	389	10	7	−1	100

TABLE A3 Regression results for factor-based logit model and F-statistics

	Sector										
	1	2	3	4	5	6	7	8	9	u_1	u_2
Constant	2.550	3.024	3.614	3.740	3.977	4.222	4.541	4.823	5.820	4.244	4.420
Factor 1	0.183	-0.049	-0.016	0.004	0.129	0.002	0.081	0.033	0.208	-0.054	-0.136
Factor 2	0.002	0.114	0.085	0.069	0.100	0.049	0.122	-0.031	-0.005	-0.060	-0.044
Factor 3	-0.096	0.028	0.049	-0.115	0.082	-0.125	0.041	-0.005	-0.058	0.047	-0.117
Factor 4	0.063	0.101	0.048	0.062	0.020	0.068	0.075	-0.043	0.089	-0.002	0.175
Factor 5	0.007	-0.077	0.142	0.043	0.008	0.012	-0.007	-0.049	0.129	0.126	-0.091
Factor 6	-0.061	0.143	0.154	0.177	0.087	0.108	0.111	-0.044	0.121	0.001	0.260
Factor 7	-0.055	-0.102	-0.078	-0.111	-0.066	-0.077	-0.134	-0.209	-0.055	-0.021	-0.122
Factor 8	0.133	0.144	0.289	0.222	0.179	0.231	0.171	0.134	0.135	0.013	0.241
Factor 9	-0.300	-0.208	-0.364	-0.337	-0.302	-0.191	-0.081	-0.100	-0.091	-0.349	0.014
Adjusted R^2	47.96	53.50	59.84	48.66	60.12	20.27	7.24	21.18	25.71	25.42	45.75
F-statistic	3.765	4.196	5.470	3.843	5.523	1.763	1.234	1.806	2.038	1.985	3.530

TABLE A4   Weights of factor-based Merton model

Sector	1	2	3	4	5	6	7	8	9	u_1	u_2
Constant	−1.45	−1.68	−1.93	−1.98	−2.08	−2.18	−2.30	−2.41	−2.75	−2.19	−2.25
Factor 1	−0.09	0.02	0.01	0.00	−0.05	0.00	−0.03	−0.01	−0.07	0.02	0.05
Factor 2	0.00	−0.05	−0.03	−0.03	−0.04	−0.02	−0.04	0.01	0.00	0.02	0.02
Factor 3	0.04	−0.01	−0.02	0.04	−0.03	0.05	−0.02	0.00	0.02	−0.02	0.04
Factor 4	−0.03	−0.04	−0.02	−0.02	−0.01	−0.02	−0.03	0.02	−0.03	0.00	−0.06
Factor 5	0.00	0.03	−0.06	−0.02	0.00	0.00	0.00	0.02	−0.04	−0.05	0.03
Factor 6	0.02	−0.06	−0.06	−0.07	−0.03	−0.04	−0.04	0.02	−0.04	0.00	−0.10
Factor 7	0.03	0.04	0.03	0.05	0.03	0.03	0.05	0.08	0.02	0.01	0.04
Factor 8	−0.06	−0.06	−0.12	−0.09	−0.07	−0.09	−0.07	−0.05	−0.04	0.00	−0.09
Factor 9	0.14	0.09	0.15	0.14	0.12	0.07	0.03	0.04	0.03	0.14	−0.01
Sector 1	0.14										
Sector 2		0.15									
Sector 3			0.12								
Sector 4				0.14							
Sector 5					0.09						
Sector 6						0.14					
Sector 7							0.14				
Sector 8								0.11			
Sector 9									0.11		
Sector u_1										0.14	
Sector u_2											0.13

CHAPTER 16

The Structuring of Collateralized Loan Obligations: A Risk Perspective

Manfred Plank and Markus Unterhofer
UBS AG

In a fully efficient and complete capital market, the benefit of issuing a collateralized loan obligation (CLO) would be very limited; the costs due to structuring and marketing would inhibit their creation in most cases. At present, however, CLOs address some important market imperfections. In the first part of the chapter, we address some of these market imperfections and give reasons why banks do securitization. Especially, we focus on synthetic securitizations and try to explain why they recently have received so much attention in the financial industry. In the second part, we present different possibilities of how the structure and the tranching of such transactions can be viewed from an economic perspective. We show various aspects of the economics of such transactions. A general outlook concludes the article.

In perfect capital markets, collateralized loan obligations (CLOs) would be of limited scope; the costs of structuring and marketing would inhibit their creation in most cases. But presently, CLOs address some important market imperfections. First, banks and certain other financial institutions have to satisfy regulatory capital requirements. This makes it worthwhile to them to securitize and sell some portion of their assets, reducing the amount of expensive regulatory capital they must hold. Second, individual loans may be illiquid, leading to a reduction in their market values. Securitization may improve liquidity, and thereby raise the total valuation for the issuer of the CLO structure. Among the sources of illiquidity that promote or limit the use of CLOs, is asymmetric information in the form of adverse selection and moral hazard problems. Finally, with the recent focus on risk-adjusted returns, the active management of credit risk has become an important motivation for securitization. Thereby, banks are able to reduce industry-specific and geography-specific concentrations in their portfolios and hence to release economic and/or regulatory capital. One of the latest and possibly most efficient means to achieve this goal are synthetic securitizations using credit derivatives to transfer credit risk without having to sell the underlying assets.

REASONS FOR SECURITIZATION AND THE EVOLUTION OF SYNTHETIC SECURITIZATIONS

Improving Liquidity and Market Transparency

Due to the relatively small size of single bank loans and the fact that borrower names are often unknown to investors, there exists only a small market of potential buyers and sellers of such assets. In order to sell illiquid assets quickly, one may be forced to sell at the highest bid among the relatively few buyers with whom one can negotiate at short notice. Searching for such buyers can be expensive and the negotiation position is certainly more difficult than in active markets with many buyers and sellers. The value of the assets is therefore significantly reduced. Potential buyers know that they will have the same selling problems in the future, resulting in even lower valuations. These illiquidity costs can be reduced through securitization into relatively large homogeneous senior CLO tranches.

With regard to adverse selection, it cannot be completely eliminated by securitization of assets in a CLO, but it can be mitigated substantially. The issuer of a CLO achieves a higher total valuation for what is sold and what is retained by designing CLO structures such that the majority of the adverse selection risk will be packed into small subordinated tranches. By the retention of the subordinated tranches by the issuer, the large senior tranches become relatively immune to the effects of adverse selection risk, resulting in a reduction of the risk premium required by an investor. Retaining a significant portion of one or more subordinated tranches that would be among the first to suffer losses stemming from poor monitoring or asset selection is a clear signal to the investor that the moral hazard risk is very limited. This in turn will also increase the willingness of investors to pay more for tranches in which they invest, and the total value to the issuer would be higher than in the case of unprioritized structures.

Cheaper Funding

Securitization as a means of collateralized lending makes sense where the stand-alone assets underlying the securitization are viewed by the market as having a better return/risk profile than the institution that holds the assets on its balance sheet. A typical example of this type are securitizations of credit card receivables where the originating institution in general does not have the large balance sheet that is necessary to hold such assets in a cost-efficient way. Nowadays this technique of raising funds is employed by a wide range of businesses with either measurable asset quality or a stream of predictable cash flows. (See the following second section for a more detailed discussion of funding issues around traditional and synthetic securitizations.)

Acceptance of Internal Data, Ratings, Models, and Processes

An additional benefit for banks issuing CLOs is the fact that the rating agencies evaluating the structure of such transactions, directly or indirectly, "approve" the bank's internal data, ratings and loss history, models and processes. On the other hand, the banks are forced to streamline their data, processes, and systems to fulfill the capital market standards. By issuing such transactions, banks enhance their reputation as leading institutions for credit assessment and portfolio management. In the long run, the good reputation could eventually result in higher ratings for the banks themselves and thereby, in better funding possibilities.

Reduction of Regulatory Capital and the Advent of Synthetic Securitizations

Banks do not only have refinancing costs, but they are also obliged to underpin their loans with regulatory capital. Shareholders are demanding a high return on equity and therefore capital is a scarce and expensive resource. By securitizing credit-risky assets and keeping a small first-loss tranche, the bank can dramatically reduce the allocation of regulatory capital. Under the – still effective – 1988 Basel Capital Accord, regulators do not differentiate between high and low credit quality assets. As a result, some large banks started to sell the better quality part of their loan portfolio, while keeping the lower quality part on their balance sheet. These banks were able to differentiate between high-quality and low-quality loans via sophisticated internal rating tools and models that allowed them to determine the economically "true" amount of capital. By securitizing the better quality assets requiring too much regulatory capital in relation to their economic risk, banks could release expensive regulatory capital. These so-called "regulatory capital arbitrage" activities were one of the reasons for the Basel Committee to reform the present regulatory capital framework with the aim to close the gap between economic and regulatory capital as much as possible.

To understand why these regulatory capital arbitrage transactions – and also those inspired by other reasons – issued recently by large banks were very often synthetic securitizations, one has to look again at the funding opportunities of a bank. Traditional securitization is quite an expensive process. Securitizing a bank's loan portfolio might cost between LIBOR + 25 bps and LIBOR + 50 bps, a level that is unattractive to an investment-grade bank that can often fund itself at LIBOR flat or even below LIBOR. The advent of synthetic securitizations was a reaction to this problem. This type of transaction allows the issuer to hold the loans on the balance sheet, while transferring at the same time the associated credit risk by means of a portfolio credit derivative. Cost reduction is one of the most significant advantages (see Tables 16.1 and 16.2 for examples) of synthetic securitizations. In addition, the structure avoids several internal legal and tax problems often caused by the transfer of assets and has a much greater flexibility than traditional securitizations. The main disadvantage of a synthetic securitization is the need for counterparty risk limits, required for the credit default swap on the senior or the super-senior tranche.

Figure 16.1 and Tables 16.1–16.2 show indicatively the superiority of synthetic securitizations over a true sale transaction, having determined the size of the tranches according to Moody's approach.[1] Even if the difference in the average market spread becomes smaller in case of a lower rated portfolio, there is a striking cost advantage of the synthetic transaction type in both cases.

The creation of a super-senior tranche is the key to the superior economics of synthetic securitizations. The reason why two positions with very similar risk profiles can demand such different spreads is that issuers of synthetic CLOs and investors in super-senior tranches have sophisticated

FIGURE 16.1   Tranching of a true sale transaction versus a synthetic securitization for a low-quality portfolio

True sale versus synthetic transaction

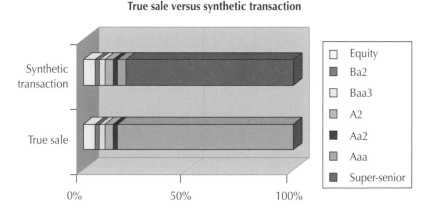

TABLE 16.1 Economics of a true sale transaction versus a synthetic securitization for a high-quality portfolio

	True sale transaction			Synthetic securitization	
Tranche rating	Market spread (basis points p.a.)	Tranche size Moody's approach	Tranche rating	Market spread (basis points p.a.)	Tranche size Moody's approach
Aaa	35	94.90%	Super-senior	10	93.70%
			Aaa	35	1.20%
Aa2	65	0.50%	Aa2	65	0.50%
A2	80	1.10%	A2	80	1.10%
Baa3	190	0.70%	Baa3	190	0.70%
Ba2	350	0.70%	Ba2	350	0.70%
Equity	–	2.10%	Equity	–	2.10%
Weighted average	38.20		Weighted average	14.78	

TABLE 16.2 Economics of a true sale transaction versus a synthetic securitization for a low-quality portfolio

	True sale transaction		Synthetic securitization		
Tranche rating	Market spread (basis points p.a.)	Tranche size Moody's approach	Tranche rating	Market spread (basis points p.a.)	Tranche size Moody's approach
			Super-senior	10	79.50%
Aaa	35	83.60%	Aaa	35	4.10%
Aa2	65	1.90%	Aa2	65	1.90%
A2	80	4.00%	A2	80	4.00%
Baa3	190	2.60%	Baa3	190	2.60%
Ba2	350	2.20%	Ba2	350	2.20%
Equity	–	5.70%	Equity	–	5.70%
Weighted average	46.34		Weighted average	26.46	

models and are therefore able to determine the adequate amount of capital for these tranches. Such models show that super-senior tranches attract far less capital than "normal" Aaa-rated tranches and, hence, are still attractive for the investor, although the spread is very low compared with traditional securitizations.

Reduction of Economic Capital and Portfolio Optimization

So far, the main motivation behind synthetic securitizations for most banks has been the desire to reduce regulatory capital. However, the new regulatory capital framework proposed by the Basel Committee at the beginning of the year 2001 has changed the motivation behind synthetic securitizations. Given the convergence of the regulatory and economic capital measures, banks will have a reduced incentive in the future to engage in synthetic securitizations in order to reduce only their regulatory capital requirements.

Due to the weaknesses of the 1988 Basel Capital Accord, major banks have not only started to exploit the arbitrage opportunities, but also to develop internal credit risk models, focusing on the "real" economic risk of a loan or portfolio of loans. A bank issuing a CLO[2] and structuring it from an economic perspective will try to transfer positions carrying a lot of economic risk; for example, due to industry-specific or geography-specific concentrations. Some banks have large concentrations in specific industries or regions that causes their loan portfolios to be highly correlated and vulnerable to the same economic upswings and downswings. By issuing CLOs, banks can get rid of the highest concentrations in their portfolios, and thereby reduce their earnings volatility and save expensive economic capital. The expected or average loss (see next section) of the securitized portfolio remains normally with the bank and is not reduced, but the bank has purchased something like an insurance against higher-than-expected losses or even extreme events.

In conjunction with portfolio optimization, it is important to emphasize that there exist at least two different types of capital that can be managed and optimized. First, regulatory capital that the bank *must* hold, calculated according to the official capital requirements. Second, economic capital that the bank *should* hold, determined via internal models and depending on the bank's desired external credit rating. Due to the fact that the current regulatory regime does not differentiate between high-quality and low-quality loans, banks easily detect that there is often a trade-off between regulatory and economic capital optimization. By securitizing the high-quality part of the portfolio, banks can release expensive regulatory capital.

But at the same time the overall credit quality of the portfolio is deteriorating, resulting in an increase in the banks' creditors risk without a corresponding compensation risk on the return side. On the other hand, by optimizing the economic capital, banks are often forced to take into the bargain that the optimization measure does not generate any value from a regulatory capital perspective. Therefore a loan portfolio manager has to evaluate each optimization measure, both from a regulatory and economic capital perspective. Figures 16.2 and 16.3 illustrate this challenge, which each loan portfolio manager is envisaging.

Portfolio managers of the most sophisticated banks have recently discovered synthetic securitizations as an efficient means to optimize their economic capital requirements of their portfolios, including the credit risk from their OTC derivative books. Examples for such deals are HAT (as discussed below) and the ALPINE transaction, both issued by UBS AG in the second half of 2000. Synthetic securitizations can be used in a much more flexible way to slice the credit risk of a given portfolio in various ways, fulfilling the credit risk management requirements, as well as meeting the investor's needs at the same time. For example, such transactions are often used to transfer the senior and mezzanine tranches and to retain the equity

FIGURE 16.2 Optimization clusters

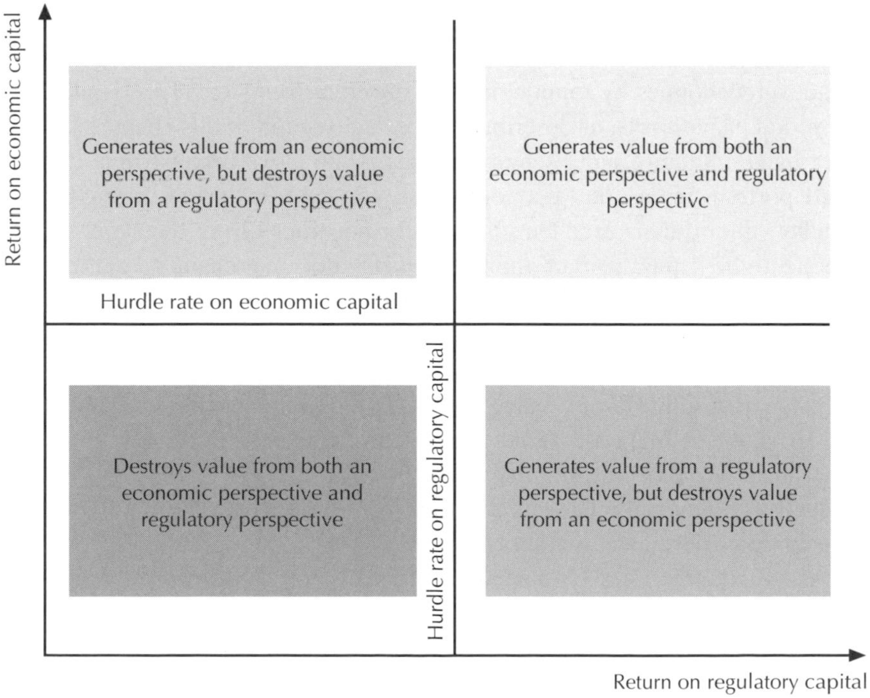

FIGURE 16.3   Optimization strategies

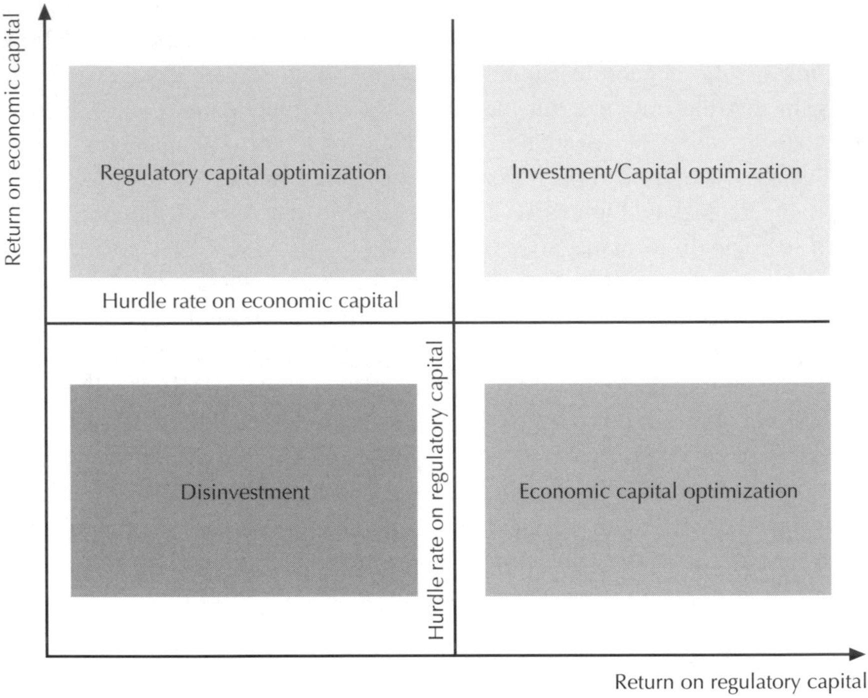

and/or super-senior tranches. Equity tranches are retained in order to achieve attractive economics by minimizing the different forms of adverse selection and moral hazard risks, as described in the first section of this chapter. On the other hand, retaining super-senior tranches is attractive because only quite a small portion of the total economic risk can be transferred through such tranches, due to their excellent quality. By not transferring the super-senior tranche to the capital market, the retained risk does not change significantly, but at the same time the risk-adjusted return is improved substantially because of the induced cost reduction. Note that the relative costs of a super-senior tranche are rather low, but due to the large volume of these tranches, they are still large in absolute terms. As we will see in the examples below (Tables 16.3 and 16.4), the selling costs of the super-senior tranche constitute 63% of the total costs for the high-quality and 30% for the low-quality portfolio, respectively. But only 10% of the total economic risk of the portfolio is transferred to the capital market by the sale.

As an example for a synthetic CLO focusing on the release of economic capital, we show the structure of the Helvetic Asset Trust (HAT) transaction, issued by UBS AG in August 2000.

FIGURE 16.4 Structure of HAT

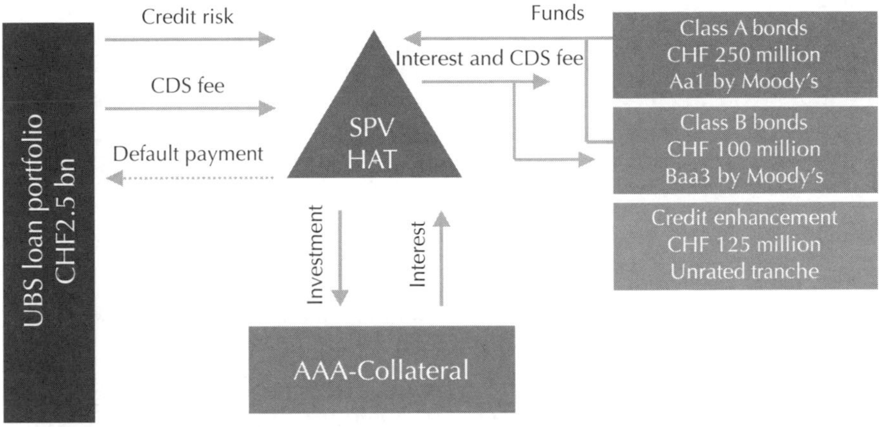

Usually, the credit default swap with an SPV covers only a certain portion of losses of the underlying portfolio. In case of HAT, the swap covers losses above the first-loss tranche up to CHF 475 million, which is the sum of the amount actually transferred to the capital market via the Class A/B bonds and the first-loss tranche. The underlying portfolio volume amounts to CHF 2.5 billion. In other securitizations, a second credit default swap is often additionally created between the originator and another (normally high-rated) bank covering the losses above the protected level of the first default swap.

As protection buyer UBS has the right to make substitutions of reference obligations at any time, provided that the substitution guidelines are satisfied. The substitution guidelines define certain restrictions, regarding, for example, maximum single-name exposure, average rating quality, geographical, and industrial concentrations and so on.[3] Within these restrictions, HAT enables UBS to dynamically change the composition of the hedged exposure, depending on the changing composition of the whole loan portfolio. Thereby, UBS can mitigate portfolio concentrations and hence release expensive economic capital. Due to the dynamic character of the reference portfolio, UBS is also able to steer a part of its SME portfolio actively. Hence, HAT increases liquidity in UBS's loan portfolio by creating the opportunity for active management of loans that otherwise would not be liquid.

SOME ASPECTS OF THE ECONOMICS OF SYNTHETIC SECURITIZATIONS

An institution that wants to calculate the economic impact of a securitization has to consider two different methodological frameworks. First, the bank has to use its own internal credit risk model to find an optimal structure and tranching and to assess the economic impact of the transaction. Second, the bank has to consider the assumptions, concepts, and models applied by the rating agencies or the transaction counterparty if no rating agencies are involved, since they eventually determine the structure and the tranching of such transactions. This makes it necessary to understand both the bank´s internal approach, as well as the approach of the rating agencies and other market participants in order to grasp the economics involved.

Internal credit risk models developed by banks during the recent years are often based on the concepts of "expected loss" and "unexpected loss". The expected loss (EL) is the amount a bank expects to lose on average over a certain period of time. It is a cost factor of doing the business that is charged to the business profit and loss in advance. Since actual losses are usually different from the expected loss, additional information is needed to assess the potential for losses of an underlying portfolio. The unexpected loss (UL) measures the volatility of actual losses around the expected loss. It is crucial for a bank not only to consider the charges for expected losses, but also to protect itself against such unexpected losses. Therefore, a bank has to calculate economic capital (ECAP) to be able to continue business as usual should such an unexpected loss occur. This cushion is a multiple of the portfolio's unexpected loss and depends on the choice of the loss distribution and on the choice of the confidence level that should be consistent with the bank's desired external credit rating.

To calculate this multiple and ECAP, many institutions choose a gamma or beta distribution as loss distribution. These distributions are chosen because they are very simple and flexible continuous distributions. But on the other hand, it has to be emphasized that these distributions are generally insufficient to give an adequate description of the loss distribution of a loan portfolio that is highly skewed and has a long and fat tail.[4]

For illustrative purposes, we use in the following a simplified variation of the CreditMetrics approach to model the loss distribution of the underlying portfolio. This approach is not used by UBS for modeling credit risk, but is used here because it is well-known, simple, and computationally superior. In order to speed-up the calculations, we made use of the fact that in well-diversified portfolios, the loss distribution can be approximated by a distribution that is completely determined by the systematic risk factors. This approach was also used recently by regulators in the New Basel Capital Accord to determine their benchmark risk weight functions.[5] The statement can be proved rigorously using the Strong Law of Large Numbers in probability theory.[6] A general application of the Strong Law of Large Numbers to credit risk modeling can be found in Plank and Plank (1999).[7]

There it is shown how this theorem can be used to speed up numerical simulations algorithms.

As an example of an approach applied by rating agencies, we use the Moody's approach due to its simplicity. (Of course, any other approach used by rating agencies or transaction counterpartys can be used as well without changing the subsequent results.) This approach is based on the concepts of the "diversity score" – a diversification measure – and the "binomial expansion technique" (BET) that can be considered as a simplified probabilistic application of a full-fledged Monte Carlo simulation. The Diversity Score D is used to build a hypothetical pool of uncorrelated and homogenous assets that will mimic the default behaviour of the original pool of correlated and inhomogeneous assets that are collateralized. Each of these assets has the same par value and the same probability of default p. The behavior of this homogeneous pool of D loans can be fully described in terms of $D + 1$ possible scenarios: no default, one default, two defaults, ... up to D defaults:

$$P_j = \frac{D!}{j!(D-j)!} \, p^j (1-p)^{D-j}. \tag{1}$$

The probability P_j that j defaults could happen is computed assuming a binomial distribution: where p represents the weighted average probability of default of the original pool. After that, the loss (expressed as a percentage) E_j under each scenario is computed for all the notes (including the first-loss tranche, even if it is unrated and retained by the originating bank), with senior tranches having priority to receive the cash flows. This is done by taking the present value of the cash flows received by the Note holders, assuming there are j defaults, and using the note coupon as the discount factor. Finally, the total expected loss for that respective Note, considering all possible default scenarios, is calculated as follows:

$$\text{Expected loss} = \sum_{j=1}^{D} P_j \cdot E_j. \tag{2}$$

The corresponding rating for this EL can then be read-off afterwards from Moody's Cumulative Expected Loss Rates table.[8]

In principle, the bank's internal model and the external rating agency view (or the view of a counterparty in bilateral transactions without the involvement of a rating agency) are not completely different. For example, Moody's uses the weighted average probability of default and the diversity score as diversification or concentration measure as main input parameters for the BET, and these parameters can easily be translated into the EL/UL framework of an internal model. However, the point is that different approaches do not translate "without friction" into each other.[9] By comparing the tranching of a CLO determined by a rating agency – after having analysed the underlying portfolio, the loss history of the bank, and other quantitative and qualitative factors – to the bank's internal credit risk model and mapping it to the internal loss distribution, one may find considerable differences (as an illustration, see Figure 16.5).

To examine the differences in more detail, we use again a high-quality and a low-quality portfolio. Figures 16.6 and 16.7[10] show that credit loss distributions are highly skewed to the right, resulting in long right-hand side tails. The shape of the loss distribution is mainly caused by the default correlation that exists between different borrowers. Comparing the loss distributions for a high-quality (Figure 16.6) and a low-quality (Figure 16.7) portfolio, it can be observed that the loss distribution of the low-quality portfolio is more skewed to the right compared to that of the high-quality portfolio. This is mainly due to the higher asset (and therefore default) correlations and the larger expected losses for low-quality portfolios.

Figures 16.6 and 16.7 not only show the loss distributions as determined by an internal model, but also the corresponding loss distributions as they are determined by the Moody's approach. An important observation is that the loss distribution of the rating agency is not as skewed as the loss distribution determined by the internal model. This can be already observed with the better quality portfolio, but the differences become even more

FIGURE 16.5 Differences internal versus external view

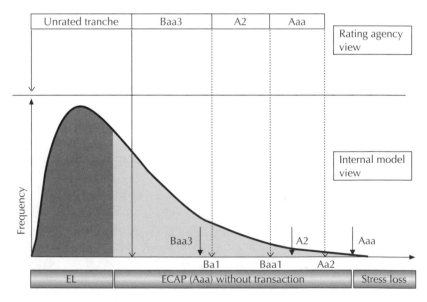

FIGURE 16.6 Loss distribution for a high-quality portfolio

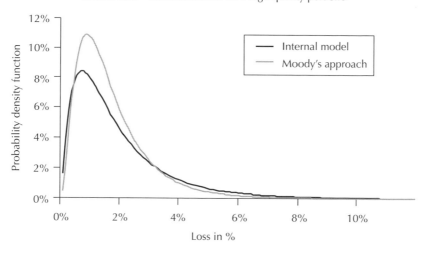

striking if the quality of the portfolio deteriorates. These differences have an important impact on the economics, the tranching of the synthetic securitizations, and the choice of the underlying portfolio.

Tables 16.3 and 16.4 show the size of each tranche for both portfolios, determined by both the internal model and the Moody's approach. In the last column, the percentage of the total economic risk covered by each tranche is shown. As expected, both models require a higher equity portion for the low-quality portfolio. The reason why the loss distribution generated by

TABLE 16.3 Tranching and economic loss allocation for a high-quality portfolio

Tranching and economic loss allocation

		Tranche size		
Tranche rating	Market spread (basis points p.a.)	Internal model	Moody's approach	Share of loss covered by tranche
Super-senior	10	93.00%	93.70%	10.00%
Aaa	35	1.50%	1.20%	17.14%
Aa2	65	0.70%	0.50%	7.14%
A2	80	1.40%	1.10%	15.71%
Baa3	190	0.80%	0.70%	10.00%
Ba2	350	0.70%	0.70%	10.00%
Equity	–	1.90%	2.10%	30.00%
Total	14.78			

TABLE 16.4   Tranching and economic loss allocation for a low-quality portfolio

Tranching and economic loss allocation

		Tranche size		
Tranche rating	Market spread (basis points p.a.)	Internal model	Moody's approach	Share of loss covered by tranche
Super-senior	10	77.10%	79.50%	10.48%
Aaa	35	5.20%	4.10%	17.90%
Aa2	65	2.40%	1.90%	8.30%
A2	80	4.80%	4.00%	17.47%
Baa3	190	3.00%	2.60%	11.35%
Ba2	350	2.50%	2.20%	9.61%
Equity	–	5.00%	5.70%	24.89%
Total	26.46			

FIGURE 16.7   Loss distribution for a low-quality portfolio

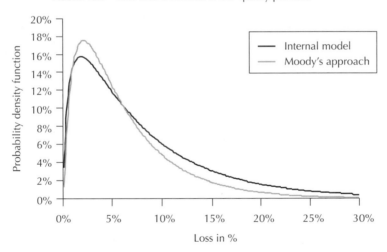

the internal model is more fat-tailed than the loss distributions generated by the BET approach is that the Moody's approach ignores the higher order correlations (i.e., probabilities of a simultaneous default of more than two borrowers) between borrowers by calibrating the binomial loss distribution. On the other hand, the Moody's approach is more conservative at the beginning of the loss distribution. This is due to the fact that Moody's performs stress-scenario analysis for the default frequency to protect investors, resulting in a generally higher expected loss for the underlying portfolio than it is assumed in the internal model. Similar differences can be observed by using different credit risk models or even by using the same credit risk model with differently calibrated input parameters.

In order to maximise economic advantage and to minimize moral hazard and adverse selection problems, most institutions retain one or more first-loss tranches. In addition, as we discussed previously, it is attractive from a risk-adjusted return perspective to retain also the super-senior tranche. As a result, only the risk of the tranches between the equity and the super-senior tranches should be transferred. With such a structure, the bank still retains a big portion of the economic risk, but the main advantage for the bank is that it is able to limit its losses, reduce thereby the volatility of earnings, and still release a considerable amount of economic capital. For the examples shown, between 35% and 50% of the economic capital is released.

With regard to the Moody's approach, the internal economics of the bank can be optimized – given a certain credit quality of a portfolio to be collateralized – by choosing obligor exposures of homogenous size in as many industries as possible. High industry and exposure concentrations should be avoided since Moody's penalizes them overproportionally through a lower diversity score. In addition, it is important to avoid inhomogeneity in the rating of the underlying assets. The scale used by Moody's to calculate the average default probability of the portfolio has a strong nonlinear structure that penalizes to a great extent the inclusion of low-rated obligors.[11]

CONCLUSION

We have mentioned that the main motivation for most banks behind synthetic securitizations has been the objective to reduce regulatory capital so far. However, the days of the old regulatory capital framework are numbered. Nowadays, loan managers are discovering more and more synthetic securitizations as an efficient and flexible tool to actively manage their credit portfolios, focusing on the "true" economic risk. By considering both the internal methodological framework and the approaches of the rating agencies in structuring transactions, banks are able to optimize the economics of such deals and to improve the return/risk profile of their loan portfolios.

Recent developments in securitization have shown that there is still a big potential for further optimization. For example, a new approach is to retain securitization principles, but without employing a bankruptcy-remote SPV.[12] The idea here is also to fence-off securitized assets from the default risk of the originator, but this objective is achieved by investing the proceeds from the sale of notes in collateral with a very high rating that can be isolated from the originator's bankruptcy. By abandoning the SPV, banks have much lower (legal) costs and shorter execution, time making the economics of such deals even more attractive.

Another remarkable and innovative approach of loan portfolio optimization is the recent deal between Royal Bank of Canada (RBC) and Swiss Re New Markets (SRNM), which provides RBC portfolio protection in times of unexpected economic downturns.[13] On this transaction, SRNM agrees to purchase RBC preference shares if RBC suffered significant losses. The deal gives RBC access to capital at times when it would find capital-raising via the debt or equity markets difficult. In the wake of the recently observed tendency of banking and insurance industry growing together, we will most probably see more novelties in the financial markets in the future.

NOTES

[1] See the section on synthetic securitizations and Appendix 16.1 for more details.
[2] Certainly, the case of not directly issuing and building up a bankruptcy-remote special purpose vehicle, is included.
[3] See HAT prospectus.
[4] See, for example, Ong (1999), chapter 8–10 for a discussion of these topics.
[5] See the New Basel Capital Accord, Consultative Document, January 2001.
[6] See Rohatgi (1975).
[7] See the bibliography for more details.
[8] See Moody's Investors Service (1996).
[9] See Koyluoglu and Hickman (1998), and Koyluoglu, Bangia, and Garside (1999).
[10] The underlying portfolio is fully ficticious and is not related to the actual UBS credit portfolio.
[11] See the Appendix 16.1 for more details.
[12] See Moody's Investors Service (2001).
[13] More information can be found in IFR, January 2001, p. 95.

APPENDIX 16.1   MOODY'S RATING MODEL

Moody's approach is based on the concepts of diversity score D, the weighted average rating factor, the weighted average recovery rate, and the binomial expansion technique. These portfolio characteristics are used by Moody's to describe the loss distribution of the actual portfolio by a hypothetical homogeneous portfolio that is built up by a pool of uncorrelated assets, each having the same face value F, the same rating, and the same maturity. Let us denote the default probability implied by the average rating, the average maturity by p, and the number of independent obligors given by the diversity score D. Under this simplified environment, the default behavior of the assets are completely determined by $D + 1$ possible loss scenarios: 0 defaults, 1 default, ..., D defaults. The probability that j defaults occur is given by the so-called binomial distribution:

$$P_j = \binom{D}{j} \cdot (\lambda p)^j \cdot (1 - \lambda p)^{D-j}.$$

λ is used as a stress factor for the default probability. The stress factor accounts for the fact that the relationship between the probability of default and the rating is far less than stable, especially for low-rated instruments. The loss distribution as described by the above formula does not explicitly address the skewness of the loss distribution. The only explicit input parameters are the diversity score D and the probability of default p. Their determination is analysed more in detail below.

The purpose of the diversity score is the derivation of a number of independent assets of identical size and rating. Moody's assumes that there are a maximum of 33 different industries and that each industry can contribute a maximum of five to the total diversity score. This implies that Moody's diversity score cannot be greater than 165.

Calculation of the Diversity Score *D*

For a portfolio with N loans in K different industries the diversity score is calculated as follows:

Step 1: Calculation of the average exposure of the underlying portfolio:

$$\overline{Exp} = \frac{1}{N} \cdot \sum_{i,j} Exp_i^j$$

where i denotes the ith loan in the jth industry.

Step 2: Calculation of the industry diversity score *IDS*:

$$IDS_j = \min\left(\frac{1}{2} \cdot \sqrt{8 \cdot EUS_j + 1} - \frac{1}{2}; 5 \right)$$

where EUS_j denotes the so-called equivalent unit score for industry j that is given by the following formula:

$$EUS_j = \sum_{i \in j} \min\left(\frac{Exp_i^j}{\overline{Exp}}; 1 \right)$$

$i \in j$ denotes all obligors in industry j.

Step 3: Calculation of the portfolio diversity score D:

$$D = \sum_j IDS_j.$$

The calculation of the diversity score shows that it can be maximized by choosing obligor exposures of equal size in as many industries as possible in order to avoid exposure and/or industry concentrations.

Calculation of the Average Rating

The average rating $\bar{R}$ of a pool of obligors is calculated in the following way:

$$\bar{R} = \frac{\sum_i \text{Exp}_i \cdot RF_i}{\sum_i \text{Exp}_i}$$

where Exp_i denotes the exposure of obligor i and RF_i denotes the rating factor of obligor i as given by Table A1.

The nonlinear rating factor scale reflects the relative riskiness of different letter ratings. The scale penalizes the presence of lower rated obligors. The resulting average rating and the exposure weighted time-to-maturity is used to look up the average obligor default probability.

TABLE A1   Moody's rating factors

Moody's rating	Moody's rating factor
Aaa	1
Aa1	10
Aa2	20
Aa3	40
A1	70
A2	120
A3	180
Baa1	260
Baa2	360
Baa3	610
Ba1	940
Ba2	1,350
Ba3	1,780
B1	2,220
B2	2,720
B3	3,490
Caa1	4,770
Caa2	6,500
Caa3	8,070
Ca	10,000

CHAPTER 17

Worst Loss Forecast in Counterparty Exposure

Sergey Lyalko and Robert Tuckett
Fidelity

O ne of the important tasks in credit risk management is forecasting the *greatest* potential loss in case of *counterparty default*. Here we build a mathematical model of exposure behavior, which gives a quantitative background for a forecast in exposure to a certain type of counterparty. "*Counterparty*" is a very generic term. Everyone you deal with is a counterparty. Let's be specific. The particular type of counterparty (CP) discussed here is a brokerage company, which sells or buys securities for big funds. This is a simplified logic of exposure and loss from the fund standpoint.

An initial contract for trade between client-portfolio and CP takes place with a *trade-price*, which at that moment is also the current market-price of the security and a price, ordered by the client fund.

The contract is considered to be fulfilled by the CP when all of the securities in the contract are traded – sold or bought. This is also referred to as trade-settlement (or settlement). The process of trading takes a certain amount of time, and depending on the type of security, country, and other details it may last from several days to several months.

Though the date of settlement is specified in the contract, it is not unusual for the trade to be settled with delay. This is the primary motivation for considering the period of settlement as a discrete random variable equal to a multiple of days.

Any CP is a company with a certain non-zero probability of bankruptcy, which is referred to as the CP's default probability. In case of default, the CP does not fulfill its Obligations, and the trade remains unsettled. In this case, the fund has to re-enter the market in order to find another counterparty for accomplishing this trade. The market situation since the initial contract will most likely have changed, and the marke price will not equal the original trade-price. The difference ($d(t)$) between these two prices may be favorable or unfavorable for the fund. For example, if the contract was to buy securities and the price went up, then, after CP default, the fund has to buy the same securities for a greater price. In this case $d(t)$ is called *replacement cost*, as the fund has to replace this amount from internal sources. From the fund's standpoint this is a loss. In these circumstances, $d(t)$ was unfavorable at the moment of CP default and therefore caused the loss. The same difference for sell transaction is favorable for the fund and won't lead to any loss. Only the unfavorable difference between trade-price and market-price is that the market price has the potential to become a loss and only it determines an exposure to the CP.

Irrespective of CP defaults, the difference between trade and market price for a particular trade exists continuously and fluctuates with market prices. As we are only concerned about losses, we introduce the random variable $RC(t)$, which is equal to the unfavorable difference between prices and equals 0 for all neutral or favorable price differences. This random variable is a function of prices, transaction type (buy or sell), and time t, and it represents potential losses or exposure to a CP. The *greatest* amount of $RC(t)$ may be defined in many different ways, as well as the historic period for determining market behavior. Though formal definitions follow, it is important to point out the basics right here. First, the random variable $RC(t)$ is not Gaussian. In our circumstances, historical data does not justify an assumption of any specific parametric distributions for it. Therefore, our approach is non-parametric. At the same time, we assume an existence of some unknown distribution function for this variable, mean, and standard deviation, which may be estimated using historical data. Second, our search for the worst loss consists of two parts. Initially, we build an expression for the mean value of the maximum of $RC(t)$, dependent on unknown distributions. Then among all possible distributions we find the one that maximizes this mean value. This approach brings us to an explicit formula of a forecast. In estimating the mean and variation estimates from historical data, we take into account that most of the trades in our consideration settle in anything from days to a couple of weeks. This allows us to restrict historical data to the most recent period in order to capture current market behavior instead of averaged through long history.

Generally, exposure for one or more trades, contracted with a big group of CPs, should be calculated on a daily basis. The following section considers one trade and then generalizes results for a group of trades.

In order to clarify some terminology, though the statistical estimate of the worst loss is actually a kind of value at risk (VaR), we reserve for it the term *replacement cost* *(RC)* to indicate the peculiarities of our situation. We are also ignoring the difference between potential (exposure) and actual (replacement) loss, since numerically they are identical.

DEFINITIONS AND ASSUMPTIONS

The main purpose of this analysis is to forecast the greatest amount of loss $RC(t)$ in an unsettled trades caused by counterparty default. Statistically, we transform it to the problem of searching for the greatest mean value of $RC(t)$. In order to make the formalization easier, we need several definitions.

Another important part of this (and any other) analysis is a set of assumptions. It is always difficult to make nonrestrictive and, at the same time, adequate assumptions. What was made clear to us is that the distribution of $RC(t)$ is not Gaussian. Other assumptions may be criticized; for example, independence of observations or the identity of their distributions. However, we believe that for the time-intervals we deal with, this is adequate. Our assumptions below are marked by A and a number.

For each trade below, we consider the interval of time from now until settlement. The number of days until settlement is denoted by n and is supposed to be adjusted for a possible delay in settlement. Our time is counted in round days, so all the formulas obtained below may be calculated for any day between *now* (0 days) and *settlement* (n days).

The justification for this approach is that although we are dealing with a continuous time process of constantly changing market prices, and $RC(.)$ is a continuous random function, most corporate reporting systems collect data as of the trading day end.

We introduce the following definitions:

- D1. Difference $d(i)$ = trade price − market price $d(i)$ is unfavorable for the fund if the trade is buy and $d(i) < 0$, or if the trade is sell and $d(i) > 0$, $i = 0, \ldots, n$.
- D2. Exposure is the amount of unfavorable net difference $d(i)$.
- D3. Settlement is an event, terminating exposure for the trade.
- D4. Default of the CP is an event, changing exposure to an actual loss.
- D5. Loss or replacement cost (RC) is the value of exposure at the moment of counterparty default. The dynamics of its value is described by the random variable:

$$RC(i) = \begin{vmatrix} -d(i) & \text{if transaction} = \text{buy}, \ d(i) < 0, \\ d(i) & \text{if transaction} = \text{sell}, \ d(i) > 0, \\ 0 & \text{otherwise} \end{vmatrix} \tag{1}$$

where $i = 0, 1, \ldots, n$. Note that $RC(i)$ is always nonnegative.

These data form a random sequence where observations may be assumed uncorrelated because of day-long intervals between them.

It brings us to the assumptions:

- A1. $RC(i)$, $i = 1, 2, 3, \ldots, n$ is a sequence of independent equally distributed random variables with unknown distribution $F(x)$.
- A2. Distribution $F(x)$ is monotonically increasing with the existing first derivative.

Though practical algorithms may implement quite different approaches, for the purposes of this context we apply the next assumption:

- A3. If the current daily exposure for the particular trade is zero, the forecast for its nominal and worst exposure is also zero.

WORST LOSS (WL)

Let's consider the earlier defined sequence: $RC(1)$, $RC(2), \ldots, RC(n)$ of random potential losses. As assumed before, each $RC(k)$ has the same distribution $F(x)$. We are interested in predicting only the greatest loss:

$$WL = \max_{k=1,n}(RC(k)). \tag{2}$$

The conventional statistical way to build an estimate for a random variable is to find its expectation – i.e., mean value. So, to estimate the worst loss, we look at the expectation $E(WL)$ of WL:

$$E(WL) = E\{\max_{k=1,n}(RC(k))\}. \tag{3}$$

Let's form the *variational sequence* from the sequence $\{RC(k)\}$ positioning elements in ascending order. This way we obtain sequence $g(1)$, $g(2), \ldots, g(n)$ of *order statistics* (see [1]) where $g(1) = \min[RC(k)]$ and $g(n) = \max[RC(k)] = WL$.

The distribution function for $g(1)$ is $F(x)$ and for $g(n)$ it is:

$$P(s(n) < x) = P(s(1) < x)) * P(s(2) < x)) * \cdots * P(s(n) < x)) = F^n(x). \tag{4}$$

So

$$E(WL) = E[s(n)] = n \int_{-\infty}^{\infty} x[F(x)]^{n-1} \, dF(x). \tag{5}$$

Transform it with $u = F(x)$ and denote for simplicity $E(WL) = E[s(n)]$ by E. Then we are looking for:

$$E = n \int_0^1 x(u)u^{n-1} \, du \tag{6}$$

where x is now a function of u. Conversion of $u(x)$ to $x(u)$ is possible as $F(x)$ is monotonically increasing.

Now our efforts will be directed to obtaining an explicit form of Equation (6) convenient for calculations. It may sound strange as Equation (6) depends upon the unknown distribution function $F(x)$, but it is exactly what we are going to do. The way is (see Equation (2) and Equation (3)) to look at Equation (6) as a variational problem. In general, this type of problem may be described as finding the curve with fixed ends that yields the maximum area under it. This is why many applied problems, expressed with integrals, may be solved with variational methods. In our context it transforms the previous to an explicit form of the function $X(.)$, which maximizes the expectation E in Equation (6). The advantage of this approach is that not knowing the distribution, we anticipate the worst one, which emphasizes our intention to estimate the greatest loss.

Let's assume that the initial mean and standard deviation for distribution $F(.)$ are known and fixed:

$$\hat{X} = \int_0^1 x(u) \, du \quad \text{and} \quad \hat{\sigma}^2 = \int_0^1 [x(u) - \hat{x}(u)]^2 \, du. \tag{7}$$

As we'll see later, these equalities represent the initial conditions for a solution of the variational problem.

Using the variational principle with Lagrangean coefficients a and b, we have to equate to 0 the first variation of x of the functional Equation (6) (see Equation (3)):

$$\int_0^1 [nx(u)u^{n-1} - ax^2(u) - bx(u)] \, du \tag{8}$$

which gives the Euler equation:

$$nu^{n-1} - 2ax - b = 0. \tag{9}$$

Then x may be derived from Equation (9):

$$x = \frac{nu^{n-1} - b}{2a}. \tag{10}$$

After substituting Equation (10) into Equation (6) and explicitly integrating, the maximum value of the expectation is given:

$$E = \frac{1}{2a}\frac{n^2}{2n-1} - \frac{b}{2a}. \tag{11}$$

In these terms, the initial expectation of $g(1)$ (which is the same as minimal CR) given the maximizing distribution, is obtained from (11) for $n = 1$:

$$\hat{x} = \frac{b-1}{2a}. \tag{12}$$

The corresponding initial variance is:

$$\hat{\sigma}^2 = \frac{1}{4a^2} \int_0^1 [n(u)^{n-1} - 1]^2 \, du. \tag{13}$$

From Equation (10) and Equation (12), after taking integral Equation (13), we have:

$$\hat{\sigma}^2 = \frac{1}{2a} - \frac{n-1}{\sqrt{2n-1}}. \tag{14}$$

Equations (12) and (14) allow us to exclude the Lagrangean coefficients from Equation (11), which gives the desired forecast for the maximum (by distribution) of the maximal value in the sequence $\{RC(k)\}$, $k = 1, \ldots, n$:

$$E(WL) = \hat{x} + \frac{\hat{\sigma}(n-1)}{\sqrt{2n-1}}. \tag{15*}$$

Equation 15* is to be considered the main result for the forecast, but in some algorithms we may need to enable it for $n = 0$. Taking into account that:

$$\frac{n-1}{\sqrt{2n-1}} < \sqrt{\frac{n}{2}} = \sqrt{\frac{n}{2}}$$

we can transform Equation (15*) into

$$E^*(WL) = \hat{x} + \hat{\sigma}\sqrt{\frac{n}{2}} \tag{16}$$

slightly increasing the forecast of the maximum, which makes us even more conservative. Here $\hat{x}$ and $\hat{\sigma}$ are the mean and standard deviation of the initial distribution $F(.)$ of $g(k)$.

INITIAL $\hat{x}$ AND $\hat{\sigma}$ ESTIMATION.

Equation (16) for the worst loss is based upon the initial mean and standard deviation for $\{RC(k)\}$. These two values are the only bridge to the past on which the forecast is built. There are a variety of methods for their estimation. For our purposes, the last observed RC is taken as an value. This is justified by the following facts: (a) RC is the latest information about the exposure; and (b) it is equal to the mean value of the last observation alone.

The standard deviation, $\hat{\sigma}$, for RC is obtained from the closest short period of historical data. In our case the length of this period is a variable and is defined for each particular market situation, but always with the intention of reflecting the latest market behavior.

AGGREGATED EXPOSURE

Approaches to aggregated risk measures depend on the particular question to be answered. Some approaches are used to estimate the real value at risk, while some others serve primarily for dynamic self-comparison. In this section we do not go into all possible variations. The measurement is of the second type, but plays an important role in daily comparative analysis.

Let's summarize $RC(i)$ (see Equation (1)) for all trades for the same broker k. This is the total exposure for this broker on day i. Denote it by $S(i, k) = RC(i, 1, k) + RC(i, 2, k) + \ldots RC(i, z_k, k)$. It may be expressed as:

$$S(i, k) = \sum_{j=1}^{z_k} RC(i, j, k) \geqslant 0 \tag{17}$$

where $RC(i, j, k)$ is RC for the jth trade of broker k on day i, z_k – the number of trades for broker k and j – the particular trade. This is an aggregated exposure on day i for broker **k**.

Suppose we have **N** brokers and their probabilities of default on a given day i are $p(i, 1), p(i, 2), \ldots, p(i, N)$. The expected loss for broker k due to default on day i is $EL(i, k) = S(i, k)p(i, k)$. We can express the *total expected loss* ELTot(i) on day i through all brokers by summing expected losses EL(i, k):

$$\textbf{ELTot(i)} = \sum_{k=1}^{N} S(i, k)p(k) = \sum_{k=1}^{N} \sum_{j=1}^{z_k} RC(i, j, k)p(k) \tag{18}$$

Usually, this amount can be calculated explicitly since we have all the needed data. At the same time, it is desirable to have a generalized measure for the duration of each trade. In other words, we would like to modify Equation (18) so that it involves the number of days to settlement for each trade. Let's denote $Pd(j, k)$ as the probability of default on the duration of the jth trade for broker k. This probability can be calculated as the probability of failure in a series of n Bernoulli trials, where n (days) is the duration of the trade. The variable *j* reflects different lengths of trades for the same broker. The *total expected loss* (TEL) is obtained as a generalization of Equation (18) with respect to the expected number of days to settlement for each trade:

$$\mathbf{TEL} = \sum_{k=1}^{N} \sum_{j_k=1}^{z_k} RC(j, k)Pd(j, k) \tag{19}$$

where $RC(j, k)$ is the last observed replacement cost for broker k in trade j and $Pd(j, k)$ accounts for a probability of default on the duration of the trade.

WORST CASE TOTAL LOSS

Now Equation (19) can be modified for an estimate of *worst case expected loss* (WCEL) by substituting Equation (16) instead of $RC(.)$

$$WCEL = \sum_{k=1}^{N} \sum_{j_k=1}^{z_k} \left[\hat{x}_{jk} + \hat{\sigma}_{jk} \sqrt{\frac{n_{jk}}{2}} \right] Pd(j, k) \tag{20}$$

where $\hat{x}_{jk}$, $\hat{\sigma}_{jk}$, n_{jk} and $Pd(j, k)$ are respectively: last (current) value of RC, standard deviation of RC, number of days until settlement, and daily probability of default for the jth trade and kth broker.

The probabilities of default used in this chapter represent a separate issue for research. For the purposes of this chapter we presume that the probabilities necessary for the above transformations, especially the Bernoulli schema, e.g., annual, quarterly, daily or n-days default probabilities, may be obtained.

EXAMPLE

The last formulas for the aggregated exposure are rather complicated, therefore we've constructed an example here which shows the calculation of the worst loss according to Equation (20).

The data for this example are presented in Table 17.1. These data do not represent any real trades and the numbers have been rounded for simplicity sake. All headers are self-explanatory. The last RC column contains the difference $d(0)$ at the moment of the forecast calculation. This is the total difference for all traded shares.

Using our symbols for variables we have: for the first broker $k = 1$, the number of trades is $z_k = z_t = 3$; the replacement costs are $\hat{x}_{11} = 10,000$, $\hat{x}_{12} = 150,000$, $\hat{x}_{13} = 0$; standard deviations are $\hat{\sigma}_{11} = 35$, $\hat{\sigma}_{12} = 25$,

TABLE 17.1 Data for an example

Counter-party	Daily default probability	Trades	Last RC ($)	Days until settlement	Standard deviation ($)
CP1	0.00003	Tr11	10,000	4	35
		Tr12	150,000	12	25
		Tr13	0	10	20
CP2	0.000007	Tr21	0	6	40
		Tr22	25,000	8	16

$\hat{\sigma}_{13} = 20$. Default probabilities depend only on the broker and number of days until settlement. As we mentioned before, using a Bernoulli success-failure schema, the probability of default during n days may be calculated as $Pd(n) = 1 - (1 - p)^n$, where p is a daily default probability for this particular broker. In our example, we have the following for the first broker and each of the trades:

$$Pd(1, 1) = 1 - (1 - 0.00003)^4 = 0.00012$$
$$Pd(1, 2) = 1 - (1 - 0.00003)^{12} = 0.00036$$
$$Pd(1, 3) = 1 - (1 - 0.00003)^{10} = 0.00030$$

Note our assumption that the last probability may remain uncalculated as the exposure and its forecast are going to be 0.

For the second broker, $k = 2$, the number of trades is $z_2 = 2$, replacement costs are $\hat{x}_{21} = 0$, $\hat{x}_{22} = 25,000$, and the standard deviations are $\hat{\sigma}_{21} = 40$ and $\hat{\sigma}_{22} = 16$. For default probabilities, we have:

$$Pd(2, 1) = 1 - (1 - 0.000007)^6 = 0.000042$$
$$Pd(2, 2) = 1 - (1 - 0.000007)^8 = 0.000056$$

Now let's calculate the internal sum of Equation (20); namely, the sum of the worst losses for all trades of the first broker:

$$WCEL(1) = (10,000 + 35*2) * 0.00012$$
$$+ (150,000 + 25*6) * 0.00036 + 0$$
$$= 55.2624$$

This is the same for the second broker:

$$WCEL(2) = 0 + (25,000 + 16*4) * 0.000056 = 1.4035$$

Now, summing across brokers, we obtain the accumulated worst expected loss, expressed by Equation (20):

$$WCEL = 55.2624 + 1.4035 = 56.6659$$

It is important to remember that this amount approximates the mean value of real *worst replacement costs*, obtained by averaging outcomes through all possible experiments with a given set of counterparties, days until settlement, and default probabilities.

NOTES

[1] David, G. *Order Statistics*, 1979.
[2] Gumbel, E. *Statistics of Extremes*, Columbia University, NY (1962).
[3] Phoa, W. "Estimating Credit Spread Risk Using Extreme Value Theory." *The Journal of Portfolio Management*, Spring (1999), 69–73.
[4] Smith, D.R. *Variational Methods in Optimization*. Dover Publications, NY (1974).

CHAPTER 18

Moving Toward Private Company Credit Risk Measurement

Justin Hingorani, Gordian Gaeta, and Shamez Alibhai
Simplex Credit Advisory Ltd

Measurement of the credit risk of unlisted companies, as opposed to risk assessment, is an increasingly crucial need for the financial community. The majority of quantitative credit risk systems have fallen short of addressing this need. In particular, attempts to develop fundamental models for private firms have been hampered by a lack of data. However, further research is warranted as fundamental models offer huge advantages over other models.

An attempt was made, using neural networks, to supplement the lack of data from public financial information and feed a fundamental, structured model (Spanjers and Heskes 2000). This contribution explores the possibilities to extend the existing Simplex Credit Advisory (SCA) fundamental and structured credit model for public companies to cover private companies. Although results are reasonable and can be used as a benchmark, further improvements will be required to develop a solid credit risk decision base from these models.

UNMEASURED PRIVATE COMPANY CREDIT RISK

Financial institutions are under growing pressure from regulators, shareholders, the general public, and senior management to improve the credit risk management of their overall portfolio. The Basel Committee on Banking Supervision blames "weak credit risk management and poor credit quality (as the) dominant cause of bank failures and banking crises worldwide" (Basel – Transparency Group 2000). Concurrently, shareholders are demanding a risk premium for stocks of financial institutions evidenced by US banks' median price/earnings ratio of 11 compared to a market median of 15 (Falkenstein 2000).

As a consequence, a broadening and deepening credit enhancement market has developed in an attempt to improve profitability and risk management. The use of credit derivatives is increasing rapidly, growing from US $40 billion in 1996 to a projected US $1,581 billion by 2002 (BBA 2001). Equally, secondary loan markets with an estimated market size of over US $120 billion are expected to double over the next few years.

Lack of private company credit risk measurement poses difficulties for institutions looking to manage or shift private firm credit risk exposures through structured products and the credit enhancement markets. Although financial institutions deploy more or less sophisticated internal ratings, they are unable to assign a credit measure that investors can rely on. Without an acceptable internal measurement system or external ratings on private company exposures, Basel's proposed regulations will impose default measures requiring institutions to set aside 100% of risk capital as a regulatory provision regardless of veridical risk (Basel 2001). This could severely damage RAROC (risk-adjusted return on capital), may motivate financial institutions to take actions not in line with prudent risk management and, in general, will do very little to improve credit risk management. This is in contrast to the Basel Committee's stated goal for credit risk management to "maximize a bank's risk-adjusted rate of return by maintaining credit risk exposure within acceptable parameters" (Basel – Risk Management Group 2000).

CLASSIFYING CREDIT RISK METHODS

A range of credit risk assessment methodologies for private companies exists in addition to the more common proprietary tools of internal scores and gradings established by a financial institution's own credit analysts. Rating agencies, credit reporting agencies, and business information reports compile and analyze financial, corporate, industry, and other information affecting or indicating a company's health and performance. They may also include a credit score or rating based on an information provider's subjective assessment.

However, a more objective and quantified approach would be desirable. To this end, we examine other methods to assess the credit risk of companies in various forms. A classification of the various models based on their inputs (factor, relative, or fundamental), the model approach (unstructured or structured), and the base of assessment (judgmental versus objective) reveal important differences (Figure 18.1).

There are generally three types of inputs. Factor models use explanatory variables, such as macroeconomic indicators, in a cause and effect

FIGURE 18.1 Credit risk assessment methods vary, based on inputs, approach, and base of assessment

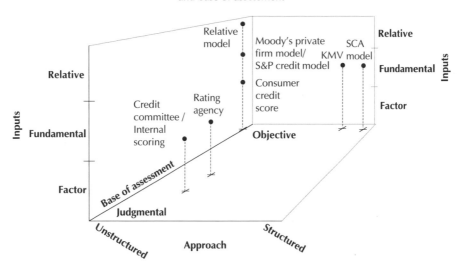

Source: Simplex Credit Advisory

framework to derive credit risk. A fundamental model determines a measure of the underlying credit risk by analyzing a company's financial data and relevant equity market information. Relative models measure credit risk on the basis of market-determined credit spread curves.

Of these three models, only the first, factor models, have been seriously considered for private companies. Although, fundamental models are now commercially available they lack adequate equity market information to be accurate for private companies. Relative models are faced with insufficient liquidity or breadth in the trading of private companies' debt instruments, if any, to provide adequate data.

Based on their approach, models can either be formulated in a structured or unstructured manner. A structured methodology poses a distinct framework to model how companies enter distress. The likelihood of a default occurring is directly calculated from the defined set of input data. The relationships between the input data are the only determinants of the outcome. The unstructured approach uses a system of equations as a mapping tool between inputs and historical rates of default. The results of such calculations are a reflection of historical patterns of default; history is the key determinant.

With respect to the nature of assessment, the move is toward a more objective base. A purely judgmental assessment uses qualitative inputs or measures based on an analyst's perceptions within a framework of experience to derive a single opinion. An objective measure combines a set of observable and quantifiable inputs into an analytical system to calculate the credit risk.

EVOLVING PRIVATE COMPANY CREDIT RISK MEASUREMENT MODELS

Commercial systems for quantifying default risk have primarily focused on listed companies. This focus seems wanting when, for example, in the United States there are about 4.5 million private companies compared to only approximately 10,000 listed ones. Some commercial providers have taken the step toward providing credit risk measures and developing automated solutions with greater objectivity for private companies. Their goal is typically to produce default probabilities rather than metrics that can only be interpreted within the context of the model.

Current commercial providers include S&P, Moody's, and KMV. S&P's CreditModel™ is a fundamental, unstructured approach that is fairly objective. It uses a neural network technology with separate models trained on S&P ratings by industry and geography. In essence, it is an automated credit score based on S&P's credit-rating experience, which introduces an element of subjectivity. Companies must have revenues of at least $100 million. Credit scores are expressed as a lower case version of S&P's rating symbols. To translate a score into a default probability a mapping to historical default rates is required.

According to S&P's documentation, the model's typical inputs include those listed in Figure 18.2 (Standard & Poor's 2000). As the approach is unstructured, separate models must be trained for different industries and geographies. Available models include North America, Europe, and Japan, with 22 sectors covered in North America.

Moody's private company model combines various adjusted financial inputs into a probit model (a regression model that transforms a result into a value between 0 and 1) trained on their proprietary database of historical private company defaults. Moody's worked with several financial institutions to consolidate data on private company defaults into a database containing 28,104 companies and 1,604 defaults. The proprietary database enabled them to take a similar approach to their public company model, calibrating a set of inputs to historical default data. By training directly on private company data they avoided any structural differences that may exist between public and private companies and their default characteristics.

Moody's inputs include 10 financial ratios and indicators calculated from 17 basic financial inputs (see Figure 18.2). Similar to the S&P model, an unstructured framework requires separate Moody's models to be trained for

FIGURE 18.2　S&P's and Moody's credit risk model inputs consist of financial ratios as indicators of default

S&P ratios	Moody's ratios
EBIT interest coverage	Assets/Consumer price index
EDITDA interest coverage	Inventories/Cost of goods sold
Pretax return on capital	Liabilities/Assets
Operating income/Sales	Net income growth
Free operating cash flow/Total debt	Net income/Assets
Funds from operations/Total debt	Quick ratio
Total debt/Capital	Retained earnings/Assets
Sales	Sales growth
Equity	Cash/Assets
Total assets	Debt service coverage ratio

Source: S&P and Moody's

different industries and geographies. However, as an initial implementation Moody's has trained a single model across various industries, US and Canadian private companies, excluding finance, insurance, and real estate industries. It can be used for private companies with assets greater than US$100,000.

KMV extends its distance-to-default metric for public companies to the private company through a mapping tool. The mapping tool uses a set of parameters to imply asset value and volatility of a private company from their database of public companies. These parameters include size, industry, and geographic characteristics, with reliance on accounting data minimized. Once asset value and volatility of a private company are determined, the KMV structured model of default calculates a distance-to-default metric. Distance-to-default is a measure of how far a company's asset value is from distress. KMV uses a proprietary historical default database to map distance-to-default measures against historical default frequencies. Thus, using this database an EDF (expected default frequency) can be generally determined for a given distance-to-default measure of a private company.

THE NEED FOR MORE STRUCTURE

One issue with unstructured models is that they rely entirely on data patterns that are anchored in history to perform forecasting, even though these patterns may not be reflective of the future. A structured approach promotes a more forward-looking, relevant result, and does not rely on any historically derived relationships of default. The necessary assumption is that the structure of the model, that is, the relationship between inputs and outputs, is a reflection of future dynamics. Of the three models mentioned, the KMV model is the closest to a structured methodology.

Further, any transparent structure on how default occurs or on a company's likelihood of default creates a framework that builds user intuition and avoids a black box approach. Intuition furthers understanding of the implications of changes in input variables on default probability results, and facilitates development of scenarios and stress tests.

Freedom from historical default data provides the flexibility for a structured model to be applied across boundaries with few adjustments. When considering multiple sectors or countries, unstructured approaches stumble; especially in emerging markets and in countries where historical default data are sparse due to poor records or government intervention prior to default. The general lack of data is of great significance for the default history of private companies and thus heavily constrains unstructured models.

A structured approach does not require an abundance of data to drive results because it does not try to imply meaningful patterns from the data. The relationships between inputs and outputs are already set by the model. With inputs derived from readily available data sources, such as equity markets and company financials, a structured method becomes highly adaptable across industries and geographies.

Therefore, in moving toward credit risk measurement of private companies, the adoption of a structured model is the goal.

APPLYING THE SCA MODEL AND A NEURAL NET

To develop a structured approach, the fundamental Simplex Credit Advisory (SCA) public company credit risk framework is used as a base. The SCA public company credit risk system uses equity volatility, market capitalization, and financial statement data as inputs into a structured model to calculate default probabilities. Market capitalization and financial data help define a company's current asset value and a future asset value at which the company can be considered to be in distress. Equity volatility is used to explain the dynamics that asset values follow over time. By simulating changes in a company's asset value into the future, defined by its volatility dynamics, and noting when it drops to distress levels, the company's likelihood of default can be calculated.

Although financial statement data can be frequently obtained for private companies, equity volatility and market capitalization does not exist. Thus if probable (surrogate) volatility and market capitalization can be implied, the public company default risk model architecture and philosophy can be leveraged to calculate default risk of unlisted companies.

The necessary input is generated by neural networks trained to estimate the volatility characteristics and hypothetical market capitalization of a given firm. The neural network approach is used because of its ability to model nonlinearities and learn from large amounts of data.

Before developing these networks two other steps first had to be taken: defining the development framework to be used, including testing and data, and examining the predictive strength of financial ratios through correlations and univariate analyses.

Defining the Development Framework

The development of the neural network can be divided into several stages. First, potential inputs are analyzed for their univariate predictive power through correlation analysis and data plots. This establishes a basis against which later neural network results can be compared. Separate neural networks are then trained on target outputs, namely volatility and market capitalization, using over 180 financial inputs for a portfolio of companies. Inputs are reduced to a useable set of 20 through backward elimination – a process where all inputs are initially included and those inputs providing the least information are removed one by one. The inputs are compared to the univariate analysis and prediction errors are analyzed for areas of improvement: testing for bias, correlation, unusual outliers, and so on. A detailed explanation of the networks and their development can be found in the contribution by Spanjers and Heskes (2000).

Financial data used to perform such analysis and train the neural networks was obtained from the AAII's (American Association of Individual Investors) US financial statement database. More than 180 financial ratios, including quarterly dollar and percentage changes in data, were calculated for over 1,700 companies. Input sets were organized along various dimensions to reduce the noise or conflicting signals that may have existed in the data set. Dimensions included geography, industry, company size, and information type. The entire data set was limited to US companies from 1996–1998. Additional training sets were used to narrow the scope by limiting sets to specific industries and/or company size. Training sets were also divided into two groups based on different input types; one solely using financial statement information and the other using a combination of financial statement and other public information such as industry volatilities and index values. Interestingly, additional industry information yielded no significant improvement in network performance so the analysis focused on using financial statement data inputs.

Testing through Univariate Analysis

The predictive value of individual financial statement ratios was equally tested. Univariate analysis provides guidance as to which ratios may yield the greatest predictive power for target outputs in a multivariate framework. It also develops intuition that can be useful in variable elimination and provides a basis of comparison for results of a multivariate analysis.

Simple univariate tests include correlation analysis and profiling. Correlations indicate a single numeric measure of relationship strength between a financial ratio input and a target output. Though such a measure serves as a guide, it is not conclusive as it only yields a linear relationship measure. Any complex nonlinear relationship that a neural network might catch between two variables will not be clearly reflected in a correlation.

Profiling involves smoothing a plot between a financial ratio and one of the target outputs. This visual measure is also univariate, providing an image of a relationship between two variables. The image develops an understanding of how two variables interact and can corroborate multivariate findings.

Figure 18.3 shows four of the financial ratios and their univariate profiles with the two target outputs: market capitalization and equity volatility. The ratios cover company size, liquidity, profitability, and leverage. Chart 1 shows a fairly linear relationship between asset size of a company and market capitalization. Unsurprisingly, Chart 2 indicates greater uncertainty for the value of smaller companies with volatility decreasing towards 20% as asset size increases. A similar relationship exists for free cash flow depicted in Charts 3 and 4. However, as free cash flow becomes more negative, market capitalization increases again. This may be explained by the fact that only larger companies can survive negative cash flow by temporarily using other funding sources.

Charts 5 and 6 show the relationship between a company's profitability relative to size (gross operating income / total assets) and the target outputs. Companies with high market capitalization, approaching US$1.5 billion, have a greater tendency to be profitable, but at a lower level in comparison to its asset size. Their average profitability ratio is less than 0.04.

Performance of companies with a market capitalization less than US$ 1.5 billion can go either way: poor performance indicated by a decreasing profitability ratio or superior performance with a ratio greater than 0.04. Volatility produces a corresponding pattern with higher volatility of under performers and lower volatility of average performers.

Charts 7 and 8 depict the relationship between leverage (total liabilities/ total assets) and the target outputs of market capitalization and equity volatility. Companies with a market capitalization of less than US$500

FIGURE 18.3   The relationship of financial ratios with volatility and market capitalization
(US companies 1996 to 1998)

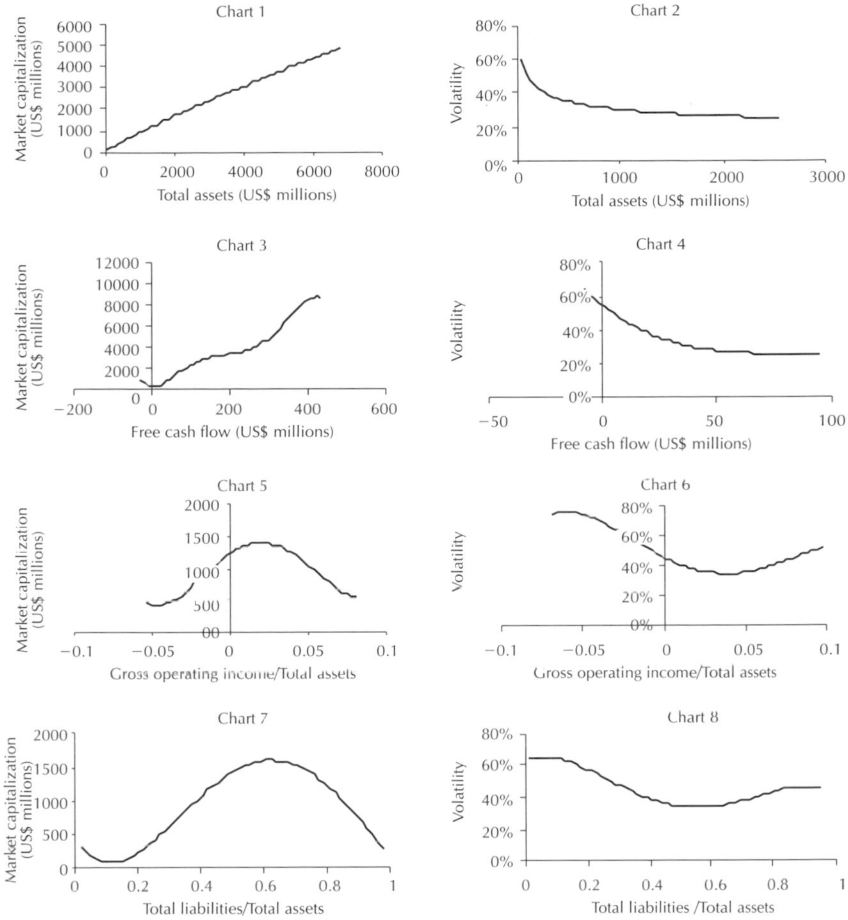

Source: Bloomberg, AAII, Simplex Credit Advisory analysis

million have low leverage. As market capitalization increases so does
leverage. Companies with a leverage approaching the ratio of 1, have assets
just over US$1 billion on average. However, they have disproportionately low
market capitalization. The volatility chart shows the greater risk of smaller
companies reflected in a higher volatility of 60% despite low leverage.
Volatility then decreases to around 35% for average leverage but increases
again for highly leveraged companies.

THE RESULTS WITHIN THE SCA FRAMEWORK

The data used in the SCA model results from neural networks that span companies in multiple industries. In related testing, individual neural networks were trained on four separate industries: services, healthcare, technology, and basic materials. However, differences in structure and results were not significant compared to a neural network trained across all four industries.

The inputs selected for the neural networks are given in Figure 18.4 for both volatility and market capitalization prediction alongside those of Moody's and S&P. Though separate neural network inputs were initially selected for volatility and market capitalization prediction, performance does not differ significantly when the market capitalization input set is used in volatility prediction and vice versa; in large part this is due to the ability of financial ratios to substitute for each other. Thus, a single input set is used for both target outputs to simplify matters.

FIGURE 18.4   Similarities emerge in comparing Moody's, S&P's, and SCA's selected financial inputs

SCA's neural network ratios	S&P's ratios	Moody's ratios
Company size		
Total assets Capital invested Cash Free cash flow	Total assets Equity	Assets/Consumer price index
Debt level or leverage		
Total debt/Capital invested Total liabilities/Total assets Long-term debt/Working capital Current liabilities	Total debt/Capital	Liabilities/Assets
Debt servicing		
Cash flow/Current liabilities Cash flow/Capital invested	Free operating cash flow/Total debt Funds from operations/Total debt EBIT interest coverage EBITDA interest coverage	Debt service coverage ratio
Profitability		
Gross operating income/Total assets Net income/Sales Net income/Total liabilities Sales Gross profit margin	Pretax return on capital Operating income/Sales Sales	Net income/Assets Net income growth Retained earnings/Assets Sales growth
Liquidity		
Quick assets/Total assets Cash/Total assets Accounts receivable turnover Free cash flow/Equity Working capital/Total assets		Quick ratio Cash/Assets Inventories/Cost of goods sold

Source: S&P, Moody's, AAII, Simplex Credit Advisory, SMART analysis

Figure 18.4 shows a number of common ratios between the neural networks and those selected by Moody's and S&P, with Moody's and the neural network covering all categories of ratios. The neural network places stronger emphasis than the other two models on debt levels while S&P emphasizes debt servicing more.

To produce a reasonable estimate of a company's default incidence likelihood, the median error for volatility predictions should be less than 5% and the median error for market capitalization predictions should be less than 10%. These target errors were arrived at by examining the sensitivity of default probabilities in the SCA public firm credit risk model to changes in volatility and market capitalization inputs.

Using the ensemble of networks and 20 financial inputs, the results are graphically depicted in Figures 18.5 to 18.7. The diagonal line in each of the figures represents a plot if predictions were 100% accurate.

The plots show that financial ratios do provide a significant amount of information on volatility and market capitalization, enabling the neural networks to determine good estimates that trend around the diagonal lines. Dispersion in the graphs indicates that individual estimates can deviate a fair degree from the correct predictions.

Ranking errors (between estimate and target) by target values shows errors become consistently negative for large target volatilities and market capitalizations   that is, underestimating – and similarly reveals small market capitalizations to be significantly overestimated. This seems to indicate some sort of bias in the neural network.

FIGURE 18.5   Resulting volatilities trend around the diagonal with a few outliers

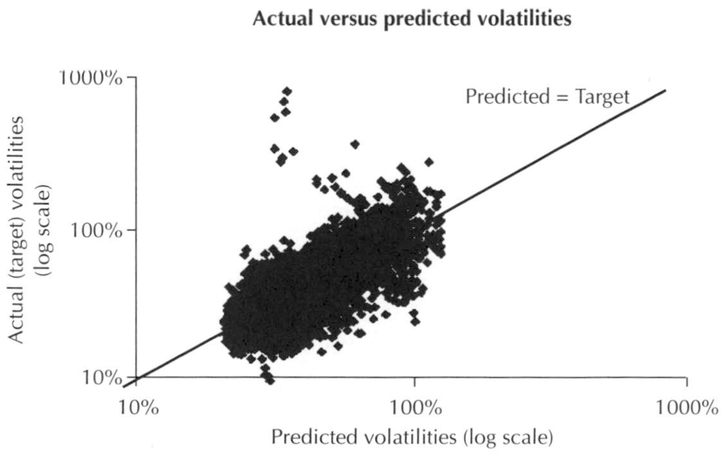

Actual versus predicted volatilities

Source: Bloomberg, AAII, Simplex Credit Advisory, SMART analysis

FIGURE 18.6   Resulting market capitalizations also trend around the diagonal

Actual versus predicted market capitalization (inset)

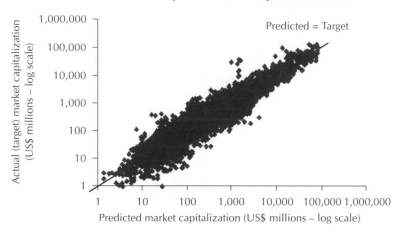

Source: Bloomberg, AAII, Simplex Credit Advisory, SMART analysis

FIGURE 18.7   An inset (zoom) of Figure 18.6 highlights deviations from the targets

Actual versus predicted market capitalization (inset)

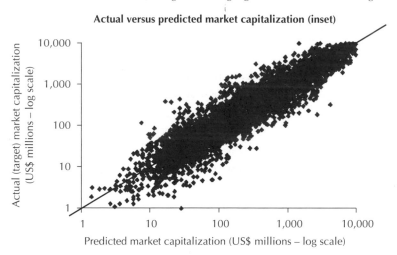

Source: Bloomberg, AAII, Simplex Credit Advisory, SMART analysis

To check for such a bias, error measures are again ranked; this time by each neural network's estimated values instead of target values. We find that the same trend does not exist for estimated values. In other words, as the estimated values increase, error measures are not consistently negative. This indicates that misestimation is not due to neural network bias, but due to the financial data providing insufficient information to enable the neural networks to detect companies with large volatilities and market capitalizations.

To quantify the dispersion of estimated values around the diagonal line, an error measurement that calculates the relative distance of a prediction from an actual (target) value is used:

$$\text{Error} = \frac{|\text{Prediction} - \text{Actual}|}{\text{Actual}}. \tag{1}$$

Overall, the error measures in Figure 18.8 show the neural networks' performance is a good start with a median error less than 20% for volatility estimates and a median error just over 35% for market capitalization.

However, these results are not sufficient to meet desired error thresholds of 5% and 10% for volatility and market capitalization, respectively. First quartile prediction errors for both target outputs extend 1.5 to 2 times desired error levels. Average errors are almost 1.75 times median errors because, as discussed above, large volatilities are greatly underestimated and small market capitalizations are significantly overestimated.

The data are, however, used to calculate default probabilities using the SCA model. For comparison, the calculated default probabilities using actual volatility and market capitalization data are defined as target default probabilities. The same calculation using data from the neural networks is defined as estimated default probabilities.

The surrogate inputs translate into default probabilities with an accuracy ratio of 0.61 of the cumulative accuracy profile of default prediction. This is just 10% points less than an AR using actual volatilities and market capitalization given by the market and well above other established models

FIGURE 18.8 Portions of the error distributions exceed desired levels

Distribution statistics for prediction errors

	Volatility	Market capitalization
Desired error level	<5%	<10%
Average error	25.44%	61.12%
Std. deviation	24.70%	106.05%
Error ranges		
Max. error	305.27%	2,854.18%
Quartile 3	33.68%	65.19%
Median	19.64%	35.28%
Quartile 1	9.21%	16.76%
Min. error	0.00%	0.05%

Source: Bloomberg, AAII, Simplex Credit Advisory, SMART analysis

(for a list of models and AR scores see Sobehart and Stein 2000). Thus the model seemingly performs well under more obvious conditions for calculating a company's default risk.

The performance is the cumulative accuracy profile (CAP) – a Moody's propagated measure – which is a graphical representation of a default risk measure's ability to distinguish between those companies in a sample that defaulted within a specified time horizon and those that did not. The horizontal axis of a CAP shows all companies in the sample ranked from highest to lowest default risk. The vertical axis indicates the percent of defaulting companies in the sample that are found as one moves from left to right on the horizontal axis (Sobehart, Keenan, and Stein 2000).

If a measure is randomly assigned to each company, with no consideration of their credit risk, and the companies are ranked according to the measure, then the CAP would be a 45-degree line. A model is shown to perform ideally if it assigns all defaulting companies the highest risk measures; that is, concentrates them on the left side of the horizontal axis.

Figure 18.9 shows the mean CAP for the target sample and the estimated sample. The target CAP outperforms the estimated CAP, particularly in higher quartiles, and both strongly outperform a random risk measure.

The strength of a CAP can be quantified with an accuracy ratio (AR). An AR measures the area between a given CAP and a random CAP – a 45-degree line. An AR of 1.0 is the area between an ideal CAP and a random CAP and an AR of 0.0 is the area between a random CAP and itself, with

FIGURE 18.9   Target CAP outperforms the estimated CAP

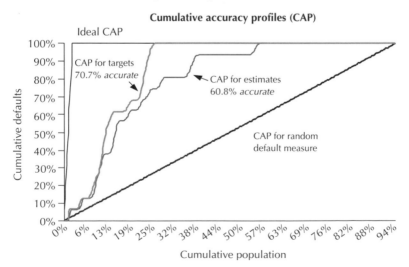

Source: Moody's, Simplex Credit Advisory analysis

all other CAPs falling somewhere in-between. Figure 18.10 contains two histograms of AR measures of the CAP samples for both the target and estimated results.

The histograms show that the mean AR for target samples is higher (0.707) than the mean AR for estimated samples (0.608) and the distributions only slightly overlap. Therefore, target default probabilities outperform estimated default probabilities.

EXPLORING ENHANCEMENTS

Based on the results of our initial analysis, improvements are required to increase the accuracy of the neural networks' estimates. Enhancements can be gained from alterations to the framework and changes to data used based on statistical patterns in model outputs and errors.

Error analysis shows that on average the networks do not predict fluctuations in market capitalization and volatility between quarters. In other words, if the volatility for a company increases from one quarter to the next there is only a 50–50 chance that a neural network's estimate of the volatility will also increase. Separate networks were trained to try to model the direction of fluctuations and improve predictions. Numerous sets of inputs and network structures were used, but none were able to produce a network that could produce predictions significantly better than 50%.

FIGURE 18.10 Target AR is significantly larger than the estimated AR

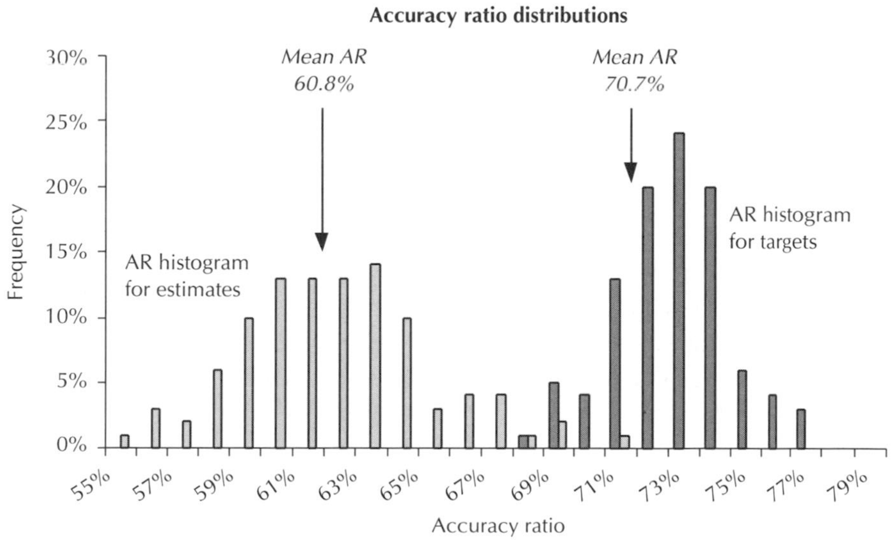

Accuracy ratio distributions

Source: Moody's, Simplex Credit Advisory analysis

Examination of outputs shows that default probabilities in the structured model are highly sensitive to equity dynamics. Thus, errors in estimation of equity dynamics greatly influence default probability results. One method for resolution would be to replace market capitalization estimates with an asset value surrogate that can be directly calculated or better approximated from financial data. From there better equity dynamics can be derived. An initial naive choice would be simply total assets with its strong linear relationship to market capitalization.

Sensitivity could be tackled by developing proxies for company value and volatility based directly on proprietary private company information. For example, incorporating the dynamics of a company's current account, or account balances, would serve as a metric for volatility.

The issue of data and ratios for private companies was examined. The financial statement database provided infrequent data on interest expenses and retained earnings. Ratios using these inputs were not sufficiently represented in the analyses. This may be especially relevant since both Moody's and S&P studies find ratios with these data items to be important indicators of a company's financial health.

Moody's has one of the most extensive databases of private company financial and default data. They noted from analysis of this database that private companies are typically smaller, with lower leverage, higher retained earnings, higher short-term debt, higher current ratios, and lower inventories than public companies with similar risk. For example, the median asset size of private companies is US$2 million and US$100 million for public companies. Plotting various ratios versus corresponding probabilities of default, Moody's also found that generally model inputs show similar relations to default in the public and private data sets but with some important exceptions (Falkenstein, Boral, and Carty 2000).

These observations and exceptions are due to structural differences between public and private companies that can significantly influence the way each type of company defaults. Public and private firms with identical financial data can produce very different default risk measures. Structural differences stem from public companies' wider access to capital markets providing them with additional sources of finance and greater flexibility. Ratios that Moody's compiled revealed differing default prediction power between public and private companies include Debt/Assets, Liabilities/Assets, Cash/Assets, Retained earnings/Assets and Short-term debt/Total debt.

The Debt/Assets and Liabilities/Assets ratios have similar initial explanatory power for public companies, but Debt/Assets is a worse indicator for private companies. This implies that non-debt liabilities – for example, accounts payable – play a more significant role as a source of financing for private companies.

As the Liabilities/Asset ratio performs similarly at estimating default probabilities for public and private companies it should be used as an input instead of Debt/Assets.

Similarly, cash plays less of a role for public companies, whereas cash is a key resource for a private company with limited avenues of finance. Cash impacts the uncertainty surrounding each company's future; for example, volatility. As a key resource for private companies, an injection of cash does a lot more to reduce their volatility than that of a public firm. Correspondingly, Moody's found Cash/Assets to be a weak predictor of default risk for public companies but the most important one for private companies. Therefore, Cash/Assets should be one of the primary inputs with roughly an inverse relationship; that is, as Cash/Assets increases, volatility decreases.

A comparison of Retained earnings/Assets shows that a far greater number of public companies have negative retained earnings than private companies. Public companies are able to sustain smaller Retained earnings/Assets due to their greater access to financing. This bifurcation of public and private companies must be considered when incorporating Retained earnings/Assets into the model.

With public companies, the Short-term debt/Total debt ratio generally increases with default probability in contrast to private companies where the ratio does not display any meaningful relationship to default probability. Moody's conjectures is that, as private firms' debt primarily consists of bank loans, there is a tendency for banks to structure debt into short-term facilities that, in substance, have long-term maturities to compensate for different regulatory capital requirements between short- and long-term financing. Hence, the distinction between short-term and long-term obligations is blurred for private companies.

The use of Short-term debt/Total debt in a model derived from public firm data for private firm credit risk would therefore result in private companies with large amounts of short-term debt as being classified with greater risk when this is not necessarily the case.

INHERENT LIMITATIONS

Performance of model results are affected by the accuracy of the underlying structure, data frequency and data quality. The structured model is a simplification of how a company enters distress with approximations made, for example, in the calculation of a company's future asset value and default threshold. Thus, private company estimations are influenced by these approximations.

In fact, a private company model will not perform as well as a public company implementation. Static data are being used to approximate dynamic inputs that fluctuate on a daily basis. A company's volatility, for example, measures the dynamics of daily changes in value. Financial data are a point-in-time measure of a company's financial progress to date and not a measure of how a company's value has fluctuated over time. Even if a time series of financial data exists, financial results are only released, at best, once per quarter. This is still infrequent relative to daily value fluctuations, thus limiting any potential accuracy.

Another limitation is the quality of private company financial data. Private companies are generally not required to publish the same level of financial data as public companies. As such, inconsistency in the interpretation and accuracy across private company financial data is far greater than for public companies. This "noise" weakens the ability of a model to estimate volatility and market capitalization from data and thus to estimate private company credit risk.

Finally, the model results raise the question as to whether public quantitative data are sufficient. Qualitative data are not used due to the inability to quantify the information for incorporation into a structured model. However, in a public company setting, investors do consider qualitative data, so this information is contained, to some degree, in equity prices and thus volatility and market capitalization. The absence of qualitative data in the neural networks for private companies may negatively affect estimates of the outputs.

Moreover, for public company, investor risk and return perceptions and preferences play a significant role for market capitalization. Larger companies generally benefit from this psychology that cannot be assessed for private companies.

CONCLUSION

The most stringent approach chosen – namely to derive surrogate equity volatility and capitalization data and predictions for private companies from financial information and to calculate default probabilities with a fundamental, structured model – has shown to provide a benchmark for credit risk measurement. However, results are consistent and accurate enough to serve as an indicator of the veridical risk for internal or external assessments.

There are inherent limitations in using only publicly available information to assess private companies. Therefore, limited improvements can be made to enhance the results by adjusting the neural networks or the models themselves. The key lies in the data, not the structure or approach.

The next step must be to use the same or a similar fundamental and structured approach with additional proprietary information that only banks have to measure credit risk. With this additional financial information, models are likely to improve significantly, perhaps performing at a higher level than current public company models. This would enable financial institutions to have an objective and abstract credit risk measure as a complement to their internal credit risk assessment processes.

CHAPTER 19

Applying a Risk Measurement Model to Opportunity Evaluation

Gordian Gaeta
Simplex Credit Advisory Ltd

In general, risk and opportunity are considered to have some form of relationship. Some people argue they are two sides of the same coin, some claim they are inversely related: the higher the risk the better the opportunity. Some languages indicate a relationship: in Chinese, for example, the character for risk is the same as for non-opportunity.

Yet, in analytical terms, we have no formalized relationship. At best we can term the relationship as nonlinear dynamics or as a chaotic system – they simply lack deterministic predictability. However, if risk and opportunity have at least structural similarities – not necessarily relationship, as the popular view would indicate, then advances in risk measurement should be somehow applicable to opportunity measurement. The analogous development of some form of independent opportunity measurement or metric with the perspective of a risk measurement system seems tempting.

To simplify the discussion and to argue for the adoption of a risk measurement-based approach, we postulate that risk and opportunity are simply different potential futures of the same starting point. As a consequence, the structure of a credit risk measurement model can be applied to opportunity analyses. Based on structural similarities, we will argue inductively, that a particular abstract risk measurement model also provides useful results as an opportunity metric.

The sample test results confirm that the abstract or objective measurement of investment return probabilities is less reliable than in risk measurement. In other words, a risk measurement derived opportunity metric cannot effectively select the best investment or indeed timing to invest.

However, as an indicator of upside stock return propensities, the model test performs well. In fact, the opportunity metric provides a seemingly true probability of a target return within a given timeframe. Similar to the use of the default probability in risk measurement, the opportunity metric provides a useful validation of an investment assessment.

In addition to the use for individual companies, the opportunity metric can be used to assess a portfolio. Such approach would describe a portfolio in abstract by probability to achieve various levels of returns and can determine objectively the optimal and range of return-probability combinations.

A GENERALIZED FRAMEWORK FOR MEASURING RISK AND OPPORTUNITY THROUGH ONE MODEL

Since the early 1900s, the subject and relationship of risk, uncertainty, and profit in enterprises and economies received considerable academic attention. Most of this literature is by economists – both quantitative and non-quantitative in outlook – and evolves mainly around macroeconomic explanations for behavior and the theory of entrepreneurship. More recently, much academic work has been devoted to a better understanding of any such form of nonlinear or simply undefinable relationships. Fractal analyses and chaos theory are but two of the areas devoted to the quantification of similar relationships.

On the other hand, there is equally good reason for ignoring the complexities of any potentially chaotic relationship between risk and opportunity, mainly because most explanations put forward lack predictive, forward-looking value. Even if past relationships can be explained more or less consistently, little exists on the application of such relationships into the future. This leads to the position or belief that risk and opportunity are different potential outcomes of the same starting point. Risk and opportunity share certain characteristics but their relationship past, present, or future has little relevance to analyzing either element independently. If risk can be measured in an abstract way as proposed in many contributions, then opportunity should equally be susceptible to abstract analysis.

Expectations and assessments of both risk and opportunity vary based on the individual value system and cognitive processes, even under perfect conditions and with full information symmetry. Thus individuals value the same situation differently and come to differing conclusions. Thus if, as we pointed out elsewhere, causal and judgmental risk assessments are flawed with poor judgment, opportunity assessments are far worse off – hardly any agreement exists among professionals. The work of stock market analysts is a vivid example as they differ significantly in their assessments.

Moreover, people in general have inconsistent perspectives on opportunity. That is they act differently to the same probability of an outcome based on factors unrelated to the opportunity itself. Betting shows clearly that often perceptions change with the magnitude of the bet and the magnitude of the potential reward without regard to the underlying risk. In financial markets, behavior is more disciplined and approaching rationality but essentially players are hostage to the same flaws in perceptions. Huge takeover deals get financed easier than small ones; large, high risk investments often find willing uptake at the detriment of, say, smaller entrepreneurial risk.

Given these uncertainties, an opportunity metric expressed in monetary values or ordinal benchmarks cannot be easily formalized. However, alternative paths for developing an independent opportunity perspective or practical benchmarks are available. Developments in credit risk measurement have added a new dimension to valuing opportunity if we can satisfy ourselves that opportunity can be structurally defined as another form of risk, namely, "upside risk".

Structural Differences and Similarities between Risk and Opportunity

Let us approach the idea from an economic perspective and define the world as two players: firstly, capitalists who invest money and take ownership of resources. They are rewarded for bearing uncertainty or taking risk. Secondly, entrepreneurs, who exploit gains from invention or innovation, more generally from untried technological possibilities, and who reform or revolutionize the pattern of production or trade. Their reward or profit comes from finding and exploiting opportunities. Often they do so by transferring the risk or part thereof to capitalists. Thus, as is argued by several leading economists, a pure capitalist is never an entrepreneur. This distinction is useful because it differentiates in the real world between taking risk and exploiting opportunities.

Without getting into an academic debate about these concepts, they suggest that predicting risk or opportunity depends on vastly different factors and thus require a different approach.

If, however, we can postulate that in the abstract opportunity is another potential future state or, say, an "upside risk", then risk assessment and measurement methods can be applied. Current risk models have largely failed. We believe the main reason for this failure and therefore any possible application towards opportunity lies in the historic causality used to assess future risk. Historic stock returns, historic volatility, historic mapping or regressions, and other historic indicators are used to predict risk. In the context of opportunity, a historic risk perspective is even more useless due to the necessarily innovative and therefore forward-looking nature of opportunity.

Risk measurement models are however increasingly recognizing this problem and have changed their logic. They are becoming more or less abstract, that is, they do not require any fuzzy input or judgment, they are objective, that is, independent of any institutional view or approach to valuing risk, and they are event based, that is, they include the unpredictable or random events.

Within such a model, the risk of the capitalist is defined as the down side propensity of a company. It measures the probability of a default or distance to a default threshold. Conversely, the "upside risk" should be the maximum (target) positive distance to the default threshold or distance to an opportunity target, say, a 30% stock return over a period of time if structural similarities between risk and opportunity measurements exist.

Applying the Same Analytical Model Treatment to Risk and Opportunity

If therefore we have a default risk model that does start from a company's value, is purely numeric, and includes random events – both positive and negative – then the model should be able to define an opportunity probability. The differences in causality and influencing factors for risk and opportunity do not matter because the model is abstract. Here risk and opportunity are just two different outcomes of forward projections. They have no apparent or relevant relationship.

Although differences in the importance of events exist – generally bad news have a greater influence on the risk and good news on the opportunity – the random event generator does not differentiate between good and bad news when imputing random events. Event analyses demonstrate that bad news occur somewhat more often and have more impact than good news. This would seem to stand to reason for our purpose. The entrepreneur's activities to innovate successfully are more complex than the capitalist's choice of action to limit the downside risk. Thus success of the entrepreneur is less likely. The random event generator mirrors this real life situation.

At company level, the measure of risk is defined as default probability, that is, the probability that a company cannot fulfill its financial obligation in at least one instance, e.g., a bond payment. The inference is that if a company's defined net asset value falls below a given threshold – typically its liabilities – default occurs. The threshold can be set at varying levels.

If such a default probability can be determined in an abstract, that is, non-causal but objective and predictive way, the upside can be established by the same approach. This would mean looking at opportunity as an "upside risk", namely, the probability that the defined net asset value of a company exceeds certain parameters. We postulate that if a company's defined asset value crosses the defined level of 30% return on asset value, an opportunity probability metric for this level can be generated. The probability of meeting this target return over a chosen period of time is established by looking at the results of multiple simulations.

Moreover, plotting the probabilities against a variety of upside levels generates a probability distribution of positive developments of a company's net asset value. This invariably long-tailed distribution can be translated into another type of opportunity indicator.

REVIEW OF MODEL ARCHITECTURE

The SCA risk model architecture applied to the opportunity measurement is derived from the traditional option-theoretic approach to valuing risk debt as developed by Black and Scholes (1973), Merton (1974), Black and Cox (1976), Geske (1977), and Longstaff and Schwartz (1995). The central tenet of the approach is that debt and equity are considered as derivatives on the firm's assets. The value of the firm's assets is modeled by using a dynamic specification. The focus is on the assets of the obligor since historical experience shows that credit losses (risk) primarily come from major declines in the value of explicit or implicit collateral. We will use this same approach and say that asset values also define the opportunity that a firm has uncovered and exploited. While this may be contested as the main measure, the premise remains that any positive development should translate into higher net asset value.

The initial debt value is derived from the obligor's financial statements:

$$DV_i = long\text{-}term\ debt + \text{MAX}(current\ liabilities - current\ assets,\ 0).$$

The netting of current liabilities with current assets is based on empirical analysis and the intuition that the primary source of settling current obligations is with current assets. If we assume that interest is accumulating on the debt, we must drift debt and asset value. However, to maintain simplicity, we assume that the value increases in debt and asset values are equal, and interest is constantly being paid off such that both drifts are zero.

Asset value is defined as the sum of the market value of debt and of equity. To maintain our simple implementation, we will use the fact that book value of debt is a good first order approximation for short-term liabilities and assume the approximation is sufficient for long-term debt. If the initial debt value provides a proxy for our debt commitments, then the company initial asset value of the obligor *(CV_i)* can be calculated as:

$CV_i = DV_i + market\ capitalization$

This initial asset value of a company reflects equity market valuations and thus provides a good proxy of the market perceived value of innovation.

Since the firm's dynamics are being derived from the equity market, there must be a method to convert these equity dynamics into asset value dynamics. The relationship between a firm's equity and asset value is affected by its degree of leverage. The gearing ratio (G) is an indicator of a firm's leverage and by multiplying the equity dynamics – drift and volatility in the econometric model – by G we are able to derive the asset dynamics. The gearing ratio is calculated as:

$G = market\ capitalization/CV_i$

For a few firms close to a default, the dynamics of debt would play a greater role in influencing asset dynamics. However, for the vast majority of firms G is sufficient for approximating asset dynamics, so for practicality debt dynamics are not considered in this implementation.

The use of an asset-based model requires calibration to historical asset values. However, the market value of a firm's assets cannot be directly observed and must be inferred from the dynamics of the asset history. Thus, the problem of calibrating the asset process decomposes into two separate issues:

1. Determining the equity parameters from market data; and
2. Determining the relationship between the asset model parameters and the equity parameters.

The return process of both the asset and equity values must be constructed to satisfy two empirically verifiable properties:

1. Large, infrequent movements in the asset price;
2. Simulated return distributions that reflect the historical return distributions.

The SCA Credit Model satisfies both above requirements by modeling the asset and equity returns series. To capture both aspects of the asset value process, diffusions, and large movements, we employ a GARCH series with a mixture of normals model for the asset return process which is simply an econometric implementation of the Merton jump-diffusion model. As the calibration is being performed on daily stock returns, the econometric model for the stock returns (log St/St_{-1}) can be formulated as a discrete-time model with t equal to one day.

Using the initial asset value and asset price movements derived from equity dynamics, a Monte Carlo simulation of the asset price dynamics is used to determine the probability that a target return threshold or opportunity level of 30% increase on asset value is reached. We found 100,000 simulations (computed using 50,000 antithetic simulations) produce sufficiently stable probabilities for the default model and have adopted the same to the opportunity metric.

Using the Monte Carlo simulation, we identify the opportunity probability. If $CV_i > O$, then opportunity has manifested itself and the simulation is stopped. If $CV_i < O$, then target return has not been achieved and the simulation is continued. After all simulations have been run, a count is done of the number of times the target has been reached. The ratio of successful simulations to total simulations reflects the propensity for a company to achieve the upside potential, i.e., its opportunity target.

If one specific target is insufficient, this model can be applied to several levels of opportunity and the resulting probabilities for each level can be graphed to provide a distribution of likelihood and amplitude of potential opportunity.

The model demonstrates two principles that describe the changing value of a firm over time. The first of these behaviors is a standard diffusion of the asset value. Large jumps in the asset value of the firm are the second aspect. These large movements, both upwards and downwards, can be caused by sudden changes in the firm's operating environment, either exogenously or endogenously induced. Thus the model is event inclusive, firm specific, predictive, and objective.

THE SAMPLE AND TEST RESULTS

The model was applied to a sample of 171 companies. These companies were composed of a random selection of businesses and industries and have the distribution, by number of companies, given in Table 19.1.

They not only cover a spectrum of industries, sizes, and origins but more importantly, they cover a complete risk spectrum. Using the SCA credit risk measurement model, the sample companies demonstrate five-year default probabilities ranging from AAA to some really shaky companies with very high default predictions. Companies are grouped roughly in line with the thresholds between historic Moody's rating for AAA, investment grade, and junk categories (see Figure 19.1).

For each company, we calculated the opportunity metric, defined as the probability to achieve a 30% increase in company value, measured by equity returns, within one year. The results show a reasonably balanced distribution of probabilities (see Figure 19.2).

Table 19.1 Sample company distribution

Country	Count	%	Industry group	Count	%
Canada	4	2.34	Advertising	2	1.2
France	28	16.37	Aerospace/Defense	4	2.3
Germany	1	0.58	Airlines	2	1.2
Italy	6	3.51	Apparel	1	0.6
Netherlands	1	0.58	Auto manufacturers	4	2.3
Sweden	3	1.75	Auto parts and equipment	5	2.9
Switzerland	2	1.17	Beverages	4	2.3
UK and Britain	54	31.58	Building materials	5	2.9
United States	72	42.11	Chemicals	9	5.3
			Commercial services	5	2.9
			Computers	4	2.3
			Cosmetics/Personal care	3	1.8
			Distribution/Wholesale	1	0.6
			Diversified finan. serv.	2	1.2
			Electric	4	2.3
			Electrical compo. and equip.	4	2.3
Industry Sector	**Count**	**%**	Engineering and construction	4	2.3
			Entertainment	1	0.6
Basic materials	17	9.9	Food	14	8.2
Communications	15	8.8	Food service	1	0.6
Consumer – Cyclical	32	18.7	Forest products amd paper	1	0.6
Consumer – Non-cyclical	37	21.6	Gas	2	1.2
Diversified	1	0.6	Hand/Machine tools	2	1.2
Energy	11	6.4	Healthcare services	4	2.3
Financial	7	4.1	Home builders	1	0.6
Industrial	36	21.1	Home furnishings	1	0.6
Technology	6	3.5	Household products/wares	1	0.6
Utilities	9	5.3	Insurance	1	0.6
			Iron/Steel	2	1.2
			Leisure time	2	1.2
			Lodging	1	0.6
			Machinery – Constr. and mining	2	1.2
			Machinery – Diversified	3	1.8
			Media	8	4.7
			Metal fabricate/hardware	2	1.2
			Mining	3	1.8
			Miscellaneous manufactur.	7	4.1
			Oil and gas producers	10	5.8
			Oil and gas services	1	0.6
			Packaging and containers	2	1.2
			Pharmaceuticals	4	2.3
			Real estate	4	2.3
			Retail	12	7.0
			Software	2	1.2
			Telecommunications	5	2.9
			Tobacco	1	0.6
			Transportation	5	2.9
			Water	3	1.8

Figure 19.1   Number and percent of sample companies by range of default probability

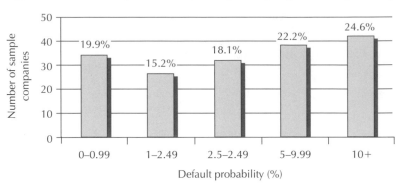

Default probability (%)

Figure 19. 2   Number and percent of sample companies by opportunity metric decile

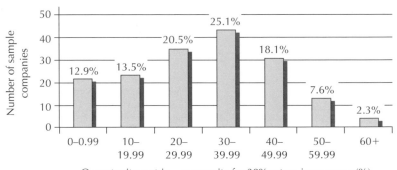

Opportunity metric – propensity for 30% return in one year (%)

When the target is lowered to 20% return, the probabilities change for the sample as a whole and as a median. However, probabilities do not change linear for each company. This means that lowering the target does make any specific company more attractive or likely to meet a certain target but companies with a reasonable chance of making 30% return have a higher probability of reaching a lower target (see Figure 19.3).

The opportunity metric does not mirror either equity dynamics or market dynamics. This metric combines and trades off the various input factors and does not follow any one factor predominantly. In particular, the analysis of one company against various target levels shows the complex trade-offs made by the model depending on the relative weight of any one factor and the random extrapolations/events that affect the results (see Figure 19.4).

At the 30% target return level that segregates more sharply between good and bad, the model shows that one quarter of the companies have less than a 20% probability to reach the target and only around 10% of the companies have more than a half chance of meeting the target. The bulk of sample companies lie in the 25–45% probability range. This seems intuitively right.

Figure 19.3   Opportunity metric for 20% and 30% target return compared – total sample

Figure 19.4   Opportunity metric distribution by return target

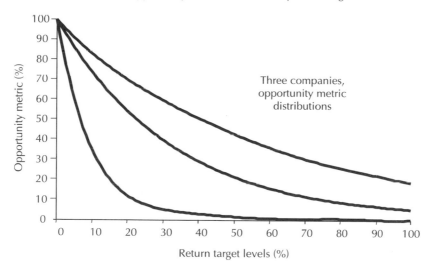

A comparison of opportunity (30% return probability) and risk (five-year default probability) shows no correlation at all (see Figure 19.5). This confirms our hypothesis that any relationship between risk and opportunity is much more complex than current models can handle.

However, the main objective of the test, is to ascertain if the model could provide an indication of the opportunity these companies provide. To this effect some investor assumptions have to be made. They relate to the level

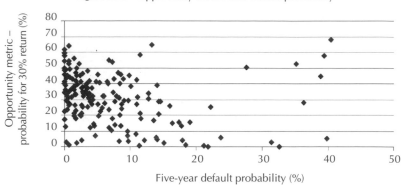

Figure 19.5 Opportunity metric and default probability

of probability that would be considered adequate for an investment. For practical reasons, we have assumed that if there is not at least a half baked chance (50%+) that the target is reached, the investment is not attractive. Of course a 25% probability of meeting the target could be sufficient for a specific investor but presumably at a lower price. Since prices are given at the time of the analysis, this latter investor would have to wait until market prices decline.

Above 50%, however, we assume that an investment can be considered at prevailing price levels. Thus the 50%+ companies were extracted from the sample. They cover a range of 50–68% probability of reaching a 30% return over one year. Their risk profile is, as expected, spread across a broad range of default probabilities (see Figure 19.6).

Interestingly, the largest number of companies are in the very low risk category and only a hand full are in the high risk segment. In fact, the majority of the low risk companies are AAA and below 0.03% default

Figure 19.6 Risk profile for 50%+ companies

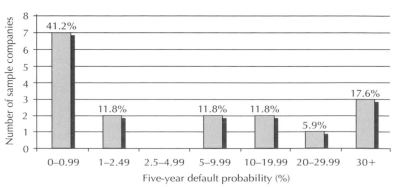

probability. This supports again the notion that risk and opportunity have little relationship.

The return analysis was conducted by calculating daily the equity market price returns starting January 2, 2001 over three sets of return periods (20, 60, 120 days) up to December 2001 or August 2002 and establishing a distribution of these returns. The upper 99% confidence interval and the average were extracted and considered for the results.

The return analyses of these 17 higher potential companies show that on average they achieved the target return based on the upper 99% confidence interval (CI) of the return distribution. This applies to the 20 day, 60 day, and 120 day equity return analyses. The shortest, 20 day return period performs best, at an average of 45.07% value increase, while the 60 days, return period performs the least with an average of 34.73%. These results mean that over some days during the return analysis period, the equity price of the company increased by at least 30% over and above the initial price.

Within each return period a significant number of individual companies achieved the target level of value increase. The results by number of companies and in % brackets of the sub-sample (17 companies with over 50% probability) are given in Table 19.2.

The lower 99% confidence interval of the distribution of all returns over the period analyzed shows none of the companies making the target. In fact, they decline considerably in value, between 47.8% and 31.6%.

Again the model results do not simply mirror equity dynamics or market volatility. They provide veridical results. Companies with at least a 50% chance of making a 30% return were in reality more successful in achieving the target than the probability would indicate. Based on an average opportunity metric of 57.16% across the sample of 17 companies, 10 companies should have made the target. In fact, over the 20 and 120 day return period, 13 and 12 companies respectively made the target.

To establish the persistence of any company making a 30% return, the number of days each company broke the 30% target level is tested for the least attractive 60 day return period. Of the seven companies making the target, they did so on average for 94 days. The shortest period was 11 days and the longest 212 days.

Table 19.2 Number of companies reaching the 30%+ target

	20 day returns	120 day returns
Upper 99% CI of return distribution	13 (76.5%)	12 (70.6%)
Average of return distribution	nil	nil

CONCLUSIONS

Opportunity analyses are significantly more complex than risk measurements. For starters, opportunity itself is defined differently for everyone. Secondly, the trade-off between probability and opportunity size is valued differently by individuals. Risk is a single concept more rational and objective with default being its manifestation but opportunity is highly subjective and multi-faceted.

However, the concept of using an abstract risk measurement model to test for opportunity probabilities or "upside risk" looks like a valid approach. The SCA model provides veridical or true sample results. This means that a 50% probability to achieve a given return in fact translates into at least 50 out of such 100 companies achieving the target result.

Moreover, results do not simply mirror company equity or market volatilities. In our model, they include random events and combine assets with equity volatility. The resulting benchmark measure – an opportunity metric – could redefine asset allocation along a spectrum of probabilities of returns. For example, investing in a 50% chance of a 35% return rather than by industry or geography could become a validating measure for investors independent of other asset allocation models.

Application of this benchmark is more difficult because company or investment selection can only be relative and timing is not considered. Thus any investor can rank companies along the opportunity metric but, contrary to the risk measure, the highest opportunity measure for a given time period does not necessarily indicate the highest potential.

ACKNOWLEDGMENTS

Many thanks to Justin Hingorani for his work on the model calculations and input on the resulting analysis.

CHAPTER 20

Credit Risk Management for Emerging Markets: Lessons from the Asian Crisis

Roman Scott
Boston Consulting Group

INTRODUCTION

The 1997–1999 financial crises in emerging markets, particularly Asia, led to massive defaults and exposed serious deficiencies in the management of credit risk in these countries. The result is that most Asian banks, from Korea to Indonesia, remain too weak to restart lending, restricting the recovery of national economies that largely depend on bank-intermediated lending for corporate investment. Other emerging markets fare no better. In Latin America – despite the lessons from earlier crises – in Eastern Europe, and in Russia, the quality of lending practices and credit risk management remains substandard. Balance sheets in these banks are building into 'accidents waiting to happen'. Even banks in Japan, among the world's largest, continue to struggle under the burden of enormous write-offs and poor new credit quality after 10 years of a protracted crisis, severely restricting access to credit in the world's second-largest economy. In addition, at about 80–90% of their total Value at Risk (VaR), credit risk for emerging market domestic banks is still a much bigger issue than market and operational risk.

The Cost of Poor Credit Risk Management

Poor credit risk management is ultimately an expensive mistake, but even more so in emerging markets. Here the deficiencies in credit risk management systems are so severe that the gap between a bank's risk assessment and its true risk has commonly led to total default – the loss of all or most capital, not just the interest due.

The economic impact on these generally poorer economies is real and severe. In Indonesia alone, banks have lost well over US$100 billion, and the taxpayer's bill for recapitalization has been US$70 billion to date. That's almost as much as the US$73 billion in public funds that Japan – a country 20 times richer than Indonesia – has used to bail out its banks. Korea has spent US$110 billion on recapitalization, and Thailand US$45 billion. These numbers are so big they are almost meaningless, but this is real money taken from taxpayers. The average Indonesian on annual earnings of US$1,000 effectively contributed one and half years of income to help bail out the banks.

The indirect costs to these economies are harder to quantify but, with most banks unable or unwilling to lend, many companies have found it difficult to obtain even basic working capital loans and trade finance. We believe the cost is at least 3–5% of GDP growth for most of these countries, which are currently stuck at growth rates of around 4–5%, rather than the 8–10% they previously enjoyed.

Practical Solutions to the Problem

Losses like these can be prevented fairly easily. The "back to basics" approach we advocate here does not depend on complex analytics or IT systems. Rather, it tries to get the underlying policies, process, and organization right, then supplements these basics with relatively simple tools that can progressively be made more complex. Many advanced, quantitative, and dynamic credit risk measurement methodologies are neither suitable nor possible in emerging markets, which usually lack data, standardised external ratings, and secondary markets for pricing – even, in some cases, a yield curve. The real difficulties in emerging markets are less about tools and techniques, and more about implementation, skills, training, and tying the credit decision process to rewards and performance measurement.

In five years of working to help "repair" damaged banks and introduce good practices into "bad" banks, we have developed a menu of simple and practical applications that will improve credit risk management in developing markets, creating a platform for introducing more advanced techniques in the future. We focus on *getting things right in the field*, not just building sophisticated models for the head office. This chapter covers the eight key "opportunities for action" we commonly find in emerging market banks. They are:

- choosing the right risk indicators;
- refining the traditional credit-rating process;
- testing the skills of line credit officers;
- validating the credit manual;

- tightening control over the organization and decision-making process;
- improving credit line monitoring, portfolio management, and early warning systems;
- enforcing true risk-based pricing;
- introducing simple board-level risk reports for non-risk experts.

The remainder of this chapter summarises our approach to each of these opportunities.

CHOOSING THE RIGHT RISK INDICATORS

Problems with Data Quality

Because many of today's advanced credit risk indicators depend on sophisticated statistical measures and IT systems, their applicability in most emerging markets is limited. The specific market and bank, not fashion, should dictate the choice of risk indicator. A simpler method designed to get 80% of the answer that actually works is a better investment than a complex system designed to get 100% that doesn't work because of the poor data quality typical of many developing markets.

Modern systems depend totally on the integrity of the input data. However, in Asia, for example, common problems include a lack of basic default data, inconsistent or arbitrary credit ratings, limited credit histories, the fact that standardized external ratings agencies cover only the few biggest corporates, and the impact on data series of the non-systemic financial shocks of the Asian financial crisis. The last of these has rendered useless all Asian default probability data before 1998.

Comparative Evaluation of Risk Indicators

Before changing its risk management approach or investing in new systems, a bank should assess the suitability of different risk indicators for its own market and specific circumstances. We use five main criteria:

1. *Accuracy*: How precise is the measurement in quantifying risk? Does it capture different dimensions of risk? Are correlations taken into account?

2. *Ability to include all risk types:* Does the measure allow the aggregation of different risk types (that is, credit with market and operational risks)? Does it capture different underlying risk parameters? (e.g., fx versus interest rates)

3. *Data availability and quality:* Are the required data available in real time? Is there a sufficiently large sample of historic data? Are all facilities and instruments covered? Is the quality of the data good (proper ratings, consistent criteria applied, and so on)?
4. *Relevance*: Is the result meaningful, intuitive, and actionable? Does it provide direction for management to take action?
5. *Understanding of method*: Can the bank master the concept and calculation technique?

Figure 20.1 provides an example of one such assessment for an Asian bank. For its credit risk measures we assessed customer and industry credit ratings, exposure measures (credit extended less collateral), portfolio concentration measures, and credit VaR. Ratings and exposure measures provide default probabilities that can be used to estimate expected future losses. However, in this case correlation within and between rating classes was not taken into account, and the rating cannot estimate unexpected losses. As a result, on the first criteria, "Accuracy", this bank's traditional rating measure was considered "deficient" in this area. The bank's credit risk measures were also specific to credit risk and could not be aggregated with market and operational risk measures to calculate overall risk (criteria 2). However, there are no problems with availability or quality of data (criteria 3), given a solid rating system and the ease of measuring exposure by industry or other categories. By contrast, credit VaR as a measure scored highly on accuracy because of the comprehensiveness of its measure of credit risk, which captured default probability distribution, net exposure, migration effect, and maximum possible loss. Unfortunately, however, the data required to assess credit VaR scored zero on quality and availability.

Figure 20.1 also shows market and operational risk indicators for the Asian bank. In this case, VaR for operational risk is as unsuitable as VaR for credit risk, again because of the lack of quality data over sufficiently long time periods. In contrast, VaR for market risk benefits from the existence of large and liquid capital markets that provide continuous pricing data for interest rate and equity instruments. We find this pattern repeated in most emerging markets: *VaR is practical for market risk assessment but inadequate for credit risk* and a distant dream for operational risk.

The Problem of Credit VaR in Emerging Markets

Data issues – in terms both of quality and length of time series – pose severe challenges for emerging market banks that want to use credit VaR. Those wishing to test the suitability of their credit VaR model should ask three questions:

FIGURE 20.1 Assessment of credit, market, and operational risks indicators for an Asian bank

Criteria	Credit risk: Rating/exposure	Credit risk: Portfolio concentration	Credit risk: VaR	Market risk: Volatility	Market risk: Sensitivity	Market risk: GAP	Market risk: Duration	Market risk: VaR	Operational risk: VaR
Accuracy of measured risk • Does the result capture different dimensions of risks? • Are correlations taken into account?	Deficient	Poor	Reasonable	Deficient	Deficient	Deficient	Nonexistent	Good	Deficient
Potential to add other risk types • Does measure allow aggregation of different risks (market, credit, operational)? • Does it capture different underlying risks parameters (e.g., interest rate, fx)?	Nonexistent	Nonexistent	Good	Nonexistent	Nonexistent	Nonexistent	Nonexistent	Good	Good
Data availability (and quality) • Real time? • Historic data (with a large enough sample)? • All instruments? • Good quality (e.g., proper ratings)?	Good	Good	Nonexistent	Good	Good	Good	Good	Good	Nonexistent
Relevance (so what?) • Intuitive and meaningful? • Actionable?	Good	Deficient	Good	Good	Deficient	Reasonable	Poor	Good	Reasonable
Understanding of methods • Risk management unit able to use data?	Good	Good	Reasonable	Good	Good	Good	Deficient	Reasonable	Deficient

Key: ● Good ◕ Reasonable ◑ Deficient ◔ Poor ○ Nonexistent

First, *is the model chosen appropriate?* To answer this, a bank must test whether the model assumptions are consistent with the statistical properties of the input data, including the default rate per industry sector over a time series, standard deviations of the default rate, and correlations between different industries.

One Asian bank estimated its credit VaR under the simplifying assumptions of a normal distribution or bell-shaped curve and the loss volatility multiples this implies. The approach works well for market risk, where loss distributions tend to be normally distributed around a mean, because the chances of making gains are roughly equal to the chances of making losses. However, credit risk is not normally distributed. The convention for credit risk is to isolate only those losses arising from loss of earnings in the event of default. Rather than the bell-shaped curve for market risk centred on zero earnings, the minimum value of the credit default distribution is zero (no default simply means no loss, not positive gain). The distribution for credit risk is sharply skewed to the left, because the most frequent losses are very small, with a long "tail" of increasingly less frequent but larger losses.

It is possible to determine an accurate multiple of loss volatility for the skewed distribution typical of credit risk. However, the sophisticated credit VaR models that provide this are derived from loss distribution patterns from more advanced – usually US – markets. The use of inappropriate data from other markets remains one of the major practical limitations to the application of credit VaR in emerging markets.

The second question banks should ask is, *is the chosen model implemented correctly?* To answer it they should check whether the correct correlation matrix (the correlation between one sector and another) is used for calculating overall VaR. Again, we have found that correlation matrices are unstable when based on insufficient data over short time series. A sample of our emerging market bank clients indicated error bars of over 30% in their calculations of portfolio VaR based on limited data and short time series.

Default means and volatility per industry are also inadequate for assessing VaR. As the composition of debtors within each industry changes, this reduces the predictive quality of past default rates. VaR calculations should instead rely on data per rating class, using the rating categories from the bank's internal rating system. This, of course, assumes that the rating system is stable and has not been substantially changed. However, most emerging market banks have indeed changed their rating systems (usually for the better) since the recent crises. Many banks in Asia have introduced them for the first time and will need several years of use to build up the required data.

The final question is, *are the data stable and accurate enough?* Useful VaR figures rely wholly on reasonably stable input data (mean, volatility of default, and correlations). This means that the definition of the default rate and its volatility must be checked. The bank must also determine whether there are sufficient points to calculate volatility, and test the stability of the defined correlation matrix based on available data. In practice, stability can only be achieved with *consistently defined data gathered over a long time*.

One Asian bank calculated volatility for each industry sector using only 13 months of data, because data before April 1999 were rendered meaningless by the crisis. How close were their figures to the actual volatility of the sectors? A Chi-square distribution test suggested that their calculated volatility using the data available resulted in an error bar of +/– 45% relative to true volatility. This translated into a VaR range of US$210 million down to US$110 million, too wide a margin to allow the bank to use the VaR measure for credit risk management. Our analysis showed that this bank would require 120 monthly data points to reach an error range of +/– 12% for this sector's VaR. As Figure 20.2 shows, this would take the bank 10 years to collect. In practical terms, the bank would need at least five years of data, taking credit VaR into the +/–17% error range, before it could use the measure for decision-making.

We recommend that most banks in emerging markets *return to the basics of traditional internal rating systems*, while developing the databases necessary for a more robust measure of credit VaR in the future (5 to 10 years) than is possible today. The fact that these kinds of databases do not yet exist in developing markets is unsurprising. Even in developed markets,

FIGURE 20.2 Confidence interval (95%) of VaR for corporate loan portfolio at an Asian bank

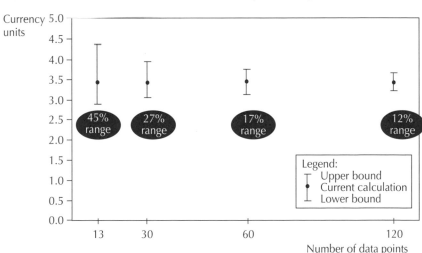

only a few top banks in countries with advanced credit databases and years of standard ratings use credit or operational VaR (Figure 20.3).

Banks in emerging markets can manage key components of credit risk, probability of default, and concentration risk using established indicators. Credit risk ratings can be used to both measure probability of default and manage default exposure if credit exposure per rating class is measured and appropriate limits are set. Concentration risk is typically managed by setting limits for segments (corporate, middle, and retail), geographies, industry sectors, and sub-sectors.

At the same time, banks should build the foundations for the future use of credit VaR. The most important next step is to begin building reliable databases using the correct definition of default and default data per rating class, aiming for a statistically significant time period that excludes non-systemic (crisis) data. While the data in the first couple of years may not be robust enough for decision-making, its existence will allow a bank to build its experience in the use of VaR and to test it against its traditional rating system.

Our research indicates that most emerging market banks will require a minimum of five years, and usually longer, before they reach the data availability and quality standards that a VaR system requires. Only at this point should they consider choosing an appropriate credit VaR model, either by purchasing software from vendors or by building the model in-house.

FIGURE 20.3   Examples of banks using credit or operational VaR

Bank	Market risk	Credit risk	Operational risk
JP Morgan, US	●	●	●
Bank of America, US	●	●	◑
Deutsche Bank, Germany	●	●	●
Credit Suisse, Switzerland	●	●	◑
Barclays Bank, UK	●	◑	○
Dresdner Bank, Germany	●	○	○
ING Barings, Netherlands	●	○	○
Shinhan Bank, Korea	●	◑	○
DBS Bank, Singapore	●	○	○

● Uses VaR   ◑ VaR and traditional measures   ○ Traditional measures

REFINING THE TRADITIONAL CREDIT RATING PROCESS

As we have seen, the traditional credit rating approach is a better option than sophisticated VaR assessment systems for most banks in emerging markets. Such banks usually have customer rating systems in place, but they tend to be incomplete, subjective, and too broadly defined to provide appropriate management of risk and price. Formal industry ratings tend to be even less developed, and limit-setting by line of business is usually inadequate. We have developed a six-step approach that modifies the traditional customer rating system for the rigours of emerging markets (see Table 20.1).

Stage 1: Financial Assessment – The First, Essential Screen

Our approach is to use financial assessment of the balance sheet and profit and loss as the first screen in the loan evaluation process, after pre-screening using industry/portfolio concentration "traffic lights" to guard against exceeding lending limits set through credit policy or the regulators (see "Improving portfolio management and monitoring" later in this chapter). The rule is that a complete financial assessment is a non-negotiable prerequisite to any further steps in credit rating. If the financial score is less than a set hurdle rate, the application is rejected immediately and no other steps are necessary.

Given the inherent credit risk in most emerging markets, we believe a conservative approach is best – if in doubt, say no. The heavy use of financials forces better discipline on credit analysts, emphasises quantitative data, and assumes that it is abnormal for a debtor to score well in other criteria (management quality, business condition, and so on), yet have bad financial results. It also frees credit analysts from performing entire credit ratings for companies that fail the financial screen.

This rules out the possibility of getting an acceptable loss expectation from a financially weak borrower but with a strong collateral structure. Such structures may appear economically attractive, but the real recovery rates banks can actually achieve in many emerging markets are typically very low, however attractive the collateral appears. Cash collateral is the exception.

Our benchmarking of international best practice supports this approach, with financial assessment typically accounting for 50–60% of the weighting in banks' customer rating systems. The broad criteria of liquidity, leverage, cash flow, and profitability are also fairly standard (unsurprisingly, given their fundamental relationship to a debtor's ability to pay). Efficiency, growth, and size are sometimes also used. The specific measures for each of the above criteria vary from bank to bank (Table 20.2), but best practice banks ensure that the financial screen is rigorously applied and heavily weighted in the final rating.

TABLE 20.1   Recommended customer-rating approach for emerging markets

① Financial criteria scoring	② Qualitative criteria scoring	③ Audits/ inspections	④ Fine tune for special conditions	⑤ Incorporate payment history	⑥ Final rating
Financial assessment pre-screen Leverage (debt/equity) — 20 Cash flow interest cover (EBITDA/ total debt, EBITDA/interest) — 15 Profitability (ROE, net income/sales) — 10 Efficiency (inventory/sales, receivables/sales) — 5 Growth (EBITDA growth, sales growth) — 5 Liquidity (current ratio, quick ratio) — 5 Total financial score pre-screen — 60 PASS/FAIL decision	—	Adjust and refine quantitative analysis for initial rating due to lack of data/transparency: • Live audits and inspections of: – factories, facilities – inventory – land • Surveys, calls on: – customers – labor – salesforces – other banks	Restricted to downgrades for conditions that are not covered in the specified categories, such as: • Force majeure event (e.g., factory fires) • Legal problems • Labor strikes • Mergers and acquisitions • Contingent/off-balance sheet liabilities	Incorporated for existing customers only Adjustments to account for delinquent debtors Missed interest and/or principal payments gives final rating of: • ≤ 3 mths – rating 7 • > 3 mths, ≤ 6 mths – rating 8 • > 6 mths, ≤ 12 mths – rating 9 • > 12 mths – rating 10	1 — Minimum risk 2 — Acceptable risk 3 — Average risk 4 — Allowable risk 5 — Marginal risk } Regular/ periodic rating evaluation 6 — Early warning 7 — Precautionary } Watch 8 — Substandard 9 — Doubtful 10 — Expected loss } Remedial
② Qualitative criteria scoring Industry rating — 20 *– Detailed in separate industry rating section* Business condition Subtotal — 10 – Market share/position — 5 – Market risks — 2.5 – Production/technology aspect — 2.5 Management Subtotal — 10 – Experience/track record — 5 – Integrity/reputation — 2.5 – Quality of financial information — 2.5					
Total score for initial rating — 100		Adjusted initial rating			Final rating

TABLE 20.2 Benchmarking of financial criteria used by Asian banks

Criteria	US bank in Asian market	Asian bank 1	Asian bank 2	Asian bank 3	Asian bank 4
Liquidity	Quick ratio	Current ratio		Current ratio	Current/Quick ratio
Leverage	Debt-to-Equity ratio	Debt-to-equity	Debt-to-equity	Debt-to-equity	Equity-to-debt
Cash flow Interest cover	EBITDA to total debt	Cash flow/total debt Cash flow/debt and payables Cash flow/sales	EBITDA to interest expense	EBITDA to interest expense	Net working capital to interest EBITDA to interest expense
Profitability	Pretax return on average capital	ROI, Net income/assets, Gross profit margin	ROAE Net profit margin	ROAE Net profit margin	ROE Net income/sales
Efficiency		Assets turnover, inventory/sales, labour, production, sales efficiency	Inventory/sales	Inventory/sales Receivables/sales	
Growth		Equity growth rate Sales growth rate			
Size	Capitalization				Sales

Selecting rating criteria and determining their weighting

Two approaches are possible for determining the criteria and the weighting for different criteria: statistical derivation or experience-based assumption. The former has the clear advantage of statistical significance and facilitates a rating system based on real correlations. Again, however, the reality is that most emerging market banks do not have a large enough database stable over time to generate good regression results, since customer data on *all* criteria and *all* default experiences are required, with at least 5–10 years of stable data. We therefore leverage our own experience and statistical database of independent financial variables that in prior work we have found to be predictive of default at a 95% confidence interval, adjusted for covariance with other independent variables. We compare this to benchmarks from international banks to derive the criteria and weights illustrated in Table 20.1. Banks can then refine their weightings over time when they have collected enough data for the statistical approach.

In our statistical tests, we find that measures of leverage (debt/equity and debt/assets) and measures of cash flow interest cover (EBITDA, the standard proxy for cash flow, to interest expense) are the most predictive, followed by measures of profitability (ROE, net margin). International benchmarks confirm this, and these factors get the highest weighting in our rating model. Liquidity, growth, and efficiency (asset and inventory turnover) measures are also useful.

Stage 2: Good Industry Ratings – A Forward-looking Perspective

In our credit rating approach for emerging markets, clients who pass the financial criteria pre-screen are then assessed against nonfinancial criteria, including an industry rating (a separate system detailed below), business condition (market share, market risks, and production/technology risks), and management quality. Benchmarking of international best practice indicates that non-financial criteria typically include a separately computed industry rating that accounts for 20–30% of the total score, and a management rating that accounts for 10–15% of the total score, although many banks choose not to include the highly subjective management rating.

Industry ratings receive inadequate attention in most banks' rating systems. Because the primary ratings are always customer-based, industry ratings are often weak, subjective – or even completely absent. However, good industry ratings are a critical element of any internal rating system and, if well designed, can be the only aspect of the risk management system that identifies *potential future problems* with businesses that may appear today to be financially sound and a good credit risk. A typical customer rating is an audit at one point in time. This backward-looking feature of credit ratings is a weakness that was exposed by the Asian financial crisis, where historic data and default statistics became meaningless overnight. Even the more quantitative customer-rating techniques such as Zeta analysis[1] focus on today's view of largely financial variables – recent and long-term profitability, interest coverage, rate of return, liquidity, leverage, and size.

Any debtor who passes the customer screening test will, by definition, be a sound company (good financials, good management, and so on), so the main credit risks are likely to be the volatile characteristics of the industry sub-sector. The semiconductor business, for example, is subject to an extreme cyclical rise and fall in margins. Industry ratings, then, are akin to assessing a healthy individual's genetic predisposition to contract a medical condition. They are "corporate DNA testing" – an assessment of the family background (sector) of an apparently healthy individual (company). This is particularly important when times are good; and helps protect the bank from dangerous overexposure to the hot sector of the moment. Portfolio limits can then be set by industry sector.

If actively monitored, industry ratings can guard against a major deficiency of customer ratings: what I call the *"market risk of credit risk"*. Customer ratings focus only on the creditworthiness of the business – in other words, its ability to pay interest and principal – hence their focus on financials and cash flow. However, external, market-related risks can turn healthy, well-run companies into bad credit risks. Recent currency fluctuations and dramatic changes in commodity prices have exposed the serious flaw in many apparently sound customer-rating systems – their inability to translate market risk into debtor credit risk for the lender. As these market shifts are often cyclical and affect whole industry sectors, we believe it makes sense to incorporate them into the industry-rating criteria and include them in periodic reviews. The objective is to generate insights into potential credit risks long before they actually happen.

Good industry ratings are hard to achieve as they must evaluate a wide range of both quantitative and qualitative criteria. Typically, three major criteria are used: industry characteristics (a broad group that includes supply, demand, and competitiveness), bad debt history for the sector, and financial performance for the sector (see Table 20.3).

For the customer and financial ratings, we used statistical methods to determine the appropriate criteria and their predictive power to set their weightings, which were compared to benchmarks. However, this is difficult to do for industry ratings in emerging markets as default data by industry sectors are virtually impossible to find. As a result, we determine the

TABLE 20.3 Recommended industry rating criteria and weightings

Maximum scores for categories	Criteria	Final rating
Industry characteristics 60	Industry structure [10] • degree of competitiveness • entry/exist barriers	
	Supply assessment [10] • degree of supplier concentration • stability of supply and prices • currency risk of supply costs • substitutability • labor supply	
	Demand assessment [20] • market prospects • degree of buyer concentration • substitutability • price stability (historic price movements and futures) • currency risk of demand prices	
	External environment [20] • dependence on government regulation • sensitivity to changes in macroeconomic factors, currency and interest rate risk, political risk	
Bad debt 20	Bad debt performance (NPL/total loan, banking sector NPL/total loan) [20]	
Industry financial performance 20	Liquidity (EBITDA/debt ratio, current ratio, quick ratio) [5] Leverage (debt/equity ratio) [5] Profitability (ROE) [5]	
Total industry score 100	Size (industry GDP as % of total GDP, credit to industry as % of total banking credit) [5]	

Final rating:

Grade	Score	Rating
A+	91–100	Very good
A	81–90	Good
B	61–80	Fair
C+	41–60	Risky
C–	20–40	Very risky

characteristics ourselves based on standard 'Porter' industry analysis (supply and demand, competitive intensity, and substitutes) and we use international benchmarks to help determine guidelines for the weighting of these factors. The choice can vary widely, and rightly so – industry ratings should be specific to the market. Our recommended weighting for emerging markets is 60% industry characteristics, 20% sector bad debt history, and 20% industry financial performance. These weightings reflect the relative advantages of both sets of measures. Industry characteristics are forward looking, as opposed to the historic data used for bad debt and financials. However, forward indicators of potential cash flow risks can be found in the historic financial data, for example margin trends, which also have the advantage of being readily available and quantitative.

We incorporate the macro-level market risks discussed above in the assessment of industry characteristics in three sub-criteria. First, in reviewing supply-side factors, we include price volatility and exchange rate risk for inputs priced in non-domestic currencies (for example, switching equipment priced in US dollars for a Thai telecom company). A similar assessment is performed for demand-side factors, particularly where product prices follow commodity cycles (pulp and paper, for example) and where export markets are subject to exchange rate risks. Finally, macroeconomic market risks (currencies, interest rates) and regulatory and political risks are included under their own headings (see Table 20.3).

Finally, we recommend banks model the sensitivity of the borrower's financial condition to a variety of "*stress tests*", including worst case scenarios that may seem improbable. Stress scenarios are run continuously to test the impact of changes in market conditions and volatility in currencies, interest rates, market prices, liquidity tightening, and even political and regulatory conditions that have the potential to affect creditworthiness. In emerging markets, currencies and interest rates are far more volatile than in the G7 countries, and domestic borrowings in international currencies tend to be unhedged. In some sectors, other, price-based risk factor "watch lists" (for example, commodity prices such as palm oil and wood pulp) should be built into early warning systems that regularly adjust the underlying credit/liquidity risk for those industry sector ratings.

Providing industry rating expertise

Industry ratings require expert and objective analyses, and are often better provided by external parties with expertise in this type of analysis. Building an internal ratings team takes time and good training. Few banks have enough good analysts with sector knowledge who are able to "think out of the box" and identify macro-level trends and risks. A good solution is to incorporate an industry expert panel of outside advisors to help refine the bank's initial analysis. Such a panel can provide mid- to long-term views on industry growth trends, supply and demand factors, and potential credit risks.

Stage 3: Audits and Inspections to Adjust and Refine Quantitative Analysis

Emerging markets typically do not have the levels of transparency and third-party corporate analysis found in the G7 nations. Aside from emphasising quantitative data, banks in these markets need to perform live audits and inspections of production facilities, inventory, and real assets such as land, as well as undertake surveys of customers, salesforces, and labour. Such investigation helps compensate for the absence of external credit-rating bureaus. Because this type of analysis broadens the traditional role of the credit analyst, it requires specific training and methods. It is also essential that the role be separated from that of the customer relationship manager. Specific training and evaluation measures are required for the assessment officers, as this is not an easy job. Desk research and legal expertise are also required to understand ownership and control networks, and the potential for multiple uses of collateral.

Stage 4: "Fine-tuning" for Downgrades Only

Our emerging markets rating system does not allow individual credit officers to make the kinds of changes commonly allowed in credit ratings systems in other markets. We have seen many internal rating systems that allow relatively uncontrolled upgrading of customers' ratings. If you provide a loophole like that, relationship managers trying to meet their business targets will surely use it. The customers who typically benefit most are those who are on the margin or who have "special relationship" privileges. Given the poor record to date of most of these banks' credit rating processes, we believe allowing this facility is dangerous. We have a simple solution – restrict such "fine-tuning" to *downgrades* only. We restrict fine-tuning to special circumstances that affect the debtor's ability to repay the loan (hence its default probability) and contingent liabilities. The former covers abnormal conditions outside the criteria used in the rating process, such as mergers with other companies, legal disputes, labor strikes, or catastrophic events such as fires or weather damage. The latter includes corporate guarantees for affiliated parties and forward contracts.

Stage 5: Adjusting for the Payment History of Existing Debtors

For existing customers, payment history provides a critical extra indicator of default potential. In our convervative model, only downgrade adjustments are made for existing customers who have missed payments. They should be based on these customers' current ratings. Table 20.1 describes our rule-based downgrades for missed payments.

Stage 6: Grading the Customer for Pricing and Risk Management

The final rating provides the *a priori* probability of default, which can be used to indicate future loss. It is vital, therefore, to mandate the use of the customer grade for pricing decisions and customer relationship management. Our rating system usually comprises ten grades, which complies with BIS benchmarks of international best practice (the most common range being 5–9 grades for non-impaired loans – we use 5 – and 4 for impaired loans – we use 5).[2] These grades can be labeled using either numbers (1 to 10) or letters (AAA down to F), whichever suits the bank.

In its basic form, a customer rating system provides a consistent, standardised method to grade customer quality from good to bad. A more precise definition of credit risk, the *probability of default*, sticks a firm number to the customer rating class. A top grade of 1 or AAA will be more precisely described by a probability of default of, say 0.1% (1 in a thousand), versus a grade 6 or B with a probability of default of, say, 5%. Probability of default is necessary for extending the use of the rating system for risk-based pricing and risk capital allocation, and is required for a bank to raise the standards of its internal rating system to that demanded under the BIS Basel II accord under their "Foundation Internal Ratings Based Approach".

Probability of default distribution can be derived using two approaches. The simplest and most accurate way is observe the actual historical default rate of companies by risk grade over time and assign these values as the probability of default expected in the future. This is the approach taken by international rating agencies such as Standard and Poor's, and all banks should aim to build up the data required (minimum five years) using a consistently applied, quantitative-based rating system such as that described above. The second approach to use when historic data are unavailable is to use statistical methods to assess the probability of default from a sample of known "good" and "bad" (defaulting) customers from the bank's current portfolio, and mathematically adjust the probability of default to reflect current population default rates. We typically use a regression model with roughly even samples of good and bad customers to get around sample limitation problems and then use Bayes theorem to adjust the default distribution to the current population default rate.

The approach is too technical to be described for the purposes of this chapter, but it performs well and is a good proxy while the bank collects sufficient data for the first approach.

Compromising the Credit Rating System
We should mention one final issue for the credit rating system, and the one we find the most frustrating. It occurs when a sound credit decision, based on a factual, well-researched credit rating, is overruled by top management, and a credit that would otherwise have been rejected is accepted. This is typically the result of political pressure and directed lending type policies, or corporate shareholders in the bank demanding access to credit for group-related companies. Events like these completely defeat the purpose of the credit rating and undermine the entire risk management process. Many emerging market banks we have worked with have a process, formal or otherwise, for accomodating 'exceptions' and authorizing loans at the highest level that do not comply with the banks' risk controls.

The solution to the problem lies largely with the entities that have created it – governments, regulators and bank owners. Allowing industrial holding companies to have group ownership of banks is a recipe for disaster, and should not be allowed by law. Government directed lending is a more complex remnant of a school of industrial policy popular in many emerging markets for more than 50 years, but rapidly losing favor now that various banking crises have exposed its true costs. At the very least, banks forced to accept such lending practices should isolate those credits and hold them in a separate book, to be underwritten by the governments concerned. The book would function as a mini state "development-bank", with the sovereign's risk rating, different lending criteria, and preferably seperate capital. Of course, the best solution is privatisation of state-owned banks and a policy of non-interference by governments in bank's credit decisions.

TESTING THE SKILLS OF LINE CREDIT OFFICERS

Robust credit rating tools are useless if they are misunderstood or incorrectly applied in the field. Implementation is the biggest problem for lenders in emerging markets. The capabilities of ordinary credit officers in the branches and regions – not the sophisticated risk measurement models in head office – determine the bank's ability to extend good credit. It's also true that part of the problem has a complex dimension: reward and punishment systems and how they support (or undermine) good credit decisions. This links to even more complex issues around basic pay levels for staff, coercion by powerful parties and corruption. Despite their intrinsic interest, these lively "soft" issues are not the subject of this chapter.

We address here a much simpler aspect of the implementation problem – inadequate skills and poor understanding of the credit assessment process among line credit and relationship management staff. The cure is also simple – intense and supportive training. However, many banks are unaware of any skills gap among their staff, and those that are tend to misunderstand their nature and magnitude. We find that most banks consistently overestimate their level of credit risk management skills, and place too much faith in good tools rather than the people that use them. Without a "wake-up call" to help them recognize the problem, banks fail to institute the changes necessary to equip their people to make good credit decisions.

The solution? We have instituted a *credit decision examination* (CDE) for line staff that provides an efficient means to identify and quantify skill levels (Figure 20.4). Passing the CDE requires a sound understanding of the bank's credit policies and processes, the limits allowed, the calculation of financial ratios required for the decision, and collateral requirements.

The CDE not only tests credit officers' knowledge of credit processes and criteria, but also provides a simulated application for a line of credit for different customer segments. The subject has to make the appropriate credit decision at the end of the exam. An individual who fails the test not only has inadequate knowledge but would, in real life, put the bank at risk when making a routine credit decision. Such risks in aggregate would result in defaults and put capital and profits at risk. In effect, the CDE measures the *operational risk* of a bank's credit risk process.

In banks we have tested we have been surprised by the high failure rates we often find – up to 25%. Remember that failing the CDE implies that in real life the credit officer is make the wrong decision, so even a 5% fail rate in the exam would have unacceptable consequences if translated into the same number as a default rate. The implications help banks institute the major training programmes necessary to redress the problem.

Finally, banks must focus their training efforts. Training programmes, usually supplied by third-party vendors, tend to be generic rather than tailored to address a bank's particular skill gaps and specific circumstances. Local examples, specific credit risks, real data problems, and familiar relationship issues with real local customers are required, based on the specific bank's internal-rating system. Learning how they do it in middle America is of limited value in Bangkok or Jakarta.

FIGURE 20.4   Sample credit decision examination (CDE) questions

PT Bigfoot is a shoe manufacturing company. It operates one production plant in Bandung that makes athletic shoes. The finance director has come to see you and is seeking a working capital loan. According to the director, "Bigfoot is a company with great business potential. In 1999, our revenue was Rp 9 billion as a result of fantastic growth. We believe that we can sustain continued high growth and triple revenue over the next two years. But in order to support this growth, we need a working capital loan of Rp 6 billion. We hope that the bank can help us with this financing requirement."

1. Please name the legal documents that must be provided to comply with   (2 points)
    the general requirement for business legality.
2. What are the minimum standards on audit quality required for the   (3 points)
    financial accounts you request from Bigfoot? How do you check these
    standards?
3. Excluding the use of a profit & loss statement, please name two ways for   (4 points)
    verifying that the revenue of Bigfoot in 1999 is indeed Rp 9 billion as
    claimed.

The collateral being proposed is: (i) a plot of land that has an area 3,000 m^2 and is located next to the Bigfoot plant. (ii) accounts receivable amounting to Rp 8 billion.

4. Please name the documents that you need to decide if this land can be   (4 points)
    accepted as collateral.
5. Who has to conduct the valuation of this plot of land?   (2 points)
6. What is the process for determining the collateral value of the accounts   (6 points)
    receivable and documents required? Name 3 (three) circumstances in
    which you would discount the accounts receivable, and what discounts
    would you apply to each?
7. Your verification concludes that the plot of land is worth Rp 1,000,000   (5 points)
    per m^2 and that the accounts receivable should be discounted by 25%
    and are worth Rp 6 billion. What is the cash equivalent value (CEV) of
    the plot of land? What is the CEV for the accounts receivable?
8. What are the ten key financial ratios to be calculated for this customer?   (10 points)
    The balance sheet is attached.
9   Using the customer rating spreadsheet model provided, input the balance   (15 points)
    sheet and P&L data required and calculate the financial rating of this
    customer. Write the rating grade on your answer sheet.
10. What are the financial covenant requirements for this customer?   (5 points)
11. The management rating for this customer has been determined as 1.   (5 points)
    What effect will that have on the financial rating?
12. What is the collateral rating for this customer? Why?   (5 points)
13. What is the overall classification rating for this customer?   (5 points)
14. Who has the authority to approve this loan?   (2 points)
15. If you were a member of the Loan Approval Committee, would you   (5 points)
    approve this loan? Why?
16. Based on the information given, would you agree with the company's   (3 points)
    assertion that its growth is sustainable?" Why?

For the remaining questions, assume that Bigfoot's loan application was approved (this does not mean that the answer to question 15 is yes and you should approve the loan).

17. In conducting effective monitoring of Bigfoot, name 3 (three) sources of   (3 points)
    information to monitor and follow its business development and credit
    development.

FIGURE 20.4   *(cont.)*

18. Name 3 (three) activities that must be done in monitoring performance   (6 points)
    for a debtor like Bigfoot.
19. Assume that the loan has been ongoing for 6 months and the activities   (3 points)
    on Bigfoot's bank accounts (revenues, cash flows, account receivables)
    have declined sharply, what do you do?
20. Assume that the loan has not been serviced for 6 months. Would you   (2 points)
    define the loan as nonperforming?
21. Describe the 3 (three) major signals of the loan early warning process   (5 points)
    that may identify possible default.

VALIDATING THE CREDIT MANUAL

The second simple flaw in implementation arises because local access to credit policies, procedures, and calculation metrics is usually embodied in a "credit manual." In theory, an up-to-date copy will sit on every credit officer's desk and all of them will thoroughly understand its content. In practice, the policies and procedures in most credit manuals bear little relationship to the sound credit risk frameworks developed in the head office. A typical example will contain fuzzy logic and confusing procedures. It will lack strict definition of current policy and provide few calculation metrics to support decision-making; that is, if you can even find an up-to-date copy in the branch office!

In a recent survey at one emerging market bank, two main reasons were cited for not using the manual. First, staff were uncertain about whether the manuals available had the latest updates and procedures required. Second, it was extremely difficult to get hold of a copy in any case. Online manuals can fix both these problems for banks with all their branches online.

Most banks' credit manuals start well (customer and industry rating and retail scoring), but are limited on pricing and portfolio management decisions, and are weaker still on collateral management and loan monitoring, and are almost useless on the early warning process and bad debt management. International best practices can be used to help set credit manual standards and evaluate the gap (see Figure 20.5), but the most important thing is to evaluate the manual according to how well it supports the credit risk management process or value chain (described later), rather than some arbitrary set of criteria.

TIGHTENING CONTROL OVER THE ORGANIZATION AND DECISION-MAKING PROCESS

Most of the literature on risk management focuses on the measurement of risk, paying little or no attention to the 'softer' issues around organizational

FIGURE 20.5 Assessment of credit manual relative to best practice (example)

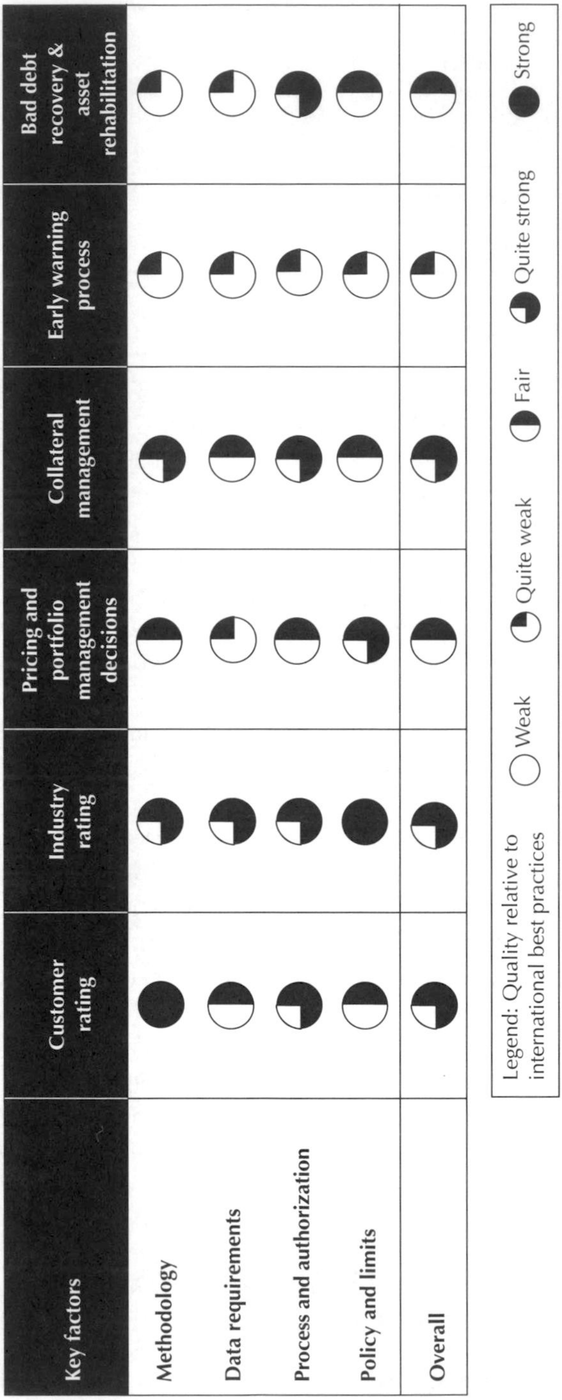

key factors	Customer rating	Industry rating	Pricing and portfolio management decisions	Collateral management	Early warning process	Bad debt recovery & asset rehabilitation
Methodology						
Data requirements						
Process and authorization						
Policy and limits						
Overall						

Legend: Quality relative to international best practices

○ Weak   ◔ Quite weak   ◑ Fair   ◕ Quite strong   ● Strong

models, roles and responsibilities, and performance evaluation systems. In practice, however, these elements are central to the effectiveness or otherwise of a bank's risk management approach. Suitable and accurate measures are vital: they determine what risk managers *know*. But organizational models and decision-making processes determine something equally fundamental to credit risk management: what risk managers actually *do*.

Three models of organization

The most widely accepted organization concept in credit risk is the *"four-eyes" principle* – the idea that for any credit decision a second, independent set of "two eyes" should provide a second opinion to the first set that usually belong to the corporate banking business unit. However, no formal rules exist on the specifics. Bankers have many questions on the principle: Do the second set of eyes have to be an independent credit officer? If so, how independent? Where do they sit: in the business unit or outside? Who do they report to? Who makes the final decision? As a result, banks have interpreted the principle in very different ways.

I have categorized the various "four eyes" organizational models observed in practice into three broad types: the *policeman model*, the *partnership model*, and the *customer-focused model*. Each of these is underpinned by a different philosophy on managing risk (see Figure 20.6).

The three models represent a continuum in terms of control over the final authority for a credit decision. At one end, the customer-focused model situates final approval or veto power in the business unit, and credit officers, while providing a second opinion, act more as analysts for the relationship managers. At the other end of the spectrum, the policeman model situates final approval or veto power in an independent credit division. The partnership model shares credit decision-making authority between the business unit and the credit organisation. All three models are widespread internationally, reflecting the fact that there is no "correct" organisational response – every bank must choose according to its own cultural and organisational constraints.

Historically, most emerging market banks' credit organizations have tended towards the customer-focused model. With credit decision-making authority vested in the business unit, they have lacked independence, leading to conflicts of interest in loan evaluations and questionable integrity in decision-making. We believe that separating credit decision-making from relationship management is a fundamental requirement in emerging market banks, achieved through the "partnership" or "policeman" model of a true "four eyes" organization, together with independently developed and

FIGURE 20.6 Organizational philosophies for managing risk

	Customer focus	Partnership	Policeman
Role of Credit Unit	• Credit evaluation done fully by Business Unit (BU) • No supervision from central risk organization • Credit analysts sit in BU, often under relationship managers	• Independent Credit Division provides ("second eyes") independent opinion to the BU proposal • Credit Officers belong to the Business Unit, responsible for analysis and evaluation, but are separated from BU relationship managers • Dotted reporting line from Credit Officers to central Credit Division	• Credit Officers belong to independent Credit Unit fully separate from BU • Head of Credit Unit reports to CEO, via Risk Director • Credit Unit responsible for evaluation and for loan performance
Role of Business Unit	• Business Unit responsible for risk-adjusted returns • No separation of credit risk and business marketing divisions	• Business Unit responsible for risk-adjusted returns • Separation of Credit Unit and BU up to division level	• Business Unit responsible for sales expansion and profitability, and customer relationship • Recommend credits, do not approve
Power of approval	• Business Unit has approval power over credit decision • Business marketing has the advantage in any credit decision	• Business Unit and Credit Unit joint approval power over credit decision • Business marketing and Credit Officers co-sign to approve credit	• Credit Unit has final approval authority • Credit Unit has the advantage in any credit decision

Extent of Business Unit control

Extent of central Credit Unit control

objective statistical tools. Banks should have a seperate risk management unit that does not report to a business unit, with an independent Chief Credit Officer at general manager level, reporting to a Director of Risk. For the highest standards of integrity over credit decisions, we advocate complete separation of the credit role from the business unit; in other words, the policeman model. This model may, however, limit growth tagets. The shift toward this model we are observing in some Asian banks suggests that the difficult lessons of the crisis have been learnt.

The Problem with the Customer-focused Model in Emerging Markets

The customer-focused model, by far the dominant model in pre-crisis Asia, undoubtedly offers more aggressive growth and client service benefits. However, in operation it tends to neglect the contingent risks. First, customer focus has to be balanced with the need to protect the bank and deposit customers from potential losses. Under this model, the credit officer and credit organisation serve the business unit, acting as analysts rather than independent credit decision-makers. Although there are "four eyes", power resides with the business unit. Second, any risk assumed to meet a customer's needs must be charged for; that is, it should be fully reflected in the price the customer pays. To say that these principles have been compromised in most emerging market banks would be an understatement.

The customer-focused model has failed in emerging markets because it depends on very high levels of objectivity, training and experience in credit decision-making from the *corporate relationship managers* themselves, backed up by performance evaluation that judges not just growth and service, but also risk. Few banks have these standards. Cultural considerations in customer relationship management also present a thorny issue. In Asia in particular – including Japan – national ways of doing business are simply not conducive to developing the objectivity required to make this model work. Few Asian relationship officers would be able to say "no" to an important and powerful customer. Fewer still would continue to say "no" under pressure to change their minds. Most would find that making a customer happy had a more positive effect on their performance evaluation than making the right credit decision. Ultimately, the customer-focused model creates a daily dilemma at work – "Do I do the right thing for the customer and say yes, or, if necessary, do I do the right thing for the bank and say no?" For most people, the right path out of a dilemma is the one of least resistance.

The problem is not exclusive to emerging market banks. Even a best practice international player like Citibank does not assume that integrity and experience guarantee its managers' objectivity and independence in the business unit controled partnership model it operates (see Figure 20.7). Citibank has strengthened the independence of its credit risk assessment by positioning senior "policeman-style" risk executives at the country and division (regional) levels. Line risk managers report both to the business unit and to these risk executives, who act as a "court of appeal" and sit on the credit committee. All credit applications flow through this risk organization, with the relationship managers acting as co-signers only. The risk managers are held accountable for the performance of the loans they accept.

Executive accountability for risk

It was clear during the Asian crisis that no one at the highest level was accountable for risk, or even for financial control and reporting, in many Asian banks. Then and now, the executive directors of most of these banks represented their major lines of business – corporate, retail, middle market, and so on – although there was often a separate treasury division managed

FIGURE 20.7   Citibank Asia model for credit analysis and risk assessment

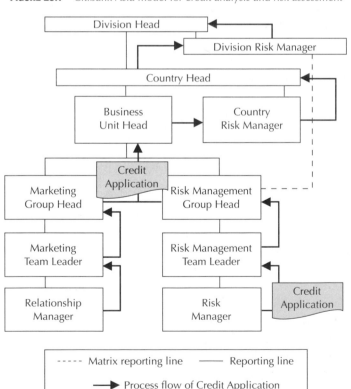

at the director level. There is therefore a clear need for each bank to create the distinct senior roles required to take accountability for managing its risk and financial position.

Three main roles, common in the international banks, are required:

- a Chief Risk Officer (CRO), responsible for setting overall risk policies (including, with the CCO, credit policy), market risk management, the integration of risk measures bank-wide and quantitative measurements such as VaR, risk capital allocation, and liaison with the regulators;
- a Chief Credit Officer (CCO), responsible for all counterparty and credit portfolio risk evaluation and management, country risk, and the systems and processes of credit control;
- a Chief Financial Officer (CFO) responsible for asset and liability management, funding, and liquidity management, as well as the usual financial and management accounting needs and tax.

Ideally, the CRO and CFO should be at director level, and the CCO can function effectively at general manger level. Each should also chair the relevant decision-making committee. At least three such committees should be a standard requirement: the policy-focused *risk management committee*, the balance sheet and liquidity focused *asset and liability committee*, and the *credit committee*, which is the highest signing authority for credit approvals.

Fitting the Organizational Model to the Situation

As in all things, the credit risk organization model that best suits a bank's specific circumstances is likely to be more successful than adherence to a purist ideal. So, while we have worked with several Asian banks to move them away from the customer-focused model toward the policeman model, the degree to which they have separated credit and relationship management varies on several dimensions (Table 20.4).

This kind of variation mirrors our conviction that a fully implemented compromise is a better outcome than failure to implement our ideal. The key is to change the status quo, to define the roles, responsibilities and process for credit decisions, and to upgrade the quality of the key players, whether they sit in the credit organization or the business unit. When working with real people in organizations with real and pressing problems, pragmatism is a more effective tool than theoretical purity.

At one Korean bank, for example, we recommended the policeman model. The result is a fully independent credit division with loan approval power reporting to a board level director, and a separate risk management

TABLE 20.4 Examples of different organization models in Asian banks restructured after the crisis

Organizing principle	Korean bank 1	Korean bank 2	Thai bank	Indonesian bank
Is there a full Credit Risk organization separate from the BUs?	Yes, Credit Management Unit (CMU) is equivalent to a BU, evaluates the credit proposal and makes decision	Partially, Credit Risk Division is part of Risk Management (RM) but does not have credit evaluation team, which sits in	Yes, Credit Division is equivalent to a BU	No, Credit Risk under BU Head. Head of Credit reports to the BU director, but "dotted line" to Risk Director
If separate, what are the responsibilities of the Credit Risk organization?	Credit policy; Risk planning and control (including exposure targets); Industry analysis; Credit evaluation	Credit policy; Portfolio management; Credit risk system development; Technology analysis	Credit policy; Credit evaluation; Loan review; Recovery and legal; Loan workout	Industry Risk Limit setting (Credit evaluation and Credit risk monitoring under BU team); Credit policy
Who is the most senior Credit Risk Manager?	CCO is a board member and is of equal seniority to BU head	CCO reports to a board member, the Chief Risk Officer	CCO is a board member and reports to the CEO	Credit Head is a General Manager, reports to Business Director and Risk Director (both are board members)
Are the line Credit Risk Analysts/Officers outside the BU?	Yes, CO and SCO are part of the CMU organization	No, CO is part of the BU but Credit Risk Division has influence through performance evaluation of the CO	Yes, the credit evaluation team of COs reports to the CCO	No, CO reports to the Head of BU and Credit, although the entire CMU sits in the BU
What is the role of the Credit Risk Officer in the credit decisions?	CO's approval needed for every loan. If he disagrees superior's (SCO) or board approval needed	COs must co-sign with RM to approve. Any dispute is resolved by the BU head	CO must sign and approve an application. Any dispute resolved by CCO	COs must co-sign application. However, BU Head can override CO if disagreement
Is the credit risk policy-maker involved in the credit decisions?	Yes, credit policy team and credit evaluation team (COs) belong to the CMU	Partially, credit policy team report to the CCO and credit evaluation team (COs) have dotted line reporting to CCO	Yes, CCO responsible for both policies and loan evaluation	Partially, COs have functional reporting to Risk Division that is also responsible for credit policy. Independent risk division can review loan files after decision is made

Abbreviations:
BU: Business Unit; CO: Credit Officers; SCO: Senior Credit Officers; CCO: Chief Credit Officer; GM: General Manager; CMU: Credit Management Unit

division responsible for risk policy, market risk, and IRM/capital allocation. But the culture, history, and skill levels of another Korean bank made it a better candidate for the partnership model. In this case, credit risk officers are located in the business units and report to the business unit head, but have a "dotted line" reporting to the risk management division, which is responsible for risk policy, market risk, and IRM/capital allocation (Figure 20.8). In this model, the credit officers co-sign the evaluation, which the relationship manager puts up to the business unit for approval.

Whatever organization model is chosen, it is critical to spend time specifying roles and responsibilities, particularly in terms of the process flow of loan applications and of credit approval limits at different levels. Finally, a conflict resolution mechanism must be designed so that disagreements can go to a "court of appeal" for speedy and authoritative resolution. Even in the partnership model described above, where the business units have final authority over the credit decision, the credit officer can appeal to the risk management unit (policies and control) for a credit review if there is a major disagreement. The credit review team should also act as the quality control check for credit organizations that are business-unit centered, sampling credit files on a regular basis to ensure compliance with risk policy.

IMPROVING CREDIT LINE MONITORING, PORTFOLIO MANAGEMENT, AND EARLY WARNING SYSTEMS

Even those emerging market banks with world-class credit rating and scoring systems tend to perform poorly at following up after deals are done. The principal issues are inadequate credit line monitoring and early warning systems for potential default, and lack of active portfolio management. A five-stage process is suggested, following international best practice (Figure 20.9).

Pricing (Stage 3) is so important an issue that it is covered separately in the next section.

Portfolio Management

Building a prudent portfolio is as important as evaluating individual loans, because several individual credit exposures often share characteristics that can result in concurrent losses. The Asian crisis painfully highlighted the risks associated with excessive concentration in certain sectors (property, construction and large, family-controlled conglomerates, to name a few), and loan types (foreign currency loans, loans against forward contracts, and so on).

FIGURE 20.8 Korean example of contrasting models chosen at two banks

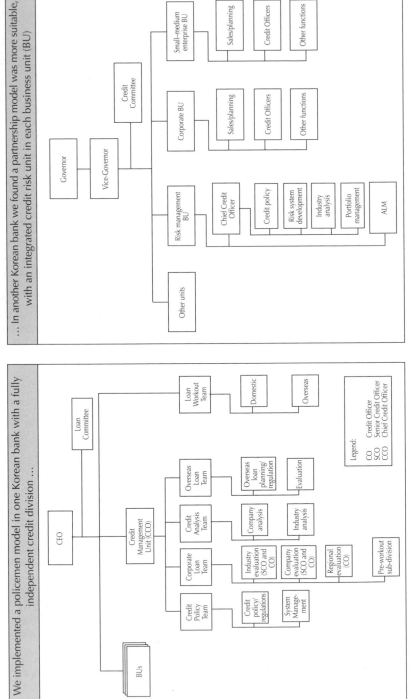

Source: BCG project experience

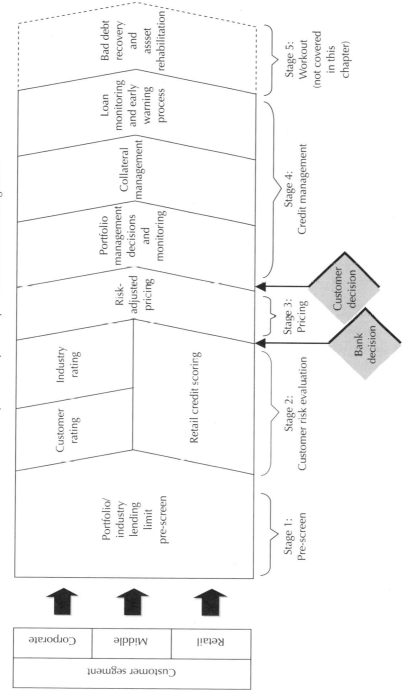

FIGURE 20.9 Credit risk process for pre- and post-decision credit management

The key principles of portfolio management – diversification to achieve a balanced portfolio, limit setting, and covariance analysis – are widely understood but rarely practiced well. This is because most banks focus on rating and monitoring individual customers and loans. Decisions tend to be made on individual credit facilities at the local level, with little attention paid to the entire portfolio at the bank-wide level. Portfolio management is usually an *ex post facto* process – someone in the head office or central risk department will analyse risk concentration after lending decisions have been made.

For many emerging market banks, only widespread default in a sector or an overall crisis will push them to readjust their exposures and portfolio limits – and by that time, it's almost always too late. To make matters worse, reactive portfolio management means that some banks overcompensate, clamping down on new credit to produce the "credit squeeze" that so often follows a crisis, sharply restricting economic recovery. The tap is either fully open or fully closed.

Covariance Analysis

As the Asian economic crisis showed, *industry sector covariance models* have limited benefits in emerging markets, as few sectors are negatively correlated (that is, move in the opposite direction to their peers). Most sectors in emerging markets are strongly influenced by the same fiscal and monetary policies and political risks. The exception tends to be export-led sectors; where demand is not dependent on the local economy, the cost base is in the local currency and the earnings are in a strong foreign currency such as the US dollar (Thai shrimp farms and Indonesian palm oil plantations are good examples).

As a result, we believe that a simple but effective exposure and limit-setting process is the most useful portfolio management approach in emerging markets. The analytic process and resulting exposure limits depend on a structured approach to industry risk that produces a rating, combined with analysis of the bank's current exposure to the sector relative to that sector's GDP contribution. Industry risk is a seperate topic summarised earlier in this chapter.

The caveat is that the poor quality of enforcement we observe must be raised for this to be effective. Most emerging markets banks have, for some years, set exposure limits by industry sector, loan type, and even region; and most regulators also impose legal lending limits. Even so, many banks routinely break the rules because of the same external pressures we described earlier for customer ratings.

Good portfolio management is a dynamic process, with the characteristics of the portfolio continually re-evaluated. A loan monitoring early warning system, the primary objective of which is to identify and take prompt action on defaulting debtors, also has a portfolio role. Common patterns in the early warning data can signal potential trouble, which should galvanise the bank to tighten limits for new loans in that sector.

Beyond "Holding-to-Maturity" Portfolio Management

In developed economies, banks are moving away from holding loans until maturity and actively managing the associated credit risk. A recent BCG global survey of risk management practices[3] shows these banks shifting their role from risk-taker to risk manager. This allows a bank to generate fee income from arranging the credit while transferring the credit risk in and out of the bank by trading on secondary markets, hedging, and securitization. The result is more active and efficient portfolio optimization.

The move from risk-taker to risk manager relies on well-developed and liquid secondary loan markets and corporate debt securities markets, as well as standardized ratings. Such sophistication is clearly a long way off in emerging markets. And, given the levels of credit, market, and political risk in many developing economies, sellers are likely to heavily outnumber those who want to buy. Banks in these countries therefore remain risk-takers, holding all loans to maturity and carrying the costs of default and the management effort of workouts. Some governments in emerging markets appear keen to encourage the development of credit derivatives and securitization. Credit derivatives, along with operational risk, provide a more fashionable topic than ratings at the latest risk management conferences in Singapore and Hong Kong, but do little to help the problems of the average Asian bank. Again, we recommend that bankers focus their efforts on getting the basics right in their internal rating systems first, to at least Basel II FIRB standard.

Integrated Management of Risk and Capital Allocation

Most banks in emerging markets have yet to integrate all risk types (credit, market, and operational) across their organizations, quantify the portfolio correlations of all risk types, allocate economic capital, and more precisely measure return on risk-adjusted capital (RORAC). All these techniques enable greater efficiency in allocating capital and managing the portfolio of risks carried by the bank, but remain unrealistic in most emerging market banks, given the problems with establishing VaR as a unifying concept, data quality in general, and limited secondary markets for pricing and trading. Integrated risk management requires the unifying, marked-to-market based concept of VaR to be extended from market risks to credit and operational risk – a data-collection process that we have shown will need at least five years to develop. In the meantime, basic RORAC measures for expected losses can be developed if the internal rating system is advanced enough to provide default probabilities as described earlier.

Collateral Management

One of the biggest problems we have seen in helping banks to restructure and clean up bad debt after the crisis is the remarkable gap between the value of collateral pledged and its actual, realizable value. The process for ensuring that collateral is always requested at sufficient levels of cover and the methodologies used for valuing collateral are both at fault.

Many banks do not even have a defined process – the customer defines the terms and nature of the collateral offered, not the bank. The first step, therefore, is to put a disciplined process in place. This should start with standards defining what collateral is acceptable and set categories for different types of collateral. Realistic values will be achieved when strict discounts are applied to the value of collateral to reflect the stability, volatility, and realizability of that value if the collateral actually had to be sold – in other words, when the real cash equivalent value of the collateral is determined.

Only cash on deposit with the bank should be considered zero risk and not discounted. Many banks apply a discounting process for collateral that shares a weakness with their pricing – *higher risk classes are not adequately discounted* relative to lower risk classes. As a result, the customers who offer the riskiest collateral have the biggest advantage with the bank, just as the riskiest customers get the best pricing deals from the bank, relative to their risk. We typically find that equity stakes in related companies and real estate are the biggest problems. In a recent example, one client bank had accepted company stock at a multiple of only 140% of the top market value at the time, in a highly volatile market. Two years later, the stock value has declined to 30% of its collateral value.

In our collateral management process, we always emphasize realistic liquidation value over the so-called market value of collateral. This means that in practice inventory, machinery, and other such nonfinancial business assets are *worthless* as collateral; and equity shares and property often have to be heavily discounted. The value of any asset is always different if you have to sell it tomorrow, and those banks that argue the benefits of waiting for better market conditions to sell rarely factor in the time cost of capital. Enforcing the most conservative view can be difficult with top customers, but, like all aspects of good risk management, it is vital to preserve the health of the bank. The gap between the customer's view of the value of an asset (usually the better of cost or the best recent market value), and the bank's view (the worst scenario liquidation value), will always be wide.

ENFORCING TRUE RISK-BASED PRICING

The pricing of credit in most emerging market banks does not reflect actual credit risk (Figure 20.10). Indeed, in the example in Figure 20.10, many of the lowest risk customers are getting the highest prices and the highest risk the lower prices! The common pattern is for *good customers to subsidize bad customers, small customers to subsidize large customers*, and *weak customers to subsidise powerful customers* – all of which is bad for risk and returns.

Unfortunately for the banks, recent experience during the various financial crises seems to indicate that the three factors are positively correlated – big is invariably powerful, and often bad. This has driven bankers away from corporate lending (the so-called "credit crunch") and into the arms of consumers in most emerging markets. Of course, in a few years time when all those unsecured credit card loans go sour these same bankers will learn that consumers are risky too!

Three factors drive the inadequate pricing of risk. First, however good a bank's loan pricing may be, competitors aggressively competing for market share or with an inadequate understanding of the price of risk may offer lower prices that force other banks either to compete or to lose business. This has always been the major problem with the pricing of credit – the best

FIGURE 20.10   Example of Korean banks pricing (indexed) relative to loan risk

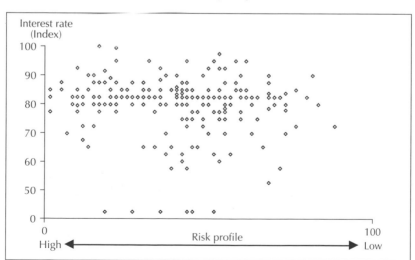

banks are forced to accept that the best prices in the market will always be offered by the least competent banks. Second, most banks price loans at a marginal rate above funding costs, either based on their average deposit cost of funds or on the prevailing interbank rate. In doing so they make inadequate provision for the costs of the bank's capital and the return required by shareholders, as well as the costs of potential default and operating costs. Finally, in many emerging markets, particularly those in Asia, cultural constraints limit true risk-based pricing, and the pricing of credit is often a better reflection of the relationship between the bank and the customer than the nature of the credit risk.

However attractive the short-term benefits, in the long-term, the *systematic underpricing of risk destroys profitability* – and maybe even the bank. If a bank believes it has no choice and is forced to accept a lower price than the risk justifies, the credit facility should at least be tied to the cross-selling of other, non-credit products than make up for the lost profitability of the credit facility. A better solution is to price correctly all the time, even if it means sacrificing some asset growth or customer relationships as a result.

In developed markets, the most efficient indicator of appropriate credit risk pricing is the spread differential above the "risk-free" sovereign debt rate demanded by the corporate bond market for different bond ratings. For example if US treasuries yield 5%, the bond market may price an A-grade bond at, say, 50 basis points above this, but it will price B-grade bonds at 350 basis points above this. The sharp increases in yield "spread" or price for more risky grades of debt in a bond market are rarely reflected in bank lending prices.

However, the price indication benefits of bond markets are typically unavailable in emerging markets. The best pricing system is therefore to use the credit risk ratings described above, coupled with their loss probability values and distribution, to set the expected default rate for each credit facility. Ideally, capital should then be allocated to cover these probable defaults and a minimum rate of return on capital priced into the loan. If, however, the loan is secured by high-quality collateral, the pricing can be adjusted downwards simply by applying the resulting capital and risk costs to the net credit exposure – the total loan amount less the true liquidation value of the collateral.

INTRODUCING SIMPLE BOARD-LEVEL RISK REPORTS FOR NON-RISK EXPERTS

The final "opportunity for action" for emerging market banks is the risk management information system and the way that a bank's risk position is presented to its top decision-makers. Most risk-reporting is designed by risk experts for risk experts. Top executives frequently misunderstand what they see, clouding vital issues and compromising decision-making. Time and time again, we hear executives confess that they do not really understand the bank's risk position because they do not understand the unreadable risk reports they receive – but most are unwilling to admit this publicly for fear of appearing ignorant.

Sophisticated software solutions are frequently unnecessary, and do not solve the problem in any case. They tend to be expensive and complex, and they demand data feeds and data quality that are unavailable in developing markets. Again, such problems are best solved initially using simple means that focus on getting the basics right.

We have designed a simple, visual, PC-based "risk dashboard" for a non-specialist audience (Figure 20.11). The dashboard, which can be integrated directly into a bank's existing risk management reporting system, provides a single page snapshot of all risk positions, and can be tiered to allow more detail for those who require it.

The single-page summary of a bank's overall risk status graphically highlights its current position on its chosen credit, market, and operational measures, with VaR as an integrating measure if the available data allow it. Executives who want further detail on a particular risk category can drill down by clicking on the summary bar for each measure. This takes them through screens detailing specific loan attributes (tenor, exposure type, facility utilization, collateral type), loan performance and limits compliance (loan growth by business segment, top NPL debtors, industry concentration, and group lending violations), and market VaR/CaR, liquidity risk positions, operational risk potential and actual losses, and finally balance sheet management positions (interest rates, average cost of funds, net interest margins, and so on).

Our premise in designing the dashboard was to provide all the risk information that a bank executive requires in only five pages of easily understood color bar graphs, something all banks should aim to do with their risk management information systems.

CONCLUSION

Although dramatic currency devaluations provided the trigger, the Asian financial crisis – and other emerging market crises before it – were banking crises above all. They were caused in the main by reckless lending to uncreditworthy businesses for speculative ventures. It is true that excess capital inflows, unrealistic currency pegs, and the optimistic "Asian miracle" investment climate of the times contributed to the crisis, but when trouble

FIGURE 20.11 Top-level screen of management risk-reporting "dashboard" (example)

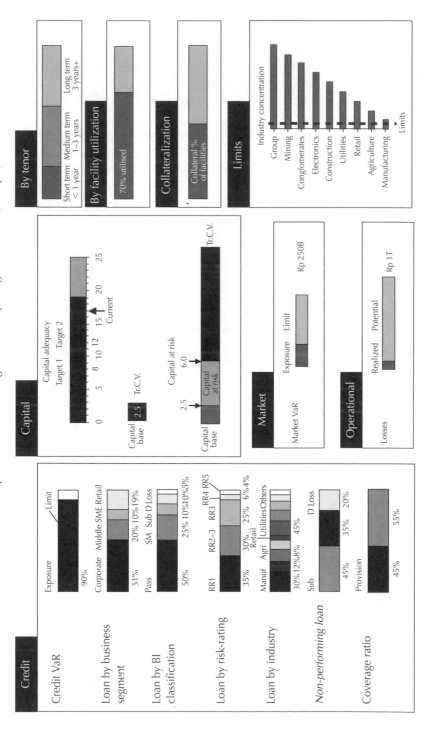

struck it was clear that most of the fundamental principles of good credit risk management had been ignored. These are principles designed to protect banks, and the result was widespread bank failure.

We have espoused here the fundamental disciplines of sound risk management. They include making credit decisions guided by robust customer and industry ratings, charging customers risk-related prices, enforcing non-negotiable lending limits, ensuring that staff in the field have the skills and the tools to do their jobs, making the credit organization independent from the business line, valuing collateral realistically, and providing a rapid response to any signs of trouble signaled by a good portfolio management system, easy-to-understand management information, and an early warning system. These are aspects of bank management that should never be compromised or half-heartedly implemented. The cost is simply too great, and depositors and taxpayers ultimately pay.

We are convinced that banks in developing markets will reap the greatest benefits from getting the basics right using traditional measures and processes, while building a platform for increasingly sophisticated credit risk management once better data are available, and experience and expertise is built. In our work we focus on what is practical, what is do-able, and what will work in these difficult markets, which means stepping back a little from the latest state-of-the-art practices and possibilities. Rather than focusing exclusively on improving measures and data, banks in emerging markets also need to look closely at what their people do and how decisions are made. They must build the right processes, organization structures, support tools, and training for their line management. Finally, implementation is everything – and that takes time, patience, and a willingness to accept a few compromises along the way.

Financial crises in emerging markets have been costly and painful for communities, governments, and businesses alike. Our hope is that by instituting the credit risk management practices we have described, banks can contribute in a significant way to rendering these crises much less destructive – or perhaps even ending them altogether.

ACKNOWLEDGMENTS

The ideas presented in this chapter owe much to the work of my Jakarta-based risk management team. I would specifically like to thank Eddy Tamboto and Sunata Tjiterosampoerno, both of BCG's Jakarta office; and Roland Bosch, of BCG's Frankfurt office. Park Sang Yong and Lee Minsup from our Seoul office contributed to my thinking on the organization of credit risk. Finally, many thanks to Rien Huizer, Asian head of risk at ABN-AMRO bank (Singapore); Jerry Ng, deputy chairman of the Indonesian Bank Restructuring

Agency; and Michael Edwards, senior financial officer at the World Bank (Jakarta) for comments and ideas on the draft of this article.

NOTES

[1] A multiple discriminant analysis model designed to differentiate a company's potential to fail, popular in the US.

[2] BIS paper on Range of Practice in Banks' Internal Ratings Systems, January 2000.

[3] Results of a Global BCG Study: "From Risk Taker to Risk Manager – Ten Principles for Establishing a Comprehensive Risk Management System for Banks", January 2001.

The SCA CreditVision Model and Demo-CD Explained

This book contains a Demo-CD of SCA's CreditVision model for interested users to test and explore the output of an abstract and event-based credit risk model in comparison with their own data sources and estimations. By nature, this demo-CD is limited in examples, but allows the user to fully modify parameters and explore the variations in output.

Below is a brief manual on how to operate the demo-CD.

OVERVIEW

SCA CreditVision's demo version contains five components: one toolbar and four screens. The four screens perform default risk analysis, plotting of default frequencies in normal and logarithmic scales and charting of stock prices and returns, respectively. The following sections provide detailed information on these, namely:

- CreditVision Toolbar;
- Default Risk Analysis Screen;
- Default Frequencies Screen with Stock Prices;
- Default Frequencies Screen with Log Scaling;
- Stock Data Screen.

CREDITVISION TOOLBAR

CreditVision's toolbar is divided into three sections. The left section provides two drop-down lists, the middle section is composed of three buttons and a drop-down menu, and the right section is a drop-down help menu. The two drop-down lists enable users to select one of the companies from the demo database. The left list displays the companies by name and the right list displays the companies by their tickers. When a company is selected all of its respective company information, financial statement data, equity market data, and default risk statistics are loaded into the corresponding areas of the system, and all appropriate charts are updated. A list can be searched by typing the full text desired in the blank area at the top of each list.

The left-most button of the middle section opens a dialog box containing various information about the user-selected company. This information includes the company's name, address, ticker, sector, industry, and a brief description of what it does. Each of the two remaining buttons jumps the user to one of CreditVision's two screens where the user can perform default risk analysis or chart stock prices and returns. The drop-down menu allows the user to select one of two screens, both of which display credit ratings for the selected company and plot its default frequencies on a normal scale. In addition, the first screen displays stock prices on the same time scale as the default frequencies and the second screen displays default frequencies on a logarithmic scale.

The right section contains a drop-down menu of help topics. The first topic takes the user to a tutorial. The second topic provides other miscellaneous information about CreditVision.

DEFAULT RISK ANALYSIS SCREEN

This is the main screen for calculating the model parameters of a selected company and computing forward-looking default frequencies.

Data contained on this sheet are divided into four sections. The top section of data contains company balance sheet and equity data needed to derive inputs for CreditVision's default risk model, which are stored in the second section from the top. The third section from the top displays equity volatility dynamics, including event risk statistics, calibrated using a given company's equity return history. The bottom section shows default frequencies resulting from CreditVision's default risk model simulations based on the model inputs given above.

The following elaborate on each of these screen components starting from the top of the screen and moving down.

FIGURE 1 The toolbar enables a user to navigate the system

FIGURE 2 The Default Risk Analysis Screen is the primary interface for default frequency calculations

AMR Corp

	12/28/01	9/28/01	6/29/01	3/30/01	12/29/00	9/29/00	6/30/00	3/31/00	
Balance Sheet and Equity Data									Clear All / Select All
Current assets ($Mil.)	6540.0	6081.0	5174.0	4573.0	5179.0	5352.0	5377.0	4999.0	
Current liabilities ($Mil.)	7512.0	8103.0	7894.0	6744.0	6990.0	7280.0	7106.0	6279.0	
Long-term liabilities ($Mil.)	19956.0	17506.0	14368.0	12557.0	12047.0	11526.0	11593.0	11613.0	
Outstanding shares (#Mil.)	154.5	154.5	154.4	153.7	152.1	150.7	150.0	149.7	Update
Market capitalization ($Mil.)	3398.6	2956.7	5578.8	5397.6	5958.9	4935.1	3964.6	4771.4	
Asset Value ($Mill.)	24326.6	22484.7	22666.8	20125.6	19816.9	18389.1	17286.6	17664.4	
Default Threshold ($Mill.)	20928.0	19528.0	17088.0	14728.0	13858.0	13454.0	13322.0	12893.0	Calculate
Gearing Ratio	14.0%	13.2%	24.6%	26.8%	30.1%	26.8%	22.9%	27.0%	
Equity Volatility Parameters (daily)									
Weighting - current returns	0.033	0.029	0.028	0.027	0.027	0.027	0.027	0.027	
Weighting - past volatility	0.949	0.958	0.956	0.959	0.957	0.956	0.955	0.956	
Unconditional equity volatility	2.4%	2.4%	2.2%	2.2%	2.2%	2.1%	2.1%	2.1%	
Initial equity volatility	3.9%	4.5%	2.3%	2.6%	2.5%	2.6%	2.9%	2.6%	Calibrate
Initial returns information	0.002	-0.029	-0.002	0.003	0.008	0.000	-0.003	0.011	Dynamics
Event Statistics (daily)									
Frequency of events	0.5%	0.4%	10.4%	10.4%	10.4%	11.2%	10.3%	10.0%	
Event size	6.211	6.022	1.891	1.878	1.902	1.902	1.929	1.904	
One Year Default Frequency	2.91%	5.27%	0.47%	0.76%	0.48%	0.55%	0.89%	0.41%	Simulate

Date Selection

The top row lists the dates to which each data set below it relates to. The check boxes beside each date allow a user to select which data sets will be affected when any of the "Calculate", "Calibrate" or "Simulate" buttons are pressed. "Clear All" clears all of the check boxes next to the dates. 'Select All' activates all of the check boxes next to the dates.

Company Data

The top section of data contains company balance sheet and equity data needed to derive inputs for CreditVision's default risk model, which are stored in the section below this. A company's data are loaded here when it is selected by a user from the drop-down lists in the CreditVision toolbar. However, a user can also manually change any of the inputs. Once a manual change has been made the "Update" and "Calculate" buttons should be pressed. The Update button re-computes the market capitalization based on the Balance Sheet and Equity Data. The "Calculate" button re-computes the asset value, default threshold, and gearing ratio based on the Balance Sheet and Equity Data.

Model Parameters

A company's asset value, default threshold, and gearing ratio are calculated from the data stored in the Company Data section above this one. They are used, along with the equity dynamics from the section below, as inputs into the CreditVision default risk model. A company's data are loaded here when they are selected by a user from the drop-down lists in the CreditVision toolbar. However, a user can also manually change any of the inputs. Once a manual change has been made the "Simulate" button should be pressed to update the default frequencies in the bottom section. The "Simulate" button computes the Default Frequencies using the asset value, default threshold, gearing ratio, equity volatility parameters, and event statistics.

A Default Frequency is the percentage of simulations, during a specified time period, where a company's asset value dropped below its default threshold. This is the primary output of CreditVision, providing a measure of default risk for a company. During simulation in the CreditVision default risk model, different paths that a company's asset value may take over time are modeled. The asset value stored in this section defines the initial point where each of these simulated paths begins. Default threshold defines the level of asset value where a company would be incapable of servicing its debt – i.e., the company is in financial distress. Gearing ratio is a company's proportion of equity market capitalization to asset value.

A company's previously simulated default frequencies are loaded here when it is selected by a user from the drop-down lists in the CreditVision toolbar.

Note that default risk calculations are fixed at 1,000 simulations for this demo version. As a consequence, the user should keep in mind that significant variations in simulation results can occur. The time horizon is also fixed at one year.

Equity Dynamics

This third section from the top displays equity volatility dynamics, including event risk statistics, calibrated by using a given company's equity returns history as displayed on the Stock Data Screen. These parameters are calculated when the "Calibrate" button is pressed and they are used, along with the model parameters from the section immediately above, as inputs into the CreditVision default risk model. A company's previously calibrated dynamics are loaded here when it is selected by a user from the drop-down lists in the CreditVision toolbar. However, a user can also manually change any of the inputs. Once a manual change has been made the "Simulate" button should be pressed to update the default frequencies in the bottom section.

The first group of data defines how a company's equity volatility changes over time during "regular" periods – i.e., an event has not occurred. Changes in volatility are calculated by using two sets of information. The first set describes how equity returns have moved today and the second set provides information on past movements in equity returns. "Weighting – current returns" is a weight that measures the amount by which changes in volatility are affected by the first information set – i.e., a weight of 0.0 means the first information set has no influence and a weight of 1.0 means the changes in volatility are completely determined by the first information set. Similarly, "Weighting – past volatility" is a weight that measures the amount of influence from the second information set.

To prevent simulations of volatility from producing unlikely values the Unconditional Equity Volatility is used to stabilize results. Unconditional Equity Volatility can be thought of as a long-run value that simulated volatilities will fluctuate around and/or tend towards over time.

Initial Returns Information and Initial Equity Volatility are used to seed the start of the volatility simulations. Initial Returns Information is used as the starting value of the first information set and Initial Equity Volatility is used as the starting value of the second information set.

Frequency of Events defines the daily likelihood of an event occurring. When an event occurs during simulation, the volatility calculated during a regular period, as described in the paragraphs above, is multiplied by the Event Size scalar to derive an event volatility.

DEFAULT FREQUENCIES SCREEN

Here the user can view plots, with the top graph, of forward-looking default frequencies (calculated using CreditVision's Default Risk Analysis Screen) versus historical default frequencies. The historical default frequencies are mapped from a given company's credit ratings, displayed on the left side of the screen, using the historical default frequencies published in the report "Default and Recovery Rates of Corporate Bond Issuers: 2001" by Moody's Investor Service, February 2002.

By using the option buttons on the right side of the graph a user can choose from two types of historical default frequencies: frequencies averaged on an annual basis and those averaged across the entire historical data set, which spans from 1983 to 2001. **Care should be taken in interpreting the results of the plots of Moody's historical default frequencies and as such, both types of averages should be considered to evaluate the difference in results**.

The first of the Default Frequencies Screens displays stock prices in the bottom graph along the same time scale as the default frequencies plot to provide a basis of comparison. The bottom graph of the second Default Frequencies Screen contains the top default frequencies graph on a logarithmic scale to magnify smaller movements and provide another comparative.

When the "Update" is pressed both plots on the current Default Frequencies Screen are updated to incorporate any changes made on any screens in CreditVision.

FIGURE 3 The first Default Frequencies Screen allows comparison between simulated default frequencies, historical default frequencies and stock prices

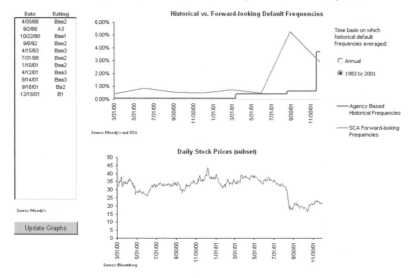

FIGURE 4 The second Default Frequencies Screen adds a comparison to default frequencies on a logarithmic scale

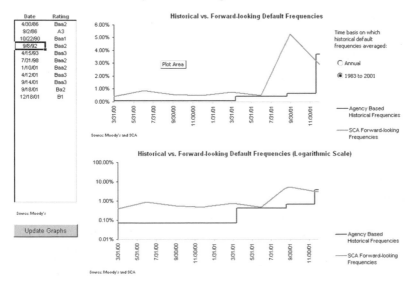

Stock Data Screen

This screen displays the stock prices and returns of a given company used to calibrate the equity volatility dynamics and event statistics shown on the Default Risk Analysis Screen. Prices and returns listed on the left side of the screen are also displayed graphically.

FIGURE 5 A display of the stock data used to calibrate volatility and event risk parameters

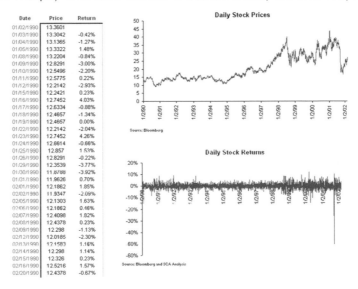

Bibliography

Aguais S and Santomero T, "Incorporating New Fixed Income Approaches into Commercial Loan Valuation," *Journal of Lending and Credit Risk Management*, 80(6): 58–65, 1998.

Aguais S, Forest L, Krishnamorthy S and Mueller T, "Creating Value from Both Loan Structure and Price," *Commercial Lending Review*, 13(2): 13–24, 1998.

Alibhai S, Gaeta G and Hingorani J, *Moving Towards Private Firm Credit Risk Measurement*, Whitepaper, Simplex Credit Advisory, 2001.

Altman E, "Financial Ratios, Discriminant Analysis and the Prediction of Corporate Bankruptcy," *Journal of Finance*, September, 589–609, 1968.

Altman E, "Measuring Corporate Bond Mortality and Performance," *Journal of Finance*, September 1989.

Altman E, *Corporate Financial Distress and Bankruptcy – 2nd Edition*, John Wiley & Sons, New York, 1993.

Altman E and Bencivenga J, *A Yield Premium Model for the High Yield Debt Market*, Salomon Brothers, 1995.

Altman E and Eberhart A, "Do Seniority Provisions Protect Bondholder's Investment?," *Journal of Portfolio Management*, 20(4): 67–75, 1994.

Altman E and Kao DL, "The Implications of Corporate Bond Ratings Drift," *Financial Analysts Journal*, 48(3): 64–75, 1992.

Altman E and Kishore V, "Almost Everything You Wanted to Know about Recoveries on Defaulted Bonds," *Financial Analysts Journal*, 52(6): 57–64, 1996.

Altman E and Kishore V, *Defaults and Returns on High-Yield Bonds: Analysis through 1997*, Special report, New York University Salomon Center, 1997.

Altman E, Marco G and Varetto F, "Corporate Distress Diagnosis: Comparisons Using Linear Discriminant Analysis and Neural Networks," *Journal of Banking and Finance*, 18: 505–29, 1994.

Altman E, Resti A and Sironi A, "Analyzing and Explaining Default Recovery Rates," ISDA, January 2002 (available from ISDA.org).

Altman E and Saunders A, "Credit Risk Measurement over the Last 20 Years," *Journal of Banking and Finance,* 1998.

Altman E, Schimpf S and Seltzer J, *The Investment Performance of Defaulted Bonds and Bank Loans and Market Outlook,* Special Report, New York University Salomon Center, 1997.

Altman E and Suggitt H, *Default Rates in the Syndicated Loan Market: 1991–1997,* Special Report, New York University Salomon Center, 1997.

Altman E and Waldman R, *Rating Migration of Corporate Bonds' Comparative Results and Investor/Lender Implications,* Salomon Brothers Inc, 1997.

Artzner P, Delbaen F, Eber JM and Heath D, "Coherent Measures of Risk," Working Paper, Institut de Recherche Mathématique Avancée, Université Louis Pasteur et CNRS, 1998.

Asarnow E, "Measuring the Hidden Risks in Corporate Loans," *Commercial Lending Review,* 10(1): 24–33, 1994.

Aziz A, "Algo Academy Notes," *Algo Research Quarterly,* 2(1): 65–72, 1999a.

Aziz A, "Algo Academy Notes," *Algo Research Quarterly,* 2(3): 65–71, 1999b.

Aziz A, "Algo Academy Notes," *Algo Research Quarterly,* 3(1): 75–85, 2000.

Basel Committee on Banking Supervision, "A New Capital Adequacy Framework," Consultative Paper, Bank for International Settlements, April 1999.

Basel Committee on Banking Supervision, *Amendment to the Capital Accord to Incorporate Market Risks,* Bank for International Settlements, 1996.

Basel Committee on Banking Supervision and the Technical Committee of the International Organization of Securities Commissions, *Recommendations for Public Disclosure of Trading and Derivatives Activities of Banks and Securities Firms,* Bank for International Settlements and the International Organization of Securities Commissions, 1998.

Basel Committee on Banking Supervision, *Credit Risk Modeling Practices and Applications,* Bank for International Settlements, April 1999.

Basel Committee on Banking Supervision, *International Convergence of Capital Measurements and Capital Standards,* Bank for International Settlements, July 1988.

Basel Committee on Banking Supervision – Risk Management Group, *Principles for the Management of Credit Risk,* white paper, Bank for International Settlements, September 2000.

Basel Committee on Banking Supervision – Transparency Group, *Best Practices for Credit Risk Disclosure,* white paper, Bank for International Settlements, September 2000.

Basel Committee on Banking Supervision, *Supervisory Risk Assessment and Early Warning Systems,* Bank for International Settlements, No. 4, December 2000.

Basel Committee on Banking Supervision, *The New Basel Capital Accord,* Bank for International Settlements, January 2001.

BCG, "From Risk Taker to Risk Manager – Ten Principles for Establishing a Comprehensive Risk Management System for Banks", January 2002.

Belkin B, Suchower S and Forest L, "The Effect of Systematic Credit Risk on Loan Portfolios and Loan Pricing," *CreditMetrics Monitor,* April: 17–28, 1998a.

Belkin B, Suchower S and Forest L, "A One Parameter Representation of Credit Risk and Transition Matrices," *CreditMetrics Monitor*, October: 46–56, 1998b.

Bishop C, "Training with Noise is Equivalent to Tikhonov Regularization," *Neural Computation*, 7:108-116, 1995.

Bishop C, *Neural Networks for Pattern Recognition*, Oxford University Press, Oxford, 1995.

Boyer B, Gibson M and Loretan M, "Pitfalls in Tests for Changes in Correlations," *International Finance Discussion Papers*, Number 597, Board of Governors of the Federal Reserve System, 1999.

Brand L and Bahar R, "Recovery on Defaulted Bonds Tied to Seniority Rankings," *Special Report Rating Performance 1997*, Standard and Poor's, August 1998.

Breiman L, "Bagging Predictors," *Machine Learning*, 24: 123–140, 1996.

British Bankers' Association, *Credit Derivatives Survey,* [online] [Available from: *http://www.bba.org.uk*], 2001.

Bucay N and Rosen D, "Credit Risk of an International Bond Portfolio: A Case Study," *Algo Research Quarterly*, 2(1): 9–29, 1999.

Burnham KP, and Anderson DR, *Model Selection and Inference*, Springer, New York, 1998.

Burton GA, *Experimental Psychology,* John Wiley & Sons, New York, 137–44, 1972.

Caouette JB, Altman E and Narayanan P, *Managing Credit Risk*: John Wiley & Sons, New York, 1998.

Carey M, "Credit Risk in Private Debt Portfolios," *Journal of Finance*, 53(4): 1363–1387, 1998.

Carty L and Fons J, *Measuring Changes in Credit Quality*, Special Report, Moody's Investors Service, 1993.

Carty L and Lieberman D, *Defaulted Bank Loan Recoveries*, Special Report, Moody's Investors Service, 1996.

Carty L and Lieberman D, *Corporate Bond Defaults and Default Rates, 1938–1996*, Special Report, Moody's Investors Service, 1997.

Cifuentes A, Choi E and Waite J, *Stability of Ratings of CBO/CLO Tranches*, Moody's Investors Service, 1998.

Cohen J, *Statistical Power Analysis for the Behavioral Sciences,* Lawrence Erlbaum Associates, Hillsdale, New Jersey, 1988.

Cox GEP and Tiao GC, *Bayesian Inference in Statistical Analysis,* John Wiley & Sons, New York, 1992.

CreditMetrics: *The Benchmark for Understanding Credit Risk, Technical Document*, 1997, New York, NY: JP Morgan, Inc.

Credit Suisse Financial Products, *CreditRisk+*, Research Report, Credit Suisse Financial Products, 1997.

Credit Suisse Financial Products, *CreditRisk+: A Credit Risk Management Framework*, Credit Suisse First Boston, 1997

Croft J, *Simplex*: *Quatitative Credit Risk Modeling*, RMG Group Report, 2000.

Crouhy M, Galai D and Mark R, *Risk Management*, McGraw-Hill, New York, 2001.

Crouhy M and Mark R, "A Comparative Analysis of Current Credit Risk Models," paper presented at the conference Credit Modeling and Regulatory Implications, London, September 1998.

Das S, (ed.), *Credit Derivatives and Credit Linked Notes – 2nd Edition*, John Wiley & Sons (Asia), 2000.

Das S, (ed.), *Credit Derivatives: Trading and Management of Credit and Default Risk*, Wiley Frontiers in Finance, John Wiley & Sons (Asia), 1998.

Das, S., (ed.), 1998. *Credit Derivatives: Trading and Management of Credit and Default Risk*. (Wiley Frontiers in Finance), New York: John Wiley & Sons.

Das, S. and P. Tufano, 1996. "Pricing Credit-sensitive Debt when Interest Rates, Credit Ratings and Credit Spreads are Stochastic," *Journal of Financial Engineering*, 5(2): 161–198.

Das S and Tufano P, "Pricing Credit-Sensitive Debt when Interest Rates, Credit Ratings and Credit Spreads are Stochastic," *Journal of Financial Engineering*, 5(2): 161–198, 1996.

David G, *Order Statistics*, John Wiley & Sons, New York, 1979.

Dembo R, Aziz A, Rosen D and Zerbs M, *Mark-to-Future: A Framework for Measuring Risk and Reward*, Toronto, Algorithmics Inc., 2000.

Dhar V and Stein R, *Seven Methods for Transforming Corporate Data into Business Intelligence*, Prentice-Hall, Upper Saddle River, 1997.

Dhar V, and Stein R, "Finding Robust & Usable Models with Data Mining: Examples from Finance," *PCAI*, September 1998.

Duda R, Hart P and Stork D, *Pattern Classification – 2nd Edition*, John Wiley & Sons, New York, 2000.

Duffie D and Garleanu N, *Risk and Valuation of Collateralized Debt Obligations*, [online] working paper, Graduate School of Business, Stanford University, [Available From: http://www.stanford.edu/~duffie/working.htm], 1998.

Duffie D and Lando D, *Term Structures of Credit Spreads with Incomplete Accounting Information*, Working paper, Graduate School of Business, Stanford University, 1997.

Duffie D and Singleton K, *Simulating Correlated Defaults*, working paper, Graduate School of Business, Stanford University, [Available from: *http://www.stanford.edu/~duffie/working.htm*], 1998.

Duffie D and Singleton KJ, *Modeling Term Structure of Defaultable Bonds*, Graduate School of Business, Stanford University, July 1, 1998.

Duffie D and Singleton K, "Modeling Term Structures of Defaultable Bonds," *Review of Financial Studies*, 12(4): 687–720, 1999.

Eales R and Bosworth E, "Severity of Loss in the Event of Default in Small Business and Larger Consumer Loans," *The Journal of Lending and Credit Risk Management*, 80(9): 58, 1998.

Efron B and Tibshirani R, *An Introduction to the Bootstrap*, Chapman & Hall, London, 1993.

Falkenstein E, "Building a Statistical Model for Middle-Market Credit Risk," *Risk Professional*, Global Association of Risk Professionals, August 2000.

Falkenstein E, Boral A and Carty LV, *RiskCalc*™ *For Private Companies: Moody's Default Model*, white paper, Moody's Investors Service – Global Credit Research, May 2000.

Falkenstein E, Boral A and Carty LV, *RiskCalc*™ *Private Model: Moody's Default Model For Private Firms*, Moody's Investors Service Special Comment, May 2000.

Finger CC, "Conditional Approaches for CreditMetrics Portfolio Distributions," *CreditMetrics Monitor*, April: 14–33, 1999.

Finger CC, *Sticks and Stones*, [online] working paper, RiskMetrics Group, [Available from: *http://www.riskmetrics.com/research/working*], 1998.

Finnoff W, "Diffusion Approximations for the Constant Learning Rate Back-propagation Algorithm and Resistance to Local Minima," *Neural Computation*, 6: 285–95, 1994.

Gaeta G, Alibhai S and Hingorani J, "Measuring the Prospects of Default Risk," *The Asian Banker Journal*, 23: 26–28, 2000.

Gaeta G and A Alibhai S, *Credit Risk Measurement*, white paper, Simplex Credit Advisory, 2000.

Geske R, "The Valuing of Corporate Liabilities as Compound Options," *Journal of Finance and Quantitative Analysis*, 12 (November), 541–52, 1977.

Ginzburg A, Maloney J and Wilner R, *Debt Rating Migration and the Baluation of Vommercial Loans*, Citibank Portfolio Strategies Group Report, December 1994.

Gordy M, "A Comparative Anatomy of Credit Risk Models," *Journal of Banking and Finance*, 24(1/2): 119–49, 2000.

Greenspan A, *Measuring Financial Risk in the Twenty-first Century*, Conference sponsored by the Office of the Comptroller of the Currency, Washington, D.C., October 14, 1999.

Grossman R and Verde M, *High Yield Industry Default Risk*, FITCH/IBCA, New York, December 1999.

Gumbel E, *Statistics of Extremes*, Columbia University, New York, 1962.

Gupton G, Finger C and Bhatia M, *CreditMetrics: The Benchmark for Understanding Credit Risk*, Technical Document, JP Morgan Inc., New York, 1997.

Gupton GM, Finger CC and Bhatia M, *CreditMetrics – Technical Document*, Morgan Guaranty Trust Co., [Available from: *http://www.riskmetrics.com/research/techdoc*], 1997.

Hamilton JD, *Time Series Analysis*, Princeton University Press, New Jersey, 1994.

Hanley A and McNeil B, "The Meaning and Use of the Area Under a Receiver Operating Characteristics (ROC) Curve," *Diagnostic Radiology*, 143 (1), 29–36, 1982.

HAT (Helvetic Asset Trust) AG, Prospectus, dated July 26, 2000.

Hayt G, "How to Price Credit Risk," *Risk*, 13(2): 60–61, 2000.

Herrity J, Keenan SC, Sobehart JR, Carty LV and Falkenstein E, *Measuring Private Firm Default Risk*, Moody's Investors Service, June 1999.

Hertz J, Krogh A and Palmer RG, *The Theory of Neural Network Computation*, Addison Welsey, Redwood, California, 1991.

Heskes T, "Balancing Between Bagging and Bumping," in: Mozer M, Jordan M, and Petsche T, (ed.), *Advances in Neural Information Processing Systems*, 9: 466–72, Cambridge, 1997.

Hoadley B and Oliver RM, "Business Measures of Scorecard Benefit," *IMI Journal of Mathematics Applied in Business & Industry*, 9: 55–64, 1998.

IFR, Swiss Re Structures Novel Credit Protection for RBC, 2001.

Iscoe I, Kreinin A and Rosen D "An Integrated Market and Credit Risk Portfolio Model," *Algo Research Quarterly*, 2(3): 21–37, 1999.

Jarrow R and Turnbull S, "Pricing Derivatives on Financial Securities Subject to Credit Risk," *Journal of Finance*, 50: 53–83, 1995.

Jarrow R and Turnbull S, "The Intersection of Market and Credit Risk," *Journal of Banking and Finance*, 24(1): 271–299, 2000.

Jarrow R, Lando D and Turnbull S, "A Markov Model for the Term Structure of Credit Risk Spreads," *The Review of Financial Studies*, 10(2): 481–523, 1997.

Jaynes ET, "Information Theory and Statistical Mechanics," *Physical Review*, 106(4): 620–630, 1957.

JP Morgan & Comapany, *CreditMetrics: The Benchmark for Understanding Credit Risk,* Technical Document, New York, NY, 1997.

JP Morgan & Company, *CreditMetrics, Technical Document,* 1997.

Kealhofer S "Managing Default Risk in Portfolios of Derivatives," *Derivative Credit Risk*, London, Risk Publications, 1996.

Keenan SC, Hamilton DT and Berthault A, *Historical Default Rates of Corporate Bond Issuers, 1920–1999*, Moody's Investors Service, 2000.

Keenan SC and Sobehart JR, *Performance Measures for Credit Risk Models*, Moody's Risk Management Services, Research Report 10–10–99, 1999.

Keenan, SC and Jobchot, JR, "A Credit Risk Catwalk," *Risk*, July 2000, 84–88.

Kender M and Waldman R, *Altman High Yield Bond and Default Study: A Decade of Assessment, Comparing 1990 with 2000*, Salomon Smith Barney, August 11, 2000.

Kim J and Finger CC, *A Stress Test to Incorporate Correlation Breakdown*, Whitepaper, RiskMetrics Group, 2000.

Koyluoglu H and Hickman A, "Reconcilable Differences," *Risk*, 11(10): 56–62, 1998.

Koyluoglu H and Hickman A, *A Generalized Framework for Credit Risk Portfolio Models*, September 1998.

Koyluoglu HU, Bangia A and Garside T, "Devil in the Parameters," *Risk*, March, S26–S30, Credit Risk Special Report, 2000.

Kreinin A, Merkoulovitch L, Rosen D and Zerbs M, "Principal Component Analysis in Quasi Monte Carlo Simulation," *Algo Research Quarterly*, 2(2): 21–29, 1998.

Kupiec PH, "Stress Testing in a Value at Risk Framework," *Journal of Derivatives*, 6: 7–24, 1998.

Lando D, *Three Essays on Contingent Claims Pricing*, PhD thesis, Graduate School of Management, Cornell University, 1994.

Lando D, "On Cox Processes and Credit Risky Securities," *Review of Derivatives Research*, 2(2/3): 99–120, 1998.

Laubsch AJ, *Risk Management: A Practical Guide*, RiskMetrics Group, New York, 1999.

Leland H, "Risky Debt, Bond Covenants and Optimal Capital Structure," *Journal of Finance*, 49: 1213–52, 1994.

Lewis A, *An Introduction to Credit Scoring*, Fair Isaac & Co., San Rafael, CA, 1992.

Li D, "The Valuation of Basket Credit Derivatives," *CreditMetrics Monitor*, April, 34–50, [Available from: *http://www.riskmetrics.com/research/journals*], 1999.

Li D, "On Default Correlation: a Copula Approach," *Journal of Fixed Income*, 9(3): 43–54, 2000.

Longin F and Solnik B, *Correlation Structure of International Equity Markets During Extremely Volatile Periods,* working paper, Department of Finance, ESSEC Graduate Business School, France, 1999.

Longstaff F and Schwartz E, "A Simple Approach to Valuing Risky Fixed and Floating Debt," *Journal of Finance*, 50(3): 789–819, 1995a.

Longstaff F and Schwartz E, "The Pricing of Credit Derivatives," *Journal of Fixed Income*, 5(1): 6–14, 1995b.

Lopez J and Saidenberg M, "Evaluating Credit Risk Models," *Journal of Banking and Finance*, 24(1/2): 151–165, 2000.

LPC Gold Sheets, *M & A Deals*, Loan Pricing Corporation, 14(23): 14, 2000a.

LPC Gold Sheets, *Investment Grade Deals*, Loan Pricing Corporation, 14(23): 8–9, 2000b.

Madan D and Unal H, "Pricing the Risks of Default," *Review of Derivatives Research*, 2(2/3): 121–160, 1998.

Mays E, (ed.), *Credit Risk Modeling: Design and Application*, Glenlake Publishing Co., Chicago, IL, 1998.

McDermott R, "The Long Awaited Arrival of Credit Derivatives," *Derivatives Strategy*, Januray 21: 19–25, 1997.

McKinsey & Co., *Credit View*, Research Report, McKinsey & Co., 1997.

McLachlan GJ and Basford KE, *Mixture Models: Inference and Applications to Clustering*, Marcel Dekker, New York, 1988.

McQuown J, *All That Counts Is Diversification*, Publicity Document, KMV Corporation, 1994.

McQuown JA, *A Comment on Market Accounting Based Measures of Default Risk*, KMV Corporation, 1993.

Mensah YM, "An Examination of the Stationarity of Multivariate Bankruptcy Prediction Models: A Methodological Study," *Journal of Accounting Research*, 22(1), 1984.

Merton R, "On the Pricing of Corporate Debt: the Risk Structure of Interest Rates," *Journal of Finance*, 29: 449–470, 1974.

Merton R, "Theory of Rational Option Pricing," *Bell Journal of Economics and Management Science*, 4: 141–183, 1973.

Moody's Investors Service, *The Binomial Expansion Method Applied to CBO/CLO Analysis*, December 1996

Moody's Investors Service, *Historical Default Rates of Corporate Bond Issuers, 1920–1998*, January 1999.

Moody's Investors Service, *Non-Bankruptcy-Remote Issuers in Asset Securitisation*, March 2001.

Nagpal K and Bahar R, "An Analytical Approach for Credit Risk Analysis under Correlated Defaults," *CreditMetrics Monitor*, April: 51–74, [Available from: *http://www.riskmetrics.com/research/journals*], 1999.

Newman D and Crawley T, *European High Yield Default Study – 2001*, Schroder Salomon Smith Barney (Europe), January 2001.

Ong MK, *Internal Credit Risk Models: Capital Allocation and Performance Measurement*, London, Risk Publications, 1999.

Parsley M, "The Launch of a New Market: Credit Derivatives," *Euromoney*, March: 28–33, 1996.

PBS, *Life on the Internet – Timeline*, [Available from: *http://www.pbs.org/internet/timeline/*], 1997.

Peters G and Altman E, *Defaults and Returns on High Yield Bonds: Analysis Through 1999 and Default Outlook for 2000–2001*, Salomon Smith Barney, January 31, 2000.

Phoa W, "Estimating Credit Spread Risk Using Extreme Value Theory," *The Journal of Portfolio Management*, Spring: 69–73, 1999.

Pierce JR, *Symbols, Signals and Noise: The Nature and Process of Communication*, Harper & Brothers, New York, 1970.

Plank M and Plank A, *Discussion Notes on Credit Risk Modelling*, University of Vienna, 1999.

Press JS, *Applied Multivariate Analysis,* Holt, Rinehart and Winston, Inc., New York, 1977.

Press W, Teukolsky S, Vetterling W and Flannery B, *Numerical Recipes in C – 2nd Edition*, Cambridge, Cambridge University Press, 1992.

Pritsker M, "Evaluating Value at Risk Methodologies: Accuracy vs Computational Time," *Journal of Financial Services Research*, 12(2/3): 201–42, 1997.

Provost F and Fawcett T, "Analysis and Visualization of Classifier Performance: Comparison Under Imprecise Class and Cost Distributions," in: *Proceedings Third International Conference on Knowledge Discovery and Data Mining*, Newport Beach, CA, August 14–17, 1997.

Refenes AP, *Neural Networks in the Capital Markets*, John Wiley & Sons, Chichester, UK, 1995.

Richeson L, Zimmerman R and Barnett K, "Predicting Consumer Credit Performance: Can Neural Networks Outperform Traditional Statistical Methods?", *International Journal of Applied Expert Systems*, 2(2): 116–30, 1994.

Rohatgi VK, *An Introduction to Probability Theory and Mathematical Statistics*, John Wiley & Sons, New York, 1975.

Roubini N, *Chronology of the Asian Currency Crisis and its Global Contagion*, [online], Stern School of Business, New York University, [Available from: *http://www.stern.nyu.edu/~nroubini/asia/AsiaChronology1.html*], 1998.

Rumelhart D, McClelland J and the PDP Research Group, *Parallel Distributed Processing: Explorations in the Microstructure of Cognition*, MIT Press, 1986.

Salomon Smith Barney Equity Research: U.S. report, January 9, 2001.

Saunders A, *Credit Risk Measurement*, John Wiley & Sons, New York, 1999.

Sellers M and Davidson A, *Modeling Default Risk: Private Firm Model*, white paper, KMV, October 1998.

Shannon C and Weaver W, *The Mathematical Theory of Communication*, University of Illinois Press, Urbana, 1949.

Shearer A and Forest L, "Improving Quantification of Risk-Adjusted Performance Within Financial Institutions," *Commercial Lending Review*, 13(4): 48–57, 1998.

Shumway T, *Forecasting Bankruptcy More Accurately: A Simple Hazard Model*, Working paper, University of Michigan Business School, 1998.

Silverman BW, *Density Estimation for Statistics and Data Analysis*, Chapman and Hall, London, 1986.

Smith DR, *Variational Methods in Optimization*, Dover Publications, New York, 1974.

Sobehart, JR, Keenan SC and Hein R, "Validation Methodologies for Default Risk Models," *Credit*, May 51–6, 2000.

Sobehart JR and Keenan SC, "Measuring Defaults Accurately," *Risk*, March 2001,

Sobehart JR, Keenan SC and Stein R, *Benchmarking Quantitative Default Risk Models: A Validation Methodology*, Moody's Investors Service Rating Methodology, March 2000.

Sobehart JR and Stein R, *Moody's Public Firm Risk Model: A Hybrid Approach to Modeling Short Term Default Risk*, white paper, Moody's Investor Services, March 2000.

Sobehart JR, Stein RM, Mikityanskaya V and Li L, *Moody's Public Firm Risk Model: A Hybrid Approach to Modeling Default Risk*, Moody's Investors Service Rating Methodology, February 2000.

Spanjers J and Heskes T, *Neural Networks for Volatility and Market Capitalization*, white paper, SMART Research BV and SNN, University of Nijmegen, December 2000.

Sprent P, *Data Driven Statistical Methods*, Chapman-Hall, London, 1998.

Standard & Poor's Corporation, *Ratings Performance 1996: Stability and Transition*, Special Report, 1997.

Standard & Poor's, *Financial Market and Economics Database*, DRI/McGraw-Hill, Lexington, MA, 1999.

Standard & Poor's, *CreditModel*^{TM}, 2000.

Standard & Poor's, *Ratings Performance 1999: Stability & Transition*, 2000.

Stevenson B, "The Intrinsic Value of a Commercial Loan: Understanding Option Pricing," *Commercial Lending Review*, 11(4): 4–22, 1996.

Swets JA, "Measuring the Accuracy of Diagnostic Systems," *Science*, 249: 1285–93, 1988.

Tavakoli J, *Credit Derivatives: A Guide to Instruments and Applications*, Wiley Series in Financial Engineering, John Wiley & Sons, NY, New York, 1998.

The President's Working Group on Financial Markets, *Hedge Funds, Leverage, and the Lessons of Long Term Capital Management*, 1999.

Tibshirani R and Knight K, *Model Search and Inference by Bootstrap Bumping*, Technical Report, University of Toronto, 1995.

Treacy WF and Carey MS, *Credit Risk Rating at Large U.S. Banks*, Federal Reserve Bulletin, Federal Reserve Board, United States, November, 1998.

Van de Laar P and Heskes T, "Pruning using Parameter and Neuronal Metrics," *Neural Computation*, 11:977-993, 1999.

Vasicek OA, *Credit Valuation*, KMV Corporation, 1984.

Wilson T, "Portfolio Credit Risk I," *Risk* Magazine, September 1997a.

Wilson T, "Portfolio Credit Risk II," *Risk* Magazine, October 1997b.

Wuffli P and Hunt D, "Fixing the Credit Problem," *McKinsey Quarterly*, 2, 1993.

Zangari P, "An Improved Methodology for Measuring VaR," *Riskmetrics Monitor*, Second Quarter: 7–25, 1996.

Zhou C, *A Jump-diffusion Approach to Modeling Credit Risk and Valuing Defaultable Securities,* Board Of Governors Of The Federal Reserve System, Finance and Economics Discussion Series, No. 1997–March 15, 1997.

Index

W

Y

Z